Ghana

the Bradt Travel Guide

Philip Briggs
updated by
Katherine Rushton

edition
4

www.bradtguides.com

Bradt Travel Guides Ltd, UK
The Globe Pequot Press Inc, USA

P9-DUM-562

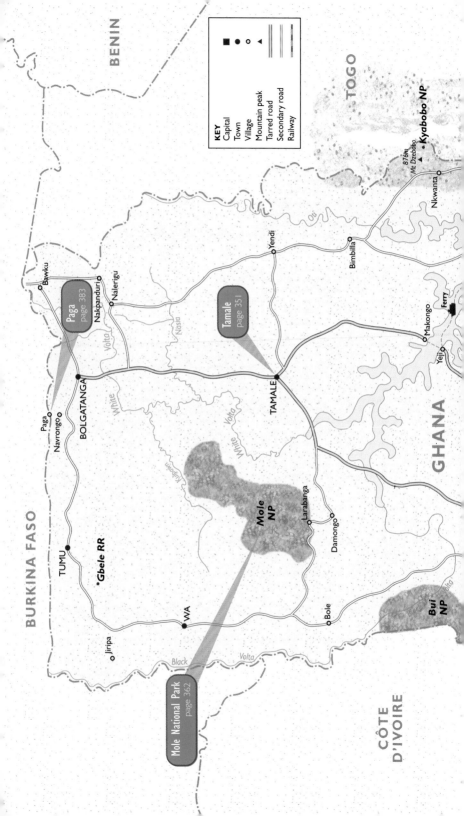

Paga
page 383

Tamale
page 351

Mole National Park
page 362

BENIN

TOGO

Kyabobo NP

876m
Mt Dzebobo ▲

Nkwanta

Ferry

Makongo

Yeji

GHANA

Bawku

Nakpanduri

Nalerigu

Yendi

Bimbilla

Oti

Volta

Nasia

BOLGATANGA

White

White Volta

TAMALE

Paga

Navrongo

TUMU

•Gbele RR

Kulpawn

Mole
NP

Larabanga

Damongo

Bole

Bui
NP

WA

Jiripa

Black

Volta

Volta

BURKINA FASO

CÔTE
D'IVOIRE

KEY
Capital ■
Town ●
Village ○
Mountain peak ▲
Tarred road
Secondary road
Railway

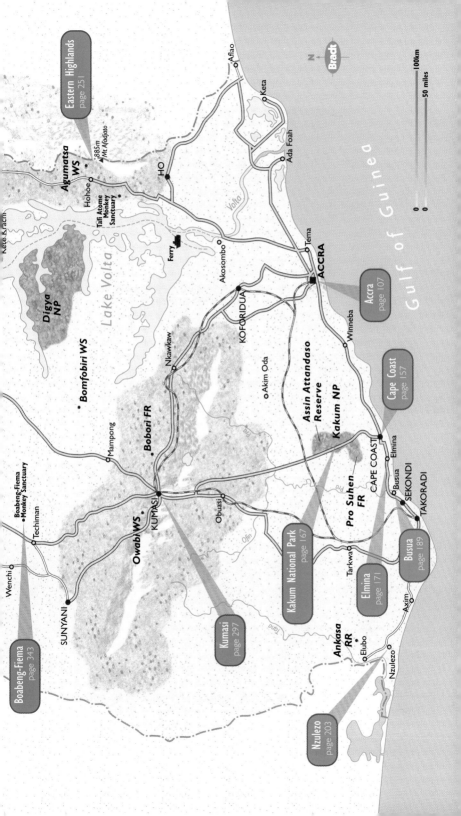

Ghana
Don't
miss...

Wildlife
Elephant, *Loxodonta africana africana*, in Mole National Park
(AZ) page 362

History
St George's Castle, Elmina
(AZ) page 176

National Parks
Kakum National Park
(AZ) page 167

Culture
Nzulezo stilt village,
Lake Amansuri
(AZ) page 203

Towns
Kumasi
(AZ) page 297

above **Market at Accra** (BA) page 128

below left **Girls eating, Accra** (SP)

below right **Orange seller, Dzemeni** (AZ) page 256

AUTHOR

Philip Briggs (philari@hixnet.co.za) is a travel writer specialising in equatorial and southern Africa. Born in Britain and raised in South Africa, he first travelled in equatorial Africa in 1986, and, since becoming a full-time writer in 1992, has spent half of his time exploring the highways and back-roads of the continent. His first book *Guide to South Africa* was published by Bradt in 1991. Subsequently, Philip has authored or co-authored several other Bradt guides, covering Tanzania, Uganda, Rwanda, Ethiopia, Malawi, Mozambique, Ghana, and east and southern Africa. He has contributed to numerous other travel guides and books, and writes regularly for periodicals such as *Travel Africa*, *Africa Geographic*, *Africa Birds & Birding* and *Wanderlust*.

AUTHOR STORY

Incredibly, a full ten years has passed since we researched the original Bradt guide to Ghana. Much has changed over the course of that decade. In the mid-1990s, Ghana – still widely associated with the series of economic and political disasters that marred its first few decades of independence – was generally thought of as a country best avoided by travellers. Today, by contrast, it is routinely cited as a nascent African success story: a genuine democracy whose relative economic health is reflected in the ease of travel conditions compared to most of west Africa.

When we first travelled around Ghana, reliable travel information was scarce, and we relied mainly on the hit-and-miss combination of instinct, serendipity, the advice of locals and a chat with the occasional other traveller. Mostly, it was hits, but the misses were spectacular. On one misinformed occasion, I recall spending 12 hours waiting for a non-existent *tro-tro* before retiring to the room where we'd spent the previous night. Elsewhere, we were forbidden from seeing the only room in the only guesthouse in the village until we paid upfront, whereupon the caretaker opened the door to reveal a squealing mass of bats flapping and crapping through the trashed ceiling – fortunately, it was early enough in the day to move on.

Of course, facilities have improved greatly since then; indeed, barely a month goes by without us receiving news of a new tourist hotel, backpacker resort or ecotourism project. And I'd like to think that this book – after four editions, still the only dedicated travel guide to Ghana – has contributed to that process. But, cheeringly, one thing that hasn't altered over the decade I've known Ghana is that it remains a singularly unpackaged destination – you'll find no snap-happy coachloads here, little in the way of prescribed tourist circuits or wallet-emptying 'must-do' excursions, and plenty of opportunity for whimsical exploration. Ghana, today as it was ten years ago, is the ideal destination for the genuinely independently minded travellers at whom Bradt guides are aimed.

UPDATER

Katherine Rushton, who updated this edition, is a full-time journalist based in London. Her first visit to Ghana was in 1999 on a gap-year placement in a village in the Volta Region. Since then she has remained involved in the village's development, returning often, and in 2003 was installed as a Queen Mother. Her other African travels have led her to Burkina Faso, Mali, Togo and Morocco.

PUBLISHER'S FOREWORD   *Hilary Bradt*

The first Bradt travel guide was written in 1974 by George and Hilary Bradt on a river barge floating down a tributary of the Amazon. It was followed by *Backpacker's Africa*, published in 1979. In the 1980s and '90s the focus shifted away from hiking to broader-based guides to new destinations – usually the first to be published on those places. In the 21st century Bradt continues to publish these ground-breaking guides, along with guides to established holiday destinations, incorporating in-depth information on culture and natural history alongside the nuts and bolts of where to stay and what to see.

Bradt authors support responsible travel, with advice not only on minimum impact but also on how to give something back through local charities. Thus a true synergy is achieved between the traveller and local communities.

* * *

We've become used to praise from readers for Philip's books. They seek us out at travel fairs to tell us, and he receives more fan letters than any other author. But the real test of a guidebook is if it's as useful to local residents as to visitors. Here's an extract from a reader in Accra: 'I have the impression that I started discovering fantastic new and unknown places only last year when I got a copy of your guide in one of the local bookshops. I am extremely grateful to you for introducing me to so many beautiful new places outside of Accra. While some guides on Ghana are far too positive and enthusiastic and thereby evoke possible disappointment on the traveller's side, other guides are too negative and almost scare any prospective traveller off. You have found the right mixture and reading your guide is a real pleasure. Even for my life here in general I found your guide useful: the big and small struggles of everyday life sometimes make me forget all the beautiful things this country has to offer. You reminded me that sometimes it is important just to take a step back and look at the greater picture and you are so right. Once again: thanks a million!'

Reprinted March 2008, Fourth edition August 2007 First published in 1998

Bradt Travel Guides Ltd
23 High Street, Chalfont St Peter, Bucks SL9 9QE, England; www.bradtguides.com
Published in the USA by The Globe Pequot Press Inc, 246 Goose Lane,
PO Box 480, Guilford, Connecticut 06475-0480

Text copyright © 2007 Philip Briggs and Katherine Rushton
Maps copyright © 2007 Bradt Travel Guides Ltd
Illustrations copyright © 2007 Individual photographers and artists (see below)
Editorial Project Manager for Bradt: Emma Thomson
Fourth edition produced by Cambridge Publishing Management Limited

The authors and publisher have made every effort to ensure the accuracy of the information in this book at the time of going to press. However, they cannot accept any responsibility for any loss, injury or inconvenience resulting from the use of information contained in this guide.
All rights reserved. No part of this publication may be reproduced, stored in a retrieval system, or transmitted in any form or by any means, electronic, mechanical, photocopying, recording or otherwise without the prior consent of the publisher. Requests for permission should be addressed to Bradt Travel Guides Ltd in the UK, or to The Globe Pequot Press Inc in North and South America.

British Library Cataloguing in Publication Data
A catalogue record for this book is available from the British Library
ISBN-10: 1 84162 205 2   ISBN-13: 978 184162 205 7

Photographs Blake Anderson (BA), Walter Callens (WC), Henrik Hartmann (HH), Sara Hebsgaard (SH), NHPA/Photoshot (NHPA), Stefania Manfreda (SM), Stig Nygaard (SN), Sarah Preston (SP), Alexander Sulzberger (AS), Ariadne Van Zandbergen www.africaimagelibrary.com (AZ)
Front cover Adobe house, Sirigu village (AZ)
Title page Woman at Nafac festival, Ho (AZ), flap-necked chameleon (AZ), pirogue in Volta estuary (AZ)
Back cover Elephants in Mole NP (SN), traditional ceremony in Bole (SH)

Illustrations Annabel Milne, Carole Vincer
Maps Redmoor Design (black & white), Dave Priestley (colour)

Printed and bound in India at Nutech Photolithographers

Acknowledgements

Many thanks to my wife, Ariadne, for her company in Ghana in 1997–98, 2000, and 2003, and for supplying many of the photographs used in this guide. Ariadne and I are both deeply indebted to John Awuah of the now defunct Ghana Airways, without whose generous support and assistance this book would never have got off the ground, as well as to Sam Osafo of Ghana International Airlines, for assistance with flights for the fourth edition research trip. I'm grateful to the many readers of previous editions who have written in with useful details (see list below), and especially to Françoise Dowsett-Lemaire and Robert J Dowsett for forwarding me the detailed ornithological reports they compiled over 2004/5, many details from which have been integrated into this fourth edition. Last, but not least, thanks to Katherine Rushton for her comprehensive update of this fourth edition – I hope that travellers who use this edition come to appreciate her efforts as much as I do.

Katherine Rushton would like to thank the Attakey family, Bill Reinecke of the Peace Corps, Tom and Jo Miles of Green Turtle Lodge, the Jones-Parry family, John Mason of the NCRC, Erik van Waveren of SNV, the Ghana Tourist Board, Comfort, Rod and Kwasi McLaren of African Rainbow, Wendy of Big Milly's Backyard, and Vic Baboo of Guestline Lodge and Vic Baboo's Café.

She is also immensely grateful to all the readers of the third edition who wrote with updates and comments, which have been incorporated into this fourth edition. A big thanks to you all: Nana Abrafi, Stefan vd Akker, Peter Allan, Carole Allsop, Scott Anderson, Joice Arends, Jonas Asendorpf, Bill and Carol Bailey, Karen Bailey, Jonathan Bates, Bruce L Billedeaux, Justice K. Boakye, Roelof Boon, Ian and Diana Bosman, Dr Ineke Bosman, Ian Bowie, Helen Brierton, Peter Bristot, Andy Brookes, David Candlin, Hilary Carnihan, Sarah Castagnola, Glen Challenger, Yanelis Chaveco, Adjoa Childs, Christina Conner-Cerezo, Marie Cobbina, Rebecca Coombes, David and Hannah Cox, Giles Cullingford, Barbra Curtis, Nicola Danby, Emma Dell, Heather Derrick, Françoise Dowsett-Lemaire, Robert J Dowsett, Paul Duke, Christiaan van der Eijk, Lisa Eller Davis, Dr Roger Fisken, Mirjam Floor, Tawiah Foster, James Fraser, Hugh Frere-Cook, Gerard van de Garde, Tanja Galetti, Steven Geerling, Sandra Gregory, Robert Gribnau, Jeremy Gustin, Lauren Hall-Lew, Anna Heywood, Manu Herbstein, Conal Ho, Fred Hodgson, Uli Hollmann, Adam Hughes, Helen Jaeger, Richard Kalayi, Tony Kaleda, Rev. Isaac Kankam-Boadu, Yorgos Kechagioglou, Chris King, Hannah Koning, Abubu Kony, Mike Kovalsky, Sjoerd 'Shorty' Krake, Marcia Ladendorff, Jason Lee, Maarten Licht, Wade Lifton, Theo van Lin, Susan Loy, Penny MacInnes, Alice and Joep Manders, Robert Maram, Juliet Martinez, Katie May, Mike Mortlock, Philippe Moseley, Daniel Nassar, Michael Newport, Mame Nyarko, Lucy Obeng, Kwabena Okyere, Peter Onderwater, Benedicte Page, Aristea Parissi, Norman Peters, Charlotte Phillips, Andrew Pittaway, Nii Quarcoo, Syreeta Quartey, Ine Reijnen, Paola Ricceri, Flavia Robin, Christopher Rompre, Tamsin

Ross Van Lessen, John Sabara, Marco Salvioni, Kate Sanger, Tim SanJule, Prosper Sapathy Melissa Schoerke, Maddy Schreurs, Amy Schwartz, Chris Scott, Maria Selby, John Selig, Dennis Shaw, Jefferson Shirley, Anne Siequien, Sandra Smeets, Toni Sonet, Charlotte Spring, Marielle van Stiphout, Aruna Subramanian, William Steel, Sharon Swyer, Allan and Julia Szczuka, Charlotte Targett, Alan Thornhill, Tim Traviss, Madeline Tyrrell, Johannes Visser, Arne Verbout, Andrea Vogel, Lilian Wassink, Laetitia van Wayenburg, Jane Wenman, Nikki Whaites, Mariusz and Karolina Wieckowski, Syerramia Willoughby, Jayne Wright, Chercher Yang, Tony Hyland, Sirichai Chongchitnan, Fabien Petitcolas, Jörg Adelberger, Andrew Fishman, Thomas Katjejowsky, Dave Pettee & Mindy Scharlin, Vicky Mugleston, Lisa Byington, Claire Meynial, Lisa Lyons, Fabio D'Atri & Francesca Rio, Jacob from Italy, Anita, John, Giles, Saxon and Jennifer (no surnames supplied).

Finally, thanks to the many travellers and Ghanaians who knowingly or unknowingly helped with research along the way.

GHANA UPDATE NEWSLETTER!

Bradt Travel Guides holds on file an update newsletter for Ghana, which is regularly revised by Philip Briggs based on feedback from readers and from other local sources. In addition to keeping travellers up to date with new developments and tourist facilities, we will strive to keep tabs on the general situation regarding hotel prices and other costs.

To obtain the free newsletter either email Bradt at info@bradtguides.com and it will be forwarded to your email address, or visit www.bradtguides.com.

The newsletter is provided as a free service and without obligation, but if you have benefited from it, we would be grateful if you could return the favour by writing to us on your return with any information that may be of use to future travellers, and, if you find the book useful, posting your comments on amazon.com and other on-line booksellers.

We believe the newsletter will provide an overdue forum by which visitors to Ghana can be made aware of any new tourist-related projects, activities, and facilities. We therefore extend an invitation to volunteers, hotel owners, and ecotourist professionals working in Ghana to contact us with any information that might be of interest to travellers.

Contents

Introduction

As travel destinations go, Ghana is difficult to flaw. When, a few years back, somebody coined the phrase 'Africa for beginners' to describe Malawi, that most laid-back of southern African countries, they might as easily have been talking about Ghana today. Doubly so. Not only can Ghana, like Malawi, be recommended without reservation to even the most nervous of first-time independent travellers for being as amiable, affordable and hassle-free as practically any country on the African continent; just as important, Ghana boasts a travel circuit so varied and compact that it might almost be seen as offering a microcosmic first taste of Africa.

The southern part of Ghana is much as you'd expect of west Africa, all lush jungle, banana plantations, and picture-postcard beaches, albeit with a unique dimension in the form of the string of 500-year-old European forts and castles that line the former Gold Coast. But the real surprises begin as you travel further north, to the game-rich savanna of Mole National Park, a setting that evokes east Africa more than west Africa, or to the deeply Muslim Burkina Faso border region, where both mood and architecture have unexpected overtones of north Africa.

For English-speaking travellers, Ghana must certainly be regarded as the obvious first port of call in west Africa. Of only five anglophone countries in the region, it's the only one that really caters for independent travellers – granted, not necessarily a major commendation from a shortlist that also includes such potential 'holiday' venues as Liberia, Nigeria, and Sierra Leone. Fairer to say that you're unlikely to meet an English speaker who's travelled in west Africa in recent years and has anything negative to say about Ghana by comparison with its more expensive (and generally less well-equipped) francophone neighbours.

What Ghana does not have is one drop-dead, big-name attraction, the sort of place that friends who've visited will say you simply have to see once in your lifetime. Zimbabwe has Victoria Falls, Tanzania has Kilimanjaro, South Africa has Cape Town, Ethiopia its rock-hewn churches. The closest thing Ghana has to offer in the not-to-be-missed stakes are the above-mentioned castles. Not quite the pyramids in terms of impact, I grant you, but nevertheless a unique and chilling memorial to an episode as sickening as any in the recorded history of Africa: the cruel trade in human life that resulted in several millions of Africans being displaced to a life of bondage in the plantations of the Americas and the Caribbean.

If Ghana lacks one truly great tourist attraction, then it is equally true that during the rapidly paced months we spent researching various editions of this guide, barely a day went by without at least one memorable highlight, be it swimming below one of the gorgeous waterfalls of the eastern highlands, the thrill of getting closer on foot to a wild elephant than I ever have in east Africa, climbing to the roof of one of the surreal mosques that dot the northwest, taking a dugout canoe through papyrus swamps to the stilted village of Nzulezu, or watching colourful mona monkeys play between the houses of Boabeng village.

Ghana is a perfect travel destination, not least because it is so mercifully free of the trappings associated with mass tourism. Nowhere in the country are you made to feel part of some tourist treadmill, and – even if it has become something of a cliché for me to say so in the introduction to my guides – Ghana really is endowed with some remarkably exciting off-the-beaten-track possibilities. There are, for instance, at least five national parks and reserves ideally suited for equipped independent travellers, yet which currently go months on end without seeing a visitor. It is my hope that, by documenting for the first time the practicalities that surround visiting many of these places, I will encourage adventurous travellers to start realising the enormous potential for exploration that lies beyond Ghana's few relatively well-established tourist trails.

There has been much talk in the last couple of years of an African renaissance and, regardless of what one thinks of such generalisations, it is Ghana along with Uganda that is most frequently cited as being at the forefront of this movement. Trailblazing of this sort is not a new role for Ghana – the former Gold Coast was the first country in Africa to have extended contact with Europeans, one of the first to be formally colonised, and in 1957 it became the first to be granted independence in the post-war era. Less prestigiously, Ghana also became one of the first African countries to slide into post-independence chaos and, while it never plummeted to the depths reached by, say, Liberia or Rwanda, the modern visitor will find it difficult to reconcile accounts of Ghana 15 years ago with the vibrant country they see today.

Ghana is indeed steeped in history and tradition, more tangibly so than most countries I have visited. Yet it is also, emphatically, a country building towards a brighter future – and this paradox, above all, makes it one of Africa's most rewarding and exciting travel destinations. As Ghanaians are so fond of saying, 'Akwaaba!' ('Welcome!') – Ghana will not disappoint.

A NOTE ON PRICING

During the production stage of this fourth edition, the Bank of Ghana announced the pending re-denomination of the cedi by a factor of 10,000 (i.e. one 'new' cedi would be equivalent to 10,000 'old' cedis) but speculation was rife that devaluation would only be by a factor of 1,000, or that the whole exercise might be postponed or abandoned. To avert confusion, we decided to quote all prices in US$ rather than in local units, at an approximate exchange rate of 10,000. However, shortly before going to print, the proposed re-denomination did go ahead as planned, by a factor of 10,000, leaving the cedi more-or-less on parity with the US$ – in other words, the US$ price quoted in this guide should be more-or-less identical to the cedi price you'll be quoted on the ground, at least until inflation kicks in.

Part One

GENERAL INFORMATION

Location Western Africa, on the Gulf of Guinea

Neighbouring countries Bordered to the west by Côte d'Ivoire (Ivory Coast), to the north by Burkina Faso, to the east by Togo and to the south by the Atlantic Ocean

Size/area 239,460km² – roughly equal to Great Britain or the state of Oregon, USA

Climate Tropical. Hot and humid in the south; hot and dry in the north

Status Republic; member of the Commonwealth; independent since 1957

Population 22.5 million (2006 est.) (2000 census: 18,845,265)

Life expectancy 59 years

Capital Accra (2005 population, 1,970,400)

Other main towns Kumasi, Takoradi, Tema, Cape Coast, Tamale

Economy Major industries include agriculture – most notably cocoa farming – bauxite and gold mining, aluminium smelting and tourism

GDP US$2,600 per capita (2006 est.)

Languages Official language is English. At least 46 African languages are spoken, with the major ones including Twi, Fante, Ewe, Ga, Dagomba, and Halisa.

Religion Predominantly Christian, but largely Muslim in the north.

Currency Cedi.

Exchange rate Until recently the cedi traded at around 9,200 to the US$, but following its re-denomination by a factor of 10,000 in July 2007 the exchange rate is practically one to one.

National airline/airport Ghana International Airlines/Kotoka International Airport, Accra

International telephone code +233

Time GMT

Electrical voltage 200/220V

Flag Horizontal stripes in red, yellow, and green (top to bottom), with a black star in the centre

National anthem 'God Bless our Homeland, Ghana'

Public holidays 1 January, 6 March, 1 May, 25 May, 4 June, 1 July, 5 December, 25 December, 26 December (see also page 61)

Background Information

GEOGRAPHY

The capital of Ghana is Accra, situated on the Atlantic coast about 25km west of the Greenwich Meridian. Population estimates for Accra vary greatly, but the current population certainly exceeds one million and is in all probability far closer to two million. The second-largest city in the country is Kumasi, the former capital of the Ashanti Empire and modern capital of the synonymous administrative region, with a population of between half and one million people, depending on which figures you believe.

Various sources quote such wildly different population figures for other large towns in Ghana that it is impossible to rank them by size, at least with any great conviction. However, based on the divergent sources and my own impressions, I would regard the ten largest towns in Ghana, in approximate descending order of population, to be: Accra, Kumasi, Tamale, Tema, Takoradi (excluding Sekondi), Cape Coast, Koforidua, Sunyani, Obuasi and Ho. Other towns with a population of around 50,000 or more include Winneba, Bolgatanga, Wa and Bawku.

HISTORY

Before entering any historical discussion, it should be stressed that Ghana, like the other modern states of west Africa, is fundamentally a European creation of the late 19th century. For this reason, it would be thoroughly misleading to write about Ghana as if it were a meaningful entity prior to the colonial era. True, as long ago as 1700, the coast of modern-day Ghana stood firmly at the epicentre of the European maritime trade out of west Africa, while the Ashanti Empire gave political and social cohesion to much of the area between the coastal belt and the Black Volta. But even as recently as 1860, few would have foreseen the eventual existence of a political state with borders approximating to those of present-day Ghana. The modern state of Ghana began to take a recognisable shape only in 1873 as the British Gold Coast colony. Even then, what are now central and northern Ghana were annexed to the colony only in 1902, while the interior to the east of what is now Lake Volta, part of German Togoland before World War I, was formally mandated to Britain by the League of Nations only in 1919.

Bearing the above in mind, I have started this history with a section offering a broad overview of west African history prior to 1500. In the sections that follow this, which focus more specifically on modern-day Ghana, I refer to the coastal belt of what is now Ghana prior to colonisation as the Gold Coast; to the interior south of the Black Volta as Ashanti; and to the interior north of the Black Volta as the northern regions (in colonial times, this area was in fact called Northern Region, though it has since been divided into three administrative regions: Northern, Upper East, and Upper West). Following this logic, I refer to Ghana in colonial times as the Gold Coast colony, and reserve use of the name Ghana to describe the

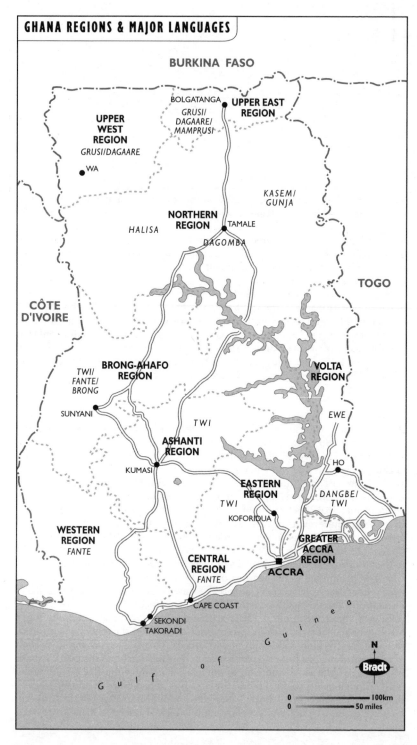

GHANA REGIONS & MAJOR LANGUAGES

BURKINA FASO

UPPER WEST REGION
GRUSI/DAGAARE

WA

BOLGATANGA
GRUSI/ DAGAARE/ MAMPRUSI

UPPER EAST REGION

KASEMI/ GUNJA

NORTHERN REGION

HALISA

TAMALE

DAGOMBA

CÔTE D'IVOIRE

TOGO

BRONG-AHAFO REGION

TWI/ FANTE/ BRONG

SUNYANI

TWI

VOLTA REGION

EWE

HO

ASHANTI REGION

KUMASI

EASTERN REGION

TWI

KOFORIDUA

DANGBE/ TWI

WESTERN REGION
FANTE

CENTRAL REGION
FANTE

GREATER ACCRA REGION

ACCRA

CAPE COAST

SEKONDI TAKORADI

G u l f   *o f*   *G u i n e a*

N

Bradt

0 ———— 100km
0 ———— 50 miles

4

ADMINISTRATIVE REGIONS

Ghana is divided into ten administrative regions, all of which to some degree have borders dating from the earliest days of colonialism. Several of the regions also have names that date from the earliest colonial times in a manner that can create some confusion to new arrivals to the country. The Western, Central, and Eastern regions as delineated by the British administration before the annexation of Ashanti in 1902 still go by those names, even though Eastern Region today lies to the west of Volta Region, and Central Region lies nowhere near the centre of modern Ghana, but on its southern coast. Likewise, the original Northern Region as delineated by the colonial authorities has since been split in such a manner that Northern Region lies to the south of Upper East and Upper West regions. It is worth being aware of this, because the regions have a high profile in Ghana today, and when most Ghanaians speak of 'eastern', 'central', or 'northern', they mean the administrative region rather than the most easterly, central, or northerly part of the country.

The ten modern administrative regions of Ghana are as follows:

	Km²	Population*	Capital	Other large towns
Ashanti	24,390	3,000,000	Kumasi	Obuasi, Tafo, Mampong
Brong-Ahafo	39,557	1,800,000	Sunyani	Techiman, Wenchi, Kintampo
Central	9,826	1,500,000	Cape Coast	Elmina, Winneba, Dunkwa
Eastern	19,223	2,200,000	Koforidua	Akim Oda, Nkawkaw, Akosombo
Greater Accra	3,245	2,500,000	Accra	Tema, Ada, Dodowa, Ashaiman
Northern	70,384	1,800,000	Tamale	Yendi, Bimbilla, Nalerigu
Upper East	8,842	1,100,000	Bolgatanga	Navrongo, Bawku, Zebilla
Upper West	18,476	800,000	Wa	Jiripa, Tumu, Lawra
Volta	20,334	1,800,000	Ho	Hohoe, Aflao, Kpando, Keta
Western	24,000	1,200,000	Sekondi-Takoradi	Tarkwa, Elubo

* Estimated by multiplying the regional population as recorded in the 1984 census by the percentage growth for that region recorded between 1970 and 1984, a calculation that should come close to the 1998 figure assuming the absence of other changing variables.

country after it gained independence in 1957. To preclude confusion between the modern state of Ghana and the ancient state from which its name is taken, the latter is referred to as Ancient Ghana. For the sake of consistency, the term 'Ancient Mali' has been used to refer to another vanished west African empire that was to bequeath its name to a modern state.

WEST AFRICA BEFORE 1500 The north-western 'bulge' of Africa can be divided into four economic units prior to 1500. The most northerly of these is the Mediterranean coastal belt of north Africa, an area that has had direct links with the other Mediterranean civilisations since ancient times, and that assimilated the influence of Islamic invaders as early as the 8th century AD, barely a century after the religion was founded. To the south of this lies the Sahara Desert, almost as large as Europe, yet devoid of permanent human settlement since time immemorial. South of the Sahara

5

is the Sahel, an ever-expanding belt of dry savanna, thinly populated except where it's crossed by large rivers, such as the Niger, Senegal, and Volta. And further south still, there is the belt of moister savanna and forest that terminates at the Atlantic coast, the area we normally think of when we refer to west as opposed to north Africa, and the area to which the modern state of Ghana belongs.

Prior to the arrival of the Portuguese on the Gold Coast in the late 15th century, there had existed for centuries a trade relationship between these four regions. Merchant caravans would cross the Sahara from north to south, bringing with them salt, fine cloth, and other luxury items that they would trade for goods such as gold, ivory and kola nuts. It is difficult to ascertain exactly when this epoch of trade started, but the available physical evidence would appear to show that a trade route across the Sahara similar to the modern one has existed since before 500BC. It can probably be assumed, too, that the spread of iron-age technology into the Sahel and areas further south before 600BC was influenced by trade routes that, for all we know, may have existed in some form or other for several millennia.

The specifics of this trade and of the societies south of the Sahel are difficult to determine prior to the 8th century AD. Some scholars suggest that there was a substantial increase in trade at around this time, based on the rather unconvincing argument that the first written record of the area south of the Sahel dates to AD773. It is just as likely that the reason no earlier records exist is linked to the rapid increase in written documentation in northwest Africa following the introduction of the Islamic faith in the 8th century AD. What is clear from this first written reference to the Sahel is, firstly, that its Arabic writer regarded it to be the 'Land of Gold', and, secondly, that it had long supported a powerful centralised trading empire that effectively acted as the 'middleman' between areas south of the Sahel and north of the Sahara.

This empire was the ancient state of Ghana, which – somewhat confusingly – lay completely to the north of its modern namesake. (Nkrumah's choice of the name 'Ghana' in 1957 was largely symbolic, as the former Gold Coast was the first African colony to gain independence from a European power; contemporary claims by some local historians that many of modern Ghana's main groupings descend from Ancient Ghana have subsequently been discredited.) Ancient Ghana was founded by Mande-speakers at some time between AD300 and AD700; at its peak, it spread for roughly 300km from north to south and 500km east to west between the rivers Niger and Senegal. The capital of Ancient Ghana at Kumbi Saleh (now a ruined city in southern Mauritania less than 100km from the Mali border) supported a population of roughly 15,000, and its emperor was able to muster an army numbering 200,000.

In AD992, Ancient Ghana was at the height of its powers, and its leadership decided to cement the hold on the trade routes out of the southern Sahara by capturing the important terminus of Awdaghast, 300km northwest of Kumbi Saleh. In the long term, this proved to be the downfall of the state, as the displaced Berbers of Awdaghast consolidated under a somewhat fanatical religious movement known as the Almoravids (meaning 'the people of the hermitage') and waged a *jihad* culminating in the capture of Kumbi Saleh in the year 1076. The Almoravids held the ancient Ghanaian capital for little more than a decade, but their brief tenure appears to have been the catalyst that caused the vast empire to fissure into several smaller and less powerful states, a situation that evidently persisted throughout the 12th century.

The beginning of the 13th century saw the emergence of a clear successor to Ancient Ghana in the omnipotence stakes, and this was the Ancient Mali empire founded by the Mandinka people of Kangaba. Accounts of the early days of this empire tend to be somewhat vague, but, so far as anybody can ascertain, the

Mandinka had by 1205 taken over large parts of what had formerly been Ancient Ghana. In 1230, the leadership of Mali was assumed by Munsa Sundiata, an inspirational expansionist who had doubled the area of Mali by the time of his death in 1255. In 1240, Sundiata captured Kumbi Saleh, and relocated the capital to the fringe of the Sahara: the exact location selected is a matter of some debate amongst historians, but it evidently proved unsatisfactory, as all later accounts place the capital of Mali at Niani in the vicinity of the Guinea and Côte d'Ivoire border.

You might reasonably wonder what bearing all the above has on modern Ghana. The best answer, in the broadest sense, is simply that it puts paid to the common misconception that this part of Africa was some sort of stagnant backwater prior to the arrival of Europeans. More specifically, the area that lies within the modern state of Ghana played a palpable role in the trade patterns of this era – it was, indeed, the empires of the Sahel that controlled the southern end of the Saharan caravan routes, but it was through a more localised trade system involving the people of the moist savanna and rainforest region that they obtained most of their trade goods. Centuries ago, Ghana was the major supplier of kola nuts to the empires of the Sahel, as well as an important source of ivory. Of more lasting significance, the rainforest belt of modern Ghana was in medieval times – as it would be in the era of coastal trade, and remains today – one of the region's richest sources of gold; the gold that not only lay at the heart of the trade route across the Sahara to Morocco, but would later be one of the factors that caused the Portuguese to set sail in search of a trade route to sub-Saharan Africa.

Another lasting effect of the cross-Sahara trade was the spread of Islam into west Africa. It is not certain when or how deeply Islam first took hold in the region, but the writings of the Arab Al-Bakri in 1067 testify to the presence of a permanent Islamic community situated roughly 10km from Kumbi Saleh. While it is clear from this that the rulers of Ancient Ghana were not converts, the fact that this community boasted 12 mosques suggests it was reasonably significant.

The rulers of Ancient Mali almost certainly *were* Muslim converts right from the empire's earliest days. As early as 1200, Mansa Uli of Ancient Mali undertook a pilgrimage to Mecca. More famous was the pilgrimage of Mansa Musa in 1324–26, when the empire would have been at its economic prime. Contemporary records state that Musa gave away so many gifts of gold that the market for the metal was seriously undermined for some time after. His visit also put Ancient Mali on the world map in the most literal sense; the west African empire first appeared by name on an Arabic map drawn up in 1339. And it is well documented that Musa returned home with several Islamic scholars who did much to entrench the exotic religion among the common people of Ancient Mali, and were responsible for designing the mud-and-stick style of mosque construction that visitors to modern Ghana will see in places like Larabanga and Wa.

Islam was the state religion of the Songhai Empire, centred to the north of what is now Burkina Faso. One of several small empires that were ruled by the Mansa of Ancient Mali following the collapse of Ancient Ghana, Songhai was revived in the mid 15th century by a leader called Sunni Ali, from his capital at the Niger River port of Gao, and it replaced Ancient Mali as the dominant Sahelian state from roughly 1464. One of the most powerful of Songhai rulers, Askia Mohammed, made the pilgrimage to Mecca in the 1490s, after which Islam was forced on the commoners of the empire. The Songhai Empire collapsed in 1591, following an attack on Gao by an army from Morocco. This event is generally seen as signalling the beginning of what many historians refer to as the west African interior's 'Dark Age', a 300-year period of economic stagnation attributable less to any one single attack than to the reorientation of trade patterns that followed the arrival of Portugal at the Gold Coast in 1471.

GHANA BEFORE 1500 On the basis of archaeological evidence, it has been established that modern-day Ghana was inhabited by humans 300,000 years ago, though current knowledge of human movements prior to this would suggest that the country has been occupied for millions of years. The earliest people to inhabit the region were hunter-gatherers, of whom little concrete can be said. It has yet to be determined when agriculture and pastoralism were adopted in the area, but this could have been as early as around 5000BC. Certainly, by 2000BC, both exotic creatures, such as cattle, and indigenous ones, such as guinea fowl, were being raised in domesticity, while archaeological findings near Kintampo demonstrate that substantial villages had been established at this time – a sure indication that hunter-gathering was no longer the predominant lifestyle in what are now Ashanti and Brong-Ahafo Regions. From around AD1000, it appears that an increased trend towards urbanisation was under way, with population centres of more than 2,000 people forming in the central and northern parts of what is now Ghana, presumably as a result of an economy that depended increasingly on trade with the great empires of the Sahel.

Oral tradition suggests that most modern Ghanaian population groups migrated to their present homeland from elsewhere in west Africa. The traditions widely agree that these migrants moved into territory occupied by the Guan, who are still regarded by other Ghanaians to be the true aboriginals of the country, though they are now assimilated into more recently arrived groups, with the exception of a few isolated Guan pockets at places such as Adokrom, Winneba, and Efutu. It is difficult to tell whether these migration traditions reflect the influx of an entire group of people who would presumably have gained territory through conquest, or whether they relate to a small group of migrants who formed a ruling class over the existing occupants of an area. What does seem reasonably certain is that the modern country's broad pattern of population had taken a recognisable shape by the late 15th century, when the Portuguese arrived at the coast.

The people of modern Ghana are generally divided into four main regional groupings, each of which shares a similar language and culture. The Mole-Dagbani of the Northern Region were possibly the first to establish their approximate modern territory; tradition has it that they migrated from the Lake Chad region in the 13th century, settling briefly at Pusiga (on the modern border with Togo) before establishing the Mamprusi kingdom at Gambaga. Other northern chieftaincies, such as Dagomba, Nanumba and Mossi, are traditionally regarded to be offshoots of the Mamprusi, and even today secession disputes in most parts of the region are referred to the Chief of Gambaga (known as the 'Nayiri'), quite possibly the oldest extant chieftaincy in modern Ghana. The only significant exception to the above generalisations regarding the people of the Northern Region is the Gonja Kingdom, which is traditionally said to have been founded by Mande migrants from Ancient Mali in the early 16th century.

As a result of its proximity to the ancient empires of the Sahel, the Northern Region has enjoyed a strong Islamic influence for centuries, though exactly when and how this exotic religion reached the area is a matter of conjecture – some sources place its arrival as early as the 13th century, while others date it to the 17th. This discrepancy in dates might be accounted for by a long delay between the establishment of the first Islamic settlements in the northern regions and a more widespread acceptance of the religion. It has been suggested that the large-scale influx of Islamic ideas into present-day Ghana was blocked for centuries by a powerful anti-Islamic kingdom in what is now Burkina Faso, but this would not have prevented Islamic traders from establishing their own settlements along the main trade routes through the region. The mud-and-stick mosques found in several villages in the northwest of modern Ghana almost certainly pinpoint some of the country's earliest Islamic settlements but, since the antiquity of these mosques is open to debate, it is difficult to draw any firm conclusions about when Islam first reached these villages.

The area to the east of Lake Volta is inhabited by the Ewe, 15th-century migrants from eastern Nigeria. Ewe society is the least centralised of any in modern Ghana; each of the roughly 130 small Ewe chieftaincies is entirely autonomous (in other words, there is no paramount chief), though the larger Anlo Kingdom based around the port of Keta is something of an exception. The other important grouping of the east is the Ga-Adangbe, which consists of the Ga people of the Accra coastal plain and the Adangbe of Ada and Somanya. The Ga and Adangbe have practically identical languages, and they share several customs, such as ritual circumcision and a defined order of child-naming, though over the centuries they have adopted a great many customs from the neighbouring Akan. Like the Ewe, the Ga-Adangbe are originally from eastern Nigeria, and it is more than probable that the Ga had settled the Accra area and gelled into a cohesive state by the time the Portuguese arrived.

The most significant population group in modern Ghana, territorially and numerically, is the Akan (see box on *The Akan*, page 28). The Akan comprise more than half the country's population and inhabit five of its ten administrative regions: Western, Central, Eastern, Ashanti and Brong-Ahafo. Although every Akan village has its own chief, political centralisation into larger kingdoms has been a recurrent feature of Akan history, from the 14th-century Bono Kingdom of Techiman to more recent entities such as Denkyira, Ashanti, and Fante. Superficially, oral traditions relating to the origin of the Akan vary greatly from one society to another, but in essence they tend to run along one of two basic themes: a migration from somewhere further north, or a sudden emergence from the sky or a hole in the ground or somewhere equally improbable. There does, however, appear to be a reasonable degree of consensus among historians that the Akan migrated to modern-day Ghana from the Sahel. Since most traditions claim Bono as the cradle of the Akan, and Bono was firmly established as a gold-mining and trading empire under King Akumfi Ameyaw I (1328–63), any migration must have occurred before the end of the 13th century. On this evidence, it seems reasonable to assume that the Akan migrated to their modern territory as a result of the dissolution of Ancient Ghana. It strikes me that those Akan societies lacking a migration tradition could be older groupings that adopted Akan culture either through long periods of association with, or colonisation by, one of the larger Akan empires.

THE GOLD COAST 1471–1665 In 1415, Portugal captured the Moroccan port of Ceuta, one first small step in an era of naval exploration that would result in the circumnavigation of Africa before the end of the 15th century. The motives that lay behind the Portuguese crown backing such a venture were manifold. Portugal believed that by sailing south around Africa they would be able to wrest control of the lucrative eastern spice trade and, although the Portuguese had no idea just how large an obstacle Africa would prove to be, they were ultimately correct in this. Religion, too, was an important factor, in that the Portuguese crown was eager to forge links with the Christian kingdom of Prester John (a legend referred to in many medieval writings, probably based on rumours emanating from Christian Ethiopia) and to spread Christianity to areas lying beyond the Islamic lands north of the Sahara. Finally, through having a foothold in Morocco, Portugal was keenly aware of the quantity of gold being transported across the Sahara, and recognised that finding a sea route to the source of the gold would be a more realistic goal than trying to take direct control of the Arabic caravan routes through the Sahara.

9

In 1471, the Portuguese arrived at the village that was subsequently named Elmina, after the Portuguese *De Costa da el Mina de Ouro* – 'the Coast of Gold Mines' (a phrase that would also give rise to the moniker 'Gold Coast') – and entered into trade with a powerful chief whose name is recorded as Caramansa. Eleven years later, with a written lease from Caramansa, the Portuguese built the castle of St George on a rocky outcrop next to Elmina. Architecturally reminiscent of the castles built by the Crusaders, St George was separated from the village by a dry moat and its strongest bastion faced inland, suggesting that the Portuguese perceived their greatest threat of attack to come not from the sea, but from the interior. St George was the first of several forts and lodges established by the Portuguese – in 1515 and 1523, respectively, they built forts at Axim and Shama, close to the mouths of the rivers Ankobra and Pra (both of which flowed from parts of the interior rich in gold), and later in the 16th century they constructed a short-lived trading lodge in what is now downtown Accra.

Elmina, however, was to remain the centre of the Portuguese gold trade throughout their 150-year tenure on the Gold Coast. The fact that Portugal found such bountiful gold at Elmina was no mere coincidence. On the contrary, Elmina's importance as a salt-production centre gave Portugal effortless access to a trade route established at least a century before its arrival, connecting Elmina to the Akan gold mines near what are now Tarkwa and Obuasi via the Empire of Eguafo. Gold was far and away the most important export from the west African coast at this time – £100,000 worth annually throughout the 16th century, or roughly 10% of the world supply – but surviving Portuguese ledgers show that there was also a thriving trade in ivory, cotton, and animal hides, while major imports included metal pots and bowls, beads, leatherware, alcoholic spirits and guns. Odd as it may seem with hindsight, the Portuguese also imported to Elmina a quantity of slaves, captured or bought in Benin during the period 1486 to 1506, and at São Tomé after 1506.

Some readers may wonder why Ghana (as opposed to, say, Senegal or Liberia) became the centre of European activities in west Africa. First and foremost, this is because Ghana is the only west African country with a coast that lies close to significant gold deposits. But this alone doesn't really explain why all but two of the roughly 60 forts and trading lodges built on the Gulf of Guinea were sited in what is now Ghana – especially as many of these forts were built to service the slave trade rather than the gold trade. Just as important as the presence of gold inland was the physical nature of the Gold Coast. Studded with large rocky outcrops rather than mangrove swamps and sprawling shallow lagoons, Ghana boasts a great many good natural harbours, easily approached by ship, but also easily guarded and protected, with ample local material for constructing fortified buildings.

It is also interesting to note that Portugal's tenure on the Gold Coast was in no respect colonialism as we think of it today. The Portuguese had no jurisdiction beyond their forts, which were built with the permission of the local chiefs on land that was formally leased for the purpose. The Portuguese did make a concerted effort to spread Christianity, but even this was restricted to the immediate vicinity of the forts. They made no serious attempt to venture inland, nor to capture the Akan gold mines, but instead traded with the local chiefs and merchants on an even footing. And, it should be noted, what is true of Portugal is largely true of the European powers that followed. The arrival of the Portuguese ushered in an era of trade that lasted more than three centuries. Only when describing events from the mid 19th century onwards is it valid to talk in terms of colonists.

The level of Portuguese trade out of the Gold Coast had probably peaked as early as 1530, its decline thereafter a result largely of the increasingly widespread Portuguese global 'empire' that spread from Goa, Malindi and Mozambique in the Indian Ocean to South America and the Caribbean. Nevertheless, Portuguese dominance of the Gold Coast was not substantially threatened in the 16th century, although it did not go entirely unchallenged. The first English ships reached the west coast of Africa in roughly 1530, and in 1542 a French ship landed at Dixcove, where it purchased 28kg of gold. From the 1550s, non-Portuguese ships were an increasingly common sight off the coast – in 1553, Captain Thomas Wyndham returned with a stash of gold that he sold for £10,000, and a few years later the coast was visited by Francis Drake as part of his successful attempt to circumnavigate the globe. The Dutch, by comparison, were latecomers, and when their first ship did arrive on the Gold Coast, blown off course *en route* to Brazil in 1593, its captain was imprisoned – though he still managed to return home with a healthy amount of gold.

That the Dutch were the first to seriously challenge Portugal's monopoly on the Gold Coast is often attributed to the tension that already existed between these two countries in Europe. In reality, economics was probably the greater factor. The first Dutch attack on Elmina was an unsuccessful naval bombardment in 1596. From that time on, between 10 and 20 privately owned Dutch ships visited the Gold Coast annually. The Portuguese responded to this influx of new traders first by attacking Dutch ships whenever possible, and secondly by punishing brutally any African caught dealing with a rival European power. The offender's ears would be cut off for a first infringement; a second offence was rewarded with execution. Possibly as a result of this cruel policy, the chief of the Asubu sent two ambassadors to Holland requesting that a fort be erected at his capital 20km east of Elmina at Moree. In 1612, the Dutch did just this, shipping skilled artisans and the requisite materials direct from Holland so that the fort would be built too quickly for the Portuguese to mount an attack during its construction.

With a secure foothold at Moree, the Dutch were positioned to mount a concerted attack on Portugal's Gold Coast possessions, especially after 1621, when the powerfully backed West India Company (WIC) was formed in Amsterdam. By 1622, some 40 Dutch ships were assigned to the Gold Coast trade. Then, in 1630, what was in effect a Dutch navy took to the Atlantic, capturing several Portuguese possessions in the West Indies and Brazil before turning its attention on the west African coast. After an aborted naval attack, Elmina fell in 1637, bombarded from the nearest hill. Shama followed in the same year, and Axim was captured by Dutch boats in 1642, effectively ending Portugal's influence in this part of the world (though Portugal would remain a major player for centuries to come in the Indian Ocean and on the coast of what is now Angola).

The Dutch capture of Portugal's Gold Coast possessions signalled the beginning of a period of intense rivalry for dominance between several European powers, some of which had little lasting impact on what is now Ghana. The Swedes, for instance, occupied Fort Carolusbourg, which they built at Cape Coast in 1653, for a mere 11 years. The Brandenburgers built Fort Gross Friedrichsburg at Pokesu (Prince's Town) in 1683, only to vacate it in 1717. Even the French, later to become so powerful in west Africa, had little influence on the Gold Coast, never occupying any one place for longer than a decade.

A more important rival to Dutch dominance was Denmark, though on the whole the Dutch tolerated the Danish presence in a tacit alliance against stronger powers. Aside from their rather obscure outpost at Keta, the Danes restricted their activities on the Gold Coast to Osu in modern-day Accra. The Danish castle at Osu grew to be one of the most impressive on the Gold Coast, and the Danes occupied it almost continuously from 1642 to 1850, when it was sold to Britain. The most significant interruption in the Danish occupation of Osu occurred in 1681–83, when the castle was captured and occupied by Portugal; part of a rather desperate last bid at recapturing some of the Gold Coast trade.

The first British 'West Africa Company', formed in 1618, met with little success – its efforts at occupying the Gold Coast climaxed in 1640 with the construction at Cormantin of a small trading lodge that burnt down shortly after it was built, possibly with the assistance of a Dutch saboteur. More successful was the snappily titled 'Company of Royal Adventurers of English Trading to Africa', established in 1660 with a royal charter and the hearty backing of the Duke of York (later King James II, and – take note, trivia lovers – rewarded for his efforts in backing the 'Adventurers' by being not only the James of Accra's James Town, but the York of the USA's New York, known as New Amsterdam until it was captured from the Dutch by his charges).

In 1665, the British company launched a concerted attack on Holland's west African possessions, capturing the forts at Takoradi, Shama, Moree and Anomabu, as well as Fort Carolusbourg at Cape Coast, which the Dutch had occupied since 1664. The British company was unable to hold on to all of its newly captured forts, so it concentrated its efforts on ensuring that Fort Carolusbourg was impregnable, converting the modest fort into a castle covering roughly three-quarters of the area it does today. The British company had its foothold on the Gold Coast, one that was strengthened with its transformation to the wealthily backed Royal Africa Company in 1672, and by the end of the century Britain had become, if anything, more economically powerful than its more established rival. The reason for this is perfectly simple: instead of trading in gold, Britain decided to enter an altogether more lucrative arena of trade. The British capture of Cape Coast in 1665 can be seen as the critical point in the process that would, by 1700, cause a Dutch official to bemoan that 'the Gold Coast had changed into a virtual Slave Coast'.

THE SLAVE COAST 1665–1807 However convenient it might be to see the trade in slaves as an abomination introduced to Africa by Europeans, there is no escaping the reality that a slave trade was in existence from the very earliest days of the trans-Sahara caravans, when people captured in the sub-Sahelian region were transported across the desert to be sold into domestic bondage in north Africa and parts of Europe. Nor can it be denied that a slave class has formed a part of practically every centralised African society on record, at least until modern times. And, while it is true that, in many past African societies, slaves have had the opportunity to climb the social ladder, it is also true that in many such societies slaves were treated as sub-human, and cruelly sacrificed to mark special occasions or entreat deities.

None of which makes Africa in any way unusual, since slavery in name or in kind has been a feature of most ancient societies until this century. It is merely worth noting that the slave trade out of the Gold Coast emerged in an environment where not only slavery but also trading in slaves were established practices, just as it should be noted that the Europeans who conducted this trade came from societies where it was customary to hold public executions for crimes as paltry as stock theft, and to burn alive witches and other perceived heretics on a stake. Viewed from the lofty moral heights of the early 21st century, there is a certain uncomfortable irony in the realisation that the very earliest form of slave trade entered into by Europeans on the Gold Coast involved not the export of slaves, but their import, as captives bought by Portuguese merchants from African sellers in Benin were sold to African buyers in Elmina.

Nevertheless, the trans-Atlantic slave trade is a singular event in human history, not simply because it operated on an unprecedented scale, but also because it was so ruthlessly well organised, and so shattering and wide-ranging in its effects. Before the arrival of Europeans, slaves were generally incidental captives of inter-tribal war, relatively few in number, and in most cases able to integrate themselves into the society that enslaved them. By the time the trans-Atlantic slave trade hit its peak, it would be an understatement to say that the capture of slaves had been transformed into the *raison d'être* for war; closer to the mark, perhaps, to say that the entire west African interior had deteriorated into a hunting ground wherein slave raiders with firearms attacked village after comparatively defenceless village, trading their booty at the coastal forts for yet more firepower. It is estimated that between 12 and 20 million Africans were transported across the Atlantic between the late 17th century and early 19th, a five-week trip in conditions so cramped and unhygienic that it was not unusual for a boat to lose half its human cargo in passage. It is impossible to tell how many more people – those who were too young or too old or too weak to be saleable – died in the course of the raids.

Most of us are familiar with the fate of the victims of these raids. Rather less well documented is the devastating effect that the slave trade had on African society. It has been noted, for instance, that many traditional industries were lost to the Gold Coast interior – iron-smelting and gold-mining are good examples – as the product of these industries became increasingly worthless by comparison with slaves, and their practitioners were taken in to bondage. Worse still was the arms race that built up between neighbouring groups, as, in the 17th century, Britain alone supplied around 100,000 guns annually to west Africa – and it is not difficult to see how this situation forced even the most unwilling of chiefs into finding slaves to trade for the firearms they needed to protect themselves. For two centuries, Africa lost a high proportion of its most able-bodied men and women to the slave trade. In return, it received items that were, at best, of no lasting value – alcoholic spirits and tobacco – and at worst entirely destructive.

In the 16th and 17th centuries, the Gold Coast was spared the worst of this. Both Portugal and, later, Holland made it policy not to buy slaves at the Gold Coast – not for any moral reason, but because they believed (correctly, as it turned out) that the slave trade would interfere with the gold trade. Instead, they concentrated their slaving efforts further south, along the stretch of coast between modern-day Nigeria and Angola. This was to change towards the end of the 17th century, firstly, because the recently arrived British had difficulty breaking into the Dutch-controlled gold trade, and, secondly, as a result of the rise of the Akwamu Empire, which at its peak controlled a 350km stretch of coast east of Accra crossing into what is now Togo, but at no point had access to the gold mines at Akan. The British and, to a lesser extent, the Danes started trading in slaves from around 1665, a situation that was rapidly exploited by the Akwamu, and the floodgates were opened in 1698, when the Royal African Company (RAC) forsook its monopoly on British trade, allowing any British boat to trade freely, provided a 10% custom was paid to the company. This policy was a failure in so far as few of the so-called 'ten-percenters' actually paid the required levy, but it did ensure that the market for slaves expanded exponentially from 1698 onwards, with Anomabu in particular becoming a major centre for 'free trade'.

In the late 17th century, two empires dominated the interior immediately north of the coast. These were Akwamu, already mentioned above, and a much older Akan empire called Denkyira, the region's main repository of gold-working skills and the centre of the gold trade to the coast. In 1701, Denkyira was conquered by the recently established Ashanti Empire of Kumasi, creating what was perhaps the most radical power shift in the Ghanaian interior since Portugal had first arrived at the coast. One result of Denkyira's defeat was that the lease papers for Elmina Castle passed into the hands of the Ashanti, who were far more interested in empire-building and trading slaves for guns than they were in such pastoral pursuits as scratching around for gold. Another was that the flow of gold to the coast, already stemmed by the emergent slave trade, dried up to such an extent that, in 1703, the governor of Elmina formally requested that Amsterdam allow him to abandon the gold trade in favour of slaves.

The threat posed by the rampant Ashanti, whose king was courted by both the major European powers almost as soon as he conquered Denkyira, appears to have been pivotal in the expansion of the Fante state in the early 18th century. Based in the area around Mankessim and Anomabu, the Fante were, in 1700, the most powerful and wealthy of perhaps 20 small Akan kingdoms running along the coast west of Accra, all of which were linked by a common culture and used to having a degree of control over trade with the Dutch and English, both of whose headquarters lay in this part of the country. Between 1707 and 1720, the Fante gradually exerted control over all these groups, including the Oguaa of Cape Coast and Edina of Elmina, using a combination of force and coercion as it became obvious to all that unity was their best weapon against an Ashanti attack. Ashanti, meanwhile, grew in power with almost every passing year, capturing Akwamu in 1730, Brong-Ahafo in 1744–45, and much of what are now Burkina Faso and the northern regions of Ghana in 1745–50. By the end of this period of expansion, Ashanti was probably bigger than Ghana is today, and, along with Fante, it was by far the most dominant power in what is now Ghana. Unexpectedly, perhaps, the two empires maintained a relatively peaceful co-existence, motivated partly by the recognition that a tacit alliance was the best way to exclude other kingdoms from the lucrative coastal trade, but also enforced to a degree by the British and Dutch, on whom they relied for weapons.

The slave trade out of the Gold Coast continued unabated throughout the 18th century. Roughly 5,000 slaves passed annually through each of the main British trading posts, Cape Coast and Anomabu, and were stored in cold, dark dungeons that are chilling to visit today. The Dutch tried in vain to revive the flagging gold trade in 1702 by building a new fort they named 'Good Hope' at Senya Beraku; ten years later, the fort was extended to include slave dungeons. Ashanti prospered, as Kumasi lay at the heart of all three major trade routes to the coast west of Accra; and, although it was forbidden for an Ashanti to enslave another Ashanti, their frequent military expeditions and slave raids ensured the flow of human cargo to the coast never abated.

As the 18th century drew to a close, the anti-slave lobby became an increasingly powerful voice in Europe, a result not only of the strengthening liberal attitudes that emerged following the industrial revolution, but also of a greater public awareness as to how the slave trade actually operated, following several publications on the subject. In 1804, Denmark abolished the slave trade, followed by Britain in 1807, the USA in 1808, and Holland, France, Portugal and Spain between 1814 and 1817. Also in 1817, several of the above nations signed a Reciprocal Search Treaty, which in effect allowed Britain to search boats captained by people of other nationalities. The slave trade was subdued by this, but it was by no means halted – it became common practice among slavers to throw all their human cargo overboard at the approach of a British naval patrol. Britain soon recognised that it would take nothing less than the abolition of slavery to end the trade, and it banned slavery throughout its colonies in 1833, followed by France in 1848, the USA in 1865 (after a bloody civil war dominated by the issue), and, finally, Brazil in 1888.

THE BUILD-UP TO COLONIALISM 1806–1902 By 1800, Britain was the major European trading power on the Gold Coast and, although the Danes were to retain a presence there until 1850, and the Dutch until 1872, developments in the 19th century, in hindsight though perhaps not at the time, show a clear trend towards British colonisation. So far as the interior was concerned, a clear pattern had emerged by 1800 wherein various Fante chieftaincies acted as middlemen between the Ashanti and British traders. This arrangement suited the British, who believed that if Ashanti were to take full control of the interior it would be able to dictate terms of trade to Britain. It suited the Fante too, since without the tacit backing of Britain they would never have had the military prowess to resist an Ashanti invasion. The arrangement was, however, less agreeable to the Ashanti, who lost out substantially by having to deal through the Fante. Nevertheless, a few minor skirmishes aside, Fante and Ashanti had a reasonably healthy relationship in the second half of the 18th century, several times combining forces against upstart states to ensure they retained their joint trade monopoly.

The relationship between the European occupants of the forts and the surrounding chieftaincies changed little in essence between the construction of St George in 1482 and 1820. Theirs was a commercial not a colonial relationship: European control barely extended beyond the forts, and even those chieftaincies closest to the forts remained autonomous political units, though inevitably they were offered a degree of protection by their well-armed European neighbours. This long-standing balance was to waver in the first decade of the 19th century, partly as a result of Britain's wish to curb the slave trade at its Ashanti roots from 1807 onwards, no less because of escalating tension between Fante and Ashanti following a military skirmish between these states in 1806.

There are two main reasons why the Ashanti attacked Fante in 1806. The first is that Fante, always more a federation of disparate states than a cohesive empire, had been weakened by internal disputes, such as the wars between Oguaa and Komenda in 1788, Anomabu and Mankessim in 1789, Oguaa and Anomabu in 1802, and Komenda and Shama in 1805. The second was the escalation of a long-standing dispute over trade with Elmina Castle. Ashanti had held the lease to the castle since 1701, for which reason they believed they had the right to trade with its Dutch occupants directly, but the Fante regularly blocked Ashanti access to Elmina in the late 18th century, and even attacked the town on a number of occasions. The above points noted, it was inevitable that sooner or later the vast Ashanti empire would decide to take direct control of the coast, and the remarkable thing is that they waited so long to try.

Between 1806 and 1874, there were nine military clashes between Ashanti and Fante, and three more were averted at the last moment. Up until 1820, these clashes were wholly internal affairs, resulting in one or other of the two dozen or so Fante states being conquered by Ashanti. The Fante, however, refused to recognise Ashanti's traditional rights of conquest, and tension between the two states meant that trade of all forms ground to a virtual halt. In this, the Fante were supported by the British, not only because Britain favoured dealing with several small competitive states over an Ashanti monolith, but also because it was eager to end the slave raids in which the Ashanti still indulged. To this end, the British parliament placed all the Gold Coast forts formerly run by its companies under Crown government in 1821. Three years later, Britain for the first time gave military support to the Fante, in a battle at the Adaamso River that ended in an Ashanti victory – one contemporary account claims that the wounded British governor was beheaded by his Ashanti counterpart, and that his head was taken to Kumasi as a trophy. In 1826, Britain and Ashanti clashed again at Akatamanso, to the north of Accra: a battle that ended in a resounding British victory. It would be three decades before another major clash took place between these powers.

By 1828, the British government was prepared to withdraw entirely from the Gold Coast, due to the high cost of maintaining the forts and the massive drop in trade following a decade of instability. In the end, however, it bowed to pressure from British merchants and the beleaguered Fante, selling the forts to a company called the London Committee of Merchants. In 1830, a new governor was installed, Gordon MacLean, who more than any other person would lay the foundation of future British rule. In 1831, MacLean pressed the humbled Ashanti into signing a tripartite treaty that required them to refrain from any further attacks on their southern neighbours. As a sign of good faith, the Ashanti left a large sum of gold with MacLean, to be returned after six years, as well as two Ashanti princes to be educated in Europe. Six years after the treaty was signed, MacLean returned the gold, and, in 1841, the princes went back to Kumasi in order to help establish a Methodist mission there, creating a new atmosphere of trust between Ashanti and the British. In addition to his role as peacemaker, MacLean made great efforts to end the slave trade; and he turned around the Gold Coast economy, ushering in a new era of 'legitimate trade' as the value of exports leapt by 275% during the first decade of his governorship, and imports by more than 300%. This remarkably successful administration ended in 1843, when the British government decided to claim back the Gold Coast forts and to install its own governor. Many of MacLean's achievements were formalised with the so-called 'Bond of 1844', a sort of proto-protectorateship over several Fante states, in exchange for which the chiefs had to pledge allegiance to the Queen of England and give up practices regarded to be barbaric, such as human sacrifices and panyarring (the seizure of a debtor's relatives, to be sold into slavery if the debt wasn't met within a specified period). MacLean himself died in 1847, and was buried in the courtyard of Cape Coast Castle. It is said that the chiefs of southern states mourned his passing for months afterwards.

The two decades that followed the MacLean administration were relatively uneventful. In 1850, the year in which the governances of Sierra Leone and the Gold Coast were finally separated, Britain bought the forts at Keta and Osu from Denmark. It is doubtful that the British saw much use for these forts at the time of their purchase, but didn't want them falling into French or Dutch hands, and perhaps hoped to have more success than Denmark in curbing the clandestine slave trade running out of Keta. (As it turned out, Osu Castle would become the seat of government in 1876, a position it has retained to this day.) In 1852, the British authorities introduced a poll tax system, which sparked a series of riots and battles (most famously, the violent Anglo-Krobo confrontation that took place on Krobo Mountain) without ever raising a great deal of revenue – it was abandoned in 1861.

The year 1863 saw renewed tension between the British and Ashanti, caused by the former's refusal to hand over refugees from Ashanti justice. In 1864, the two armies clashed once again. The battle went the way of the Ashanti, largely because so many British troops died in an outbreak of fever or dysentery brought on by unusually heavy rain. It also signalled the beginning of a rush of events that would conspire to make the period 1867–74 of unparalleled decisiveness in the history of the Gold Coast.

The rush started in 1867, when Britain and Holland arrived at the mutual conclusion that every aspect of their increasingly unprofitable administrations would be improved were Britain to control a continuous strip of coast east of Cape Coast, and the Dutch a strip of coast to the west of Elmina. The two countries signed the so-called 'Fort Exchange Treaty', much to the consternation of several Fante states, long allied to a nearby British fort and now suddenly forced to live alongside the Dutch, whom they regarded as foes due to their involvement with the Ashanti who still held the lease to Elmina fort. King Aggrey of Cape Coast led a protest against the treaty, and was arrested by the British and exiled to Sierra Leone. The arrest of Aggrey, along with widespread dissatisfaction with the new status quo, triggered the formation of the Fante Confederation. Founded at Mankessim in 1868, this was the first formal alliance incorporating all the Fante states from Axim to just east of Accra, and, although it was to prove short-lived, the movement had some success in preventing the Dutch from occupying forts they had traded with Britain. In 1871, Britain arrested the confederation leaders and imprisoned them for a month. In the following year, Holland finally limped away from the Gold Coast, selling its remaining possessions to Britain. In 1873, the Fante Confederation disbanded, having lost direction after the Dutch evacuation of the coast – and in any case riddled with leadership squabbles. By this stage, the British parliament was of the opinion that it would have to take one of two approaches to the governing of the increasingly fractious Gold Coast: in its own words, a 'very evil choice' between following the Dutch and withdrawing completely, or pursuing an active policy of territorial expansion and colonisation. On 24 July 1874, Britain formally declared the Gold Coast a Crown colony.

The withdrawal of Holland from Elmina proved to be the trigger of the notorious Anglo-Ashanti War of 1873–74. Fearing that Britain wouldn't honour the ancient lease, the Ashanti occupied Elmina in 1873. Britain responded with a naval bombardment that flattened the old town to the west of the castle, leaving around 20,000 people without a home. In 1874, British troops entered Ashanti for the first time, defeating its army at Bekwai and – after the Ashanti king refused to accept their initial terms of treaty – burning Kumasi to the ground. The treaty of Fomena, signed in Adanse towards the end of 1874, forced the Ashanti to renounce all claims on territories lying to the south of their core state, most of all Elmina. At the same time, several vassal states to the north (for instance Gonja, Bono and Dagomba) took advantage of the defeat to assert their independence from Ashanti, and so an empire that had once been larger than modern Ghana was reduced to an area similar in size to present-day Ashanti Region.

In its earliest incarnation, the Gold Coast colony was a fraction of the size of modern Ghana, with an identical coastline, but barely extending more than 50km inland. So it might have remained were it not for the so-called 'Scramble for Africa', initiated in the late 1870s when Belgium and France entered into a race for control of the Congo. By 1888, most of the modern states of Africa had more or less taken shape, though not Ghana, presumably because its most interesting asset, the Gold Coast, had been British long before the scramble started. By the 1890s, however, both France and Germany were eyeing the interior of what is now Ghana. As a result of this, Britain extended its borders to cover the whole of the modern Western and Central provinces in 1893, while the northern border was settled with France in 1898, and the eastern border with Germany agreed in 1899 (though the latter was to move further east exactly 20 years later, when the League of Nations divided German Togoland between Britain and France).

In the 1890s, Britain's attention turned once again to Ashanti, which it was desperate not to let fall into German or French hands. In 1891, British protectorateship was offered to Ashanti, and soundly rejected by the recently installed King Prempreh I. Britain decided it would have to install a British resident in Kumasi to prevent the French from doing the same, and so it was that, in 1896, a British military expedition (whose numbers, incidentally, included the future Lord Baden-Powell, just in case you ever wonder why the Scout movement regularly comes up as a topic of small talk with students in this part of the country!) entered Kumasi without firing a shot. Prempreh, along with many other members of the royal family, was arrested and imprisoned in Elmina Castle before being exiled to Sierra Leone, and, later, the Seychelles. Britain then demanded that the remaining Ashanti elders in Kumasi hand over the Golden Stool (not so much the symbol of the king as its embodiment, handed down from generation to generation), a request that had been anticipated to the extent that they had a fake stool ready to hand to Britain (the fake is now on display in the Prempreh II Museum in Kumasi).

In 1900, the Ashanti rose one last time against British colonisation in the war named after its main instigator, Yaa Asantewaa, the Queen Mother of Ejisu. After heavy loss of life on both sides, Ashanti was defeated again in 1901, and yet another contingent of dignitaries, Yaa Asantewaa among them, was imprisoned and exiled to the Seychelles. On 1 January 1902, Ashanti was formally annexed to the British Gold Coast colony, along with the territories that today make up Ghana's three northern regions.

GOLD COAST COLONY 1902–57 The Gold Coast, like most other British colonies in Africa, was run along the system of indirect rule, a sharp contrast to the French and Portuguese systems whereby African colonies were – in theory, if not in practice – run as an extension of the so-called 'mother' country. The basic principle underlying indirect rule, as patented by Lord Lugard, first in Uganda and later in Nigeria, was that traditional chiefs would continue to rule locally as before, but under the supervision of the colonial administration. The motivations for adopting this system were twofold. Firstly, Britain believed that the Gold Coast would be better served in the long run if it developed a system of government rooted in its own traditions rather than one imposed entirely from outside. More to the point, perhaps, the lack of funding and shortage of European manpower created by Britain's insistence that all colonies should be economically self-sufficient would have made it impossible for most colonial governors to rule in any other manner. Indirect rule was, in the words of eminent Ghanaian historian Albert Adu Boahen (1932–2006), 'in reality, the most indirect way of ruling directly'. It was also, doubtless, the cheapest.

The core problem with indirect rule as it was administered in the Gold Coast is that it undermined the very institution it was nominally designed to protect. A traditional chief in pre-colonial Ghana was not, as might be supposed, a hereditarily determined autocrat, but an appointee of the council of elders. And the elders who appointed a chief had not only a right to veto any ruling he made, but the customary right to remove him from the stool. Prior to the colonial era, then, the authority of the chief was rooted in the council of elders over whom he presided. Under Britain, the authority of the chief came from the colonial administration, a situation that was bound to become a problem the moment that the administration tried to enforce an unpopular ruling through the chief.

The first steps towards indirect rule took place in 1883, when all chiefs in the Gold Coast (then only a fraction of what is now Ghana) were required to apply for recognition by the colonial administration. The policy took a more formal shape with the formation of so-called 'Native Authorities', comprising a paramount chief and his main sub-chiefs; an institution that, to its credit, paved the way for the modern regional and district councils of Ghana. In reality, Britain often tried to appoint a chief who was wholly unacceptable to his subjects. The clearest example of this occurred in Ashanti, where King Prempreh I and many other important chiefs were held in exile from 1896 until 1924, while the British authorities attempted to gain recognition for a dummy king of their choosing. Even when Prempreh I was returned to the stool in 1926, it was as King of Kumasi rather than King of Ashanti. Only in 1935 did Britain come full circle and restore the Ashanti Confederacy Council that it had abolished following the Yaa Asantewaa War in 1901, at the same time allowing the recently enstooled King Prempreh II to assume his full traditional role.

Resistance to colonial rule emerged as early as 1897, when the Aboriginal Rights Protection Society successfully blocked a bill that would have made all physically unoccupied territory in the colony the property of the colonial administration. It appeared in a more orchestrated form in the wake of World War I with the formation of the National Congress of British West Africa (NCBWA) by the Gold Coast barrister, Casely Hayford. The formation of the NCBWA is widely seen as the beginning of a formal split between educated nationalists, who were excluded from government under the system of indirect rule, and the uneducated and generally conservative traditional chiefs who gained from it. The inaugural meeting of the NCBWA took place in Accra in 1920, bringing together a total of 20 nationalist delegates from the Gambia, Nigeria, Sierra Leone, and, of course, the Gold Coast. The delegates drew up a list of demands; notably, that the government should provide equal job opportunities for Africans and Europeans with equivalent qualifications, that at least half of the legislative council in all countries should be freely elected, and that the colonial administration should cease interfering in the selection and removal of traditional chiefs. An NCBWA delegation was sent to London to present these demands to the Colonial Secretary, but was refused an appointment. Nevertheless, a great many changes along the lines suggested by the organisation had been set in place by the time of Casely Hayford's death in 1930, by which time the organisation was close to disintegration.

It was World War II, however, that proved decisive in ending the colonial era in the Gold Coast as elsewhere in Africa. In the Gold Coast specifically, at least 65,000 African volunteers were shipped to fight in the European war (mostly in east Africa and Burma), where they were exposed on a daily basis to the democratic and anti-imperialistic ideals of the Allied Forces. The Atlantic Charter signed by Roosevelt and Churchill stated categorically that the signatories would 'respect the right of all peoples to choose the form of government under which they will live'. Churchill would later retract the statement insofar as colonies were concerned, but the American government affirmed that by 'all people', they meant *all* people. When these African servicemen returned home after the war, they had high hopes of benefiting from the democratic ideals for which they had been obliged to fight. Instead, in at least 50,000 cases in the Gold Coast alone, the ex-servicemen returned home to unemployment, not to say a capital city whose population had increased threefold as a result of short-lived employment opportunities created by the European war.

In the Gold Coast more than any other British colony, the immediate post-war period saw events move with remarkable speed and purpose. In 1946, Governor Burns responded to the mood of the time with a new constitution that allowed 18 of the 30 seats in the colony's Legislative Council to be elected, 13 by the Provincial Council of Chiefs of the southern Regions and Ashanti, and five by the small number of registered African voters in Accra, Cape Coast, and Sekondi. In 1947, the United Gold Coast Convention (UGCC), formed by Dr J B Danquah, demanded 'self-government within the shortest possible time' and objected to the new constitution on the valid grounds that the Provisional Council of Chiefs was seen as a stooge organisation by most commoners, that the electoral roll in the above-mentioned cities was laughably unrepresentative, and that the Northern Region had no vote at all. November 1947 saw the return from 12 years in the USA and UK of the nationalist and pan-Africanist Dr Kwame Nkrumah, invited home by Danquah to act as Secretary General to the UGCC.

On 28 February 1948, colonial officers opened fire on a peaceful march organised by ex-servicemen to deliver a petition to the governor. Three marchers were killed, including the leader of the ex-servicemen, and another 12 died in the rioting that followed. This event proved decisive in the history of modern Africa. The Gold Coast was Britain's 'model colony', the most prosperous, educated, and organised of them all, and the administration reasoned that if this could happen in the Gold Coast, then colonialism in Africa was surely doomed. Even before 28 February 1948, Britain had generally seen self-government as the end goal for its colonies, but it had been thinking ahead to a time decades, perhaps even centuries away. After 28 February, that time span changed to one of years.

In the short term, however, the colonial administration put the UGCC leadership in jail, hoping that would help quieten things down. On his release in July 1949, Nkrumah formed the new and more radical Convention People's Party (CPP) – motto, 'self government now'! – and set about organising a series of strikes and boycotts that peaked in January 1950, with the aim of making the colony ungovernable. Nkrumah was once again thrown in jail, but the colonial administration backed down by installing a new constitution that allowed 36 seats in the government to be elected by the African population. In the 1951 election, the CPP won 33 of the seats, and Nkrumah was released to enter government. In March 1952, Nkrumah became the Gold Coast's first African prime minister. He then set about writing a new constitution that gave the Gold Coast virtual self-government after the 1954 election, in which the CPP won 79 out of 104 seats. Nkrumah then lobbied for full independence from Britain, but this was held up while the UN resolved the so-called 'Ewe Question' (a legacy of the split of the Ewe homeland when the former German Togoland was divided between Britain and France by the League of Nations in 1919) with a referendum that went in favour of the British section becoming part of independent Ghana. In the election of July 1956, the CPP won 74 out of 104 seats on a pro-independence ticket. Britain had no choice but to acquiesce to popular demand, and so, on 6 March 1957, the former Gold Coast colony became independent Ghana. It was the first African colony to be granted independence in the post-war era, and its name was adopted from the most ancient of west African empires; in the words of Nkrumah, 'as an inspiration for the future'.

GHANA 1957–81 Ghana's pioneering status as the first independent former colony in Africa is pivotal to understanding much of what occurred in the country under Nkrumah, who evidently perceived himself as a spokesman not merely for his country, but for the far broader goal of liberating Africa from colonial rule. It is for this reason that the grassroots development of agriculture and the mining era were often ignored in favour of frittering away the country's financial reserves on a variety of grand schemes and empty gestures. Nkrumah's role as an African statesman cannot be denied – he was, for instance, the prime mover behind the formation of the Organisation of African Unity (OAU) in 1963, and he frequently gave generous financial support to other newly independent countries. But nor can one ignore a level of economic mismanagement and wastefulness that resulted in Ghana having accumulated a foreign debt of US$1 billion by 1966, despite having had foreign reserves ten times greater than its foreign debt at the time of independence. Characteristic of the Nkrumah era was the construction of an enormously expensive OAU Headquarters in Accra, one that was never to be used after the OAU decided to base itself in Ethiopia instead.

The Nkrumah government did have several far-reaching successes, eg: the vast improvement in the country's transport network between 1957 and 1966 – notably the laying of the 'new' Kumasi–Tamale road and surfacing of several other major trunk routes, and the construction of Akosombo Dam and a deepwater harbour at Tema. Another success was the expansion of an education system that already ranked among the best in Africa, resulting in a fivefold to twentyfold increase in enrolment at every level from primary school to university. And if Nkrumah's biggest failings were in the development of the crucial agricultural sector, then the 60% drop in the externally determined cocoa price during his rule must be cited as an important mitigating factor. It is also the case that post-independence Ghana was something of a victim of the cold war mentality – Nkrumah's espoused policy of African socialism, not to say his strong diplomatic ties with the Eastern Bloc, made him an increasingly unpopular figure in the West, so that many Western governments were unwilling to provide Ghana with the support they might otherwise have given.

On the political front, the Nkrumah regime followed a path that, in hindsight, feels naggingly familiar. In July 1958, the Preventative Detention Act was passed in response to the formation of the opposition United Party under the leadership of Dr Kofi Busia, allowing for the detention without trial of perceived political opponents for a period of up to five years. In July 1960, following a national referendum, Ghana was decreed a republic with Nkrumah elected as executive president. Shortly after the presidential election, Nkrumah's main opponent for the presidency, J B Danquah, was placed in detention, where he would eventually die, as would another former ally of Nkrumah's, Obetsebi Lamptey. It is estimated that, by this time, the jails of Ghana held some 3,000 political detainees, a number that would increase dramatically following the attempted assassination of the president in 1962. It was this harsh repression of criticism, combined with the elevated status given to the Presidential Guard of the normal military, that would result in Nkrumah's downfall. On 24 February 1966, while the president was away in Hanoi, control of the country was assumed by the military. Nkrumah never returned home, and he died of cancer in exile in 1972.

Between 1966 and 1969, Ghana was ruled by the military National Liberation Council under the leadership first of Lieutenant General Joseph Ankra, and later (and more briefly) Brigadier Akwasi Afrifa. This regime did much to restore democracy by releasing all political detainees and allowing a reasonable degree of free speech and a free press. It also restored Ghana's credibility in the West by breaking ties with the Eastern Bloc and initiating a widespread policy of privatisation. In May 1969, in line with a freshly drawn-up Bill of Rights, political parties were legalised. The election held a few months later was won by the Progress Party (PP) under Dr Kofi Busia, recently returned to the country after having fled to exile in 1959.

Busia's most notable contribution to the country was a remarkable drive towards rural improvement, eg: by building several new clinics and hospitals, drilling boreholes, and installing electricity in many places. By and large, the Busia regime maintained a policy of free speech and a free press, but these democratic ideals were undermined somewhat by their inconsistent application – at one point, for instance, Busia made it a criminal offence to mention Nkrumah by name, a response to the increasing lionisation of the former president. Busia's biggest failings were on the economic front and, although much of this can be blamed on a legacy of mismanagement left by former regimes, it would be an economic decision – the devaluation of the cedi by 44% – that triggered the coup which removed him from power on 13 January 1972.

The six-year presidency of General Ignatius Acheampong started out well enough, but all the initial grand talk of economic self-reliance and democracy soon deteriorated into a more familiar scenario. Acheampong's gross economic mismanagement and stubborn refusal to take advice regarding the freeing of the exchange rate resulted in an annual inflation rate of 130%, prompting an economic collapse that was exacerbated by two severe droughts during the early years of the regime. The repression of political activity continued with the mass detention of perceived political opponents. Meanwhile, the national coffers were drained by the regime, nepotism was rampant, and the level of corruption soared so high it caused one prominent Ghanaian to coin the term 'kleptocracy' – rule by thieves. Amid an increasing level of civil unrest and widespread cries for a return to civilian rule, the military sacked Acheampong in 1978, and installed in his place

Lieutenant General Akuffo. The ensuing months saw the unveiling of a new constitution, as well as a lift on the six-year-old ban on political parties, and an election date was set for 1979.

On 4 June 1979, exactly two weeks before the scheduled election date, power was seized in a coup led by Flight Lieutenant Jerry Rawlings, a 32-year-old Ghanaian of mixed Scottish descent. Rawlings vowed that the election would go ahead, but that before power was transferred to the victor it was essential to purge corruption from the military and civil service. In the bout of bloodletting that followed, a great many civil servants were removed from office, tax offenders were forced to pay their debts, and several high-ranking members of the military were executed publicly by firing squad, among them three former heads of state: Afrifa, Acheampong, and Akuffo. Remarkably, on 24 September, a week ahead of schedule, civilian rule was restored when Rawlings handed power to the newly elected People's National Party under President Hilla Limann. The initial popularity of this government, however, was soon offset by the country's continued economic slide, and within a year the new government had become as corrupt as any before it.

GHANA: THE RAWLINGS YEARS AND BEYOND 1982–2001 On 31 December 1981, Ghana suffered its fourth coup in 15 years, as power was seized once again by the popular figure of Jerry Rawlings. The constitution was abolished, parliament was dissolved, political parties were banned, and a number of prominent figures were jailed, President Limann among them. Rawlings installed a Provisional National Defence Council comprising three civilians and four military men, and at a local level he replaced councils with People's Defence Committees (later called Committees for the Defence of the Revolution). The next few years were marked by two clear trends. The first was unprecedented economic growth (a result of Rawlings's massive devaluation of the cedi), large-scale paring down of the civil service, privatisation of several state assets, and improved payments at the grassroots of the crucial cocoa industry. The second trend was one of repeated political instability, including several attempted coups and the unravelling of alleged assassination conspiracies against Rawlings, as well as a great many strikes and protests.

Things came to a head in 1989, when universities nationwide were closed for four months after protests and rioting, and Rawlings had introduced severe press restrictions. An attempted coup against the government was foiled in September, and, a few months later, one of its instigators was found hanged in his cell, prompting an international outcry led by Amnesty International as well as providing a rallying point for the many Ghanaians who wanted a return to civilian rule. In December 1990, Rawlings announced that a new constitution would be put in place within a year – it would, in fact, be enacted in April 1991, following a 92% approval among the 44% of the population who turned out for the national referendum. In May 1991, Rawlings endorsed the implementation of a multi-party system; the next month, he passed amnesty on all political detainees, and six opposition groups were granted legal status. The most important of these were Dr Limann's People's National Convention (PNC) and Dr Boahen's New Patriotic Party (NPP), while Rawlings announced that he would retire from the military as per the new constitution and stood as president for the National Democratic Congress (NDC).

The election was held in two phases. The presidential elections in November 1992 saw Rawlings poll a clear majority of 58%, almost twice as many votes as his closest rival Boahen, who polled 30%. The election was declared substantially free and fair, but this was contested by the NPP and PNC who decided to boycott the constituent elections held on 29 December 1992 in protest. As a result, the NDC took 189 out of a possible 200 seats, with only a 29% poll recorded.

Rawlings's years as an elected president saw many positive developments on the economic front, as well as an increased level of political freedom with the release of political detainees and the re-emergence of a free press. The government managed to weather two major storms during Rawlings's first term. The first of the crises to beset Ghana in recent years was an outbreak of ethnic violence in the northern regions, which originated from a land dispute between the Konkomba and Nunumba of the Bimbilla district in February 1994. Within months, the violence had spread to many parts of the north, leaving as many as 6,000 people dead and a further 100,000 displaced as 200 villages were razed. The second was an attempt to replace the existing sales tax with a new VAT system in February 1995, an unpopular decision that resulted in widespread rioting, the death of five people in Accra, and – eventually – the reinstatement of the familiar sales tax system. The above events notwithstanding, Rawlings was voted back into power in December 1996, defeating John Kufuor's New Patriotic Party (NPP) with a diminished, but still comfortable, majority of 133 seats.

Most observers agree that Ghana's days of coup and countercoup are long since gone, a view supported by the momentous election of December 2000, which ushered in the first transfer of power from one elected leader to another in Ghanaian history. It also marked the end of an era, as Rawlings stepped down after 18 years in power, having served his maximum of two presidential terms as stipulated in the 1991 constitution. In the first round of Ghana's Election 2000, neither of the two main parties seized enough seats to assume outright power, but in run-off elections that followed a few days later, John Kufuor, the leader of the former opposition NPP, defeated Rawlings's handpicked successor, Vice President John Atta Mills, by a substantial margin. Despite some fears to the contrary, the election took place in a peaceful atmosphere; both the result and the process by which it was obtained drew widespread international praise. Kufuor and Rawlings appeared together on television shortly after the election, to demonstrate their mutual commitment to smooth transition. 'We need to co-operate to find solutions to the economic problems that are going to beset this country for the next years to come,' Rawlings said generously. Kufuor's response was: 'We welcome very much your constructive criticism, because that is the essence of multi-party democracy.' Kufuor was re-elected as leader of the NPP in 2004, and the party won 128 out of 230 seats in election in the same year. The NDC won 94.

But Ghana does indeed face severe economic problems and one does not envy Kufuor the task that lies ahead. Despite boasting one of the highest growth rates in Africa throughout the 1990s, the country is in the midst of a currency crisis that saw the sudden but rapid devaluation of the cedi to the order of 200% against the US dollar during 2000. Although experts tie this crisis to a drop in international gold and cocoa prices, as well as the rise in international fuel prices, the reasons for the scale of devaluation are difficult to identify. According to government estimates, inflation in Ghana is around 10%, but local expatriates pin it at up to 27%. The truth is probably somewhere between the two, but the re-denomination of the currency in July 2007 – which involved dropping four zeros and reintroducing the pesewa (100th of a cedi) – is expected to bring it slightly lower.

The government has said it intends Ghana to be a 'first-world' country by 2020, but although these expectations are clearly misplaced, Ghana remains strikingly economically vibrant by comparison to most parts of Africa. With the co-operation of his predecessor, and in the sustained atmosphere of political freedom, stability and economic growth that has characterised Ghana in recent years, Kufuor has inherited the presidency of a country whose outlook is as bright as it has been at any time since independence.

MUSIC

West Africa is well known for its vibrant and largely self-contained music scene, and for many years Ghana was perhaps the leading innovator when it came to styles that combined traditional African sounds with foreign influences. More recently, Ghana has by and large relinquished its status as innovator to its francophone neighbours; nevertheless, a practically incessant backdrop of music remains a notable feature of travelling in urban parts of the country, and visitors will find themselves exposed to a rich variety of unfamiliar sounds.

The most popular music to have emerged out of Ghana is highlife, a term that covers a broad spectrum of homegrown styles fusing traditional percussive beats with various European, American, and even Caribbean influences. Highlife, developed in the 1920s along the ports of what was then the Gold Coast, was first recorded in the late 1930s, reaching a popular peak in the period 1950–70. Its leading practitioners included E T Mensah, the African Brothers International Band, and, more recently, Alex Konadu and Koo Mino's Adadam Band.

Less easy to hear are the myriad traditional musical styles that hark from all around the country, generally drum-based in the south, more reliant on fiddles and other string instruments in the far north. It is in the north, though, that you are most likely to hear the peculiar 'talking drum', an instrument associated with the Sahel, as well as colourfully robed ensembles of Dagomba drummers (one of which we encountered by chance at a funeral in Bolgatanga).

Within Ghana, locally recorded music is largely drowned out by a plethora of exotica, not only the familiar contemporary Western hits, but also vibrant guitar music from the Congo and other parts of francophone Africa, as well as reggae – the South African

ECONOMY

Ghana is a country of great mineral and natural wealth, for which reason it has been an important centre of trade since prehistoric times. Skipping briefly through subjects covered more fully in the above history section, Ghana is thought to have been the main west African producer of kola nuts (sharp tasting and mildly narcotic, favoured by Muslims who are forbidden from drinking alcohol, and available in any Ghanaian market today) prior to the 15th century, at which time it also supplied amounts of gold and salt to Islamic traders in the Sahelian region to its north. From 1471 until the late 17th century, the Gold Coast supplied roughly 10% of the world's gold, as the empires of the south entered into a maritime trade with Portuguese and, later, Dutch traders. From the late 17th until the early 19th century, this trade in gold and other natural assets was swamped by the nefarious trans-Atlantic slave trade, operated by British and Dutch traders out of the Gold Coast and by several other European powers elsewhere off the west coast of Africa.

The roots of the modern Ghanaian economy can be traced to Britain's attempts to re-establish what they termed 'legitimate trade' after the slave trade was legally abolished in 1807. The main problem facing Britain in this regard was that many traditional trade-related skills, such as gold-mining, were lost during the era when slaves were the main item in demand by European merchants. In any case, the powerful Ashanti empire of the interior had been built largely on the slave trade, so that it was in both their interest and that of many European merchants to continue operating a clandestine trade in slaves, one that continued out of the Gold Coast at least until Britain's first defeat of Ashanti in 1826.

The first important item of legitimate trade to emerge in the 19th century was palm oil, used for cooking and in the manufacture of detergents, and exported reggae singer Lucky Dube is quite possibly the most popular recording artist in the country. Traditional Ghanaian music is most likely to be encountered by chance, at a street funeral or similar public festival, though in the north you could ask whether there is a specific day when music will be performed for the chief. The Academy of African Music and Arts on Kokrobite Beach near Accra is regarded to be one of the best places in west Africa to hear and learn about traditional and contemporary Ghanaian music.

Cassettes of popular Ghanaian recording artists – admittedly not always of the highest quality sound-wise – can be bought for next to nothing in lorry parks and markets in most substantial towns. The selection can be daunting; perhaps the simplest way to go about choosing a few cassettes as mementos of your trip is to make a habit, when you hear something you like in a bar or on a *tro-tro*, of asking somebody what's playing.

The most useful practical handbook to exploring Ghanaian and other contemporary and traditional African music forms is the Rough Guide's comprehensive tome, *World Music*. In London, Stern's African Record Centre in Covent Garden (☎ +44 (0)20 7387 5550) boasts an extensive catalogue of African recordings. Good starting points include E T Mensah's *All for You*, effectively a 'greatest hits' package, and various artists' compilations (*Akomko*, *Giants of Dance Band Highlife*, *I've Found My Love* and *The Guitar and the Gun*), several of which are available on CD. For a broader overview of contemporary African music, try Stern's *Guide to Contemporary African Music*, or the informatively packaged three-CD compilation *Africa Never Stands Still*, also available through Stern's.

from the Gold Coast as of 1820. This was of necessity a small-scale trade harvested from wild palms (the oil palm still cannot be properly cultivated), but plantations were slowly established in many areas, notably in what is now the interior of Eastern Region, and the emergent industry had the important effect of restoring respectability to agriculture after a century in which cultivation had been seen by many Africans as work fit only for slaves. By 1850, palm oil was the principal export from the Gold Coast, and by the 1880s it accounted for almost 75% of export revenue raised by the recently established Gold Coast colony. At the peak of the palm-oil era in 1884, some 20,000 tonnes of pure oil and twice that of palm kernels were exported, mostly to Germany.

Two other relatively important crops that took hold in the 19th century were cotton and rubber. The former never became an export crop due to infestations of disease and insects, but the crop was generally adequate to supply local needs, sometimes with a bit to spare for export. Rubber trees, by contrast, had been grown and tapped in the forest zone since the 17th century, but it was only in the 1870s that rubber was cultivated on a large scale, when its global importance soared as a result of the invention of the pneumatic tyre. In 1880, the Gold Coast exported a mere 0.05 tonnes of rubber. By 1886, that figure had increased to 692 tonnes, and by the early 1890s rubber was a bigger earner than palm oil, and the Gold Coast had become the world's third largest supplier. In the early 1900s, however, the bottom fell out of the rubber market; prices slid, and the industry in the Gold Coast collapsed, never to recover.

Perhaps the pivotal moment in Ghana's future economic development came in 1879, when Tetteh Quarshie returned home to the Gold Coast from Fernando Po with a few cocoa seedlings that he planted in his garden in Mampong. The climate and soil of the Gold Coast proved ideal for growing cocoa, and the crop was exported from 1891. By the turn of the century, cocoa had replaced rubber as the colony's biggest earner of foreign revenue, and by 1935 the Gold Coast was supplying half the world's cocoa. Cocoa remains to this day Ghana's most important agricultural earner (though it lies second on the production table after neighbouring Côte d'Ivoire), and the failure of the annual crop due to disease has, along with the rise and drop of the internationally determined cocoa price, often had a major influence on the country's politics. This is largely because the cocoa industry still favoured the small-scale farmer – it has been estimated that in 1951 roughly 500,000 people were employed by the cocoa industry, or earned their primary income from cocoa production.

Much of Ghana's modern transport infrastructure dates to the colonial era, and there is little doubt that in this regard, if no other, Ghana was reasonably well served by its colonists, particularly by Gordon Guggisberg, the governor from 1919 to 1927. By the end of World War II, the Gold Coast had some 10,000km of roads (about one-third of the present road network), and all its present rail systems had been constructed – the Tarkwa–Sekondi line was completed as early as 1901 and extended to Kumasi in 1903, while the Accra–Kumasi line was finished in 1927. Under Guggisberg, the colonial administration provided a solution to the country's lack of a natural deepwater harbour with the construction of an artificial one at Takoradi in 1928. It was extended in 1956 as the colonial era drew to a close and is still the most important harbour in the country.

Two major engineering projects that were first mooted in the colonial era, but only brought to fruition later, largely at the instigation of Nkrumah, were the

TRADITIONAL FESTIVALS

A notable feature of Ghanaian society, and one that is of great interest to travellers, is the enormous number of local festivals that take place in various parts of the country throughout the year. Few travellers are likely to deliberately select the dates of their trip to Ghana to coincide with any one particular festival, but it's certainly worth taking note of any festivals that will take place while you are in Ghana and making the effort to be in the right place at the right time, bearing in mind that accommodation may be in relatively short supply in some areas during the most important festivals.

If you are visiting Ghana in early May, do try to get to Winneba for the first weekend of the month in time for the renowned Aboakyir deer-hunting festival, one of the most ancient in the country, described in detail in the section on Winneba (page 148).

Most other festivals in coastal parts of Ghana take place during the European autumn. The most important annual festival in Greater Accra region, celebrated in the capital as well as in other Ga towns such as Prampram, is Homowo, which literally means 'mocking hunger'. It takes place in August and September, the months that normally yield the largest harvest of fish and grain. A similar festival, called Damba, takes place in the Northern Region, centred around Tamale, during the same months.

The most important festival on the Fante calendar is the colourful Oguaa Fetu Afahye (the last word literally means 'adorning of new clothes'), on the first Saturday of September, when local chiefs and asafo companies dressed in full traditional regalia lead processions through the streets of Cape Coast.

The main festival in Anomabu is the five-day-long Bontungu, in which a variety of drumming and dancing rituals are held to bring God's blessing for the forthcoming year.

In Elmina, the Bakatue festival takes place a bit earlier in the year, on the first Tuesday of July, the beginning of a new fishing season. Characterised by a variety of processions and competitions, this festival is said to pre-date the arrival of the Portuguese at Elmina 500 years ago, making it one of the most ancient in Ghana.

development of Tema as a deepwater harbour close to Accra, and the linked construction of a dam on the Volta at Akosombo, the latter not only important to the transport network of the north and east, but also capable of producing enough electricity for the whole country, as well as for export to neighbouring countries.

Just as important to economic development as a healthy transport infrastructure is good education, and here again the colonial administration was unusually forward-looking, with primary school attendance reaching 300,000 by 1951, and secondary school attendance 7,700. By the time of independence, the Gold Coast had 29 teacher-training colleges as well as a highly regarded university and a number of trade colleges. The adult literacy rate at this time stood at roughly 25% – nothing to shout about by Western standards, perhaps, but remarkable by comparison with many other African countries at the end of the colonial era.

It is difficult to be so positive about the colonial administration's development of the mining industry – not because the colony's great mineral wealth was left unexploited, but because the industry was structured in such a manner that very little of the significant profit it raised would stay in the colony. Formal gold mining in the Gold Coast started at Tarkwa in 1877 and at Obuasi two years later, and it was also soon discovered that the colony had significant deposits of several other minerals, notably diamonds and manganese. By 1951, the year in which Nkrumah's CPP entered government, annual gold exports exceeded £8 million annually, with manganese and diamonds close behind at around £7 million and £6 million, respectively. For the sake of comparison, the value of cocoa exports in this

In Volta Region, the whole of September is given over to the Yam Festival, and two other important festivals take place during November. In Anloga, near Keta, on the first Saturday of the month, Hogbetsotso (pronounced Hobejojo) or the 'Exodus' Festival, commemorates the escape of the Ewe people from a tyrannical ruler in what is now Togo. It is marked by processions of traditionally dressed chiefs as well as lively drumming and dancing (note that a similar festival called the Godigbeza takes place in nearby Aflao every April). Later in November, the Agumatsa Waterfall Festival in Wli traditional area is also characterised by dancing, drumming and colourful costumes.

There is a small festival in Kumasi and other parts of Ashanti twice during each of the nine 42-day cycles, or *adae*, into which their annual calendar is divided. It is difficult to give dates for these, since they change from year to year (as astute mathematicians will realise, 9 × 42 does not equal 365), but basically the festival days fall on every sixth Sunday, and then the 17th day after that, always a Wednesday.

The most important annual festival in Ashanti is Odwira, a week-long affair that climaxes on Friday with a procession through town to the palace. The Odwira generally takes place during the ninth *adae* of the calendar, which falls in September. Among the most lively celebrations are those in Kumasi, Akwapim, Akrapong, Akuapem, and Akwamu. Visitors to northern Ghana might want to note the following festival dates:

22 January	Kpini Kyiu Festival	Wa
7 March	Kyiu Sung Festival	Upper East and West Regions
14 May	Don Festival	Wa, Bawku, Bolgatanga
11 June	Dzimbi Festival	Upper East and West Regions
1–12 November	Daa Festival	Tongo
9 November	Sabre Dance Festival	Lawra
15 November	Kobina Festival	Lawra
28 November	Boarim Festival	Tongo
1 December	Fao Festival	Navrongo

The most numerically significant of Ghana's four ethno-linguistic groupings, the Akans of the southern and central part of the country embrace several dozen culturally similar and historically allied peoples, the best known of whom are probably the Ashanti of the Kumasi area and the Fante of the central coast. Most travellers to Ghana will come into regular contact with several Akan cultural institutions, as the country's two main travel circuits pass almost exclusively through Akan territories. Even those who travel further afield – into the Ewe heartland of Volta Region, for instance – will soon recognise the Akan influence over the cultural and political organisation of many of their neighbours.

Every Akan village has its chief, whose position is not purely hereditary. Most, although generally of matrilineal aristocratic birth, are selected by a Council of Elders for their perceived capabilities and may be stripped of their powers if they do not perform satisfactorily or indulge in tyrannical behaviour. Practically throughout Ghana the power of the chief is denoted by his possession of the royal stool, which is typically made of wood and blackened after the death of the monarch (notable exceptions being the famous golden stool of Ashanti and the silver stool of Mampong). Akan chiefs are referred to as having been enstooled when they ascend to power and destooled should they lose that position. In many Akan territories, a traditional hierarchy of chiefs is maintained – the King of Ashanti, for instance, is considered paramount to the chiefs of such vassal states as Mampong and Jauben, who in turn preside over several small local chieftaincies. It is customary in Akan societies as well as in other parts of Ghana for visitors to a village to pay their respects to the chief, a custom that is still enforced in villages receiving few foreign visitors.

Most Akan societies show remarkably similar political structures. Every chief is served by a Council of Elders, a body to which he must refer all important matters and which has the power to destool him. Another very important figure is the queen mother, a misleading title since she will not necessarily be the mother of a queen, but serves as spiritual mother to the chief. She will work closely with the Council of Elders in selecting a new chief, will sit in on all council meetings, and preside over all births and menstruation rites. Other key figures include the Akyeame, the chief's official spokesman and carrier of a royal staff, and the Adontenhene, the leader of the main military body. Some Akan societies are divided into several asafo, military companies that play an important role in defence as well as in the arts (see box on *Posuban shrines*, page 144), and is one of the few Akan institutions to follow purely patrilineal lines of inheritance.

The basic unit of traditional Akan society is the extended family, an institution that is maintained along matrilineal lines, evidently on the basis that one can always be certain of the identity of a child's mother. In modern Ghana, patrilineal inheritance lines are now assuming greater importance, and (in urban areas particularly) the nuclear family is valued more highly by many than the extended one. Traditionally, the Akan regard every person to be comprised of three parts: blood, semen and soul. Blood, the most significant, is inherited from the mother as a signifier of family. Semen is the father's contribution, and determines personality and other individual attributes. The soul is believed to be the part of God that enters each child at birth.

year was a massive £60 million, and timber, the second most important agricultural export, stood at £5 million.

At the time of independence in 1957, Ghana had one of the strongest economies in Africa, with foreign revenue reserves ten times greater than the foreign debt. By 1966, the situation had practically reversed, with foreign debt in the region of US$1 billion. The reasons for Ghana's economic decline in the decades immediately following independence, and particularly between 1966 and 1981, are

Interestingly, the Akan regard a person's soul to be linked to the day of the week on which they were born. For this reason, most Ghanaians' first name is not a given name, but one determined by their day of birth. It is the child's second name that is chosen by the parents eight days after birth, and is normally that of a respected family member, in the belief that the child will have some of the attributes of the person after whom it has been named. Names associated with the day of birth are as follows:

Day	Male	Female
Sunday	Kwasi	Akosua, Asi, Ese
Monday	Kwadwo, Kojo	Adwoa, Ajao
Tuesday	Kwabena, Kobina	Abena, Araba
Wednesday	Kwaku	Akua
Thursday	Yao, Ekow	Yaa
Friday	Kofi	Afua, Afia, Efua
Saturday	Kwame, Kwamena	Ama

The religious beliefs of the Akan are too complex to do justice to here. Briefly, all Akan societies believe in one omnipotent God, but also pay homage to any number of minor local deities (some villages in Ghana have more than 70 local shrines, which may take the form of trees or rocks or any other natural feature) and like most African societies place high emphasis on the veneration of ancestors. Many Akan villages have a totem, often a particular type of animal that may not be killed or eaten by members of that village. Selection of the totem is often bound up in the oral history of that village. The people of Baobeng-Fiema, for instance, believe the sacred monkeys descend from villagers transformed into monkeys by the magical powers of a king who died before he could return them to human form.

At some point visitors are likely to encounter one of the most remarkable aspects of Akan society: its colourful and vibrant funerals. Unusually, Ghanaian societies tend to separate the burial ceremony from the actual funeral – generally by at least three months, but sometimes by as long as two years! At the risk of great oversimplification, burial is generally a quiet and dignified moment, though often preceded by wailing and singing, and is followed by at least nine days of quiet mourning and fasting by close relatives. The funeral itself was traditionally held on a Monday or Thursday several months after the person died, but is now most often held on a Saturday for pragmatic reasons. The general tone is one of celebration rather than mourning, marked by exuberant drumming and dancing, not to say heavy drinking – on attending a Ghanaian funeral, you can't help but feel that it displays an altogether more convincing belief in some sort of afterlife than its sombre Christian equivalent.

For a good overview of Akan culture, I recommend Peter Sarong's book *Ghana in Retrospect* (Ghana Publishing Company, 1974), which is readily available and inexpensive in most Accra bookshops.

clearly linked to the political instability of that era, though exacerbated by external factors such as the 60% drop in the cocoa price during the Nkrumah era. More important here and now is that Ghana has undergone more than a decade of substantial economic growth since productivity reached a post-independence nadir in the early 1980s. Many people – not just Ghanaians – regard the country to be the most promising economic prospect in Africa at the moment. Real gross domestic product (GDP) growth since 1984 has typically hovered at around 5%, and an ambitious plan for the next 25 years has set a goal of roughly 8% per annum.

Despite a marked increase in industrialisation in recent times, agriculture remains at the heart of the economy, contributing almost 50% of GDP and directly or indirectly supporting 80% of the population. Cocoa remains the most important crop in export terms and, although output dropped from over 500,000 tonnes annually in the early 1960s to 158,000 tonnes in 1983, it has recently risen back above the 300,000 tonne mark. Other important crops include cassava, plantains, coco yams, yams, maize, groundnuts, millet, rice, sorghum, and sugar cane.

In recent years, mining has become the most important source of foreign revenue: renewed development in the goldfields of the south means Ghana is now Africa's largest gold exporter after South Africa, with production rising from 17,000kg in 1990 to more than 35,000kg in recent years, while diamond exports have topped 700,000 carats annually since 1991. After gold and cocoa, tourism has recently risen to become the country's third largest earner of foreign revenue, generating an income of US$233 million in 1995 by comparison with US$19 million ten years earlier – an increase of greater than 1,000% in one decade!

LANGUAGE

English is the official national language, and it is widely spoken as a result of the country's long links with Britain and an unusually high standard of education from colonial times to the present day. A total of at least 46 African languages and 76 dialects are spoken in Ghana, generally divided into the Akan, Mole-Dagbani, Ewe and Ga language groups. Twi is the main Akan tongue, first language to roughly half the population, including both the Ashanti and Fante, and widely spoken elsewhere in central and southern parts of the country.

RELIGION

Freedom of religion is a constitutional right in Ghana and, while no official figures seem to be available, it is thought that about 60% of Ghanaians are Christian and at least 25% Muslim. Minority religions include Hinduism, Buddhism, Bahai, and various traditional faiths. Although Islam is a minority religion on a national level, it is the predominant faith in the north, having reached west Africa via the trans-Sahara trade routes as early as the 8th century AD. It has been practised in what is now northern Ghana for at least 500 years, probably longer.

Christianity dominates in the southern and central parts of the country. Catholicism was first introduced at the coast by the Portuguese in the late 15th century (the first public mass was said at Elmina in January 1482), but its influence dwindled after the Portuguese withdrew in 1637. Christianity in modern Ghana dates mostly to the latter half of the 19th century. Catholicism, now the most widespread and popular denomination, was reintroduced to the south with the establishment of a French mission at Elmina in 1880, and it arrived in the north in 1906, when the White Fathers opened a mission in Navrongo. The Presbyterian Church reached Ghana in 1828, with the foundation of a Swiss mission at Danish Osu Castle. After initial setbacks as several missionaries were claimed by malaria, Presbyterianism spread into much of what is now Eastern Region in the 1840s. The separate Evangelical Presbyterian Church, established by German missionaries in the 1850s, has had its stronghold in what is now Volta Region for almost 150 years. The Methodist Church, formerly the Wesleyan Mission, is almost as widespread as Catholicism – it was established around British castles in the 1830s and spread largely through the pioneering work of the Reverend Thomas Birch Freeman, who served in the Gold Coast and Ashanti from 1838 to 1890. In

RELIGIOUS SLOGANS

One of the more idiosyncratic ways in which Ghanaians like to demonstrate their faith is by naming their businesses after religious sayings. Cumulatively, it can start feeling like you are trapped in a world designed by an evangelical Hallmark copywriter, but their unintentional humour can also make for some light relief on long journeys. Here are some of the best:

- Innocent Blood Restaurant
- Holy Spirit in Charge Communication Centre
- Trust in God Hair Saloon
- Solace of My Desire Spot
- Jesus Loves Fashion
- Consuming Fire Fast Food
- Blood of Jesus Hair Care.

And a few non-religious ones for good measure:

- No Rush in Life Taxi Services
- Observers are Worried Chop Bar
- Fred's Tact Shop
- Let's All Crap for Jesus (I think they meant 'clap')
- No Condition is Permanent Vulcanising Service (for *Star Trek* cultists?)
- Snob Against Cornmill (eh?)
- Mary Immaculator Rewinding Service (double-eh?!).

addition to denominations familiar to most Europeans, a large number of American churches have been established in Ghana, most significantly the AME Zion Church, which spread out of Keta from 1896, as well as more recent ones. Roughly 60% of the present population of Ghana is Christian, though Christian slogans and music are so prevalent that you might easily think that should be 150%!

Despite Ghana being the most flagrantly Christian country that I've ever visited – exasperatingly so at times, at least for a crusty old rationalist such as myself – various traditional beliefs and customs have also retained an unusually high profile in the country. It's difficult to establish whether this is essentially a case of Christians and traditionalists existing alongside each other, or whether it's simply that a significant number of Ghanaians somehow manage to adhere to what appear to be two contradictory systems of belief. Either way, it makes for an interesting if occasionally bemusing cocktail of faiths to the outsider. 'To more religious visitors,' Bruce Billedeaux recommends that, 'visiting a local church service will be very rewarding, as the services have a great African feel.'

INTERCHANGE

Spirit of Ghana

- Tailor-made itineraries for independent travellers
- Flexible packages
- Special interest group tours (bring your own group looking at bird-watching, ancestry trail etc.)

For brochure and further information please call
020 8681 3612
or visit your local travel agent

INTERCHANGE (ESTD. 1973)
INTERCHANGE HOUSE
27 STAFFORD ROAD, CROYDON, SURREY CR0 4NG
Fax: 020 8760 0031
Email: interchange@interchangeworldwide.com
www.interchangeworldwide.com

AITO 2429

2

Natural History

GEOGRAPHY AND CLIMATE

GEOGRAPHY Ghana is, in essence, flat and low lying. Almost half of the country lies at an altitude of below 150m, and nowhere does it top an altitude of 1,000m. The far south of the country is dominated by the low-lying coastal plain that runs between 100km and 150km inland of the Atlantic coastline, except near Accra, where the Akwapim Mountains around Aburi rise from the coastal plain only 20km inland. At the heart of the country is the low-lying Volta Basin, Ghana's most important drainage system, stretching from around Tamale in the north to the Volta mouth at Ada. Much of it is now submerged in the 8,500km² Lake Volta, the world's largest artificial body of water.

The Volta Basin is flanked by mountains to the east and west. The eastern highlands, part of the Togo–Atakora range that stretches through to Benin, reach altitudes in excess of 900m near the Togolese border. The county's highest peak, Mount Afedjato, is part of this range. The highlands to the east and west of the Volta Basin are characterised by a high number of waterfalls, most famously the Wli Falls near Hohoe, reputedly the highest waterfall in west Africa.

CLIMATE The combination of low altitude and proximity to the Equator gives Ghana a typical tropical climate. Daytime temperatures are high throughout the country, approaching or topping 30°C on most days. Temperatures do drop at night, more noticeably in the relatively dry north than the humid south, but visitors from cooler climes will generally consider most parts of Ghana to be hot both day and night. The only really temperate parts of the country are the highlands flanking the Volta Basin, where temperatures can be genuinely cool after dusk.

Owing to its equatorial location, Ghana does not experience the strong seasonal changes to which most Europeans and North Americans are accustomed. Temperatures are reasonably consistent throughout the year, and in many parts of the country the average temperature for the northern hemisphere winter months is actually higher than for the summer months – Accra, for instance, experiences its hottest temperatures from November to January, despite lying in the same hemisphere as Europe. The main seasonal factor to be aware of is rain, which falls almost exclusively during the European summer, peaking in May and June. The rains in the south tend to start earlier than in the north (often in early March) and to dry up a little between June and October, then start again in earnest – indeed, northerners consider southerners to enjoy two wet seasons a year. Rainfall figures are highest in the forested southwest, where some areas regularly experience in excess of 2,000mm per annum, and are lowest in the north and the plains immediately around Accra, where it is very unusual for as much as 1,000mm of rain to fall in a calendar year.

A noteworthy phenomenon in this part of the world is the Harmattan winds, which blow from the northeast during the dry season, bringing dust from the

Sahara and reducing visibility to as little as 1km. Generally, the winds come in late November or early December and continue until some time in March. The Harmattan will have little effect on most tourists, but it is a nightmare for photographers and will cause disappointment to those who've come to admire the scenery in mountainous areas.

VEGETATION Most of southern Ghana for about 250km inland of the Atlantic is naturally covered in rainforest and, while clearing for cultivation and logging activities have left few areas of true rainforest intact outside designated reserves, southern Ghana remains very lushly vegetated. For most visitors to Ghana, exposure to the rainforest is limited to a day trip to **Kakum National Park** (see page 167), noted for its unique and spectacular canopy walkway, but there are countless other opportunities for more adventurous travellers to explore Ghana's forests, ranging from a number of relatively accessible reserves close to Kumasi to a handful of obscure national parks suited to self-sufficient hikers.

The central and northern parts of the country support savanna habitats, gradually becoming drier and more sparsely vegetated as you head further north. In conservation terms, Ghana's most important savanna habitat is Mole National Park, easily visited as an overnight trip from Tamale.

WILDLIFE

Like other west African countries, Ghana lacks the vast conservation areas and huge herds of wildlife still to be found in most countries in eastern and southern Africa. Several large mammals typically associated with Africa do not occur in west Africa, eg: rhino, zebra, wildebeest, and gorilla, while many other large mammal species have been driven to extinction in Ghana in historical times, notably giraffe, cheetah, and, probably, African hunting dog. Within Ghana, the status of several other large mammal species, including lion, is highly vulnerable.

For all that, Ghana still offers some great opportunities for game viewing, with a wide variety of large mammals present, and monkeys, in particular, well represented and easily observed. The following overview of the more interesting mammals to be found in Ghana is designed to help readers who are not carrying a field guide of any sort, but it should also be useful to those carrying a continental guide and seeking more specific information about the distribution and status of various mammal species within Ghana.

Ghana boasts 15 integrated protected areas, which are managed by the Wildlife Division, and cover a total area of 13,489km² (5.66% of the total land area). These are Ankasa Conservation Area, Bia Conservation Area, Kakum Conservation Area, Bui National Park, Digya National Park, Kyabobo National Park, Mole National Park, Gbele Resource Reserve, Kalakpa Resource Reserve, Shai Resource Reserve, Kogyae Strict Nature Reserve, Agumatsa Wildlife Sanctuary, Boabeng-Fiema Monkey Sanctuary, Bomfobiri Wildlife Sanctuary and Owabi Wildlife Sanctuary. The Wildlife Division is also responsible for five coastal wetland areas designated under the RAMSAR Convention, as well as the zoological gardens in Kumasi and Accra. For more information see www.wildlife-ghana.org/WWF-Webpage/protectedAreas.

PREDATORS The **lion** (*Panthera leo*) is Africa's largest predator, and the animal everybody hopes to see on safari. It is a sociable creature, living in prides of five to ten animals and defending a territory of between 20km² and 200km². Lions hunt at night, and their favoured prey is large or medium-sized antelope. Most of the hunting is done by females, but dominant males normally feed first after a kill.

When not feeding, lions are remarkably indolent – they spend up to 23 hours of any given day at rest – so the anticipation of a lion sighting is often more exciting than the real thing. Lions naturally occur in any habitat but desert and rainforest, and they once ranged across much of the Old World; these days, they are all but restricted to large conservation areas in sub-Saharan Africa (one remnant population exists in India). In Ghana, a small population of lions remains in Mole National Park, though few tourists see them. There may also be lions present in some other relatively unexplored conservation areas.

The powerful **leopard** (*Panthera pardus*) is the most solitary and secretive of Africa's large cats. It hunts using stealth and power, often getting to within 5m of its intended prey

Leopard

before pouncing, and it habitually stores its kill in a tree to keep it from hyenas and lions. Where the two co-exist, the leopard can be distinguished

Leopard

Cheetah

from the superficially similar cheetah by its rosette-like spots, lack of black 'tear marks', and more compact, powerful build (though current information suggests that cheetahs are extinct in Ghana). Leopards occur in all habitats, favouring areas with plenty of cover, such as riverine woodland and rocky slopes, and there are many records of individuals living for years undetected in close proximity to humans. The leopard is the most common large feline, occurring in many forests, but you'd be extremely fortunate to see one.

Of the smaller cats, the **serval** (*Felis serval*) built rather like a miniature cheetah, with black-on-gold spots giving way to streaking near the head, is seldom seen, but widespread and quite common in moist grassland, reed beds, and riverine habitats. The **caracal** (*Felis caracal*) closely resembles the European lynx with its uniform tan coat and tufted ears, and it favours relatively arid savanna habitats. The not-dissimilar **golden cat** (*Felis aurata*) lives in forested areas, lacks ear tufts, and has a spotted underbelly. The markedly smaller **African wild cat** (*Felis sylvestris*) ranges from the Mediterranean to the Cape of Good Hope and is similar in appearance to the domestic tabby cat.

Caracal

The endangered **African hunting dog** (*Lycaon pictus*), distinguished by a cryptic black, brown and cream coat, is now very rare in west Africa and for all practical purposes extinct in Ghana, with occasional reports in the north probably reflecting vagrants that wandered across the border from a neighbouring country. The **side-striped jackal** (*Canis adustus*) occurs sparsely in northern Ghana and is listed for Mole National Park. Far smaller and less sociable than the wild dog, it is the only jackal species recorded for Ghana and has an indistinct pale, vertical stripe on each flank and a white-tipped tail.

African hunting dog

The **spotted hyena** (*Crocuta crocuta*), probably the most common large predator in Ghana, has a bulky build, sloping back, brown-spotted coat, powerful jaws, and dog-like expression. Contrary to popular myth, hyenas are not exclusively scavengers: the spotted hyena, in particular, is an adept hunter capable of killing a large antelope. Nor are they hermaphroditic, an ancient belief that stems from the false scrotum and penis covering the female hyena's vagina. Sociable animals, and fascinating to observe, hyenas live in loosely structured clans of about ten animals, led by females who are stronger and larger than males. The north African **striped hyena** (*Hyaena hyaena*), pale brown with several dark vertical streaks and a blackish mane, may occur in the very far north of Ghana.

A great many small nocturnal predators occur in Ghana. The **African civet** (*Civettictus civetta*) is a bulky, long-haired creature with a rather feline appearance, primarily carnivorous, but also partial to fruit, and widespread and common in many habitats but very rarely seen. The smaller, more slender **tree** or (**two-spotted**) **palm civet**, *Nandinia binotata*, is an arboreal forest animal with a dark-brown coat marked with black spots. The **small-spotted genet** (*Genetta genetta*), **Hausa Genet** (*Genetta thierryi*), **panther genet** (*Genetta pardina*), and **Johnston's Genet** (*Genetta johnstoni*) are Ghanaian representatives of a taxonomically confusing genus comprising perhaps ten species, all very slender and rather feline in appearance, with a grey to gold-brown coat marked with black spots and a long ringed tail.

African civet

The **ratel** or **honey badger** (*Mellivora capensis*), black with a puppyish face and grey-white back, is an opportunistic feeder best known for its symbiotic relationship with a bird called the honeyguide, which leads it to a beehive, waits for it to tear open the hive, then feeds on the scraps. The **Cape clawless otter** (*Aonyx capensis*) is a brown fresh-water mustelid with a white collar.

Six mongoose species occur in Ghana, most of them diurnal, terrestrial, and reasonably common – all six have, for instance, been recorded in Mole National Park. The **marsh mongoose** (*Atilax paludinosus*) is large, normally solitary, with a very scruffy brown coat, often seen in the vicinity of water. The **Egyptian** or **large grey mongoose** (*Herpestes ichneumon*) is also large and often associated with water, but its grey coat is grizzled in appearance, and it is most often seen in pairs or family groups. Restricted to rainforest habitats, where it is often quite common, the **cusimanse** (*Crossarchus obscuras*) is a small, sociable mongoose with a shaggy brown coat, almost always seen in family groups. The **white-tailed mongoose** (*Ichneumia albicauda*) is a large, solitary, brown mongoose, generally found in savanna country and easily identified by its bushy, white tail. The **slender** or **pygmy mongoose** (*Galerella sanguinea*) is another solitary inhabitant of the savanna, but very much smaller and with a uniform brown coat and blackish tail tip. The

Gambian mongoose

Gambian mongoose (*Mungos gambianus*), dark brown with the distinctive combination of pale throat and black cheek stripe, is the most sociable mongoose found in savanna country, occurring in groups of up to 30 animals.

PRIMATES The **common chimpanzee** (*Pan troglodytes*), along with the bonobo (*Pan paniscus*) of the southern Congo, is more closely related to man than to any other living creature. The chimpanzee lives in large troops based around a core of related males dominated by an alpha male. Females aren't firmly bonded to their core group, so emigration between communities is normal. Primarily frugivorous, chimpanzees eat meat on occasion and, though most kills are opportunistic, stalking of prey

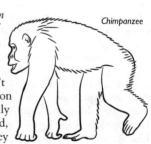
Chimpanzee

is not unusual. The first recorded instance of a chimp using a tool was at Gombe Stream in Tanzania, where modified sticks were used to 'fish' in termite mounds. In west Africa, chimps have been observed cracking open nuts with a stone and anvil. In the USA, captive chimps have successfully been taught sign language and have created compound words such as 'rock-berry' to describe a nut.

The chimpanzee is naturally a widespread and common resident of the African rainforest, but numbers are in rapid decline throughout its range, with a wild population estimated at several million in the early 20th century now thought to be around 150,000, thanks mainly to deforestation, hunting for bushmeat, and the slaughter of adults to capture youngsters for the pet trade. No reliable figures are available for Ghana: a 1997 estimate placed the population at 1,500-plus based on limited data, but recent reports suggest it is now much rarer than that figure suggests, possibly even on the verge of local extinction, despite having been accorded full legal protection since the 1970s. The main population centre is in the southwestern rainforest, where a small but viable population is known to occur in Ankasa, but its status in other reserves is uncertain. There are no habituated chimps in Ghana, and they are most unlikely to be seen by tourists.

The **anubis** or **olive baboon** (*Papio anubis*), a powerful terrestrial primate distinguished from any monkey by its much larger size, inverted 'U'-shaped tail, and distinctive dog-like head, is fascinating to watch from a behavioural perspective. It lives in large troops that boast a complex, rigid social structure characterised by matriarchal lineages and plenty of intra-troop movement by males seeking social dominance. Omnivorous and at home in almost any habitat, the baboon is the most widespread primate in Africa. It is quite frequently seen in Ghana, especially in Mole National Park and the Shai Hills.

Vervet monkey

The **green monkey** (*Cercopithecus aethiops*) is a type of vervet monkey, probably the world's most common monkey super-species, and the most widespread representative of the *Cercopithecus* guenons, a taxonomically controversial genus associated with African forests. The vervets are atypical guenons in that they inhabit savanna and woodland rather than true forest, spending a high proportion of their time on the ground. For this reason, vervets are more likely to be confused with the much larger and heavier baboon. However, the green monkey's light-grey coat and white forehead band should be diagnostic – as should the male's garish blue genitals. The green monkey is common in most Ghanaian reserves.

The terrestrial **patas** or **red monkey** (*Erythrocebus patas*), larger and more spindly than the vervet, has an orange-tinged coat and black forehead stripe. Essentially a monkey of dry savanna, the patas occurs in northern Ghana, and can quite easily be seen alongside the green monkey in Mole National Park.

Patas monkey

Probably the easiest to see of Ghana's true forest monkeys is the **mona monkey** (*Cercopithecus mona*), of which six long-recognised races are now regarded by some authorities to be distinct species on the basis of recent chromosome studies. The most widespread mona in Ghana is **Lowe's monkey** (*Cercopithecus (m.) lowei*), a pretty and cryptically coloured grey, white, and black guenon distinguished by the pale stripe over its eye. Lowe's mona is the common monkey at Baobeng-Fiema Monkey Sanctuary, and it occurs in most Ghanaian rainforests, where it is offered some protection against hunting. It is replaced in Tafi Atome in the east by the **true mona** (*Cercopithecus (m.) mona*),

Mona monkey

which is similar in overall appearance, but can be distinguished by the prominent white discs on its hips, easily seen when it moves away from the observer.

Two other distinctive species of forest guenon occur in Ghana. The **lesser spot-nosed monkey** (*Cercopithecus petaurista*) is a small guenon easily distinguished by its prominent white nose. Though widespread in Ghana's forests, the lesser spot-nosed monkey is most likely to be seen on Monkey Hill in Takoradi, where a small and relatively habituated troop survives within a few hundred metres of the city centre. Much rarer is the beautiful, white-bearded, orange-rumped **Roloway's Diana monkey** (*Cercopithecus diana roloway*), which may now be locally extinct in Kakum, but survives in the Ankasa and Bia resource reserves near the Ivorian border, where it is rarely seen.

The **western** or **Geoffrey's black-and-white colobus** (*Colobus vellerosus*) is a beautiful jet-black monkey with bold white facial markings and a long white tail, widespread where it hasn't been hunted to extinction, and easily seen at Baobeng-Fiema Monkey Sanctuary. Almost exclusively arboreal, it is capable of leaping distances of up to 30m, a spectacular sight with its white tail streaming behind. The Miss Waldron's bay race of **western red colobus** (*Procolobus badius waldroni*) is a distinctly red, long-limbed forest monkey formerly restricted to a few forests in southwestern Ghana. It is now officially regarded to be extinct in Ghana, though recent reports suggest a relic population survive in the remote Krokosua Hills Forest Reserve near the Bia Resource Reserve. The smaller and duller **olive colobus** (*Procolobus verus*), an olive-grey monkey distinguished by two light grey patches on its forehead, occurs in several forests in southern Ghana, including Kakum National Park, but is most likely to be seen on Monkey Hill in Takoradi.

The one other forest monkey to occur in Ghana, the **sooty mangabey** (*Cercocebus atys*), is the only west African representative of a genus that's more widely represented in the central African rainforest. It is the only uniform dark-grey monkey to occur in Ghana, where it is confined to western forests such as Bia and Ankasa. The race found in Ghana, *Cercocebus atys lunulatus*, has a small white collar, and is sometimes referred to as the white-naped or white-checked mangabey.

Also present in Ghana are a few species of nocturnal **bushbaby**, often quite easy to locate if you know where to find them and have a good spotlight. The **Demidoff's bushbaby** or **dwarf galago** (*Galagoides demidoff*) is found in the southerly rainforests of Kakum and Ankasa, while the **northern lesser bushbaby** (*Galagoides senegalensis*) is found in the savanna regions to the north, and is very common in Mole. In 2005, **Thomas's bushbaby** (*Galagoides thomasi*) was discovered in the forested hills east of the Volta. The **potto** (*Perodicticus potto*) is a sloth-like nocturnal primate of rainforest interiors, also most easily located with the aid of a spotlight.

ANTELOPE The **roan antelope** (*Hippotragus equinus*) is the largest plains antelope found in Ghana, with a shoulder height of 120–150cm. It is a handsome horse-like creature, uniform fawn-grey with a pale belly, short decurved horns, and a light mane. It occurs in several savanna reserves and is the common antelope of Gbele Resource Area near Tumu in the north. The roan is quite likely to be seen by visitors spending a few days in Mole National Park.

The **Defassa waterbuck** (*Kobus (ellipsiprymnus) defassa*) is another very large antelope, easily recognised by its shaggy brown coat, white rump, and the male's large, lyre-shaped horns. It is normally seen in small family groups grazing near water, and is almost certain to be seen in the vicinity of the hotel at Mole National Park. The closely related **kob** (*Kobus kob*) is a beautiful, red-gold antelope with a white throat, but otherwise few distinguishing features. It is probably the most common large antelope in Ghana and family herds are almost certain to be seen by visitors to Mole National Park and Shai Hills.

Roan antelope

The **western hartebeest** (*Alcelaphus buselaphus*) is a large, ungainly antelope readily identified by the combination of large shoulders, sloping back, red-brown or yellow-brown coat, and smallish horns in both sexes. It is resident in several savanna reserves in Ghana, but quite rare everywhere.

Defassa waterbuck

Kob

Secretive and scarce, the **bongo** (*Tragelaphus euryceros*) is a very large, stocky, and clearly striped rainforest species, isolated populations of which occur in several Ghanaian reserves, including Kakum National Park. It is highly unlikely to be seen by a casual visitor. A far more common and widespread resident of forest and thick woodland, though also quite secretive, the **bushbuck** (*Tragelaphus scriptus*), is an attractive, medium-sized antelope. The male is dark brown or chestnut, while the much smaller female is generally a pale reddish brown. The male has relatively small, straight horns. It can be seen in just about any Ghanaian forest or game reserve, and is quite frequently observed in Shai Hills and Mole National Park.

Hartebeest

Bushbuck

Less common, the **Bohor reedbuck** (*Redunca redunca*) is a plain, light fawn, medium-sized antelope generally seen in pairs in open country near water. The **oribi** (*Ourebia ourebi*) is rather like a miniature reedbuck, uncommon in grassland habitats. Even smaller, the **common** or **grey duiker** (*Sylvicapra grimmia*) is an anomalous member of the duiker family in that it occurs in savanna and woodland rather than true forest. Distinguished by the black tuft of hair between its small horns, it is the only small, grey antelope likely to be seen in non-forested habitats in Ghana.

Reedbuck

The forest duikers are a taxonomically confusing group of 12 to 20 species restricted to the rainforests of Africa. Six species occur in Ghana, all of them widespread (all but the red-flanked, for instance, occur in Kakum National Park), but secretive and rather unlikely to be seen in the wild by tourists. The largest of these is the nocturnal **yellow-backed duiker** (*Cephalophus leucogaster*), a bushbuck-sized antelope with a blackish coat and yellow patch on its back, which occurs sparsely in most true rainforests, including Kakum National Park.

Common duiker

Three of Ghana's remaining duiker species are also rather large by the standards of the family, with a shoulder height of up to 55cm. The most distinctive of these, the **black duiker** (*Cephalophus niger*), with a thick off-black coat and red forehead and throat, is realistically likely to be seen clearly only at Owabi Wildlife Sanctuary outside Kumasi. More widespread, the **bay duiker** (*Cephalophus dorcas*), red-brown with a wide, black, dorsal stripe, would be difficult to tell apart at a glance from **Ogilby's duiker** (*Cephalophus ogilbyi*), which is similar, but has a narrower dorsal stripe.

The most common forest antelope in Ghana, **Maxwell's duiker** (*Cephalophus maxwelli*), is a small, grey duiker with a distinctive, pale eye stripe, likely to be seen in any forest in southern Ghana. Similar in size to Maxwell's, but with colouring closer to the bay duiker, the **red-flanked duiker** (*Cephalophus rufilatus*) is best distinguished from members of its genus by habitat and distribution, since it is essentially a species of forest fringe and woodland that differs from all other forest duikers in that it occurs only in the northern half of Ghana.

Also occurring in the Ghanaian rainforest, the **royal antelope** (*Neotragus pygmaeus*) is a common, but infrequently observed, brown antelope with a red throat collar, which, with a shoulder height of up to 28cm, is regarded as the world's smallest horned ungulate. More closely related to European deer than any antelope, the **water chevrotain** (*Hyemoschus aquaticus*) is an odd, hare-sized nocturnal creature with a brown coat and white stripes and spots, generally associated with wet habitats within rainforests.

Recently there have also been sightings in the Avu Lagoon of the **sitatunga** (*Tragelaphus spekei*) – the world's only aquatic antelope, which is adapted to swimming with widely splayed hoofs and a thick oily coat that repels water. This rare mammal was previously thought to have been extinct from Ghana for over 20 years.

OTHER MAMMALS The **African elephant** (*Loxodonta africana*) is the world's largest land animal, and both the savanna and smaller forest species occur in Ghana. It is an intelligent, social animal, and often very entertaining to watch. Female elephants live in closely knit clans in which the eldest female plays matriarch over her sisters, daughters, and granddaughters. Mother–daughter bonds are strong and may last for up to 50 years. Males generally leave the family group at around 12 years to roam singly or form

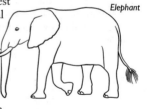
Elephant

bachelor herds. Under normal circumstances, elephants range widely in search of food and water, but when concentrated populations are forced to live in conservation areas, their habit of uprooting trees can cause serious environmental damage. Elephants are widespread and common in habitats ranging from desert to rainforest and, despite heavy poaching, they are still present in several national parks and reserves. Mole National Park, with a population of between 500 and 800 elephants, is the best place to see them.

Characteristic of Africa's large rivers and lakes, the **hippopotamus** (*Hippopotamus amphibius*) is a large, lumbering animal that spends most of the day submerged, but emerges at night to graze. Strongly territorial, herds of ten or more animals are presided over by a dominant male who will readily defend his patriarchy to the death. Hippos are present in Mole National Park, but not within day-walk distance of Mole Motel (see page 366), and they are very common in the part of the Volta River protected by Bui National Park.

The **West African manatee** (*Trichechus senegalensis*) is an unmistakable large, grey, hairless mammal, related to the marine dugong, but entirely restricted to fresh-water habitats. Increasingly very rare, manatees are still seen from time to time on Lake Volta and the Volta estuary area near Ada.

African buffalo

The **African buffalo** (*Syncerus caffer*), frequently but erroneously referred to as a water buffalo (an Asian species), is a distinctive ox-like animal that lives in large herds on the savanna and occurs in smaller herds in forested areas. It is common and widespread in sub-Saharan Africa, and historically both the black savanna race and the smaller, redder, forest race occur in Ghana, though the latter is now very rare and possibly extinct. The country's largest buffalo population, of roughly 1,000 animals, is found in Mole, but buffalo also occur in some forest reserves and in Kalapka Resource Reserve near Ho.

The rather endearing **warthog** (*Phacochoreus africanus*) is grey in colour with a thin covering of hairs, wart-like bumps on its face, and rather large upward-curving tusks. Africa's only diurnal swine, the warthog is often seen in family groups, trotting off briskly with its tail raised stiffly (a diagnostic trait) in a determinedly nonchalant air. In Ghana, it occurs in most savanna reserves, though is only likely to be seen in Mole National Park, where it is common. The **red river hog** (*Potamoccoerus porcus*) is a larger forest swine, common but primarily nocturnal, and regarded by some authorities to be a race of the east Africa bushpig, from

Warthog

which it is readily distinguished by a decidedly red coat and clear white stripe along its back. Larger still, the **giant forest hog** (*Hylochoerus meinertzhageni*), a very hairy, dark-brown swine that weighs up to 250kg, is a fairly common but difficult-to-observe nocturnal resident of most rainforests in Ghana.

The **aardvark** (*Orycteropus afer*) is a singularly bizarre insectivore, quite common in dry savanna country and unmistakable with its long snout and huge ears, but rarely seen due to its nocturnal habits. Equally distinctive, **pangolins** are rare nocturnal insectivores with armour-plating and a tendency to roll up in a ball when disturbed. Spiky rather than armoured, several **hedgehog** and **porcupine** species occur in the region, the former generally no larger than a guinea pig, the latter generally 60–100cm long.

One small mammal species that you're quite likely to encounter in the right habitat is the **rock hyrax** (*Procavia capensis*), a rodent-like creature more closely related to elephants and often seen sunning itself in rocky habitats. Probably more numerous in Ghana, but less easily seen, the similar looking **tree hyrax** (*Dendrohyrax dorsalis*) is a nocturnal forest creature that announces its presence with an unforgettable shrieking call.

Rock hyrax

Of the great many squirrel species present in Ghana, all but one are essentially restricted to forest and woodland. The exception, a widespread inhabitant of the northern savanna, is the **unstriped ground squirrel** (*Xerus*  *inauris*), a terrestrial animal with a white eye-ring, silver-black tail, and the characteristic squirrel mannerism of holding food in its forepaws while standing on its hind legs. Occasionally seen at Kakum and in other forests, the **anomalures** (also known as flying squirrels) are large rodents with a flap of skin stretched between their front and hind legs, enabling them to glide for quite significant distances through the canopy.

Ground squirrel

Also common in Ghana, the **savanna cane-rat** (*Thryonomys gregorianus*) is a large grizzled-brown rodent that can be as heavy as 8kg and is associated with marshes and elephant grass. Known locally as the grass-cutter, it is prized as bushmeat by Ghanaians of all religious groups, and is reputedly very low in cholesterol, though many westerners find it an acquired taste (like gamy mutton or goat meat). Commercial grass-cutter farming is rapidly catching on in Ghana, and makes for a more ecologically sound option than farming non-indigenous stock.

REPTILES
Nile crocodile The order Crocodilia dates back at least 150 million years, and fossil forms that lived contemporaneously with dinosaurs are remarkably unchanged from their modern ancestors, of which the Nile crocodile (*Crocodylus niloticus*) is the largest living reptile, regularly growing to lengths of up to 6m. Widespread throughout Africa, the Nile crocodile was once common in most large rivers and lakes, but it has been exterminated in many areas in the past century – hunted professionally for its skin as well as by vengeful local villagers. Contrary to popular legend, Nile crocodiles generally feed mostly on fish, at least where densities are sufficient. They will also prey on drinking or swimming mammals where the opportunity presents itself, dragging their victim underwater until it drowns, then storing it under a submerged log or tree until it has decomposed sufficiently for them to eat. A large crocodile is capable of killing a lion or wildebeest, or an adult human for that matter, and in certain areas, such as the Mara or Grumeti rivers in Tanzania, large mammals do form their main prey. Today, large crocodiles are mostly confined to protected areas throughout Africa. In Ghana, they are most easily observed at Paga or any of several other ponds countrywide where they are held sacred by locals.

Snakes A wide variety of snakes is found in Ghana, though – fortunately, most would agree – they are typically very shy and unlikely to be seen unless actively sought. One of the snakes most likely to be seen on safari is Africa's largest, the **rock python** (*Python sebae*), which has a gold-on-black mottled skin and regularly grows to lengths exceeding 5m. Non-venomous, pythons kill their prey by strangulation, wrapping their muscular bodies around it until it cannot breathe, then swallowing it whole and dozing off for a couple of months while it is digested. Pythons feed mainly on small antelopes, large rodents, and similar. They are harmless to adult humans, but could conceivably kill a small child. A slumbering python might be encountered almost anywhere in Ghana.

Of the venomous snakes, one of the most commonly encountered is the **puff adder** (*Bitis arietans*), a large, thick resident of savanna and rocky habitats. Although it feeds mainly on rodents, the puff adder will strike when threatened and it is rightly considered the most dangerous of African snakes, not because it is especially venomous or aggressive, but because its notoriously sluggish disposition means it is more often disturbed than other snakes. The related **Gabon viper** (*Bitis gabonica*) is possibly the largest African viper, growing up to 2m long, very heavily built, and with a beautiful cryptic geometric gold, black, and brown skin pattern that blends perfectly into the rainforest litter it inhabits. Although highly venomous, it is more placid and less likely to be encountered than the puff adder.

Several cobra species, including various **spitting cobras** (*Naja* spp.), are present in Ghana, most with characteristic hoods that they raise when about to strike, though they are all very seldom seen. Another widespread family is the mambas, of which the **black mamba** (*Dendroaspis polylepis*) – which will attack only when cornered, despite an unfounded reputation for unprovoked aggression – is the largest venomous snake in Africa, measuring up to 3.5m long. Theoretically, the most toxic of Africa's snakes is said to be the **boomslang** (*Dispholidus typus*), a variably coloured and, as its name – literally 'tree snake' – suggests, largely arboreal snake that is reputed not to have accounted for one known human fatality, as it is back-fanged and very non-aggressive.

Most snakes are in fact non-venomous and not even potentially harmful to any other living creature much bigger than a rat. The **mole snake** (*Pseudaspis cana*) is a common and widespread grey-brown savanna resident that grows up to 2m long and feeds on moles and other rodents. The remarkable egg-eating snakes (*Dasypeltis* spp.) live exclusively on birds' eggs, dislocating their jaws to swallow the egg whole, then eventually regurgitating the crushed shell in a neat little package. Many snakes will take eggs opportunistically, for which reason large-scale agitation among birds in a tree is often a good indication that a snake (or small bird of prey) is around.

Lizards All African lizards are harmless to humans, with the arguable exception of the giant monitor lizards that could, in theory, inflict a nasty bite if cornered. Two species of monitor occur in west Africa, the **water** and **savanna monitor** (*Varanus niloticus* and *V. exanthematicus*), the latter growing up to 2.2m long and occasionally seen in the vicinity of termite mounds, the former slightly smaller, but far more regularly observed by tourists in moist habitats. Their size alone might make it possible to fleetingly mistake a monitor for a small crocodile, but their more colourful yellow-dappled skin precludes sustained confusion. Both species are predatory, feeding on anything from bird eggs to smaller reptiles and mammals, but will also eat carrion opportunistically.

Visitors to Ghana will soon become familiar with the **common house gecko** (*Hemidactylus mabouia*), an endearing, bug-eyed, translucent white lizard, which, as its name suggests, reliably inhabits most houses as well as hotel rooms, scampering up walls and upside-down on the ceiling in pursuit of pesky insects attracted to the lights. Also very common in some hotel grounds are various *Agama* species, distinguished from other common lizards by their relatively large size of around 20–25cm, basking habits, and almost plastic-looking scaling – depending on the species, a combination of blue, purple, orange, or red, with the flattened head generally a different colour to the torso. Another common family are the skinks: small, long-tailed lizards, most of which are quite dark and have a few thin black stripes running from head to tail.

Tortoises, terrapins and turtles (*With help from Tricia Hayne*) These peculiar reptiles are unique in being protected by a prototypal suit of armour formed by their heavy exoskeleton. The most common of the terrestrial tortoises in the region is the leopard tortoise (*Testudo pardalis*), which is named after its gold-and-black mottled shell, can weigh up to 30kg, and has been known to live for more than 50 years in captivity. Several species of terrapin – essentially the fresh-water variant on the theme – are resident in west Africa, all somewhat flatter in shape than the tortoises, and generally with a plainer brown shell. They might be seen sunning on rocks close to water or peering out from roadside puddles, and in rare instances might reach a length of almost 1m.

Turtles – the saltwater equivalent of terrapins – live largely in the water, coming ashore only to nest, and unlike their landlubber cousins they are unable to retract either their heads or their flippers into their shell for protection. The world's eight species of marine turtle are all protected under the Convention on International Trade in Endangered Species (CITES), and four are known to nest on the beaches and lagoons of the Ghanaian coast. The most common of these are the **green turtle** (*Chelonia mydas*), so-called because its fat is a greenish colour, the **olive ridley turtle** (*Lepidochelys olivacea*), and the **leatherback** (*Dermchelys coriacea*), which can reach a length of greater than 2m. Also indigenous to these waters is the very rare **hawksbill turtle** (*Eretmochelys imbricata*), whose exquisite shell is the source of traditional 'tortoiseshell', long coveted for ornamental purposes and an important trade item since Ancient Egyptian times.

Turtles do not nest until they are at least 25 years old, when they lay their eggs deep in the sand. The eggs take around 60 days to hatch, at which time the hatchlings make their way towards the sea, attracted by the play of moonlight on the waves. The green turtle, the most likely of the five species to be seen by visitors, lays between 300 and 540 eggs per season in the wild, nesting every three or four years, with the eggs hatching from May to September. In captivity, these figures increase, with up to 1,700 eggs in total laid over several batches in a season. In their first year, the hatchlings grow up to 2.7kg, and they can be expected to weigh up to 24kg by the time they are three or four. Green turtles may live to be centuries old, and can weigh in excess of 200kg. Turtles are cold-blooded animals, requiring warm water to survive. In fact, water temperature affects the sex of the hatchlings: at 28°C, a balance between male and female is to be expected; cooler than that, and males will dominate; hotter, and there will be a predominance of females.

Sadly, female turtles – which go into a trance for several hours while they lay eggs – are routinely captured as food by local villagers, and the egg sites are also often disturbed. This problem is being countered in some areas by public awareness campaigns, in which tourist interest can play a major role. Among the best sites for turtle-spotting in Ghana are the Songor Lagoon and Volta estuary at Ada Foah (see page 222), the Sukuma Lagoon near Keta (see page 213), and the beaches around Busua (see page 189) and Old Ningo (see page 215), but they might be seen on any sandy and reasonably deserted beach – November to March is the best season.

BIRDS *Adam Riley* Although Ghana has of recent times been seldom visited and explored by birders, it is a country with great birding potential. Its obvious advantages as a politically stable, English-speaking nation with friendly people are complemented by a decent network of national and regional parks and eco-tourism facilities, with the cherry on the top being the fabulous Kakum canopy walkway (see page 169). These factors, combined with the wide variety of habitats within this small country, make Ghana a very worthwhile birding destination. The two main climatic zones (dry north and wet south) spawn several distinct habitat biomes, including the southwestern Guinea–Congo forest zone, the southeastern coastal savanna, the central and northern Guinea Savanna, and the far northeastern dry Sudan Savanna.

Ghana's premier birding region is its lowland forests, which fall within the Upper Guinea forest block. This stretches from Guinea to Ghana and harbours 15 endemic species, of which 14 are globally threatened. Ghana is currently the only safe country in which this internationally recognised Endemic Bird Area can be visited. Kakum National Park provides a superb opportunity for sampling the avian delights of this threatened lowland forest biome. Other reserves that protect lowland forests and are recognised as Important Bird Areas by BirdLife International are Ankasa Resources Reserve & Nini-Suhien NP, Atewa Range FR

CHAMELEONS

Common and widespread, but not easily seen unless they are actively searched for, chameleons are arguably the most intriguing of African reptiles. True chameleons of the family Chamaeleontidae are confined to the Old World, with the most important centre of speciation being the island of Madagascar, to which about half of the world's 120 recognised species are endemic. Aside from two species of chameleon apiece in Asia and Europe, the remainder is distributed across mainland Africa. In Ghana, you're most likely to come across a chameleon by chance when it is crossing a road, in which case it should be easy to take a closer look at it, since most chameleons move painfully slowly and deliberately.

Chameleons are best known for their capacity to change colour, a trait that has often been exaggerated in popular literature and which is generally influenced by mood more than the colour of the background. Some chameleons are more adept at changing colour than others, with the most variable being the common chameleon, *Chamaeleo chamaeleon*, of the Mediterranean region, with more than 100 colour and pattern variations recorded. Many African chameleons are typically green in colour, but will gradually take on a browner hue when they descend from the foliage in more exposed terrain, eg: while crossing a road. Several change colour and pattern far more dramatically when they feel threatened or are confronted by a rival of the same species. Different chameleon species also vary greatly in size, with the largest being Oustalet's chameleon of Madagascar, known to reach a length of almost 80cm.

A remarkable physiological feature common to all true chameleons are their protuberant round eyes, which offer a potential 180° vision on both sides and are able to swivel around independently of each other. Only when one of them isolates a suitably juicy-looking insect will the two eyes focus in the same direction as the chameleon stalks slowly forward until it is close enough to use the other unique weapon in its armoury. This is its sticky tipped tongue, which is typically about the same length as its body and remains coiled up within its mouth most of the time, to be unleashed in a sudden, blink-and-you'll-miss-it lunge to zap a selected item of prey. In addition to their unique eyes and tongues, many chameleons are adorned with an array of facial casques, flaps, horns and crests that enhance their already somewhat fearsome prehistoric appearance. Another oddity is the spectrally pale nocturnal colouring, which shows up clearly under a spotlight and makes it clear why these creatures are regarded with both fear and awe in many local African cultures.

(Forest Reserve), Bia NP, Boin Tano FR, Boin River FR, Bosumtwi Range FR, Bura River FR, Cape Three Points FR, Dadieso FR, Draw River FR, Ebi River Shelterbelt FR, Fure River FR, Jema-Asemkrom FR, Mamiri FR, Mount Afadjato-Agumatsa Range Forest, Nsuensa FR, Pra-Suhien FR, Subri River FR, Tano-Anwia FR, Tano-Ehuro FR, Tano-Nimiri FR, Tano-Offin FR and Yoyo River FR. Sadly, only 11% of Ghana's forests remain intact, and even within reserves, logging, illegal hunting, and forest destruction continues.

Within Ghana, a remarkable 180 species, many of them beautiful and highly sought-after avian gems, are restricted to these forests. Some of the key birds that occur here are white-crested tiger-heron, Congo serpent eagle, the dashing long-tailed hawk, white-breasted guineafowl (an Upper Guinea Forest Endemic – UGFE – and very rare), white-spotted flufftail, the strange Nkulengu rail, yellow-billed turaco, black-throated coucal, rufous fishing owl (UGFE and very rare), brown nightjar, brown-cheeked hornbill (UGFE), the huge yellow-casqued and black-casqued wattled hornbills, Bates's swift, chocolate-backed kingfisher, western wattled cuckoo-shrike (UGFE and very rare), green-tailed bristlebill (UGFE), yellow-bearded greenbul (UGFE), rufous-winged illadopsis (UGFE), white-necked rockfowl or picathartes (UGFE and very rare), Sharpe's apalis (UGFE), black-headed rufous warbler (UGFE and very rare), and copper-tailed glossy starling (UGFE).

Kakum National Park is arguably the best site for these rarities as well as for other forest species. Lower-storey bird parties are composed of greenbuls, sunbirds, flycatchers and warblers, while ground-dwelling species include the elusive Nkulengu rail, the white-spotted flufftail, no less than three illadopsis, and several specialised ant-attending species. An extended session on Africa's only rainforest canopy walkway offers the possibility of a plethora of canopy dwellers including crowned and Cassin's hawk-eagles, the fabulous great blue, guinea and yellow-billed turaco, the giant black casqued and yellow casqued wattled hornbills, and the diminutive dwarf hornbills, as well as various cuckoos, woodhoopoes, barbets, honeyguides, bush-shrikes, and weavers.

Another excellent forest birding site is the Atewa Range, which is situated on the South Volta Scarp and is one of the only higher-lying forests in Ghana. Atewa is managed as a logging reserve, but is still covered in extensive forest. The birding is extremely productive and all the more exciting for the rediscovery of the extremely

WEAVERS

The weavers of the family Ploceidae, which also incorporates the closely related sparrows, are a quintessential part of Africa's natural landscape, common and highly visible in virtually every habitat from rainforest to desert. The name of the family derives from the intricate and elaborate nests – typically, but not always, a roughly oval ball of dried grass, reeds, and twigs – that are built by the dextrous males of most species.

It can be fascinating to watch a male weaver at work. First, a nest site is chosen, usually at the end of a thin hanging branch or frond, which is immediately stripped of leaves to protect against snakes. The weaver then flies back and forth to the site, carrying the building material blade by blade in its heavy beak, first using a few thick strands to hang a skeletal nest from the end of a branch, then gradually completing the structure by interweaving numerous thinner blades of grass into the main frame. Once completed, the nest is subjected to the attention of his chosen partner who will tear it apart if the result is less than satisfactory, and so the process starts all over again.

All but 12 of the 113 described weaver species are resident on the African mainland or associated islands, with roughly 30 represented within Ghana alone. Most of these species are placed in the genus *Ploceus* (true weavers), which is surely the most characteristic of all African bird genera. *Ploceus* weavers are typically slightly larger than a sparrow, and display a strong sexual dimorphism. Males are generally very colourful, but females, with a few exceptions, tend to be drab buff- or olive-brown birds, with some streaking on the back, and perhaps a hint of yellow on the belly.

Most male *Ploceus* weavers conform to the basic colour pattern of the 'masked weaver' – predominantly yellow, with streaky back and wings, and a distinct black facial mask, often bordered orange. Several Ghanaian weaver species fit this masked weaver prototype more or less absolutely, and a similar number approximate it rather less exactly, eg: by having a chestnut-brown mask, or a full black head, or a black back, or by being more chestnut than yellow on the belly. Identification of the masked weavers can be tricky without experience – useful clues are the exact shape of the mask, the presence and extent of the fringing orange, and the colour of the eye and the back.

The various species of golden weaver are also brilliant yellow and/or light orange with some light streaking on the back, but they lack a mask or any other strong rare white-necked rockfowl near Asumura. Atewa is also a good site for the dazzling but elusive blue-headed bee-eater, as well as the western bronze-naped pigeon, the impressive great blue turaco, Narina trogon, little green woodpecker, square-tailed saw-wing swallow, black-capped apalis, olivaceous and dusky crested-flycatcher, chestnut and red-cheeked wattle-eye, brown and the endangered rufous-winged illadopsis, Bates's sunbird, many-coloured bush-shrike, and green-backed twinspot.

In a broad belt across the centre of Ghana lies an extensive tract of pristine, broad-leaved Guinea woodlands and in this zone is our next base, the vast **Mole National Park**. The beautiful oriole warbler, violet turaco, several species of kingfisher, bee-eaters, rollers (including blue-bellied), barbets (including bearded), sunbirds, starlings, and seed-eaters will certainly create a riot of colour! The lodge at Mole National Park is a superb place for birds associated with the drier northern woodland. Seedeaters abound, including mixed flocks of lavender and orange-cheeked waxbill, red-cheeked cordonbleu, red-billed and bar-breasted firefinch, pin-tailed and long-tailed paradise-whydah, chestnut-crowned sparrow-weaver, grey-headed sparrow, and yellow-fronted canary. The rocky escarpment harbours family groups of stone partridge, double-spurred francolin, freckled nightjar, Abyssinian ground-hornbill, rock-loving and Dorst's cisticola, white-fronted black-chat, and cinnamon-breasted bunting.

distinguishing features. The handful of forest-associated *Ploceus* weavers, by contrast, tend to have quite different and very striking colour patterns, and although sexually dimorphic, the female is often as boldly marked as the male. The most aberrant among these is the common Vieillot's black weaver (*Ploceus nigerrimus*), the male of which is totally black except for its eyes, while the black-billed weaver (*Ploceus melanogaster*) reverses the prototype by being all black with a yellow facemask.

Many *Ploceus* species are gregarious breeders forming single or mixed species colonies of hundreds, sometimes thousands, of pairs, often in reed beds or other waterside vegetation (**Hans Cottage Botel** is a good site; see page 170). Most weavers don't have a distinctive song, but they compensate with a rowdy jumble of harsh swizzles, rattles, and nasal notes that can reach deafening proportions near large colonies. One more-cohesive song you will often hear seasonally around weaver colonies is a cyclic 'dee-dee-dee-Diederik', often accelerating to a hysterical crescendo when several birds call at once. This is the call of the Diederik cuckoo (*Chrysococcyx caprius*), a handsome green-and-white cuckoo that lays its eggs in weaver nests.

Most of the colonial weavers, perhaps relying on safety in numbers, build relatively plain nests with a roughly oval shape and an unadorned entrance hole. The nests of certain more solitary weavers, by contrast, are far more elaborate. Several weavers, for instance, protect their nests from egg-eating invaders by attaching tubular entrance tunnels to the base – in the case of the spectacled weaver, sometimes twice as long as the nest itself. The Grosbeak weaver (a peculiar, larger-than-average brown-and-white weaver of reed beds, distinguished by its outsized bill and placed in the monospecific genus *Amblyospiza*) constructs a large and distinctive domed nest, which is supported by a pair of reeds and woven as precisely as the finest basketwork, with a neat, raised entrance hole at the front. By contrast, the scruffiest nests are built by the various species of sparrow- and buffalo-weaver, relatively drab but highly gregarious dry-country birds likely to be seen in Mole National Park and elsewhere in the north (there's a large white-billed buffalo weaver (*Bubalornis albirostris*) colony in central Wa, marked on the map; see page 388).

The moist woodland surrounding the swamp below the lodge is home to some special birds, in particular the highly desirable oriole warbler, one of west Africa's most beautiful birds. In fact, colourful birds are here the rule rather than the exception. Even the most hardened birder will be dazzled by one gem after the next: Bruce's green-pigeon, violet turaco, rose-ringed parakeet, blue-breasted and gray-headed kingfisher, red-throated and northern carmine bee-eater, Abyssinian, rufous-crowned, broad-billed and blue-bellied roller, bearded barbet, western violet-backed, green-headed, scarlet-chested, beautiful and splendid sunbird, sulphur-breasted and gray-headed bush-shrike, and greater blue-eared, lesser blue-eared, bronze-tailed, purple and long-tailed glossy-starling.

Other target species in these woodlands are white-throated francolin, vinaceous dove, green woodhoopoe, black scimitar-bill, yellow-fronted tinkerbird, greater and lesser honeyguide, fine-spotted, gray and brown-backed woodpecker, fanti sawwing, white-breasted and red-shouldered cuckoo-shrike, yellow-throated greenbul, African thrush, Senegal eremomela, northern crombec, yellow-bellied hyliota, several species of overwintering palearctic warblers, northern black, African blue, European pied and swamp flycatcher, white-crowned robin-chat, brown-throated wattle-eye, Senegal batis, blackcap and brown babbler, white-winged black-tit, spotted creeper, African golden oriole, northern puffback, yellow-billed shrike, brubru, white helmetshrike (this race topped with an

BUTTERFLIES

Ghana's immense wealth of invertebrate life is largely overlooked by visitors, but is perhaps most easily appreciated in the form of butterflies and moths of the order Lepidoptera. An estimated 1,000 butterfly species, including several endemics, have been recorded in Ghana, as compared to roughly 650 in the whole of North America, and a mere 56 on the British Isles. Several forests in Ghana harbour 400 or more butterfly species, and one might easily see a greater selection in the course of a day than one could in a lifetime of exploring the English countryside. Indeed, I've often sat at one roadside pool and watched 10–20 clearly different species converge there over the space of 20 minutes.

The Lepidoptera are placed in the class Insecta, which includes ants, beetles, and locusts among others. All insects are distinguished from other invertebrates, such as arachnids (spiders) and crustaceans, by their combination of six legs, a pair of frontal antennae, and a body divided into a distinct head, thorax, and abdomen. Insects are the only winged invertebrates, though some primitive orders have never evolved them, and other more recently evolved orders have discarded them. Most flying insects have two pairs of wings, one of which, as in the case of flies, might have been modified beyond immediate recognition. The butterflies and moths of the order Lepidoptera have two sets of wings and are distinguished from all other insect orders by the tiny, ridged wing scales that create their characteristic bright colours.

The most spectacular of all butterflies are the swallowtails of the family Papilionidae, of which roughly 100 species have been identified in Africa. Named for the streamers that trail from the base of their wings, swallowtails are typically large and colourful, and relatively easy to observe when they feed on mammal dung deposited on forest trails and roads. The west African giant swallowtail, *Papilio antimachus*, a black, orange and green gem with a wingspan of up to 20cm, is probably the largest butterfly in the world, but it's seldom seen as it tends to stick to the forest canopy.

The Pieridae is a family of medium-sized butterflies, generally smaller than the swallowtails and with wider wings, of which almost 100 species are present in Ghana, enormous, floppy crest), red-headed weaver, black-faced and black-bellied firefinch, and brown-rumped and Cabanis's bunting.

Raptors are particularly prolific in Mole and regularly encountered species include white-backed, white-headed and hooded vulture, short-toed and brown snake-eagle, bateleur, several species of migrant harrier, lizard buzzard, Wahlberg's, martial and long-crested eagle, Ayres' and African hawk-eagle, lanner falcon, and African hobby.

Another excellent northern site is the large Tono Dam, home to a healthy population of waterbirds where you may see a variety of herons, egrets, waders, and waterfowl. Furthermore, it supports one of Africa's most sought-after birds, the seasonally resident Egyptian plover or crocodile bird. Other target species around Tono include Gabar and dark chanting-goshawk, grasshopper buzzard, Beaudouin's snake-eagle, Stanley and white-bellied bustard, black-headed lapwing, Forbes's plover, four-banded sandgrouse, swallow-tailed bee-eater, rufous-rumped and sun lark, rufous cisticola, pygmy sunbird, piapiac, chestnut-bellied starling, bush petronia, speckled-fronted weaver, red-winged pytilia, African silverbill, and white-rumped seedeater.

Nocturnal excursions around Tono Dam often yield sightings of the incredible standard-winged nightjar. The male of the species has a 50cm-long bare feather shaft ending in the so-called 'standard' – a large feather vane off each wing – an impossible-sounding combination making for one of the world's most unusual

several as seasonal intra-African migrants. Most species are predominantly white in colour, with some yellow, orange, black, or even red and blue markings on the wings.

The most diverse family of butterflies in Africa is the Lycaenidae, which accounts for almost 500 of the 1,500 species recorded continent-wide. Known also as Gossamer Wings, this varied family consists mostly of small to medium-sized butterflies, with a wingspan of 1–5cm, dull underwings, and brilliant violet blue, copper, or rufous-orange upper wings. The larvae of many Lycaenidae species have a symbiotic relationship with ants – they secrete a fluid that is milked by the ants and are thus permitted to shelter in their nests.

Another well-represented family is the Nymphalidae, a diversely coloured group of small to large butterflies, generally associated with forest edges or interiors. The Nymphalidae are also known as brush-footed butterflies because their forelegs have evolved into non-functional brush-like structures. One of the more common and distinctive species is the African blue tiger, *Tirumala petiverana*, a large black butterfly with about two dozen blue-white wing spots, often observed in forest paths near puddles or feeding from animal droppings.

The family Charaxidae, regarded by some authorities to be a subfamily of the Nymphalidae, is represented in Africa by roughly 200 species. Typically large, robust, strong fliers with one or two short tails on each wing, the butterflies in this family vary greatly in coloration, and several species appear to be scarce and localised since they inhabit forest canopies and are seldom observed.

Rather less spectacular are the grass-skipper species of the family Hersperiidae, most of which are small and rather drably coloured, though some are more attractively marked in black, white, and/or yellow. The grass-skippers are regarded as forming the evolutionary link between butterflies and the generally more nocturnal moths, represented in Ghana by several families of which the most impressive are the boldly patterned giant silk-moths of the family Saturniidae.

birds, particularly during its display flight. Other nocturnal species include greyish eagle-owl, African scops-owl, northern white-faced owl, barn owl and long-tailed and plain nightjar. Adam Riley's company, **Rockjumper Birding Tours** (\Vf *(+27) 33 342 8346;* e *info@rockjumper.co.za; www.rockjumper.co.za*), specialises in guided birding tours to Ghana and elsewhere in Africa.

Explore Africa in your own home...

If you are planning a trip to Africa, or just like to learn more about it, *Travel Africa* magazine is the ideal read for you. Published in the UK, each edition comprises at least 120 pages of travel ideas, practical information and features on Africa's attractions, wildlife and cultures.

SPECIAL OFFER! Subscribe for four issues (one year) and we'll give you an extra issue **FREE!** Phone, fax or email us or subscribe online using our secure server. Quote BRADT in the gift voucher box to make sure you get your free issue...

www.travelafricamag.com tel: 01844 278883
email: subs@travelafricamag.com 4 Rycote Lane Farm, Milton Common, OX9 2NZ, UK

3

Planning and Preparation

For a list of books and websites useful in planning a trip to Ghana, please see Appendix 3, *Further Reading* page 407. Aspects of trip preparation related to health and safety are covered in detail in the *Health* section, page 91.

WHEN TO VISIT

In most respects, the best time to visit Ghana is during the northern hemisphere winter. The months of October through to April are not significantly hotter or cooler than other times of the year, but they are a great deal more comfortable since humidity levels are lower. More importantly, these months form the dry season, which means there are fewer mosquitoes (and correspondingly there's a lower risk of contracting malaria), dirt roads are in better condition, and there is less likelihood of you or your luggage being drenched in an unexpected storm. The dry season is particularly suitable for those with a strong interest in natural history, since game viewing is best when the grass is low and resident bird populations are supplemented by all sorts of Palaearctic migrants.

The main disadvantage of the dry season, particularly from December through to February, is that visibility is seriously impeded by sands blown from the Sahara by the Harmattan winds. This won't greatly affect most travellers, but the beaches lose much of their beauty, people who plan on doing a lot of hiking will miss the best of the mountain scenery, and serious photographers will find the dull ambient light and grey skies not at all conducive to getting decent pictures.

RED TAPE

Check well in advance that your **passport** hasn't expired and will not do so for a while, since you may be refused entry on a passport that's due to expire within six months of your intended departure date.

Visitors of practically all nationalities require a **visa** to enter Ghana. There is some talk of Ghana following the recent initiative of several other African countries and creating the facility for one to purchase a visa upon arrival by air or at a land border, but until such times as this happens, visas must be applied for in advance at a Ghanaian embassy or high commission. Most embassies require applicants to fill in the application form in quadruplicate and send it in, together with four identical passport-sized photos (two, if you hand it in in person), an air ticket, a letter of introduction (for business travellers only), your passport, and a fee of US$30–60 (£30–40 in the UK), depending on whether you want a single-entry visa (valid for one stay of up to 60 days from the date of entry) or a multiple-entry visa (valid for any number of visits of up to 60 days in duration within 6 or 12 months of the date of issue). Visas typically take three days to issue if you hand in and collect the application personally, but will take around ten days by post. As with many developing countries, journalists are likely to face a considerably longer wait.

Should you want to stay in Ghana for longer than 60 days, you will have to apply for a visa extension once you are in the country (normally a straightforward process) and to pay an additional US$10 for every extra 30 days, regardless of whether you have paid for a single- or multiple-entry visa. It's worth knowing that a visa extension in Accra might take two weeks to process, whereas it shouldn't take more than 48 hours at any other regional capital – although a considerably more attractive option might be to buy a multiple-entry visa and then to cross into one of the neighbouring countries and get an extra 60 days on your return.

We've had reports of travellers having visas issued in January stamped a year behind – eg: a visa issued on 3 January 2004, but accidentally dated 3 January 2003 – which effectively means it will have expired on the date of issue! It's an easy mistake, and most (but not all) border officials will be reasonable about it, but best to check your visa is dated correctly when you collect it.

Visas forms for the UK and US can be downloaded from the respective high commission websites, ie: www.ghana-com.co.uk and www.ghana-embassy.org.

E GHANA HIGH COMMISSIONS, EMBASSIES AND DIPLOMATIC REPRESENTATIVES

Algeria Rue Parrnentier-Hydra, Algiers; ℡ 02 60 64 44/ 60 64 76

Australia (Perth) PO Box 169, 13 Numerella St, O'Malley, ACT 2606, Perth, Western Australia; ℡ 02 62902110 or 02 62867738; f 08 9316 2254; e ghcomaus@grapevine.com.aus or ghcomaussies@post.com

Australia (Sydney) Ste 1404, Level 14, 370 Pitt St, Sydney, NSW 2000; ℡ 02 9283 2961

Belgium 7 General Wahisin Laan, B-1030 Brussels; ℡ 02 705 82 20

Benin BP 488, Cotonou RPB; ℡ 30 07 46

Brazil Shis QL 10, Conj 08, Casa 02, PO Box 07-0456, Brasilia; ℡ 061 248 6047/9

Bulgaria PO Box 38, 113 Sofia; ℡ 02 70 65 09

Burkina Faso BP 212, Ouagadougou 01; ℡ 30 76 35

Canada 1 Clemow Av, The Glebe, Ottawa, Ontario K1S 2A9; ℡ 613 236 0871–4; f 613 236 0874

China 8 San Li Tun Lu Rd, Beijing 100600; ℡ 10 6532 1319/6532 1544/6532 2012 (switchboard); f 0086 10 65323602; e ghacan@public.bta.net.cn

Côte d'Ivoire BP 1871, Abidjan; ℡ 33 11 24

Denmark ℡ 039 628222; f 039 621652; e ghana@ mail.dk; www.ghanaembassy.dk

Ethiopia PO Box 3173, Addis Ababa; ℡ 01 71 14 02

France 8 Villa Said, Paris; ℡ 01 45 00 09 50

Germany Stavanger Strasse 17 & 19, 10439 Berlin; ℡ 0 30 447 9052; f 0 30 447 9053; e ghanembonn@ aol.com

India 50-N Satya Marg, Chanakyapuri, New Delhi 110021, India; ℡ 011 6883298, 6883315 & 6883338

Italy 4 Via Ostriana, 00199, Rome; ℡ 06 8391200

Japan PO Box 16, Tokyo; ℡ 3 5410 8631/2/3; f 3 5410 8635

Liberia PO Box 10-0417, 1000 Monrovia 10; ℡ 261477, 261355, 261098

Netherlands ℡ 070 3384 384/5; f 070 3062 800; www.ghanaembassy.nl

Nigeria 21/23 King George V Rd, PO Box 889, Lagos; ℡ 01 630015, 630934

Russia 14 Skaterny Pereulok, Moscow; ℡ 095 202-1870/ 71, 202-1890

Switzerland 11 Belpstrasse, 3000 Berne; PO Box 3007; ℡ 031 381 7852; f 031 381 4941

Togo BP 92, Lome; ℡ 21 31 94 or 21 26 02

UK 104 Highgate Hill, London N6 5HE; ℡ 020 8342 7500/8686; f 020 8345 8570/8566; www.ghana-com.co.uk; *Trade Section* 102 Park St, London W1Y 3RT; ℡ 020 7493 4901

USA 3512 International Drive NW, Washington DC 20008; ℡ (New York) 212 832 1300 or (Washington DC) 202 686 4520, *passport section* ℡ 202-6864503; www.ghanaembassy.org/index.html

In theory, it's compulsory to have a valid **yellow fever vaccination certificate** to enter Ghana, but in practice this document is seldom asked for.

In case you might want to drive or hire a vehicle in Ghana, do organise an **international driving licence** (any AA office will do this for a nominal fee).

For security reasons, it's advisable to detail all your important information on one sheet of paper, photocopy it, and distribute a few copies in your luggage, your money-belt, and amongst relatives or friends at home. The sort of things you want to include on this are your travellers' cheque numbers and refund information, travel insurance policy details and 24-hour emergency contact number, passport number, details of relatives or friends to be contacted in an emergency, bank and credit card details, camera and lens serial numbers, etc.

Should your passport be lost or stolen, it will generally be easier to get a replacement if you have a photocopy of the important pages.

Something that you no longer need to be concerned about, at least in our experience, is having policemen ask you to produce your passport on a whim.

GETTING THERE

✈ **BY AIR** The national carrier, **Ghana International Airlines** (GIA), flies between Accra and London and Johannesburg, replacing Ghana Airways, which went out of business in 2004. Some passengers have reported delays of many days, but reliability is likely to improve considerably following the acquisition of a second aeroplane in 2006. One major advantage of flying with GIA is the enormous luggage allowance: 46kg at time of writing, compared to around 23kg on most other carriers.

Other airlines with scheduled flights to Accra include Afriqiyah Airways, Alitalia, Atlantic Express Airlines, British Airways, Egypt Air, Emirates, Ethiopian Airlines, Kenya Airways, KLM, Lufthansa, Virgin Nigeria and Royal Air Maroc.

Flights from the US and Canada tend to be expensive, so North Americans with more time than money may find it cheaper to fly to London and organise a ticket to Africa from there. Travellers who want to see the north of Ghana, but are tight for time, might also consider pushing on through to Ouagadougou in Burkina Faso and flying out of there.

There are dozens upon dozens of travel agents in London offering cheap flights to Africa, and it's worth checking out the ads in magazines like *Time Out* and *TNT* and phoning around before you book anything. The following include Ghana specialists:

Africa Travel Centre 21 Leigh St, London WC1H 9EW; ✆ 0845 450 1520; f 020 7387 1211; e info@africatravel.co.uk; www.africatravel.co.uk
Alpha Holidays Ste 406, 71 Bond Way, Vauxhall, London SW8 1SQ; ✆ 020 7793 1667; f 020 7793 1985; e info@alphaholidays.com; www.alphaholidays.com
Interchange 27 Stafford Rd, Croydon, Surrey CR0 4NG; ✆ 020 8681 3612; f 020 8760 0031; e interchange@interchange.uk.com; www.interchangeuk.com

STA 117 Euston Rd, London NW1 2SX; ✆ 0871 468 0619; f 020 7388 0944; www.statravel.co.uk. There are 40 STA branches in the UK specialising in cheap round-the-world-type tickets.
Trailfinders 194 Kensington High St, London W8 7RG; ✆ 020 7938 3939; f 020 7937 9294; www.trailfinders.com. Also specialise in cheap round-the-world tickets.

Unless it's absolutely unavoidable, don't even think about flying to Ghana on a one-way ticket and organising your ticket out once you are there. For starters, you may hit serious problems with airport immigration officials if you don't arrive on a return ticket, and, secondly, flights out of Accra are very expensive, so you'll almost certainly end up paying double what you would for a cheap return.

🚐 **OVERLAND FROM EUROPE** There are two overland routes between Europe and Ghana. Both start in Morocco and involve crossing the Sahara, one via Algeria and the other via Mauritania, then continue through Mali and Burkina Faso. The Algeria option has been impassable for some years now, but the situation with either route is highly changeable and you should seek current advice. For readers based in the UK, the best way to gauge the situation would be to get in touch with the many overland truck companies that advertise in magazines such as *TNT* and *Time Out*. And, frankly, unless you've a reliable 4×4, joining an overland truck trip is almost certainly the best way of doing this difficult route, especially if you have thoughts of continuing through the Democratic Republic of the Congo (formerly Zaire) to east Africa. Operators who offer overland trips by truck in and through Ghana include:

Dragoman Overland Camp Green, Debenham, Stowmarket, Suffolk IP14 6LA; ✆ 01728 861133; f 01728 861127; e info@dragoman.co.uk
Explore Worldwide Nelson Hse, 55 Victoria Rd, Farmborough, Hants GU14 7PA; ✆ 01252 319448;

e info@exploreworldwide.com. Offer overland trips by truck in & through Ghana.
Guerba Expeditions Wessex Hse, 40 Station Rd, Westbury, Wiltshire, BA13 3JN ✆ 01373 826611; f 01373 858351; e info@guerba.co.uk

Travellers visiting Ghana overland from Europe will presumably want to carry a regional or continental guide. If you are taking your own vehicle, then the *Sahara Handbook* by Chris Scott (Trailblazer, 2001) is the essential companion, while *Africa Overland* by Siân Pritchard-Jones and Bob Gibbons (Bradt Travel Guides, 2005) is very useful when it comes to general planning. It might also be worth investing in a regional guide to west Africa, or even a more general guide to Africa; but bear in mind that the wider the scope of the guide, the skimpier it is on individual detail.

WHAT TO TAKE

There are two simple rules to bear in mind when you decide what to take with you to Ghana. The first is to bring with you everything that you could possibly need and that might not be readily available when you need it. The second is to carry as little as possible. Somewhat contradictory rules, you might think, and you'd be right – so the key is finding the right balance, something that probably depends on personal experience as much as anything. Worth stressing is that most genuine necessities are surprisingly easy to get hold of in Ghana, and that most of the ingenious gadgets you can buy in camping shops are unlikely to amount to much more than deadweight on the road. If it came to it, you could easily travel in Ghana with little more than a change of clothes, a few basic toiletries, and a medical kit.

CARRYING LUGGAGE Assuming that you'll be using public transport, you'll want to carry your luggage on your back, either in a backpack or in a suitcase that converts into one, since you'll tend to spend a lot of time walking between bus stations and hotels. Which of these you choose depends mainly on your style of travel. If you intend doing a lot of hiking, you definitely want a proper backpack. On the other hand, if you'll be doing things where it might be a good idea to shake off the sometimes negative image attached to backpackers, then there would be obvious advantages in being able to convert your backpack into a conventional suitcase.

My preference, before travelling with a photographer made it impractical, was a robust 35cl daypack. The advantages of keeping luggage as light and compact as possible are manifold. For starters, you can rest it on your lap on bus trips, avoiding extra charges for luggage, arguments about where your bag should be stored, and the slight but real risk of theft. A compact bag also makes for greater mobility, whether you're hiking or looking for a hotel in town. The sacrifice? Leaving behind camping equipment, a sleeping bag, and paring down your toiletries and wardrobe. Do this, and it's quite possible to fit everything you truly need into a daypack, and possibly even a few luxuries – I've always travelled with binoculars, a bird field guide, and at least five novels – and still keep the weight down to around 8kg. Frankly, it puzzles me what the many backpackers who wander around with an enormous pack and absolutely no camping equipment actually carry!

If your luggage won't squeeze into a daypack, a sensible compromise is to carry a large daypack in your rucksack. That way, you can carry a tent and other camping equipment when you need it, but at other times reduce your luggage to fit into a daypack and leave what you're not using in storage.

Travellers carrying a lot of valuable items should look for a pack that can easily be padlocked. A locked bag can, of course, be slashed open, but in Ghana you are still most likely to encounter casual theft of the sort to which a lock would be a real deterrent.

CLOTHES Take the minimum, bearing in mind that you can easily and cheaply replace worn items in Ghana, or, even better, get them made to measure. In my opinion, what you need is one or possibly two pairs of trousers and/or skirts, one pair of shorts, three shirts or T-shirts, one light sweater, maybe a light waterproof windbreaker during the rainy season, enough socks and underwear to last five to seven days, one solid pair of shoes or boots for walking, and one pair of sandals, thongs, or other light shoes.

When you select your clothes, remember that jeans are heavy to carry, hot to wear, and slow to dry. Far better to bring light cotton trousers and, if you intend spending a while in montane regions, tracksuit bottoms which will provide extra cover on chilly nights. Skirts are best made of a light natural fabric such as cotton. For reasons of protocol, women may prefer to keep their shoulders covered and wear a skirt that goes below the knees in the Muslim north – it's by no means necessary, since Ghanaians are relatively relaxed about dress codes, but single women in particular might find that a dress draws much less attention than skimpier attire.

T-shirts are lighter and less bulky than proper shirts, though the top pocket of a shirt (particularly if it buttons up) is a good place to carry spending money in markets and bus stations, since it's easier to keep an eye on than trouser pockets. One sweater or sweatshirt will be adequate, since no part of Ghana lies at an altitude above 1,000m, so night-time temperatures are almost invariably comfortable to sweaty. There is a massive used-clothing industry in Ghana, and at most markets you'll find stalls selling jumpers of dubious aesthetic but impeccable functional value for next to nothing – you might consider buying such clothing on the spot and giving it away afterwards.

Socks and underwear must be made from natural fabrics. Bear in mind that re-using sweaty undergarments will encourage fungal infections, such as athlete's foot, as well as prickly heat in the groin region. Socks and underpants are light and compact enough that it's worth bringing a week's supply. As for footwear, genuine hiking boots are worth considering only if you're a serious off-road hiker, since they are very heavy whether on your feet or in your pack. A good pair of walking shoes, preferably made of leather and with good ankle support, is a good compromise. It's also useful to carry sandals, thongs, or other light shoes.

Getting clothes made from local fabrics is also quick and relatively inexpensive. The markets sell all sorts of cotton-based cloth by the yard (slightly shorter than a metre) and the vendors will be able to take you to reliable local seamstresses.

CAMPING EQUIPMENT The case for bringing camping equipment to Ghana is compelling only if you intend hiking or visiting some of the more obscure reserves where there is no other accommodation. In most other situations, rooms are cheap and campsites few and far between, so this isn't a country where camping will save huge sums of cash. The main argument against carrying camping equipment is that it will increase the weight and bulk of your luggage by up to 5kg, all of which is deadweight except for when you camp.

If you decide to carry camping equipment, the key is to look for the lightest available gear. It is now possible to buy a lightweight tent weighing little more than 2kg, but make sure that the one you buy is mosquito-proof. Other essentials for camping include a sleeping bag and a roll-mat, which will serve as both insulation and padding. You might want to carry a stove for occasions when no firewood is available, as is the case in many montane national parks where the collection of firewood is forbidden, or for cooking in a tropical storm. If you do carry a stove, it's worth knowing that Camping Gaz cylinders are readily available only in southern Ghana (which is where you're most likely to do most of your camping and open-air catering). A box of firelighter blocks will get a fire going in the most unpromising conditions. It would also be advisable to carry a pot, plate, cup, and cutlery.

OTHER USEFUL ITEMS Many backpackers, even those with no intention of camping, carry a **sleeping bag** – but a much better plan in this climate would be to carry a **cotton sheet** or **sheet-sleeping bag**, something you can easily make yourself or have run up cheaply when you arrive in Accra. For the most part, the bedding in local lodgings will be far cleaner than any sweaty rag you haul around with you, but it can be a relief if faced with super-synthetic sheets on a humid night, or something less than sanitary.

If you're interested in natural history, it's difficult to imagine anything that will give you such value-for-weight entertainment as a pair of light compact binoculars, which these days needn't be much heavier or bulkier than a pack of cards. Binoculars are essential if you want to get a good look at birds (Africa boasts a remarkably colourful avifauna even if you've no desire to put a name to everything that flaps) or to watch distant mammals in game reserves. For most purposes, 7×21 compact binoculars will be fine, though some might prefer 7×35 traditional binoculars for their larger field of vision. Serious birdwatchers will find a 10× magnification more useful.

Some travellers like to carry their own **padlock**, though in Ghana there are few circumstances where you are likely to need one, unless you have a pack that is lockable. A combination lock might be the best idea, since potential thieves in Ghana are far more likely to have experience of picking locks with keys.

All the **toilet bag** basics (soap, shampoo, conditioner, toothpaste, toothbrush, deodorant, basic razors) are very easy to replace as you go along – so there's no need to bring family-sized packs – but women planning on longer stays might want to stock up on some **heavy-duty**, **leave-in conditioner** to minimize sun-damage to their hair. Those staying outside Accra and Kumasi should also carry enough **tampons** and/or **sanitary pads** to see them through, since these items may not always be easy to find. If you wear **contact lenses**, be aware that the various cleansing and storing fluids are not readily available in Ghana and, since many people find the intense sun and dry climate irritates their eyes, you might consider reverting to glasses. Some readers have recommended daily disposable contact lenses to save the hassle and risk of re-using. Most budget hotels provide **toilet paper** and many also provide **towels**, but it is worth taking your own with you to make sure you don't get caught short. If you plan eating at local stalls, it might be worth bringing a **cheap plastic bowl**, just in case you're not too great with eating with your fingers!

Other useful items include a **torch**, a **penknife**, and a compact **alarm clock** for those early morning starts – or you could use a **mobile phone** with an alarm clock. They do make obvious targets for thieves but are nigh on essential if you are based in a city and plan on having a social life. A pack of wet- or **facial cleansing-wipes** can help maintain a semblance of cleanliness on long, dusty journeys, and **anti-bacterial gel** is a good way of making sure you don't make yourself sick with your own grime if you're eating on the move. If you're interested in what's happening in the world, you might also think about carrying a **shortwave radio**. Some travellers carry **games** – most commonly a pack of cards, less often chess or draughts or travel Scrabble. A **universal sink plug** will get around the fact that many baths in Ghana don't come with a plug – useful for doing the laundry if not for bathing in – and a twisted **no-peg washing line** is great for hanging them out. Some people wouldn't travel without a good pair of **earplugs** to help them sleep at night (or through morning mosque calls in the north) and a **travel pillow** to make long bus journeys that bit easier to endure.

You should carry a small **medical kit**, the contents of which are discussed in *Chapter 4* (see page 93), as are **mosquito nets**. Two items of tropical toiletry that are surprisingly difficult to get hold of in Ghana are **mosquito repellent** of a type suitable for skin application, and **high-factor sunscreen**. In both cases, you are advised to bring all you need with you. One could spend a day in Accra unsuccessfully trying to get hold of mosquito repellent, though aerial repellents and mosquito coils can be bought almost anywhere. Only a few pharmacies in Accra stock sunscreen (*eg: the Pillbox Pharmacy off Cantonments Rd*), and finding anything stronger than Factor 6 is nigh on impossible. **Canesten** for fungal infections, though available in Ghana, is expensive.

$ MONEY

ORGANISING YOUR FINANCES There are three ways of carrying money: hard currency cash, travellers' cheques, or a debit/credit card. These days, most travellers prefer to carry a card as their primary source of funds, but this has several limitations in Ghana. For one, very few tourist facilities outside the capital accept any form of card, which means that it is difficult to make direct payments to hotels and restaurants, etc. Most large towns and cities will have at least one bank with an ATM that takes international cards (Hohoe was one of the few exceptions when this fourth edition was researched), but this facility may not be available during a power cut or if the only machine in town happens to be out of service.

Where an ATM is present and functional, it is normally possible to draw up to US$90 per transaction in local currency against a Visa card and make upwards of five transactions daily, though this sort of thing is subject to regular change and may vary from one bank to the next. As a rule, larger transactions can be made over the counter. Be aware, however, that the *only* type of card accepted by most such facilities in Ghana is Visa, though MasterCard and American Express are accepted in some central Accra banks and major hotels. What's more, many establishments that advertise Visa facilities don't actually accept card payments, or offer poor exchange rates, or levy hefty surcharges.

Put this all together, and it's little wonder than on most recent trips in Africa, I've bumped into at least one person who's strayed a bit too far off the beaten track with only a credit card for support. It pays to be conservative in your assumptions about where you'll be able to use a card, as the one thing you want to avoid is a situation where you need to have money transferred or drafted across to west Africa. Furthermore, we have received several reports of credit/debit card scams in Ghana. Sometimes this has involved direct theft of a card, but more frequently hotel staff have simply copied a card number from a client and used it to make a fraudulent payment. Some readers have reported having had their details used within a couple of hours of making a credit card payment, and this has happened at some of the larger and more reputable hotels.

Bearing the above in mind, the best overall option for Ghana will depend to some extent on how long you'll be there, your style of travel, and whether you'll spend most of your time in cities or in the sticks. If you are spending one week only in Ghana, all in Accra, then you should be fine with a Visa card and nothing else. If you will spend weeks exploring in more remote areas, a card will be close to useless. Most people's travel plans fall between these extremes, however, and a sensible compromise would be to carry perhaps half of what you expect to spend in the form of cash or travellers' cheques, and to withdraw the remainder from ATMs as you go along. Bearing in mind the vulnerability of cards to fraud, it is probably wise to avoid paying hotel bills directly by card, while carrying a second debit or credit card (and keeping it apart from the rest of your funds) provides some insurance against theft or loss of your primary card.

It's advisable to make sure that the money you bring with you is in a healthy mix of denominations of US$100 and below. The advantage of travellers' cheques over cash is that can be refunded if they are lost or stolen, but it is increasingly difficult to change travellers' cheques except at larger banks, rates are often poor as compared to cash, and the only widely recognised brand is American Express (we've had a few reports of people having real problems changing Thomas Cook travellers' cheques). In order to facilitate a refund in the case of theft, you should keep the proof of purchase separate from the cheques, as well as noting down which cheques you have cashed.

The advantage of hard currency cash (especially US dollars) over cards or travellers' cheques is that it is so readily changeable into local currency in almost any circumstance. For this reason, it's advisable to bring a proportion of your money in cash, say around US$200–300, since you are bound to hit situations where travellers' cheques won't be accepted (the bureau de change at the airport, for example). Furthermore, cash gets a better exchange rate, especially large denomination bills – but this won't be much consolation if all your money is stolen, so it's inadvisable to carry cash only.

Carry your hard currency and travellers' cheques, as well as your passport and other important documentation, in a money-belt – one that can be hidden beneath your clothing rather than the sort of fashionable, externally worn type, which, in some circumstances, will serve as a beacon rather than protection. Your money-belt should be made of cotton or another natural fabric, and everything inside the belt should be wrapped in plastic to protect it against sweat.

In theory, any excess local currency can be changed back into dollars when you leave Ghana, provided you can provide proof of purchase from a bank or other licensed foreign exchange bureau. In practice, the banks at the airport will often refuse to offer this service, which leaves you stuck with spending your leftover cedis in unexciting duty-free shops, which tend to charge high dollar rates and to offer a poor rate of exchange when spending local currency! If you have excess cash, your best bet is to exchange it at one of the foreign exchange bureaux in town before you head to the airport.

COSTS AND BUDGETING Ghana is not an expensive country in which to travel. So far as travel basics go, **accommodation** for one or two people will probably average out at around US$5 per day for the cheapest room, US$8 per day for a self-contained room, and from US$20 per day for air-conditioned comfort.

For **food**, expect to spend around US$2 per day per head if you eat street food only, and around US$5 if you eat once daily in a restaurant.

Depending on how often and how far you travel, **public transport** shouldn't come to more than US$4 per day per head, while a charter taxi ride in most towns costs no more than US$2.50.

The main thing you need to add to the above on a daily basis is **liquid**. Unless you restrict yourself to tap water (not advisable) or the slightly chemical-tasting but perfectly acceptable water in sachets, you'll spend a fair bit of money just keeping your thirst quenched in Ghana's hot climate – say US$2 per head daily if you stick to bottled mineral water and soft drinks, perhaps US$4 daily if you add on a couple of beers.

Put this together, and you're looking at a rock-bottom budget of US$10/15 daily for one/two people (considerably more for any nights you spend at Mole National Park, unless you camp there). To travel in reasonable comfort, eat and drink what you feel like within reason, and take the odd taxi, a budget of around US$20/30 for one/two people would be about right. If you want air conditioning, two solid meals, and the rest, I'd budget on US$40/50 for one/two people.

The above reckoning excludes one-off expenses such as entrance fees to museums or guiding fees in parks, factors that tend to create the occasional expensive day, markedly so for those on a tight budget. In countries such as Tanzania, where national park fees and safari costs are very high, I've sometimes found it a useful budgeting device to separate one-off expenses from the more predictable day-to-day costs. As a rule, you'll have relatively few major one-off expenses in Ghana, though tips and guide fees, etc, can start to add up in some places. If you are very tight for cash, rather than allocating yourself a budget of, say, US$15 per day, it might work better to aim for a daily budget of US$10 and set aside the rest for one-offs.

LONDON, ACCRA, LONDON
The **right price,** *the* **right choice**

GHANA
INTERNATIONAL AIRLINES
Experience it. Believe it.

www.fly-ghana.com

4

Travelling in Ghana

i TOURIST INFORMATION

There is a regional office of the **Ghana Tourist Board** in each of the country's ten regional capitals. On the whole, these offices are helpful and well worth visiting if you want to check up on new developments in the region, though our experience has been that staff are sometimes surprisingly ignorant about even the most important local attractions, and often have a tendency to invent a plausible but inaccurate answer to a query rather than admit that they don't know.

A useful source of information about wildlife reserves and ecotourism in Ghana is the **Nature Conservation Research Centre** (NCRC) website (*www.ncrc-ghana.org*).

REGIONAL TOURIST OFFICES

Accra Regional Admin Office, Barnes Rd, PO Box 3106, Accra; ☎ 021 23 1817

Bolgatanga (Upper East) Information Services Dept, PO Box 395, Bolgatanga; ☎ 072 3416

Cape Coast (Central) Jackson Rd, PO Box 847, Cape Coast; ☎ 042 32062

Ho (Volta) SIC Bldg, PO Box 568, Ho; ☎ 0756 22431

Koforidua (Eastern) SIC Bldg, PO Box 771, Koforidua; ☎ 081 23209/32128

Kumasi (Ashanti) National Cultural Centre, PO Box 3065, Kumasi; ☎ 051 26242/22421

Sekondi-Takoradi (Western) Third Flr, SIC Bldg, PO Box 781, Takoradi; ☎ 031 22357

Sunyani (Brong Ahafo) Regional Admin Office, PO Box 802, Sunyani; ☎ 061 7108

Tamale (Northern) Regional Admin Office, PO Box 1053, Tamale; ☎ 071 22212

Wa (Upper West) Ministry of Trade and Industry, PO Box 289, Wa; ☎ 0756 22431

PUBLIC HOLIDAYS

Although several public holidays are recognised in Ghana, the only major impact they will have on tourists is that banks and government offices are closed and the volume of public transport decreases to a level you'd expect on a Sunday. There are four variable-date public holidays: the Christian Good Friday and Easter Monday, the Muslim Eid il Fitr and Eid il Adel.

In addition, the following fixed-date public holidays are recognised:

1 January	New Year's Day
6 March	Independence Day
1 May	May Day
25 May	Africa Unity Day
4 June	June 4 Anniversary
1 July	Republic Day
5 December	Farmers' Day
25 December	Christmas Day
26 December	Boxing Day

FARMERS' DAY

Ama Branford-Arthur

Farmers' Day was instituted in 1984, after a particularly bad period of drought and hunger the previous year, when it hardly rained, there was a very bad harvest, widespread bush fires, and many Ghanaians starved. To compound the problem, Nigeria deported a great number of Ghanaians who were working in that country, who arrived to swell the population.

I remember that at that time, *kenkey*, a staple food of many Ghanaians, was not allowed to be cooked at the *kenkey* seller's house, so great was the demand. The trick was to arrive early, buy as many uncooked balls as you were allowed, and then to take them home and cook them yourself. These were the early days of Jerry Rawlings' revolution, which started on 31 December 1981, and the economy was in serious trouble – it's amazing that the drought didn't cause it to collapse entirely.

In 1984, the IMF and the World Bank stepped in to help, but, more fortunately, it rained. The harvest was much better, and so Farmers' Day was instituted to thank the hardworking and often un-rewarded farmers for their efforts. It was not initially a holiday, though. Indeed, I believe it was not until 1995 that it was declared a national holiday.

Farmers from all over the country are assessed by visits to their farms from extension officers of the Ministry of Agriculture, who evaluate their farming methods, acreage, diversity of products and their yield. Winners are chosen in each category by a central committee. There are two sets of best farmers – those that are entered at the national level, and those that win at the regional level.

A couple of weeks before Farmers' Day proper, all the national-level farmers are invited to Accra. Accompanied by 'chaperones' from the ministry, they tour the sights, go on the Akosombo Lake, visit the president, and are royally wined and dined. Note that none of them know, at this stage, who will be chosen National Best Farmer.

On the actual day, all the winning farmers are taken to the durbar grounds, which have been different each year. The event is broadcast on national television. Starting in reverse order, and with appropriate prizes, each of them is honoured. The crowning moment is the unveiling of the National Best Farmer (NBF), with an impressive reeling off of her/his achievements by the MC. When s/he is called to the podium, he/she receives from last year's NBF a traditional sword, symbolising a passing on of the responsibility for feeding Ghana's very hungry population.

When the awards first started, the NBF received a pair of Wellington farming boots, a set of cutlasses, a power tiller, and 12 yards of wax cloth. Prizes have expanded to include a visit to the Royal Agricultural Festival in Kew, UK, and pick-up trucks. Last year, the NBF was awarded a two-bedroom house in the town of his choice by the Agricultural Development Bank. In times when the farmer has received a pick-up truck, the president has been his driver, driving him around the durbar grounds to the cheers of the crowd. Throughout the year, whoever won will take part in programmes and discussions, and past NBFs have set up training for young people.

If the holiday falls at the weekend, the 'free day' shifts to the following Monday. One reader adds that: 'on two occasions during our six months in Ghana, public holidays were announced at short notice – both on Mondays! If you're travelling when this happens, public transport will be minimal and banks are closed, so keep your ear to the ground.'

$ MONEY

The unit of currency is the cedi (pronounced 'seedy'), named after the Twi for cowry shell (visible on a C200 coin). The cedi was re-denominated by a factor of 10,000 as this book went to print, and pesewas (cent-like divisions made obsolete by years of heavy devaluation) were restored. It is likely that old and new notes will exist alongside each other for some time to come, and the locals will take some time to think in terms of 'new' cedis. The move follows years of steady devaluation. During the early 1990s, the value of the cedi fell by roughly 100%, but then held reasonably steady at between 2,000 and 2,500 cedis to the US dollar until late 1999, after which it has devalued a further 200% to approach C7,000 to the dollar within the space of one year. Over the six years prior to publication of the fourth edition of this book, the trend has been one of steady but undramatic devaluation against all major currencies. As this book goes to print, exchange rates are around C0.92 to the US dollar, C1.25 to the euro and C1.85 to the British pound sterling.

FOREIGN EXCHANGE The most widely recognised and exchangeable foreign currency is the US dollar, although the euro is fast catching up, and the pound sterling is often just as exchangeable but tends to fetch a slightly poorer rate. US dollar, euro, and pound sterling banknotes can be exchanged for local currency in practically any town or border post, often at a bank or a private bureau de change (forex bureau), though smaller bills often fetch a poor rate compared to US$50/100 bills. In Accra, Kumasi, and, to a lesser degree, the other regional capitals, there's generally a choice of places to exchange hard currency cash and the rate may vary by as much as 10%, so it's worth shopping around; you will also find some other world currencies accepted. In smaller towns, your options will probably be limited to one bank or forex bureau, so you'll have to take whatever rate you're offered.

In towns where there are no banks, or if you want to exchange money outside the normal banking hours of 08.30 to 14.00, you'll rarely have a problem finding a private individual to exchange your US dollars. There is always a danger of being conned in such a situation, however – particularly when you deal with 'professional' money-changers at borders who occasionally deal in counterfeits – so I would advise against changing significantly more money than you need to get to the next town with banking facilities.

The situation is less straightforward with **travellers' cheques**, which are not accepted by private foreign exchange bureaux, while even the larger banks outside Accra have to get rates on a daily basis from the capital, a procedure that becomes less reliable the further north you go. If you are carrying mostly travellers' cheques, you should probably rely on being able to exchange money only in the regional capitals. North of Kumasi, you may be held up a day or two waiting for the rates to be faxed up. The simple solution to all this is to carry enough US dollars in the form of cash. One reader wrote in to suggest that 'since Ghana is a very safe country it might be a good idea to have only plain dollars instead of travellers' cheques, which are quite hard to change and you get a bad rate', but I cannot recommend going that far – if you are robbed, cash is not replaceable; travellers' cheques are.

The three main banks with foreign exchange facilities are the Commercial Bank of Ghana, Barclays, and the Standard Chartered. In general, they offer a lower rate of exchange for cash than the private foreign exchange bureaux. When we were in the country, the best exchange rate for travellers' cheques was invariably at the Standard Chartered Bank, which normally charges no commission. Travellers' cheques can be exchanged only on production of your passport and most banks also ask for a local address (although a hotel address should suffice if you say you are staying for a few days). Some might also insist you show the proof of purchase (ie: the receipt you received when you bought the cheques), in which case do bear in mind that most issuing companies will not fulfil the guarantee of refund if the proof of purchase is stolen along with the cheques!

If you are changing a large sum of money and are offered 'old' cedi banknotes, do check that the bank or forex bureau can give you the bulk of your local currency in large notes. The new C20,000 or C10,000 notes are best, and even C5,000 is acceptable, but it's not unusual to have to accept local currency in C2,000 bills – which works out at almost 500 banknotes per US$100! It's also worth thinking about how and where you will carry your newly acquired pile of bank notes after a major transaction. You don't want to be walking around the streets of Accra with a few hundred US dollars worth of cedis and nowhere to conceal them.

SMALL CHANGE Prior to re-denomination in July 2007, the largest bill was the C20,000 note (around US$2) – yet finding small change (or as locals call it, 'balance') even for 'old' C5,000 notes was an ongoing problem for Ghanaian traders. Indeed, travellers were frequently unable to make a purchase for, say, C100 because nobody could find change for an 'old' C500 note! This scenario is bound to persist under the new denominational regime, and the simple solution is to keep a reasonable balance of small bills and coins on you at all times. Bear in mind that tro-tro conductors and taxi drivers *always* seem to be able to find change, so never use your last small bill on a taxi or tro-tro ride, but rather give them a big bill and get change from them. And if you are in a hurry and don't have the right amount when you buy something like a Coke, then pay before you start drinking so the vendor has time to find change. In general, you can rely on vendors who run off and get change to return again!

PRICES With few exceptions (basically a handful of upmarket hotels in Accra), pretty much everything in Ghana can be paid for in the local currency. In many situations, attempting to pay for something in anything but cedis would create complete confusion. Prices are quoted in dollars to avoid confusion during the build up to, and the follow on from, the re-denomination of the cedi in July 2007 (see page x).

A **government levy** of 15% is charged on all accommodation and restaurant meals in Ghana. At the lower end of the price range, hotels, and restaurants generally include the levy in any advertised price, hence the frequency with which one comes across room rates so pedantically precise that they are seemingly designed to do nothing but waste time in a country where finding small change is a constant precipitator of mini-crises. By contrast, most upmarket hotels and restaurants quote prices exclusive of the levy, so that a room quoted at US$40 will actually cost you US$44.80. Where I am aware of the latter situation, I've raised figures accordingly to reflect what the room will actually cost.

BARGAINING AND OVERCHARGING Tourists to Ghana do sometimes need to bargain over prices, particularly in Accra, but generally only in reasonably predictable circumstances, such as when chartering private taxis, organising guides, or buying curios and to a lesser extent other market produce. Prices in hotels, restaurants, shops, and public transport are generally fixed, and overcharging in such places is too unusual for it to be worth challenging a price unless it is blatantly ridiculous.

You're bound to be overcharged at some point in Ghana, but it is important to keep this in perspective. Some travellers, after a couple of bad experiences, start to haggle with everyone from hotel owners to old women selling fruit by the side of the road, often accompanying their negotiations with aggressive accusations of dishonesty. Unfortunately, it is sometimes necessary to fall back on aggressive posturing in order to determine a fair price, but such behaviour is also very unfair on those people who are forthright and honest in their dealings with tourists. It's a question of finding the right balance, or, better still, looking for other ways of dealing with the problem.

The main instance where bargaining is essential is when buying curios. What should be understood, however, is that the fact a curio seller is open to negotiation does not mean that you were initially being overcharged or ripped off. Curio sellers will generally quote a price knowing full well that you are going to bargain it down (they'd probably be startled if you didn't) and it is not necessary to respond aggressively or in an accusatory manner. It is impossible to say by how much you should bargain the initial price down. Some people say that you should offer half the asking price and be prepared to settle at around two-thirds, but my experience is that curio sellers are far more whimsical than such advice allows for. The sensible approach, if you want to get a feel for prices, is to ask the price of similar items at a few different stalls before you actually contemplate buying anything.

In fruit and vegetable markets and stalls, bargaining is often the norm, even between locals, and the most healthy approach to this sort of haggling is to view it as an enjoyable part of the African experience. There will normally be an accepted price band for any particular commodity. To find out what it is, listen to what other people pay and try a few stalls. A ludicrously inflated price will always drop the moment you walk away. When buying fruit and vegetables, a good way to get a feel for the situation is to ask for a bulk discount or a few extra items thrown in. And bear in mind that when somebody is reluctant to bargain, it may be because they asked a fair price in the first place.

Above all, don't lose your sense of proportion. No matter how poor you may feel, it is your choice to travel on a tight budget. Most Ghanaians are much poorer than you will ever be, and they do not have the luxury of choosing to travel. If you find yourself quibbling with an old lady selling a few piles of fruit by the roadside, stand back and look at the bigger picture. There is nothing wrong with occasionally erring on the side of generosity.

BUSINESS The first port of call for anybody thinking of establishing a business in Ghana should be the **Ghana Promotion Investment Centre**, PO Box M193 Accra; ☎ 021 665125/6/7/8/9; f 021 663801.

GETTING AROUND

CAR HIRE AND DRIVING Of the established international companies, Hertz and Europcar have desks in some of the hotels in Accra (eg: Novotel, Golden Tulip, Labadi Beach).

The head office for **Hertz** is on Nima Maamobi Highway (*PO Box 15119, Accra North;* ☎ *021 223389/220510/776499;* f *021 775009*). They normally offer the car with driver (you pay his expenses), or you can ask for what they call 'self drive', where you pay quite heavy full-cover insurance charges. Either way, it is more expensive than Europe due to the lack of competition, and there are no small cars.

For a better price, contact the **Niagara Hotel** in Accra (see page 118), which can arrange sensibly priced car hire with a driver. They currently offer an excellent deal, particularly suitable for people who want to explore the Greater Accra area from the capital, which includes a 4×4 vehicle with driver, plus a double room at the hotel, for US$110 per day.

VOLUNTEERING IN GHANA

Dominic Durose

Volunteer projects in Ghana offer an amazing opportunity for individuals to live, work, and have fun in a new and exciting country; having lived in Accra for six months myself, working in an advertising firm with i-to-i Volunteer & Work Abroad (*www.i-to-i.com*), I can thoroughly recommend the experience. However, there are a few things that are worth considering before you leave.

To begin with, it can often feel restrictive and unsettling living in a new and unfamiliar environment, so much so that there can be the temptation to neglect your placement. It is important to think carefully before you depart about the things that you wish to achieve as a volunteer, as this can go a long way to ensuring your time in Ghana is as beneficial to both yourself and your placement as possible.

This is not to say that volunteer projects are all work and no play; the laid-back lifestyle in Ghana lends itself to flexibility. If I wanted an afternoon off to do a little relaxing at the beach, or even a couple of weeks to explore the wilds of Ghana, my placement was more than happy to accommodate me.

The working style in Ghana is very different to that in the West, with a much more relaxed approach to working hours and productivity. It can be frustrating when things appear to be at a standstill, but be patient; once you get used to the rhythm and pace of life you'll tend to find that things have a way of running smoothly of their own accord.

During the first few weeks, you are certain to feel the effects of culture shock to one degree or another. Nevertheless, as you begin to settle into your placement you will learn to accept the differences in your new environment, and who knows, you may even prefer them.

The fact that I was living with other volunteers served as an ideal parachute to settle me into Ghanaian life. Many of them had been in the country for a few months already and had acquired local knowledge that was invaluable in helping me through those first few disorientating weeks. I found that socialising with the Ghanaian people I was working with was hugely beneficial too; after all, they were the people guaranteed to be with me for the entirety of my placement.

Overall, volunteering in Ghana was a fantastic experience, one that I will cherish for the rest of my life. For me, it was the little things that mattered most: the greeting of a bread seller as I walked to work and the friendly shouts of the local schoolchildren as I joined in their game of football. Becoming part of my community is something that, although it wasn't easy, brought me the most enormous amount of satisfaction during my stay.

Elkhart Car Enterprise (☏ *021 546521;* f *021 245792;* e *elkhart44fire@ yahoo.com*) has also been recommended. Another promising set-up is **Afrocentric Ventures** (☏ *022 206011 or 024 698760;* e *enquiries@afrocentric-ventures.com; www.afrocentric-ventures.com*), based in Tema's Westgate Hotel, which rents out a range of 4×4s at very reasonable prices.

An affordable alternative to renting a vehicle formally is to charter a taxi driver for one or more days – which, if you choose the right driver, means you also have a guide, interpreter, and evening companion for the bar. The rate for this sort of service is highly negotiable, and it will depend on the distance you want to travel, the number of days, and whether fuel and the driver's meals and room are included, but at worst you should be looking at around US$25 daily, exclusive of extras such as fuel – and a lot less in rural areas or the north of the country! If you want to rent a taxi as a **private charter** on a one-off basis, bank on a fee of around US$5 per hour inclusive of fuel and unlimited kilometres.

Petrol stations are plentiful (even if it's just a man with a few barrels by the roadside) and fuel is very cheap by any standards. There are **tolls** on most major roads, often at bridges, charging nominal fees. Official road signs exist, usually at junctions, and have white text on a green background. Otherwise, there is little indication of distances or route confirmation on the roads.

Unusually for a former British colony, Ghana drives on the right-hand side of the road (except on dual carriageways, where two-way traffic has been known to flow down *both* sides!). Ten years ago, the state of Ghana's roads was appalling. In recent times, however, there has been large-scale upgrading of all the main routes, most of which are now surfaced. You could easily drive the entire coastal road from Aflao to Elubo in a saloon car, as you could the main north–south road from Accra to Paga via Kumasi and Tamale. In fact, there are now very few parts of the country that aren't accessible to practically any carefully driven vehicle – as evidenced by the ancient Peugeot taxis that cover the most unlikely of routes throughout Ghana. All the same, it would be prudent to seek local advice repeatedly as you move around the country, particularly if you visit more remote areas during the rainy season.

If you've never driven in Africa before, be aware that the general approach to driving is quite different to that in more developed countries. Ghanaians tend to be complete maniacs on the road, and visitors should be very cautious, particularly if they are also adapting to driving on the right-hand side of the road. In addition to a heart-stopping approach to overtaking, you will have to contend with potholes, pedestrians, and domestic animals on the road, as well as insane levels of traffic in Accra and Kumasi during rush hour. And be acutely aware that it's customary not to slow down on a blind curve, but to race around it hooting wildly – if you don't hoot back, it will be assumed that no vehicle is coming! Driving at night is inadvisable, not so much for security reasons, but because the general chaos on the road is exacerbated by a lack of street lights and many vehicles without headlights.

Foreigners may drive for up to 12 months in Ghana on an international or foreign driving licence.

BY PUBLIC TRANSPORT

Rail A triangle of railway lines connects Accra, Kumasi, and Takoradi. The Kumasi–Takoradi route is the only one that has functioned in recent years, however, and the passenger service along this line was withdrawn in 2006 due to high fuel prices, leaving the commuter train from Accra to Nsawam as the only remaining passenger service with two trains a day running in each direction (working days only). Updated timetables and info about Ghana railways can be found at www.fahrplancenter.com/GhanaTimings.html.

Road All major roads through Ghana are covered by a variety of public transport, divisible into three broad categories: buses, tro-tros and taxis. By comparison with many African countries, getting around Ghana's roads is very straightforward, though the standard of driving leaves a great deal to be desired on the safety front.

In small towns and villages, there is generally one place from where all public transport leaves, referred to by Ghanaians as the 'station' or 'lorry station' – lorry evidently being a term used interchangeably with tro-tro, bus, or any vehicle larger than a saloon car. In larger towns, there will often be several different stations, each serving a set of destinations in one direction. **STC**, **Metro Mass**, **City Express** and other company buses may well leave from a different station to the one used by private tro-tros. This can become very confusing, and, while I've tried to indicate the most important stations in most large towns, I'd advise readers to do things the easy way: cough up a taxi fare (in most towns, for less than US$2) and ask the driver to take you to the right place. The convention is to ask for the 'station' for the destination you want – in other words, should you be looking for transport to Mampong, then ask to be taken to Mampong Station. The exception is where you want a specific bus company, such as STC, when you should ask for the STC station.

Most buses and tro-tros charge an extra fee for large luggage, such as a backpack. On STC buses, you are charged formally according to the weight of the luggage going in the hold, a two-phase procedure that entails having your luggage weighed and being issued with a baggage tag, then going to a separate kiosk to pay the fee – which, for a normal rucksack, should be less than US$0.50. On other services, the charge is negotiable, and there are no hard and fast rules about how to handle it. In most cases, the fee is legitimate, and is also charged to local people, but travellers might well be overcharged sometimes, and may occasionally be asked for a luggage fee where a local wouldn't be. I was more inclined to accept the legitimacy of the fee when I was asked for it upfront rather than at the end of the trip, and when the sum seemed proportionate.

Buses As a rule, the safest and most efficient way of travelling is by bus. This is particularly the case when you travel directly between two major centres, eg: from Accra to Kumasi or Accra to Takoradi, since the recently privatised **State Transport Company** (STC) runs regular, reasonably reliable, direct bus services along most major surfaced routes. STC buses typically cover around 80km per hour with one or two scheduled 15-minute meal breaks, and blaring Nigerian films to keep you entertained (or aggravated) through the trip. Most STC buses will drop off passengers along the way, provided that they are prepared to pay full fare – in other words, the Accra–Kumasi bus will drop you at, say, Nkawkaw, but you must pay the same fare as you would to get to Kumasi. STC buses run to fixed departure times and can be booked in advance. On regular routes, such as between Accra and Kumasi, or Accra and Takoradi (buses virtually every hour throughout the day), it's often possible to pitch up at the STC bus station and buy a ticket for the next bus leaving, but this can't be relied on completely, and buses may well be booked solid over long weekends and holiday periods, such as the week before Christmas or Easter weekend. One word of caution: if you're inclined to nod off on long journeys, don't make the same error as the researcher of this edition and mistake a drop-off stop for a scheduled stop... it's quite a disconcerting thing to watch your bus pull away with your luggage still on it!

On practically every major route in the country, even those where there is no STC bus, a cheaper service is provided by the **Metro Mass** and/or **City Express** lines. Run by the government, these lines are just as safe as the STC, but they are generally slower, partly because they stop for passengers more often, and partly because the buses are older. Metro Mass and City Express buses generally pick up and drop passengers as required, and fares are charged accordingly. Bus fares in Ghana are very reasonable. A ticket for the STC bus between Accra and Kumasi, for example, costs about US$7–8 for a 250km ride that takes four to five hours. Metro Mass and City Express buses are slightly cheaper for comparable distances.

Tro-tros 'Tro-tro' is the catch-all term for pretty much any licensed passenger vehicle that isn't a bus or a taxi, ranging from comfortable and only slightly crowded minibuses to customised, covered trucks with densely packed seating, a pervasive aura of sweat, and bugger all chance of finding an escape route should you be involved in an accident.

Tro-tros cover the length and breadth of Ghana's roads and you will have little choice but to depend on them when you travel between smaller towns – but I would strongly advise you to use buses wherever possible, not so much because tro-tros are slower or less comfortable than buses (though generally they are both), but because the risk of being involved in a fatal accident is so much greater. Road accidents occur with alarming frequency in Ghana, and ending up in one of them is a very real danger – far more so than malaria, snake bites, or all the other tropical threats visitors usually worry about. Where tro-tros are the only option, go for the larger models referred to as 207s or 209s; try and avoid the converted Ford vans, which were never really designed to carry people.

Most tro-tros leave when they are full, and on all main roads you'll rarely wait more than 30 minutes for a vehicle heading in your direction. Taken together, they form a surprisingly efficient network – the updater of this edition never had to wait more than 15 minutes for a vehicle across the entire country.

But be warned that many of the touts whose task it is to fill up tro-tros have a quite neurotic need to physically 'see' bums on seats. It can take all your powers of persuasion to convince them that if they could only use their imagination and pretend you are sitting in your seat, then you could stand outside while you wait for the vehicle to fill up rather than having to practise being uncomfortable in a sweaty, cramped, motionless vehicle for half an hour. And even when you think that you've had an incandescent moment of cross-cultural communication, as the tout appears to light up with recognition of the good sense of your position, he'll be edging up to you two minutes later hissing 'you sit, white man, you sit!' One blessing is that the Ghanaian government is starting to crack down on over-crowded vehicles, although it is still common on rural routes where there are fewer police checks.

Only on routes where there is very little transport do you need to think in terms of set departure times, and in such circumstances you should definitely check the situation the day before – it may, for instance, be the case that all the transport leaves before 06.00. It is also worth being aware that many tro-tros don't run on Sundays, particularly in Christian parts of the country, which means you'll generally wait longer for something to leave along main roads and may be delayed for hours or find that nothing is going at all along minor routes. Where possible, I would avoid travelling on a Sunday, though we frequently did and usually got where we wanted to in the end.

Fares on tro-tros are cheaper than on buses. Typically, you can expect to pay around US$2 per 100km on a good road, and a little more on an inferior road because the journey takes longer. In many places, you have to buy a ticket at the booth of the **Private Transport Union** (or the GRPTU of TUC to give its full set of initials) for that specific route, and even when you just pay the conductor (known as the 'mate') on the road, fares are fixed and overcharging is not a significant concern. As with buses, some tro-tros will charge the full fare to passengers alighting along the way. If you're going to be picking up tro-tros en route (which most travellers will), it is worth getting to know a few of the many hand signals used to indicate where you want to go. Universal signs include jabbing the air with your index finger to indicate that you want to go 'far', making the same gesture downwards to demonstrate a short trip, or using your thumb to sideways to point in the direction you will eventually want to turn or 'branch'.

Taxis I've never seen a country with so many taxis as Ghana, and I'd not be surprised to be told that they account for more than 80% of the vehicles on the road. Typically battered old Peugeots with orange wings, Ghanaian taxis can be split into two systems of operating: **dropping** and **shared** (or 'line') taxis. The dropping system is essentially the one we are familiar with, where you charter a taxi privately, with the major difference being that Ghanaian taxis are not metered, so a

Anna Heywood

Practically speaking, cycling is probably easiest in the far north and in the far south, for rather different reasons. A dry climate, flat landscape, and plenty of tarmac characterises the north, and we found 125km a day was not unreasonable. As we pedalled south, the landscape became more spectacular and we were glad of the shade as we toiled up hills set in incredibly lush and jungly surroundings. After leaving Mole National Park, we encountered some very rough roads – corrugations and deep gravel made the going pretty tough. Once south of Kumasi, however, the roads were good again and the fairly flat coastal strip made for some very scenic cycling.

The east is perhaps a mixture of the two – hilly, but well-surfaced roads and spectacular scenery means it is definitely an area to explore on two wheels. We found the northern and eastern regions to be less hard-going in human terms – friendlier reactions from locals and less of the hassle typical of coastal tourist resorts. Areas we would particularly recommend against are Kumasi and Accra, where traffic volumes are high, and driver patience low. Like the locals, you may feel that pulling off onto the verge is the safest option on narrow roads when a vehicle approaches.

Ghana is a fantastic place to indulge in a spot of birdwatching, and perhaps cycling is the ideal way to appreciate the birdlife without having to set off on specific twitching expeditions. On the quiet forest roads, we found birds to be abundant and unperturbed by a passing cyclist. But be warned that craning to watch birds means you can't hole-in-the-road watch so closely, which can be rather dangerous! Cycling in Ghana, you'd be wise not to let your eyes stray from the road at all, in fact – judging by the abundance of tangled tro-tros and rusting wrecks on the verges, it was miraculous that we didn't witness a single crash in almost two months of cycling.

It pays to double-check your information for less-used routes – maps can be wrong, and even relying on a single source of local information is risky. Ghanaians have, in general, no sense of distance – so as not to disappoint, they will tell you how many

price must be agreed in advance. The shared taxi system is like a mini tro-tro, where a taxi plies a specific route at a fixed fare, either picking up passengers along the way, or else filling the vehicle at a recognised terminal, and is often the most convenient way to get around quickly and cheaply.

Whichever system you use, taxis in Ghana are quite inexpensive, and it is well worth making use of them. In most parts of the country, a dropping taxi will charge between US$1 and US$2 for a ride within a town (the price is a little higher in Accra), and a fare on a passenger taxi within any given town may be less than US$0.10 and will rarely be more than US$0.30.

Passenger taxis are often the main form of transport between two nearby towns, notably in the part of Ashanti northeast of Kumasi. They also often cover short roads between a junction and a nearby town, especially along the coast, where many towns and villages lie a few kilometres south of the main road. Officially these taxis should take four passengers, but on routes where the drivers think they can get away with it, the convention is still six: two in the front and four in the back. It will often be assumed by taxi drivers that any foreigner prefers a private taxi, so always specify when you want a 'passenger' not a 'dropping' vehicle. In most towns, you can normally assume that any empty taxi that stops for you will be offering you a 'dropping' service to wherever you like at a negotiable fare, whereas a vehicle that already has passengers will be offering you a lift in a specific direction at a fixed fare.

There may often be circumstances where you do want to use a private taxi. In Accra, for instance, it's barely worth figuring out the passenger taxi routes if you're kilometres it is to a certain place, but it rarely bears any relation to the real distance! Where settlements are close together, or the road a fast one, it doesn't matter too much, but, at the end of a long day on the piste, it can be demoralising to find yourself 10km from your destination... then *still* 10km from your destination...

As well as a willingness to give directions, the Ghanaians we encountered displayed a keen curiosity and surprise at our decision to explore their country by bike. It was assumed that we were too poor to afford other forms of transport and we were treated with great kindness on several occasions. Following a hold-up and robbery near Larabanga in the North, we were badly shaken but unhurt. Pedalling madly back to the village and safety, we were surrounded by a crowd of about 50 shocked and outraged villagers within minutes. Despite the sorry circumstances, this episode led to a display of real concern and kindness on the part of the villagers, who went out of their way to help us retrieve our possessions and apprehend the culprits. Shouts from the roadside – 'who are you', 'where are you going' – can seem rude and abrupt, but it's only a first impression. Typically, the Ghanaians we got to know were exceedingly helpful and welcoming.

It's easy to burn 4,000 calories in a long day in the saddle, so finding and eating food took on great importance for us on our journey. We were happy to find that good cycling grub – especially for veggies – was easy to come by in Ghana. Some of the culinary colonial relics – British-style white bread, shandy, baked beans, Horlicks – provoked a bout of homesickness as well as a heightened appreciation of tasty indigenous cuisine! The fruit was perhaps the best thing – we found ourselves screeching to a halt by a roadside stall to fill our bar bags with pineapple, or papaya, or bananas several times a day. By eating fresh produce, and staying in cheap hotels or camping, we found cycle-touring to be a really cheap way to explore Ghana. With our own transport, we had none of the hassles associated with tro-tro travel, and the added flexibility and slow pace meant we felt we got a real insight into the life of this very beautiful country.

only spending a night or two there. When you arrive in a town with luggage, it is often pleasant to catch a taxi to a hotel. Likewise, you may consider it a waste of time to wait an hour for a passenger taxi to fill up when, for instance, it is covering a 6km road at a cost of 10 pesewas per person, and you could charter the whole thing for 60 pesewas. And note that in such circumstances it would be perfectly acceptable to pay the difference where the taxi is partially full – using the example above, if two passengers each paying 10 pesewas were already sitting in the taxi when you arrived, you could offer to pay 40 pesewas to make up the full fare.

Shared taxi fares, like those for other public transport, are fixed by the government for specific routes, often at rates that make it difficult for the taxi-driver or owner to make any significant profit. Dropping fares, by contrast, are not fixed and are thus perceived to be negotiable. You might ask a cab driver how much a passenger fare is and he'll tell you it's C1, then when you ask how much to charter the same taxi on the same route he'll ask ten times as much. It's very difficult to come up with a rule of thumb for determining the right dropping fare – you might ask two different taxi drivers for the same route and one will ask half what the other does – but you'll quickly get a feel for what seems reasonable, and should bear in mind that the dropping fare between two spots should work out at between four and six times the passenger fare.

By plane Of the two companies operating commercial domestic flights in Ghana, **Antrak** (✆ *021 777134 or 051 41296 or 071 91075;* e *reservations@antrakair.com;*

www.antrakair.com) is usually regarded as the most reliable. Twice-daily services run between Accra and Kumasi, twice-weekly services run from Accra to Ouagadougou in Burkina Faso, and four flights a week connect Accra and Tamale for US$146 – a very appealing solution to travellers who are tight for time, but keen to see the north.

CityLink (✆ *021 785725 or 051 39267 or 024 4335152;* f *021 785843;* e *info@flycitylink.com; www.flycitylink.com*) is a newer set-up and operates between Accra, Kumasi, Sunyani and Tamale in two brand-spanking new planes for slightly cheaper prices (US$125 Accra–Tamale, compared to US$146 with Antrak), but flights are frequently cancelled if there are too few passengers.

All Accra flights fly to and from Kotoka International Airport.

By boat Several ferry services operate on Lake Volta, of which the most extensive is the weekly ferry service between Akosombo and Yeji, details of which are under Akosombo on page 242. There are also local 'short-hop' ferries between Yeji and Makongo, Kpando and Agordeke, and Ekye and Adowso.

ACCOMMODATION, EATING AND DRINKING

ACCOMMODATION Accra, Kumasi and the major coastal resorts boast a selection of hotels suitable to most tastes and budgets, ranging from international-class skyscrapers to simple local resthouses and church-run establishments. Elsewhere in the country, the majority of hotels are simple and unpretentious places, geared primarily to the local market, and generally present reasonable value for money – although they will take the biggest slice out of your budget proportionally speaking.

For the most budget-conscious travellers, rooms typically start at around US$5–7 in smaller towns and in the north, perhaps 50% higher in larger towns and along the coast. Even at the bottom end of the price range, you'll seldom need to stay in real dumps of the sort you find in many other parts of Africa – the cheapest hotels generally have fans, electricity, and acceptable washing facilities. In most towns, US$9–12 will get you a self-contained room with a fan, while for US$15–20 you can expect to find a room with air conditioning, television, running hot water and a fridge. Note that in Ghana, rooms with en-suite toilet and bath are generally referred to as self-contained.

One quirk to watch out for, particularly if you are travelling as a couple, is that a single room in Ghana is often a room with a double bed, while a double room is actually a twin (ie: with two beds). Occasionally, and more bizarrely, you'll also find that by single room the hotel actually means a double room sharing toilet and shower facilities, while a double room has exactly the same bed, but is self-contained. Generally, a couple will first be shown a room with two beds, presumably because it's the most expensive option, so if your preference is to share a bed, then ask to look at a single room first. If you're having trouble making your meaning clear, Ghanaians often talk about big and small beds – you're less likely to be misunderstood if you ask for a room with one big bed as opposed to asking for a double room. Single travellers might also take note that when I went out looking at hotels on my own, my request to see a room at a hotel where no prices were advertised almost invariably resulted in my being shown the most expensive option, often one with two large double beds – quite what the receptionist imagined I would want to do with this prairie-like expanse of soft mattress, I don't know!

It is customary in Ghana for hotels to supply guests with an under-sheet only. Many hotels will supply you with a sheet to sleep under upon request, but many won't. Most of the time in Ghana you don't really need a top-sheet to keep you warm, but it can be pleasant to have something to break the direct effect of a fan and to help keep off mosquitoes. And then there are some people who just hate sleeping without some sort of cover. My wife, Ariadne, advises, 'if you're in that category, bring a sheet or similar with you'.

There are relatively few opportunities for camping in Ghana and, accommodation being as cheap as it is, I think that for most people the hassle of carrying a tent and other camping equipment will outweigh the advantages. The major exception is if you expect to spend a lot of time visiting remote wildlife reserves and national parks, many of which are only realistically accessible to people with camping equipment.

Accommodation entries for the fourth edition of this guide have been categorised under four headings: **upmarket**, **moderate**, **budget** and **shoestring**. This categorisation is not rigid, but should nevertheless help travellers isolate the range of hotels in any given town that best suits their budget and taste. Broadly, upmarket hotels are 3- to 5-star affairs that meet international standards and typically quote rates in US dollars. Moderate hotels are typically 1- or 2-star lodgings that approach, but don't quite meet, international standards, and are still comfortable enough for most tourists, offering a range of good facilities such as air conditioning (AC), DSTV (see page 89), en-suite hot showers and toilet. Budget accommodation mostly consists of ungraded hotels aimed largely at the local market, which definitely don't approach international standards, but are still reasonably comfortable and in many cases have air conditioning and en-suite facilities. Shoestring accommodation consists of the cheapest rooms around, usually unpretentious local guesthouses or church-affiliated hostels. The categorisation has been decided on the feel of the hotel as much as the price; it is often relative to the other options in that town, and there are many borderline cases.

✖ FOOD We found the food in Ghana to be refreshingly tasty, or perhaps that should more accurately be distinctly spicy, since it is the ubiquitous and liberal use of a hot, red type of powdered pepper that distinguishes Ghanaian cuisine from the bland local food served in most parts of eastern and southern Africa.

Among the great many starch-based staples you're likely to encounter in Ghana, the most popular are *fufu*, *kenkey*, *banku*, *akple*, *tuo zafi* (TZ), *omo tuo* (rice balls), boiled rice, and fried yam or plantain. Particularly popular in the south, *fufu* is made of cassava, plantain, or yam, mashed until the starch breaks down and it becomes a gooey ball, then cooked with no water to form an even gooier one. It is normally served submerged either in a light soup, or with palm oil, or groundnut sauce. Almost identical to each other in taste and slimy texture are *banku* and *akple*, both made of fermented maize and cassava, and often eaten with *okro* stew for double helpings of that gelatinous feel! *Akple* is particular to the Volta Region while *banku* is found throughout Ghana. Much nicer, in my opinion, is *kenkey*, also made of fermented maize, but much firmer than *banku* or *akple* for being boiled in a removable wrapping of plantain leaves before being served with a spicy tomato sauce or similar. Largely restricted to the north, *tuo zafi* is a millet or maize-based porridge. Fried yam, often sold at markets, is not dissimilar in taste and texture to potato chips – though, when bought on the street, it often has a lingering, petroleum-like taste, presumably a result of using the same oil for too long – and is great eaten with spicy tomato relish, or soft green *palava sauce* made from spinach-like cocoyam leaves.

Other dishes worth trying include *red-red*, a delicious concoction of rice and beans cooked in lots of red palm oil, *kalawole* (pronounced keliweli), soft, deep-fried cubes of plantain liberally seasoned with ginger, pepper and salt, and *titale*, which is very smilar to *kalawolei*, but mashed with flour and deep-fried as fritters. Most travellers find Ghanaian staples to be an acquired taste, and it's probably fair to say that, while you wouldn't want to travel in Ghana without trying *fufu* or *kenkey*, you're unlikely to miss them when you return home.

Local food can be eaten in small restaurants known as '**chop bars**', where you will generally be served with a plate of *fufu*, or *kenkey*, or rice along with a portion of meat or vegetable stew. Another typical chop bar dish is *jollof* rice – rice fried up in red palm oil (again!) with chicken or meat cooked into it. A more interesting way of eating local food, and dirt cheap, is on the street. Most towns have at least one place where vendors sell a huge variety of dishes from informal stalls, often near the lorry station or the market. One advantage of eating on the street is you can try a bit of this or that, rather than be confronted with one specific dish. In addition to the usual staples, street vendors often sell grilled poultry (chicken, or, in the north, guinea fowl), spicy beef or goat kebabs, delicious sweet fried plantain with pepper seasoning, smoked fish, hard-boiled eggs stuffed with chilli and tomato relish, and deep-fried doughnut-like balls called *bo froot*. The Ghanaian equivalent of cheese – 'wagashee' phonetically – is a fried cow's cheese that can be found on the street, and is great for those craving dairy products. Sugar *kenkey* is sold in smaller bundles than savoury *kenkey*, and is sort of like semolina/tapioca, but more solid and eaten with super-hot pepper sauce.

Fresh fruit and vegetables are widely available, with a degree of regional and seasonal variety. The most characteristic fruits are probably pineapples, coconuts and oranges, the latter skinned in a way that makes it easy to suck the liquid out without getting sticky fingers. Other unexpected pleasures for the sweet of tooth are the locally manufactured Kingsbite chocolate – not a complete surprise when you consider that Ghana is one of the world's major cocoa producers, but unexpectedly good all the same. As for vegetables, tomatoes, onions and yams are available practically everywhere, but most others are mainly restricted to the south and the larger towns of the north.

When it comes to **breakfast**, you'll pay a small fortune for an egg, bread and tea in your hotel, so head rather for one of the tea stalls that are to be found in most markets and lorry stations. These places serve fresh, tasty tomato and onion omelettes, as well as bread and hot drinks. Note, however, that, in Ghana, 'tea' seems to be a blanket term covering all hot drinks, so instead of asking for tea or coffee, you should ask by brand name for Lipton (tea), Nescafé (coffee) or Milo (a chocolate malt drink). Bread, meanwhile, comes in three forms. The ordinary loaves, squarish but often with a pattern baked in, are known simply as 'bread', and are quite unpleasantly sweet. Better to eat with eggs or other savoury food is tea bread, a slightly crustier loaf that's often not much bigger than a large roll. You'll normally be able to find fresh tea bread somewhere around the market or lorry station, though you may want to resist any offer to have it smothered in margarine, since this is most often rancid. Butter bread is light and soft, and frequently easier to find than tea bread.

Finally, most towns of substance have at least one restaurant serving exotic dishes, most often straight Western chicken or steak with chips or rice. Quite why, I don't know, but there are a large number of Chinese restaurants in Ghana, and many of the more Westernised places and superior chop houses serve Chinese-style fried rice and spring rolls. A meal in a proper restaurant generally costs around US$4–6 per head excluding drinks, so it is a lot more expensive than eating on the street or in chop bars. If you are not carrying a lot of cash on you, remember to check the small print of the menu before you order, since many restaurants quote prices exclusive of the **government levy** and **service charge** – so that you actually pay around 15% more than the stated price.

Vegetarianism is a concept unfamiliar to Ghanaians, and few restaurants offer many (or any) vegetarian option. One vegetarian reader notes: 'soy beans are available at markets throughout the country, and make an excellent soy milk if blended with water and a sweetener, like honey or sugar, then sieved – most chop bars, hotels and restaurants will offer their blender for use'. Another reader adds: 'my biggest piece of advice for vegetarians is come prepared with protein bars, nutritious spreads, like Marmite, so you get plenty of iron and B vitamins, and multivitamins. Vegetarians should always think ahead when a Sunday or a public holiday is approaching, as many places are shut – we spent a few Sundays with some stale bread and whatever else we could get our hands on, which wasn't much'.

DRINKS Starting with the familiar, most of the usual brand name sodas are widely available in Ghana's fridges, including Pepsi and Coca-Cola. Locally bottled minerals are very cheap by any standards, though as a tourist you may sometimes be urged to waste your money on imported tins of the same drinks for twice the price. In addition to the international brands, there are a few uniquely Ghanaian minerals available, most memorably Pee Cola – Pee being a common surname in Ghana, in case you're wondering.

They say that the sound of the African bush is the piercing cry of the fish eagle. Well then, the sound of the Ghanaian bus station is indisputably the banshee wail of *Aaaaiiiiiiiswuhtuh*, emitted in best announcement voice by hordes of generally pre-pubescent girls. What they are selling is ice water: sealed plastic bags that contain chilled clear water and cost next to nothing. Two types of ice water are available. The more ubiquitous, often available even in small villages, comes in an unmarked bag and holds water from an undetermined source. The other type, often referred to as 'pure water', is labelled, factory-sealed, and contains genuine mineral water and is really very cheap at US$0.03 in the south, rising to US$0.04 in Tamale and US$0.05 further north. We drank both varieties without ill effect, which could well have been a triumph of luck over judgement. More sensible readers will probably prefer to stick to the labelled 'pure water' – or the slightly less chemical-tasting, but considerably more expensive, 1.5-litre bottles of still mineral water that are widely available, though rarely chilled. For a change of flavour, you can spice up the water with a sachet of *Tang*, a powdered orange or mango drink with added vitamins. At most bus stations, you'll also see men trundling around with a selection of Fan Ice products, which include great strawberry frozen yoghurts in sachets, frozen chocolate milk, ice cream and a refreshing citrus-based drink called Tampico. Bottled pure orange and pineapple juice from Accra is also widely available at bars and restaurants catering to tourists. Also worth trying are the surprisingly good, sweetened Kalyppo fruit juices that come in 250ml packs. I never acquired much of a taste for Bruna, a fizzy, locally bottled fruit punch, but we both liked its Togolese equivalent, called Cocktail de Fruits, which is widely available in 750ml bottles in the Togolese border area. A cheap, refreshing, and highly nutritious drink is fresh coconut juice. You'll often see street vendors selling piles of coconuts, particularly along the coast – just ask them to chop one open and you can slurp down the liquid.

The most widespread alcoholic drink is lager beer, which is brewed locally and generally pretty good. A standard 750ml bottle costs anything from US$1 to US$3, depending on where you drink, but be aware that the recently introduced small bottles (375ml) are often relatively overpriced, especially at tourist hotels that don't stock large beers. Five brands of bottled beer are available, Gulder, ABC, Star and Club, all with an alcohol level of around 5%, and Stone Lager, which is a little bit stronger at 5.7%. In the south, inexpensive draught beer or Bubra is widely available. Also widely available are litre boxes of Don Garcia red and white wine, which sell for around US$3 per carton and are very drinkable at the price. Local bars in Ghana are also called '**spots**', and they can generally be distinguished a mile away by the blue-and-white picket fences that customarily enclose bars.

If you're interested in trying local tipples, several are available, all very cheap and generally rather potent. *Pito* is a type of millet beer, similar to the local beer brewed in villages in many parts of Africa, and most easily located in the *pito* bars that can be found in most towns, especially in the north. Palm wine, easily located on the coast, is called *ntunkum* in its mildest form and *doka* when it is older and stronger. *Akpeteshie* is a fiery spirit distilled from palm wine. It's frequently offered to visitors when they visit a village chief – the correct protocol is to spill a few drops on the ground in honour of the ancestors before you swig it down. Another popular drink is the locally bottled Schnapps, which many chiefs prefer as a libation to money!

Smoking *Based on information by Carole Allsop and Tony Kaleda* Smoking is pretty uncommon in Ghana, and often associated with fast or immoral living by the Ghanaian middle classes – although it is better understood on foreigners. As such, it's not easy to find cigarettes in small towns, and you will usually have to ask for an ashtray in bars. Some cigarettes are readily available in cities and larger towns, with the most popular brands being Rothmans and 555s, which both cost around US$1 a pack. You can also try Tusker, which I am told is very cheap, but also very rough. Marlboro cigarettes are rarely available, but, when you can find them (there is one stall around the corner from the Niagara Hotel on Farrar Av in Accra), they are still pretty inexpensive at US$2 a pack. Loose tobacco is very hard to find so roll-up fans should bring their own tobacco with them.

CULTURAL ETIQUETTE

Ghana, like any country, has its rules of etiquette, and while allowances will normally be made for tourists, there is some value in ensuring they don't have to be made too frequently!

Visitors to the north of Ghana should bear in mind is that it is considered highly insulting to use your left hand to pass or receive something or when shaking hands – a common custom in Muslim countries. If you eat with your fingers, it is customary to use the right hand only throughout Ghana.

Greeting procedures tend to be more formalised in Ghana than in modern Western societies, especially in small towns and villages, and elderly people in particular should be treated with special respect. If you need to ask somebody directions, or anything else for that matter, it is considered very rude to blunder straight into interrogative mode without first exchanging greetings – even when shopping. At village level, it is polite for strangers to say hello to anybody they pass along the way.

It is customary to visit the chief of any village where you intend to stay overnight or to do any local sightseeing. In practice, this is no longer necessary in many villages, and where the custom has been continued in places that regularly receive tourists it tends to feel a bit showy. Only when you travel in really out-of-the-way areas is a visit to the chief likely to feel like a matter of etiquette over commerce, and here you should be especially careful to observe protocol. You will be expected to pay tribute in the form of kola nuts, a bottle of Schnapps or money (the equivalent of about US$2 is normally fine). In return, you may receive a glass of *akpeteshie* (local gin), and it would be rude to refuse unless you use the excuse that you don't touch alcohol. Before drinking the gin, pour a few drops on the ground

TAKING IT EASY

Conal Ho

Having lived in Ghana for some time, I would advise Westerners to takes things as light-heartedly as they can. Laugh at ridiculous situations and act in a humorous way when you find yourself in a situation that seems ridiculous, or you are being asked ridiculous questions. For instance, there are times when the traveller can find the calls of 'Obruni! Obruni!' tiring. Of course it is silly, but if you lightly call back 'Bebeni! Bebeni!' (which means 'black person'), people will generally like the fact that you can speak a few Twi phrases and enjoy you being funny with them too.

I think the most important single point of etiquette is ALWAYS to greet someone first and ask them how things are going. I typically begin with the salutation 'Sister', 'My friend', 'Auntie', 'Uncle' or 'Brother' as applicable. Then, after they answer and return the greeting, you can start asking them for a favour, begin bargaining, or enquire about the price of something. Greetings are the first and foremost single point of etiquette to learn in Ghana, especially for many Westerners who may not find it intuitive to greet their waiters or hotel clerk before asking something.

as a tribute to the forefathers. You should always take off your hat or cap in the presence of a chief (or any old person), and should never sit with your legs crossed in his presence.

INTERACTING WITH GHANAIANS Ghana has a reputation as the friendliest country in west Africa, a title that is patently absurd, but certainly not unjustified. Taken as a whole, Ghanaians do seem to be remarkably affable and friendly both among themselves and in their dealings with tourists, and I find it difficult to think of any other African country where I felt so safe or unhassled. First-time visitors to Africa, or at least those with a white skin, may be surprised at the amount of attention they draw by virtue of their conspicuous foreignness – symptoms of which range from having every passing taxi in Accra blare its horn at you to being greeted by mobs of exuberant children chanting *obruni* as you walk past. At times, this can be exhausting, but I cannot recall an incident of this type that was underscored by anything approaching malice. Put simply, Ghana is an amazingly welcoming country, and although you'll sometimes encounter people who treat all Westerners like a walking ATM, they are the exception, not the rule. You'd have to be extraordinarily unlucky to experience anything that could be described as seriously threatening or unpleasant. If you do feel mobbed by Ghanaians asking you 'one thing' or who want to 'take you as a friend', a good way of moving on is to enthusiastically wave goodbye or just say 'later'. Generally, Ghanaians will happily accept your promise without any real expectation that you will stick to it, and you will be able to make an exit without their facing the social humiliation of having you shake your head or say no. If hassle starts to become more intrusive and less good-humoured – and certainly if a Ghanaian touches you without permission – it is perfectly acceptable and nearly always more effective to make a big fuss of saying no.

WOMEN TRAVELLERS It is difficult to imagine a country where women have less to fear on a gender-specific level, and women travelling alone will often find themselves the subject of great kindness from the strangers who want to see that they are safe.

The most hassle you are likely to face is heightened levels of flirtatiousness from many Ghanaian men, with the odd direct proposition and a million marriage proposals thrown in. They can be persistent, but barring the marriage part, it's nothing that you wouldn't expect in any Western country, or – probably with a far greater degree of persistence – from many male travellers.

If may sometimes help to pretend you have a husband at home or waiting for you in the next town – in which case, a wedding ring is accepted as 'proof' – but be aware whilst you are fabricating that he is almost worthless without having given you some 'issue', or children. Being married without offspring attracts the twin reactions of vigorous proposals from 'better' men, and sorrowful looks based on the assumption that your husband is impotent or, to call it by that most mystifying of Ghanaian euphemisms, 'without portfolio'. If anyone does overstep the mark – by touching you, for instance – do make a fuss and slap the offending hand away to underscore that it is not acceptable.

It would also be prudent to pay some attention to how you dress in Ghana, particularly in the more conservative Muslim north where covered shoulders and skirts or trousers that come below the knee are advisable. It's not that Ghanaians would be deeply offended by women travellers wearing shorts or other outfits that might be seen to be provocative, but it pays to allow for local sensibilities, and under certain circumstances revealing clothes may be perceived to make a statement that you don't intend. Even in the south, where heart-stoppingly tight clothes are the order of the day, try and keep your midriff and the area just below covered, as this is where Ghanaian women often wear their beads and is seen as highly sexual.

More mundanely, tampons are not readily available in smaller towns, though you can easily locate them in Accra and Kumasi. If you're travelling in out-of-the-way places, it's advisable to carry enough to see you through to the next time you'll be in a large city, although, in an emergency, sanitary pads are available in most towns of any size. It is also worth bearing in mind that travelling in the tropics can sometimes cause women to have heavier or more regular periods than they would at home – often alarmingly so. This is quite normal, but any pharmacist will be able to recommend something to stem the flow if necessary.

For the experiences of two readers of the second edition of this book, see *Perspectives from Women Travellers* box (page 82).

GUIDES AND TIPPING One aspect of travel in Ghana that can become mildly enervating is the constant stream of guides and wannabe guides that tend to attach themselves to travellers. This is not something that's unique to Ghana, I grant you, but it is certainly more prevalent in Ghana than in many other African countries, so it is worth thinking through your attitude to this in advance. There is no doubt in my mind that using guides is in principle a good thing, since it ensures that tourism provides an income to local people, but there is also a line to be drawn; basically, that the guide should in some way contribute to your experience.

Starting positively, there are many situations where a guide is an unambiguously worthwhile investment, eg: when visiting game reserves (where it is not permitted to walk without an armed guide), or at many historical sites (where knowledgeable guides are generally provided by request only). In such clear-cut circumstances – basically, where you are allocated a guide by an institution – you *will* normally pay a fee, but since this will not go directly to the guide (who in all probability is poorly paid), it is proper and customary to tip. It's difficult to give an exact guideline for tipping, since this depends on group size and the quality of service, but at current exchange rates a figure of around US$0.30 per group member per hour feels about right. Another way of looking at it would be to tip around half of what you paid as an actual fee, bearing in mind the guide fees in Ghana are generally very reasonable.

The guide situation becomes more ambiguous when it isn't institutionalised. Even here, though, there are some reasonably straightforward scenarios. At places such as Bonwire or Tongo, for instance, visitors are normally approached by a cluster of prospective guides on arrival. There is no reason why you should take one on in such circumstances but, once you've selected somebody who seems a good bet and you've agreed a fee, you'll be left in peace by the other guides, and the one you've chosen will generally be able to add a great deal of insight to what you see. One cautionary note in this sort of situation is that guides will often agree to a fee, but then when you pay them this amount they go on a major sulk because you haven't tipped them. Personally, I don't see any valid reason why an additional tip should be given to a private individual with whom you've already agreed a fee, and nine times out of ten, when people sulk, they are simply chancing it.

The right approach to this sort of situation – particularly when the guide comes up with the old 'you pay whatever you like' line – is to talk through costs at the negotiation stage. Stress to the guide that whatever fee is agreed is final and inclusive of a tip. Check, too, what other fees must be paid – it's not unusual to agree to a guide fee thinking that it covers the full excursion, only to find that the village chief also wants his fee, the caretaker his fee, the guy who thrusts himself unbidden into the middle of your photo his modelling fee, etc. This may feel like nit-picking to our Western mentalities, but Africans are accustomed to negotiation and will not be offended if it is conducted in good humour. The reality is that most of us in most situations are more comfortable when we get a full quote than when there are hidden extras (think of taking your car to a garage!). The overwhelming argument in favour of clarifying things at the outset is that it will decrease the likelihood of bad feeling later.

Now for the difficult bit, difficult because it is so riddled with ambiguity. This might aptly be described as people who are under the illusion (or think that *you* are under the illusion) that they are a guide. One type is the person who, for instance, greets you at the bus station, asks you where you are going, follows you there, then demands a fee for being your guide. Then there are those who attach themselves to you in a manner that is nothing short of intrusive, butting into your conversation and prattling on about themselves in a way that can only be described as self-absorbed, and then expect you to give them a guide fee or a tip when finally you part ways – penance, presumably, for having been too polite to have told them to bugger off and annoy somebody else in the first place. It's pretty easy to refuse in this sort of situation, but there is a whole hazy area in between. For instance, you meet a perfectly likeable guy, get chatting, wander around together for a while, then suddenly find that he is dropping broader and broader hints in the direction of payment for an imagined service. It is easy enough to explain and understand this behaviour, and I don't see any point in reiterating the obvious here. The point is whether tourists should allow guilt or whatever else to make them feel obliged to pay somebody for no other reason than that they have been asked, and the person who asked is poorer than they are. Be generous with genuine beggars. Be generous when tipping genuine guides. By all means, slip a small note to the person who cleans your room, and shrug your shoulders over a few pesewas change. But before you give money to a random individual who in all probability befriended you for the express purpose of financial gain, think – if not about those travellers who will follow in your wake, then certainly about the type of relationship you would like to see develop between the people of Ghana and the tourists who, collectively, are already the country's third-biggest source of foreign revenue. Having said all that, do not suspect every Ghanaian is always after your money. Many are genuinely trying to help and I have often been struck by how far some Ghanaians will go out of their way to show you directions, without so much as hinting at a tip and with no other obvious gain.

On a less ardent note, it is not customary to tip for service in local bars and chop bars, though you may sometimes want to leave a tip (in fact, given the difficulty of finding change in Ghana, you may practically be forced to do this in some circumstances), in which case 5% would be very acceptable and 10% generous. Most restaurants catering to Western palates automatically add a 5% or 10% service charge to the bill, and this (in theory) goes to the waiter, but it can do no harm to give a cash tip if you feel the service was good.

PLEASE GIVE ME... are the opening three words (with the 'please' often omitted) of many a one-line interaction with children in Ghana and elsewhere in Africa. Usually, the sentence finishes with a request for one of three things: money, a pen or an address. In general, I suggest you answer the first two in the negative. Children who ask for money are not necessarily especially needy, more likely just chancing it, and every tourist who accedes to such a request with a pittance is guilty of reinforcing behaviour that has a far greater effect on people's dignity than on their well-being – it is notable that swarms of children asking for money is a phenomenon associated with areas where you find the greatest numbers of tourists, not the worst levels of poverty. And be aware that children who ask tourists for pens are no more worthy than their money-grabbing peers, just a great deal more sophisticated – they know that the average liberal Westerner is more likely to part with a pen than with cash. Finally, there's no need to be rude when fobbing off what are basically light requests; far better to do something that makes the children laugh, like pulling a silly face or something else unexpected.

EDUCATION AND THE 'TREE' SCHOOL

Tricia Hayne

Near the fishing village of Nyanyano, some 23 miles west of Accra, there is a school that, today, has around 500 pupils. Not so extraordinary in an area where schools are now burgeoning, except that this school was the inspiration of just one man. Almost ten years ago, Dave Mustill came across a group of children sitting under a tree, singing. This was an ordinary school day, but, during the heavy rains, school was cancelled. Struck by the unfairness of the situation, Dave set about giving these children a roof over their heads – and so was born 'The Lord is My Shepherd Educational Centre'.

Although the government aims to make primary school compulsory, the reality is that, at best, 80% of children receive any formal education. The children here are among the lucky ones. Their fees, from around US$2.30 a week, include their tuition, lunchtime meal and transport – it takes two minibuses over an hour to bus children from the outlying villages to and from school. Infants start from as young as two years old, often coming across English – the language of education throughout Ghana – for the first time. While many of the older children are prepared for the west Africa exams that enable them to go on to senior school, the less academic are trained in dressmaking and carpentry, giving them a viable trade and raising money from the sale of their work to boost funds. As well as a hall, modern classrooms and a library, there is a science room, and a privately run computer room where children and teachers can learn the basics. The school also runs its own plant nursery and has both a stationery shop and a hairdressing salon, the profits from which are ploughed back. And, most important of all, school doesn't stop when it rains.

For further information contact Dave Mustill, 61 Malden Hill Gardens, New Malden KT3 4HX, United Kingdom; ☎ 020 8949 2864. Cheques should be made out to 'Ghana School Project'.

The address business – a request you can expect at least a dozen times a day, though we had it far less in 2003 than on previous trips – is an odd one. For years, I mostly handed out fake addresses when I travelled in Africa, simply because it became too complicated to explain that I'd never get around to writing to the hundreds of people who asked for my address on every trip. Recently, however, it occurred to me that even though I'd also often given out my genuine address, mainly to people with whom I'd actually become friendly, I have only once ever had a response (and this, bizarrely, five years after the event from a person who described a meeting I couldn't recall in a place I'd never visited!). In Ghana, as an experiment, I gave my genuine address to hundreds of people. I've yet to have one response. My only explanation is that we're dealing with the African equivalent of autograph hunting – it is the address itself, not the writing, that is the point of the exercise. One reader responded to these comments in the first edition by saying they had handed out their address regularly and received a huge volume of mail. A reader of the second edition notes: 'My father and I returned from Ghana three weeks ago. We gave out business cards. In your *Ghana* guide, it was referred to as the equivalent to autograph collecting and generally you didn't hear from anybody although it was mentioned somebody did … can you add us to the ones that do! So far we have received a dozen calls, 14 emails and four letters. Thought you might like to know.' Hmmm, perhaps the key here is to have illegible handwriting!

I should probably clarify, just in case anybody thinks I'm being a monster, that the above comments about giving money and pens apply only to children (or occasionally adults) who ask for things purely because you are a Westerner. I see no harm whatsoever in giving money to a genuine beggar (in other words, somebody who was begging before you came on the scene) and would actively encourage generosity towards those who obviously have no other means of sustaining themselves – I was struck by the ease with which salaried Ghanaians give to beggars, and would suggest that if they can do it, then so can we.

SAFETY

THEFT The level of crime against tourists is remarkably low in Ghana, and I can't recall meeting or hearing from travellers who have been robbed, outside of a few very specific places along the coast. The main centre of crime, not unexpectedly, is Accra, where muggings and drive-by thefts are definitely on the increase, though certainly not anything like the problem they are in many other African capitals. Other spots that have experienced spates of tourist attacks are Kokrobite Beach, the footpath between Busua and Dixcove, and the beach between Axim and Ankobra.

My feeling is that Ghana – even Accra – is as safe as anywhere in Africa, and I've never felt uneasy walking around by day or night. But even in a relatively safe African country, tourists are easy game for whatever criminal element exists. As things stand, it would be wholly inappropriate to be anything but relaxed and open in your dealings with Ghanaians; you certainly oughtn't to be ruled by fear. Nevertheless, the risk of being pickpocketed or mugged does exist, and the basic common-sense precautions appropriate to travelling in any African country are worth repeating here:

- Most casual thieves operate in busy markets and bus stations. Keep a close watch on your possessions in such places, and avoid having valuables or large amounts of money loose in your daypack or pockets.
- Keep all your valuables and the bulk of your money in a hidden money-belt. Never show this money-belt in public. Keep any spare cash you need elsewhere on your person.

Helen Beecher Bryant wrote: 'I spent several months during 2002 teaching English and French in a preparatory school in Ghana, then travelling around during the school holidays. I was 19 at the time, though always claimed to be at least 24 when questioned, as 19 sounds very young. I loved travelling alone – people always wanted to talk with the "white lady" and there wasn't a single journey where I didn't make several friends. Obviously, you have to be sensible about giving personal information, and I very rarely gave personal contact details.

'I found Ghanaians immensely protective of the lone *obruni*. They would walk me to hotels and places to eat, tell me where the transport was (though never when it would depart!), and they even bargained with taxi drivers for me at times. *En route* to Akosombo in a minibus, there was a near-fatal crash and we all had to pile out of the minibus. I had no idea where I was, and a friendly man called Mr Happy paid for a taxi to take me to Akosombo!

'The number of marriage proposals was ridiculous; I was single at the time, but always claimed to have a boyfriend waiting for me in whichever town or village I was heading for. Even then, they want to know what colour he is. I never had to produce my fake wedding photo and didn't bother with a fake ring. People tend to believe what you say.

'Although I had many hair-raising experiences on public transport, I was never threatened in any way whilst travelling alone. It is important to be sensible and to look confident, however scared you feel. The people are fascinated by your wish to see their country, particularly in the smaller towns and certainly in rural places; they all want to know why you are there and how they can keep in touch with you. They will often go out of their way to help you and often don't expect anything back as they do in the

- I feel that a button-up pocket on the front of the shirt is the most secure place for money, as it cannot be snatched without the thief coming into your view. It is also advisable to keep a small amount of hard currency (ideally, cash) hidden away in your luggage, just in case you lose your money-belt.
- Where the choice exists between carrying valuables on your person or leaving them in a locked room, I would tend to favour the latter option, particularly after dark, but obviously you should use your judgement and be sure the room is absolutely secure. Remember that some travellers' cheque companies will not refund cheques that are stolen from a room. If you do decide to carry large sums of money, or other valuables, with you after dark, then use taxis, don't walk around.
- Leave any jewellery of financial or sentimental value at home.
- Avoid quiet or deserted places, such as unlit alleys by night, or deserted beaches by daylight, particularly if they lie close to or within a major urban area. When in doubt, take a guide, though preferably one who has been recommended to you by your hotel or by other travellers.
- Particularly in large cities, Westerners carrying a daypack or handbag or external money-belt are often targeted by bag-snatchers and other thieves. Ideally, carry as little baggage as possible when you're out and about.

OTHER PRACTICALITIES

ELECTRICAL DEVICES Electricity is 220V AC at 50 cycles. Stabilisers are required for sensitive devices and adaptors for appliances using 110V. Batteries are useful during power cuts.

tourist areas of Mali, like Mopti and Timbuktu. However, I was usually genuinely grateful and happily bought whoever had helped me a drink or a few oranges.'

Alexandra Fox wrote: 'I think it may be helpful, for the benefit of single female travellers, to mention something about the amount of hassle they should be prepared to expect from men in Ghana. Nearly everywhere I went (even around the village where I was staying), I was approached by men wanting to talk to me. Usually within 20 seconds, they would be telling me that they were in love with me! I managed to clock up around 32 marriage proposals in three months, and although at times you just had to laugh, at other times I found it incredibly tedious. I never got to the bottom of why they were so keen to declare their love to any white girl they met; however, one Ghanaian told me that it could be because in order to get Ghanaian women to go out with you, you have to tell them you love them so they take you seriously. The way I found to deal with it, though, was to start counting them so I would say, for example, "You are number 22; when I've been through the first 21 husbands then I'll move on to you." This seemed to work as it made them laugh, and gave me an easy exit. Although the unwanted attention was annoying at times, I didn't, however, feel overly threatened by any of them, and not all Ghanaian men are the same.

'Something else for the girls: if you've ever wanted to have your hair braided, get it done while you're in Ghana. I have fairly long hair and found having it braided much cooler in the hot weather as, although there is a lot of artificial hair braided into your own natural hair, it enables more air to get to your scalp so feels less hot. I had it done just before coming home – a hairdresser in my village came to my house to do it, it took her five hours, and she only charged me the equivalent of US$3.50.'

PUBLIC TOILETS For those unused to travel in the developing world, it should be noted that public toilets in Ghana, as in most other parts of Africa, leave much to be desired by Western standards. Often, few such facilities are available – in many rural areas, specific stretches of beach or patches of wasteland serve as communal dumping grounds – and where they do exist, they tend to be dirty and may not have running water. Restaurants, hotels, and bars are your best bet if you are caught short, though smaller chop shops and drinking spots won't normally have a toilet. Many bus stations have public toilets that are kept reasonably clean by virtue of charging a small fee for use and toilet paper. It's still a good idea always to carry some toilet paper around with you though, as not all toilets will have it. One reader suggests: 'when you need to use the loo urgently, a bank is a great place – maybe the staff takes pity on a wandering *Obruni*, but not once have I been turned down!'

Among Ghanaians, it seems to be perfectly acceptable to urinate publicly – men pretty much anywhere, women more generally in rural areas than in towns – a solution more likely perhaps to appeal to male travellers than females. To be sure of not offending anybody, it's a good idea to ask a local person of the same gender where you can urinate. Nobody will find this strange – in my experience, Ghanaians are not at all coy about this sort of thing (I've often asked for a toilet in a bar and been asked bluntly – sometimes with graphic miming gestures – whether I need to urinate or the other thing). What will create total confusion is if you resort to euphemisms or more informal, slangy terms – most Ghanaians will not know what is meant by a rest room or a piss!

ASKING DIRECTIONS There is no polite way of saying it: most Ghanaians are utterly clueless when it comes to estimating distance or time in any measure more

Gordon Rattray; www.able-travel.com

Many of Ghana's highlights – such as the coastal forts and the Kakum rainforest canopy walkway – are going to present a challenge to people with mobility problems, but don't let this exclude the country from your travel wish list. Depending on your ability and sense of adventure, most obstacles are surmountable, and Ghanaians are well known for their friendliness and hospitality. If you need help, you will receive it.

PLANNING AND BOOKING There are, as yet, no operators who run specialised trips to Ghana for disabled people. Having said that, most travel companies will listen to your needs and try to create an itinerary suitable for you. For the independent traveller, it is possible to limit potential surprises by contacting local operators and establishments by email in advance (see eg: *Regional tourist offices*, page 61).

ACCOMMODATION In general, it is not easy to find disabled-friendly accommodation in Ghana. Only top-of-the-range lodges and hotels have 'accessible' rooms, and, even here, I've yet to hear of anywhere with grab-handles, roll-under sinks and a roll-in shower. Occasionally (more by accident than through design), bathrooms are wheelchair accessible, but where this is not the case, you should be prepared to be lifted, or do your ablutions in the bedroom.

GETTING THERE AND AROUND

By plane Accra's Kotoka international airport has assistance and wheelchairs available for those who need help entering or leaving an aircraft. Smaller provincial terminals are not as well equipped, so unless you are at least partially ambulant, you will need to be prepared to compromise.

By buses and trains There is no effective legislation in Ghana to facilitate disabled travellers' journeys by public transport; therefore, if you cannot walk at all, then both of these

objective than 'far' and 'not far'. Travellers, particularly those needing directions off the beaten track, will have to allow for this.

One regular and reasonably straightforward area of confusion is the difference between miles and kilometres, measurements that many Ghanaians seem to see as interchangeable. It's always better to ask for a distance in miles, the measure still used by most people, even though signposts generally show distances in kilometres. If you're not familiar with one or other system of measurement, you can convert distances using the equation that five miles is roughly equivalent to eight kilometres, while three feet (or a yard) is basically the same as one metre – imprecise equations, I grant you, but more than adequate for practical travel purposes. Another way of verifying distances is to ask both the distance and the time – in reasonably flat conditions, a reasonably fit walker will cover 5km (3 miles) in one hour.

That said, it's difficult to figure out how a bar worker who not only speaks good English, but also has the capacity to make drawing a pint of draught look as exhausting as running a marathon, can say that a hotel 2km distant is three minutes' walk away. Or how people living at Larabanga and Mole, not to say various books, can come up with estimates as divergent as 3km and 10km for the road between Larabanga and Mole Motel. Or how a signpost at Vane reads 'Amedzofe 5km' when the two towns are less than 3km apart by road. We hit this sort of problem on a daily basis, and found it difficult to escape the conclusion that a lot of Ghanaians simply say whatever figure first comes into their head – not with options are going to be difficult. You will need to ask for help from fellow passengers to lift you to your seat, it will often be crowded, and it is unlikely that there will be an accessible toilet.

By car Distances are great and roads are often bumpy, so if you are prone to skin damage you need to take extra care. Place your own pressure-relieving cushion on top of (or instead of) the original car seat and if necessary, pad around knees and elbows.

It is possible to hire self-drive vehicles, but I know of no company providing cars that are adapted for disabled drivers. If you're not sticking to the main roads, you will need to use a 4x4 vehicle, which will be higher than a normal car making transfers more difficult. Drivers/guides are normally happy to help, but are not trained in this skill, so you must thoroughly explain your needs and always stay in control of the situation.

HEALTH Doctors will know about 'everyday' illnesses, but you must understand and be able to explain your own particular medical requirements. Rural Ghanaian hospitals and pharmacies are often basic, so it is wise to take as much essential medication and equipment as possible with you, and it is advisable to pack this in your hand luggage during flights, in case your main luggage gets lost. Ghana can be hot; if this is a problem for you, then try to book accommodation with fans or air-conditioning, and keep a cooling aid, such as a plant-spray bottle, with you.

SECURITY The usual security precautions apply (see pages 81–2), but it is also worthwhile remembering that, as a disabled person, you are even more vulnerable. Stay aware of who is around you and where your bags are, especially during car transfers and similar. In Africa, these activities often attract onlookers and the confusion creates easy pickings for an opportunist thief.

the deliberate intent of misleading visitors, but either to oblige you with the information they think you want to hear, or because the measurements that are so important to us mean very little to somebody who has lived in a small town all their life and 'knows' how far one place is from another without ever having had reason to translate that knowledge into hours or kilometres.

It goes without saying that a great deal more interrogation about distances is required when you're researching a travel guide than when you are using one. Still, two points ought to be passed on to readers. The first, particularly if you are hiking, is to ask at least three or four people how far away somewhere is, to use some judgement in interpreting the answers, and to accept that you'll probably never know for sure until you walk there yourself. The second is that I've had to 'guestimate' a great many walking distances in this guide, but they are informed and generally based on first-hand experience, and – unlike many of the short distances that are quoted so emphatically by other books, by people you meet, and even on some maps – they will not be wildly out.

BRIBERY AND BUREAUCRACY For all that you read about the subject, bribery is not the problem it is often made out to be, and I've heard of no specific incident where a traveller to Ghana was asked for a bribe. Don't worry about it!

As for the tendency to portray African bureaucrats as difficult and inefficient in their dealings with tourists, this says a great deal more about Western prejudices than it does about Ghana. Sure, you come across the odd unhelpful official, but

PHOTOGRAPHIC TIPS

Ariadne Van Zandbergen

EQUIPMENT Although with some thought and an eye for composition you can take reasonable photos with a 'point-and-shoot' camera, you need an SLR camera if you are at all serious about photography. Modern SLRs tend to be very clever, with automatic programmes for almost every possible situation, but remember that these programmes are limited in the sense that the camera cannot think, but only make calculations. Every starting amateur photographer should read a photographic manual for beginners and get to grips with such basics as the relationship between aperture and shutter speed.

Always buy the best lens you can afford. The lens determines the quality of your photo more than the camera body. Fixed fast lenses are ideal, but very costly. A zoom lens makes it easier to change composition without changing lenses the whole time. If you carry only one lens, a 28–70mm (digital 17–55mm) or similar zoom should be ideal. For a second lens, a lightweight 80–200mm or 70–300mm (digital 55–200mm) or similar will be excellent for candid shots and varying your composition. Wildlife photography will be very frustrating if you don't have at least a 300mm lens. For a small loss of quality, tele-converters are a cheap and compact way to increase magnification: a 300 lens with a 1.4× converter becomes 420mm, and with a 2× it becomes 600mm. Note, however, that 1.4× and 2× tele-converters reduce the speed of your lens by 1.4 and 2 stops, respectively.

For photography from a vehicle, a solid beanbag, which you can make yourself very cheaply, will be necessary to avoid blurred images, and is more useful than a tripod. A clamp with a tripod head screwed on to it can be attached to the vehicle as well. Modern dedicated flash units are easy to use; aside from the obvious need to flash when you photograph at night, you can improve a lot of photos in difficult 'high contrast' or very dull light with some fill-in flash. It pays to have a proper flash unit as opposed to a built-in camera flash.

DIGITAL/FILM Digital photography is now the preference of most amateur and professional photographers, with the resolution of digital cameras improving the whole time. For ordinary prints, a 6 megapixel camera is fine. For better results and the possibility to enlarge images, and for professional reproduction, higher resolution is available up to 16 megapixels.

Memory space is important. The number of pictures you can fit on a memory card depends on the quality you choose. Calculate in advance how many pictures you can fit on a card and either take enough cards to last for your trip, or take a storage drive on to which you can download the content. A laptop gives the advantage that you can see your pictures properly at the end of each day and edit and delete rejects, but a storage device is lighter and less bulky. These drives come in different capacities up to 80GB.

then such is the nature of the beast everywhere in the world. In Ghana, we encountered nothing but friendliness from almost every government official we had dealings with. This, I can assure you, is far more than most African visitors to Europe will experience from officialdom.

A factor in determining the response you receive from African officials will be your own attitude. If you walk into every official encounter with an aggressive, paranoid approach, you are quite likely to kindle the feeling held by many Africans that Europeans are arrogant and offhand in their dealings with other races. Instead, try to be friendly and patient, and accept that the person to whom you are talking may not speak English as fluently as you, or may struggle to follow your accent. Treat people with respect rather than disdain, and they'll tend to treat you in the same way.

Bear in mind that digital camera batteries, computers, and other storage devices need charging, so make sure you have all the chargers, cables, and converters with you. Most hotels have charging points, but do enquire about this in advance. When camping, you might have to rely on charging from the car battery; a spare battery is invaluable.

If you are shooting film, 100 to 200 ISO print film and 50 to 100 ISO slide film are ideal. Low ISO film is slow, but fine grained and gives the best colour saturation – but will need more light, so support in the form of a tripod or monopod is important. You can also bring a few 'fast' 400 ISO films for low-light situations where a tripod or flash is no option.

DUST AND HEAT Dust and heat are often a problem. Keep your equipment in a sealed bag, stow films in an airtight container (eg: a small cooler bag), and avoid exposing equipment and film to the sun. Digital cameras are prone to collecting dust particles on the sensor, which results in spots on the image. The dirt mostly enters the camera when changing lenses, so be careful when doing this. To some extent, photos can be 'cleaned' up afterwards in Photoshop, but this is time-consuming. You can have your camera sensor professionally cleaned, or you can do this yourself with special brushes and swabs made for the purpose, but note that touching the sensor might cause damage and should only be done with the greatest care.

LIGHT The most striking outdoor photographs are often taken during the hour or two of 'golden light' after dawn and before sunset. Shooting in low light may enforce the use of very low shutter speeds, in which case a tripod will be required to avoid camera shake.

With careful handling, side lighting and back lighting can produce stunning effects, especially in soft light and at sunrise or sunset. Generally, however, it is best to shoot with the sun behind you. When photographing animals or people in the harsh midday sun, images taken in light but even shade are likely to be more effective than those taken in direct sunlight or patchy shade, since the latter conditions create too much contrast.

PROTOCOL In some countries, it is unacceptable to photograph local people without permission, and many people will refuse to pose or will ask for a donation. In such circumstances, don't try to sneak photographs as you might get yourself into trouble. Even the most willing subject will often pose stiffly when a camera is pointed at them; relax them by making a joke, and take a few shots in quick succession to improve the odds of capturing a natural pose.

Ariadne Van Zandbergen is a professional travel and wildlife photographer specialising in Africa. She runs The Africa Image Library. For photo requests, visit www.africaimagelibrary. co.za or contact her on ariadne@hixnet.co.za.

PHOTOGRAPHIC ETIQUETTE The unwritten law of photography in Africa is that anybody you actually want to photograph will refuse permission, while it is often practically impossible to take a photo of a static subject without having 20 snotty brats leaping uninvited into the frame. Seriously, though, the question of photographing people is a sticky one, especially in Muslim parts of the country, and the first rule at all times is to **ask permission** and accept gracefully if it is refused, no matter how much it hurts. It is not customary in most parts of Ghana to pay to take a photograph, and I must admit that I'd be sad to see such a custom develop. That said, there are a few instances (the *kente* weavers at Bonwire leap to mind) where you will be expected to pay to photograph a particular subject. One rather nice way around this is to carry a few photographs of you, your friends and family, and your home town, to distribute in exchange for taking a picture of them.

When somebody does agree to let you photograph them, your next question will often be how to go about it without every nearby child leaping into the frame. If you have a point-and-shoot, the answer is to take the picture as quickly as you can. On the other hand, if you have a camera that requires a certain amount of fiddling around, then you may have to compromise by first taking a group photo, and then trying to clear the frame of extraneous kids, bearing in mind that if they then decide to line up behind you, there's a good chance that the photograph will be spoiled by their shadows. Another thing to bear in mind is that people often pose very stiffly when you point a camera at them and relax only when the flash goes off, so it may help to take two shots in quick succession, hoping that the second one will capture a more natural pose. As a rule, you can forget about taking good photos of Africans without fill-in flash, since their skin is very dark by comparison with the bright light.

You should be conscious that until recently there were strict photographic restrictions in Ghana, and that even now you could get in trouble by pointing a camera at any sensitive subject, such as a bridge, dam wall, prison (which includes several of the old coastal forts) or military installation. In general, however, you can photograph what you like, though you may sometimes encounter individuals who will feel a need to interfere in what you're doing. Mostly, they're just playing to the crowd, but that doesn't mean you shouldn't recognise when you'd be better off standing down. One way to counter this type of thing is always to ask somebody standing around whether it's OK to 'snap' (as they say locally) whatever subject takes your fancy – once somebody has given you the nod, they will generally back you up should somebody else make a problem, though here again you should be sensitive to not letting anything ugly develop.

One last thought, if you're not particularly keen on photography, is this: why not leave your camera at home and buy a few postcards before you leave? Ultimately, cameras are heavily intrusive, and trying to get good photos of people will often create more frustration than pleasure.

For more technical tips about photography, see the photography box (page 86).

➲ MEDIA AND COMMUNICATIONS

NEWSPAPERS Several English-language newspapers are printed in Ghana, of which the well-established *Daily Graphic* is probably the best and will gives you a good grounding in what are the hot debates during your visit. The weekly *Graphic Sport* is of great interest to ardent followers of African football, but coverage of other sports is, at best, cursory. Other titles include the well-respected *Ghanaian Times*, and a whole range of deliciously sordid tabloids, ranging from the just about respectable *P&P* to the *Daily Parrot*, which once gave its front page to the memorable headline, 'Woman Dies Whilst Doing it'. In Accra, you can buy imported newspapers at a highly inflated price – far better to spend a cosy hour catching up on international news in the air-conditioned confines of the British Council in Accra or Kumasi, both of which have a pile of English newspapers from three to four days old.

TELEPHONE If you're going to be in Ghana for more than a couple of weeks, it is probably worth bringing a mobile phone with you and buying a SIM card on arrival. The major networks are Areeba, Tigo, Onetouch and Kasapa, with the first two the most popular, but which will be best for you depends very much on where you are staying. The levels of coverage, even in rural areas, is actually quite astonishing, but out-of-the-way places are usually covered by just one provider, which more or less determines who you go with.

Ghana's fixed-line telephone system is reasonably efficient. From overseas, it's one of the easiest African countries to get through to first time. The ringing tone is a single short tone followed by a longer pause, and the engaged tone is equal lengths on and off. International calls out of Ghana can be made at official telecommunication centres, and a bit more expensively (but with less queuing) at many upmarket hotels and at private telecommunication centres offering IDD (International Direct Dialling) – the latter are usually available even in small towns. Cheapest, and most efficient of all, is to use a phone booth that takes phonecards. A 50-unit card, usually purchasable from one of the vendors near a public phone booth, costs US$2 and lasts around three minutes for calls overseas. Dialling overseas, the country code should be preceded by 00.

Dialling into Ghana, the international code is +233. Major area codes are as follows:

Accra	021	Koforidua	081
Ada	0968	Kumasi	051
Akosombo	0251	Navrongo	072
Axim	0342	Sunyani	061
Bolgatanga	072	Takoradi	031
Cape Coast	042	Tamale	071
Dunkwa	0372	Tema	022
Ho	091	Wa	0712
Hohoe	0935	Winneba	041
Keta	0966		

POST Ghana's international post service is cheap and reasonably reliable, but often very slow. One reader who worked in Ghana for a while reckons that sending mail from Ghana to Europe (Holland, England, and Belgium) was generally about six times faster than the other way around (about one week to Europe, but up to eight weeks from Europe).

RADIO AND TELEVISION The Ghana Broadcasting Corporation produces a reasonable television service by African standards, though it's nothing to shout about by any other. The state-owned radio service, by contrast, is quite exceptional, with some good news and issue coverage and an eclectic mix of music – except on Sundays when it's hijacked by God. You can pick it up on 95.7 FM. Travellers with short-wave radios can pick up the BBC World Service on 15400kHz throughout most of the day and 17830kHz between 08.30 and 23.30 – programme details are available from the British Council in Accra (see page 132). Voice of America broadcasts from 03.00 to 22.30, but the frequency changes regularly throughout the day. The African schedules of the BBC World Service are also available on 101 FM in Accra. The last few years has seen a boom in commercial radio stations, most of which seem to combine chat shows with local and international music (dominated by reggae and contemporary R&B).

An increasing number of hotels in the middle to upper price range, as well as many bars catering to expats and tourists, subscribe to a South African satellite multi-channel pay service called **DSTV**. The package varies from one hotel to the next, but it generally includes M-Net, which shows reasonably current movies and serials, as well as Movie Magic (mostly one- to two-year old movies), BBC World, CNN and Supersport, the latter showing a good selection of current sporting

4

events, with an inevitable bias to sports popular in South Africa (football, cricket, rugby) and events involving South African teams.

INTERNET AND EMAIL The internet has caught on in Ghana in a big way, making communication with home far easier and cheaper than it was even a couple of years ago. There must be dozens of internet cafés in Accra, concentrated in Osu and, to a lesser extent, Adabraka, the two suburbs where most travellers stay, and there are private internet cafés in most other substantial towns, including Kumasi, Tamale, Cape Coast, Takoradi, Ho and Hohoe.

Rates are very reasonable, especially in Accra and other large towns, where you're typically looking at C100–150 per minute – US$1 or less per hour. Servers are generally rather slow by comparison to Europe or North America, but this is improving. It's worth setting up a Yahoo account before you go, as, at the time of writing, this is by far the quickest and most reliable free email provider in Ghana – much better than Hotmail, which can get seriously frustrating.

5

Health and Safety

with Dr Felicity Nicholson

This is the chapter that always gives me the creeps when I read a travel guide, and I'm quite sure that some readers will question the sanity of travelling to Ghana by the time they finish it. Don't let it get to you – with the right vaccinations and a sensible attitude to malaria prevention, the chances of serious mishap are small. It may help put things in perspective to point out that, after malaria, your greatest concern in Ghana should not be the combined exotica of venomous snakes, stampeding elephants, gun-happy soldiers or the Ebola virus, but something altogether more mundane: a road accident.

Road accidents are very common in many parts of Ghana so be aware and do what you can to reduce risks: try to travel during daylight hours, always wear a seatbelt and refuse to be driven by anyone who has been drinking. Listen to local advice about areas where violent crime is rife, too.

PREPARATIONS

TRAVEL INSURANCE Don't think about travelling without a comprehensive medical travel insurance policy, one that will fly you home in an emergency. The **ISIS** policy, available in Britain through STA (✆ *0870 1 606070*), is just one of several inexpensive policies and has a good reputation.

IMMUNISATIONS Preparations to ensure a healthy trip to Ghana require checks on your immunisation status: it is wise to be up to date on **tetanus**, **polio**, and **diphtheria** (now given as an all-in-one vaccine, Revaxis, that lasts for ten years) and **hepatitis A**. Immunisations against meningococcus and rabies may also be recommended.

Proof of vaccination against **yellow fever** is needed for entry into Ghana from all travellers. The World Health Organization (WHO) recommends that this vaccine should be taken for Ghana by those over nine months of age, although proof of entry is only officially required for those over one year of age. If the vaccine is not suitable for you, then obtain an exemption certificate from your GP or a travel clinic.

Immunisation against **cholera** may also be recommended for your trip to Ghana. This is now given as the oral vaccine (Dukoral), and, ideally, two doses should be taken between one and six weeks apart at least one week before you go for those over six years of age. Children between the ages of two and six should receive three doses.

Hepatitis A vaccine (Havrix Monodose or Avaxim) comprises two injections given about a year apart. The course costs about £100, but may be available on the NHS (in the UK); it protects for 25 years and can be administered even close to the time of departure. Hepatitis B vaccination should be considered for longer trips (two months or more), or for those working with children or in situations where contact with blood is likely. Three injections are needed for the best protection and can be given over a three-week period if time is short. Longer schedules give more sustained protection and are therefore preferred if time allows. Hepatitis A vaccine can also be given as a combination with hepatitis B as 'Twinrix', though two doses are needed at least seven days apart to be effective for the hepatitis A component, and three doses are needed for the hepatitis B.

The newer injectable typhoid vaccines (eg: Typhim Vi) last for three years and are about 85% effective. Oral capsules (Vivotif) are currently available in the US (and soon in the UK); if four capsules are taken over seven days, it will last for five years. They should be encouraged unless the traveller is leaving within a few days for a trip of a week or less, when the vaccine would not be effective in time.

Meningitis vaccine (ideally containing strains A, C, W and Y, but if this is not available then A+C vaccine is better than nothing) is recommended for all travellers, especially for trips of more than four weeks (see *Meningitis*, page 101).

Vaccinations for rabies are ideally advised for everyone, but are especially important for travellers visiting more remote areas, particularly if you are more than 24 hours from medical help, and definitely if you will be working with animals (see *Rabies*, page 101).

Experts differ over whether a BCG vaccination against tuberculosis (TB) is useful in adults; discuss this with your travel clinic.

In addition to the various vaccinations recommended above, it is important that travellers should be properly protected against malaria. For detailed advice, see page below.

Ideally you should visit your own doctor or a specialist travel clinic (see page 94) to discuss your requirements, if possible at least eight weeks before you plan to travel.

MALARIA Along with road accidents, malaria poses the single biggest serious threat to the health of travellers in most parts of tropical Africa, Ghana included. It is unwise to travel in malarial parts of Africa whilst pregnant or with children: the risk of malaria in many parts is considerable and these travellers are likely to succumb rapidly to the disease. The *Anopheles* mosquito that transmits the parasite should be assumed to be present at all altitudes below 1,800m, a category that includes all of Ghana.

Malaria prevention There is not yet a vaccine against malaria that gives enough protection to be useful for travellers, but there are other ways to avoid it; since most of Africa is very high risk for malaria, travellers must plan their malaria protection properly. Seek current advice on the best antimalarials to take: usually mefloquine, Malarone or doxycycline.

If **mefloquine** (Lariam) is suggested, start this two-and-a-half weeks (three doses) before departure to check that it suits you; stop it immediately if it seems to cause depression or anxiety, visual or hearing disturbances, severe headaches, fits, or changes in heart rhythm. Side effects, such as nightmares or dizziness, are not medical reasons for stopping unless they are sufficiently debilitating or annoying. Anyone who has been treated for depression or psychiatric problems, has diabetes controlled by oral therapy, or who is epileptic (or who has suffered fits in the past) or has a close blood relative who is epileptic, should probably avoid mefloquine.

In the past, doctors were nervous about prescribing mefloquine to pregnant women, but experience has shown that it is relatively safe and certainly safer than the risk of malaria. That said, there are other issues, so if you are travelling to Ghana whilst pregnant, seek expert advice before departure.

Malarone (proguanil and atovaquone) is as effective as mefloquine. It has the advantage of having few side effects and need only be continued for one week after returning. However, it is expensive and because of this tends to be reserved for shorter trips. Malarone may not be suitable for everybody, so advice should be taken from a doctor. The licence in the UK has been extended for up to three months' use and a paediatric form of tablet is also available, prescribed on a weight basis.

Another alternative is the antibiotic **doxycycline** (100mg daily). Like Malarone, it can be started one day before arrival. Unlike mefloquine, it may also be used in travellers with epilepsy, although certain anti-epileptic medication may make it less effective. In perhaps 1–3% of people, there is the possibility of allergic skin reactions developing in sunlight; the drug should be stopped if this happens. Women using the oral contraceptive should use an additional method of protection for the first four weeks when using doxycycline. It is also unsuitable in pregnancy, or for children under 12 years.

Chloroquine and proguanil are no longer considered to be effective enough for Ghana but may be considered as a last resort if nothing else is deemed suitable.

All tablets should be taken with or after the evening meal, washed down with plenty of fluid and, with the exception of Malarone (see above), continued for four weeks after leaving.

Despite all these precautions, it is important to be aware that no anti-malarial drug is 100% protective, although those on prophylactics who are unlucky enough to catch malaria are less likely to get rapidly into serious trouble. In addition to taking anti-malarials, it is therefore important to avoid mosquito bites between dusk and dawn (see *Avoiding insect bites*, page 100).

There is, unfortunately, the occasional traveller who prefers to 'acquire resistance' to malaria rather than take preventive tablets, or who takes homeopathic prophylactics thinking these are effective against killer disease. Homeopathy theory dictates treating like with like so there is no place for prophylaxis or immunisation in a well person; *bona fide* homoeopaths do not advocate it. Travellers to Africa cannot acquire any effective resistance to malaria, and those who don't make use of prophylactic drugs risk their life in a manner that is both foolish and unnecessary.

PROTECTION FROM THE SUN Give some thought to packing suncream. The incidence of skin cancer is rocketing as Caucasians are travelling more and spending more time exposing themselves to the sun. Keep out of the sun during the middle of the day and, if you must expose yourself to the sun, build up gradually from 20 minutes per day. Be especially careful of exposure in the middle of the day and of sun reflected off water, and wear a T-shirt and lots of waterproof suncream (at least SPF15) when swimming. Sun exposure ages the skin, makes people prematurely wrinkly; and increases the risk of skin cancer .Cover up with long, loose clothes and wear a hat when you can. The glare and the dust can be hard on the eyes, too, so bring UV-protecting sunglasses and, perhaps, a soothing eyebath.

PERSONAL FIRST-AID KIT A minimal kit contains:

- a good drying antiseptic, eg: iodine or potassium permanganate (don't take antiseptic cream)
- a few small dressings (Band-Aids)
- suncream
- insect repellent; anti-malarial tablets; impregnated bed-net or permethrin spray
- aspirin or paracetamol
- antifungal cream (eg: Canesten)
- ciprofloxacin or norfloxacin, for severe diarrhoea
- tinidazole for giardia or amoebic dysentery (see below for regime)

- antibiotic eye drops, for sore, 'gritty', stuck-together eyes (conjunctivitis)
- a pair of fine-pointed tweezers (to remove hairy caterpillar hairs, thorns, splinters, coral, etc)
- alcohol-based hand rub or bar of soap in plastic box
- condoms or femidoms
- needle and syringe kit with accompanying letter from health-care professional
- a digital thermometer (for those going to remote areas).

MEDICAL FACILITIES

There are private clinics, hospitals and pharmacies in most large towns, and doctors generally speak fluent English. Consultation fees and laboratory tests are remarkably inexpensive when compared to most Western countries, so if you do fall sick it would be absurd to let financial considerations dissuade you from seeking medical help.

Commonly required medicines, such as broad-spectrum antibiotics and Flagyl (though Tinidazole is easier to take, it is not generally available in Ghana), are widely available and cheap throughout the region, as are malaria cures and prophylactics. It is advisable to carry all malaria-related tablets (whether for prophylaxis or treatment) with you, and only rely on their availability locally if you need to restock your supplies.

If you are on any medication prior to departure, or you have specific needs relating to a known medical condition (eg: if you are allergic to bee stings, or you are prone to attacks of asthma, which may be exacerbated by the high dust levels), then you are strongly advised to bring any related drugs and devices with you.

TRAVEL CLINICS AND HEALTH INFORMATION

A full list of current travel clinic websites worldwide is available from the **International Society of Travel Medicine** on www.istm.org. For other journey preparation information, consult www.tripprep.com. Information about various medications may be found on www.emedicine.com. For information on malaria prevention, see www.preventingmalaria.info.

UK

Berkeley Travel Clinic 32 Berkeley St, London W1J 8EL (*near Green Park tube station*); ☎ 020 7629 6233
Cambridge Travel Clinic 48a Mill Rd, Cambridge CB1 2AS; ☎ 01223 367362; e enquiries@ cambridgetravelclinic.co.uk; www.cambridgetravelclinic. co.uk. *Open Tue–Fri 12.00–19.00, Sat 10.00–16.00.*
Edinburgh Travel Clinic Regional Infectious Diseases Unit, Ward 41 OPD, Western General Hospital, Crewe Rd South, Edinburgh EH4 2UX; ☎ 0131 537 2822; www.link.med.ed.ac.uk/ridu. Provides inoculations & antimalarial prophylaxis & advises on travel-related health risks. Travel helpline, ☎ 0906 589 0380; *open weekdays, 09.00–12.00.*
Fleet Street Travel Clinic 29 Fleet St, London EC4Y 1AA; ☎ 020 7353 5678; www.fleetstreetclinic.com. Vaccinations, travel products, & latest advice.
Hospital for Tropical Diseases Travel Clinic Mortimer Market Bldg, Capper St (off Tottenham Ct Rd), London

WC1E 6AU; ☎ 020 7388 9600; www.thehtd.org. Offers consultations & advice, & is able to provide all necessary drugs & vaccines for travellers. Runs a healthline (☎ 0906 133 7733) for country-specific information & health hazards. Also stocks nets, water purification equipment, & personal protection measures.
Interhealth Worldwide Partnership Hse, 157 Waterloo Rd, London SE1 8US; ☎ 020 7902 9000; www.interhealth.org.uk. Competitively priced, one-stop travel health service. All profits go to their affiliated company, InterHealth, which provides health care for overseas workers on Christian projects.
MASTA (Medical Advisory Service for Travellers Abroad) Moorfield Rd, Yeadon LS19 7BN; ☎ 0870 606 2782; www.masta-travel-health.com. Provides travel health advice, anti-malarials and vaccinations. There are over 25 MASTA pre-travel clinics in Britain; call or check online

for the nearest. Clinics also sell mosquito nets, medical kits, insect protection, & travel hygiene products.

NHS travel website www.fitfortravel.scot.nhs.uk Provides country-by-country advice on immunisation & malaria, plus details of recent developments, & a list of relevant health organisations.

Nomad Travel Store/Clinic 3–4 Wellington Terrace, Turnpike Lane, London N8 0PX; ☎ 020 8889 7014; travel-health line (office hours only) ☎ 0906 863 3414; e sales@nomadtravel.co.uk; www.nomadtravel.co.uk. Also at 40 Bernard St, London WC1N 1LJ; ☎ 020 7833 4114; 52 Grosvenor Gdns, London SW1W 0AG;

☎ 020 7823 5823; and 43 Queens Rd, Bristol BS8 1QH; ☎ 0117 922 6567. For health advice, equipment, such as mosquito nets & other anti-bug devices, & an excellent range of adventure travel gear.

Trailfinders Travel Clinic 194 Kensington High St, London W8 7RG; ☎ 020 7938 3999; www.trailfinders.com/clinic.htm

Travelpharm The Travelpharm website, www.travelpharm.com, offers up-to-date guidance on travel-related health & has a range of medications available through their online mini-pharmacy.

IRISH REPUBLIC

Tropical Medical Bureau Grafton St Medical Centre, Grafton Bldgs, 34 Grafton St, Dublin 2; ☎ 1 671 9200; www.tmb.ie. A useful website specific to tropical

destinations. Also check website for other bureau locations throughout Ireland.

USA

Centers for Disease Control 1600 Clifton Rd, Atlanta, GA 30333; ☎ 800 311 3435; travellers' health hotline 888 232 3299; www.cdc.gov/travel. The central source of travel information in the USA. The invaluable *Health Information for International Travel*, published annually, is available from the Division of Quarantine at this address.

Connaught Laboratories PO Box 187, Swiftwater, PA 18370; ☎ 800 822 2463. They will send a free list of specialist tropical-medicine physicians in your state.

IAMAT (International Association for Medical Assistance to Travelers) 1623 Military Rd, 279, Niagara Falls, NY14304-1745; ☎ 716 754 4883; e info@iamat.org; www.iamat.org. A non-profit organisation that provides lists of English-speaking doctors abroad.

International Medicine Center 920 Frostwood Drive, Ste 670, Houston, TX 77024; ☎ 713 550 2000; www.traveldoc.com

CANADA

IAMAT Ste 1, 1287 St Clair Av W, Toronto, Ontario M6E 1B8; ☎ 416 652 0137; www.iamat.org

TMVC Ste 314, 1030 W Georgia St, Vancouver BC V6E 2Y3; ☎ 1 888 288 8682; www.tmvc.com

AUSTRALIA, NEW ZEALAND, SINGAPORE

TMVC ☎ 1300 65 88 44; www.tmvc.com.au. 31 clinics in Australia, New Zealand & Singapore, including: *Auckland* Canterbury Arcade, 170 Queen St, Auckland; ☎ 9 373 3531 *Brisbane* 6th Flr, 247 Adelaide St, Brisbane, QLD 4000; ☎ 7 3221 9066

Melbourne 393 Little Bourke St, 2nd Flr, Melbourne, VIC 3000; ☎ 3 9602 5788 *Sydney* Dymocks Bldg, 7th Flr, 428 George St, Sydney, NSW 2000; ☎ 2 9221 7133

IAMAT PO Box 5049, Christchurch 5, New Zealand; www.iamat.org

SOUTH AFRICA AND NAMIBIA

SAA-Netcare Travel Clinics P Bag X34, Benmore 2010; www.travelclinic.co.za. Clinics throughout South Africa.

TMVC 113 D F Malan Drive, Roosevelt Park, Johannesburg; ☎ 011 888 7488; www.tmvc.com.au. Consult website for details of other clinics.

SWITZERLAND

IAMAT 57 Chemin des Voirets, 1212 Grand Lancy, Geneva; www.iamat.org

FURTHER READING Wilson-Howarth, Dr Jane, and Ellis, Dr Matthew, *Your Child Abroad: A Travel Health Guide* (Bradt Travel Guides, 2005) and Wilson-Howarth, Dr Jane, *Bugs, Bites & Bowels* (Cadogan, 2006).

Dr Jane Wilson-Howarth

Long-haul air travel increases the risk of deep vein thrombosis. Although recent research has suggested that many of us develop clots when immobilised, most resolve without us ever having been aware of them. In certain susceptible individuals, though, clots form on clots, and, when large ones break away and lodge in the lungs, this is dangerous. Fortunately, this happens in a tiny minority of passengers.

Studies have shown that flights of over five-and-a-half-hours are significant, and that people who take lots of shorter flights over a short space of time can also form clots. People at highest risk are:

- those who have had a clot before – unless they are now taking warfarin
- people over 80 years of age
- anyone who has recently undergone a major operation, or surgery for varicose veins
- someone who has had a hip or knee replacement in the last three months
- cancer sufferers
- those who have ever had a stroke
- people with heart disease
- those with a close blood relative who has had a clot.

Those with a slightly increased risk include:

- people over 40
- women who are pregnant, or have had a baby in the last couple of weeks
- people taking female hormones, the combined contraceptive pill, or other oestrogen therapy
- heavy smokers
- those who have very severe varicose veins
- the very obese
- people who are very tall (over 6ft/1.8m) or short (under 5ft/1.5m)

COMMON MEDICAL PROBLEMS

TRAVELLERS' DIARRHOEA Travelling in Ghana carries a fairly high risk of getting a dose of travellers' diarrhoea; perhaps half of all visitors will suffer, and the newer you are to exotic travel, the more likely you will be to suffer.

By taking precautions against travellers' diarrhoea, you will also avoid typhoid, paratyphoid, cholera, hepatitis, dysentery, worms, etc. Travellers' diarrhoea and the other faecal-oral diseases come from getting other people's faeces in your mouth. This most often happens from cooks not washing their hands after a trip to the toilet, but even if the restaurant cook does not understand basic hygiene, you will be safe if your food has been properly cooked and arrives piping hot. The most important prevention strategy is to wash your hands before eating anything. You can pick up salmonella and shigella from toilet door handles and, possibly, bank notes.

The maxim to remind you what you can safely eat is: PEEL IT, BOIL IT, COOK IT, OR FORGET IT. This means that fruit you have washed and peeled yourself, and hot foods, should be safe, but raw foods, cold cooked foods, salads, fruit salads that have been prepared by others, ice cream and ice are all risky, and foods kept lukewarm in hotel buffets are often dangerous. That said, plenty of travellers and expatriates enjoy fruit and vegetables, so do keep a sense of perspective: food served in a fairly decent hotel in a large town or a place regularly

A deep vein thrombosis (DVT) is a blood clot that forms in the deep leg veins. This is very different from irritating but harmless superficial phlebitis. DVT causes swelling and redness of one leg, usually with heat and pain in one calf and sometimes the thigh. A DVT is only dangerous if a clot breaks away and travels to the lungs (pulmonary embolus). Symptoms of a pulmonary embolus (PE) include chest pain that is worse on breathing in deeply, shortness of breath, and sometimes coughing up small amounts of blood. The symptoms commonly start three to ten days after a long flight. Anyone who thinks that they might have a DVT needs to see a doctor immediately who will arrange a scan. Warfarin tablets (to thin the blood) are then taken for at least six months.

PREVENTION OF DVT Several conditions make the problem more likely. Immobility is the key, and factors like reduced oxygen in cabin air and dehydration may also contribute. To reduce the risk of thrombosis on a long journey:

* Exercise before and after the flight.
* Keep mobile before and during the flight; move around every couple of hours.
* Drink plenty of water or juices during the flight.
* Avoid taking sleeping pills and excessive tea, coffee and alcohol.
* Perform exercises that mimic walking and tense the calf muscles.
* Consider wearing flight socks or support stockings (*see www.legshealth.com*)
* Ideally, take a meal each week of oily fish (mackerel, trout, salmon, sardines, etc) ahead of your departure. This reduces the blood's ability to clot and thus DVT risk. It may even be worth just taking a meal of oily fish 24 hours before departure if this is more practical.

  If you think you are at increased risk of a clot, ask your doctor if it is safe to travel.

frequented by expatriates is likely to be safe. If you are struck, see box (page 98) for treatment.

EYE PROBLEMS Bacterial conjunctivitis (pink eye) is a common infection in Africa; people who wear contact lenses are most open to this irritating problem. The eyes feel sore and gritty and they will often be stuck together in the mornings. They will need treatment with antibiotic drops or ointment. Lesser eye irritation should settle with bathing in salt water and keeping the eyes shaded.

If an insect flies into your eye, extract it with great care, ensuring you do not crush or damage it, otherwise you may get a nastily inflamed eye from toxins secreted by the creature. Small elongated red-and-black blister beetles carry warning colouration to tell you not to crush them anywhere against your skin.

PRICKLY HEAT A fine pimply rash on the trunk is likely to be heat rash; cool showers, dabbing dry, and talc will help. Treat the problem by slowing down to a relaxed schedule, wearing only loose, baggy, 100%-cotton clothes, and sleeping naked under a fan; if it's bad, you may need to check into an air-conditioned hotel room for a while.

SKIN INFECTIONS Any mosquito bite or small nick in the skin gives an opportunity for bacteria to foil the body's usually excellent defences; it will surprise many

TREATING TRAVELLERS' DIARRHOEA

Dr Jane Wilson-Howarth

It is dehydration that makes you feel awful during a bout of diarrhoea, and the most important part of treatment is drinking lots of clear fluids. Sachets of oral rehydration salts give the perfect biochemical mix to replace all that is pouring out of your bottom but other recipes taste nicer. Any dilute mixture of sugar and salt in water will do you good: try Coke or orange squash with a three-finger pinch of salt added to each glass (if you are salt-depleted, you won't taste the salt). Otherwise, make a solution of a four-finger scoop of sugar with a three-finger pinch of salt in a 500ml glass. Or add eight level teaspoons of sugar (18g) and one level teaspoon of salt (3g) to one litre (five cups) of safe water. A squeeze of lemon or orange juice improves the taste and adds potassium, which is also lost in diarrhoea. Drink two large glasses after every bowel action, and more if you are thirsty. These solutions are still absorbed well if you are vomiting, but you will need to take sips at a time. If you are not eating, you need to drink three litres a day plus whatever is pouring into the toilet. If you feel like eating, take a bland, high carbohydrate diet. Heavy, greasy foods will probably give you cramps.

If the diarrhoea is bad, or you are passing blood or slime, or you have a fever, you will probably need antibiotics in addition to fluid replacement. A dose of norfloxacin or ciprofloxacin repeated twice a day until better may be appropriate (if you are planning to take an antibiotic with you, note that both norfloxacin and ciprofloxacin are available only on prescription in the UK). Ciprofloxacin is considered to be less effective in Ghana.

If the diarrhoea is greasy and bulky, and is accompanied by sulphurous (eggy) burps, one likely cause is giardia. This is best treated with tinidazole (four × 500mg in one dose, repeated seven days later if symptoms persist).

travellers how quickly skin infections start in warm humid climates, and it is essential to clean and cover even the slightest wound.

Creams are not as effective as a good drying antiseptic, such as dilute iodine, potassium permanganate (a few crystals in half a cup of water), or crystal (or gentian) violet. One of these should be available in most towns.

If the wound starts to throb, or becomes red and the redness starts to spread, or the wound oozes, and especially if you develop a fever, antibiotics will probably be needed: flucloxacillin (250mg four times a day) or cloxacillin (500mg four times a day). For those allergic to penicillin, erythromycin (500mg twice a day) for five days should help. See a doctor if the symptoms do not start to improve within 48 hours.

Fungal infections also get a hold easily in hot, moist climates, so wear 100%-cotton socks and underwear, and shower frequently. An itchy rash in the groin or flaking between the toes is likely to be a fungal infection. This needs treatment with an antifungal cream such as Canesten (clotrimazole); if this is not available, try Whitfield's ointment (compound benzoic acid ointment) or crystal violet (although this will turn you purple!).

MALARIA: DIAGNOSIS AND TREATMENT Even those who take their malaria tablets meticulously (see page 92), and do everything possible to avoid mosquito bites, may contract a strain of malaria that is resistant to prophylactic drugs. Untreated malaria is likely to be fatal, but even strains resistant to prophylaxis respond well to prompt treatment. Because of this, your immediate priority upon displaying possible malaria symptoms – including a rapid rise in temperature (over 38°C), and any combination of a headache, flu-like aches and pains, a general sense of disorientation, and possibly even nausea and diarrhoea – is to establish whether you have malaria, ideally by visiting a clinic.

Diagnosing malaria is not easy, which is why consulting a doctor is sensible: there are other dangerous causes of fever in Africa, which require different treatments. Even if you test negative, it would be wise to stay within reach of a laboratory until the symptoms clear up, and to test again after a day or two if they don't. It's worth noting that if you have a fever and the malaria test is negative, you may have typhoid or paratyphoid, which should also receive immediate treatment.

Travellers to remote parts of Ghana would be wise to carry a course of treatment to cure malaria, and a rapid test kit. With malaria, it is normal enough to go from feeling healthy to having a high fever in the space of a few hours (and it is possible to die from falciparum malaria within 24 hours of the first symptoms). In such circumstances, assume that you have malaria and act accordingly – whatever risks are attached to taking an unnecessary cure are outweighed by the dangers of untreated malaria. Experts differ on the costs and benefits of self-treatment, but agree that it leads to over-treatment and to many people taking drugs they do not need; yet treatment may save your life. There is also some division about the best treatment for malaria, but either Malarone or Coarthemeter are the current treatments of choice. Discuss your trip with a specialist either at home or in Ghana

OTHER INSECT-BORNE DISEASES Malaria is by no means the only insect-borne disease to which the traveller may succumb. Others include sleeping sickness and river blindness (see box, *Avoiding insect bites*, page 100). Dengue fever is rare in Ghana but there are many other similar arboviruses. These mosquito-borne diseases may mimic malaria, but there is no prophylactic medication against them. The mosquitoes that carry dengue fever viruses bite during the daytime, so it is worth applying repellent if you see any mosquitoes around. Symptoms include strong headaches, rashes and excruciating joint and muscle pains and high fever. Viral fevers usually last about a week or so and are not usually fatal. Complete rest and paracetamol are the usual treatment; plenty of fluids also help. Some patients are given an intravenous drip to keep them from dehydrating. It is especially important to protect yourself if you have had dengue fever before, since a second infection with a different strain can result in the potentially fatal dengue haemorrhagic fever.

BILHARZIA With thanks to Dr Vaughan Southgate of the Natural History Museum, London, and Dr Dick Stockley, The Surgery, Kampala Bilharzia, or schistosomiasis, is a disease that commonly afflicts the rural poor of the tropics. Two types exist in sub-Saharan Africa: *Schistosoma mansoni* and *Schistosoma haematobium*. It is an unpleasant problem that is worth avoiding, though can be treated if you do get it.

The parasite is common in almost all water sources in Ghana, even places advertised as 'bilharzia free'. The most risky shores will be close to places where infected people use water, wash clothes, etc. It is easier to understand how to diagnose it, treat it, and prevent it if you know a little about the life cycle. Contaminated faeces are washed into the lake, the eggs hatch, and the larva infects certain species of snail. The snails then produce about 10,000 cercariae a day for the rest of their lives. The parasites can digest their way through your skin when you wade or bathe in infested fresh water.

Winds disperse the snails and cercariae. The snails, in particular, can drift a long way, especially on windblown weed, so nowhere is really safe. However, deep water and running water are safer, while shallow water presents the greatest risk. The cercariae penetrate intact skin, and find their way to the liver. There, male and female meet and spend the rest of their lives in permanent copulation. No wonder

As the sun is going down, don long clothes and apply repellent on any exposed flesh. Pack a DEET-based insect repellent (roll-ons or stick are the least messy preparations for travelling). You also need either a permethrin-impregnated bednet or a permethrin spray so that you can 'treat' bednets in hotels. Permethrin treatment makes even very tatty nets protective and prevents mosquitoes from biting through the impregnated net when you roll against it; it also deters other biters. Otherwise retire to an air-conditioned room or burn mosquito coils (which are widely available and cheap in Ghana), or sleep under a fan. Coils and fans reduce rather than eliminate bites. Travel clinics usually sell a good range of nets, treatment kits and repellents.

Mosquitoes and many other insects are attracted to light. If you are camping, never put a lamp near the opening of your tent, or you will have a swarm of biters waiting to join you when you retire. In hotel rooms, be aware that the longer your light is on, the greater the number of insects will be sharing your accommodation.

Aside from avoiding mosquito bites between dusk and dawn, which will protect you from elephantiasis and a range of nasty insect-borne viruses, as well as malaria (see page 92), it is important to take precautions against other insect bites. During the day, it is wise to wear long, loose (preferably 100% cotton) clothes if you are pushing through scrubby country; this will keep off ticks and also tsetse and day-biting *Aedes* mosquitoes which may spread viral fevers, including yellow fever.

Tsetse flies hurt when they bite and it is said that they are attracted to the colour blue; locals will advise on where they are a problem and where they transmit sleeping sickness.

Minute pestilential biting blackflies spread river blindness in some parts of Africa between 19°N and 17°S; the disease is caught close to fast-flowing rivers since flies breed there and the larvae live in rapids. The flies bite during the day, but long trousers tucked into socks will help keep them off. Citronella-based natural repellents (eg: Mosi-guard) do not work against them. However, since the introduction of the Control Programme in 1974, this terrible disease has largely been eradicated from Ghana and other affected countries, and the various agencies involved are determined to remain vigilant to avoid its return.

Tumbu flies or putsi, often called mango flies in Ghana, are a problem where the climate is hot and humid. The adult fly lays her eggs on the soil or on drying laundry, and when the eggs come into contact with human flesh (when you put on clothes or lie on a bed), they hatch and bury themselves under the skin. Here, they form a crop of 'boils' each with a maggot inside. Smear a little Vaseline over the hole, and they will push their noses out to breathe. It may be possible to squeeze them out, but it depends if they are ready to do so as the larvae have spines that help them to hold on. In putsi areas, either dry your clothes and sheets within a screened house, or dry them in direct sunshine until they are crisp, or iron them.

Jiggers or sandfleas are another flesh-feaster, which can be best avoided by wearing shoes. They latch on if you walk barefoot in contaminated places, and set up home under the skin of the foot, usually at the side of a toenail where they cause a painful, boil-like swelling. They need picking out by a local expert.

you feel tired! Most finish up in the wall of the lower bowel, but others can get lost and can cause damage to many different organs. *Schistosoma haematobium* goes mostly to the bladder.

Although the adults do not cause any harm in themselves, after about 4–6 weeks they start to lay eggs, which cause an intense but usually ineffective immune reaction, including fever, cough, abdominal pain, and a fleeting, itching rash called 'safari itch'. The absence of early symptoms does not necessarily mean there is no infection. Later symptoms can be more localised and more severe, but the general symptoms settle down fairly quickly and eventually you are just tired. 'Tired all the time' is one of the most common symptoms among expats in Africa, and bilharzia, giardia, amoeba and intestinal yeast are the most common culprits.

Although bilharzia is difficult to diagnose, it can be tested at specialist travel clinics. Ideally, tests need to be done at least six weeks after likely exposure and will determine whether you need treatment. Fortunately, it is easy to treat at present.

Avoiding bilharzia

- If you are bathing, swimming, paddling, or wading in fresh water that you think may carry a bilharzia risk, try to get out of the water within ten minutes.
- Avoid bathing or paddling on shores within 200m of villages or places where people use the water a great deal, especially reedy shores or where there is lots of water weed.
- Dry off thoroughly with a towel; rub vigorously.
- If your bathing water comes from a risky source, try to ensure that the water is taken from the lake in the early morning and stored snail-free; otherwise, it should be filtered, or Dettol or Cresol added.
- Bathing early in the morning is safer than bathing in the last half of the day.
- Cover yourself with DEET insect repellent before swimming: it may offer some protection.

HIV/AIDS The risks of sexually transmitted infection are extremely high in Ghana, whether you sleep with fellow travellers or locals. About 80% of HIV infections in British heterosexuals are acquired abroad. If you must indulge, use condoms or femidoms, which help reduce the risk of transmission. Condoms are widely available in Ghana; however, it is always best to bring your own reputable brand, eg: with the British Kitemark. If you notice any genital ulcers or discharge, get treatment promptly since these increase the risk of acquiring HIV. If you do have unprotected sex, visit a clinic as soon as possible; this should be within 24 hours, or no later than 72 hours, for post-exposure prophylaxis.

MENINGITIS This is a particularly nasty disease as it can kill within hours of the first symptoms appearing. The tell-tale symptoms are a combination of a blinding headache (light sensitivity), a blotchy rash, and a high fever. Immunisation protects against the most serious bacterial form of meningitis, and the tetravalent vaccine ACWY is recommended for Ghana by British travel clinics, but if this is not available, then A+C vaccine is better than nothing.

Although other forms of meningitis exist (usually viral), there are no vaccines for these. Local papers normally report localised outbreaks. A severe headache and fever should make you run to a doctor immediately.

There are also other causes of headache and fever, one of which is typhoid, that occur in travellers to Ghana. Seek medical help if you are ill for more than a few days.

RABIES Rabies is carried by all mammals (beware the village dogs and small monkeys that are used to being fed in the parks) and is passed on to man through a bite, scratch, or a lick of an open wound. You must always assume any animal is rabid, and seek medical help as soon as possible. Meanwhile, scrub the wound with soap under a running tap, or while pouring water from a jug. Find a reasonably clear-looking source of water (but, at this stage, the quality of the water is not important), then pour on a strong iodine, or alcohol solution of gin, whisky, or rum. This helps stop the rabies virus entering the body and will guard against wound infections, including tetanus.

Pre-exposure vaccinations for rabies is ideally advised for everyone, but is particularly important if you intend to have contact with animals and/or are likely to be more than 24 hours away from medical help. Ideally, three doses should be taken over a minimum of 21 days, though even taking one or two doses of vaccine is better than none at all. Contrary to popular belief, these vaccinations are relatively painless.

If you are bitten, scratched, or licked over an open wound by a sick animal, then post-exposure prophylaxis should be given as soon as possible, though it is never too late to seek help, as the incubation period for rabies can be very long. Those who have not been immunised will need a full course of injections. The vast majority of travel health advisors, including WHO, recommend rabies immunoglobulin (RIG), but this product is expensive (around US$800) and may be hard to come by – another reason why pre-exposure vaccination should be encouraged.

Tell the doctor if you have had pre-exposure vaccine, as this should change the treatment you receive. And remember that, if you do contract rabies, mortality is 100% and death from rabies is probably one of the worst ways to go.

TETANUS Tetanus is caught through deep, dirty wounds, including animal bites, so ensure that such wounds are thoroughly cleaned. Immunisation gives good protection for ten years, provided you do not have an overwhelming number of tetanus bacteria on board. If you haven't had a tetanus shot in ten years, or you are unsure, get a tetanus toxoid injection and a tetanus booster as quickly as possible. Keep immunised and be sensible about first aid.

TICKBITE FEVER African ticks are not the rampant disease transmitters they are in the Americas, but they may spread tickbite fever and a few dangerous rarities in Ghana. Tickbite fever is a flu-like illness that can easily be treated with doxycycline, but as there can be some serious complications it is important to visit a doctor.

Ticks should ideally be removed as soon as possible as leaving them on the body increases the chance of infection. They should be removed with special tick tweezers that can be bought in good travel shops. Failing that you can use your finger nails: grasp the tick as close to your body as possible and pull steadily and firmly away at right angles to your skin. The tick will then come away complete, as long as you do not jerk or twist. If possible douse the wound with alcohol (any spirit will do) or iodine. Irritants (eg: Olbas oil) or lit cigarettes are to be discouraged since they can cause the ticks to regurgitate and therefore increase the risk of disease. It is best to get a travelling companion to check you for ticks; if you are travelling with small children, remember to check their heads, and particularly behind the ears.

Spreading redness around the bite and/or fever and/or aching joints after a tick bite imply that you have an infection that requires antibiotic treatment, so seek advice.

SNAKEBITE Snakes rarely attack unless provoked, and bites in travellers are unusual. You are less likely to get bitten if you wear stout shoes and long trousers when in the bush. Most snakes are harmless and even venomous species will dispense venom in only about half of their bites. If bitten, then, you are unlikely to have received venom; keeping this fact in mind may help you to stay calm. Many so-called first-aid techniques do more harm than good: cutting into the wound is harmful; tourniquets are dangerous; suction and electrical inactivation devices do not work. The only treatment is antivenom. In case of a bite that you fear may have been from a venomous snake:

- Try to keep calm – it is likely that no venom has been dispensed.
- Prevent movement of the bitten limb by applying a splint.
- Keep the bitten limb BELOW heart height to slow the spread of any venom.
- If you have a crêpe bandage, wrap it around the whole limb (eg: all the way from the toes to the thigh), as tight as you would for a sprained ankle or a muscle pull.
- Evacuate to a hospital that has antivenom. At the time of writing this is only known to be available in Kampala/Uganda. Many centres have an Indian antivenom that does not include the most common biting snakes in Ghana.

And remember:

- NEVER give aspirin; you may take paracetamol, which is safe.
- NEVER cut or suck the wound.
- DO NOT apply ice packs.
- DO NOT apply potassium permanganate.

If the offending snake can be captured without risk of someone else being bitten, take this to show the doctor – but beware since even a decapitated head is able to bite.

SAFETY

WATER STERILISATION You can fall ill from drinking contaminated water, so try to drink from safe sources, eg: bottled water, where available. If you are away from shops and your bottled water runs out, make tea, pour the remaining boiled water into a clean container and use it for drinking.

Alternatively, water should be passed through a good bacteriological **filter** or purified with iodine or the less-effective chlorine tablets (eg: Puritabs).

WILD ANIMALS The dangers associated with African wild animals have frequently been overstated in the past by the so-called 'Great White Hunters' and others trying to glamorise their chosen way of life. In Ghana specifically, there are few situations in which you would be likely to encounter potentially dangerous large mammals. Furthermore, most wild animals fear us far more than we fear them, and their normal response to human contact is to flee. The likelihood of a tourist in Ghana being attacked by an animal is very low, but it may be worth giving a quick overview of the situation with certain animals.

The need for caution is greatest near water, particularly around dusk and dawn, when **hippos** are likely to be out grazing. Hippos are responsible for more human fatalities than any other large mammal, not because they are aggressive but because they tend to panic when something comes between them and the safety of the water. If you happen to be that something, then you're unlikely to live to tell the tale. Never consciously walk between a hippo and water, and never walk along riverbanks or though reed beds, especially in overcast weather or at dusk or dawn, unless you are certain that no hippos are present.

Watch out, too, for **Nile crocodiles**. Only a very large croc is likely to attack a person, and then only in the water or right on the shore. Near towns and other settlements, you can be fairly sure that any very large crocodile will have been disposed of by its potential prey, so the risk is greatest away from human habitation.

There are only a couple of places in Ghana where a hiker might stumble across an **elephant** or **buffalo**, the most dangerous of Africa's terrestrial herbivores. Elephants almost invariably mock charge and indulge in some hair-raising trumpeting before they attack in earnest. Provided that you back off at the first sign of unease, they are most unlikely to take further notice of you. If you see them before they see you, give them a wide berth and bear in mind they are most likely to attack if surprised at close proximity. If an animal charges you, the safest course of action is to head for the nearest tree and climb it. Black rhinos are also prone to charging without apparent provocation, but they're now very rare except in a few reserves where walking is forbidden.

There are campsites in Africa where **green monkeys** and **baboons** have become a pest. Feeding these animals is highly irresponsible, since it encourages them to scavenge and may eventually lead to them being shot. Monkeys are too small to progress much beyond being a nuisance, but baboons are very dangerous and have often killed children and maimed adults with their vicious teeth. Do not tease or underestimate the strength of a baboon. If primates are hanging around a campsite, and you wander off leaving fruit in your tent, don't expect the tent to be standing when you return.

The dangers associated with large **predators** are often exaggerated. Most predators stay clear of humans and are likely to kill accidentally or in self-defence rather than by design. Lions are an exception, but it is uncommon for a lion to attack a human without cause – in the highly unlikely event that you encounter one on foot, the important thing is not to run, since this is likely to trigger the instinct to give chase. A slight but real danger when sleeping in the bush without a tent is that a passing hyena or lion might investigate a hairy object sticking out of a sleeping bag and decapitate you through predatorial curiosity. In areas where large predators are still present, sleeping in a *sealed* tent practically guarantees your safety – provided that you don't sleep with your head sticking out, or at any point put meat in the tent.

MARINE DANGERS The currents off many parts of the Ghanaian coast are highly dangerous, and swimmers risk being dragged away from shore by riptides, strong undertows and whirlpools, particularly during the rainy season and in windy weather. It is common for those swimmers who underestimate the dangers associated with these currents to drown. Quite simply, you should never swim in the sea without first asking local advice, perhaps not at all if you are a weak swimmer, and you are advised against going into water deeper than your waist without some sort of flotation device. If you are ever caught in a riptide or whirlpool, it is generally advisable not to immediately fight the current by swimming to shore, but to save your strength by floating on your back or swimming parallel to shore until the tide weakens, and only then to try to get back to land.

The coastal residents of Ghana evidently view beaches in a less aesthetic way than we do. It is customary in most seaside towns and villages for the beach to serve as a communal toilet. While this may not constitute a health threat in most circumstances, dodging between freshly deposited turds does tend to take the edge off a pleasant stroll on the sand, and imagining what the last tide washed away would certainly put me off swimming. Fortunately, most beaches that are regularly visited by tourists are no longer put to the, um, traditional use.

Don't swim or walk barefoot on the beach, or you risk getting coral or urchin spines in your soles or venomous fish spines in your feet. If you tread on a venomous fish, soak the foot in hot (but not scalding) water until some time after the pain subsides; this may be for 20–30 minutes in all. Take your foot out of the water to top up, otherwise you may scald it. If the pain returns, re-immerse the foot. Once the venom has been heat-inactivated, get a doctor to check and remove any bits of fish spine in the wound.

Part Two

ACCRA

YOU now have the opportunity to find GHANA in West Africa with all the general and background information that you need to know. All at your fingertips.

Probably the most exciting feature of TRAVELagenda is that you can now choose your dream holiday through photography. Simply select what you would like to see by either subject, location or a keyword and then relate the photos to fully interactive maps, which will show you the location of tourist attractions and events.

TRAVELagenda has been created by experienced travellers and other informed personnel on a totally independent basis. All of this will help you get the most out of your desire and enthusiasm to visit Ghana, without risk.

Open your mind and check out what's on offer.

A new agenda for a new holiday, business or investment experience !

www.travelagenda.org

6

Accra

It is tempting to introduce Accra as Ghana's historical capital, or something similarly portentous. This is, after all, a city that started life in the 15th century, when the Ga people who still live in the area settled on the west side of Korle Lagoon to found a small village from where they traded with passing Portuguese ships. Later in the same century, near what is now Brazil Lane, the Portuguese built a lodge that was burnt to the ground by locals shortly after it was constructed. No traces of this lodge remain, but modern Accra can still lay claim to three fortified buildings dating from the mid 17th century – Dutch Fort Ussher, British Fort James, and Danish Osu Castle. Furthermore, in 1877, when what are now Nairobi, Johannesburg and Addis Ababa were no more than tracts of empty bush, Accra became the capital of the British Gold Coast colony.

Knowing the above, Accra has to be classed as something of a disappointment. Two of the three old forts, the city's most obvious draw cards, at least on paper, are closed to the public and their whitewashed stone exteriors patrolled by camera-sensitive military personnel. Osu Castle, the seat of government since colonial times, cannot even be approached closely, since the surrounding streets are barricaded on all sides. And the smaller Fort James now serves as a prison – approachable, yes, but wholly untouchable. Alone among Accra's historical buildings, **Fort Ussher** (see page 133) and the colonial-era **lighthouse** near Fort James (see page 133) offer an informal welcome to the curious visitor – ask nicely and you may even be allowed to climb the 82-step spiral staircase for a gull's-eye view over old James Town and Ussher Town.

Accra is a modern city, emphatically so, with a population of over the two million mark and an urban landscape of giddy incongruity – scruffy lanes lined with open sewers and colonial-era homesteads lead to untended open spaces, grandiose Independence monuments and arches, dazzling modern skyscrapers, and run-down concrete blocks harking from the headiest days of Soviet town planning. The more you try to pin Accra down, the more elusive it seems, and it is in this respect – the way in which the former Danish outpost of Osu, say, still feels like a separate entity to Ussher Town, or Adabraka – that Accra is, if not a historical city, then certainly a city whose modern schizophrenia reflects its distant past.

We found Accra rewards casual exploration – punctuated in this drenching humidity by frequent stops to sip the juice from a decapitated coconut or gulp down a chilled soft drink. Tourist attractions, it is true, are few and far between, but both **James Town** and **Osu** have a certain faded charm, while the frenzied central market area and – even more – Adabraka are vibrantly, brashly modern without ever feeling in any way threatening. Add to this any number of garden bars, inexpensive restaurants and live music venues, and Accra in all its modernity becomes as likeable and absorbing as most African cities.

Not the least of Accra's attractions is its amiability. Hectic it may be, chaotic in places, but as far as visitors need be concerned, there must be few developing world cities of comparable size with such a safe and relaxed mood. I arrived in Accra with defences formed by years of east African travel. Within 24 hours, I realised how wholly inappropriate these defences were. The closest thing to hassle that we encountered in Accra was the relentless horn blowing of taxi drivers (can any city be patrolled by such a high proportion of empty taxis?) to whom a white pedestrian evidently spells custom. Yet, remarkably, the selfsame taxi drivers were always happy to point us to a shared taxi if that's what we wanted, rather than try to hustle us into an overpriced charter ride.

In summation, those who have only a short time in Ghana would probably be well advised to spend as little time as is necessary in a city that has little to offer in the way of targeted sightseeing. For those with the time to enjoy Accra – well, enjoy…!

GETTING THERE AND AWAY

BY AIR All international flights arrive at the recently renovated **Kotoka International Airport**, which is one of the most centrally located international airports that I'm aware of in an African capital, a mere 4km from Sankara Overpass and roughly 500m east of Liberation Avenue.

Assuming that your passport and visa are in order, and you have an onward ticket, the immigration and customs procedures are quick and straightforward. Until recently, immigration wouldn't stamp more than 30 days in your passport, regardless of what visa you had or how long you intended to stay. These days, they seem automatically to grant visitors a 60-day stamp, but you might want to check this should you intend to spend longer than a month in Ghana. It is also theoretically possible to buy a visa at the airport (at an inflated fee), but I wouldn't want to chance it myself, as travellers have been refused before and sent straight back home at vast expense. There has also been the very occasional report of immigration officials asking for extra fees on arrival. It's unlikely to happen, but if it does, stick to your guns and say no.

There is only one place to **exchange foreign currency** (but not travellers' cheques) at the airport, before customs in the luggage hall, and while the rate isn't particularly great, it makes sense to change enough money into local currency to get a taxi to your hotel and see you through to the next banking day. If you fly in during the wee hours of the morning, then you shouldn't expect foreign exchange facilities to be open, and will probably be glad of having a few spare US$1 bills rather than relying on the taxi drivers to provide you with change.

As soon as you leave the terminal building, expect to be mobbed by taxi drivers. As things stand, there would be nothing to prevent you from pushing past them all and hopping into a passenger taxi in the direction you want to go, though it's probably fair to say that if any one public transport route in an African capital is likely to attract light fingers, then it's the one from the airport. My inclination after a long flight and loaded down with luggage would be to save your first acquaintance with Accra's bemusing public transport routes for later in the day. A passenger **taxi** from the airport to anywhere in central Accra really shouldn't cost more than US$4, if that, but you'll be asked a lot more and, again, while you certainly ought to negotiate the fare, this probably isn't the moment to get overtly confrontational.

A couple of years back, there were a few incidents of Westerners picking up a dropping taxi from the airport after dark, being rear-ended, and then being held up at knifepoint by the occupants of the rear car when they stopped to assess the damage. I've not heard of anything of the sort recently, but it might still be wise to instruct your driver to stay on main roads (eg: pass through the junction near '37' and on to Sankara if going into the city centre) as these sort of robberies mostly occurred in less populated areas.

HOTEL 'HIJACKING' BY DRIVERS

Chris Scott

You have done your homework preparing for your trip to Ghana using the Bradt Travel Guide and the internet. You have made your hotel bookings over the net and you have arrived in Ghana. To get to your hotel, you charter a more expensive, less hassle, airport taxi found to the left of the exit to 'Arrivals', or a public taxi found across the road from 'Arrivals' in the public parking area. You give the driver the name of your hotel only to receive a comment to the effect that the hotel is closed temporarily for some reason or another and such and such hotel is a better choice. This is a scam. Many drivers have made prior arrangements with certain hotels to get hefty commissions when they bring tourists. Insist on your hotel-whatever.

Or... you have chartered a car hire company to take you around to major centres outside Accra. You are approaching a certain city and the driver says he will call on his mobile, or yours, the hotel you have booked over the internet to ask for directions. Often the driver will feign the call and then give you some excuse why you can't go there – 'they are fully booked', 'they are overbooked' – and then take you to the hotel where, again, he would collect a big commission. Insist on talking to the hotel yourself, or, better still, call the night before to confirm your reservation.

Should your flight be scheduled to arrive after dark (which nearly all of them do), it might be wise to make an advance booking at a mid- to upper-range hotel, depending on your budget: the Granada, Shangri-La and Golden Tulip are all close to the airport. Be aware that many hotels graded three-star or above have a shuttle service to and from the airport, but you ought to check whether this is the case when you book (or get your travel agent to check it), and should also ascertain until what time it runs. (Balanced against the argument for booking a hotel in advance is that on three recent occasions when we've flown into a west African capital scheduled to arrive after dark, various delays meant we actually arrived the next morning, so that a pre-paid hotel booking would have been a waste of money.)

Airlines

✈ **Alitalia** Ring Rd Central; ☎ 021 229813 or 221549; f 021 220759; airport ☎ 021 772766

✈ **American Airlines** Valco Trust Hse, behind USIS; ☎ 021 231804/5; f 021 231806

✈ **British Airways** Horizon Plaza, 60 Liberation Rd; ☎ 021 214996; f 021 214976; airport ☎ 021 779998

✈ **Cathay Pacific** Trust Tower, Asylum Down; ☎ 021 238364 or 020 8138244 or 024 231875; e cathayp@its.com.gh

✈ **Egypt Air** Ring Rd East (near Danquah Circle); ☎ 021 773538 or 777826. Airport ☎ 021 776586

✈ **Ethiopian Airlines** Cocoa Hse, Kwame Nkrumah Av; ☎ 021 664856/7

✈ **Ghana International Airlines** Opposite Alliance Française, Liberation Rd; ☎ 021 213555; reservations ☎ 021 221000 or 777406

✈ **KLM & Kenya Airways** Ring Rd Central; ☎ 021 224050 or 241560; airport ☎ 021 775729/6509

✈ **Lufthansa** Ring Rd Central; ☎ 021 243893/6; airport ☎ 021 762372 or 779052

✈ **Middle East Airlines** Kojo Thomson Rd; ☎ 021 228437 or 230867; airport ☎ 021 775492

✈ **Nigeria Airways** Danawi Bldg, Kojo Thompson Rd; ☎ 021 249798

✈ **South African Airways** Millennium Heights, Liberation Link Rd opposite Alliance Francaise; ☎ 021 783676/7/8; airport ☎ 021 770319

BY ROAD There are numerous different bus and tro-tro stations in Accra, some serving specific lines, and others a specific cluster of destinations. The most important stations to travellers are the main **STC Station** on Ring Road, **Kaneshie Station** on Winneba Road about 1km northwest of Lamptey Circle, and **Tudu Station** in the city centre north of Makola Circle.

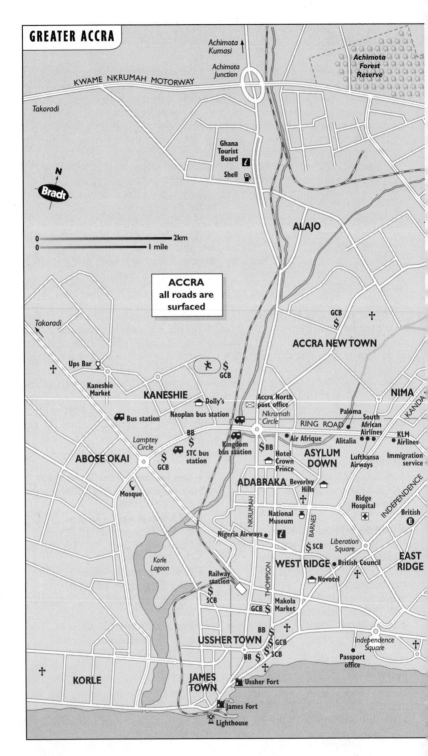

GREATER ACCRA

Achimota
Kumasi

Achimota
Junction

Achimota
Forest
Reserve

KWAME NKRUMAH MOTORWAY

Takoradi

Ghana
Tourist
Board

Shell

N

Bradt

Takoradi

0   2km
0   1 mile

ACCRA
all roads are
surfaced

ALAJO

GCB
$

ACCRA NEW TOWN

Ups Bar

Kaneshie
Market

KANESHIE

Dolly's

Bus station

Neoplan bus station

$
GCB

Accra North
post office

Nkrumah
Circle

NIMA

Paloma

South
African
Airlines

KLM
Airlines

RING ROAD

KANDA

BB
$

Lamptey
Circle

ABOSE OKAI

STC bus
station

$
GCB

Kingdom
bus station

$ BB

Air Afrique

Alitalia

Immigration
service

Hotel
Crown
Prince

ASYLUM
DOWN

Lufthansa
Airways

Mosque

ADABRAKA

Beverley
Hills

Ridge
Hospital

British

NKRUMAH

National
Museum

Nigeria Airways

BARNES

INDEPENDENCE

Korle
Lagoon

Railway
station

$
SCB

GCB $

Makola
Market

SCB

WEST RIDGE

Liberation
Square

British Council

Novotel

EAST
RIDGE

THOMPSON

BB

GCB

Independence
Square

USSHER TOWN

BB

SCB

Passport
office

KORLE

JAMES
TOWN

Ussher Fort

James Fort

Lighthouse

110

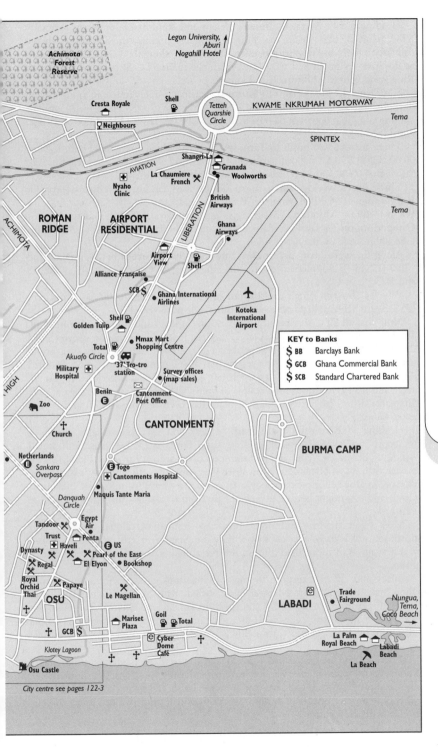

Legon University,
Aburi
Nogahill Hotel

KWAME NKRUMAH MOTORWAY

Achimota
Forest
Reserve

Cresta Royale

Shell

Tetteh
Quarshie
Circle

Tema

Neighbours

SPINTEX

Shangri-La

Granada

Woolworths

AVIATION

La Chaumiere
French

Nyaho
Clinic

British
Airways

Tema

**ROMAN
RIDGE**

**AIRPORT
RESIDENTIAL**

Ghana
Airways

ACHIMOTA

LIBERATION

Airport
View

Shell

Alliance Française

SCB $

Ghana International
Airlines

Kotoka
International
Airport

Shell

Golden Tulip

Total

Akuafo Circle

Mmax Mart
Shopping Centre

Military
Hospital

'37' Tro-tro
station

HIGH

Survey offices
(map sales)

Benin

Cantonment
Post Office

Zoo

CANTONMENTS

Church

BURMA CAMP

KEY to Banks		
$ BB	Barclays Bank	
$ GCB	Ghana Commercial Bank	
$ SCB	Standard Chartered Bank	

Netherlands

Sankara
Overpass

Togo

Cantonments Hospital

Danquah
Circle

Maquis Tante Maria

Tandoor

Egypt
Air

Trust

Penta

Haveli

US

Dynasty

Pearl of the East

Regal

El Elyon

Bookshop

Royal
Orchid
Thai

Papaye

Trade
Fairground

Nungua,
Tema,
Coco Beach

OSU

Le Magellan

LABADI

Goil

Mariset
Plaza

Total

GCB $

La Palm
Royal Beach

Labadi
Beach

Klotey Lagoon

Cyber
Dome
Café

La Beach

Osu Castle

City centre see pages 122-3

Heading out of Accra, the most efficient and comfortable option is generally STC, assuming that you are travelling a reasonable distance (the STC buses charge full fare to their end destination, even if you 'drop' along the way). All STC buses to destinations north and west leave from the main STC Station, which lies on Ring Road between Nkrumah and Lamptey Circle.

STC runs 13 buses daily to **Kumasi**, leaving roughly once an hour during daylight hours – normal buses cost US$6, while the express video buses with air conditioning that depart at 04.00, 05.30, 07.30, 09.00, 11.00 12.30, 13.00 and 16.00 cost US$7.50.

There are also two buses to **Tamale** every day, which annoyingly both leave at 09.00 (US$12.50 for the ordinary vehicle, or US$17.50 with AC) and two buses to Sunyani at 05.00 and 16.00, taking around eight hours (US$9).

Three buses weekly run to most destinations far north: vehicles leave for **Bolgatanga** at 08.00 on Monday, Wednesday and Saturday (US$20 with AC), for **Wa** at 09.00 on Mondays, Wednesdays, and Saturdays (US$16), and the bus for **Ouagadougou** in Burkina Faso leaves one hour later, at 10.00 (US$28 plus CFA500 payable on the other side).

Along the west coast, eight buses daily leave for **Takoradi** between 04.00 and 17.30 (US$5–6), supplemented by four buses daily to **Cape Coast** (07.30, 09.30 and 16.30, cost US$4).

Vehicles also run direct to **Abidjan** in Côte d'Ivoire at 04.00 daily, and cost US$15 plus CFA9,000 payable on the other side of the border.

Note that all STC services are cut back on Sundays and some don't run at all. To check current timetables and fares, ring the helpful information office (↘ *021 221414/912/932*). Tickets are best booked a day or two in advance, but you should usually be safe arriving without a reservation 30–60 minutes before the scheduled departure time, except over long weekends and other holiday periods. If you are stuck at the STC terminus for a couple of hours, the canteen serves a range of tasty Ghanaian dishes (the red-red and plantain has been recommended) and is very good value.

Heading to **Kumasi** or **Takoradi**, a new and very comfortable mode of transport is **City Express**. These are large Ford or Dodge vans with tinted windows, blasting air-con, and half the seats of an ordinary tro-tro. They are a bit pricier than STC, but much faster, since they travel directly and don't stop along the way to drop off or pick up people. In Accra, they leave from Kwame Nkrumah Circle and you might be able to pick one up from Kaneshie – just ask for the 'City Express'.

Most other tro-tros and other buses to destinations along the coast and north towards Kumasi also leave from Kaneshie Station on a fill-up-and-go basis – you'll rarely wait more than 30 minutes for a vehicle for wherever you want to go to.

Buses and other transport to most destinations east of Accra leave from Tudu Station near Makola Market. These include daily STC buses to **Ho** (11.30; US$3.20), **Hohoe** (16.00; US$4) and **Kpandu** (15.00), and two daily to **Aflao**. For some destinations east, eg: Shai Hills and Prampram, you may have to pick up a tro-tro from Tema Station (just south of the Novotel) to Ashaiman and change vehicles there.

Wherever you are going, hail a taxi to take you to the right station – the drivers know exactly from where vehicles leave for even the most obscure destinations, and, at around US$2, it will save you immense hassle and asking around. Likewise, when you arrive in Accra, it really is worth the small price of a taxi to get to your hotel swiftly and simply.

Accra is serviced by a remarkably cheap and efficient system of tro-tros, passenger (shared) taxis, and dropping (charter) taxis, though getting to grips with the main routes used by passenger vehicles takes time and a certain degree of trial and error. In my opinion, travellers who are spending only a couple of days in Accra may as well stick to dropping taxis, which can be picked up practically anywhere and at any time. You're unlikely to have to pay more than US$2 for a daytime trip within the bounds of Ring Road, though you may sometimes have to negotiate to get a fair price, and fares do seem to be higher on days when traffic is particularly heavy. Dropping taxis to places outside Ring Road – La Beach, the STC bus station, Accra Zoo or the airport – will cost more, but are still very cheap by international standards.

Passenger taxis and tro-tros are even cheaper – around US$0.20–0.30, depending on the exact route – and we've neither heard nor experienced anything to suggest there is any serious need to worry about pickpockets and other petty thieves on public transport. In fact, the presence of a whole minibus of Ghanaians (who will get noisy if something happens that they don't like) actually seems to work as insurance against getting ripped off. Once you are reasonably well oriented to Accra, the system is quite easy to assimilate.

The most important local transport hub is **Nkrumah Circle** and the adjacent stations under the Nsawam Overpass, from where you can safely assume you'll find a shared taxi or tro-tro to anywhere in central or Greater Accra, at the worst involving one change of vehicle. Shared taxis to the Novotel Hotel (via Farrar Av & Barnes Rd) and to Osu leave from the south side of the circle, while those to Sankara Overpass, '37', the airport, La Beach and Nungua leave from the station next to the overpass. Minibuses heading right down Nkrumah Road to James Town can generally be picked up by waiting on the west side of Nkrumah Road immediately south of the circle. Tro-tros to destinations slightly further out of town, eg: Legon University, generally leave from the northwest side of the circle.

The most important station in the city centre for local tro-tros is **Tema Station** on Independence Avenue below the Novotel Hotel, where you can pick up transport to coastal destinations in the direction of Tema as well as northeast along Independence Avenue to Sankara Overpass and along Liberation Avenue past the airport and on to Aburi.

Outside Ring Road, a landmark worth knowing is **'37' Station** at Akuafo Circle on the junction of Liberation Avenue and Gifford Road, where you'll pick up shared taxis to most destinations, including Nkrumah Circle (via Sankara Overpass), Osu (via Cantonments Rd & Danquah Circle) and Nungua (via Burma Camp Bypass & La Beach).

It's worth getting to know some of the signals and calls most frequently used by tro-tro mates within Accra. When they shout 'Accra!', it means they are heading to the central Tema Station. When they shout 'circle', they will be heading to Nkrumah Circle – there is also a sign to show you're going to the circle, which involves rotating your hand in small circles with your index finger pointed downwards. The trendy part of Cantonments Road running through Osu south of Danquah Circle is often referred to as 'Oxford Street' by taxi drivers and tro-tro mates. Other signs – used in Accra and throughout Ghana – are briefly explained in the *Travelling in Ghana* chapter (see page 69).

If you use 'dropping' taxis, be aware that their drivers seldom know the names of streets or of places of touristic interest. This includes the likes of the National Culture Centre, National Museum, Asylum Down, and important traffic connections like Kanda Overdrive, Liberation Circle and Independence Avenue!

When this happens, the driver may show some uncertainty, but that doesn't prevent him from taking you just anywhere, so be prepared and have your maps at hand.

ORIENTATION Central Accra is bounded to the south by the Atlantic Ocean and to the west by Korle Lagoon. In other directions, it is bounded by Ring Road, which starts at the old Winneba Road on the seafront immediately west of Korle Lagoon, before running northeast via Lamptey Circle to Nkrumah Circle, then east from Nkrumah to Sankara Overpass (still sometimes referred to as Sankara Circle, which it was prior to the construction of the overpass), and then southeast from Sankara overpass via Danquah Circle to the junction with Labadi Road near the seafront.

Tourists who spend some time in Accra will probably come to regard Nkrumah Circle as the city's most significant landmark. Not only is it the local transport hub of the city, but it also marks the intersection between Ring Road and Nkrumah Road, the latter the main north–south thoroughfare through Accra's commercial heart of Adabraka (in the north), Ussher Town and James Town (on the seafront). Running parallel to and east of Nkrumah Avenue, Kojo Thompson and Barnes roads are arguably the city's second and third most important north–south thoroughfares, the former well supplied with budget accommodation, the latter effectively the eastern border of the most built-up part of the city centre, and notable for two important landmarks, the National Museum and Novotel Hotel.

The suburbs that lie within Ring Road can be divided into three broad clusters. In the west are the three central suburbs mentioned above, essentially the commercial city centre. Of these, Adabraka is the main haunt of budget travellers since it is dotted with cheap accommodation, bars and restaurants, while the older suburbs of Ussher Town and James Town are of some historical interest. To the west of this, bounded roughly by Barnes Road to the west and an imaginary north–south line running between Sankara Overpass and Independence Square, lies a cluster of more spacious, green suburbs comprising, from north to south: Asylum Down, North Ridge, East Ridge, West Ridge and Victoriaborg. The main thoroughfare through this part of Accra is Independence Avenue, which connects Sankara Overpass on Ring Road to the seafront at the south end of Barnes Road. The most easterly suburb is Osu (aka Christiansborg), another old part of town focused towards Osu Castle and bisected by Cantonments Road, an important commercial centre notable for its many restaurants.

Several important trunk roads fan out from Ring Road. The main road to Winneba and the West Coast leaves Ring Road at Lamptey Circle, the main road to Nsawam, Kumasi and the north leaves from Nkrumah Circle, while Liberation Road, which leaves from Sankara Overpass, heads past the airport to Tetteh Quarshie Circle and the Kwame Nkrumah Highway for Tema and other destinations east of Accra. At the very southeast of Ring Road, Labadi Road heads to La Beach, Coco Beach and Tema via the coast.

MAPS The *KLM/Shell Ghana Road Map* (with Accra on the flip side) is sometimes available in Accra's bookshops and upmarket hotels. For other requirements, head to the map sales office in the **Department of Surveys** (⊕ *09.00–16.00, Mon–Fri*) on the junction of Airport and Gifford roads, about 500m from '37' Station. Don't buy the 1:1,000,000 one-sheet map of Ghana, which so far as I can see is identical to the KLM/Shell map, but much more expensive and lacking Accra on the flip. Far more useful is the set of four 1:500,000 sheets, which together cover the whole country, while for hikers and walkers, there are more detailed 1:50,000 sheets covering most parts of the country. These maps cost around US$8 each and have proved to be reasonably reliable in my experience.

Be aware, however, that most maps of Ghana contain some curious omissions, inclusions, displacements and misspellings (one example is the substantial junction town of Ashaiman, only 20km from Accra, which is not shown on any map that I've seen), suggesting they are rather less current than the legend '8th edition Jan 1994' on the 1:500,000 maps would have you believe. Some maps also use unusual or archaic spellings for some towns and villages, so exercise a certain amount of judgement in deciding how far they are to be trusted.

TOURIST INFORMATION

The Regional Tourist Office is a bit of a trek out of the town centre, but quite easy to locate, along an apparently anonymous side road to the west of Barnes Road between the major intersections with Liberia and Castle roads. The people who work here are reasonably friendly, but making friends is about the only purpose that a visit is likely to serve.

A far better source of current information about Accra is the excellent book *No More Worries: The Indispensable Insiders' Guide to Accra*, compiled and published by the North American Women's Association and sold at most large bookshops and upmarket hotels for the equivalent of US$15–20. Geared primarily at people spending a while in Accra rather than the casual visitor, it provides a useful combination of detailed listings and commonsense advice on everything from swimming in the sea to hiring a domestic servant.

Also recommended is the Accra Visitor Centre (AVC), a new private enterprise on Ring Road Central, a short distance east of the Nsawam Overpass, whose multilingual staff can offer local advice and services as well as maps, postcards, handicrafts, and other souvenirs. To find out more, visit www.strictlyaccra.com or e bentsifi@hotmail.com.

The Nature Conservation Research Centre (NCRC), the organisation responsible for setting up the majority of Ghana's best eco-tourism projects, has plans to open an information and booking office in the centre of Accra under the banner 'Greet'. For more details check the website: www.ncrc-ghana.org.

EMBASSIES AND HIGH COMMISSIONS It might be worth noting here that if you intend travelling more extensively around west Africa, you'll probably save quite a sum of money (and passport-page wastage) by obtaining a *Visa Conseil de l'Entente*, a single visa that costs US$50 and allows entry to five different countries (Côte d'Ivoire, Burkina Faso, Niger, Togo and Benin) within two months of a selected date. The catch with this visa is that its existence is not actively publicised by several of the embassies concerned, presumably because it's more profitable to sell a one-country visa – indeed, in late 2003, we spoke to several of the relevant embassies in Johannesburg and visited four in Accra to be told either than no such visa existed or that there were no forms left! Fortunately, the Togo High Commission in Accra proved to be the exception, and issued us the visa in three hours – things might change by the time you read this, but it's definitely worth phoning around the relevant embassies in Accra to check.

E **Algeria** 22 Tito Av; ☎ 021 776719; f 021 776828
E **Australia** 2 Second Rangoon Close, Cantonments; ☎ 021 701296/3 or 021 777080; f 021 776803
E **Austria** resident in Abidjan; ☎ 021 220640 for limited consular services in Accra
E **Belgium** Independence Av (between 37 Military Hospital & Flagstaff House); ☎ 021 762281/2

E **Benin** 3 Switchback Lane; ☎ 021 774860; f 021 774889
E **Bulgaria** 3–5 Kakramadu Rd, East Cantonments; ☎ 021 772404; f 021 774231
E **Burkina Faso** 772/3 Farrar St, Asylum Down; ☎ 021 221988/36
E **Canada** 42 Independence Av; ☎ 021 228885 or

228566 or 773791; **f** 021 773792

🇪 **China** 6 Agostino Neto Rd; ☎ 021 777073; **f** 021 774527

🇪 **Côte d'Ivoire** (Ivory Coast) 9 18th Lane, Osu; ☎ 021 774611/2; **f** 021 773734

🇪 **Denmark** 67 Dr Isert Rd; ☎ 021 226972 or 229830; ☎ 021 228061

🇪 **Finland** Consular services in Shangri-La Hotel; ☎ 021 772178

🇪 **France** 12th Rd, off Liberation Av; ☎ 021 228571/04 or 774080; **f** 021 778321

🇪 **Germany** 6 Ridge St, North Ridge; ☎ 021 221311/26; **f** 021 221347

🇪 **Greece** c/o Embassy of Spain

🇪 **Guinea** 4th Norla St, Labone; ☎ 021 777921; **f** 021 760961

🇪 **India** 9 Ridge Rd, Roman Ridge; ☎ 021 775601/2; **f** 021 772176

🇪 **Ireland** 5th Circular Extension, Labone; ☎ 021 772866 or 779774

🇪 **Italy** Jawaharlal Nehru Rd; ☎ 021 775621/2; **f** 021 777056

🇪 **Japan** 8 Tito Av; ☎ 021 775616 or 765060/1; **f** 021 775951

🇪 **Liberia** 10 West Cantonments Rd; ☎ 021 775641/2 or 775987

🇪 **Mali** Bungalow # 1, Liberia Rd (opposite Ministry of Trade & Industry; near National Theatre); ☎ 021 663276; fax 021 666942

🇪 **Mauritania** c/o Embassy of France

🇪 **Netherlands** 89 Liberation Rd; ☎ 021 773644 or 231991/2; **f** 021 773655

🇪 **Niger** E104–3 Independence Av; ☎ 021 224962 or 229011

🇪 **Nigeria** Tito Av; ☎ 021 776158/9; **f** 021 774395

🇪 **Norway** Cola Av (off Ring Rd, near Ghana Cement); ☎ 021 220101/44

🇪 **Portugal** c/o Embassy of Spain

🇪 **Russia** 13th Lane Ring Rd East (opposite Chicken Licken'); ☎ 021 775611; **f** 021 772699

🇪 **Senegal** c/o Embassy of France

🇪 **South Africa** Klottey Crescent, North Labone; ☎ 021 764501 or 762380; **f** 021 762381

🇪 **Spain** Drake Av Ext; ☎ 021 774004/5; **f** 021 776216

🇪 **Sweden** 11th Lane, Osu; ☎ 021 773145; **f** 021 773175

🇪 **Switzerland** 9 Water Rd, North Ridge; ☎ 021 228125; **f** 021 223583

🇪 **Togo** Togo House, Cantonments Circle; ☎ 021 777950/4521

🇪 **United Kingdom** 1 Abdul Gamel Nasser Av; ☎ 021 221665 or 221715

🇪 **United States of America** Ring Rd East, Osu; ☎ 021 775347/8/9; **f** 021 776008

WHERE TO STAY

There are several hundred hotels and guesthouses scattered in and around Accra, ranging from half-a-dozen with world-class facilities to innumerable budget hotels aimed primarily at the local market. What follows is a representative selection of some of the best places in each range; it is bound to be less than fully comprehensive, and readers are invited to let me know about any new finds. Note that those luxury hotels that cater mainly to business travellers on expense accounts (eg: Golden Tulip, Labadi Beach, and La Palm) sometimes offer weekend rates of about half the advertised price, including a full breakfast and buffet dinner – they won't always mention these rates, so ask!

LUXURY: US$100 AND ABOVE

🏠 **Accra Novotel** ☎ 021 667546; **f** 021 667533. Part of the French Novotel chain, this 4-star hotel lies on the southern end of Barnes Rd, & its height makes it something of a landmark in the city centre. Very much a businessman's hotel, the Novotel is the obvious choice if you plan on doing a lot of walking around the city centre, but the atmosphere is negligible & the rooms are not as plush or spacious as those at Accra's other 4- & 5-star hotels. Facilities inc a swimming pool, tennis court, business centre, outstanding restaurant, curio shop, & DSTV in all rooms. *US$158/178 sgl/dbl inc a good buffet b/fast, & executive rooms are available at US$286.*

🏠 **Coconut Grove Regency Hotel** ☎ 021 225155 or 226310 or 238414; **f** 021 230140; **e** regency@ coconutgrovehotels.com.gh; www.coconutgrovehotels. com.gh. Part of a chain with sister establishments in Elmina & Obuasi, the Coconut Grove in Cantonments offers reliable accommodation & good service in pleasant leafy grounds. Facilities inc a swimming pool, an excellent restaurant & bar – which hosts regular dancing nights – business centre & conference hall. *US$85/95/120 for a sgl/dbl/suite.*

🏠 **Fiesta Royale Hotel** ☎ 021 517411; **f** 021 51755; **e** reservations@fiestaroyalehotel.com. Opened in Oct 2003, this ostentatious out-of-town hotel, which stands in large grassy grounds on Nkrumah Highway between Quarshie Circle & Achimota, seems designed more for business travellers than for tourists. Nevertheless, it's a good if perhaps overpriced semi-urban option, with a large swimming pool area, full business facilities, & AC rooms with DSTV. *US$150/180 sgl/dbl, or US$210–230 for a chalet.*

⌂ **Golden Tulip Hotel** (230 rooms) ☎ 021 775360; **f** 021 775361; **e** info@goldentulipaccra.com; www.goldentulipaccra.com. This 4-star hotel, part of the Dutch chain, lies out on Liberation Rd towards the airport & is the only hotel in Accra to approach the standard set by the two beach hotels listed below. It is well situated for access to the city centre & the airport, & the facilities are easily the equal of the Labadi – swimming pool (open to non-residents for US$5), tennis courts & mini-golf course, good restaurants, DSTV & in-house movie channel, an excellent curio & bookshop, a mini art gallery, & a business centre. Drawbacks inc the relatively uninspiring grounds & the distance from the beach. *US$226/242 sgl/dbl inc a good buffet b/fast, or up to US$425 for a suite.*

⌂ **Hotel Shangri-La** ☎ 021 776993/4; **f** 021 774873; **e** shangri@ncs.com.gh; www.shangri-la.gh.com. Situated on Liberation Rd, a short distance past the airport, the venerable 3-star Shangri-La is superb value for money following extensive renovations. The attractive common areas make tasteful use of natural materials & ethnic art & crafts, & are centred around a palm-fringed fountain & large illuminated swimming pool (open to non-residents for US$4.50). Facilities are comparable to those of the hotels listed above, & inc a business centre, book & imported newspaper stall, gymnasium, sauna, tennis court, horse riding, & a superb restaurant known for its pizzas. *Self-contained dbl chalets with AC, fridge, DSTV, & large private safe costs US$100–170, depending on room size.*

⌂ **Labadi Beach Hotel** ☎ 021 772501/6 or 021 772531; **f** 021 773110; **e** contact@labadibeach.com; www.labadibeach.com. It isn't difficult to see why Labadi Beach is the only established hotel in Ghana to be awarded a 5-star grading. The most striking feature of

the hotel is the rare attention to detail noticeable not only in the architecture & the lush landscaped gardens (complete with large reed-fringed dam & adult & children's swimming pools), but also in the standard of service. The location, too, is a major boon, adjacent to one of the country's most attractive & lively public beaches, practically opposite the Trade Fair grounds, & yet only 10 mins by taxi from the city centre. Facilities inc tennis courts, sauna & health club, an excellent business centre, a poorly stocked curio & bookshop, 3 highly regarded restaurants, a free hourly airport shuttle, & 15-channel DSTV in every room. According to a Ghanaian resident of 10 years, the hairdressing & beauty salon here is very good & reasonably priced. The rooms are as good as any available in the capital, with the bathrooms in particular less cramped than is often the case in international-class hotels – indeed, Labadi Beach Hotel has hosted both Tony Blair & Queen Elizabeth II in recent years. *US$185/200/450 sgl/dbl/suite inc an outstanding buffet b/fast. The pool is open to day-visitors for US$9 pp.*

⌂ **La Palm Royal Beach Hotel** ☎ 021 771666 or 771700 or 7010353; **f** 021 771717; **e** lapalmres@ gbhghana.com; www.goldenbeachhotels.net. Situated 200m from Labadi Beach Hotel, the recently opened La Palm is Accra's only other 5-star hotel, overlooking La Beach, but without direct access to the shore. The hotel grounds are centred around a first-class swimming pool area, & the communal areas & rooms are tastefully decorated with a contemporary look. Facilities inc an excellent restaurant – which serves a fabulous all-you-can-eat buffet on Sun for US$13 – DSTV in all the rooms, & a good shop selling curios, books, & newspapers. La Palm is the flagship hotel for the Golden Beach chain, & effectively serves as its head office. *US$200 for a standard dbl or US$300–500 for a suite.*

⌂ **Nogahill Hotel** ☎ 021 500121/2 or 506141; **f** 021 501002. This small 3-star hotel is situated on First Link Rd in the suburb of East Legon, close to Osu & the airport. Facilities inc a swimming pool, international restaurant, pizza restaurant & confectionery, & DSTV in all rooms. *US$110/140 sgl/dbl.*

UPMARKET: US$60–85

⌂ **Airport View Hotel** ☎ 021 769594 or 780341/2; **f** 021 780342; **e** airporthotel@africaonline.com.gh. The distinguishing feature of this blandly smart hotel on Liberation Av is its proximity to the airport, which makes it convenient for early or late departures & arrivals. *Self-contained dbl/twin rooms with AC & DSTV US$90/100.*

⌂ **Akwaaba Beach Guesthouse** ☎ 024 4280028 or 021 717742; **e** akwaaba21@hotmail.com; www.akwaaba-beach.de. Small, very friendly, &

individualistic, this Swiss-owned guesthouse in Nungua forms a great alternative to the bland modern hotel blocks that are more typical of this price range. It is set in attractive green grounds that run down to a small but sandy private beach, & boasts a great rooftop bar/restaurant serving continental food for around US$7 per plate. *Self-contained dbls with fan/AC cost US$50/75, & an apartment with kitchenette & lounge is available for around US$130.*

♠ **Blue Royal Hotel** ✆ 021 783075; f 021 783076; e blueroyalghana@yahoo.com. There is an internet café onsite. Probably the smartest of the several hotels in this range scattered around central Osu, the new Blue Royal is very acceptable value too: *US$59/69 for a large sgl/dbl semi-suite with AC, DSTV, & sitting area.*

♠ **Byblos Hotel** ✆ 021 782250; e bybloshotel@ hotmail.com. If it's nightlife you're after, this new hotel on Osu's Embassy Lane is difficult to beat for a combination of comfort, price & location. The attached Venus Cocktail Bar & Grill is attractively decorated & a good place for a drink or meal on the pavement. Dishes start at around US$3.50 for Lebanese mezze, & rise to US$6.50 for steak or US$28 for lobster thermidor. *Self-contained sgls/dbls with DSTV, AC & fridge cost US$50/80, or cheaper for longer stays.*

♠ **DutcHotel Nshonaa** (67 rooms) ✆ 021 711111/8; f 021 711110; e info@dutchotel.com; www.dutchotel.com. This excellent new multi-storey hotel on Beach Drive lies on an attractive rocky stretch of coast about 1km east of the new Coco Beach Hotel & 1.5km from the coastal road to Tema. Dutch-owned & managed, the facilities inc a neat swimming pool area, live music at w/ends, a children's playground & a good restaurant serving continental dishes. *From US$70 for a standard self-contained dbl with AC & DSTV, to US$100 for a large dbl suite.*

♠ **El-Elyon Hotel** ✆ 021 774421/784620; f 021 774620; e elelyon@africaonline.com.gh. This small and appealing 2-star hotel is situated in the lively suburb of Osu, on 18th Lane opposite the Côte d'Ivoire Embassy. The downstairs restaurant serves good Ghanaian & continental dishes for around US$5. The rooms & facilities approach those of more expensive hotels, so it seems fairly priced at: *US$60/75/80/90 sgl/dbl/twin/suite for an attractively furnished self-contained room with AC & DSTV & b/fast.*

♠ **Frankie's Hotel** ✆ 021 773567; f 021 773569; e frankies@frankiesghana.com; www.frankiesghana. com. This smart new hotel in the heart of fashionable Osu, & attached to the long-serving restaurant of the same name, is ideally placed for nightlife & eating out. The Frankie's complex also hosts an internet café & serves up delicious pastries for b/fast, plus moreish ice creams at any time. The rooms are very clean, with modern furnishings, but they are relatively small & perhaps overpriced: *US$60/85 sgl/dbl.*

♠ **Granada Hotel** ✆ 021 775343 or 775293; f 021 774880; e granada_hotel@hotmail.com. A good bar & Chinese restaurant is attached. This 2-star multi-storey hotel on Liberation Rd is not as classy as the neighbouring Shangri-La, but it is certainly cheaper. *Dbl with AC, DSTV & fridge US$60, suite US$120.*

♠ **Gye Nyame Hotel** ✆ 021 223321 or 223211; e gyenyamehotel@hotmail.com. Set in Asylum Down's Fifth Crescent, just off Ring Rd, this small & sparklingly clean hotel is a pleasant escape but it feels relatively overpriced at: *US$50/60 for a self-contained sgl/dbl with AC.*

♠ **Hotel Paloma** ✆ 021 228700; f 021 231815; e reservations@paloma-gh.com; www.paloma-gh.com. Situated on the north side of Ring Rd, between Nkrumah Circle & Sankara Overpass, the recently refurbished Paloma Hotel is regularly recommended by readers. Rooms are all large & comfortably furnished, with DSTV, AC & hot water, & there are also suites with kitchenettes. The complex also hosts a good selection of popular restaurants, inc the AC Champs sports bar dominated by a flat-screen TV, & an outside area serving decent salads & the usual Ghanainan & continental standards at reasonable prices. There is often live music at w/ends. *Good value for money at US$65/85 sgl/dbl inc b/fast or US$100 for a chalet suite.*

♠ **Mariset Plaza** ✆ 021 774434; f 021 772085. Situated at the southern end of Osu, just off Labadi Rd, this large 3-star hotel inc a swimming pool. *Self-contained dbl rooms with DSTV & AC for US$82/88 sgl/dbl.*

♠ **New Coco Beach Resort** ✆ 021 717235/6/7/9; f 021 717231; e newcocobeach@yahoo.com; www.newcocobeachresort.com. Sold & rebuilt almost from scratch since the second edition of this guide was published, the 75-room New Coco Beach Hotel has a superb beach-front location in Nungua, roughly 10km from central Accra & 500m along a signposted junction off the coastal road to Tema (any taxi heading towards Tema can drop you at the junction) – although be warned that the trip can take up to 2 hours during heavy traffic. Facilities inc a swimming pool right above the beach (open to non-residents for US$3), a children's playground, a well-equipped business centre, a gym, massage parlour & hair salon, & live music at w/ends. MasterCard is accepted. A decent restaurant serves Western & Ghanaian dishes on the beach, or you could try the Billy Jane restaurant opposite, which serves good pizzas & fish, although service tends to be slow. *It is one of the best deals in its price range anywhere in Greater Accra, charging US$70–75/85–90 for a smart self-contained sgl/dbl with DSTV & AC or US$115–140 for a chalet.*

♠ **Niagara Hotel** ✆ 021 230118; f 021 230119; e niagara@ighmail.com. The Niagara Hotel on Kojo Thomson Rd in Adabraka is one of the most popular hotels in this range, as much for the excellent & responsive management as for the comfortable rooms. It is a good hotel to contact as a first base in Accra, as the management responds quickly to emails (a rarity in Ghana) & can also arrange reasonably priced car hire. The Al Basha restaurant next door (with AC) serves delicious

Lebanese food. *Good value at US$66/88 for a sgl/dbl with hot water, AC, DSTV & beds big enough for a football team.*

🏠 **Niagara Plus Hotel** ☎ 021 772402; e niagara@ ighmail.com. Owned by the same family as its popular namesake in Adabraka, the newer Niagara Plus on 14th Av is one of the better deals in the Osu area. The shady garden restaurant serves inexpensive pasta & Lebanese dishes. Discounts are available for volunteers. *US$46/60 for a smart sgl/dbl/family-room with hot water, AC & DSTV.*

MODERATE: US$30–55

🏠 **Adeshie Hotel** ☎ 021 221307; e adeshiehotel@ freeghana.com. Situated on Ring Rd about 100m from the Paloma Hotel & Shopping Arcade. A restaurant is attached & there are plenty of other options for eating out in the immediate vicinity. *Very reasonably priced at $46 for a self-contained dbl with AC & DSTV.*

🏠 **Afia African Village** (27 chalets) ☎ 021 681465; www.afiavillage.com. Just next door to the Riviera Beach, the new Afia is a gem of a find, combining tourist-class accommodation with delicious home-cooked food & plenty of African character. The set-up is run by a Ghanaian jazz fan & his friendly Australian wife, who serve up hearty meals & chilled drinks – inc wine by the glass – in the open Tribes restaurant, which overlooks the rocky coast. Comfortable accommodation with all mod cons is offered in 27 chalets overlooking the rocky shore, where a swimming pool & second restaurant are also planned. Other facilities inc a brilliantly stocked antiques shop, which sells artefacts the couple have collected themselves from all over west Africa. *US$50/56 sgl/dbl occupancy, or US$95 for a 2-room suite.*

🏠 **Ghalebon Guesthouse** ☎ 021 778897. Conveniently located on Osu's 14th Av, this small, low-key, & quiet

🏠 **Penta Hotel** ☎ 021 774529; f 021 7760812. This is a pleasant 2-star hotel, centrally located in Osu. The associated 'Chez Aboud' restaurant specializes in Middle Eastern cuisine in the US$4.50–10 range, & the attached Hemmingway bar is a pleasant but expensive place for a drink. *US$60/70 for a comfortable self-contained sgl/dbl with AC & DSTV.*

guesthouse seems pretty good value. *US$40/50 for a clean self-contained dbl/twin with AC, fridge & DSTV.*

🏠 **Grisfarm Hotel** ☎ 021 774602 Also situated in Osu, one street north of Embassy Rd, this friendly little hotel has a cheap restaurant, & is right next door to a more expensive Indian restaurant. Credit cards are not accepted for guests staying less than one month – ignore the MasterCard sign on the door! *US$48/54 for a very clean self-contained dbl/suite with AC, fridge & TV.*

🏠 **Pink Hostel** ☎ 021 256710; f 021 256712; e phostel@idngh.com. This comfortable lodging on Fifth Av in Asylum Down – not quite as pink as the offices opposite – is a popular first stop for moderately priced tour groups & NGOs, though occasional reports of theft from rooms should probably be heeded. The self-contained rooms, though rather small, are very clean & neat, & come with AC & DSTV. Good meals are available in not 1 but 2 restaurants, serving Ghanaian dishes for around US$2 or Western cuisine from US$3.50. *Decent value at US$40/50 sgl/dbl, or US$17 for a bunk bed in the AC dormitory.*

BUDGET: US$10–25

🏠 **Avenida Hotel** ☎ 021 221354. Back when it opened in 1948, this substantial hotel on Kojo Thompson Rd, Adabraka, was one of the fanciest in town. There has been little money invested in upkeep since then, but the staff are earnest & friendly & although the large rooms are shabby, they are clean & well equipped. The spotless kitchen serves decent food in a cavernous canteen-style dining room, & there are plans to build a pool in 2008. *Expect to pay US$15/23 for a self-contained sgl/dbl with fan or US$18/27 with AC, TV & fridge.*

🏠 **Avenue Club Hotel** ☎ 021 222679; f 021 2340136. Although the lively outdoor bar at this rather seedy hotel on Farrar Rd doesn't bode well for a peaceful night, the self-contained rooms with AC, TV & fridge seem fair value at: *US$23/31 for a dbl/twin.*

🏠 **Beachcomber Guesthouse** ☎ 021 712986; e melvrnasenso41@hotmail.com. This relaxed beach-front guesthouse lies in Nungua, about 10km from central Accra along the coastal road to Tema, & a few hundred metres from the well-known Coco Beach Resort. The small grassy grounds run down to a rocky stretch of beach where swimming is not recommended, but you can swim in the pool at Coco Beach for a fee of US$3. *Dbl chalets with a tiled floor, hot water, fridge & fan feel a little expensive at US$30 (booking is recommended), although the enormous apartments with kitchen & living room are excellent value for groups at US$45 a night.*

🏠 **Beverley Hills Hotel** ☎ 021 224042; f 021 242532. Owned & managed by a feisty former journalist, this small hotel on the junction of Farrar & Samora Machel Avs is worth a visit for the kitsch value of the rooms alone. Cold drinks & good Ghanaian & continental dishes are served in the outside restaurant at the front. Colour-coded suites with AC, DSTV & fridge (US$32) are festooned with fake flowers & posters decorated with roses & pledges of eternal love. *Cheaper rooms are equally tacked-up & cost upwards of US$22.*

🏠 **Crystalline Hostel** ✆ 021 304634; m 027 743 9745 or ✆ 024 384 1339; e crystalhostel@ yahoo.com or crystalhostel@hotmail.com; www.crystalhostel.com. Universally praised by readers who have stayed there & situated in the suburb of Darkuman, about 10 mins by tro-tro from Kaneshie Market. The hotel is run by the amiable Quaynor family & has comfortable rooms with a fan & cold shower centred around a grassy compound. Non-central, but they do arrange airport pick-ups & there is a tro-tro station close by. Vegetarian & meat-based meals are available by advance order; there are kitchenettes for guests who like to prepare their own meals. Nearby are cloth shops, chop stalls, 2 internet-reliable cafés, a good book stall (3 books for US$1) & curious but friendly locals. The hotel also arranges short- and long-term volunteer placements at relatively affordable prices. *Rooms with TV, fridge & en-suite shower & toilet cost US$15/20 sgl/dbl, & a dormitory bed is US$7.50.*

🏠 **Hansonic Hotel** ✆ 021 300849 e hcottage@ yahoo.com; www.hanscottage.com. Under the same management as Cape Coast's Hans Cottage Botel (see page 170), this inexpensive set-up is far from central, lying more than 1km northwest of Kaneshie Market. There is a travel agent next door called Akwaaba Tours, where a car & driver can be arranged at a fair price. The hotel is situated in a lively area with several good bars, & the large self-contained rooms are good value at: *US$10/15 for a sgl/dbl with fan & TV or US$25 with AC.*

🏠 **Hotel President** ✆ 021 223343. Of several inexpensive lodgings clustered around Adabraka &

neighbouring Asylum Down, this bright purple multi-storey hotel on Farrar Av is probably the best overall value. The rooms can be a bit grubby, however, & the b/fast isn't great. There's a good patio bar & affordable restaurant attached. *Balconied dbls with TV, private bath & fan/AC cost a very reasonable US$16/21.*

🏠 **Hotel St George** ✆ 021 224699 or 220935. Situated on Chatfield Rd in Adabraka, this small, smart hotel is excellent value at: *US$20/24 for a large, sparklingly clean sgl/dbl with AC, TV, fridge & hot water.*

🏠 **Joska Lodge** ✆ 021 774808 or 777468. Expensive anywhere else but a pretty good deal by Osu standards, this ordinary hotel just beyond the Niagara Plus charges: *US$25 for small but clean self-contained dbls with AC.*

🏠 **KorkPalm Hotel** ✆ 021 226797; f 021 223424; e korkpalmhotel@yahoo.com. There is a spotless restaurant attached, which serves delicious fruit milkshakes & good Ghanaian & continental dishes inside or on the outside terrace. This justifiably popular hotel next to the Burkina Faso Embassy in Asylum Down charges: *US$18/30 for a smart, self-contained sgl/dbl with fan, or US$34 for a dbl with AC.*

🏠 **Marymart Hotel** ✆ 021 221011; e marymart@ ghana.com. Boasting a convenient location on Ring Rd immediately east of Nkrumah Circle & the Nsawam Overpass, this friendly & clean hotel offers clean dbls with fan & common showers for similar prices to the Beverley Hills Hotel (see above).

🏠 **Riviera Beach Hotel** ✆ 021 662400. This odd concrete block on the beach-front near Independence Sq could not be described as beautiful, but it has an appealing air of faded grandeur all the same. The outside terrace – overlooking a vast & empty swimming pool that was the centre of Accra's expat activity through the 1960s – is perfectly positioned to catch the evening breeze. *Large self-contained rooms with fan all cost a sgl rate of US$20.*

SHOESTRING: US$10 & UNDER

🏠 **Akuma Cultural Village** ✆ 021 660573. This beach-front set-up could be fantastic, but is quite frankly ruined by neglect. It's worth keeping an eye out for a change of ownership, but steer clear until then.

🏠 **Amomomo Beach Garden** ✆ 024 648703; e sharonswyer@hotmail.com. Owned & managed by a former British volunteer & her Ghanaian husband, this popular beach-front lodge started life a couple of years ago as a vegetarian restaurant & subsequently expanded to become a backpacker-style guesthouse. The vegetarian food is very reasonably priced, & good washed down with fresh fruit juice or one of the local brews on offer. It also offers drumming & dancing lessons, shows nightly movies in an open-air cinema, &

holds a reggae night on the first Sat of every month. It is situated behind the Cambridge Prep School in the suburb of Korle Gonno, which lies about 10 mins' drive from the city centre along what is effectively an eastern extension of High St – ask tro-tros heading in this direction to drop you at White House junction. *Accommodation in self-contained beach huts costs around US$8/11 sgl/dbl, & is generally comfortable although there has been the occasional reader complaint about cleanliness.*

🏠 **Ampax Hotel** ✆ 021 244636. This popular hotel a few doors down from the Korkpalm in Asylum Down offers clean & spacious self-contained rooms at around half the price of its competitor. *Expect to pay around US$8 for a dbl.*

☐ **Calvary Methodist Guesthouse** ☎ 021 679319.
Arguably the best-value central budget option in Accra, this Christian hostel lies on Barnes Rd near the junction with Castle Rd, opposite the National Museum. There's a communal lounge with TV, & inexpensive meals are served, though there are plenty of other eateries within walking distance. *Recently refurbished self-contained sgl/dbls with fan cost US$5/7, while those with AC cost US$8.50/10.*

☐ **Date Hotel** ☎ 021 228200. In Adabraka, on Adama Rd, this small lodge is decent value. There used to be occasional reports of theft from the rooms, but the problem seems to have abated in recent years. *US$8/9 for large but basic (& occasionally musty) sgls/dbls with fan & common showers, or US$11/14 for a self-contained dbl/twin.*

☐ **Hotel Crown Prince** ☎ 021 225381. Situated in Adabraka, at the junction of Castle & Kojo Thompson roads (opposite the empty lot that used to be the Hotel de California), the Crown Prince has a pleasant atmosphere & helpful, friendly staff. Try & get a room away from the main courtyard bar which turns the music full blast from as soon as the sun comes up. *The rooms are shabby but convincingly clean & inexpensive at US$7/9 sgl/dbl, although the shared showers are usually flooded.*

☐ **Hotel de California** ☎ 021 226199. The Hotel de California used to be one of Accra's most likeable budget lodges. but it sadly lost most of its charm & cleanliness along with a relocation in 2002, when the original building was knocked down. It remains a good

spot to meet travellers however, & is often fully booked. *Dingy rooms using unappealing common showers cost US$6/8/9 sgl/dbl/trpl, while self-contained dbls cost US$10.*

☐ **Lemon Lodge** ☎ 021 227857. This long-serving hotel, situated next door to the KorkPalm Hotel in Asylum Down, remains one the best budget choices in Accra. The number of rooms is limited so it's worth ringing in advance. Otherwise, if it's full, the nearby Asylum Down & Mavis hotels are also very comfortable & similar in price. *US$9/10 for a clean twin/dbl with fan & common showers.*

☐ **Salvation Army Hostel** ☎ 021 776971. At the end of Embassy Rd in Osu. The cheapest acceptable option for sgl travellers, with the bonus of a brilliant location for nightlife & eating out. Officially speaking there is a 22.30 curfew, but it's easy enough to get round with a little polite pleading. To avoid confusion upon departure, do make sure you get a receipt when you pay. *US$5 pp for a bed in a 5- or 6-bed dormitory.*

☐ **YMCA** ☎ 021 679319. Situated on Castle Rd, about 500m east of Kojo Thompson, the YMCA is a good place to meet travellers. *The dbl rooms are excellent value at US$9/11 with fan/AC.* Sweaty male-only dormitory accommodation is also available (*US$2.50 pp*), but cannot be recommended. The nearby **YWCA** (women only) is much more basic, & little used by travellers – *but with beds priced at US$2 it could be a good fall back for those on a tight budget.*

✕ WHERE TO EAT AND DRINK

Accra is a pretty good city for eating out, with a diverse range of restaurants to suit all budgets. The main cluster of cheaper bars and restaurants is in Adabraka, between Nkrumah Circle and the Hotel Crown Prince, while many of the more upmarket restaurants are clustered on and around Cantonments Road in Osu. Because of this, and bearing in mind that, all else being equal, most people would prefer to eat within walking distance of their hotel rather than to cross town, I've clumped restaurants and bars by area rather than by cost or type of cuisine.

ADABRAKA This is the best part of town for cheap eating and drinking, with a good selection of restaurants serving meals for less than US$3, as well as a great many bars. Our favourite place in the area is the **White Bell** on the junction of Farrar Avenue and Kojo Thompson Road. The only open-sided first-floor bar in this part of town, there's usually a good breeze here, not to say cold beer and a reasonably eclectic music selection, although it can get a bit overly loud. Above all, the food is varied (even if a significant proportion of the menu is usually unavailable), inexpensive and reliably good – everything from vegetable or chicken curry with rice to a cheeseburger with chips, and nothing much more than US$5.50 – and it stays open from mid-morning through until about midnight.

Five minutes' walk away, the dining hall at the **Hotel President** lacks atmosphere, but the food is good, the price is certainly right at around US$3.50 for a chicken or steak dish, and you can ask to be served in the pleasant garden bar.

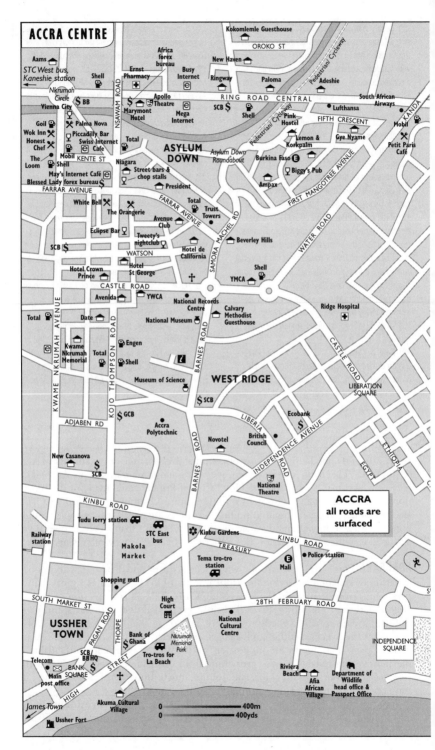

ACCRA CENTRE

Kokomlemle Guesthouse
OROKO ST
Aams
STC West bus,
Kaneshie station
Shell
Africa forex bureau
Ernst Pharmacy
New Haven
Busy Internet
Ringway
Paloma
Adeshie
Nkrumah Circle
Vienna City
BB
Apollo Theatre
Marymont Hotel
Mega Internet
RING ROAD CENTRAL
SCB
Shell
Pink Hostel
FIFTH CRESCENT
Lufthansa
South African Airways
Goil
Wok Inn
Honest Chef
Palma Nova
Piccadilly Bar
Swiss Internet Cafe
Total
Lemon & Korkpalm
Gye Nyame
Mobil
Petit Paris Café
The Loom
Mobil
Shell
KENTE ST
ASYLUM DOWN
Asylum Down Roundabout
Burkina Faso
Biggy's Pub
May's Internet Café
Blessed Lady forex bureau
Niagara
Street bars & chop stalls
President
Ampax
FARRAR AVENUE
FIRST MANGOTREE AVENUE
White Bell
The Orangerie
Eclipse Bar
Tweety's nightclub
FARRAR AVENUE
Total
Trust Towers
Avenue Club
SCB
WATSON
Hotel de California
Beverley Hills
WATER ROAD
Hotel Crown Prince
Hotel St George
Shell
YMCA
Avenida
CASTLE ROAD
YWCA
Total
Date
National Records Centre
National Museum
Calvary Methodist Guesthouse
Ridge Hospital
Kwame Nkrumah Memorial
Engen
Total
Shell
Museum of Science
WEST RIDGE
LIBERATION SQUARE
KWAME NKRUMAH AVENUE
KOJO THOMPSON ROAD
BARNES ROAD
SAMORA MACHEL RD
CASTLE ROAD
SCB
GCB
ADJABEN RD
Accra Polytechnic
LIBERIA
Ecobank
British Council
Novotel
INDEPENDENCE AVENUE
ETHIOPIA
New Casanova
SCB
BARNES ROAD
National Theatre
EGYPT
KINBU ROAD
ACCRA all roads are surfaced
Tudu lorry station
STC East bus
Kinbu Gardens
KINBU ROAD
Railway station
Makola Market
TREASURY
Tema tro-tro station
Mali
Police station
Shopping mall
SOUTH MARKET ST
High Court
28TH FEBRUARY ROAD
USSHER TOWN
PAGAN ROAD
THORPE
Bank of Ghana
Tro-tros for La Beach
Nkrumah Memorial Park
National Cultural Centre
INDEPENDENCE SQUARE
Telecom
SCB/BB HQ
BANK SQUARE
Main post office
Riviera Beach
Afia African Village
Department of Wildlife head office & Passport Office
James Town
HIGH STREET
Akuma Cultural Village
0   400m
0   400yds
Ussher Fort

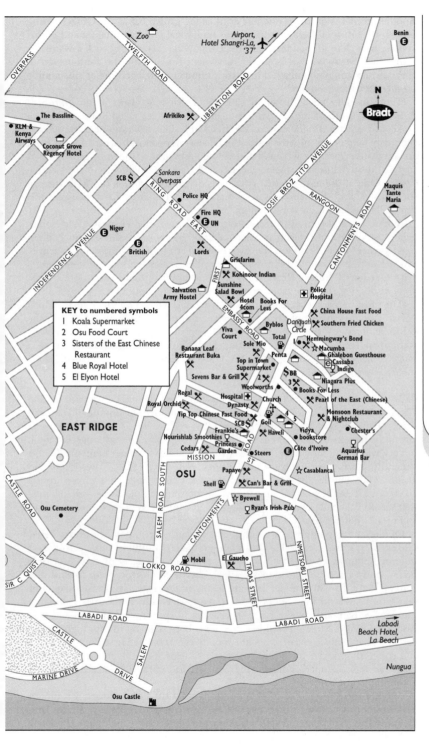

KEY to numbered symbols
1 Koala Supermarket
2 Osu Food Court
3 Sisters of the East Chinese
   Restaurant
4 Blue Royal Hotel
5 El Elyon Hotel

EAST RIDGE

OSU

Another nearby spot for an outdoor drink is the garden bar at the **Club Avenue Hotel**, though food here is restricted to traditional Ghanaian staples and grilled kebabs. Also close to the President Hotel, following Farrar Road back towards the White Bell, **Strawberry's** is a lively pavement bar offering the combination of cheap drinks and good music. There are a number of delicious *jollof* rice stands on this stretch of road too.

There used to be a cluster of eating and drinking places along Nkrumah Avenue just south of the Circle, but most of these were razed to the ground to make way for the bright orange **Vienna City**. The entertainment complex – reputedly (and believably) the biggest in Ghana – is open 24 hours and veers from an acceptable place to eat, drink, and play pool by day, to a den of prostitutes at night – mostly clustered around the attached Caesar's Nightclub or the sizeable casino. One of the few restaurants to have survived the cull is the **Wok Inn**, an inexpensive and low-key Chinese restaurant with tasty food (spring rolls especially) and arctic air-conditioning.

A few doors down away from Nkrumah Circle, the **Honest Chef** serves generous portions of chicken and rice for US$3.50 cooked in a reassuringly clean open kitchen. Dishes can be taken away or eaten at a bar facing the culinary action. On the northeast side of Nkrumah Circle, the spotlessly clean, air-conditioned **City Gardens Chinese Restaurant** serves a variety of Chinese and other take-away dishes, but there are tables at which you can eat if you want.

The most upmarket place to eat in this part of town is **The Orangerie**, which has an extensive menu of Ghanaian, Italian and other continental dishes in the US$3.50–9 range – the prawns and grilled tilapia in pepper sauce are particularly recommended. The excellent Lebanese restaurant in the **Niagara Hotel** serves a range of kebabs and other grills in the US$5.50–8.50 range, as well as delicious mezze at around US$3 each.

OSU Accra's main cluster of mid- to upper-range restaurants lies on and around Cantonments Road – aka 'Oxford Street' – in the suburb of Osu south of Danquah Circle. Bank on spending anything from US$7–12 per head for a main course at any of the better restaurants in this area, but there are also a few cheaper 'fast food' outlets, where you can eat well for less than US$5. The smarter restaurants in Osu generally open for lunch and/or dinner only (typically 12.00–15.00 and 16.30–23.00), but the cheaper fast-food places tend to operate all day from around 10.00 until 23.00. If you're feeling peckish at an unusual hour, it's worth knowing that Vasili's Bakery (see below) in the Osu Food Court serves coffee, bread, pastries and pies 24 hours a day.

Of the cheaper options, a recommended starting point is **Southern Fried Chicken** on Danquah Circle. This might on the face of things come across as an inferior Kentucky clone, but it actually serves a good variety of very affordable pizzas, curries and burgers alongside the greasy fried chicken, with most dishes coming in at US$4.50 or under. Less appetising and more generic fast-food options on Oxford Street include **Seers** and **Papaye Fast Foods**, the former serving up inexpensive hamburgers, the latter specialising in spicy grilled chicken and fish. Also on Oxford Street, **Frankie's** has long been known for its high-quality pastries, cakes and ice cream, while the more recently opened first-floor restaurant and coffee shop serves an excellent variety of salads and grills in the US$3.50–5 range, as well as superb burgers (the best she had ever had outside the States, according to one reader).

Another inexpensive fast-food favourite is the **Osu Food Court**, a southern African implant that hosts branches of **Chicken Inn** (fried chicken), **Pizza Inn**, **Creamy Inn** (ice creams), **Vasili's Bakery** (delicious coffee and cakes) and a new internet café. Up on the roof, the smart, Zimbabwean-owned **Monsoon** restaurant serves pricey but fantastic game meat indoors or out (upwards of US$13 a dish; reservations are recommended) as well as excellent Japanese-made sashimi and sushi, hand rolled to order for around US$1 a piece.

There are some good cheaper eats behind the food court, including the **Sunshine Salad Bar** on Embassy Road, which was repeatedly recommended by readers of the last edition for its enormous fresh salads (notably free of salad cream) from around US$3.50. On the other side, behind Viva court, the well-signposted **Buka** restaurant specialises in African food and is the perfect place for new arrivals to sample top-notch Ghanaian cuisine, often to live music. Another good starting point is **Country Kitchen**, near the Salvation Army Hostel, which offers standard menus between US$2 and US$5 or charges around US$3 for à la carte *fufu*.

As is so often the case in Ghana, there is also a proliferation of Chinese restaurants, of which the most affordable sit-down option is probably **Tiptop Chinese Fast Food**. The varied menu offers generous portions at US$5 or less – although the take-away only **China House Fast Food** on the north side of the circle is cheaper still. The **Sisters of the East** on 15th Lane serves superior Chinese cuisine in the US$5.50–7 bracket, and gives you the choice of eating indoors or in the open courtyard it shares with the popular **Mapee's Jazz Club** (live music at weekends) and **New Connection Club** (occasional live music, plus darts and pool). Highly recommended but very expensive is the **Dynasty Restaurant** on Oxford Street itself. There are also three good Indian restaurants in this part of town, all of which are pretty pricey – the **Haveli Restaurant** down an unmarked side road opposite the Dynasty Restaurant, the better **Tandoor Restaurant** near the Byblos Hotel, or the **Heritage Indian** signposted off Salem Road opposite Papaye.

Apart from Monsoon, top quality game meat is available at **El Gaucho** – a top-flight steakhouse on Abebresem Street that flies its meat in from South Africa. The excellent steaks and tapas are supplemented by seafood and game dishes such as ostrich, zebra, kudu, springbok and crocodile, priced between around US$9 and US$16. The **Indigo Club**, off Danquah across from the US Embassy, recently opened a very good rooftop restaurant serving mostly continental dishes in the US$7–13 range. The somewhat less pricey **Restaurant Sole Mio** and **Mama Mia** – tucked off a side street behind Dynasty – both serve excellent Italian dishes, while **Cedars Restaurant** specialises in Lebanese food.

For something completely different, **Ryan's Irish Pub**, a smart yellow and green establishment popular with expats, sustains an Irish country bar atmosphere remarkably convincingly – you could easily forget you're in Africa after half an hour here. Various grills are served at moderate to high prices, and there's a popular weekend barbecue.

Good places for a drink include **Bywel Bar** (staggeringly popular on Thursday nights when the live band comes), the Venus Cocktail Bar at the **Byblos Hotel**, and (cheaper) the anonymous pavement bar on Oxford Street close to the junction with Mission Road. Another drinking hole that's popular with expatriates and Ghanaians alike is the **Fusion Bar** close to the Elf Garage on Embassy Road, while the nearby **Connections Nightclub** has been recommended as one of the best in town. A new recommendation is the **Maquis Tante Maria** opposite Cantonments Police Station, which is done in the style of an Ivorian maquis and serves excellent Ghanaian and other west African food in the US$3–5.50 price range – the Senegalese rice with red-red is particularly good. Rooms are available, but tend to be invaded by mosquitoes.

ELSEWHERE IN ACCRA The excellent **Restaurant La Pergola** lies on Liberation Avenue, right behind the Elf garage between Akuafo Circle and the Golden Tulip Hotel, and serves Ghanaian and other African meat and fish dishes in the

6

US$3.50–4 range. Further out on Liberation Road, past the airport, the restaurant at the **Hotel Shangri-La** has long had the reputation of serving the best pizza in Accra, as well as a variety of grills in the US$7-plus range. The nearby **Alliance Française**, off Liberation Road, is popular with the expat crowd for the free cultural performances (usually drumming, dancing or theatre) on Wednesday nights – food costs around US$2, but tends to run out early, so arrive by 19.00 if you want to eat. Back on Liberation Road, immediately north of the Sankara Overpass, the **Afrikiko Restaurant** consists of a shady garden bar and restaurant, with live music every night (no cover charge), chilled draught beer, and a variety of good salads, burgers and fish dishes in the US$5.50–7 range. The **Canadian High Commission Restaurant** on Independence Avenue, almost immediately south of the same overpass, has good, inexpensive meals and sandwiches (lunchtime only).

On Ring Road, about halfway between Nkrumah Circle and Sankara Overpass, the **Paloma Shopping Centre** boasts a cluster of restaurants, including the **Paloma Restaurant**, which does the usual grills and pizzas and has live music most nights. In the same centre, **Champs Sports Bar** serves good Mexican food, and is the place to watch major international sporting events courtesy of DSTV, as well as American films on Sunday nights. Nearby, the **Bus Stop Restaurant** serves inexpensive Western dishes and ice cream, while **Ivy's** is a well air-conditioned upmarket coffee house, gift shop and bistro. **Le Petit Paris** is an excellent new bakery and coffee house in North Ridge immediately south of Ring Road and very close to the KLM/Air Kenya office.

Among the few places in central Accra where you can eat overlooking the sea are the open-air restaurant of the **Riviera Beach Hotel**, and the excellent **Tribes** restaurant at Afia African Village next door. Alternatively you could try the splendid **Osekan Bar**, which consists of an open-air bar/restaurant/nightclub carved into the cliffs west of Akuma Village: to get there from High Street, walk towards the sea from Bank Square along a side road adjacent to a large insurance building and across from the Standard Chartered Bank. Also on High Street, opposite the Telecom Centre, the **Wato Bar** is a wooden, colonial-era two-storey building, painted green and surrounded on three sides by a shady veranda, where you can drink cheap chilled beers, eat spicy kebabs and watch Accra go by.

Less central, the **Labadi Beach** and **La Palm hotels** both have excellent upmarket restaurants overlooking La Beach, while the beach itself houses quite a number of inexpensive bars, restaurants and stalls selling freshly grilled kebabs and chicken (but keep an eye on valuables as it's also a favourite with thieves). Still further afield, a great place to eat at the seaside is the sprawling **Next Door Restaurant**, which lies on the coastal road towards Nungua/Tema perhaps 5km past the Labadi Beach Hotel, and can readily be reached by public transport heading to Nungua. Next Door serves a wide selection of international dishes – though the Ghanaian specialities are the best bet – accompanied by the sound of crashing waves and live music in the evening at weekends.

☆ ENTERTAINMENT AND NIGHTLIFE

BOWLING There's a brand new, extraordinarily modern bowling alley on the Teshie–Nungua road right next door to Next Door. *Games cost about US$5.*

CINEMAS Highly recommended is **Ghana Films**, located at TV3 near the Afrikiko Restaurant, and the Alliance Française, which sometimes shows Ghanaian and other African movies for around US$1 a ticket. For Western movies, head to Champs Sports Bar in the Paloma Centre on Sunday night, or Amamomo Beach Gardens any evening, when movies are screened outdoors.

With thanks to Holger Tills of Tills No 1 Hotel

Accra is an excellent place to go partying, particularly at weekends, but the most popular venues vary depending on the night of the week. Here are some current recommendations:

☆ **Afrikiko** A short distance from the town centre along the airport road, this is a good place to eat & drink on any evening, but best on Tue & Sat when popular salsa dancing lessons are given at 20.00.

☆ **Alliance Française** North of the city centre off Liberation Rd, this popular venue invites renowned musicians from all over west Africa to perform on a Wed evening from about 18.00. Early birds can order food, & the evening attracts a nice mix of Ghanaians & expats.

☆ **Amamomo Beach Gardens** This friendly beach-front lodge aimed at backpackers holds a lively reggae night on the first Sat of every month.

☆ **Bassline Jazz Club** Situated close to the KLM office near Sankoma Overpass, this jazz club is more a place for listening to music than for dancing, but it hosts good live jazz or blues most nights except Sun, generally starting at around 22.00. A recent report suggests it might have closed.

☆ **Byewell** In Osu, this popular bar hosts live music from 21.00 on Thu & Sat nights, & theatre performances on Fri nights.

☆ **Champs** This is a Sports Bar type of set-up in the Paloma Centre, with karaoke nights every Fri, film shows on Sun night, & large-screen coverage of major international sporting events.

☆ **Chester's Place** Situated in Osu, this lively bar has live music every Wed night from 21.00 onwards, including a good line in jazz.

☆ **Fusions** Situated in Osu, close to the Byblos Hotel, this relaxed night café is open daily & busiest in the wee hours over the weekends & on Wed (the latter is karaoke night). Films are shown at 21.20 on Sun.

☆ **GBC Club** On Liberation Av near Flagstaff Hse, this club peaks on Fri when there's live music from 21.00.

☆ **Golden Tulip Hotel** Normally a rather staid upmarket hotel, the Golden Tulip is a good place to see live jazz on Fri & Sat nights.

☆ **Jokers** Lively pub in Labadi, with pool tables & casino, that keeps going until 04.00 – but note we've had a few reports of muggings outside here late at night.

☆ **Jump Sports** Busy club near Nkrumah Circle, open until around 02.30 seven days a week, with live music nightly except Tue.

☆ **Macumba** One of Accra's oldest & most popular nightclubs, albeit an unabashed pick-up joint teeming with hookers, the Macumba is open from Wed to Sat, when it generally gets busy after midnight.

☆ **Next Door** About 10km out of town on the Tema road, this is a beach-front restaurant & bar, particularly worth visiting on Fri & Sat nights, when there is normally either live music or a highlife disco.

☆ **Tiptoe Café** On 42nd St, close to Nkrumah Circle, this aptly named bar stays open when everything else has closed – the place for a pre-dawn nightcap!

☆ **Ups** A short distance from the city centre in Kaneshie, this bar plays great highlife music, particularly on Wed night.

☆ **Waikiki** Another long-serving & popular nightclub, situated in Adabraka close to Nkrumah Circle, this has a reputation as something of a pick-up joint & is also busiest after midnight.

The Surfer's Inn (☎ *021 505111;* e *dktgh@Ghana.com*) at American House in East Legon is a great if less than central option for watching recent DVDs or videos – any movie costs US$2 to watch on-site, and good affordable food and drinks are available.

More centrally, at **Video Nut Plaza** (☎ *021 768282 or 768448*) on Orphan Crescent in Labone, you can rent a room complete with couches and cushions and your choice of DVD for US$7–9.50 per room. The biggest room could comfortably seat 10 people. Drinks and snacks are also available, and you can order Chinese food from a nearby restaurant, which will be delivered for a small additional fee.

New movies are also shown at the 1,600-seat **International Conference Centre** on Fridays, Saturdays, and Sundays (the programmes are listed in newspapers). At the time of research, there were also talks of building a big new cinema at Teteh Quarshie Circle.

GYM/SPORT The Aviation Centre on the road between the airport and Cantonments post office is a great place to work out for anyone in Accra for a while. Monthly membership is about US$25, well below the US$100 you can expect to pay at most other places.

SWIMMING A nominal entrance fee of US$0.50 is charged to swim at the public beach at La, which is popular with locals and lined with bars and restaurants. For a swimming pool, the pick is the one at the Shangri-La Hotel, where non-hotel residents pay US$4.50 to swim. The other upmarket hotels charge around US$5 to non-residents.

SHOPPING

A good place for general curio shopping is the market at the National Cultural Centre on the seafront on 28th February Road. Here you can buy just about anything from genuine *kente* and other local cloths to carvings, masks and statues from all over Ghana and elsewhere in west Africa. It's also a good place to pick up colourful dyed shirts and cheaper trinkets such as imitation *kente* wallets and bead necklaces, although the atmosphere can get pushy and you'll need to bargain pretty hard to get a fair price.

Unless you're tremendously pressed for time, you may prefer to do your curio shopping in a more haphazard way. Most curios sell primarily to Ghanaians, not to tourists, and for all but the most esoteric requirements (face masks, for instance) you'll find that there are stalls selling interesting items all over the city – around '37' and the Golden Tulip Hotel, on Ring Road next to Danquah Circle, and on La Beach, for instance. Alternatively, the main markets – Makola in the city centre and Kaneshie on Winneba Road – also stock a wide range of textiles and beads, and although the markets are generally more busy than the National Cultural Centre, the stall owners are not as dependent on the tourist dollar, so the atmosphere is less pushy. Another place to get crafts and curios is the African Market in Osu, close to the Sotrec Supermarket. Started by a Peace Corps volunteer several years ago, it's not overly inexpensive and items are typically not up for bargain (all have sticker prices). It's a nice place to browse to get an idea of what you can get as souvenirs in Ghana. Some of the profits reputedly go to support local artists.

For more serious buyers, a group of skilled craftsmen operate out of the Trade Fair Centre opposite La Palm Hotel. Finally, if your budget is up to shipping it home, surely the ultimate in Ghanaian souvenirs must be your very own fantasy coffin, carved *posuban*-style in whatever shape you like (elephant, boat, minibus, whale, uterus!). Get measured up or just go window shopping at Isaac Adjetey Sowah's shop or one of the many other celebrated coffin makers in Teshie on the Tema road.

For those with a more serious interest in high quality Ghanaian art, it is recommended that you pay a visit to The Loom – the oldest and probably the best art gallery in Accra (and in the whole country). Some paintings can be bought for as little as the equivalent of US$15–20, but it is also suitable for people willing to spend more for quality work. Located just down the road from the Wok Inn on Adabraka's Nkrumah Avenue, The Loom also sells souvenirs, craftwork and postcards, has very helpful and reliable staff, and absolutely no bargaining is involved. Other recommendations include the nearby Step In Gallery, on the south side of Farrar Avenue between the junction with Kojo Thomson Road and Trust Towers, or – for traditional carvings and artefacts – the gallery at Afia African Village.

SUPERMARKETS There are a number of good supermarkets in Accra, selling a variety of imported goods ranging from breakfast cereals to Californian wine, though only those in Osu and the city centre are likely to be of great interest to travellers. One of the best is the new multi-floor Maxmart, on Liberation Road opposite the Golden Tulip Hotel, which not only sells a superb range of imported foodstuffs but also has a good appliance section and attached coffee bar and bakery. In Osu, the Koala Supermarket on Cantonments Road, close to Danquah Circle, is regarded as one of the best supermarkets in the city centre, with a good ground-floor bakery and probably the best selection of imported goods, though sometimes at inflated prices. Also in Osu, Sotrec Groceries has been recommended as the best for fresh bread and meat, while the Ghana Supermarket has an excellent selection of imported wines and spirits, and Tip Top In Town stocks a good range of imported food items at reasonable prices. In the city centre proper, the best range of goods is probably at Multistores on High Street. If you are looking for vegetarian products and herbal teas, try Relish Health Foods on the corner of 11th Lane and 6th Street in Osu.

SAFETY

Accra is one of the safest capital cities in Africa, and violent crime against tourists remains reassuringly unusual, certainly by comparison to the likes of Nairobi, Lagos or Johannesburg. That said, no city is entirely free of crime, and Westerners, being relatively wealthy and conspicuous, inevitably form a target for whatever casual criminal element might exist in a developing world capital. And, unfortunately, anecdotal information, including readers' letters, would appear to suggest that this element is on the increase in Accra (associated, say some residents, with an influx of criminals from Nigeria and of small arms from Liberia and Sierra Leone).

The most common form of crime against tourists appears to be bag snatching, often from a passing vehicle and generally after dark – the beach resorts of La and Nungua, to the east of central Accra, and Oxford Street and surrounds in central Osu, have been identified as hotspots for this sort of thing. Rather more unusual, but certainly not unheard of, nocturnal hold-ups at knifepoint or gunpoint are most likely to happen along quiet roads abutting popular night spots such as Adabraka or Osu, or around the Tudu lorry station. Should you be unfortunate enough to be held up like this, the risk of being injured is very slight, provided that you comply with your assailants' demands.

The most effective measure against crime is to avoid attracting the attention of criminals in the first place. If possible, never carry a daypack or other bag, especially after dark, and if you must do so then wear it on the opposite side of your body from the street, with the entrance facing your body. Wearing expensive (or for that matter cheap) jewellery might also attract the interest of robbers, as would flashing around any other valuables. In Accra, as elsewhere in Africa, I would strongly advocate that travellers carry on their person only as much cash as they will need for any given excursion, especially at night. All travellers (but especially women) are advised against walking around alone after dark, particularly in known trouble spots or along quiet unlit roads, as this will increase their appearance of vulnerability.

In my experience, the above warnings notwithstanding, there really is very little about Accra to strike serious fear into the heart of any traveller who adheres to the same commonsense rules of urban survival that one might follow in any unfamiliar modern city. Anybody can be unlucky, but on the whole Accra remains as safe and hassle-free as any African capital I've visited.

OTHER PRACTICALITIES

AMERICAN EXPRESS The sole agent for American Express is Scantravel, in Enterprise House on High Street, Ussher Town (⊕ *08.00–17.00 Mon–Fri*).

BEAUTY AND HAIR SALONS An excellent place for waxing and manicures, etc, in Osu is the X'Quisite Beauty Centre, next to l'Argo Restaurant, which offers Western standards at very reasonable rates (US$12 for a 1½-hour mani-pedi).

For women's haircuts and other beauty treatments, Bellitas (near Haveli's in Osu), Eden (in the Shangri-La Hotel), Janet's (in the Golden Tulip) and Regina's (near Danquah Circle) have been recommended. There's also a barber shop for men in the Golden Tulip Hotel.

CAR HIRE Recent recommendations are **Ghana Vacations** (*Castle Junction, 28th February Rd, Kinkawe, Osu, Accra;* ⟍ *021 763811*) and **Akwaaba Tours Ghana Limited** at the Hansonic Hotel (⟍ *021 313273*). Expect to pay around US$50 per day for a car with driver, excluding fuel.

FILM DEVELOPMENT Print film can be developed at numerous photography shops in Accra, but many travellers have reported that the quality is very low – under most circumstances it's probably advisable to wait until you get home before developing anything. One place that has been recommended by readers is **Flash Photo Lab** on Danquah Circle (⟍ *021 773377/776228*), which produces good work using Fuji film paper and also stocks a good selection of print film. **Laser Photo**, on the east side of Kwame Nkrumah Avenue about four blocks south of the intersection with Castle Road, has also been recommended.

FOREIGN EXCHANGE The best banks for changing foreign currency and travellers' cheques are Barclays and the Standard Chartered Bank, with the latter generally offering the best rates for cash or travellers' cheques. Both have head offices on Bank Road, 100m from the High Street Post Office in Ussher Town, and branches in Adabraka and Osu. Barclays also has a large branch at Nkrumah Circle.

Generally, you'll get a better exchange rate for hard currency cash at any of the dozens of forex bureaux dotted throughout the city (the Blessed Lady Forex Bureau and a couple of others on Farrar Road in Adabraka seem to generally offer a slightly better rate than their peers in Osu and elsewhere in the city), but few forex bureaux accept travellers' cheques. In an emergency, there is a forex bureau in most of the upmarket hotels, though rates tend to be very poor and most will change only for hotel residents. At cheaper hotels, the receptionist or manager can probably arrange for you to change a small sum outside banking hours.

Visa cards can be used to settle bills at the most expensive hotels and restaurants, though in practice you might find that many mid-range hotels displaying the facility to accept Visa and/or MasterCards will do so only when the, um, machine is working (for which, read 'as good as never'), and you will need to keep a close eye on your account as it is not uncommon for card details to be stolen and used at even reasonably upmarket hotels.

Visa cards can also be used to draw cash from ATMs outside most branches of Barclays and the Standard Chartered Bank. Other credit cards, including MasterCard, are next to useless in most circumstances. The Social Security Bank behind the National Theatre handles Diners Club cards, and Scantravel (see *American Express*, above) handles American Express.

HOSPITALS AND MEDICAL FACILITIES

✚ **37 Military Hospital** Liberation Rd near Akuafo Circle and '37' Station; ☎ 021 776111–4; 777595. The trauma facility here is the best in Accra; it also has good after-hours facilities, including a 24-hour X-ray laboratory & pharmacy.

✚ **Beaver Dental Clinic** 7 Roman Rd, Roman Ridge; ☎ 021 771785 or 024 324639. Reliable, modern dental clinic run by UK-trained dentist.

✚ **Ernst Chemist** Ring Rd, near Sankara Overpass; ☎ 021 229293. Well-stocked chemist in Adabraka.

✚ **Gakals Opticals** ☎ 021 777077. Reliable for replacement glasses or contact lenses; situated on Oxford St opposite Frankie's Hotel.

✚ **Korle Bu Hospital & Chemist** ☎ 021 665401. Good hospital with 24-hour pharmacy service.

✚ **Medlab** SGS Hse, 14 Ridge Rd; ☎ 021 776844 or 773994; ☉ 08.00–17.00 Mon–Fri only. This is the best laboratory in Accra, & also has branches in Osu's Akai House Clinic (☎ 021 763822 or 027 546488).

✚ **North Ridge Hospital** Castle Rd near African Liberation Square; ☎ 021 227328. Doctor available at all hours.

✚ **Nyaho Clinic** Aviation Rd, Airport Residential Area; ☎ 021 775341/5291

✚ **Trust (SSNIT)** Clinic Cantonments Rd 500m south of Danquah Circle; ☎ 021 776787/7137/1694. Reputable clinic for consultations & minor ailments, with 24-hour malaria testing facilities & a convenient location in Osu.

MEDIA AND COMMUNICATIONS

BOOKS Books For Less, off Embassy Road, sells a vast stock of secondhand paperbacks, presumably imported from the USA and showing a strong bias towards contemporary American crime and other genre bestsellers, for around US$2.50–3. A similar selection of secondhand novels can also be bought at the stalls on the southeast side of Nkrumah Circle, on Pagan Road near the central post office, at '37' taxi station near Akuafo Circle, and the bookshop at Legon University.

Accra is the best place in the country (if not anywhere in the world) to pick up historical and other works about Ghana. If casual browsing and bargaining is the way you prefer to make your purchases, then head to the cluster of bookshops and stalls on and around Pagan Road, where you can often pick up the most unlikely books for next to nothing. The bookshop at **Legon University**, open on weekdays and Saturday mornings, stocks all sorts of oddities, with probably the best range of historical books I could find in Accra.

The best bet for new books at Western prices is **Vidya Bookstore**, previously known as Riya's Bookstore (*18th Lane, Oxford Street, Osu [past Elyon Hotel and next to TNT Couriers]; PO Box 6667, Accra;* ☎ *023321 781005/762704;* f *0023321 225123;* e *vidyabookstore@gmail.com*). Ask for Heena Karamchandani. Vidya stocks a good range of contemporary adult and children's fiction, as well as a good selection of non-fiction (including maps and travel guides for Ghana, west Africa and other destinations), magazines, greetings cards and gift stationery. It offers an ordering service and claims to be able to import any book or magazine.

For travel guides, maps, and new books, you could also try the **EPP Book Services** on Abafun Crescent – which you can reach by using any transport heading between '37' Station and La Beach – or there is a second branch opposite the Trade Fair Centre near the Labadi Beach Hotel.

INTERNET There are dozens of internet cafés scattered around Accra, with more opening the whole time. Servers tend to be reasonably fast, though this can vary greatly from one day to the next, and rates (often charged by the minute) are very good – working out at significantly less than US$1 per hour.

The best internet facility in Accra is undoubtedly Busy Internet (*www.busyinternet.com*), which lies on Ring Road Central between the Nsawam Overpass and Paloma Shopping Centre near Barnett's Furnishers, and is said to be the largest privately held technology centre in Africa. The fastest internet café in Accra, it is open 24 hours and offers fully serviced offices, a restaurant and bar, a copy centre, teleconferencing, DVD movies and all sorts of other goodies.

Of the rest, the Cybercafé in the Paloma Centre is one of the best; it opens from 07.00 until 23.00 daily except on Sundays when it closes an hour earlier. Other cafés include Yankee Ventures opposite the Paloma Centre, a cybercafé on Kojo Thompson Road opposite the Niagara Hotel, the Communications Centre on Castle Road close to the Hotel de California, and five or six cafés along Osu's Oxford Street in the vicinity of Frankie's Hotel.

NEWSPAPERS Ghana (like most African countries) must be approached with a certain spirit of sacrifice for those of us whose morning ritual is based around a pot of fresh coffee and an equally fresh newspaper. So far as the coffee is concerned, Nescafé is generally the only solution, but a cheap fix on the newspaper front is provided by the gloriously air-conditioned reading room in the British Council on Liberia Road, liberally stocked with British newspapers from three days to one month old, and open from 09.00 to 17.00 Monday to Wednesday and 09.00 to 12.00 Thursday to Saturday. Otherwise, various Ghanaian newspapers are readily available throughout Accra. If you look around, you can also pick up the American weeklies *Time* and *Newsweek*, as well as one- or two-day-old British newspapers, the latter often at inflated prices.

POST *Poste restante* addressed to Accra should be collected between 08.00 and 16.30 from the Central Post Office on High Street, near the seafront in Ussher Town. International mail posted in Accra will arrive at its destination more quickly than mail posted from other towns in the country, but it will still most likely take up to two weeks. Mail posted from the post office in the airport is reputedly a bit quicker. For express and courier services, contact DHL on North Ridge Crescent; ☏ 021 227035.

TELEPHONE International telephone calls can be made from the telecommunication offices near the Central Post Office on High Street, on Cantonments Road, and on Nkawam Road just north of Nkrumah Circle. Only a little more expensive, but considerably more time effective, are the dozens of communication centres that offer local and international telephone and fax facilities in Osu, Adabraka and elsewhere. There are also plenty of payphones throughout the city, everywhere except Osu.

WHAT TO SEE

As mentioned in the introduction to this chapter, Accra is not especially rich in sightseeing. There is, however, a fair amount to busy yourself with in and around the city. A walking tour through the city centre, perhaps making some use of taxis, would be a good way to occupy a morning, followed perhaps by an afternoon visit to the National Museum, taking lunch at the adjacent Edvy Restaurant. Less centrally, La Beach, Coco Beach and Next Door Restaurant are perhaps the most obvious tourist attractions for sun-worshippers, though the excellent Du Bois Centre and more mundane Accra Zoo will attract some.

In addition to the places listed below, there are quite a number of places covered along routes in the regional chapters which make for realistic **day trips** (or, using public transport, overnight trips) from the capital. On the west coast, I would lump anywhere as far as Apam in this category, and some people even visit Cape Coast and/or Elmina as a day trip from Accra. (On the whole, though, the west coast is more suited to overnight than day trips, not least because of the heavy traffic getting out of Accra in this direction.) Other easy targets for day trips include anywhere along the east coast as far as Ada, and most places covered in the chapter *Inland of Accra* (see page 231).

CITY CENTRE Although Accra is well suited for random exploration, the following 'highlights' in and around the city centre are described along a rough route that starts in **James Town** and follows the main road along the seafront east as far as **Independence Square** or **Osu Castle**, before turning back inland past the **National Theatre** and British Council to the **National Museum**, a total distance of roughly 6km.

This is a longer distance than you might think in a city that's not only very busy, but also really hot and sweaty. One look at the map, however, and you'll see that several shorter variations are possible. You could also make use of a taxi part of the way – a charter along the 2km run from Independence Square to the National Museum shouldn't cost more than US$2.

It's also worth mentioning to new arrivals in Ghana that a walk of this length will seriously dehydrate you should you not drink a lot. One of the most refreshing and healthy drinks on offer is coconut juice – keep an eye out for the coconut vendors who hang out all over the city centre and will cut a fresh coconut for a pittance.

James Town The most atmospheric part of Accra, James Town is a pleasure to walk around, though admittedly the colourful small markets, colonial-era shops and houses and strong sense of community are offset by the open sewers, public shitting grounds and accompanying smells – and a few readers have said they felt a little threatened. A highlight is the whitewashed 30m high colonial-era lighthouse – you might be allowed to climb to the top for a tip, though recent reports are that the caretaker is asking around US$5 per person for the privilege! If this jars, a climb to seventh floor of the City Car Park will give you a partial view for free. Also worth visiting is the old fishing harbour on the beach below Fort James, the second largest harbour in Ghana until the construction of Tema, which is a riot of colourful traditional pirogues in the early to mid morning after the fishermen come in. Shared taxis from James Town to Nkrumah Circle leave from in front of the lighthouse, and you can also pick up a charter taxi here. People here can be very funny about photography – it is difficult to say whether this is because it is forbidden to take pictures of Fort James, or just plain contrariness. Tourists are now expected to report to the office at the entrance to the harbour before they stroll around – expect to be asked around US$3 per party to be shown around by a security officer.

Ussher Town From James Town, follow High Street northeast and you'll soon cross the ill-defined border into Ussher Town, which is centred around the Dutch-built Fort Ussher (located on your right when walking up High Street, about 500m past Fort James) and, more than any other part of Accra, lays claim to being the true city centre. Even before you reach Fort Ussher, look out for Brazil Lane, the seaward end of which is the former site of a long-vanished Portuguese Lodge, built above the cliff in the late 15th century.

Until the mid 1990s, Fort Ussher, like nearby Fort James, served as a prison, and although it is not formally open to tourism, there is a plan to convert it into a museum à la Alcatraz or Robben Island within the next five years. Until such time as that happens, the caretaker is usually willing to show interested visitors around, according to Wiktor Moszczynski, who writes: 'We were rewarded with an extraordinary tour. We were shown the cell where Kwame Nkrumah was imprisoned. The enclosed area where prisoners were hanged was surrounded by condemned cells on the first floor. In the two main prison blocks, every cell door was opened, and it looked as if nobody had entered them since the last prisoners left. Some of the wall and cell-door paintings were works of consummate artistry, some deeply religious, some quite erotic. The prison mosque and chapel were in adjoining rooms under what had once been one roof – now caved in – and the chapel wall had an extraordinary painting of a powerful armed angel.'

Past Fort Ussher, I would turn left from High Street along Bank Lane, a large square around a parking lot where you'll see not only several old buildings, the main banks, and the Central Post Office, but also Fam's Mobile Foods, which has acquired a deserved reputation along the overland truck routes of Africa for its cheap, tasty burgers. At the end of Bank Lane, turn right into Pagan Road, where the pavement spills over with stalls (this is an excellent place to pick up cheap secondhand novels and cassettes of Ghanaian music) until you reach Makola Square, from where you can join the throngs that mass around Makola Market, the largest open-air market in Accra and a good place to buy beads and fabrics. Then turn back down Thorpe Road to High Street.

Those who like colonial architecture should visit the Train Station on the north side of Ussher Town, which is possibly the best preserved 19th-century building in Accra. It looks closed and locked up, but if you slip though the gate you will find a generally un-crowded place with the railway station on the left and the railway offices on the right. Another interesting building of the same era is the Holy Trinity Cathedral, which was designed by Sir Aston Webb, architect of London's Victoria & Albert Museum, and built in 1895–96.

Nkrumah Mausoleum Set in attractive gardens on the seafront side of High Street between the junction of Thorpe and Barnes roads, the current resting place of Kwame Nkrumah is an altogether colder and more ostentatious affair than its quaintly low-key precursor in Nkrumah's home town of Nkroful on the west coast. Students of African history in particular shouldn't miss the adjoining museum, which contains photos and other artefacts relating to Ghana's first president. Before heading on from here, you might think about walking the few hundred metres south to the superbly located Akuma Village or Osekan Bar for a cliff-top drink or meal overlooking the Atlantic Ocean.

National Cultural Centre At the intersection with Barnes Road where High Street becomes 28th February Road, you'll see to your left the National Cultural Centre (or Arts Centre), somewhat misleadingly named – at least from a tourist's point of view – since by day it amounts to nothing other than Ghana's biggest craft market. It is a good place to buy practically any type of curio, though readers appear to be split evenly as to whether the level of hassle and pushiness is acceptable or not. There is some talk of the cultural centre being moved to accommodate the site of a new hotel development. To the right of the cultural centre are two art galleries, one seemingly for show only, the other with paintings for sale at negotiable prices.

Independence Square Also known as Black Star Square, this conglomeration of Soviet-inspired monuments to pan-Africanism and Ghanaian independence, constructed under Nkrumah, is a stark anachronism, not least – ironically – because of the absolute lack of African influences apparent in its angular design. The thematic centrepiece of the square is Independence Arch; the adjective that springs to mind is ugly (one reader points out: 'I thought the real irony was that, viewed from the right angle, the set of curving arches at the back of the stadium look an awful lot like the McDonald's logo!'). The parade ground between the square and the sea is a barren concrete eyesore, at least when void of the 30,000

THE AGORSOR CULTURAL GROUP, A TRADITIONAL JAZZ BAND FROM ACCRA

Flavia Robin

During May 2004, I decided to take unpaid leave to volunteer as a teacher at various orphanages in Accra, a task that was utterly rewarding in every respect. In order to get a deeper insight into Ghanaian art and culture during my stay in Accra, I took up *djembé* lessons with local masters, attended local dancing classes, went to traditional jazz performances, and was initiated into the rich heritage of Ghanaian artwork by various painters, in short: I had the time of my life! You might be wondering how I got the chance to enjoy these fascinating activities. In August 2003, I had the opportunity to attend the exhibition/show of the exciting Ghanaian painter, dancer, and flutist Kofi Agorsor at the Golden Tulip Hotel in Accra. This versatile artist didn't just impress me: other Africa connoisseurs, diplomats, and hotel guests were equally taken with Agorsor's paintings, his exuberant Atentenben solos and the catching traditional jazz rhythms (Kpanlogo, Fumgbe Fumgbe, Gahu, Otufo, Agbadza, etc.) of his music group, not to forget the ecstatic dancers defying gravity in hip swivelling motion. Most guests were touched by the fact that Kofi Agorsor recruited most of the 14 music group members out of local orphanages, which he supports by selling his paintings, and he strives to preserve the rich west African cultural heritage (local dialects and music traditions of Ghana). A CD of his recent music show 'Amlima' (mystery) is currently in production. Contact Kofi Agorsor at ℡ + 233 244 74 55 16 or e agorsoratelier@hotmail.com in La-Accra, or at the Legon University Campus, where he and his band rehearse every day from 10.00 to 18.00. Entry is free, but a small contribution to one of his orphanage projects in Accra would be highly appreciated.

people it is intended to accommodate, though it would take a hard heart to be wholly unmoved by the enclosed Flame of African Liberation, lit by Nkrumah himself in 1961.

Osu Castle Also known as Christiansborg Castle, this is one of the three main castles on the Ghanaian coast, and it has a more chequered history of occupation than the others. The original castle, much smaller than the modern one, was constructed by Denmark shortly after they bought a piece of land from the chief of Accra in 1661. It was briefly occupied by the Portuguese after the Danish commander was killed in a mutiny in 1679, returned to Denmark four years later, captured by the chief of Akwama in 1693 and sold back to Denmark barely a year later (though the keys of the original castle were never returned to the Danes and remain the hereditary property of the chief of Akwama to this day). After that, the castle remained the Danish coastal headquarters for 150 years, during which time it was greatly expanded, before being sold to Britain along with four other Danish forts in 1850.

The seat of government from 1876 to the present day, Osu Castle etched its name indelibly into the modern African history books on 28 February 1948. This was the day when an anti-colonial demonstration outside the castle, initiated by recently returned veterans of World War II, was fired upon by colonial police, who killed three demonstrators and injured another 237 – a landmark event not only in the history of Ghana, but in the change in tide that led to almost all of Britain's African colonies being granted independence over the subsequent 15 years.

As already mentioned, Osu Castle may not be visited without special permission, and the surrounding roads are cordoned off to prevent close access. The best views of the castle are from the Riviera Beach Hotel and Independence Square. Photography from any angle is absolutely forbidden.

National Theatre (℡ *021 663449/3559; US$0.50 (or US$0.80 if you want a guided tour) to get into the lobby unless you have a ticket for a performance. Performances are almost all on Fri, Sat & Sun, either afternoon or evening – midweek they're a rarity.*) Built by China and opened in 1992, this impressive modern building is host to regular plays and dance performances, and it's well worth checking if there'll be anything on while you are in town. In any case, you might want to look in to see the small ethnographic display of traditional instruments and carvings.

The tour is worth it just for the information about the huge ceremonial male and female drums displayed in the lobby, each decorated with features specific to individual Ghanaian tribes. The theatre restaurant (the Courtyard) is good – serving Ghanaian and Chinese food in cool, airy surroundings with cheerful tablecloths and napkins and good service. (*US$4–5 for a (big) main course.*)

National Museum Even if you explore the city centre no further, do pop into the National Museum on Barnes Road. (⊕ *09.00–18.00 daily except Mon, and charges an entrance fee of US$1 plus a nominal extra for photography.*)

Most of the displays here are ethnographic in nature, with some excellent examples of traditional crafts ranging from an elaborately carved *oware* board to several *akyeamepoma* (the decorated staffs used by royal spokesmen). There are also reasonable displays at Larabanga mosque and Cape Coast castle.

The Edvy Restaurant in the museum grounds does fair meals in leafy surrounds for around US$4 (*not open evenings*), and it serves cold drinks of all types. The lunchtime buffet on Wednesday has been recommended. The architect of the National Museum, built in 1960, was Sir Denys Lasdun, who also designed the National Theatre in London.

FURTHER AFIELD
Accra Zoo Fifteen minutes' walk from Sankara Overpass, Accra's small zoo is hardly an exemplar, and many visitors find it depressing, which it is – particularly when you see highly sociable animals such as monkeys locked away in confined isolation. On the other hand, as is often the case in small African zoos, most of the enclosed animals were orphaned, injured, or born in captivity, and are also the only opportunity the average city-born Ghanaian would ever get to see them at all. More unusually, most of them do seem to be in good physical condition. The only real alternative to the animals' current situation is death (most would die horribly, of starvation or at the hands of a predator, were they to be released into the wild) and it strikes me as somewhat assumptive to transpose our feelings about captivity on to other creatures (lions, for instance, spend up to 23 hours of the day lazing around even in their natural state). This is a good place to see a fair cross-section of Ghana's large mammals and, who knows, perhaps leaving an extra donation might be a more appropriate response to its downfalls than indignant condemnation.

Coco Beach Further out of town, about 20 minutes' walk and signposted from the Tema Road at Nungua, near Teshie, this is a good beach, based around a popular upmarket resort. In addition to the good bar and restaurant, there's live music here most weekends. It's worth stopping in Teshie to look at the fantastic coffin shop – sculpted in shapes from beer bottle to snails to polished uteruses – and the excellent arts and crafts gallery on the opposite side of the road. Note that the Nungua area has acquired something of a reputation for bag-snatching and other robberies aimed at Westerners.

Du Bois Centre Situated at 22 First Circular Road, Cantonments (021 773127 ⊕ w/days 08.00–17.00), this is the former home and now burial place of the prominent American pan-Africanist Dr William E Burghardt Du Bois, leader of all the Pan-African congresses between 1919 and 1927, vocal anti-segregationist and later communist, and prolific writer and speaker. Visitors are welcome to the centre, which now serves as a research institute and library for students of pan-Africanism, as well as being a memorial to Du Bois himself. The Du Bois Centre is most easily reached by taking a shared taxi east from '37' Station along Gifford Road, and hopping off after about 1km, roughly 100m after passing Awak Stadium to your right.

Kaneshie Market This large market lies along the Winneba Road about 1km past Lamptey Circle, next to the synonymous tro-tro station. In terms of what you can buy, it differs little from Makola Market in the city centre, but it is generally quieter and less frequented by tourists, so the pressure to buy is minimal. On the second floor south of this market is an excellent African bead section. Some of the beads are quite old. There are a number of sellers and the prices are quite reasonable.

La Beach This is Accra's best swimming beach, situated in front of the Labadi Beach Hotel, and easily reached by using a shared taxi or tro-tro from Nkrumah Circle or Tema Station to Nungua. In addition to the beach itself, which is reasonably safe for swimming depending on the strength of the undertow, there are several shady outdoor bars here, a couple of cheap restaurants, and at least two pool tables, warped ingeniously by the constant exposure to the sun. Thursday night is the best time to come partying here. Entrance costs US$0.50 and you should keep an eye on your belongings as it's a favourite spot for casual theft.

University of Ghana Situated 14km from Accra along the Aburi Road, this is the oldest university in Ghana, set in attractive grounds that include a mellow **botanical garden** (behind the Department of Zoology), which is of special interest to birdwatchers. In addition to boasting a good bookshop, the university is home to the superb **Balme Library**, whose unparalleled hoard of colonial-era books and documents is of great interest to Ghanaphiles. (⊕ to the public 08.00–16.00 Mon–Sat.)

Even more worthwhile perhaps is the recently renovated **Museum of Archaeology**, which has a remarkable collection of ancient beads as well as displays about bead-making, human prehistory, the first known sub-Saharan agricultural settlement at Kintampo, the early trading town of Begho, the Akan kingdoms, Koma statues and finds from excavations in Elmina. To get there, catch a tro-tro from the station located on the northwest side of Nkrumah Circle. After entering the main gate, keep going straight to reach the library or bookshop, but turn right at the roundabout for the Department of Archaeology and the museum. Hungry visitors should ask for the **Bush Canteen**, which serves up a good basic meal for less than US$1. (⊕ w/days only.)

Hot on Africa!
Just some of our destinations for serious explorers...

Bradt Guides are available from all good bookshops,
or by post, phone or internet direct from

Bradt Travel Guides Ltd
Tel: +44 (0)1753 893444

www.bradtguides.com

Part Three

THE COAST WEST OF ACCRA

It is hardly surprising that Ghana's coast lies at the centre of its tourist industry. But what is remarkable – I daresay unique – is that such a magnificent chunk of tropical coastline should support a tourist industry based almost entirely around historical sightseeing. The reason for this is not that the beaches of the west coast fail to live up to every archetype of white-sanded, palm-fringed tropical nirvana – many of them do, even if riptides and currents pose a potentially fatal threat to swimmers in several places. No, it is that Ghana, alone in Africa, bears tangible physical evidence of an episode as barbarous and shameful as any in the recorded history of the continent: the trans-Atlantic slave trade.

For the sake of historical accuracy, I think it important to stress that the west coast of Ghana is scarcely unique in having supported a substantial slave trade before 1850. On the contrary, the large-scale trade in human lives arrived much earlier at several other parts of the west African coast, whereas Ghana remained relatively immune as a result of its importance to the international gold trade. Even in the mid-18th century, by which time the slave trade out of Ghana had peaked, a greater volume of slaves was being exported annually from French Dahomey alone than from the entire coast of what is now Ghana.

What makes Ghana different to any other part of west Africa is simple. Elsewhere along the coast, trade was generally conducted out of makeshift buildings of which nothing is left today. In Ghana, by contrast, the slave trade was run out of a string of solidly built forts and castles, many constructed at the height of the gold-trading era and later adapted to include slave dungeons. The most substantial of these castles and forts are still standing today, the scratched walls of their dank dungeons a graphic reminder of two centuries of cruelty and despair, from the Fort of Good Hope in the east to Fort Apollonia in the west, via the imposing whitewashed castles that dominate the beach-fronts of Cape Coast and Elmina.

The west coast of Ghana is neatly divided in two by the twin towns of Cape Coast and Elmina, which lie 15km apart, roughly halfway between Accra and the Côte d'Ivoire. Formerly the Gold Coast headquarters of Britain and Holland, respectively, Cape Coast and Elmina today form the main tourist focus in the region, their fully restored castles holding immense historical significance and impact. Both towns, however, warrant further exploration, as in different ways they both retain something of the mood of an older Africa, not merely in terms of historical buildings, but in their tangible sense of community. An added attraction of Elmina is that it boasts what is perhaps the country's most impressive selection of *posuban* shrines (see box on page 144).

While the immediate vicinity of Cape Coast and Elmina could hardly be described as heaving with tourists, the area does support a tangible tourist industry, and it is thus accorded its own chapter. Subsequent chapters cover the relatively untrammelled stretches of coast between Accra and Cape Coast, and west of Elmina. Both of these areas are largely ignored by the tourist industry, and thus offer rewarding pickings to independent travellers. True, the relatively upmarket beach resorts at places such as Ankobra, Biriwa, and Fete do attract a steady trickle of well-heeled custom, and Busua sometimes hosts a busy backpacker scene. But such places are the exception on a coast that's dotted with strange, time-warped backwaters such as Senya Beraku, Apam, Anomabu, Shama, Sekondi, Prince's Town, Axim, Beyin and Nzulezu stilt village.

7

Towards Cape Coast

Many visitors to Ghana will experience the coastal belt between Accra and Cape Coast as little more than a blur of small junction towns and erratically weaving taxis, framed by the window of an STC bus or tour coach. This is because the main coastal road connecting Accra and Cape Coast, for most of its length, lies just far enough inland that it offers few obvious indications that it runs along the coast at all. And yet, connected to the main road by a series of short feeder roads, this stretch of coast is scattered with a tantalising array of time-warped small towns, run-down forts and palm-fringed beaches, all of which are bypassed by the overwhelming majority of visitors to Ghana.

Whether one chooses to explore this area will be a question of temperament and available time. It would be an exaggeration to claim that any of the forts has an impact commensurate to that of the immense castles at Elmina or Cape Coast, or that the region boasts any upmarket resort better than Elmina's Coconut Grove, or one natural attraction comparable to Kakum National Park near Cape Coast. Frankly, if you have only a couple of days available to explore the coast, then the case for hopping on to that STC bus or tour coach direct to Cape Coast or Elmina is strong.

It is different altogether for travellers with time on their hands, or a yen for getting off the beaten track. If it is beaches you are after, they don't come much better than **Fete**, a small town which lies only an hour's drive from Accra (see page 146). For the historically minded, **Senya Beraku**, **Apam** (see page 150) and **Anomabu** (see page 153) are obvious highlights, the first two offering accommodation in centuries-old forts, the last the site of a fine upmarket beach resort. Closer to Accra, the attractive **Kokrobite Beach** (see below) is the site of a private music academy, and recommended to those who wish to learn more about Ghanaian music. Also of interest are the relatively substantial towns of **Winneba** and **Saltpond** (see pages 147 and 151), the former offering some of the cheapest beach-front accommodation in the country, and the isolated Biriwa Beach Resort between Anomabu and Cape Coast.

KOKROBITE BEACH

Located no more than 25km west of Accra by road (though the heavy traffic on the western outskirts of the capital can make it feel a lot further), Kokrobite Beach is perhaps best known as the site of the **Academy of African Music and Arts Ltd** (AAMA) (see page 144), founded by the internationally known Ga percussionist Moustapha Tettey Addy. More recently, Kokrobite – or, more specifically, the admirably laidback **Big Milly's Backyard** (see page 144) – has become entrenched as a popular alternative base to Accra itself, particularly with volunteers working upcountry and long-haul travellers looking for a few days' respite from the bustle of urban west Africa.

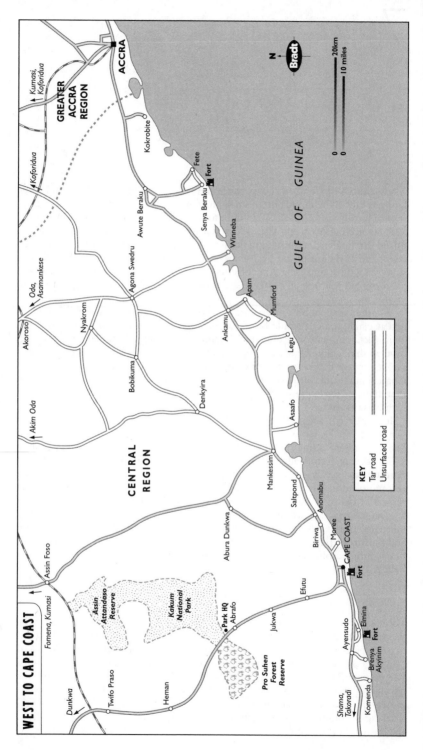

WEST TO CAPE COAST

KEY
Tar road
Unsurfaced road

N Bradt

GULF OF GUINEA

GREATER ACCRA REGION

CENTRAL REGION

ACCRA

← Kumasi, Koforidua

← Koforidua

← Oda, Asamankese

Akim Oda →

Kokrobite

Fete
Fort

Senya Beraku

Awute Beraku

Agona Swedru

Winneba

Apam

Mumford

Ankamu

Legu

Nyakrom

Akoroso

Bobikuma

Denkyira

Asaafo

Mankessim

Saltpond

Anomabu

Moree

Biriwa

CAPE COAST

Fort

Abura Dunkwa

Assin Foso

Fomena, Kumasi →

Dunkwa →

Twifo Praso

Heman

Assin Attandaso Reserve

Kakum National Park

Pro Suhen Forest Reserve

Park HQ
Abrafo

Jukwa

Efutu

Ayensudo

Elmina
Fort

Brenya
Akyinim

Komenda

Shama, Takoradi →

0   20km
0   10 miles

142

Kokrobite is a good place to spend time if you'd like to be instructed in African drumming or music, while AAMA and/or Big Milly's host a popular drumming and dancing show most Saturday nights. For Accra residents, it's also an excellent and conveniently close chill-out venue, dominated by a beach that would be thoroughly idyllic were it not for a potentially dangerous undertow (ask before you swim) and a burgeoning reputation as a crime hotspot. Indeed, for several years now, we have received regular reports from readers who were robbed or mugged on Kokrobite Beach. This situation might conceivably change following Big Milly's recent initiative to pay former criminals to perform security patrols, but two muggings reported to us in the first two months of 2007 would suggest otherwise. For the time being, you're advised to ignore any local reassurances with respect to safety, and to assume that carrying any valuables (money, jewellery, camera, mobile phone, etc) onto the beach is likely to attract the interest of thieves.

Situated some 5km east of Kokrobite as the crow flies, the Densu River Delta – composed of about 100km² of palm-fringed dunes, fresh-water lagoons and mangrove swamps – was declared a Ramsar Wetland Site in 1992, though much of the area is mined commercially for salt. Ecologically, the delta is of significance both as a turtle breeding site and for supporting immense seasonal colonies of marine birds, most notably the rare roseate tern (flocks of 500 have been recorded), but also the likes of common tern, Sandwich tern, little tern, black tern, royal tern and spotted redshank. For birdwatchers, a good access point to the delta is the bird observation post 3km away and signposted from the small town of Mendkrom on the main Accra–Cape Coast road a short distance east of the Kokrobite junction.

Of greater interest to most travellers, in particular those who won't have the opportunity to visit Tafi Atome or Boabeng-Fiema, is the **Solo Forest Monkey Sanctuary** at Bortianor, some 4km from Kokrobite. This new community-run sanctuary consists of a sacred grove of tall trees bisected by a small stream and inhabited by a troop of semi-habituated monkeys, which can be visited for US$3 per person. When we visited at midday there was no sign of the monkeys, but we were told they are more easily located before 08.00 or after 16.00 when they come to the stream to drink. From the description we were given, they are probably mona monkeys, but we couldn't confirm this.

GETTING THERE AND AWAY To get to Kokrobite, those with private transport should follow the coastal road west of Accra for approximately 22km before turning left at the signposted junction for Kokrobite. Using public transport, there are normally direct tro-tros between Kaneshie Station in Accra and Kokrobite, though they may take ages to fill up. Alternatively, any other vehicle heading towards Winneba from Kaneshie Station or Malam Junction can drop you at the police barrier near the junction for Kokrobite, from where it is 7km to the beach – shared taxis cost US$0.50, though you might have to charter a taxi. If you are arriving after dark, it may be worth paying the extra for a drop in to your hotel.

To visit the Solo Forest Monkey Sanctuary, ask any transport heading along the feeder road between Kokrobite and the junction with the main Accra–Cape Coast road to drop you at Bortianor, where fees must be paid and a guide arranged at the Tsokomey Nature Centre, 100m from the feeder road. The walk to the sanctuary takes no more than five minutes.

Unique to Ghana's central coastal region, *posubans* are the eye-catching and often elaborately decorated concrete shrines that dot the urban landscape of many Fante settlements, reaching something of a garish zenith in such ancient trading centres as Elmina, Anomabu and Mankessim.

These shrines are the work of *asafo* companies, the patrilineal military units that are a feature of most Akan societies. *Asafo* companies are traditionally responsible for the defence of their town, but these days they are perhaps more significant for their ceremonial function and for their activity and influence in the arts and local politics. Most towns in the region boast at least five rival companies, and some boast up to 12. Each company is identified by number, name, and location, with Number One Company generally being the longest established unit in any given town, as well as the most important and influential in terms of links to the chieftaincy. In Anomabu, for instance, a new chief is always sworn in at the *posuban* built by Number One Company, which is adorned with a symbolic padlock and key.

Many *posubans* originated as storage houses, used to hold not only arms but also the company regalia, and they are often decorated in a manner that is both richly symbolic and – to the outsider – decidedly cryptic. The extent of this decoration varies enormously from town to town. You could easily walk right past most of Cape Coast's *posubans* without noticing them, since at best they are decorated by one small mural. In Elmina and Mankessim, by contrast, the most important shrines are multi-storey affairs decorated with up to ten life-size human forms, and complex enough in their symbolism to keep you guessing for several hours.

Perhaps the most surprising thing about the *posubans* of the Ghanaian coast is how little they owe to any other African artistic tradition – unique to the area these *posubans* may be, and ancient too by all accounts, but were you to show a picture of a typical shrine to most Europeans, they'd be hard pushed to guess in what continent it

WHERE TO STAY
Moderate

Korkor Inn 027 5180406. Right next door to Big Milly's, this new hotel offers suites with kitchen, AC & a sea view – although the hospital-like cleanliness comes with matching sterile atmosphere & deafeningly loud music late into the night. *Suites US$50.*

Budget

Academy of African Music and Arts (AAMA)
027 7380854; e addy2000gh@yahoo.com; www.afrikamusika.de. This perennially popular resort on the road out of Kokrobite towards Langma, though arguably in decline, is recommended to anybody with a strong interest in African music, especially drumming. Founder Moustapha Tettey Addy, now evidently semi-retired, restricts himself to smiling benignly in the background while his staff & musicians do the heavy work, but drumming & dancing lessons taken by understudies are available at US$8 pp per hour, while more specialised drum & xylophone lessons with master instrumentalists cost US$15–20 pp per hour. *Comfortable self-contained rooms in a great beach-front location cost US$11/13 sgl/dbl, whilst an attached restaurant serves adequate seafood for US$4.50–9.50 a plate.*

Big Milly's Backyard 024 607998, 042 206961 or 028 5053010; e bigmilly2000@hotmail.com. Also known as Wendy's Place, this justifiably popular budget resort, run by an Anglo-Ghanaian couple, is one of the few places close to Accra – indeed anywhere along the Ghanaian coast – that bears comparison to the myriad beach-front backpacker lodges dotted around southern Africa. An on-site restaurant & bar serves excellent b/fasts (the cinnamon toast & the spicy 'eggs *sambal*' are particularly recommended), as well as good seafood, fruit juices & cocktails. Other facilities inc a book swap service, safe, professional massages, & a number of handpicked traders selling batik, beads & other handicrafts in the compound. Visitors can also enjoy cultural shows around a beach bonfire on Fri nights, as well as live music performances on Sat nights –

had been photographed. One renowned shrine in Anomabu just about conjures up Africa by depicting lions and leopards (sitting somewhat incongruously alongside a whale and several surreal antelope-like creatures), which cannot be said for the best-known *posuban* in that town, several metres long and built in the shape of a European warship. Other famous shrines in the region are dotted with European sailors (clad in blue and white) and overgrown clocks, while one startling shrine in Elmina depicts the story of Adam and Eve. It's the sort of thing that's bound to annoy arty ethno-purists, though personally I find it fascinating to see this strange melding of exotic and indigenous influences in a town such as Elmina, a place where Africa and Europe have, after all, been rubbing shoulders for more than five centuries.

Despite vigorous questioning of local elders, I was unable to establish when, why, and how these elaborate *posubans* were constructed. Most of the shrines I saw look as if they took their present form in the post-Independence era. It is my understanding (and I'm open to correction on this) that the actual sites of the shrines are often centuries old, but that the shrines themselves are resculpted every few decades to reflect changes in fashion and any recent additions to the long list of symbols and proverbs boasted by each *asafo*. One of the few shrines to reflect their age directly is the one in Saltpond, which is dated 1685.

Details of important individual shrines are given under the town where they are found. For most short-stay visitors, the obvious place to go *posuban* viewing is Elmina, though the selection found in Anomabu is arguably more varied and interesting, while the main shrine in Mankessim (traditionally regarded as the first capital of Fante) is probably the largest and most elaborate in the country, and the one in Saltpond among the most bizarre. Most of the shrines lie on main roads so viewing them is free, but a donation of around US$1 per shrine will be expected if you want to take photographs.

---

although the latter incurs a cover charge (US$1.50) for those eating outside the premises. There have been a few reports of rival hotels passing themselves off as Big Milly's, so double check the signboard if your lodging does not meet this description! A wide variety of accommodation ranges from the luxurious self-contained 'Sahara suite', which sleeps 4 for US$49 & offers AC, fridge & hot water, to self-contained dbls at US$17, or sgl/dbl/trpl/quadruple rooms with fan & common showers at US$7/12/20/26. Shoestring options inc camping at US$2.50 pp (own tent) or US$3 pp in an open loft-style dorm.

🏠 **Dream Hotel** ☎ 028 8246177. This pleasant lodge is situated just opposite Big Milly's & accommodates a lot of its spill-over. Clean, self-contained dbl/trpl for US$15/30 with fan, or US$25/35 with AC.

Shoestring

🏠 **Blackstone Hotel** Around the corner from Big Milly's, this little hotel offers adequate sgls with common bath for US$6, although reports of theft from rooms should probably be heeded. Good local dishes can be provided on request. US$6.

🏠 **Kokrobite Garden Restaurant** ☎ 024 6785746. Next door to Blackstone, this Italian-run haven offers what is easily the best-value accommodation in the area, with two stylish dbl bungalows priced at US$8 inc fan and b/fast. An attractive house for larger groups was also under construction at the time of the last update, & should be up & running by the time you read this. Other facilities inc Thai massage & an excellent restaurant serving real Italian coffee, pizza & other Italian dishes for US$4–6 a plate. Mobile reception is poor but reservations can be made by SMS. US$8 for dbl bungalow inc fan & b/fast.

✖ **WHERE TO EAT** Big Milly's, **AMAA**, and the **Kokrobite Garden Restaurant** all serve good food at sensible prices, although the latter – which one reader ranks as 'the best thing' about Kokrobite – is closed on Mondays.

Also worth a try is the misleadingly named **Ocean View Garden and Restaurant** (✆ *021 766405/028 232440*) on the road towards AMAA, which was set up by former employees of the Kokrobite Garden Restaurant and serves a carbon-copy menu together with lobster thermidor and a range of fish dishes.

Further along, the green **Calabash Restaurant** offers 'continental' and Ghanaian dishes for around US$3 a plate, although the music is overly loud and there are only two outside tables.

FETE AND SENYA BERAKU

Roughly 40km southwest of Accra as the crow flies, the somewhat isolated twin towns of Fete and Senya Beraku form an obvious first port of call for unhurried travellers heading west from the capital. Set only 6km apart, and connected to each other by a dirt road covered by regular shared taxis, these two small towns are both attractive travel goals, albeit for very different reasons.

The main point of interest in the sleepy town of Senya Beraku is the 18th-century **Fort of Good Hope**, which boasts a dramatic cliff-top position overlooking a beach covered in colourful fishing boats and reportedly safe for swimming. The town itself is larger than you might expect, unbelievably run-down and populated by perhaps the noisiest children in Ghana. Nevertheless, it is not without some curiosity value, notably a clutch of old churches and – bizarrely – a group of cracking concrete graves that date from the early 20th century and stand right in the middle of a road (or at least what appears to have been a road before it was eroded to its present topographic state).

Senya Beraku first attracted the interest of Holland in the 1660s when a small trading lodge was built there, to be abandoned shortly afterwards. In 1704, the Dutch returned to the site, and with the permission of the Queen of Agona they started work on what would turn out to be the last fort they were to build in west Africa. Originally a very small, triangular construction designed to facilitate a low-key trade in gold, the Fort of Good Hope – would it be too heavy-handed to note the irony? – ended up serving almost exclusively as a slave-trading centre. In 1724, the fort was extended to cover more or less its present area, and a large slave dungeon was built into the southwest bastion. The Fort of Good Hope was handed to Britain as part of the 'fort exchange' treaty of 1868, and apparently fell into disuse at some point during the colonial era, since by the time of independence it was a partial ruin. In the 1980s, the fort was restored as a joint historical monument and resthouse.

If Senya Beraku, with its combination of beautiful coastal setting, grandiose European fort, slave dungeons, crumbling buildings, eroded streets and abject poverty, could be seen to encapsulate much of what is disturbing about modern Africa, Fete's attractions are altogether more uncomplicated. This, in a nutshell, is prime sun 'n' surf territory. The small town sprawls over a low hill down to two attractive sandy beaches, both of which now host a good resort hotel, and it is rapidly establishing a deserved reputation as an isolated **upmarket beach retreat** the equal of anywhere along the coast.

GETTING THERE AND AWAY Both Senya Beraku and Fete lie roughly 15km south of the main road between Accra and Winneba. Either town is reached via a reasonably good dirt road, leaving the main road about 2km west of Awutu Beraku. This road passes through the small town of Ojobi (notable for its bright pink church) and then about 5km before reaching the coast it forks, with the left fork going directly to Fete and the right fork directly to Senya Beraku. The best place to pick up public transport heading this way is not at the junction itself, but at Awutu Beraku, where regular shared taxis leave for both Senya Beraku and Fete. It is advisable to pick up a taxi heading specifically to the town you want to visit: although the occasional shared taxi runs along the 6km road directly connecting Senya Beraku to Fete, you might be in for a long wait. The alternative is to hire a charter taxi (this shouldn't cost more than US$2 one way) or to walk; the latter is a reasonably attractive option in one direction, provided that you're not carrying luggage.

If you are coming direct from Accra, tro-tros to Senya Beraku leave reasonably regularly from Kaneshie Station.

WHERE TO STAY AND EAT
Upmarket

Tills No I Hotel 027 7550480 or 021 304890; f 027 558247; e tillsbeach@yahoo.com; www.till.net/TillsNo1. Set on a beautiful beach 500m from Fete town, Tills is not quite as plush as it once was, but it nevertheless offers very good value for money in its price range, & is reportedly receiving renewed attention under new management in early 2007. The restaurant serves excellent seafood & grills in the US$5–10 range, while facilities & activities inc beach & indoor games, mini-golf, canoe trips, fishing, drumming & dancing lessons, as well as minibus excursions with a driver. *Rooms are priced at US$45/54 for a standard sgl/dbl,*

or US$63 for a suite (all with hot shower, AC, satellite TV, fridge, & b/fast inc).

Whitesands Beach Resort 021 773070/774226 or 024 4311888; f 021 774064; e whsands@ighmail.com. Sadly for travellers & less well-heeled expats, the beautiful Whitesands resort is being remodelled as a members-only club – open to Accra residents seeking weekend escape for US$800/1,200/1,600 a year for a sgl/dbl/family room. Those that can stomach the price tag will be rewarded with Hopi Indian architecture, an infinity pool overlooking the private beach & a bar that could compete for interior decoration prizes in any Western city.

Shoestring

Anthill Hotel 024 4834994 The only other accommodation in Senya Beraku lies behind the taxi station, & doubles as a very friendly sewing & catering school for girls. Acceptable dbl rooms range from cupboard- to ballroom-proportions, & cost US$8 regardless of size. Prices are likely to rise in line with planned renovations & installation of private bath facilities. Meals & corner fans can be supplied on request. *US$8*

Fort of Good Hope 024 3184766 Oddly, when you consider the shabbiness & isolation of Senya Beraku itself, this easily ranks as the most organised of the various forts now serving as a resthouse along the Ghanaian coast. Facilities inc a communal lounge, clean shared toilet & shower, gift shop, bar with fridge, &

restaurant serving chicken or fish with fried rice or chips for around US$3.50. The staff, too, seem unusually well-tuned to the needs of travellers. Bearing in mind that this fort at one point served as a slave dungeon, the very slickness of this operation (slick, that is, by Ghanaian standards) does teeter on the edge of tastelessness. Then again, you could argue that any economic uplift offered to this town by tourism must outweigh historical sensitivities. Still, it's difficult to imagine that anybody would want to hold their wedding reception here, though the facility is advertised. A tour of the fort is free to lodgers, or US$0.50 to other visitors. *Comfortable dbl rooms with electric light & fan cost US$12 pp.*

WINNEBA

The largest coastal settlement between Accra and Cape Coast, Winneba is the traditional capital of the Afutu, whose King Ghartey IV was the prime initiator behind and president of the Fante Confederation of 1868–73. Winneba was also the site of a reasonably important British fort from 1673 until 1812, when the town was evacuated by its settler community following an Ashanti invasion in which the British commander was tortured to death (for decades after this, passing British ships fired a broadside when they passed the site of the fort). Traces of the old fort can be seen in the Methodist church built on the same site by missionaries in the late 19th century. Otherwise, Winneba's compact town centre has the atmosphere of a historical port, all winding alleys, malodorous fishy markets and fading

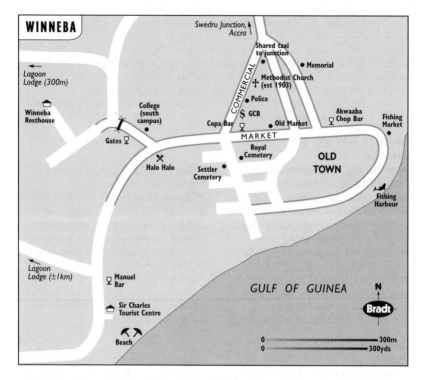

Swedru Junction,
Accra

Shared taxi
to junction

● Memorial

Methodist Church
✝ (est 1903)

● Police

Lagoon
Lodge (300m)

⌂ Winneba
Resthouse

College
(south
campus)

$ GCB

Copa Bar

Akwaaba
Chop Bar

Fishing
Market

Gates ⍭

Old Market

MARKET

Halo Halo

Settler
Cemetery

Royal
Cemetery

OLD
TOWN

Fishing
Harbour

Lagoon
Lodge (±1km)

Manuel
Bar

GULF OF GUINEA

N

Bradt

Sir Charles
Tourist Centre

Beach

0 ————————— 300m
0 ————————— 300yds

colonial buildings, but no individual buildings of great historical interest, so far as I am aware.

For travellers, Winneba is most attractive for its busy **fishing harbour** and the expansive beach that lies immediately to its west. You might want to take a look at the old European and royal cemeteries, which face each other about 300m from the fishing harbour, and hopefully you'll have more luck than us trying to locate the worthwhile *posuban* shrine that reportedly lies between town and beach.

The one time of the year when Winneba changes status from diverting backwater to must-visit is on the first weekend of May, when it hosts the **Aboakyir Festival**. This 300-year-old festival, probably the most famous in the country, is centred on the 'deer hunt', in which Winneba's two oldest *asafo* companies, dressed in full traditional regalia, compete to be the first to hunt down and capture alive an antelope using only their bare hands. The festival carries on throughout the weekend, climaxing twice: on Saturday, when the deer hunt takes place amid much noise and colour until one or other company wins; then at 14.00 on Sunday when the captured animal is sacrificed to the oracles at the Pemkye Otu fetish.

Immediately west of Winneba, the **Muni-Pomadze Ramsar Site**, designated in 1992, is dominated by the vast Muni Lagoon, which extends over 30km² when full, but also incorporates two forest reserves as well as the traditional hunting ground used in the Aboakyer Festival. It is an important birdwatching site, notable in particular for large seasonal colonies of black, roseate, common, royal and little tern, as well as being the only known Ghanaian haunt of the localised Puvel's illadopsis. Less esoterically, the palm-fringed beach that divides the lagoon from the open sea regularly hosts breeding turtles between August and March. To reach the Ramsar Site, follow the coastal road west out of town for about 1km past the

Sir Charles Tourist Centre until you reach a makeshift wildlife office on the right-hand side. The rangers here will guide visitors to a nearby bird observation post, from where with good binoculars a variety of terns can be seen, especially towards dusk. The rangers are also willing to go turtle tracking after dark – there is no formal charge, but a tip will be expected.

As for facilities, Winneba has a brand new and very well-organised internet café called Teddy's Net, on Commercial Road, across the road from the shared taxi stand to the junction. If you're in Winneba for a few days, you might also want to visit **Radio Peace**, one of seven community radio stations in Ghana.

GETTING THERE AND AWAY Winneba lies about 6km south of the main road between Accra and Cape Coast. You can get a bus direct to Winneba from Kaneshie Bus Station in Accra, but otherwise, coming from most directions, it's easier to catch a bus or tro-tro to Winneba junction (also known as Swedru junction) from where regular shared taxis make their way to the old town centre (*US$0.30*).

WHERE TO STAY
Budget

Hunters Lodge (9 rooms) ☎ 0432 22318. Situated halfway between Swedru junction & Winneba just before Right Step Spot, this is an unexpectedly plush set-up. All rooms are self-contained with AC, DSTV, fridge & hot shower & there is a pleasant outdoor bar. Counting against this otherwise excellent hotel is the bland setting & the distance from the beach. *From US$20 (sgl with dbl bed) to US$26 (suite).*

Lagoon Lodge ☎ 0432 22435 or 020 816 2031/4; e lagoonlodge@yahoo.co.uk or lagoon_lodgegh@yahoo.com; www.lagoon-lodge-winneba.com. Situated midway between the lagoon & the beach within the southern campus of the University College of Education, this is by far the best lodge in Winneba, & it has been praised by numerous readers as one of the best-value & friendliest establishments anywhere on the coast. The self-contained rooms are large, bright & spotless, while 4 connecting rooms are available upstairs for families & groups. The bar, which overlooks the Muni Lagoon, is perfectly positioned to catch the sunset, & a good restaurant serves seafood & local dishes in the US$4.50–6 range. The energetic & friendly Ghanaian owner is an excellent source of local travel advice, & can direct you to the beach, about 10 mins' walk away. Booking is recommended. *US$9/17/30 sgl/dbl/quadruple.*

Shoestring

Ernst Home Lodge (3 rooms) ☎ 0432 22222; e mensahadka@yahoo.com. The most central accommodation in Winneba, this simple but homely new guesthouse is owned & managed by a welcoming Ghanaian who lived for several years in the UK. The lodge is 10 mins' walk from the town centre on Commercial Rd, just off the map, but to the right if arriving from Swedru junction. *Around US$4.*

Sir Charles Tourist Centre ☎ 024 755051. Winneba's longest-serving tourist hotel is a run-down & brutally ugly chalet complex set right above the beach about 1km from the town centre. On previous visits, the rooms have seemed habitable – & it seems churlish to quibble with a price of US$3.50/4.50 for a self-contained dbl/twin – but who knows what they look like now? With admirable frankness, the staff advised the most recent updater of this guide that the key holder had gone to sleep & that Lagoon Lodge would be a far better bet. Assuming you do manage to secure lodging, a severely limited menu (fish with rice or yam) is served in an absurdly vast circular dining hall, at moderate prices. Outside, the pink & blue 1970s architecture does something to undermine the beachfront location, but fortunately, the beach stretches west for a few kilometres, & is very beautiful once you wander 50m away from the resort. *US$3.50/4.50.*

Winneba Resthouse ☎ 0432 22208. Altogether less aesthetically confrontational, the Winneba (or 'Army') Resthouse lies within the College of Education Southern Campus off the road between the town centre & the Sir Charles. This place has a great view, perched on a hilltop facing a beach & hill-forest to the West of town where the antelope is caught during the Winneba deer festival. It's a little run-down, but the large self-contained dbl rooms with fan are fantastic value. The only drawbacks are the distance from the beach (a good 10-min walk) & that first priority is given to military personnel. Food is available on request. *US$4.*

✕ WHERE TO EAT Most of the hotels listed above serve food of some sort, though only Lagoon Lodge stands out, in particular for seafood. A great place to eat and/or get a drink is **Halo Halo!**, a spot located on Market Road between the two south gates to the University of Education at Winneba. A number of spots on the road into town also serve good grilled meats; of the bars in the city centre, the Pee Spot warrants a special mention for its unfortunate name alone.

APAM

Memorable for its picturesque fishing harbour laden with colourful pirogues, Apam would perhaps be my first choice were I in a position to stay in only one place between Accra and Cape Coast. The centrepiece of the town is **Fort Leydsaamsheid** ('Fort Patience'), built by the Dutch in 1697, captured by the British in 1782, returned to the Dutch three years later, then finally handed back to Britain in 1868. Now a resthouse (see below), this must be about the smallest extant fort on the Ghanaian coast, and the cramped dimensions of the prison cell suggests that it was never used to store slaves to any serious extent, if at all. The most impressive thing about the fort is its position, perched on top of a sharp little hill, which offers the potential for some fantastic photos of the town and harbour to one side, or the pretty, secluded beach to the other. The US$2 entrance fee seems a bit steep given the lack of information or evidence of repairs, but is probably negotiable. Also of interest, a somewhat timeworn three-storey *posuban* opposite the tro-tro station depicts several biblical figures – many of which have been accidentally decapitated! Several other buildings in Apam strike me as being of some antiquity, including the turn-of-the-century Methodist church and the house belonging to Chief Quaye.

GETTING THERE AND AWAY Apam lies about 15km south of the main Accra–Cape Coast road. Regular shared taxis run from Ankamu junction or Winneba junction to the town. Both are easily reached by tro-tro from either direction.

🏠 WHERE TO STAY
Budget

🏠 **La Plage** Out along the road towards Mamford & about 100m beyond a bizarre corkscrew-shaped palm, this weird hotel is a fine example of unrealised potential. Its self-contained, beachfront chalets would rank as a bargain, were it not for the concrete bar & attendant building-site atmosphere, & the apparent lack of plans for change. A good alternative only if the Lynnbah is full & you can't face a night in the fort. *US$10.*

🏠 **Lynnbah Guesthouse** ✆ 024 635 9680/ 028 707 5779 Situated about 1km from the tro-tro station & accessed through open fields to the right of the road into town, this smart & homely little guesthouse has clean, dbl rooms priced between US$15 & US$20 depending on whether they have AC. Facilities inc a good outdoor bar, communal sitting room with TV & meals available on request. Arriving by public transport, you'll probably need a taxi to find it. *US$15–20.*

Shoestring

🏠 **Fort Patience Resthouse** (4 rooms) There are 4 tiny, cells-turned-bedrooms on the top floor of the fort, each of which contains one sgl bed & offers stunning views over the harbour. No food is available. The only facilities are bucket showers, but, still, they're not bad value at: *US$2 pp – which is also the price of entrance to the fort.*

✕ WHERE TO EAT You can buy a fair selection of food and drinks around the market and tro-tro station, and a restaurant has opened recently right behind the tro-tro station. One reader warns: 'Avoid the Candle Nite Spot and Bar, near the fort opposite the church, where the bartender tried to remove his Osama bin Laden-supporting customers and friends to let us pay double the price we agreed before for breakfast.'

MANKESSIM

The frantic junction town of Mankessim may not be much to look at today, but it is widely regarded as the focal point from which the Fante expanded into much of what is now south-central Ghana. The Fante tradition is that Mankessim was founded by three priests who went by the name of Obunumankuma, Oson, and Odapagyan, an event that evidently occurred at least half a century before the Portuguese reached the Ghanaian coast. Mankessim has had its moments in more recent history too: it was here in 1868 that the chiefs of the Akan states of south-central Ghana met to form the Fante Confederation, of which Mankessim served as *ipso facto* capital under the presidency of King Ghartey IV of Winneba until the confederation disbanded in 1873.

The most likely reason you'd want to stop at Mankessim is to see the famous **posuban** that lies about 500m from the central traffic circle along the same road as the tro-tro station. This must be about the largest shrine of its sort in Ghana, a peculiar three-storey construction adorned with around a dozen life-sized human sculptures (see page 144). You might also want to ask about visiting a sacred shrine called **Nananompow** – Grave of the Fathers – traditionally thought to be both where the three founding fathers of Fante were buried, and the seat of the Fante gods. The most interesting days to visit Mankessim are Wednesday and Saturday, when there is a good market.

GETTING THERE AND AWAY Mankessim is an important transport hub, easily reached by tro-tro from Winneba, Cape Coast and points in between.

WHERE TO STAY AND EAT
Moderate

🏠 **Manna Heights Hotel** ✆ 042 33856 or 020 8110400/04; e mannaheights@mannaheightshotel.com. This large & impressive hotel is perched on an isolated, breezy hilltop about 3km from Mankessim, & reached via a signposted, unmade turn-off from the Saltpond road. The lack of sea views & distance from the beach suggest it is not aimed specifically at tourists, but otherwise it has to rank as one of the best deals in its range near the Ghanaian coast, & would make a useful base from which to explore the area. Facilities inc a swimming pool, tennis courts, & excellent restaurant offering dishes from US$4.50. *Large, smart self-contained rooms with DSTV, AC & a hot bath cost between US$45 & US$70 inc b/fast.*

Budget

🏠 **Royal Palace Hotel** ✆ 024 2620586. The only accommodation within the town limits, this central & reasonably priced hotel lies about 300m from the Accra tro-tro station next door to the Top Oil filling station. Acceptable rooms are all self-contained with fan. No food is served, but the nearby Aponkye Nkrakra Chop Bar serves good local dishes, whilst the Marknes Spot just next door is a lively place for a drink. *US$6.50 for a sgl or US$7.50–13 for a dbl, depending on the size of the bed.*

SALTPOND

Saltpond is often regarded as Mankessim's coastal twin, lying about 8km to its southwest and about 1km from the main road towards Cape Coast. Very few travellers pop into Saltpond, but it's an interesting enough place. The narrow roads and colonial architecture are reminiscent of a smaller version of Cape Coast, and there's a very pretty beach. Of historical interest, 200m from the hospital is a stunning *posuban* shrine that dates to 1687 and is decorated with perhaps a dozen life-sized human statues as well as a menagerie of dragons and vultures.

At Abanze, on the Cape Coast road about 2.5km from Saltpond, lies **Fort Amsterdam**, which dates to 1631 and was the first fort built by the British on the

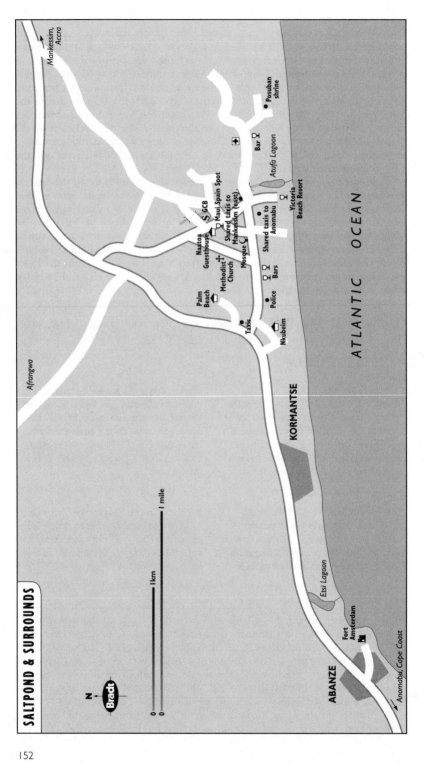

SALTPOND & SURROUNDS

Mankessim, Accra

Afrangwa

N

Bradt

1 km

1 mile

0

0

Posuban shrine

Bar

Atufa Lagoon

Victoria Beach Resort

GCB

Maui Spain Spot

Shared taxis to Mankessim (east)

Naatoa Guesthouse

Shared taxis to Anomabu

Mosque

Methodist Church

Palm Beach

Police

Bars

Taxis

Nkubelim

KORMANTSE

ATLANTIC OCEAN

Etsi Lagoon

ABANZE

Fort Amsterdam

Anomabu, Cape Coast

Gold Coast. The original fort was destroyed in an attack by the people of Anomabu in 1811, to be restored as recently as 1951. Perched on a hilltop, Fort Amsterdam affords excellent views over a busy fishing beach and the Etsi Lagoon to the village of Kormantse, from which its alternative name of Fort Cormantin derives. The slaves held in Fort Amsterdam, sold mainly to the Caribbean plantations, became known as Cormantins – a name that reportedly travelled to the West Indies. Among the prominent Afro-Americans to have traced their roots to Kormantse is Louis Armstrong.

GETTING THERE AND AWAY Shared taxis connect Saltpond to Mankessim and Anomabu. From elsewhere, disembark from public transport at Saltpond junction then walk or hire a taxi for the last 1km or so to the town centre.

WHERE TO STAY AND EAT
Budget
⌂ **Palm Beach Hotel** ☎ 031 46683 or 042 33328. Looming untidily over Saltpond junction, this high-rise concrete block is something of an eyesore, only partially redeemed by the fabulous views it offers over the town & beach. Assuming that you can get past the architectural insensitivity & a general aura of gloom, the rooms here are actually reasonable value. There's no restaurant, but the rooftop bar would be a nice place to sit in the evening. *US$12 for a self-contained dbl with AC, TV, fridge & balcony, or US$22 for a chalet.*

Shoestring
⌂ **Naatoa Guesthouse** ☎ 020 9274518 or 020 9043901. This small & airy first-floor hotel in the town centre has acceptable self-contained rooms with fans. There is a communication centre but no restaurant. Several nearby places sell cheap chop, while the Victoria Beach Resort looks good for a drink; disco on Fri & Sat. *US$12 dbl, or US$15 for a dbl with AC & fridge.*

⌂ **Nkubeim Hotel** ☎ 024 4758858. Situated back near the junction, this family-run guesthouse has clean but basic rooms. The management is very friendly, but likely to subject visitors to speaker-distorting gospel music. *Self-contained dbl US$12/20 with fan/AC. Family rooms sleeping 4 people cost US$30.*

ANOMABU AND BIRIWA

The small seaside town of Anomabu, situated about halfway between Mankessim and Cape Coast, was an important trading centre before Britain settled at Cape Coast, when it served as the coastal trade outlet for the Fante Empire based at Mankessim. Anomabu has a strong history of independence, despite having been settled intermittently by various European powers. In 1630, the Dutch built a fort at Anomabu, only to abandon it in 1664 due to pressure from Britain. After the British constructed Fort Charles on the beach in 1674, Anomabu became perhaps the biggest slave emporium on the Gold Coast, dealing mainly with the freelance 'ten-percenters'. Britain left Anomabu in 1731, largely as a result of disagreements with the local traders, and destroyed the fort so that it couldn't be captured by a rival power. The French then settled at Anomabu for a period, attracted by the established trade in slaves, but they were expelled by Britain in 1753.

Anomabu today has more to occupy visitors than first impressions might suggest. Away from the somewhat mundane main road, the skyline is dominated by a large, sandstone church and the fort, constructed by the British over the foundations of the older Fort Charles in 1756. One of the most solidly constructed pre-20th-century buildings anywhere on the Gold Coast, Anomabu's fort was extended upwards by one storey during the reign of William IV, since when it has been known as Fort William. Until recently, it served as a prison, and entrance and photography were forbidden, but it is unoccupied at the time of writing, and rumour has it that it will soon open to the public as a museum.

Adjacent to Fort William, there's a substantial ruin which, according to one knowledgeable local, actually predates the fort. About 100m further east, on a beach dotted with coconut palms and (be careful!) fresh turds, there's a sanded-up swimming pool in the rocks, probably dating to the 18th century – a good spot from where to take a discreet snap of the fort. Look out to sea and you'll see the rock after which Anomabu is named – seasonally the site of a breeding colony of gulls.

Several of Ghana's most notable *posuban* shrines lie in Anomabu. There are in all seven shrines in the town, one built by each of the seven *asafo* companies, and all are easy to find. Don't miss the shrine belonging to Company Three, an improbable assemblage of sculpted animals ranging from a cheetah to a whale, adorned with several smaller carvings of animals in grotesque proportions. This shrine is situated about 50m from the main road facing the Ebenezer Hotel behind a contorted strangler *ficus* tree that's one of the most impressive of the town's 70-plus gods. There are also three substantial *posuban* shrines tucked away in the tight network of alleys lying immediately west of the fort, notably the shrine built by Company Seven, shaped like a European ship and the size of a small house. The oldest shrine, built by Company One, is not as impressive to look at, but it is of special importance as the site where a new village chief must be sworn in – symbolised by the lock and key depicted on the shrine.

You're free to wander around Anomabu and look at the shrines, but you'll be expected to pay if you take photos. (See also *Posuban shrines* box on page 144.)

Alongside the main road next to the Ebenezer Hotel is a small memorial, erected to commemorate Anomabu's most famous son, George Ekem Ferguson (born Ekow Atta in 1864), a trained geographer and natural linguist who was perhaps the single most important pioneer in expanding Britain's knowledge of the Ghanaian interior before his death in battle near Wa at the age of 33.

The small, rather nondescript fishing village of **Biriwa**, a few kilometres west of Anomabu, is best known for its superb beach – popular with hippies in the 1970s, but these days used almost exclusively by patrons of the Biriwa Beach Hotel (see *below*). It also boasts an impressive cluster of the fish-smoking ovens that are typical of the area, dominating a slope on the landward side of the road.

GETTING THERE AND AWAY Anomabu is bisected by the main coastal road between Mankessim and Cape Coast, and tro-tros heading between these towns will drop you right in front of any of the hotels. When you leave it's easy to find a seat in a passing tro-tro in either direction – just walk outside to the main road. From Accra or Takoradi, you could take the STC bus which stops at the Ebenezer Hotel for a break – but you'll have to pay the full fare even if you disembark here.

WHERE TO STAY AND EAT
Upmarket

Biriwa Beach Hotel ☎ 024 4446277 or 027 554 4711 or 042 33222 390611; e info-ghana@ecowas.net; www.africannaturetours.com. Positioned on a high bluff overlooking Biriwa's fantastic beach, this German-owned hotel started life about 20 years ago as a restaurant, since when it has expanded to become one of the most homely upmarket retreats in Ghana. Architecturally it is a little dated, but all the rooms are comfortable. The restaurant remains outstanding, & is well worth a special stop if you're travelling from Accra to somewhere further west – the varied menu reflects not only the proximity to the sea, but also the German ownership – & there are plans to re-establish a second restaurant on the beach itself. Other facilities inc free internet access to guests, & a good souvenir shop filled with curios from across west Africa. A variety of day trips can be arranged with Africa Nature Tours, which operates out of the hotel, as can 1- or 2-week trips around northern & eastern Ghana. AC & *bath for US$45/50 sgl/dbl (no sea view) or US$54/60 (sea view).*

Moderate

Anomabu Beach Resort ☎ 021 221111 or 042 91562; **f** 021 230806; **e** anomabu@hotmail.com; website: www.anomabubeach.com. Strung out along a palm-lined beach to the west of the town centre, this exceptionally beautiful resort combines considerable comfort with an appealing organic aesthetic that has few if any peers on the Ghanaian coast. The resort is very child-friendly, & attracts expats from all over francophone west Africa for their family holidays, thanks to a relatively safe swimming beach with lifeguards, & free body-board hire. Future plans inc a paddling pool & a games room. In the evening, the raised wooden restaurant is a great place to catch the breeze & serves excellent meals priced at around US$2 for Ghanaian fare, or closer to US$10 for fish, beef or lobster. Portions are enormous – with the grilled fish cooked especially well – & reasonably priced wine is served by the glass or bottle. A second, more upmarket restaurant should be under construction by

the time you read this. *The accommodation is arranged in two 'villages', one offering large mud-clad & thatched dbl bungalows with a fan at US$27, & the other larger, smarter self-contained units with AC for US$50 or family bandas with two bedrooms & a kitchen at US$100. Standing tents are available at US$15 per dbl & camping costs US$6 pp – although the management doesn't seem overly keen on taking shoestring guests.*

Weda Lodge ☎ 024 4806958 or 020 814 1435. This large hilltop villa would be a gem of a find in any other spot, but suffers somewhat by its proximity to the Anomabu Beach Resort. Well run, clean & extremely friendly, the new guesthouse has 5 spacious self-contained dbl bedrooms costing US$26 with fan or US$32 with AC, TV & fridge. A varied menu offers dishes between US$3.50 & US$7.50, though it is tempting to eat by the beach at the resort, 10 minutes' walk away.

Budget

Ebenezer Rest Stop & Hotel ☎ 024 4721598 or 027 6185084. Situated along the main coastal road towards the centre of Anomabu town, this friendly, 1-star hotel offers large self-contained sgls with hot water & private balcony for US$8/12 fan/AC, or US$20 to US$25 for dbls with AC. The ground-floor restaurant serves excellent & inexpensive chop. *US$8/12; US$20/25*

Hotel Mariesabelle ☎ 042 92024. To the right of the main road as you enter town from Accra, this slightly cheaper & very friendly hotel charges US$8/12 for decent self-contained sgls/dbls with fan. The restaurant here serves good meals for around US$2 & ice-cold drinks, best enjoyed on the breezy rooftop balcony. *US$8/12*

MOREE

This large village (or should that be small town?) about 5km northeast of Cape Coast is the site of **Fort Nassau**. This was the first fort built by the Dutch on the Gold Coast, using bricks brought from Holland, and it served as their headquarters from its construction in 1612 until the capture of Elmina Fort in 1637. Now a substantial ruin, Fort Nassau is clearly visible on a hill above the town, where the standing walls are interspersed with the circular, mud, fish-smoking ovens so characteristic of this part of the coast. More engaging than the ruined fort, however, is the view from the hill: on one side, Moree stretches out in all its corrugated-iron-roofed glory; on the other side is a beach as beautiful as any in Ghana, dotted with typically colourful fishing boats.

GETTING THERE Moree lies only 2km from the main Accra road (though it feels so isolated that it could be 200km). At the junction, you'll find some of the most dilapidated taxis in Ghana waiting to trundle down to Moree in blissful, pothole-dodging lethargy. Alternatively, direct shared taxis between Moree and Cape Coast take about 15 minutes.

WHERE TO STAY There is no formal accommodation in Moree, but you could ask about a room in a private house, or try camping on the beach.

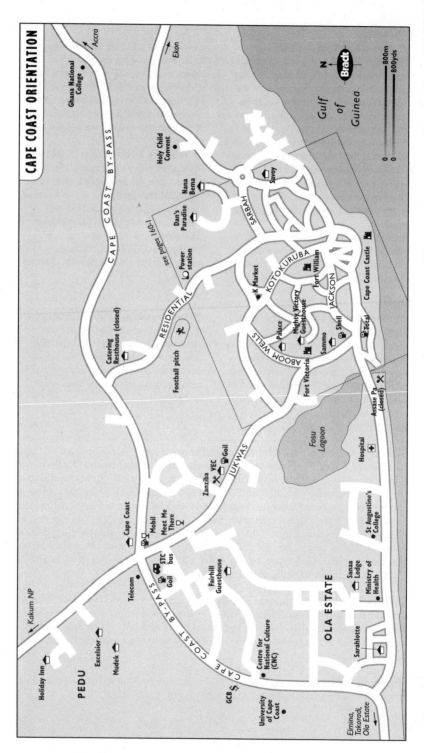

Accra

Ekon

Gulf of Guinea

N

Bradt

0   800m
0   800yds

Kakum NP

PEDU

Holiday Inn

Excelsior

Mudek

Telecom

Ghana National College

CAPE COAST BY-PASS

Holy Child Convent

Catering Resthouse (closed)

RESIDENTIAL

Football pitch

Power station

see pages 160-1

Dan's Paradise

Nana Bema

Savoy

SARBAH

Cape Coast

Mobil

Meet Me There

STC bus

Goil

Fairhill Guesthouse

GCB

University of Cape Coast

CAPE COAST BY-PASS

Centre for National Culture (CNC)

Elmina, Takoradi, Ola Estate

Sarahlotte

OLA ESTATE

Ministry of Health

Sanaa Lodge

St Augustine's College

Zanziba

VEC

Goil

JUKWAS

Fosu Lagoon

Hospital

K Market

KOTOKURUBA

Mighty Victory Guesthouse

Palace

ABOOM WELLS

Fort Victoria

Sammo

Shell

Fort William

JACKSON

Total

Assase Pa (closed)

Cape Coast Castle

8

Cape Coast, Elmina and Surrounds

While Ghana might have a less clearly defined tourist circuit than many African countries, the twin towns of Cape Coast and Elmina – situated less than 15km apart – form its obvious focal point. In addition to some great beaches, notably those at Brenu, Ampenyi and Coconut Grove, the region is notable for the castles at Cape Coast and Elmina, the largest and best-preserved buildings of their type in west Africa – and in the case of **Elmina Castle**, the oldest extant European building of any type in Africa. While historical sightseeing and lazing on the beach are the core tourist activities in this area, both of its major towns are lively and rewarding social centres, bound to be enjoyable to any who want to absorb themselves in the intricacies of modern urban Africa. For natural-history lovers, meanwhile, the regional highlight is likely to be **Kakum National Park**, renowned for its 40m-high canopy walkway, but also the most accessible place to seek out Ghana's elusive forest fauna.

CAPE COAST

The first capital of Britain's Gold Coast colony and modern capital of Ghana's Central Region, Cape Coast is steeped in history. Architecturally, it has little in common with the old Swahili towns of Africa's east coast; in atmosphere, however, the streets and alleys of the town centre share with, say, Lamu or Mombasa, a comfortable, lived-in feel, and a genuine sense of community – this is one of those towns where the distinction between administrative, business and residential districts is so blurred as to be meaningless. Cape Coast is a fascinating town to explore, its relative antiquity reflected not only in an endlessly surprising range of architectural styles spanning three centuries, but also in the organic shape of the old town, with roads hugging the curves of low hills.

Cape Coast was probably founded in the early 15th century. Its English name is a derivation of *Cabo Corso* – Short Cape – the name given to it by the Portuguese captains Joao de Santarem and Pedro de Escobar in 1471. Two contradictory traditions relate to the origin of Cape Coast's vernacular name, Oguaa. One tradition holds that Oguaa is a derivation of the Fante word *Gua* (market) and that Cape Coast was originally founded as a market town. The other explanation is that it derives from that of the village's founder, a hunter from Efutu remembered by the name Egya Oguaa.

While the truth of the local traditions is difficult to verify, we do know that by the time the British captains John Lok and William Towerson reached the Gulf of Guinea, in 1555 and 1556 respectively, Oguaa was a fishing village of roughly 20 small houses enclosed within a reed fence and presided over by a chief who went by the rather intriguing name of Don Juan. Nothing more is heard of Oguaa for two generations, until 1610, when a Portuguese lodge was built at an undetermined site on the outskirts of the village, which by that time probably extended from the beach north to what is now Jackson Street.

The rapidly growing village changed hands several times in the 17th century. In 1652, the abandoned Portuguese lodge was occupied by Swedes, then a mere six years later it was captured by the Danes, who signed a treaty with the Efutu paramount chief allowing them to construct a larger, triangular fort at nearby Amanful. The new fort fell briefly into the clutches of the Dutch – the dominant European power in the region at that time, with large forts at nearby Moree and Elmina – before it was taken over by Britain following the Anglo-Dutch War of 1664–65. From that time onwards, Cape Coast was Britain's headquarters on the Gulf of Guinea, and from 1672 onwards the British begin work on expanding and converting the fort to become modern-day Cape Coast Castle.

By the late 17th century, Cape Coast had grown from a small fishing village to one of the largest and most important trading ports along the coast. In 1693, the paramount chief of Efutu moved his capital from the inland village of Efutu to what is now Victoria Park, on the west side of Cape Coast Castle. Two years later, a visitor estimated the number of houses in the small town to exceed 500, and it is clear that by this time the modern town centre had more or less assumed its present shape.

Cape Coast's importance derived from its position as the link between the maritime trade routes of the European powers and the terrestrial trade routes through to the Sahel. Throughout the 18th century, Cape Coast's economy was dominated by its role at the heart of the trans-Atlantic slave trade – at any given time before 1807, when trading in slaves was abolished by the British parliament, there would have been up to 1,500 captured individuals awaiting shipment in the dungeons of the expanded Cape Coast Castle.

Following the re-establishment of legitimate trade from the Gulf of Guinea in 1821, all British castles along the coast were formally taken over by the British Crown and placed under the governor of Sierra Leone. Cape Coast served as the administrative headquarters of Britain's castles from 1828 until 1874, when it became the first seat of government of Britain's Gold Coast colony. Three years later, this role was assumed by Accra, and although Cape Coast has hardly slid into backwater status since, one still senses that the town centre would be instantly recognisable to a time traveller from the Victorian era.

GETTING THERE AND AWAY Three **STC buses** daily run directly between Accra and Cape Coast, leaving from the STC station next to the Goil garage on the Cape Coast bypass at 04.00, 11.00, and 13.00 (12.00 and 15.00 on Sun). Tickets cost US$4 and the trip takes roughly three hours in either direction, though the exact timing will depend greatly on how quickly the bus gets through the outskirts of Accra. The STC buses between Accra and Takoradi also pick passengers up at Cape Coast arriving every one or two hours from 06.30, and charging US$2–2.50 for a seat. There are also two buses daily between Takoradi and Kumasi, which pick up passengers at Cape Coast at 06.00 and 14.00 for US$6.50, though whether you get a seat on one of these depends on luck as no advance tickets are available at this stop.

There are also regular tro-tros from Cape Coast to most main coastal towns from Takoradi to Accra. Tro-tros to Accra and other destinations along the Accra road east of Cape Coast generally leave from the vicinity of the main lorry station on the junction of Sarbeh and Residential roads. Tro-tros to Kakum National Park leave from Kotoka Station near Kotokuraba Market. Tro-tros to Takoradi and points west along the coast leave from in front of Joyce Lovers Spot at the Elf garage at the junction of Elmina and Jukwa roads, or can be caught en route opposite the STC station.

Shared taxis to Elmina leave every few minutes from Commercial Road, about 50m from the Barclays Bank, and cost about US$0.40 per person – if you're in a rush, you can pay for the extra two or three seats and go straight away.

WHERE TO STAY
Upmarket

🏠 **Heaven's Executive Lodge** ☎ 042 30330/34999. Situated a few kilometres from the town centre along the main Accra road, this small family-run lodge is reputedly popular with local business travellers & was recommended to me by several Ghanaians. The accommodation is indeed very smart & comfortable – all rooms have dbl bed, AC, DSTV, fridge & phone – but it's no better than the lodges listed in the moderate bracket & seems steeply priced. The location counts against it too – though bonus points are due for the rare correct use of an apostrophe, which should keep the proofreader off my back! *US$55–65.*

🏠 **Sanaa Lodge** (30 rooms) ☎ 042 32570; f 042 32898; e lodgenaa@hotmail.com or

csmall1926@aol.com. This ostensibly upmarket monolith has definitely seen better days, but it remains the smartest option in Cape Coast. It lies a couple of kms west of the bridge across the Fosu Lagoon on a rise near the Ministry of Health. All rooms have AC, bath with an erratic hot water supply, DSTV, fridge & balcony, & rooms high enough to see over the utilitarian block in front have an attractive view over the beach in the distance. Facilities inc a large swimming pool, hairdressing salon, gift shop, conference centre & a good poolside grill, restaurant & cocktail bar. The service receives mixed feedback. *From US$60/75 sgl/dbl to US$85 for a family room, with group discounts available on request.*

Moderate

🏠 **Cape Coast Hotel** ☎ 042 32919. Although it lacks character & has an indifferent location on the main Accra road, the Cape Coast Hotel is a very pleasant tourist-class set-up & quite exceptional value for money at a negotiable US$35 for a large self-contained dbl with AC, fridge, DSTV, balcony & hot bath, or US$45 for a suite. There is a good outside bar but it is a good 30-minute walk from town, though you can easily pick up a shared or charter taxi at the traffic circle. *Negotiable; US$35, US$45.*

🏠 **Fairhill Guesthouse** ☎ 042 33322; f 042 33323. This homely but rather out-of-the-way hotel has very

good self-contained dbls for US$25–30 with b/fast, AC, hot water, fridge, TV & video (there's a library of videos to watch) & comes highly recommended for its helpful staff. It is a bit difficult to find, perched on an isolated hill in the marshy area to the west of Fosu Lagoon, but is clearly signposted along a 1.4km track which begins next to the Goil garage on the Cape Coast. Without private transport, you're advised to get a taxi to drop you off with your luggage, though once you know the way it's only 10 mins' walk from Jukwa Rd where you can pick up shared taxis to the town centre. *US$25–30.*

Budget

🏠 **Dan's Paradise Lodge** ☎ 042 32942. Cape Coast's oldest hotel (known locally as Dan's P) seems intent on growing old disgracefully, functioning in its dotage more as a leery annex to the popular weekend disco held on the ground floor than as a hotel in its own right. A kitsch art deco exterior is complemented by spectacularly tasteless décor (think crimson carpets & pillow-strewn beds large enough to sleep a rugby team), while the decidedly dodgy plumbing led one reader to complain of 'sparks flying from the shower head when the water was turned on'. It's not without some curiosity value, though you couldn't put a price on it: *Self-contained dbls cost US$10 at the time of the third edition, but although the hotel was clearly still functioning when this edition was researched, no-one was around to say how much it costs.*

🏠 **Fespa Hotel** ☎ 042 35886; e apsef2002@ yahoo.com. This new hotel, which lies on a shared taxi route along Jukwas Road between the town centre & the STC bus station, has received favourable mentions by a few readers. The Solace Spot around the corner

serves good chop & cheap drinks. *Twin rooms with fan cost US$9.50, sharing a bathroom, while self-contained dbls with AC cost US$12–16.*

🏠 **Mighty Victory Hotel** ☎ 042 30135. This relatively new hotel, though slightly more expensive than some of the competition, is the best budget pick in town & has been praised as such by numerous readers. The staff are very friendly & an inexpensive restaurant is attached. It's an easy walk to the centre of town. *Clean & airy, self-contained rooms with crisp white sheets, hot water & a powerful fan cost US$16/20 sgl/dbl, while similar rooms with AC cost US$25.*

🏠 **Oasis Beach Resort** Owned by a German-Turkish woman, this beach-front restaurant now also offers rooms & seems good value for money. The central location is very convenient & perfect for watching the fishermen go by & for swimming (leaving all your stuff in your room), though the sea can be quite dangerous here. *US$20 for a small self-contained dbl bungalow with fan (b/fast excluded), or US$6 pp for a more basic room using shared facilities.*

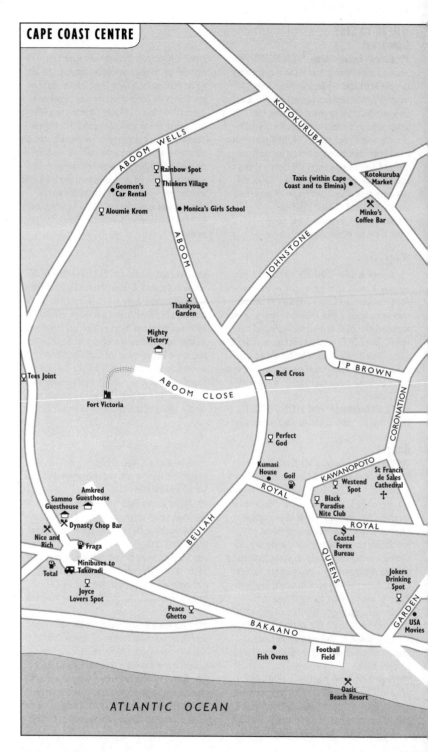

CAPE COAST CENTRE

KOTOKURUBA

ABOOM WELLS

Rainbow Spot

Thinkers Village

Geomen's
Car Rental

Aloumie Krom

Monica's Girls School

Taxis (within Cape
Coast and to Elmina)

Kotokuruba
Market

Minko's
Coffee Bar

ABOOM

JOHNSTONE

Thankyou
Garden

Mighty
Victory

J P BROWN

Tees Joint

ABOOM CLOSE

Red Cross

CORONATION

Fort Victoria

Perfect
God

Kumasi
House

Goil

KAWANOPOTO

St Francis
de Sales
Cathedral

ROYAL

Westend
Spot

Amkred
Guesthouse

Sammo
Guesthouse

Black
Paradise
Nite Club

Dynasty Chop Bar

BEULAH

ROYAL

Nice and
Rich

Fraga

Coastal
Forex
Bureau

QUEENS

Total

Minibuses to
Takoradi

Jokers
Drinking
Spot

Joyce
Lovers Spot

GARDEN

Peace
Ghetto

BAKAANO

USA
Movies

Fish Ovens

Football
Field

Oasis
Beach Resort

ATLANTIC OCEAN

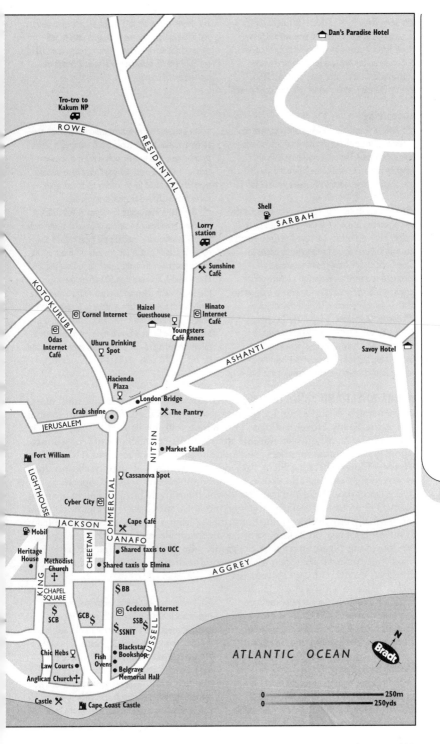

Dan's Paradise Hotel

Tro-tro to
Kakum NP

ROWE

RESIDENTIAL

Shell

SARBAH

Lorry
station

Sunshine
Café

KOTOKURUBA

Cornel Internet

Haizel
Guesthouse

Hinato
Internet
Café

ASHANTI

Savoy Hotel

Odas
Internet
Café

Uhuru Drinking
Spot

Youngsters
Café Annex

Hacienda
Plaza

Crab shrine

London Bridge

The Pantry

JERUSALEM

NITSIN

Market Stalls

Fort William

Cassanova Spot

LIGHTHOUSE

Cyber City

COMMERCIAL

Mobil

JACKSON

Cape Café

Heritage
House

CHEETAM

CANAFO

Shared taxis to UCC

Methodist
Church

Shared taxis to Elmina

AGGREY

KING

CHAPEL
SQUARE

BB

SCB

GCB

Cedecom Internet

SSB

SSNIT

RUSSELL

Chic Hebs

Fish
Ovens

Blackstar
Bookshop

ATLANTIC OCEAN

Law Courts

Belgrave
Memorial Hall

Anglican Church

Castle

Cape Coast Castle

N

Bradt

0 ———————— 250m
0 ———————— 250yds

Savoy Hotel 042 32805/416; f 042 32804;
e savoyhotel@yahoo.com. The time-warped Savoy Hotel has long been a favourite with budget travellers, & it continues to offer very comfortable central accommodation at cheaper rates than the Mighty Victory. There is a good internet café next door, as well as a decent restaurant that can be persuaded to serve you in the balcony bar overlooking the street. *Self-contained dbls with fan & hot water are good value at US$12 or US$18 with AC, while a variety of suites & chalets are available at US$23–60.*

Shoestring

Amkred Guesthouse 042 32868. Just next door to Sammo's, this dark but pleasant little hotel seems like pretty good value. The bedrooms themselves are generally clean but some of the bathrooms are questionable. *Large, self-contained rooms for US$9.50/12 sgl/dbl with fan, or US$15 with AC.*

Red Cross Hostel 024 32395. With its reasonably central location opposite the turn-off to the Mighty Victory Hotel, the unfussy but clean Red Cross Hostel vies with Sammo's as the best shoestring option in Cape Coast. Secure triple rooms set around a concreted courtyard are subject to a bizarre pricing structure: *US$6 for sgl occupancy or a couple, US$7 for two people of the same gender, & US$8 for trpl occupancy.*

Sammo Guesthouse 042 33242. This pink 3-storey building, which lies conveniently close to a tro-tro station & only 10 minutes' walk from Cape Coast Castle, has been for some years been the most popular local cheapie. Sammo's receives mixed but mostly positive reviews from travellers, & although the accommodation is a bit run-down & cramped, it is still fantastic value. The breezy rooftop bar is an excellent spot for a drink & meal, & a good place to meet other travellers. *US$3.50/6 for an ordinary sgl/dbl with fan & shared bath or US$7–8 for a self-contained dbl.*

Sarahlotte Guesthouse (6 rooms) 042 32871. If you don't mind being a little out of town, this extremely friendly guesthouse is probably the most relaxed budget option in Cape Coast. It lies opposite the beach in Ola Estate, about 4km from the town centre along the Elmina road, & no more than 500m from the intersection with the main Takoradi–Accra highway. The family which runs the place is happy to prepare meals, or you could eat in town – all shared taxis & tro-tros between Cape Coast & Elmina run right past it. *From a dbl with shared bath & fan for US$9 to a small self-contained dbl with fan, TV & fridge for US$14.*

✖ **WHERE TO EAT AND DRINK** In addition to the restaurants listed below, most of the smarter hotels in and around Cape Coast serve good food. Of the more central places, the **Savoy Hotel** has a good restaurant, with meals in the US$2–3 range which can be served outside. Another attractive place is the **Sammo Guesthouse**, whose breezy rooftop bar offers good food and a nice view over town. The **Mighty Victory Hotel** offers excellent fish and lobster dishes at slightly cheaper than average prices, although the spotless indoor dining room lacks atmosphere.

For street food, head to Ntsin Road, which positively buzzes at night, exuding the aura of sociability and community typical of Cape Coast. During the day, you can normally buy fresh coconuts for drinking from a vendor who stands in front of the Mobil garage on Jackson Street, while pineapples and other fruits are sold by vendors along Ntsin Street near the castle. The orange and white Dynasty Fast Food chop bar just outside Sammo's is recommended for particularly fine omelette breakfasts served with fresh bread.

✖ **Aloumie Krom Garden Bar and Restaurant** Some distance from the town centre, this drinking hole is set in a closed courtyard, so it can get rather stifling, but otherwise it's a good place for a chilled beer & local meal.

✖ **Baab's Juices** Since springing up close to the site of the old Coconut Delight, this vegetarian snack and juice bar a few steps from London Bridge has attracted warm recommendations from a number of readers. The menu incs fresh fruit smoothies, vegetable pies, & soya, tofu & wheat kebabs. Of great interest to travelling vegetarians, it also has a health food shelf selling packaged goods such as tofu, wheat chunks, powdered soy milk, brown sugar, honey & molasses.

✖ **Cape Café** (aka **Women's Centre**) This popular & well-established restaurant off Commercial St opens from 08.00 to 20.00 to serve a good range of local & Western meals & pizzas for around US$4.50 a plate. It's a bit gloomy & no alcohol is available, but the room is well ventilated & the service is friendly, & all proceeds are directed towards providing shelter for the homeless. An attached shop stocks excellent quality local fabrics.

✗ **Castle Restaurant** This popular restaurant, with its breezy beach-front location overlooking the waves crashing against Cape Coast Castle, re-opened in early 2002 after having being razed by fire a few years earlier. It's an excellent spot for a drink, & the extensive menu is reasonably priced, with most dishes in the US$3.50–4.50 range or slightly more for fish. Service can be slow but otherwise reader feedback has been generally positive, with one person rating it as 'definitely the best all-round package in Ghana'.

✗ **Courthouse Canteen** Situated in the Court Building less than 100m from the entrance to Cape Coast Castle, this canteen serves substantial portions of inexpensive local cuisine in a functional but perfectly adequate setting with clean toilets.

✗ **Hacienda Plaza** This popular outdoor nightspot next to the Crab Shrine & London Bridge seems to change hands (& name) with every edition of this book, but can always be relied upon for a cold drink, if not some simple food & blaring highlife. The current management offers good kebabs for around US$3 a plate.

✗ **Oasis Beach Resort** Situated practically next door to the Castle Restaurant, this central beachfront restaurant & w/end nightclub has a similarly attractive setting, as well as a good music system & an extensive cocktail menu making it an excellent place to watch the sunset over a drink. The food is similar in price & standard to the Castle, with pizzas, burgers & steaks between US$2.50 & US$4, or fish dishes for US$6.50, but the perennially slow service has come in for plenty of stick from readers.

WHAT TO SEE

Cape Coast Castle (*Set aside around 2 hours to see it properly. US$6.50 for non-Ghanaians, US$4 for students, and including an emphatically recommended 45-minute tour, while photography attracts an additional US$0.50 charge*) This World Heritage Site is reputed to have been one of the largest slave-holding sites in the world during the colonial era, where Ghanaians – many of them traded to the British by Ashantes in return for alcohol and guns – were stored before being cramped into returning merchant ships and deported to a life of captive labour. Sited on the edge of town overlooking a rocky stretch of coast with crashing waves, this white-washed building is far more attractive than you feel a place with its history ought to be. But once below ground, in the claustrophobic dungeons which saw tens of thousands of Ghanaians during the peak of that barbaric era, it is a grim and sobering place indeed.

Once inside, the museum houses an absorbing sequence of displays charting the origin and mechanisms of the slave trade, the scale of the resultant diaspora, and its aftermath in the hands of inspirational black leaders such as Marcus Garvey and Martin Luther King. But, ultimately, it is the time you spend in the slave dungeons that cuts most closely, their stone walls still marked by the desperate scratching of those imprisoned within them. There are three dungeons in all, all grimly efficient in design. The oldest was built before 1790 on the southeastern bastion, and was followed with the male dungeon below Dalzel's Tower in 1792. The female dungeon is on the eastern wall, near the exit to the sea that bore the grim nickname 'Door of No Return'. A couple of years ago, a symbolic invitation was issued to two descendants of slaves that saw them return through the door of no return, thus effectively breaking the chain. There is a sign on the other side, now, that says 'Door of Return'.

The castle itself – a squat, solid fortress of ramps and stairs and parapets – is thought to stand on the site of the Swedish Fort Carolusborg, built from wood in 1653 and fortified with stone the next year (note that there is little foundation for the claim that the original Portuguese lodge at Cape Coast stood on this site). After Cape Coast was captured by Britain in 1665, the fort was expanded to be comparable in size and strength with the nearby Dutch fort at Elmina, and in the 1680s the slave dungeons were constructed in such a way that they were accessible only from the seaward side of the fort. A second phase of expansion, prompted in part by the notorious leakiness of the roof, took place roughly between 1760 and

1795. By the end of this period, the castle had assumed its modern, loosely pentagonal shape, and practically no traces of the original Swedish fort remained.

Those buried in the courtyard of the castle include the Reverend Philip Kwakwe (1741–1816), a native of Cape Coast who became the first Anglican priest of African origin. Also buried here are the novelist Letitia Elizabeth Landon (1802–38) and her husband George MacLean (1801–47), governor of Cape Coast from 1830 until 1843 and Judicial Assessor of the town from 1843 until his death.

Around the old town Several of the hills in Cape Coast have been fortified at some point in their history. Only two such out-forts now survive, forts Victoria and William, both part of a chain of lookout posts which were used for signalling purposes, and both of which are still clearly visible from the governor's rooms at the castle. Fort Victoria, to the northeast of the castle, was constructed in 1837 on the site of a ruined fort built in 1712 and formerly known as 'Phipp's Tower'. On Dawson's Hill, Fort William is now a lighthouse and has been since 1855, but it was constructed over the older Smith's Tower, built of mud and stone in 1820. Both forts are in good condition and welcome visitors.

Otherwise, the centre of Cape Coast may lack individual landmarks, but it is certainly well endowed with Victorian-era buildings, especially along Commercial and Jackson streets and Beulah Lane – and there is even a bust of Queen Victoria standing in her namesake park to prove it. Many of these old buildings are solidly constructed brick homes with an enclosed upper-floor balcony. The area around Dawson's Hill is one of the best-preserved parts of the old town, with Coronation Street in particular boasting several two- and three-storey buildings architecturally characteristic of Cape Coast in the mid to late 19th century. Particularly notable is the now derelict building near the junction with Commercial Street, built as a hotel in the 1880s and later a convent.

Possibly the oldest unfortified building in Cape Coast is the three-storey former Government House opposite the Methodist church off Jackson Street. It is known that this building was leased to the government by one Caroline Jackson in 1850, but it is unclear how much older it actually is – it seems reasonable to assume it was built before or during the period 1817–22 (when John Hope-Smith was governor), and it may conceivably have been built in the late 18th century. Government House has recently been restored and re-named Heritage House. It now houses the tourist information office, as well as an internet café and drinking spot.

Near to this, on Royal Lane, the former Convent of St Mary is perhaps the best-preserved building of its kind in Cape Coast. Originally built by an Ashanti prince in around 1850, this building was bought by a community of nuns in 1891 and served as a convent until 1975, since when it has been only intermittently occupied. It currently houses the Coast Forex Bureau.

There are a few *posuban* shrines in Cape Coast, but none is very impressive. At the centre of the traffic circle on the junction of Ashanti and Commercial roads there is a small *posuban*-like sculpture of a crab. Although recently placed there, this statue has a great significance as the crab is one of the important symbols of Cape Coast – one tradition has it that the village was first founded because of the good crab meat available, and that it was originally called Kotokuraba ('Crab Village'), still the name of the town's main market and the nearby tro-tro station.

Near the above junction, London Bridge is a rather odd and unimposing little bridge dating to the late 19th century and appropriately garnished with painted Union Jacks and the like – it's worth crossing if only to have a fruit juice at Baab's juices.

Gramophone Records Museum and Research Centre Established in 1994 as a non-profit organisation by musicologist Kwame Sarpong, this unique museum contains a vast collection of recordings made solely in Ghana by principally Ghanaian musicians, and is well worth visiting if you are interested in Ghanaian/highlife music. The core collection consists of 18,000 highlife recordings from the mid 1960s and earlier on 78rpm shellac discs, representing more than 700 different artists, but there are also more than 2,500 old vinyl recordings.

At present, the museum is based at Cape Coast Centre for National Culture on the Cape Coast bypass, but it may be relocated to Fort St Jago in Elmina in the near future. The museum is in the process of developing a website, in conjunction with UNESCO, entirely dedicated to Ghanaian culture and cultural issues, which will serve as a useful resource for future travellers. There is also a plan to digitalise many of the key recordings for an online archive. For more details, contact Mr Sarpong at sarpongkwame@yahoo.com.

Castle View Fishers' Association (✆ *34057*) Located directly opposite the Castle, this association has bought its own very large canoe and outfitted it with lifejackets and fishermen who are willing to be available to take people out to sea. The cost per person will be about US$10, and trips will leave either from the Door of No Return to see Cape Coast Castle or leave from there to go over to Elmina Lagoon.

Women in Progress Workshops (✆ *024 0467 or 042 36883; www.womeninprogress. org; costs range from US$12–18 pp*) This is an NGO developed by a former Peace Corps volunteer, working with local women to improve their handcrafts for export and local sale. It has developed several different half- to full-day workshops – concentrating on batik-making, Ghanaian cuisine, dancing/drumming (run by the only woman master drummer in Ghana), fishing, village life/smoking fish, helping with nets, etc.

Assin Manso This small town, which lies about an hour from Cape Coast along the Kumasi road, was formerly an important stop along the slave-trade routes of the 18th and 19th centuries. It is located on the banks of the Ndonkor Nsuo ('Slave River'), where slaves were bathed and checked for fitness before being taken to the coast for shipment out of Africa. As a symbolic gesture, the bodies of two slaves – Samuel Carson from the USA and a woman known as Crystal from Jamaica – were flown to Ghana in July 1998 to be re-buried here. Visitors are welcome to see the graves and to wander along the riverbank. Regular tro-tros leave in this direction from Kotokoruba Station in Cape Coast, and they will drop you outside the large building which serves as the seat of the traditional council, where it would be courteous to pay your respects before you look around.

In early 2004, a new Visitors Centre with toilets and public-use spaces was being built at Assin Manso by the Ministry of Tourism, the first step in a major rehabilitation of this site scheduled over the next year or two. Recommendations for development include interpretive displays that build on those at Cape Coast Castle stories, a juice bar using locally produced fruits, a shop selling batik and other garments made by a local women's sewing co-op, and drumming displays. Long-term plans include improving the river area with a boardwalk. The Chief's Palace will also have at least one room open to display paraphernalia related to the Throne, and two simple rooms using a shared bath will be made available to overnight guests for around US$5–10, with meals also available. An entrance fee will be charged to go to the local community.

SHOPPING
Bookshops The excellent Black Star Bookshop, 30m from the castle on Commercial Street stocks an unexpectedly extensive range of new imported

8

paperbacks – most of which cost around US$3.50–4 – along with some secondhand titles which can be bought for US$1–2.50 or exchanged for a nominal fee. A somewhat more limited selection of cheap paperback novels can be found just up the road at the Methodist Bookshop.

Two excellent and inexpensive books giving a historical background to Cape Coast are sometimes available at the Castle curio shop. These are the *Cape Coast and Elmina Handbook*, edited by Kwame Arhin of Legon University (Institute of African Studies, 1995) and *Cape Coast in History* by James Erskine Graham Jr (Anglican Printing Press, 1994). Here, you can also ask about the useful *Central Region Tourist Map* with large maps of both Cape Coast and Elmina on the reverse. A second branch of Black Star Bookshop recently opened opposite the Elmina Beach Resort near Elmina.

Curios In the same building as the relocated Cape Café (see page 162), **Global Mama's** is a shop connected to Women in Progress. It sells beautiful handmade and batik clothing for kids and adults, not to mention a few more other fun things. It's pricey by Ghanaian standards.

OTHER PRACTICALITIES

Car rental Geoman's Car Rental (↘ *042 31187 or 020 8159433;* e *geomans117@hotmail.com*) on Aboom Wells Road offers chauffeured day trips to Kakum National Park for US$50 per group, for a decent vehicle including driver and fuel but not park fees. It can also arrange transfers to Takoradi (*US$50/100 one-way/return*), Busua (*US$80/160*), Accra (*US$100/180*) and various other towns around Ghana, as well as straightforward daily rentals at US$8 per hour within town or US$80 per day further afield, excluding fuel and driver's expenses. Self-drive rental is available, but at a high premium due to the insurance costs. Reader feedback has been pretty positive, although it seems to be worth agreeing an exact itinerary in advance, as well as who will be paying for the driver's lunch.

Foreign exchange All the major banks are represented, with the Standard Chartered on Chapel Square normally offering the best rate of exchange for cash and travellers' cheques, no commission charged. Barclays Bank, on Commercial Road, generally offers a poorer rate, but you can draw local currency on a Visa card at the ATM outside. A second Visa ATM also recently opened at the SG-SSB bank about 25m closer to Cape Coast Castle. There are several forex bureaux dotted around town, of which Coast Forex on Royal Road offers the best rate for cash, though at the time of writing it was no better than the bank rate.

Internet There are now several internet cafés in Cape Coast, although all of them can be pretty slow at times. The best is probably Ocean View (*042 45782 or 042 40020*), a large, airy, second-floor room on Commercial Road, with plenty of computers. Several other services lie just north of the Crab Shrine, with Odas and Cornell internet cafés on Kotokoruba Road, and Hinato internet café on Residential Road. There is also an internet café in Heritage House, the same building that houses the tourist office.

Tourist information The regional tourist office in Heritage House is probably the best source of up-to-date information about Cape Coast and other places in Central Region, though the not unfamiliar prevailing attitude seems to be that all the answers must be in the handful of pamphlets and maps they stock. It's not that you'll meet with an unhelpful response, it's just that it doesn't appear to have occurred to anybody involved that tourists visit a tourist information office to get information.

DOMAMA ROCK SHRINE

Consisting of a cool three-storey-high natural cavern formed by one large rock balanced on three others, the Domama Rock Shrine is associated locally with a paramount deity known as Bosom Kese. A community-based ecotourist project has recently been set up in the area, offering both a guided visit up a near-vertical rock face to the sacred cavern for around US$1 per head, and canoe trips on the 500m wide, forest-fringed Pra River for US$2 per head (except during the dry season or on Wednesdays). The river offers good fishing, birding and butterfly-viewing. A seven-bedroom guesthouse has been constructed to accommodate tourists. Accommodation cost US$3 per night, and local meals can be prepared on request.

Domama is most easily visited as an extension of a trip to Kakum. From the main national park entrance and canopy walk, drive north for a further 8km or so to Ankaako junction, where a left turn will lead to Atobiase junction after about 15km. Turn right here, and you will reach Domama after approximately 5km. Using public transport from Cape Coast, head to Kotokraba Bus Station and ask for one of the tro-tros that ply the route through to Atobiase junction. The road to Domama is often in very poor condition during the rainy season. Pre-booking is not necessary for guided tours, but it is recommended that accommodation reservations are made in advance. These and other enquiries are best directed to the Friends of the Earth Society in Takoradi (❭ *031 21050;* e *friends@africaonline.com.gh*).

In February 2003, Sue Randell wrote: 'Domama was well worth visiting, but you need to be prepared. We arrived at the guesthouse at midday and picked up a Dutch couple who had been waiting for a taxi or lift for two hours. They had arrived by tro-tro, but couldn't get any further. It was a 15–20-minute drive, on a difficult road, to the start of the walk. I recommend long trousers and/or insect repellent for the hour's walk to the shrine through the forest. The walk to the river is quite long too, but not as difficult. The river trip was spectacular, but the canoe boys took a while to come. Beware of overloading the canoe: we had to help keep balance and bail out. In the rainy season it becomes very deep and some parts are dangerous then. We got out while the boys went round one stretch of 'white water', but had to stay in for another. Not for the faint-hearted. We got back at about 16.30, so don't leave it too late to start. Take your own water.'

KAKUM NATIONAL PARK

Less than an hour from Cape Coast by private vehicle or tro-tro, Kakum National Park – along with the contiguous Assin Attandaso Game Production Area and Pra Suhien Forest Reserve – protects what is among the most extensive rainforest habitats in Ghana, covering a total area of 607km², as well as possibly the most accessible to casual visitors. The predominant vegetation type in Kakum is moist, semi-deciduous forest, which like any true rainforest is characterised by high rainfall figures (peaking between May and December) and a humidity level averaging around 90%. Unfortunately, however, much of the forest protected in Kakum is no longer in pristine condition, as a result of extensive logging, particularly between 1975 and 1989, though some logging still occurs to this day. In addition to harbouring a great wealth of plant and animal species, Kakum is also an important watershed – the rivers that rise in the forest provide water to more than 130 towns and villages, Cape Coast among them.

The diversity of Kakum's flora is such that there are parts of the forest where the number of plant species per hectare comfortably exceeds 200. This vegetation is divided into five broad layers. The sparsely vegetated floor of the forest interior is

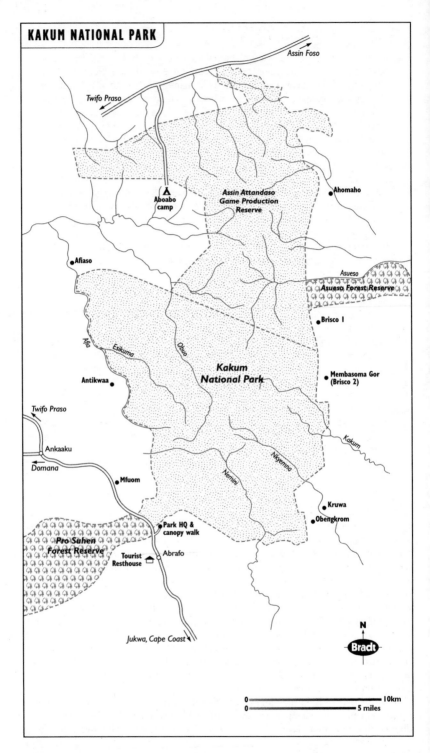

KAKUM NATIONAL PARK

Assin Foso

Twifo Praso

Aboabo camp

Assin Attandaso
Game Production
Reserve

Ahomaho

Afiaso

Asueso

Asueso Forest Reserve

Brisco 1

Afia

Esikuma

Obuo

Kakum
National Park

Membasoma Gor
(Brisco 2)

Antikwaa

Twifo Praso

Kakum

Ankaaku

Domana

Nkyenno

Mfuom

Nemini

Kruwa

Obengkrom

Pro Suhen
Forest Reserve

Park HQ &
canopy walk

Tourist
Resthouse

Abrafo

Jukwa, Cape Coast

N

Bradt

0 ——————— 10km
0 ——————— 5 miles

dominated by herbaceous plants, above which a layer of shrubs reaches up to about 4m. The upper three layers together form the canopy: the lowest layer consists of spreading trees reaching a height of around 18m, above which lies the main closed canopy of larger trees, typically around 40m high, and then finally there are the emergent trees, many of them very old, reaching a height of up to 65–70m.

The Kakum complex of reserves protects at least 40 large mammal species, including the country's densest population of forest elephant, as well as giant forest hog, six types of duiker, bushbuck, bongo, various flying squirrels, leopard, spot-nosed monkey, Diana monkey, mona monkey, and black-and-white and olive colobus. None of these mammals is likely to be seen by day visitors, but it is possible to arrange overnight camping trips to Antikwaa Camp, where elephants are encountered with some frequency. Checklists of the park's large mammals, birds and reptiles, together with detailed notes and line drawings of the more common and interesting species, are included in Roell, Helsens and Nicolet's 124-page *Field Guide to the Kakum National Park*, available at the headquarters for around US$3 – though do note that the bird checklist in this field guide is incomplete and includes several erroneous species.

Kakum is an excellent place to see forest birds, with a checklist of 266 confirmed and another 50 unconfirmed species, though to see even a tiny proportion of these you would need to spend a couple of days in the area and do some early-morning guided walks – the Aboabo section is particularly recommended for birdwatching. Kakum harbours eight bird species of global conservation concern (white-breasted guineafowl, brown-cheeked hornbill, yellow-casqued hornbill, yellow-footed honeyguide, green-tailed bristlebill, yellow-throated olive greenbul, rufous-winged illadopsis and copper-tailed glossy starling) as well as seven other forest hornbill species. The best birding guide is Robert Akwesi Ntakor, who comes highly recommended.

The main tourist attraction at Kakum is the much-publicised canopy walk, which was constructed in 1995 with the support of USAID, and remains, to the best of my knowledge, unique in Africa. The canopy walk consists of a 350m-long, 40m-high wood-and-rope walkway suspended between seven trees and broken up by a number of viewing platforms. It's a little gimmicky – and gets busy at weekends when some tourists feel frogmarched across it – but it is undoubtedly good fun and offers a rare opportunity to actually look into the forest canopy, a breathtaking experience in itself (though emphatically *not* for those with a poor head for heights), and one that will immediately excite birdwatchers. Given the popularity of the attraction, you'll get the most from the experience by being at the headquarters as soon as possible after the opening time of 08.00, or better still, if you spend the night in Abrafo, you can arrange the previous afternoon to be met by a guide before 08.00, when everything is quiet and the forest is at its most atmospheric. Timing aside, the extent to which you'll enjoy the canopy walk will probably depend greatly on whether the fee (US$9 per person for non-Ghanaians, US$2.50 for Ghanaians or US$5 for volunteers and students with proof of their status) is small change or relatively expensive within the context of your travel budget.

Before heading out on the walk, it's worth spending a few minutes looking around the informative natural-history displays in the information centre. The extent to which the canopy walk dominates thinking around the park headquarters can become mildly irritating (recent comments include 'a regular tourist-mill', 'not worth visiting' and 'more of a tourist gimmick than an interesting sight'), but this richly diverse forest has so much more to offer than one novelty, and those with the time and an interest in natural history are encouraged to think about doing a more general walk. In theory this will cost US$4 per person for the first hour plus US$1 per extra hour, and you can arrange on the previous afternoon to be met

HANS COTTAGE BOTEL

042 91456/7 or 0244 322522; f *042 91457;* e *hcottage@yahoo.com;*
www.hansbotel.com

This very attractive and original set-up, situated at Efutu about 8km from Cape Coast centre along the road to Kakum National Park, is not only an excellent place to spend a night or two, but is well worth visiting as a day trip from Cape Coast, and would make a convenient brunch stop *en route* back to Cape Coast after a morning walk at Kakum. The centrepiece of the 'botel' is a double-storey wood-and-thatch restaurant built on a stilted platform over a small lake and connected to the shore by several wooden walkways.

The main attraction here is the dozen or so crocodiles resident in the lake, easily lured to the surface by throwing bread in the water to attract the fish on which they feed. The lake also supports a plethora of colourful agama lizards and a varied avifauna. Aurally, things are dominated by the ceaseless chattering and swizzling that emanates from various weaver colonies around the lake (we identified village, orange weaver and Vieillot's black weaver), but several types of kingfisher also appear to be resident, and herons and egrets are well represented – patient photographers with adequate lenses could find it very rewarding.

The rooms form a separate unit about 100m from the platform, centred around a residents-only swimming pool. Different types of room are available to suit most budgets, all including breakfast: a smart self-contained room with AC, fan, DSTV and hot water costs US$35/50 single/double, while suites cost US$95 and at the lower end of the scale self-contained rooms with fan cost only US$25/35 single/double and 'backpacker' doubles with fan using hot communal showers cost US$20. Camping is permitted at US$5 a head, although breakfast is not included. Feedback about the accommodation is variable, with some readers complaining that it is overpriced, but few would dispute that the restaurant is a great place to sit. It serves a good variety of reasonably priced meals for around US$5, as well as chilled drinks of every variety, though it can be a little slow, so people using it as a lunchtime stop should allow at least 90 minutes. An internet café with six computers can be used for free by hotel residents and for a fee by day visitors.

Hans Cottage Botel lies to the left of the main Kakum road at Efutu. Coming from Cape Coast, you can't really miss it if you have private transport or are sitting in the left side of a tro-tro. To find a tro-tro from Cape Coast heading in this direction, go to Kotoka Station.

before 08.00 the next day – the early morning is the best time to see birds and monkeys (though not butterflies, of which 400 species have been recorded in the area, since they tend to peak in activity in the mid to late morning). In practice, according to some readers, the only way the guides will actually agree to do a guided walk is if it is tagged on to the canopy walk, presumably for financial reasons.

Recent developments at Kakum include an overnight stay on a camping platform close to the park headquarters (see *Where to stay*), as well as guided night walks, which cost the same as other guided walks.

A more alluring option still is to overnight at a little-visited tree platform, two hours into Kakum from Mosomagor, a village perched on the edge of the park 40km from Cape Coast along the Assin Foso road. A nominal entrance fee covers a tour of the village itself, and additional fees are charged for guided day and evening hikes into the forest or to the platform. The very friendly village is also famed locally for its Nyamebekyere Kukyekukyeku Orchestra, which plays traditional music on wind instruments crafted from local bamboo. Performances can be arranged for US$15 for up to five people, and musical lessons are also available. A mosquito net is provided and in the dry season no tent is required, but it is best to make any arrangements a few days in advance; for contact numbers and details of accommodation in the village see *Where to stay* below.

GETTING THERE AND AWAY The Kakum National Park headquarters is clearly signposted along the Jukwa road roughly 33km from Cape Coast. You can easily get there either by chartering a shared taxi or by using a tro-tro heading to Jukwa from Kotoka Station in Cape Coast. With an early start, you can be at the headquarters when it opens at 08.00.

WHERE TO STAY AND EAT There is no accommodation within walking distance of the park headquarters, but travellers with their own tent can **camp** on a tree platform ten minutes' walk away for the cedi equivalent of US$5 per person. Camping equipment (net, sleeping bag and mat) can also be hired at an additional US$3 per person. Fires aren't permitted at the campsite, so you will have to eat at the restaurant in the park headquarters.

The **restaurant** at the park headquarters has improved greatly of late, serving a variety of local and continental dishes in the US$4–6 range, as well as cold drinks and beer. Anyone staying overnight on the tree platform should bring their own food however, as the restaurant closes quite early.

It would be possible to use **Hans Cottage Botel** (see opposite) as a base from which to explore Kakum. There is no real logistical advantage in doing this, as opposed to heading there as a day trip directly from Cape Coast, but the atmosphere of the Hans Cottage does seem more in keeping with that of Kakum than does anywhere in Cape Coast. At **Mosomagor** village on the eastern side of the park, a small local resthouse charges about US$4 per person for basic accommodation. Meals can be provided. It is also possible to walk out to a tree platform two hours from the village and sleep in the forest at a charge of US$8 per person. For more details, contact the Ciltad/Agoro Project Management (*PO Box 711, Cape Coast;* ✆ *042 30265/7;* f *042 30264;* e *ghcr@ghana.com*).

Another alternative for the future will be the **Monkey Forest Resort** (*www.monkeyforestresort.com*), currently being constructed by a Dutch couple about two kilometres from Kakum park entrance. The plans are for a group of ten huts set around a swimming pool, overlooking the village of Frami and with a small zoo attached.

ELMINA

Situated on the thin strip of land that separates the shallow Benya Lagoon from the Atlantic, Elmina is a fascinating and strikingly attractive small town, at least the equal of nearby Cape Coast in terms of historical sightseeing, though often overlooked by tourists in favour of its larger neighbour. The town started life as a fishing and salt-producing village roughly 700 years ago and, despite having served as first the Portuguese and later the Dutch headquarters in west Africa, an overgrown fishing village is basically what Elmina remains today, the rich harvest of the surrounding ocean supplemented by the production of salt from the brackish lagoon. Back in its economic heyday, however, Elmina lay at the heart of the west African gold trade.

Known by the Portuguese as *Aldea das Duas Partes* ('Village of Two Parts' – a reference to the lagoon), Elmina has probably gone by its modern name only since the Dutch took over in 1637. Nevertheless, the name Elmina is almost certainly derived from a Portuguese term which referred to this whole stretch of coast – *Da*

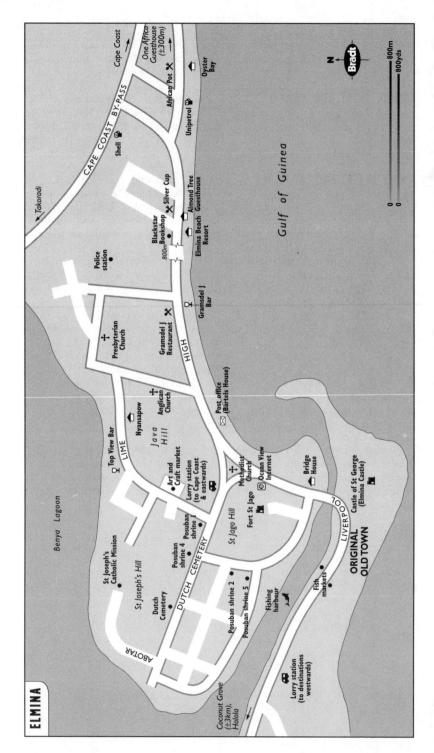

ELMINA

Benya Lagoon

Takoradi →

CAPE COAST BY-PASS

Cape Coast

One Africa Guesthouse (±300m) →

African Pot ✕

Oyster Bay

Unipetrol

Shell

Silver Cup ✕

Blackstar Bookshop

Almond Tree

Elmina Beach Guesthouse Resort

800m

Police station

Presbyterian Church

Gramsdel ✕ Restaurant

Gramsdel Bar

HIGH

Gulf of Guinea

Top View Bar

LIME

Nyansapow

Anglican Church

Java Hill

Art and Craft market

Lorry station (to Cape Coast & eastwards)

Post Office (Bartels House)

Methodist Church

Ocean View Internet

Bridge House

St Joseph's Catholic Mission

St Joseph's Hill

Dutch Cemetery

Posuban shrine 4

DUTCH CEMETERY

Posuban shrine 1

St Jago Hill

Fort St Jago

ABOTAR

Posuban shrine 2

Posuban shrine 5

Fishing harbour

Fish markets

LIVERPOOL

Castle of St George (Elmina Castle)

ORIGINAL OLD TOWN

Coconut Grove (±3km), Holola

Lorry station (to destinations westwards)

N

Bradt

0   800m
0   800yds

Costa de el Mina de Ouro ('The Coast of Gold Mines') – though some sources suggest, without any apparent foundation, that Elmina is derived from the Arabic phrase *el mina* ('the harbour').

Traditional accounts suggest that Elmina has been settled since at least 1300, when it was chosen as the capital of Kwaa Amankwaa, the founder of the Edina state, originally a matrilineal chieftaincy though its monarch was selected on patrilineal lines after 1680. The site was probably chosen because of the Benya Lagoon, an excellent venue for salt production. An important trade route developed in prehistoric times between the salt mines of Elmina and the goldfields of the Bono Empire (around what are today Tarkwa and Obuasi), and it was due to this that the Portuguese were able to buy gold with such ease when they first landed at Elmina in 1471.

Our best idea of Elmina's wealth and political set-up prior to the arrival of the Portuguese comes from a contemporary account of a meeting held in 1482 between the Portuguese captain Diogo de Azambuja and King Caramansa (probably an erroneous transcription of the common Edina royal name Kwamina Ansah). The narrator writes that Caramansa 'was seated on a high chair dressed in a jacket of brocade, with a golden collar of precious stones ... his legs and arms covered with golden bracelets and rings ... and in his plaited beard golden bars' and that 'his chiefs were all dressed in silk [and] wore rings and golden jewels on their heads and beards'. The same account goes on to describe the king as a man 'of good understanding, both by nature and by his dealing with the crews of the trading ships' and that 'he possessed a clear judgement ... as one who not only desired to understand what was proposed to him, who not only listened to the translation of the interpreter, but watched each gesture made by Diogo de Azambuja; and while this continued, both he and his men were completely silent; no-one as much as spat, so perfectly disciplined were they'.

In 1482, with the permission of Caramansa, the Portuguese began work on the earliest incarnation of the Castle of St George, a rather humble building by comparison with the modern castle. Within five years, several Portuguese traders had settled around the fort, and Elmina had been elevated to city status by the king of Portugal. Elmina remained the Portuguese centre of operations for more than 150 years, though their grip on the fortress gradually waned towards the end of this period. In August 1637, St Jago Hill was taken by the Dutch and the castle was bombarded by cannons, forcing a Portuguese surrender that effectively ended their period of influence in west Africa.

From 1637 until 1872 (when Holland sold all her Gold Coast forts to Britain), Elmina was in many respects the Dutch equivalent to Cape Coast. The Castle of St George was substantially expanded shortly after the Dutch took possession of it, and it was further renovated and expanded throughout their centuries of occupation. In 1665–66, a second fort was established on St Jago Hill, ensuring that no other rival power could take Elmina with the same ease as the Dutch had. A French trader, describing Elmina in the 17th century, wrote that it was 'very long, containing about twelve hundred houses, all built with rock stones [and] divided into several streets and alleys'. Old maps show that the small town centre had assumed much of its modern shape by the late 18th century, perhaps earlier. It would appear that the town has seen surprisingly little development since being abandoned by the Dutch, partly because the British were already well ensconced at nearby Cape Coast, but more significantly perhaps because its very location between ocean and lagoon precluded the sort of expansion that has taken place in Cape Coast since the late 19th century.

Much of Elmina's fascination today lies in the way the former Portuguese and Dutch capital has returned to its fishing-village roots. There is something decidedly odd about watching the colourful pirogues sail in and out of the lagoon, much as they might in any other small Ghanaian port, except that it is happening right in front of what is the oldest European building in west Africa. And this is the sort of paradox that one repeatedly encounters in a town which has a mood so inherently African juxtaposed against an urban landscape moulded almost entirely by exotic influences. Elmina's apparent contradictions are epitomised by the large *posuban* shrines that lie to the east of St Jago Hill, monuments unique to this part of Ghana, yet which – on the basis of appearance alone – could as easily have come from practically anywhere in the world.

Over recent years, Elmina has witnessed a marked increase in the number of pseudo-guides, children seeking sponsorship/addresses and other hangers-on who lurk around the grounds of Elmina Castle playing 'guess the nationality' with passing tourists. There's not – as yet – anything overtly intimidating about this scene, but it does threaten to head that way if nothing is done to curb it. Even as things stand, should you make the mistake of letting one hanger-on entice you into conversation, you can expect to be swarmed by his buddies, while if you don't, then you're likely to find yourself on the receiving end of some low-key verbal abuse and accusations of racism etc. These guys hang around the castle with the express purpose of befriending gullible tourists, then guilt-tripping them into handing over cash or presents or an address. Whatever you do, and no matter how convincing the yarn you are spun, don't under any circumstance reinforce this cynical behaviour by allowing yourself to be persuaded to part with cash or other donations.

It's also worth noting that, hotels aside, Elmina boasts surprisingly few tourist facilities – if you want to exchange money or to browse the internet, you'll need to head back to Cape Coast.

GETTING THERE AND AWAY Elmina lies about 2km off the main Takoradi–Accra road, and it's connected to Cape Coast by a regular stream of tro-tros and shared taxis charging about US$0.40 for a seat. In most circumstances, your best bet in heading to Elmina is to catch public transport to Cape Coast, then use a local vehicle to Elmina – there are regular STC buses to Cape Coast, as well as tro-tros from Takoradi. The same is true when you leave Elmina – you can pick up a shared taxi to Cape Coast from Chapel Square, and find transport on from there (bearing in mind if you are heading to Takoradi that you'll pass Takoradi Station on your way into Cape Coast).

WHERE TO STAY
Upmarket

⌂ **Coconut Grove Beach Resort** ☏ 042 401003/5 or 020 8171960 or 024 4333001 or 042 91213; e grovehotel2000@yahoo.com; www.coconutgrovehotels.com.gh. Set on a superlative palm-lined beach about 3km west of central Elmina, Coconut Grove is rightly regarded to be one of the country's premier beach resorts – although once through the gates there is little evidence you are in Africa let alone Ghana. The rooms are large & attractively furnished, with hot showers, DSTV & fridge. The spacious landscaped grounds incorporate a golf course & a large swimming pool close to the beach, which is open to non-residents for US$4 a day. Other facilities inc an internet café, horseriding on the beach for US$10/hour, & a variety of watersports. An excellent

restaurant serves meals for around US$7–16. All prices rise over the Christmas & Easter peak periods. *From US$81/92 (sgl/dbl) with a garden view, to US$132 for a detached suite with kitchenette, & US$150–161 for 2-bedroom family suites with a sea view.*

⌂ **Elmina Beach Resort** PO Box 100, Elmina; ☏ 042 40010 or 042 40011 or 042 40012; f 042 33714/34359; e elbr@gbhghana.com; www.goldenbeachhotels.net. Formerly part of the international Best Western chain, now merged into the Ghanaian Golden Beach Hotels group, this plush, international-standard unit lies about 1km northeast of the town centre on a ruggedly rocky stretch of coast. The building is fairly bland from the outside, but with its elegant décor, blasting AC throughout, smart & helpful staff & aura of breezy trans-Atlantic efficiency, Elmina Beach Resort feels very much like a world-class, business hotel. In addition to a great swimming-pool area, the hotel has good conference facilities, an excellent restaurant serving meals around US$10, & DSTV in every room. *Standard rooms cost US$72/79 sgl/dbl B&B while rooms with an ocean view cost US$87/94 & suites start at US$118.*

Moderate

🏠 **Almond Tree Guesthouse** \ 024 4281098; \f 042 91057; e bookings@almond3.com; www.almond3.com. This family-managed guesthouse on the outskirts of town offers brightly decorated rooms. The colourful garden & terrace restaurant has a sea view, & specialises in Jamaican, Ghanaian & vegetarian cuisine, while activities on offer inc African drumming & dancing, tie-dye & batik, traditional storytelling & head-wrapping. It's a promising spot that has attracted some good reviews from readers of the last edition – but one rather worrying report of theft from rooms, which resulted in an arrest. *From US$23 for a sgl with shared bath & fan, to US$35/45 for a self-contained dbl with fan/AC.*

🏠 **Coconut Grove's Bridge House** \ 042 40045 or 024 454/332; Web booking details as for Coconut Grove Beach Resort. The opening of this hotel in early 2000 means that finally there is some decent tourist-class accommodation in Elmina's historic old town. Better still, it is housed in one of the town's oldest buildings, with a patio bar facing the fishing harbour & castle. It is comfortable rather than luxurious, but the air-conditioned rooms with DSTV are decent value, & the setting – assuming you want to soak up the nocturnal atmosphere of the old town – really is unbeatable. The hotel runs a daily shuttle between Bridge House & the beach resort, where residents have free access to all facilities. A good restaurant serves a selection of dishes from the beach resort menu at considerably lower prices. *US$41/52/63 sgl/dbl/trpl.*

Budget

🏠 **One Africa Guesthouse** (10 huts) \ 020 8195483 or 042 40021. This super-friendly beach hotel offers clean accommodation in roomy huts, all daubed in bright rasta colours. The compound is situated behind the defunct Harmony Beach Hotel, about 200m from the main Cape Coast road, & overlooks an attractive, rocky stretch of coastline within walking distance of a safe swimming beach. I liked the pan-Africanist theme of this place – the chalets are decorated with some great photographs of ethnic folk from all around the continent, & each one is named for an eminent Africanist pioneer such as Yaa Asantewaa, Marcus Garvey & Malcolm X. Shame, then, that it's all lent a somewhat spurious air by the sign at reception dedicating the lodge to the decidedly non-heroic personage of 'His Excellency Robert Mugabe'! *US$32 per hut.*

Shoestring

🏠 **Fort St Jago** Rumours that this hilltop fort will one day be converted to a resthouse have been doing the rounds for longer than a decade, & were still doing so in late 2003, but there remains no sign of rumour translating into reality.

🏠 **Holola Guesthouse** \ 024 3380293. The only alternative to the Nyansapow is this small, very friendly guesthouse, which lies in the suburb of Bantoma about 1km from Elmina Castle along the Pershie road. The self-contained rooms are of a similar standard to the Nyansapow, & slightly cheaper at US$7 for a sgl or US$25 for a quadruple, but the inconvenience of its location, not to say the quantity of mosquitoes that breed in the neighbouring salt flats, make it something of a last resort. *US$7–25.*

🏠 **Nyansapow (Hollywood) Hotel** \ 042 40250. While Elmina boasts a wide range of tourist-class accommodation, travellers on a budget are poorly catered for – the one exception being this long-serving central lodge set around a large, open courtyard. It's rather basic, but priced accordingly & quite popular, by default as much as anything else. There is a bar on the ground floor & b/fast is available on request, but there is no restaurant for other meals. *US$8.50–15 sgl/dbl for a clean self-contained room with fan & running water.*

❌ **WHERE TO EAT** By comparison to Cape Coast, bespoke restaurants are somewhat thin on the ground in Elmina and – unless you want to try one of the many chop stalls around the market – the best options for eating out are the smarter hotels.

The **Coconut Grove Beach Resort** has the most attractive location and serves excellent food for around US$7 for chicken dishes or around US$12 for fish, while its less luxurious relative, the **Bridge House**, stands as the best place to eat in the town centre. Rice-based standards are priced around US$5.50 and fish dishes range from US$6.50 for grilled red snapper or US$14 for generous servings of lobster. The filling snacks at the **Elmina Beach Resort** are also very good value at around US$2.50 per plate.

Elmina Castle Restaurant The winning combination of a historical setting, breezy location, and meals in the US$4–7 range make this a great town-centre choice. Service is slow, but it does at least come with a smile. Be warned that it often closes up at dusk when custom is slow, so do warn them in the afternoon if you plan on taking an evening meal there.

Mabel's Table This excellent bar and restaurant, situated right on the beach beside the One Africa Guesthouse, is popular with Ghanaians seeking a cold beer by the sea. Rice and fresh fish or rice and chicken cost less than US$2 for a large plate. Ring 042 33598 to place an advance order.

WHAT TO SEE If you are interested in a guided walking tour of Elmina, these start at the tourist office behind the Presbyterian Church, and follow three possible routes tailored to individual interest. Otherwise, the obvious place to start a self-guided walk of Elmina is **St George's Castle**, perched on a rocky promontory between lagoon and ocean. the whitewashed castle is now maintained as a historical monument and museum, and there is an entrance fee of US$4 for non-Ghanaians, plus an additional fee of US$0.50 for cameras. The castle is if anything more architecturally impressive than its Cape Coast counterpart, much of it four storeys high, and it offers excellent views across to the beach and over the town. Founded in 1482, St George's Castle is the oldest extant colonial building in sub-Saharan Africa, though it has been so extensively rebuilt and extended over the centuries that even its mid-17th-century shape is radically different to its modern one. (I think you could convincingly argue that the 'oldest building' tag hangs more meaningfully on the small Church of Senhora Baluarte on Mozambique Island, barely altered in architectural terms since it was constructed in 1522.)

The original St George, a small rectangular fortress, was sufficiently substantial to withstand three Dutch naval bombardments, before it was captured as a result of the bombardment from the top of St Jago Hill. The modern fort must cover about ten times the surface area of the original; the only recognisable relic of pre-Dutch times is the former Portuguese chapel, converted by the Dutch to an auction hall for slaves, now a museum with displays that concentrate on local history rather than the slave trade. In the castle, you can attend free rehearsals of the Butwaku traditional drum and dance ensemble. There are rehearsals in the west wing of the castle every night between 17.00 and 18.00. The ensemble also offers drum and dance lessons for foreigners – contact butwaku@hotmail.com for further details.

You may want to linger awhile at the pretty **fishing harbour** and fish market directly in front of the castle, or on the small bridge from where dozens of colourful pirogues can be seen every morning, making their way in and out of the sheltered Benya Lagoon. Entrance to the fenced part of the fishing market costs US$0.05 for locals, but although you may not be charged at all, some enterprising ticket collectors ask tourists for anything up to US$0.50 as a photographic fee. If this happens, insist on a receipt (a wad of US$0.05 stubs might not be of much use in itself, but it should prevent the ticket collector from pocketing your cash) and be warned that, fee or no fee, photography is barely tolerated within the market – best perhaps to leave your camera behind! Immediately east of the castle and the harbour, between lagoon and ocean, lay the **original old town**, depicted in several paintings and lithographs before it burnt to the ground in 1873 as a result of a British naval bombardment.

To get from the castle and fishing harbour to what, I suppose, has to be termed the modern **old town**, you must follow Liverpool Street north over the bridge across the lagoon mouth. During Elmina's prime in the early 19th century, this area is where the wealthiest citizens lived, many of them mulattos or prosperous Dutch merchants who married Elmina women and settled in the town. Immediately after you cross the bridge, you'll see a cluster of these houses running up the right side of Liverpool Street, large double-storey buildings now trimmed of many of their more ornamental touches. Built in the 1840s, this cluster of buildings consists of Bridge House (partially destroyed during heavy rains in 1981, more recently renovated as a hotel), Quayson House, the twin Viala Houses and Simons House (now a complete ruin).

From here, a left turn into the road that runs alongside the north bank of the lagoon will, after no more than 20m, bring you to the steep and easily found path to the top of **St Jago Hill**. A wonderful panoramic view over the fishing harbour and the town centre is to be had from the top of this hill. It also provides an excellent vantage point over St George's Castle, something that was exploited by the Dutch in 1637 when they dragged four cannons to its peak and bombarded the castle, forcing a Portuguese surrender. **Fort St Jago** was built on top of the hill in 1665–66, so that the Dutch could be certain that they wouldn't lose possession of the castle in a manner similar to the one they had used to gain it. The resultant relatively modest fortified garrison post was named Fort Coenraadsburg by its Dutch constructors, but for reasons that are unclear it is generally known today by the older Portuguese name for the hill. Though several extensions were made after 1666, the essential shape of the fort is little changed since that time.

When you walk back down to the base of St Jago Hill, turn right, following the road that runs alongside the harbour away from Liverpool Street before curving inland. Here, over the space of perhaps 200m, is Elmina's main concentration of *posuban* **shrines** (see also page 144). The first two, on the left side of the road a few metres after it curves inland, belong to Asafo Companies Five and Two. The shrine built by Asafo Company Five is a double-storey affair with several life-sized figures carved on the ground floor and – strikingly – a ship with three naval officers on the upper one. Number Two Shrine consists of four life-sized carvings of people surrounding an older man in a bright blue robe and flanked by two aeroplanes. Most impressive, however, is the shrine built by Asafo Company Four at the junction with Dutch Cemetery Street, which depicts a variation on the story of Adam and Eve (although several of the life-size figures have been decapitated in recent years as a result of poor maintenance). Unlike in smaller towns, it isn't normally a problem to photograph the shrines in Elmina without being asked for a payment.

Turn left into Dutch Cemetery Street if you want to nose around the old **Dutch Cemetery**, inaugurated in 1802 and moved to its present site at the base of St Joseph's Hill four years later. Well maintained, the graveyard boasts several marble tombstones (one of which marks the grave of Governor Hagenblom, who was murdered in 1808) as well as a large, neo-classical cenotaph dating to 1806. The cemetery is normally padlocked, but if you ask around – and are prepared to offer a dash or two – then it shouldn't be difficult to locate the caretaker. Turn back along Dutch Cemetery Street, passing the shrines built by Asafo Companies Two and One, and you can take a left turn into Lime Street. This is the site of **Dolphin House**, built in the late 19th century by the merchant Fred Dolphin at the foot of the road running to the top of St Joseph's Hill. Once distinguished by its multi-arched façade, Dolphin House had become very run-down prior to collapsing entirely in late 1999. Walk up this hill to see a clutch of impressive mission buildings, including a large **Catholic church** dating from the 1880s, and a view over the salt ponds in Benya Lagoon.

When you walk back to Dutch Cemetery Street, turn left and follow it to Chapel Square, at the intersection of Liverpool and High streets and marked by an attractive Methodist church. A left turn into High Street will bring you to what is perhaps the best-maintained building of its vintage in Elmina, the stone **post office**. This was built some time between 1825 and 1850 as the domestic dwelling and trading quarters of the merchant C H Bartels (son of Governor Bartels), and it later served as a hospital during the colonial era.

Definitely worth a visit, the new **Elmina-Java Museum** (*www. elwininternational.com*) focuses on the history of the 3,080 Ghanaian men who were recruited by the Dutch from 1831–72 to serve in the Royal Netherlands East Indies Army (KNIL). Exhibits include photographs, documents and other artefacts related to the lives of the soldiers and their descendants in Indonesia, Netherlands and Ghana. The museum also has extensive displays about the history of Elmina itself, the story of two Ashanti princes sent to the Netherlands in the early 19th century, and on the Genealogy of the Ulzen family for ten generations. Many interesting aspects of the cross-cultural mixing are explored (like why batik is so common in Ghana) and the curator gives an excellent tour. It is situated on the highway at Nippon junction, one block west of Elmina Junction.

TOWARDS TAKORADI

The stretch of coast between Elmina and Takoradi has three obvious highlights: the beach resorts at **Brenu Akyinim** and **Ampenyi**, both of which can be visited as a day trip from Elmina, and – closer to Takoradi – the off-the-beaten-track town of **Shama** with its historic fort.

BRENU AKYINIM AND AMPENYI The small village of Brenu Akyinim, 15km west of Elmina, is known for its attractive and reasonably safe swimming beach, a substantial chunk of which has been fenced off to form the Brenu Beach Resort, charging an entrance fee of US$0.50 for adults or US$0.30 for children, which ensures that the villagers do their ablutions elsewhere. Swimming is not advisable unless you check current conditions with the locals, but Brenu is a great place to lounge in palm-fringed, white-sanded perfection, and facilities are suited to those on a budget. Brenu forms an easy goal for a day trip out of Elmina.

A bit further west lies the village of Ampenyi and Ko-Sa Beach. This beach is as pretty as any on the Ghanaian coast, and although it is less popular than Brenu, it boasts a natural rock pool where swimming is reliably safe and pleasurable.

Getting there and away In a private vehicle, you need to first head out along the Takoradi road for about 15km until you reach Ajensudo junction, where the respective turn-offs to Brenu and Ampenyi lie about 500m apart and are signposted. The distance between the main road and either beach is about 5km and the roads are in good nick.

There is no direct public transport between Elmina and Brenu Akyinim (and note that 'Akyinim', pronounced 'Achinim', is also, rather confusingly, the name of a suburb in Elmina) or Ampenyi. This means you will first need to catch a tro-tro to Ajensudo junction; any westbound transport from Elmina will oblige. Here you'll find a few shared taxis to Brenu and Ampenyi. These taxis can fill up a bit slowly, but since the full fare for four passengers works out at little more than US$1 you could always treat yourself. Expect to pay around US$6.50 to charter a taxi from Elmina or Cape Coast. Travelling between Brenu and Ampenyi, the alternatives are to charter a car back via the junction, or take a 20-minute walk straight from one to the other along the beach.

Where to stay and eat
Upmarket
⌂ **Alberta's Palace Beach Resort** (20 bungalows) ◟ 024 387937. This new, I-star resort shares one of the loveliest beach locations in Ghana with Ko-Sa guesthouse, but has sadly done little to harmonise with its surrounds. Accommodation comes in the shape of

bungalows set around an enormous, bare courtyard, replete with an outdoor bar populated by plastic chairs & blaring hi-life. Each chalet comprises 3 comfortable rooms with fan, DSTV & a shared lounge. *US$50 per bungalow.*

Budget
⌂ **Ko-Sa Cultural Centre** ◟ 024 4375432; e ko-saguesthouse@gmx.net; www.ko-sa.com. Situated right on the beach at Ampenyi, this popular & eco-friendly German-run lodge, though arguably a touch overpriced, has won awards for its environmental & social consciousness in both Germany & Ghana. A variety of accommodation is available, ranging from local-style clay-&-thatch huts using clean communal showers & toilets for US$12–19 dbl & 4-person rooms with a fan at US$25, to smarter self-contained rooms &

bungalows with fan, sleeping up to four people, at US$35–45. Facilities inc a good book-swap service, solar electricity, drum & dance lessons, guided beach walks to Elmina & excursions to the Beposo farmer's market nearby (Tue & Fri). An onsite restaurant specialises in vegetarian meals priced between US$3–6.50 (yam burgers with sugar or tomato relish are the house speciality), although the slightly grumpy owner gets cross if non-residents use it for all their meals. *US$12–19; US$25; US$35–45.*

Shoestring
⌂ **Brenu Beach Resort** ◟ 024 4158675 or 024 6493819. The beach is supervised by a lifeguard. Until a few years ago, this totally gorgeous beach resort in Brenu was just a restaurant, serving excellent seafood dishes at around US$4–6 for a main course, as well as minerals & alcoholic drinks. Accommodation was recently added, however, in the form of an uninspiring block of small but clean rooms, offered with fan & common cold showers for: *US$12/16/18 sgl/dbl/twin. Camping is permitted at US$5 pp.*

⌂ **Esteem Kofi & Adjoa Motel** ◟ 024 4541288; e adjoachilds@yahoo.com. Situated at Ajensudo junction, this friendly new guesthouse offers an excellent budget deal, though it's rather difficult to

come up with a good reason why any traveller would want to stay over at the junction itself. The vast self-contained rooms with dbl bed, tiled floor & sofa are good value, depending on size, & a good open-air restaurant is attached. Just a shame about the location! *US$18–27.*

⌂ **Samaland** ◟ 024 4374493. This bizarre, locally run resort alongside Ko-Sa has been under construction since the last edition, & is finally due to open in 2007. Rooms are arranged in a mini village of alpine-style guesthouses named after saints or the owners' children. *The price for a small, self contained chalet with AC is likely to be around US$20.*

OLD KOMENDA The mouth of the Komenda River was a focal point of Anglo-Dutch rivalry in the 17th and 18th centuries, as testified by two ruined forts on the opposite banks. Fort Vreedenburg was built by the Dutch in 1682, and Fort English by the British five years later. The substantial remains of the British fortress can still be seen in Old Komenda, a sleepy, small fishing port which also boasts an attractive old Wesleyan church and lies 5km south along a signposted turn-off from the main Cape Coast–Takoradi road. The fort aside, there is nothing to Old Komenda that couldn't be seen or done at dozens of other small ports along the Ghanaian coast, but it's an attractive enough backwater, practically unvisited by tourists, and in the right frame of mind it could be a worthwhile place to hang out for a few days.

Regular shared taxis run between the Cape Coast–Takoradi road and the town centre, from where you'll probably need to charter a private taxi to track down what appears to be the only accommodation in town – the clean and friendly but rather gloomy three-storey **Graceland Guesthouse** (◟ *024 861720*), where carpeted self-contained dbls with fan start at US$5. Sadly, we could find no trace of the Monarch Guesthouse, signposted as a beach resort at the junction, but unheard of in the town itself.

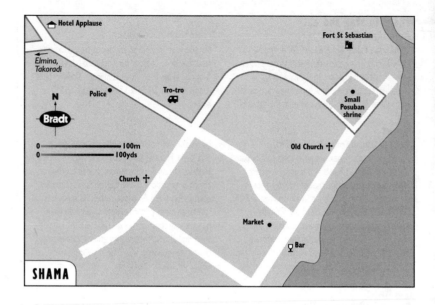

SHAMA This small, out-of-the-way town makes for a diverting overnight excursion en route between Cape Coast and Takoradi. Shama is the site of Ghana's third-oldest fortified building, the **Fortress of St Sebastian**, built and named by the Portuguese in 1523. In 1640, the all-but derelict fort was captured by the Dutch, who completely rebuilt it following a brief British occupation in 1664. The ground plan today is almost identical to the Portuguese original, but an extra storey was added by the Dutch. Later in the fort's career, strong buttresses were constructed to prevent the soft foundation rock from being washed away – hence the high semi-circle of steps leading to the main entrance.

Shama's fort is well maintained and looms imposingly above the central market. Entrance costs US$2 inclusive of a guided tour – though you might be asked extra to take photographs, and some readers report unprecedented levels of hassle from local children all clamouring for a 'dash'. So far as we could see, the only other building of any great vintage in Shama is the Methodist church built opposite the fort in 1893. Also of interest is the fish market on the mouth of the Pra River, a short walk to the east of the town centre. During the gold-trading era, Shama was renowned for the seaworthy canoes that were crafted on an island a short distance upstream of the Pra mouth, and even today it is possible to organise a canoe ride up the river from near the market.

Getting there and away Any tro-tro heading between Cape Coast and Takoradi can stop at Shama junction. A steady flow of shared taxis ply the 4km road to Shama.

Where to stay and eat

⌂ **Hotel Applause** ☎ 031 23941. This rather smart 3-storey hotel seems misplaced in the shabby low-rise surrounds of Shama. The self-contained dbls with fan, balcony & shower are great value, while the revitalised rooftop bar & restaurant offers great views over the town & decent meals for around US$3. *Dbl US$6–9.*

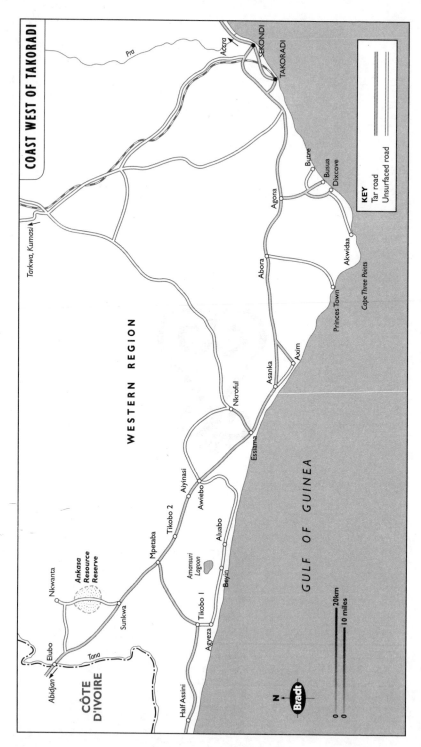

COAST WEST OF TAKORADI

KEY
Tar road
Unsurfaced road

WESTERN REGION

CÔTE D'IVOIRE

Ankasa Resource Reserve

GULF OF GUINEA

Cape Three Points

Pra
Accra
SEKONDI
TAKORADI
Butre
Busua
Dixcove
Agona
Akwidaa
Abora
Princes Town
Tarkwa, Kumasi
Axim
Asanka
Nkroful
Esiama
Aiyinasi
Awiebo
Tikobo 2
Mpetaba
Aluabo
Amansuri Lagoon
Beyin
Sunkwa
Tikobo 1
Nkwanta
Elubo
Agyeza
Tana
Abidjan
Half Assini

N
Bradt

20km
10 miles
0
0

9

Sekondi–Takoradi and the West Coast

The coastline of Ghana's Western Region sees relatively few tourists by comparison to the areas covered in the preceding two chapters, but it is no less worthwhile. The twin city of Sekondi–Takoradi, regional capital and gateway to the west coast, is admittedly of less inherent interest than Cape Coast or Elmina, but it is still an amenable place to spend a night or two, boasting a bustling central market, a pretty beach, the historical Fort Orange, and – unexpectedly – the opportunity to see wild monkeys within a few hundred metres of the city centre.

The beaches to the west of Takoradi are arguably the most stunning in Ghana, none more so than the palm-lined slices of tropical nirvana at the blissfully isolated Ankobra or Lou Moon beach resorts near **Axim**. The beaches in and around **Busua** – though less beautiful – are excellent for swimming, and lined with a row of resorts and guesthouses to suit all budgets, whilst the supremely chilled-out Green Turtle and Safari Beach resorts near **Akwidaa** tend to play havoc with even the most rigid of travel itineraries.

For the historically minded, there are **old colonial forts** at Dixcove, Princes Town, Axim and Beyin, the last of which forms the normal base from which to visit the unique stilt village of **Nzulezo** (see page 203).

For nature lovers, the coast around Princes Town presents some interesting rambling opportunities, while extensive new developments at the **Ankasa Resource Reserve** (see page 205) have elevated this formerly neglected tract of rainforest to one of the country's prime hiking and birding destinations.

SEKONDI–TAKORADI

The twin cities of Sekondi–Takoradi together form the third-largest urban conglomeration in Ghana, with a total population of roughly 300,000. Takoradi (often shortened to 'Tadi') is the more populous, modern and industrialised of the two cities, which lie about 10km apart on the coast roughly halfway between Accra and the Côte d'Ivoire border. Takoradi is also the main transport hub in the southwest of Ghana, connected to Kumasi by a daily train service, and with good road links in all directions, as well as an excellent selection of hotels and restaurants.

Formerly an obscure fishing village, Takoradi was earmarked for development as a harbour in 1920, and officially opened as such in 1928, to become the most important port in the country until the development of Tema. The compact city centre, emanating from a circular central market, has a busy, modern feel, without approaching the chaotic atmosphere of, say, Kumasi. South of the city centre is a more verdant suburban area and golf course, running down to an adequate swimming beach.

Takoradi inspires mixed reactions in travellers. One reader wrote that he 'found the level of *"obruni"* catcalls and general interference reached quite staggering

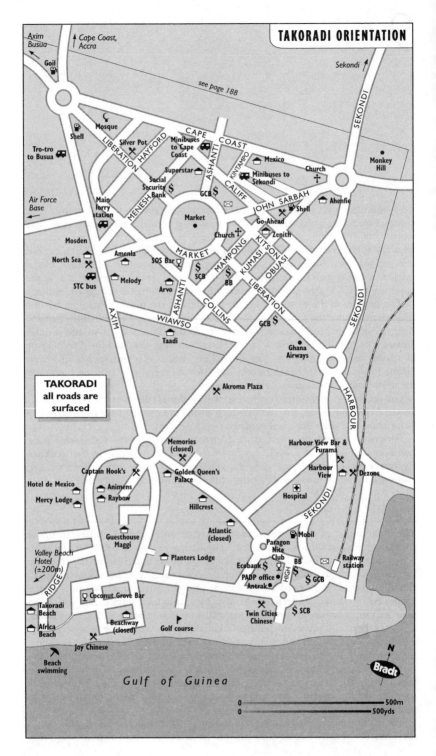

TAKORADI ORIENTATION

Axim Busua

Cape Coast, Accra

Sekondi

SEKONDI

Goil

see page 188

Mosque

Shell

Silver Pot

LIBERATION

HAYFORD

CAPE COAST

Minibuses to Cape Coast

ASHANTI

KINTAMPO

Mexico

Church

Monkey Hill

Tro-tro to Busua

Superstar

CALIFF

Minibuses to Sekondi

Social Security Bank

GCB

JOHN SARBAH

Ahenfie

Air Force Base

Main lorry station

MENESH

Market

Go-Ahead

Shell

Zenith

Mosden

Church

KITSON

KUMASI

OBUASI

North Sea

Amenla

SOS Bar

MARKET

MAMPONG

LIBERATION

STC bus

Melody

Arvo

SCB

BB

ASHANTI

COLLINS

WIAWSO

GCB

AXIM

Taadi

Ghana Airways

TAKORADI
all roads are surfaced

HARBOUR

Akroma Plaza

Memories (closed)

Harbour View Bar & Furama

Captain Hook's

Golden Queen's Palace

Harbour View

Dezoos

Hotel de Mexico

Animens

Raybow

Mercy Lodge

Hillcrest

Hospital

SEKONDI

Guesthouse Maggi

Atlantic (closed)

Mobil

Valley Beach Hotel (±200m)

Planters Lodge

Paragon Nite Club

RIDGE

Ecobank

BB

Railway station

Takoradi Beach

Coconut Grove Bar

PADP office

HIGH

GCB

Antrak

Africa Beach

Beachway (closed)

Golf course

Twin Cities Chinese

SCB

Joy Chinese

Beach swimming

N

Gulf of Guinea

Bradt

0 ——————— 500m
0 ——————— 500yds

levels... I got more attention just wandering around here than as a tourist in Istanbul's Grand Bazaar, or in fact anywhere else I've visited', while another said he 'found it one of the most amenable places I went in Ghana, and the only place in the country where I went for a few days without being asked for money or seeing another "*obruni*"'. But fair to say that Takoradi seldom inspires affection in travellers, and while one recent letter characterising the city centre as a rat-infested, smelly dump does seem unduly harsh, the reality is that the city is of interest primarily as a well-equipped staging post for forays to more inherently attractive places.

Sekondi, in direct contrast to its upstart twin, is visibly steeped in history. A solid Dutch fort was built there in 1690 over the foundations of a lodge built 50 years earlier, and the town has served as the administrative capital of Western Region and an important naval base from the very earliest colonial times right up to the modern day. Very few travellers make the 20-minute tro-tro ride from Takoradi to Sekondi, but those who do will be amply rewarded. The Dutch Fort Orange is still in use as a lighthouse, and the family who lives there generally lets visitors wander around the fortifications, which offer a great view over the town (though some travellers reported being refused entry in 2003). The railway station is a fine piece of colonial architecture, while the harbour, with its backdrop of green hills, is bustling with colourful fishing boats. Above the harbour, the quarter still referred to locally as the 'European Town' is a compact jumble of crumbling turn-of-the-century buildings, with an atmosphere as rich as it is depressing.

On the fringes of central Takoradi, a three-hectare patch of forest on Monkey Hill supports tenacious populations of the localised olive colobus monkey and more widespread spot-nosed monkey. A census in 1999 counted 12 colobus and 41 spot-nosed monkeys, suggesting that neither species is likely to persist indefinitely within this suburban enclave unless the local authorities recognise its tourist potential and accords the hill formal protection as a nature sanctuary. In the meantime, it is easy to visit Monkey Hill informally, ideally at around 17.00, when the odds of seeing both types of monkey are better than even – though one report in early 2007 suggests the olive colobus are now most often seen in the early morning. The turn-off to the top of the hill lies about 100m from Sekondi Circle (the roundabout north of the Ahenfie Hotel) along New Takoradi Road.

GETTING THERE AND AWAY Direct **STC buses** between Accra and Takoradi take roughly four hours in either direction and cost US$5–6 depending on whether they have air conditioning. The first bus out of Accra leaves at 05.00, after which there is one bus every hour until 17.00, whilst buses out of Takoradi leave throughout the day at 02.30, 02.35, 04.30, 09.30, 11.30, 13.00, 14.30 and 17.30. It's advisable to arrive at the STC station about 30 minutes before the bus departs to be sure of getting a ticket.

There are also two STC buses daily to Kumasi via Cape Coast, leaving at 04.00 and 12.00 (07.00 and 14.00 on Sundays) charged at US$6–8 a seat and taking around five hours. Two buses run daily to Tema at 06.30 and 13.30, for US$6–7, and one bus goes directly to Bolgatanga every Friday at 08.00, with seats costing US$15–22. It's advisable to book on all but the Accra buses at least a day ahead of travel.

Direct **tro-tros** run between Takoradi and practically every town of substance on the coast west of Accra. Tro-tros to Elubo, Beyin, Half Assini, Dunkwa and most other points west of Takoradi leave from the lorry station on the opposite side of Axim Road to the STC station, though those to Agona junction (for Busua and Dixcove) and Axim now leave from a newer station on the same side of Axim road as the STC station, but about 500m further north towards the main traffic circle at the junction with the Elubo road. Tro-tros to Cape Coast and other points east of Takoradi leave from the station at the corner of Cape Coast and Ashanti roads. Tro-tros to Sekondi leave from a back road off Kintampo Road.

For details of the daily train service to Kumasi, see *Getting there and away* under Kumasi on page 300.

WHERE TO STAY Despite its low profile as a tourist centre, Takoradi boasts Ghana's largest concentration of hotels outside of Accra and Kumasi, including a couple of dozen mid-range places that cater primarily to cruise passengers and local businessmen, as well as expatriates from the nearby mining towns over the weekend. The following listings, though selective, are far from comprehensive; readers are welcome to pass on new recommendations.

Upmarket

Africa Beach Hotel 031 25148/26455; f 031 21666; e africa_beach@yahoo.co.uk. Oddly, this is the only real beach resort among Takoradi's myriad hotels, for which reason alone it ranks as the first choice in this price range. The attractive hotel grounds are dominated by a large swimming pool overlooking a rocky beach, & an open bar/restaurant which often hosts live music at weekends. Spacious clean self-contained chalets with AC & DSTV. *Sgl/dbl US$45–55/55–60.*

Hillcrest Hotel 031 22277; f 031 24381; e hillcresthotelgh@yahoo.com. This bland international 3-star hotel is situated between the city centre & beach, close to the disused Atlantic Hotel. What it lacks in character is compensated for by the facilities, which inc a business centre, a swimming pool, AC & DSTV in all rooms, & a dependable restaurant. *Dbl US$70.*

Planters Lodge 031 22233; f 031 22230; e planters@africaonline.com.gh. Set in large grounds separated from the beach by the golf course, Planters Lodge is the most ambient upmarket hotel in Takoradi. Comfortable Swiss-style chalets with AC & DSTV. Facilities inc a tennis court, business centre & excellent restaurant, as well as a tempting swimming pool (open to non-residents at US$5 a day) & a large, glass-walled poolside bar. *Dbl US$60 w/day, US$55 w/end, or US$100 for 2-night stay over Fri & Sat.*

Raybow International Hotel 031 22072/25438/26929; f 031 23960; e info@raybowhotel.com; www.raybowhotel.com. This smart hotel doesn't offer much in the way of character or setting, but it's an attractive & – in the best possible sense of the word – modern set-up, well suited to business & other upmarket travellers. The mini-suites have a huge bed, sofa, DSTV, & kitchenette, & are good value. Internet & other business facilities are available, & a swimming pool is under construction. *Sgl/dbl from US$50/65, US$120 for a 2-bedroom chalet.*

Takoradi Beach Hotel 031 21021/22504; f 031 21022; e info@takoradibeachhotel.com; www.takoradibeachhotel.com. The recent addition of a tempting swimming pool notwithstanding, this bland multi-storey monolith, separated from the beach by the Africa Beach Hotel, is a popular conference venue but is unlikely to appeal greatly to tourists. *Sgl/dbl/twin US$60/70/75 with AC & DSTV, or suite US$95–145.*

Moderate

Animens Hotel 031 24676; e animenshotel@yahoo.com. This bright & cheerful 3-storey block isn't bursting with character but it's probably the pick in this range. The attached restaurant offers good local & continental dishes at US$5–6, which can be taken in the pleasant courtyard. Recommended. Clean rooms with AC, DSTV, fridge & hot water. *Sgl/dbl US$25/30 B&B.*

Guesthouse Maggi 031 22852. A sign outside this popular & friendly suburban hotel proclaims 'public liability insurance' as one of its qualities, but far more notable still are the red carpets that run down each corridor, & ostentatious décor of the rooms. Small but comfortable dbls with AC, DSTV, fridge, hot shower & b/fast are passable value. Internet & limited conference facilities available. *Dbl US$22–41, sgl with fan US$14.*

Melody Hotel 031 24109/28875; f 031 28874. This popular pink hotel opposite the STC bus station is another good bet, with large rooms, AC, fan, TV, hot bath & fridge. The restaurant serves good meals, with several Indian dishes available. *Dbl US$35.*

Mercy Lodge 031 21803; e mercy-lodge@yahoo.com. Situated opposite the Raybow, this has variously sized self-contained rooms with AC, DSTV & hot water. It would be good value were it not for the overly fussy mausoleum-cum-boarding house décor. *Dbl US$28–39.*

Superstar Hotel 031 23105. This friendly set-up has large, clean rooms, from self-contained dbl with fan to executive suite with fridge, DSTV & AC. The décor leaves something to be desired, but it offers a good central compromise between cost & quality. A very speedy internet café with lots of computers is situated opposite. *Dbl from US$18, suite from US$35.*

Budget

Ahenfie Hotel 031 21267; e info@ ahenfiehotel.com; www.ahenfiehotel.com. This large, sludgy green block on the northern edge of the city centre has 57 rooms & a good many more are planned. Small self-contained rooms with fan, or larger rooms with AC & TV available. Facilities inc parking, a good restaurant, garden bar, & disco where – take note – 'all shirts must be tucked into trousers except jumper'! *Small sgl/dbl from US$11/16, larger sgl/dbl US$25/28.*

Golden Queen's Palace 031 23463. Assuming you can put up with the garish décor, this friendly suburban set up (formerly the Western Home Hotel), is fair value. *Dbl with AC & DSTV, common shower US$15, or self-contained dbl US$18–21.*

Harbour View Hotel 031 23576; f 031 24944. This relatively central hotel, on Sekondi Road above the harbour, sounds nicer than it is, but rooms are reasonably priced. A good outdoor bar & restaurant are in the same complex. *V. basic sgl US$6, sgl/dbl with fan & TV US$7/8, lg self-contained dbl with AC & TV US$15.*

Hotel de Mexico 031 21644. This relatively respectable hotel offers the cheapest lodging in an expensive part of town. Ground floor rooms are currently in better state than those on the first floor, but renovations are planned. The management insists on keeping room keys when guests go out, but may well leave them unattended at the desk. *Dbl US$12–16.*

Hotel You 84 031 22945. Situated opposite the central market, this somewhat enigmatically named hotel is excellent value, with AC, hot water & DSTV. The ground-floor restaurant has been replaced by a well-stocked supermarket. *Self-contained dbl US$18.*

Mosden Hotel 031 22266. This small hotel on the first floor of the Mankessim White House bills itself as 'the convenient choice', & so it is for anybody arriving at night or leaving early in the morning by STC bus, since it stands next door to the station. Otherwise, the slightly musty rooms feel a touch overpriced. *US$13–18 with hot bath, fan & TV, or US$20 with AC.*

Taadi Hotel 031 23778/31104. This comfortable, friendly 1-star hotel has a convenient location on the southern outskirts of the city centre. Recommended. *Self-contained dbl with fan & TV US$17–20, suites from US$22.*

Shoestring

Amenla Hotel 031 22543. Probably the best of the central cheapies, the Amenla Hotel has a pretty little interior courtyard decorated with artificial flowers, & charges reasonable rates for dark but clean rooms. The notices 'politely instructing' guests to keep noise levels down are ignored by the staff. *Sgl/dbl with fan US$7/8, self-contained dbl US$9.*

Beachway Hotel Situated 20 minutes' walk from the city centre, the Beachway – a creaky, four-storey colonial building with large balconies facing the beach – was the most attractive budget hotel in Takoradi prior to closing in 2002 as a result of a family dispute. The building is still there, set in leafy grounds near the golf course, but whether or when it will re-open is unclear.

Hotel Arvo 031 21530. Situated around the corner from the Amenla, & slightly more run-down, is this popular backpackers' fallback. Most rooms are reasonably clean but one or two are pretty grim, so look at a few to check you have a good deal. *Sgl/dbl with fan & common showers US$5.50/6.50, self-contained dbl US$7.50–8.50.*

Zenith Hotel 031 22359. Notable more for its idiosyncratically decorated courtyard than for the large but rather run-down rooms, the pink, multi-storey Zenith Hotel is about the cheapest option in central Takoradi & decent value. The central courtyard is a popular venue for local funerals, with all the deafening music that comes with them. *Sgl/dbl with common showers US$6–7, with private bath US$9.*

WHERE TO EAT AND DRINK Most of the upmarket and moderate hotels listed above have good restaurants serving continental and/or Chinese dishes in the US$3-plus bracket – Africa Beach Hotel is probably the most attractive, if only for its beach-front location.

Akroma Plaza This smart AC restaurant, which lies a short distance south of the city centre towards the beach, serves a wide selection of grills, curries, burgers, pizzas & Chinese dishes. *US$3–5.*

Ambassador Kitchen Situated on Liberation Rd a block up from the Silver Pot, this serves a similar range of dishes at similar prices, but seems a less comfortable place to sit.

Bocadillos Don't let the Spanish name fool you: this casual new restaurant just south of Takoradi centre is known for its very good croissants, pain au chocolat & baguettes above all else. But the varied menu also extends to tasty (if lurid) ice creams, pizzas & local food. *Good-value meal deals, inc US$4 English b/fast.*

Captain Hook's 031 27085. This German-owned restaurant on Beach Road is undoubtedly the smartest

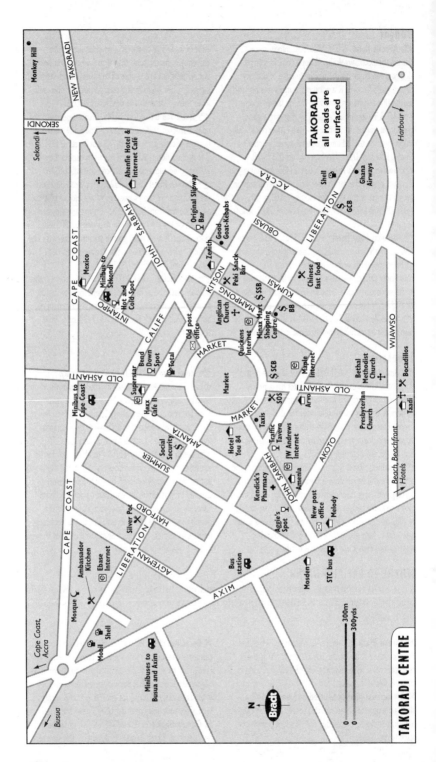

TAKORADI
all roads are
surfaced

TAKORADI CENTRE

in Takoradi, specialising in top-notch seafood & grills. Although the prices seem steep if you've been in Ghana for a while, both the food & décor are good enough to leave the restaurant packed at w/ends. *Main courses upwards of US$10.*

✕ **Joy Chinese Restaurant** This briskly managed, Chinese-run restaurant can add up to be relatively expensive, with rice charged separately to the main dishes, & the management has a reputation for hijacking any tips given to the waitresses. But it has to be said that the food is excellent & it boasts a fabulous beach-front location 100m or so from the defunct Beachway Hotel.

✕ **North Sea Restaurant** As long as you can cope with the freezer-like AC, this upmarket new restaurant is a great spot for top notch sea food, as well as pizzas, smatterings of Lebanese cuisine & serious meat dishes.

It is also very conveniently placed for late afternoon departures from town, right next to the STC bus station, whilst happy hour on Friday evenings makes a good excuse to raid the well-stocked bar. *US$8–16.*

✕ **Silver Pot Restaurant** This excellent establishment serves local, continental & Ghanaian dishes in a comfortable, AC dining room – giving a considerable boost to the number of options in the centre of town. Highly recommended. *US$3–5.50.*

✕ **Twin Cities Chinese Restaurant** ✆ 031 23888. Situated at the eastern end of the golf course, this strange eatery feels more like the front room of a family house than a conventional restaurant, but the food is excellent & moderately priced. The service is friendly & relatively quick, & also extends to deliveries. *Main courses less than US$4.*

ENTERTAINMENT
Cultural shows An excellent dance group named Kundum Obrenpong goes around to the different hotels in the area to perform. They are easy to contact to arrange for performances: PO Box 1056MC, Takoradi, Ghana. (They are based in the northern part of Takoradi in the section of town called Astoria.)

Deep-sea fishing The marlin fishing is exceptional, & although fees are out of the range of most travellers to Ghana, they are good value in comparison to the usual price tags worldwide. Excursions can be arranged through the owner of Captain Hook's restaurant – at US$850 per day! – albeit for 3–4 persons. He also does a slightly cheaper inshore charter for 4–6 people and whale-watching trips can be arranged during humpback season between July and December.

Swimming Day visitors will be asked a fee of around US$5 to use the swimming pools at the Hillcrest Hotel, Africa Beach Hotel, Takoradi Beach Hotel or Planter's Lodge.

OTHER PRACTICALITIES
Foreign exchange All the major banks are represented, with the Standard Chartered as usual offering the most favourable rates. Case Forex Bureau on John Sarbah Road and Esam Forex opposite the Amenla Hotel are two of the best places to exchange cash quickly – rates for cash are slightly but not significantly lower than in Accra or Kumasi.

Internet There are now several internet cafés dotted around the town centre. The most reliable is probably Ebase, on Liberation Road next to the Ambassador Kitchen, which is open 24 hours a day seven days a week.. Other good cafés include the one in the building in front of the Ahenfie Hotel, and Quickens and SSB Internet on Liberation Avenue opposite the Barclays Bank, but these don't keep the long hours and charge slightly more than Ebase.

BUSUA AND SURROUNDS

Only 20km east of Takoradi, the village of Busua lies on a beach that is widely regarded as among the best and safest in Ghana, for which reason this small fishing village has played host to a steady influx of backpackers since the 1960s. Recent years have seen Busua attract a marginally more upmarket crowd than in its hippy

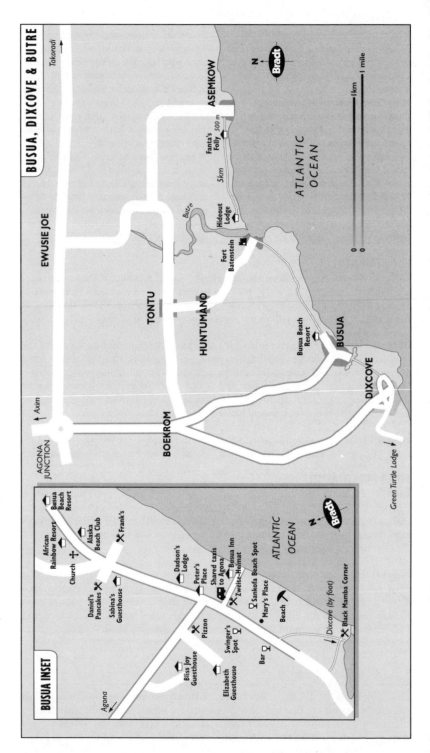

BUSUA, DIXCOVE & BUTRE

BUSUA INSET

190

heyday, particularly following the refurbishment of the long-serving Busua Beach Resort. But it is also true that the village has never before been blessed with so many affordable lodgings and restaurants, most of which are run by locals rather than out-of-town businessmen. The beach remains magnificent, the village and fishing harbour in particular are very colourful, and the friendly, backpacker-oriented atmosphere makes it tempting to label Busua as west Africa's answer to the legendary Twiga Lodge in Kenya and Cape Maclear in Malawi. Busua, in a nutshell, is a great place to chill out for a few days.

Twenty minutes' walk from Busua, **Dixcove** is more a small town than a village, a compact settlement of run-down alleys and crumbling colonial-era buildings, which impart a definite sense of – well, if not history exactly, then certainly historical continuity. Like many other Ghanaian ports, Dixcove has long been the site of a European fort, but was probably settled by local fishermen for centuries before that. In 1692, Dixcove (or Dick's Cove as it was then known) was chosen by the British as the site of a fort, construction of which was completed in around 1696. For the best part of two centuries, Dixcove Fort was the only British property in the Dutch-controlled part of what is now the Ghanaian coast, for which reason it is said to have survived more attacks than any other fortress on the Gold Coast. The fort was captured by the Dutch in 1868 and renamed Fort Metalen Kruiz, only to be returned to Britain in 1872 along with all other Dutch forts on the Gold Coast. Oddly, however, the Dutch name stuck and it is known as Fort Metal Cross today. The fort is the obvious focal point for visits to Dixcove, and the caretaker will lead an informative tour by request, as well as arrange rooms for travellers – no formal accommodation exists. It is also interesting to watch the colourful fishing boats on the busy beach.

About 3km east of Busua as the crow flies, the small fishing village of **Butre** can be reached along a fairly direct footpath from Busua, or by road directly from Agona junction. Butre lies on a wide sandy swimming beach in a large bay adjacent to a small river estuary and protected by a well-wooded peninsula. The main point of historical interest is the substantial but somewhat overgrown ruin of Fort Batenstein, perched on a tall hill above the village and reached via a short, steep footpath. Originally constructed by the Dutch in 1656, Batenstein was rebuilt in the 18th century, abandoned due to slow trade between 1818 and 1829, and was eventually handed over to Britain in 1872, after which it fell into disuse. The views from the fortifications are exceptional. For a negotiable fee, villagers in Butre can take visitors by canoe upriver to the site of a derelict British palm-oil factory near Sese. Until recently, there was no accommodation in the vicinity of Butre, but that changed in 2003 with the opening of Hideout Lodge, an excellent budget retreat set on a nearby beach.

The substantial fishing village of **Akwidaa**, bisected by the Ezile Estuary, lies about 10km southwest of Dixcove as the crow flies. Also known as Ezile or Akodaa, the village boasts a couple of clean, quiet and beautiful palm-lined beaches, one of which is the site of the idyllic Green Turtle Lodge. It is possible to arrange canoe trips with local fishermen into the mangrove swamps upriver, where a large variety of birds as well as monkeys are likely to be encountered, especially towards dusk and shortly after dawn. Of minor historical interest is the ruined Fort Dorothea (or Fort Akodaa), situated on a rock promontory immediately south of the old town centre.

The deserted **Nunu Busua Island**, in the bay below the village, can be visited by boat from Busua. There isn't a lot to see on the island, but there's nothing stopping you from camping overnight and peering at the mainland if the mood takes you. Swimming out to the island cannot be recommended – even if the tides don't put you off, the proliferation of stinging jellyfish should! If you want to boat to the island, arrange it from the village itself – first visiting the chief (with the customary bottle of Schnapps) if you want to camp overnight – as arrangements made via the hotels are very costly.

GETTING THERE AND AWAY Dixcove and Busua lie no more than 2km apart and roughly 20km east of Takoradi as the crow flies. To reach either town, follow the main Elubo road east of Takoradi to the junction town of Agona, then take the left turn signposted for Busua Beach Resort. This road splits at Asane, about 6km south out of Agona, with the left fork reaching Busua after another 4km and the right fork reaching Dixcove after about 5km. So far as I'm aware, no tro-tros connect Takoradi directly to Dixcove and Busua, but there are regular tro-tros from Takoradi to Agona for US$0.50, from where tro-tros run every hour or so to both Dixcove and Busua.

There is no direct road between Busua and Dixcove. If you want to travel between the two, you have three options: to catch a tro-tro back to Agona and change vehicles there, to charter a private taxi between the two, or to walk. The two towns are connected by a 1.5km footpath, which takes about 15–20 minutes to cover. The path leaves Dixcove from alongside the fort and Busua from the opposite side of the estuary next to the fishing harbour. Do be aware that you'll have to wade through the estuary at Busua, which is safe enough at low tide when the water is thigh height, but dangerous at high tide, according to some locals. Of greater concern perhaps are several recent reports of robberies along this footpath, on which basis it would be extremely risky to walk between Busua and Dixcove with luggage or any valuables on your person, or without a local guide recommended to you by another traveller or a hotel/restaurant owner.

Butre lies 3km east of Busua and can be reached along a direct footpath which follows Busua Beach for about 500m before ascending low cultivated hills that offer some lovely views over the ocean. There are also reasonably regular shared taxis connecting Agona junction to Butre along the signposted dirt road that forks left from the Busua road just south of Asane. Should you have your own vehicle, head along this road for about 3km, then turn right at Tentum (aka Tontu) and you will reach Butre after another 4km.

To get to Akwidaa by private vehicle, turn right at the taxi station as you enter Dixcove and follow this road for about 10km, passing Green Turtle Lodge to your left about 1km before entering the village. Reasonably regular tro-tros from Agona junction or Dixcove to Akwidaa can drop passengers at Green Turtle Lodge.

It is also possible to hike between Dixcove and Akwidaa. The more straightforward route is to follow the roughly 12km-long road via Achowa, but this runs inland and offers little in the way of scenic interest or shade. An alternative but slightly longer route passes through Mediya, an ancient and interesting village, dotted with the clearly visible remains of many old buildings, which lies about 4km from Dixcove by road. Onwards from Mediya, an interesting bush track leads to Chavane across thick, overgrown farmland and a series of small and rather precarious bamboo bridges, as well as a dark, shaded passage where many butterflies and birds can be seen and heard. En route to Chavane, Breman is a small village where you can witness the palm-oil production process. From Chavane, the road continues to Kwamanfokrom through a rubber plantation, the management of which is willing to offer information on request. From Kwamanfokrom, it is a further 5km to Akwidaa by road.

WHERE TO STAY
Upmarket
African Rainbow Resort \ 031 32149;
e africanrainbow@gmail.com or arr@africaonline.
com.gh; www.africanrainbowresort.com. This relatively

new resort, which opened in early 2003, has rapidly acquired an enviable reputation thanks largely to the hospitable & attentive attitude of the Canadian-Ghanaian owner managers. The 3-storey block – designed by their architect son with a view to being naturally airy – offers 12 spacious self-contained rooms, each with their own private balcony looking over the road to the sea. Rooms have DSTV, minibar, fan & hot water, & the price includes a good b/fast. The restaurant has excellent pizzas & other continental dishes in the US$4–10 range, which are routinely served on the ground floor but can be taken to the rooftop bar for a small extra charge. There is also an indoor bar with a great sound system & pool table, as well as a well-stocked curio shop & kayak for hire. The only real drawback to this place is the lack of a private beach, but the Alaska Beach Club & Busua Beach Resort both lie within metres of the gate. A private taxi is available for day trips, as well as transfers from Agona junction, Cape Coast & Accra. *Sgl/dbl US$45/50, or US$60/65 with AC. Extra mattress US$1.*

Budget
🏠 **Alaska Beach Club** 📞 020 7412660. Boasting an idyllic beach-front location adjacent to Busua Beach Resort, the Alaska Beach Club is the most inherently attractive budget option in Busua itself, & its relaxed lively atmosphere has made it a perennially popular hangout for volunteers & budget travellers. Unfortunately it's also the spot that seems to have garnered the most polarised comments in Ghana, with some travellers rating it as a superb place to stay, & others complaining of a noisy bar, rude management, dirty rooms & – more worryingly – frequent theft from the rooms. There has been a change of management fairly recently so these problems may have abated, but you could be better off using this one as a great hangout, by day or night, & take a room elsewhere. If you do decide to stay, accommodation rates are very reasonable. Two twin rooms could sleep 4, at a push. The attached restaurant serves pizzas for US$4.50–8.50 (small/large), as well as sandwiches, salads & Ghanaian dishes from US$2.50. *Dbl with common bath US$8.50, 2 twins US$15, self-contained dbl US$20.*

🏠 **Black Mamba Corner** 📞 024 67106271 or 024 6427495. Situated on the western outskirts of town, this highly recommended German-run eatery recently attached 2 secluded dbl chalets with a shared bath & their own, private stone beach. The set up is reached across a new footbridge & then up a bushy footpath guarded by 4 lively dogs; once there, you can expect to eat fabulously well, choosing (with considerable advance notice!) from a large & ambitious menu & served on a shady terrace. *Dbl chalet US$12.*

🏠 **Bliss Joy Lodge** 📞 020 8885154. Set about 100m back from the beach off the Agona road, this rather dingy little guesthouse is a friendly place, but seems a

🏠 **Busua Beach Resort** 📞 031 93307/8/9; 📠 031 21858; 📧 busua@gbhghana.com. This popular resort re-opened in all its newly renovated glory in late 1996, since when it has acquired a justified reputation as one of Ghana's top beach hotels, & more recently been bought out by the Golden Beach Hotels Group. Set in large landscaped grounds, right on the beach, it has excellent watersport facilities inc jet ski hire, as well as a swimming pool, curio shops, tennis court, 35-seat tourist coach for hire, restaurant & a three-hole golf course. By international standards, Busua Beach Resort is good value, with plush self-contained rooms with ocean view, AC & DSTV. Budget rooms available, theoretically aimed at backpackers. Be warned that prices more or less double at Christmas. *Dbl/twin US$70/80, suite US$90, budget room with fan US$20 pp, extra mattress US$12.*

touch overpriced. Dbl rooms are large but grimy and use common showers. Some are slightly smarter with AC. Internet access is advertised at a steep 5 cents per minute, but the service is – to put it kindly – somewhat erratic. *Dbl US$8–15.*

🏠 **Busua Inn** This French-owned beach-front restaurant also offers some accommodation, in three large & exceedingly comfortable self-contained rooms, prices depending on whether they have hot water, AC & a sea view. The most expensive room also enjoys a terrace overlooking the sea, which is available for use by the other guests if the AC room is unoccupied, as well as by restaurant customers if the hotel is empty. Another plus is the excellent French-influenced menu, which includes pain au chocolat & crepes, as well as many more complicated dishes priced around US$6.50, which need to be ordered in advance. *US$17, US$23 & US$35.*

🏠 **Dadson's Lodge** 📞 024 4947326. This long-serving & popular budget lodge is the first place you'll pass, on your right when walking from the tro-tro park in Busua towards Busua Beach Resort. The building itself is a fairly uninspiring double-storey structure, but the management seems friendly & the rooms fairly priced. The large indoor restaurant on the ground floor serves an extensive range of dishes at US$2.50–3.50. *Sgl/dbl with fan & common shower US$7/9, self-contained suites US$12.*

🏠 **Fanta's Folly** 📞 024 3213677; 📧 pbreuillot@ hotmail.com. This newly established lodge just above the beach 1km west of Asemkow, is run by a charming French-Nigerian couple, & has been widely praised by readers for their delicious French-style home-cooking. Accommodation is provided in comfortable, colourful, individually designed chalets or in a first-floor flat using common showers, which caters for up to 4. Camping is permitted, with discounts negotiable for groups, & monkey-spotting canoe trips can be arranged into the mangroves behind the resort. Some food can be rustled up on the spot but you're best off ordering up to a day in advance. Count on paying around US$2.50 for a salad, US$6–8.50 for most main courses (like carpaccio & ossobucco) & US$11 for lobster. To reach Fanta's Folly on public transport, take a tro-tro from Angona junction direct to the Asemkowk, & ask to be dropped 1km early where a new dirt road has been signposted. Alternatively, you could go to Butre & walk 2.4km east along the beach. *Chalets: dbl US$20, 2 dbls US$35 & 2 sgls & 1 dbl US$40. Flat US$40. Camping US$3 pp.*

🏠 **Green Turtle Lodge** 📞 024 893566; e greenturtlelodge@yahoo.co.uk. Set on a beautiful palm-lined beach 1km east of Akwidaa, this relaxed new eco-lodge is a devil for disturbing travel plans, as people who arrive often find they never want to leave. The place is run by an infectiously enthusiastic young English couple, committed to keeping the environmental impact of the lodge at a minimum, & prices within the range of most backpackers. Dormitory accommodation is available, or large, cool clay bungalows with mosquito netted beds (inc some bamboo 4-posters) using common showers/self-contained. The open-air Calabash Kitchen offers simple but imaginative dishes using seasonal produce, together with a mean cocktail menu, wines & the usual beers, whilst the communal lounge/bar has comfortable sofas for relaxing, table football, a book-swap service & a range of board & beach-games. The lodge itself – which was traditionally constructed, using mostly local, sustainable materials – runs on solar power & has self-composting toilets that rely on ash to keep away the nasty smells. It has also worked hard to ensure good relations with the community by employing people from Akwidaa, & runs a turtle rescue service that compensates fisherman who break their nets with accidental leatherback catches, so that they don't have to sell the animal for meat (see box). Green Turtle can also arrange a variety of excursions inc canoe trips through the mangroves, hiking & biking trails through the Cape Three Points Forest Reserve to Prince's Town's Woodstock resort (complete with baggage transfer), & trips further afield to good surfing spots, the Nzulezu Stilt Village & Ankasa Forest Reserve. The tour company Soul of Africa Trails operates from the lodge. W/ends & holidays get very busy, so it's worth making a reservation by SMS. *Dormitory: US$4 pp. Bungalow: dbl US$10–20.*

🏠 **Hideout Lodge** 📞 020 7369258 or 020 7357039; e contact@hideoutlodge.com; www.hideoutlodge.com. Set on a forest-fringed sandy beach just across a small river from the village of Butre, this excellent lodge pairs a Rasta-vibe with one of the most attractive hang-out spots anywhere in Ghana. Accommodation consists of 6 low-ceilinged dbl huts, each with fan, private bathroom & porch, or 2 5-bed dormitories. Camping is permitted, but a more tempting alternative for budget travellers is a spot in the open loft overlooking the sea. The beach-front bar/restaurant serves good pasta, salads, & local dishes at around US$3 a plate. The lodge is reached from Butre across a small wooden footbridge, from where it is a 5-minute walk, or along a newly built dirt road signposted from Asemkow. For most visitors, the main attraction is the opportunity to chill out on a remote, pristine beach, but it's also worth arranging an early morning canoe trip 45 minutes upriver to look for monkeys, birds & crocodiles (US$5 pp). *Dbl hut US$15, bed in dorm US$4 pp. Camping US$2 pp, or in loft US$3.*

🏠 **Safari Beach** 📞 024 6651329 or 027 7723274; e safaribeachlodge@yahoo.com. Just along the beach from the Green Turtle, Safari Beach is a similar proposition with a more upmarket feel & corresponding prices. Accommodation is provided in spacious, self-contained round huts, all with mosquito-netted 4-posters & individually decorated with a tremendous eye for detail, together with artefacts collected by the American owners from their journeys in other parts of Africa. Smaller, cheaper rooms with outside showers are available, which typically accommodate 3 people. Overlanders are welcomed at US$5 a vehicle. But a bigger attraction still is the lodge's ambitious gourmet menu, inspired by the owners' travels in Asia & rated by some French tourists to be as good as anything they could get at home. Happily, there is a well-stocked bar & an impressive wine list to match. Expect to pay around US$10 for 3 courses without drinks. The lodge also offers a tempting curios shop, stocked with African artefacts & restored colonial furniture, & can arrange transfers with the Mighty Victory Hotel in Cape Coast. *Hut US$35, smaller room US$7 pp.*

Shoestring

🏠 **Elizabeth's Guesthouse** 📞 020 292263493. Another former homestay, this little upstairs guesthouse would feel slightly overpriced, were it not for the super-friendly management & the inclusion of a fruit & pancake b/fast. Rooms are small & basic & share a sgl shower & dingy common toilet. *Sgl/dbl US$7/9.*

🏠 **Fort Metal Cross** The eccentric English owner of this fort in Dixcove is renovating the building, reportedly with a view to creating an upmarket hotel complete with staff in colonial uniforms. Whilst the tastefulness of this enterprise is questionable, the fort is bound to benefit from some TLC & could make a very interesting overnight stay.

⌂ **Sabina's Guesthouse** 📞 020 9263437. This simple, family-run guesthouse evolved from a homestay set-up

started about ten years ago, providing basic but reasonably clean rooms, some of which have fans. The cheaper sgls will be attractive to budget-conscious solo travellers, except during the rainy season when the roof leaks, but the more expensive dbls seem poor value by comparison to Dadson's Lodge. Inexpensive meals are available on request. *Sgl/dbl US$5/7.*

✗ **WHERE TO EAT** Of the hotels listed above, **Black Mamba Corner** is the most special place to eat, offering a vast choice of freshly cooked, generous dishes at a few hours or preferably a day's notice (US$7–9 a plate), or pizzas and salads on the spot. **Busua Inn**, **Busua Beach Resort** and **African Rainbow Resort** also have good restaurants serving Western-style dishes from around US$4 upwards, and the latter – with its roof-top bar or downstairs pool table – is a good place to hang out in the evening. Cheaper food is available at **Dadson's Lodge** and the **Alaska Beach Club**. The food at both **Hideout Lodge** and **Fanta's Folly** is also recommended, but you're unlikely to eat at either place unless you sleep there too.

✗ **Daniel the Pancake Man** The pioneer among Busua's improbable cast of specialist name caterers (Joseph the Lobster Man, Frank the Juice Man et al), the friendly Daniel has recently opened a new restaurant close to Sabina's Guesthouse. In addition to preparing his 'world-famous' pancakes, Daniel serves great fruit juice & a vast menu of main dishes at very reasonable prices. Joseph the Lobster Man meanwhile has shifted his brand to Waters the Lobster Man after he was copied by too many impostors!

✗ **Hidden Treasure** This newly opened restaurant, located adjacent to Dadson's Lodge, consists of just 2 intimate front tables & serves moderately priced local & Western meals such as roast chicken & grilled lobster, though you should order half a day before you want to eat. It also offers bonfires & drumming & dancing lessons. *Meals from US$3–6.*

✗ **Sankofa Beach Spot** This pleasant if rather cramped bar is a good place to enjoy a drink on the beach –

food can be arranged by advance order through Joseph/Waters the Lobster Man next door!

✗ **Zweite Heimat** This shack opposite the main junction is really nothing more than a chop bar, but the scrawlings of dozens of visitors on the walls testify to the quality of its food. Serves Ghanaian & fish dishes, with more expensive shrimp pizza & lobster. If you want to stay put, the outside table makes for a nice people-watching spot, but there are 2 more inside if it rains. Nana Yaw, who runs the joint, is also a self-styled source of free tourist information, & although he has no official mandate he does seem genuinely helpful. A second, indoor branch of Zweite Heimat is planned along the street to the west of town, & an associated guesthouse is currently under construction on top of the hill to the left before you enter. *Most dishes US$4–7, rising to US$10. Generally cheaper to take away.*

THE COAST BETWEEN AKWIDAA AND AXIM

The coastal strip west of Akwidaa and east of Axim has stagnated economically since the 1970s, when a crippling outbreak of a disease known as Cape St Paul's Wilt struck the extensive coconut plantations on which the local economy was based. It is, however, a region of great natural, historical and cultural importance, centred on arguably the most scenic stretch of coast anywhere in the country. Unfortunately, tourist facilities in the region are currently rather limited, with the only formal accommodation in the region being available at Prince's Town, where several rooms are available to travellers. Several other villages along the coast could be visited as day trips in a private vehicle, or using the tro-tros that connect them to the main Takoradi–Axim road.

The area is of particular interest to adventurous hikers who could, at present, walk between most coastal villages using an existing network of local footpaths. Following an ecotourism assessment in early 1999, the NCRC has come up with

TURTLE CONSERVATION

Jo Miles, Green Turtle Lodge

Marine turtles are ancient reptiles, or 'living dinosaurs', that have been swimming through our oceans for one hundred million years. Marine turtles survived while dinosaurs became extinct, but since their decline in the 20th century, they are now on the brink of extinction, with all but one of the world's seven species now listed on the IUCN (International Union for the Conservation of Nature and Natural Resources) Red List, three of them being classified as Critically Endangered. Three species of marine turtle exist in Ghana and can be found nesting on many of Ghana's beaches. These are the leatherback, the green turtle and the olive ridley. The leatherback is the largest of all marine turtles: the length of their shell can be up to 178cm and they can weigh up to 900kg.

In the 20th century, there became a global market for turtle meat and eggs, which were seen as a delicacy in the West and thus valued highly along with turtle shells. This demand led to mass hunting of the sea turtles and their eggs. However, the biggest cause of death to sea turtles and, therefore, the biggest threat to them becoming extinct is commercial fishing. Huge boats, far out at sea with enormous nets, trawl the ocean for shrimps and fish. Unfortunately, sea turtles get caught and trapped in these nets. Thousands of turtles can be killed in only a few weeks when the trawling occurs in nesting season. These international threats to turtles are being mirrored in Ghana where fishermen using nets can accidentally catch a turtle that becomes entangled in the net. There is also hunting of turtles nesting on the beaches and poaching of eggs, both of which are seen as a rich source of protein. In Ghana during the nesting season, from August to March, about 1,300 sea turtles venture onto the beaches to lay their eggs. Unfortunately, about 60% of these turtles are caught by fishermen and more than one million of their eggs are destroyed by man and domestic animals. In recognition and co-operation with international efforts at turtle conservation, Ghanaian law states that it is illegal to catch or kill sea turtles and to sell their meat or eggs.

The Wildlife Division of Ghana and Ghana Wildlife Society are working hard on several conservation projects undertaking research, public awareness, and protection of nesting turtles and their eggs. Eco-tourism projects offer night hikes to observe nesting turtles, the payment for which goes directly into a turtle conservation fund. Current turtle conservation projects in Ghana are trying to involve and employ local people from the villages where turtles have been nesting for years, whilst educating them about the importance of protecting the endangered turtles. To change long-standing beliefs and behaviours is a process that takes time. Introducing, for the first time, the idea of conservation, preserving rather than killing and eating sea turtles to make a living or feed one's family, requires a major shift in beliefs and behaviours. This is not something that will happen overnight. However, movement towards this is a positive step and something that tourists visiting nesting beaches can support and help sustain.

For more information about how you can get involved in turtle conservation during your visit to Ghana contact **Green Turtle Lodge** (☎ *0244 893566;* ✉ *contactus@ greenturtlelodge.com; www.greenturtlelodge.com*).

the concept of a Heritage Trail through the region, which will run from Butre to the Ankasa Resource Reserve via Busua, Dixcove, Akwidaa, Cape Three Points, Prince's Town, Egyambra and Axim. The idea is to link the region's various natural and cultural sites by supplementing local footpaths with some new and more scenic trails, all of which will be signposted and serviced by a series of community-managed ecotourist lodges and campsites. This, it is hoped, will not only attract tourism to a neglected corner of Ghana, but also ensure that the economic, environmental, and social benefits of this tourism are spread throughout the rural communities involved.

In the second edition of this guide, I stated that the Heritage Trail was still just a gleam in the eyes of the NCRC, and predicted that few if any tangible developments would occur in the immediate future. Whilst this prediction has been proved correct, and there remains no immediate prospect of further NCRC involvement in the area, it does seem likely that the Heritage Trail will see some development over the next few years through the collective impetus of the owners of the African Rainbow Resort, Green Turtle Lodge and Ellis Hideout, all of whom have expressed a strong interest in developing the area. Until such time as that happens, however, local footpaths open to adventurous travellers already cover many legs of the mooted trail.

The major problem facing travellers along several stretches of this trail is that formal accommodation between Akwidaa and Axim exists only at Prince's Town. It should, however, be possible to camp in most villages with the permission of the local chief. Given this, and the lack of a formal tourist infrastructure, it is recommended that you engage the services of a local guide and buy the appropriate 1:50,000 survey sheets in Accra (0402A1 and 0403B2).

CAPE THREE POINTS Situated about halfway between Akwidaa and Prince's Town, Cape Three Points is the most southerly point in Ghana, and the site of a 19th-century lighthouse. The panoramic views from the low cliffs around the lighthouse are stunning, and whales sometimes come close to shore between November and January. At the base of the cape lies a small fishing village and a clean sandy beach that completely justifies the bumpy ride there.

About 3km inland of the cliffs, the Cape Three Points Forest Reserve, demarcated in 1949, extends over 51km² of low hills to protect what is probably Ghana's most extensive remaining patch of near-pristine coastal forest. Undeveloped for tourism, this small reserve is regarded as having a biodiversity rating as high as that of Ankasa, and more than half of its area has been unaffected by commercial logging. Cape Three Points is reputedly still home to small populations of several large mammal species, including the endangered Diana monkey, white-crested sooty mangabey and bongo antelope. More than 160 bird species are known, including spot-throated ibis, crowned eagle, chocolate-backed kingfisher, great blue turaco, yellow-billed turaco, blue cuckoo-shrike, five hornbill species (including the rare yellow-casqued hornbill) and possibly white-breasted guineafowl, though the density of the canopy makes birdwatching somewhat more challenging here than at Ankasa or Kakum. The forest at Cape Three Points is among the least ecologically compromised in Ghana, and is not under any great pressure from subsistence hunters, though the recent discovery of alluvial gold within its boundaries might pose a limited medium-term threat.

GETTING THERE AND AWAY An extension of the road between Agona junction and Akwidaa continues on to Cape Three Points, passing within 1km of the forest boundary at Tumentu. For hikers, the scenery from this 10km stretch of road is somewhat monotonous, but at present no coastal footpath exists as an alternative. Shared taxis between Agona and Akwidaa don't normally continue to Cape Three Points, but it should be possible – and not dauntingly expensive – to charter one of them to take you there.

In the other direction, Cape Three Points is linked to Prince's Town by a well-marked and scenic footpath that leads to Aketechi then follows the sandbar dividing the ocean from the 2.5km-long Ehunu Lagoon. This walk takes about two hours, which means that one could visit Cape Three Points on foot as a round day trip from Prince's Town, possibly breaking up the walk by canoeing across the lagoon. Canoes are probably best arranged from Prince's Town, as the villagers at Aketechi on the eastern side of the lagoon reputedly ask exorbitant fees.

An alternative route between Akwidaa and Prince's Town offers the opportunity to walk inside the Cape Three Points Forest Reserve. To do this, however, it is essential to be accompanied by a knowledgeable local guide, as there are many tracks in the forest and one might otherwise get lost – Green Turtle Lodge in Akwidaa can supply further information. The hike involves a 3–4km walk through cultivation to the forest boundary near Tumentu. The trail within the reserve is about 8km long, shady, and of great interest to butterfly and bird enthusiasts, with the small possibility of encountering monkeys. The trail leaves the forest close to Aketechi, from where one can follow the footpath alongside the lagoon, or try to arrange a canoe.

 WHERE TO STAY AND EAT There is no formal accommodation, but it is normally possible to stay at a room in the lighthouse. A proper eco-lodge is likely to open as and when the Heritage Trail is established.

PRINCE'S TOWN

Rather isolated, yet easily the best-equipped stop for tourists along this stretch of coast, Prince's Town is notable not least for having acquired a list of aliases worthy of the most notorious of gangsters – Prince's Terre, Princess Town and Prusi for starters. Set on an attractive and largely unspoilt stretch of coast on the eastern bank of the Nyila River mouth, Prince's Town is visited by very few travellers, partially as a result of its distance from the main Takoradi–Elubo road. The centrepiece of the small town is Fort Gross Friedrichsburg, a near ruin at the time of independence, but now fully restored and functioning as a resthouse.

Fort Gross Friedrichsburg has a rather unusual history. It is the only fort in Ghana with Germanic associations, built as it was by the Brandenburg Africa Company, a latecomer to the European struggle for dominance of the Gold Coast, formed in 1682 as a representative of Prince Friedrich of Brandenburg. After landing at the village then known as Pokesu in 1683, the Brandenburgers were ceded the promontory on which the fort now stands, in exchange for which they offered the village protection against the Dutch and other slave raiders. By the 1690s, Fort Gross Friedrichsburg had become the most important smuggling centre on the coast, simply because the officials received so few ships from Brandenburg that they were forced to trade illicitly with other nations to make a profit.

In 1716, the Brandenburgers abandoned their fort to John Connie, an Ahanta chief who had already acquired the nickname 'King of Prince's Terre' for his role at the centre of a trade network so powerful that it caused a temporary decline in the fortunes of nearby Dutch ports such as Dixcove and Axim. Over the next decade, the fort was the centre of a series of military clashes between the Dutch and John Connie, and word of the Ahanta chief's victories over a European power made him something of a folk hero in the slave plantations of the Caribbean (Connie is evidently the source of the John Canoe festivals that have been celebrated in the region ever since). Gross Friedrichsburg was finally captured by the Dutch in 1724 and re-named Fort Hollandia; it remained under Dutch control for almost 150 years before being handed to Britain as part of the treaty signed in 1872. Despite all this, the most striking thing about the fort today is how little it looks like a military building – on first glance, it could easily be mistaken for an old colonial governor's residence or something similar.

Aside from the fort, Prince's Town forms the base for several interesting day trips, normally arranged through the fort's caretaker. The most popular goal in the area is the crocodile pond at the village of Egyambra, which lies about a two-hour walk from Prince's Town, and can also be reached by a boat along the Kpani River. Although Egyambra can be visited independently of an overnight stay at Prince's Town (see *Egyambra*, page 200), Prince's Town is currently the most popular and probably the easiest base from which to visit it.

Immediately east of Prince's Town lies the beautiful Ehunu Lagoon, a 2km² expanse separated from the ocean by a narrow, sandy – and practically uninhabited – beach that is reputedly safe for swimming. Canoe trips on the lagoon can be arranged with the caretaker at the fort for around US$3 per person; there is a good chance of seeing black-and-white colobus monkeys from the boat, especially in the early morning, and you can also ask to be taken to a bamboo forest and a traditional palm-wine distillery. It is also possible to walk from the lagoon on to Cape Three Points, which lies about two hours each way from Prince's Town, or into the Cape Three Points Forest Reserve – both possibilities are elaborated on under the *Getting there and away* section for Cape Three Points.

GETTING THERE AND AWAY Prince's Town is 18km from Abora junction on the main Takoradi–Elubo road and is signposted. Any vehicle heading between Agona and Axim can drop you at the junction, where you'll probably be in for a long wait – there's not a lot of transport, but you should get through eventually, except perhaps after heavy rain when the road has in the past tended to become impassable.

Details of the hike from Cape Three Points and to Egyambra are covered under those headings.

WHERE TO STAY

Fort Gross Friedrichsburg contains four dbl rooms with a fan for about US$4 pp, & a communal bucket shower is available. Recent reports suggest that the rooms in the fort are very dirty & crawling with spiders, as well as being subject to nocturnal visits by drunken locals! Meals can be prepared with advance notice, or there are a couple of chop shops in the village.

Two other private options exist. The first is a 3-bedroom **German-owned house** with a garden & living-room on the beach near the fort, which can be rented in its entirety for around US$20 per night – excellent value, especially for a group. This can be arranged through the fort's caretaker, who can also prepare inexpensive meals.

Woodstock ☎ 027 644 33 50 or 024 6170771; e contact@woodstockghana.com;

www.woodstockghana.com. Set up in 2006 by a pair of young Swedish overlanders, this idyllic resort was still under construction as this edition went to print. Accommodation is provided in a series of stilted huts, built along a palm-fringed stretch of beach flanked by the Ehunu Lagoon on one side & the Atlantic on the other. There are dormitory beds or self-contained dbls with mosquito nets & hot water. There is an attached camping area built with overlanders in mind. The Face bar offers good food & a choice of drinks, as well as a book swap & board games. The lodge can also organise a number of canoe & hiking tours, including an overnight trek through Cape Three Points Forest Reserve to Green Turtle Lodge, complete with luggage transfer. *Dormitory: US$4 pp, self-contained dbl US$22.*

The other option is an **anonymous beach camp**, also German-owned, which consists of four small but comfortable stilted houses without electricity, situated on the beach between the river mouth & the cemetery. The houses cost around US$9 each, & food can be prepared on request. Further details can be obtained from the caretaker at quarshiejohn@yahoo.com.

EGYAMBRA

Situated about 6km west of Prince's Town as the crow flies, Egyambra (aka Agyembrah) is of interest mainly for a sacred crocodile pond, which offers a similar but less publicised experience to the one at Paga on the Burkina Faso border. For a negotiable fee of around US$5–10, the fetish priest at the pond will call a crocodile to be fed, chanting as he pours a (traditional?) bottle of coke into the water. When the crocodile arrives, it feeds on one (of two) chickens provided by the visitor. At this time, there is an opportunity to take photographs, but the crocodile soon disappears back into the water with the chicken in its mouth. In addition to the fee, each party of visitors must provide a chicken, a cockerel and two bottles of coke.

GETTING THERE AND AWAY A rough 15–20km road connects Egyambra to the main Takoradi–Axim road at Anyame. Public transport along this road leaves from Axim and Agona junction (near Busua) and is reasonably frequent. Since the crocodile ceremony takes place only in the morning, travellers wanting to experience it should get an early start.

A more popular option is to visit Egyambra by foot or canoe as a day trip from Prince's Town, something that is easily arranged with the caretaker at Fort Gross Friedrichsburg. From Prince's Town, one can, for a small fee, hire a canoe up the Kpani River as far as Miamia, passing on the way through mangrove swamps teeming with birds. You can also walk along the beach to Miamia, which will take about one hour, with views over the sea and the river and mangroves. It is possible to stop off at the *akpeteshie* distillery on the riverbank between Prince's Town and Miamia to observe the distilling process. The beach at Miamia is very beautiful and perfect for swimming, as the sea is very calm, but it is kept clean only on the eastern part where several private villas have been built. From Miamia, a roughly 1.5km trail continues to Egyambra via the beach and then around a rocky outcrop surrounded by a mass of brightly coloured flowers, all the while offering good views of the sea.

Keen hikers – especially those who travelled to Egyambra by canoe – could think about continuing westward on foot towards Axim, a roughly 10km walk along the beach, with the option after roughly 7km of staying overnight at the superb Axim Beach Resort. The trail towards Axim follows a lovely coastline of palm-lined beaches, shady lagoons, interesting rock formations, and small fishing villages (where one should greet the locals). It would be advisable to take a guide along this route, which is currently used by few tourists.

 WHERE TO STAY AND EAT Egyambra currently has no accommodation, though there is probably nothing stopping you from asking permission to camp, and there are a few chop bars.

AXIM

The largest town on the coast west of Takoradi, Axim (pronounced more like *Azsim*) is also the site of Ghana's second-oldest fort. The triangular Fort São Antonio dates to the Portuguese era, and although its exact year of construction is not on record, most authorities reckon it to be around 1515. Positioned on an outcrop, with excellent natural protection in the form of a few small rocky islands and a reef, the fort was captured by Holland in 1642 and remained under Dutch control until it was handed to Britain in 1872. Unlike St George's Castle in Elmina, nominally the oldest European building in Africa, the basic shape of Fort São

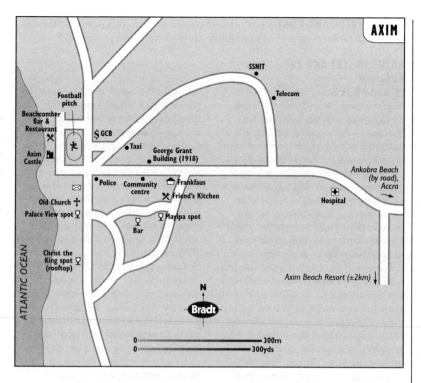

SSNIT

Telecom

Football
pitch

Beachcomber
Bar &
Restaurant

$ GCB

Taxi

George Grant
Building (1918)

Ankobra Beach
(by road),
Accra

Axim
Castle

Police Community
centre

Frankfaus

Friend's Kitchen

Hospital

Old Church ✝

Palace View spot

Mayipa spot

Bar

ATLANTIC OCEAN

Christ the
King spot
(rooftop)

Axim Beach Resort (±2km)

N

Bradt

0 — 300m
0 — 300yds

Antonio's bastions has changed little since the 16th century. The three-storey
building that rises above the main fortifications was added during the period of
Dutch occupation, but is recognisable from an etching dating from 1682.

Axim was once one of the busiest trading posts anywhere on the west African
coast. In the late 17th century, more gold was traded through Fort São Antonio
than any other Dutch fort, and in the 18th century the surrounding area became
an important source of cotton and timber. In the colonial era, Fort São Antonio was
used as a regional administrative centre, and it continued to house government
offices until early 2000. Since then, the offices have been moved elsewhere and the
fort has opened up formally to tourism, though plans that it will become a
resthouse have yet to be realised.

Aside from the fort, which is one of the most impressive in Ghana, there is
little about Axim today that betrays its historical significance. In the first edition
of this guide I described the town as 'the most characterless port in Ghana,
chronically run-down and rather unwelcoming', an assessment which, in
hindsight, seems unduly harsh. It helps, of course, that the town's most important
tourist attraction is now open to the public, especially as the vantage point offered
by the fort over the beach-front is thoroughly arresting. But on revisiting Axim, I
found it to be a rather interesting town: friendly, atmospheric and refreshingly
untouristed.

Whatever else one might think about Axim, there is no denying it lies close to
two beaches of almost breathtaking perfection. These are Ankobra Beach, about
3km northwest of town, and Awangazule Beach, a similar distance to the southeast.
Both of these beaches are serviced by comfortably rustic and reasonably priced
resorts (see *Where to stay* on page 202); either one of them alone is worth coming
this far west of Takoradi to stay at.

GETTING THERE AND AWAY Regular tro-tros connect Axim to Takoradi in the east, to Essiama to the west, and to most other towns along the west coast.

🏠 WHERE TO STAY AND EAT
Moderate

🏠 **Ankobra Beach Resort** 📞 031 92321/3 or 024 3592294; e ankobra_beach@hotmail.com. Situated about 500m south of the main Takoradi–Elubo road, from where it is clearly signposted about 5km west of the Axim turn-off, Ankobra Beach Resort is surrounded by a small pine wood on a beautiful beach close to the mouth of the Ankobra River. In addition to having an attractive layout, the resort places a strong emphasis on cultural & historical excursions, for instance to the various slave forts & Nzulezo stilt village near Beyin. Accommodation is in rustic but comfortable detached & semi-detached bungalows, strung out over several hundred metres through the tall palms. Best value for large parties is a 4-person 'family bungalow' with a fan & its own veranda. The open-air restaurant is atmospheric & the food excellent. If you are reliant on public transport, any tro-tro heading along the main road can drop you at the signposted junction, from where it's a 5-minute walk to the resort. Note that while the beach at Ankobra is safe, we have had reports of travellers wandering along the beach between Ankobra & Axim being mugged. *Family bungalow: US$43. Village room: dbl US$37, sgl US$17.*

🏠 **Axim Beach Resort** 📞 020 8121753 or 024 4885920 or 024 3211068 or 031 92397; e info@aximbeach.com; www.aximbeach.com. Planted on a rocky promontory to the southeast of Axim, this resort overlooks a pristine & virtually uninhabited expanse of palm-fringed swimming beach stretching eastwards towards the Awangazule Lagoon. It's the stuff of desert-island fantasies, but the swift expansion of the resort & the recent addition of TVs in every room seem rather defeat the point. Accommodation is decorated in tasteful African style, with a choice of sgl attic room, twin room in a block, circular self-contained chalets with fans & solar-heated showers, and 'family huts' for 4 people. There is also a 6-man volunteer chalet for hire

(30% discount to accredited volunteers) & a new 8-man 'Sunset Villa', which comprises 5 inter-linked huts. Although the resort itself has been widely praised by readers, we've received a few negative reports about the open-air restaurants, which serve a variety of local & continental dishes for around US$6. The resort lies along a roughly 2km dirt road, signposted from the feeder road between Axim & the Takoradi–Elubo road about 1km out of central Axim (close to the hospital). If you don't have private transport, you can charter a taxi cheaply from Axim town. *Sgl from US$9, twin US$23, chalet US$37–47, family hut (for 4) US$75–90, 6-man chalet US$120, 8-man villa US$180.*

🏠 **LouMoon Lodge** 📞 020 8241549 or 024 4424497; www.loumoonlodge.com or www.loumoon.net. This very special resort occupies what is probably the most perfect beach spot in Ghana – a picturesque bay bisected by an isthmus, with rocks & wavy waters on one side, & a turquoise-looking glass sea on the other. Happily, the Belgian couple who run the place – & were still finishing construction when this book was researched – have managed to do it justice, with beautifully finished modern buildings that make imaginative use of natural materials & work hard to harmonise with the surrounds. Accommodation ranges from a 2-man travellers' room to an executive suite, or an AC chalet on the isthmus – which becomes an island when the tide comes in – each with glass walls on two sides so you wake up looking out onto the sea. At the centre of the lodge is an airy loft-style bar & restaurant, where the owners plan to offer a set menu for every meal. Facilities at the lodge inc volleyball, canoeing & mountain biking in the surrounding forest. To get there, take a tro-tro from Axim junction to the small fishing village of Agyan; LouMoon is one bay along, accessed along a dirt road. *Dbl (inc b/fast) US$41, suite US$102, chalet US$136.*

Budget

🏠 **Frankfaus Hotel** 📞 0342 22291. The only accommodation in Axim town, this reasonably comfortable double-storey building lies roughly 100m uphill from the tro-tro station & main traffic circle. *Sgl with common shower US$12, self-contained dbl with fan US$15.*

🏠 **Fort São Antonio** Plans are afoot to turn this attractive Portuguese fort into a guesthouse & restaurant, offering 6 rooms at moderate prices. It has

to be said that this was also the case when the second & third editions of this book were researched, but the caretaker assures me that this time the money is ready.

If the fort restaurant does get up & running, it would have to serve very bad food indeed before a dinner on one of its balconies became an unattractive option. In the meantime, the **Beachcomber Bar** just next door is a safe bet.

For local eats, try the **Friend's Kitchen** around the corner from the Frankfaus Hotel. There's no shortage of places to sink a beer or two: the **Christ The King spot** near the post office is notable not only for its monumentally improbable name, but also for having a balcony (facing away from the sea, sad to say) while an **anonymous open-air beach-front bar** next to the fort has a lively, inclusive atmosphere underscored by happy, blaring music.

NKROFUL

This small town 4km north of the main Takoradi–Elubo road is noted as the birthplace of Kwame Nkrumah, Ghana's first president, and the site of the small mausoleum where the former president was buried after his death in 1972. Frankly, this Nkrumah Mausoleum is a rather underwhelming sight by comparison with the vast Nkrumah Mausoleum in Accra (which in any case is where Nkrumah's body now lies). It is easy enough to find, however, lying within the bright pink information centre – children, lots and lots of them, will show you how to get there, not to say drape themselves over the memorial and shove their way in front of the camera, etc.

If you want to visit the mausoleum, ask any vehicle travelling along the main road to drop you at Essiama, from where regular and inexpensive shared taxis go directly to Nkroful. There is now a rather good budget hotel in Nkroful, the **B & Q Guest Inn** (0342 22377), where clean, smart self-contained doubles cost US$9 with fan only or US$11 with air conditioning and TV. A restaurant and bar are attached.

You could also stay in Essiama itself. The **Motel de Miegyina**, which lies behind the Goil garage on the Axim side of the main junction, could hardly be cheaper at US$4 for a basic double. Rather nicer is **Maggie's Guesthouse**, 100m further up the road, which has double rooms with air conditioning for around US$17 and serves good meals on request. For those who enjoy getting off the beaten track, Essiama is worth exploring, notably the road to the beach, which is lined with substantial but decaying residences built by miners in the 1920s and 1930s.

BEYIN, NZULEZO AND THE AMANSURI WETLANDS

The seaside village of Beyin is the site of Fort Apollonia, the last fort to be built by Britain on the Gold Coast, constructed in 1770 with the permission of the Nzema chief, Amenihiya. Fort Apollonia was built in a different manner from any other fort in the country, with a substantially stronger seaward bastion that not only served a defensive purpose, but also contained the cells used to store slaves. Beyin's fort was built to endure, using rock quarried from a site 10km away. It has retained its original shape, despite having been shelled during the war between the British and the French, and having been abandoned for long periods of time. It was renovated in the late 1950s, and converted to a resthouse in the 1970s, in which capacity it still serves at the time of writing. Following a recent agreement reached between the Ghana Museums & Monuments Board and the University of Pisa in Italy, however, the fort is scheduled for conversion to a historical and ethnographical museum dedicated to the Nzema people of the area. The fort aside, Beyin also has an attractively sandy beach, one of the few sites in Ghana where the spectacular European oystercatcher is regularly observed.

Arguably one of Ghana's travel highlights, and certainly a more singular experience than Fort Apollonia, is an excursion to **Nzulezo stilt village** (aka Mzulezo), which lies on the fresh-water Lake Amansuri about 5km from Beyin. Supporting a population of roughly 500 people, Nzulezo is one solid construction raised above the water, consisting of a central wood and raffia walkway with perhaps two dozen individual houses on either side of it. Quite why the people of Nzulezo decided to build their village above the water is an open question – especially as they are not primarily fishermen but agriculturists, whose fertile fields lie about 1km north of the lake. One legend has it that it was built about 500 years ago by refugees from modern-day Nigeria, who were chased there by another tribe during a war. The villagers welcome tourists, except on Thursdays, which are sacred, but it's probably also worth trying to avoid Sundays, when the boatmen may refuse to travel to the village instead of going to church. A recent development at Nzulezo is a small guesthouse catering for overnight stays.

Nzulezo can only be reached by dugout canoe and the one-hour ride there is as rewarding as the village itself, passing through the **Amansuri Wetland**, the largest stand of intact swamp forest in Ghana. The canoes follow the Amansuri River through areas of marsh and open pools fringed by raffia palm thickets and lush jungle until it opens out on to the reflective black water of the lake itself. It's a lovely trip, especially in the early morning cool, and you should see plenty of birds. Pygmy goose and African jacana are abundant on the lily-covered pools, while purple and squacco heron are often flushed from the reeds; purple gallinule and black crake creep through the fringing vegetation; hornbills and plantain-eaters draw attention to themselves as they cackle and chuckle in forest patches, and a variety of colourful bee-eaters, rollers and kingfishers perch silently on low branches. Indeed, keen birdwatchers and photographers could happily spend an additional morning on the water without visiting the village. Note that it is hot out on the water, and there is no shade once on the lake, so remember to take bottled water, wear a shady hat and liberally slap on the sunblock.

GETTING THERE AND AWAY Beyin lies along the dirt road that follows the coast southwest from Awiebo junction on the main Takoradi–Elubo road. Coming from Takoradi, a few direct minibuses leave daily from Busua Station (the first one goes at around 09.00) and take three to four hours. It's often easier and quicker, however, to do this trip in short hops, catching any Elubo-bound transport as far as Awiebo, then picking up a shared taxi to Beyin itself. Heading towards Elubo, there are a few direct vehicles daily, but if nothing is going, you could catch a vehicle bound for Half Assini as far as the village known as 'Tikobo One' and there pick up a shared taxi to Elubo.

All visits to Nzulezo and the Amansuri Wetland must be arranged through the Ghana Wildlife Society (GWS), which has implemented a project for the sustainable development of the lagoon and promotion of its attractions for ecotourism (✆ *031 92310; www.ghanawildlifesociety.org*). Half the attraction of this excursion is the canoe trip there, which lasts roughly an hour in each direction and is charged at US$6 per person return, with discounts for students, Ghanaians and large groups, and about US$1 for a camera. All the money is directed towards six communities in the area and according to the GWS you will not obliged to pay any further fees – but reality is quite different and you are likely to be asked for around US$2 per group which is recorded in a book, as well as for a tip by the boatman on the return journey. A number of travellers report feeling pressured and one notes that 'the boat guides feigned disgust at my tip because it was "not large enough"'– but many travellers still write to say this was the highlight of their trip. The stilt village is open every day including Sundays, and the canoe service is available between 08.00 and 15.00, with later trips possible if you plan to stay at the village overnight.

WHERE TO STAY AND EAT Despite rumours to the contrary, **Fort Apollonia** is still functioning as a resthouse at a cost of US$3 for a basic room. The established alternative is the new **Apollonia Beach Guesthouse**, which consists of a row of attractively situated raffia-palm huts, also at around US$5 apiece. There's a bar with an electric fridge next to the fort, and local food such as fried yam and *kenkey* is available at stalls along the main road. Far more promising, however, is the new **Beyin Beach Resort** (↘ *024 218 8240 or 027 513 9186;* e *Ninasarpong@ hotmail.com*), which opened in early 2007 and has already received positive feedback from one reader. It is conveniently located on the plot next to the Ghana Wildlife Department (where you pay for the canoe ride to Nzulezu) and currently consists of four big wooden chalets and a restaurant, all built using natural materials, with more units likely to be added in the near future. Rates are US$30/50 for a double/family chalet (though cheaper rooms are planned) and a wide selection of food is available, including toasted sandwiches, pizzas, fresh fish, jacket potatoes and croissants.

The only accommodation in Nzulezu itself is the friendly and exceedingly popular new **Homestay Bar & Resthouse** (aka Steve's Place), which consists of five basic but clean stilted rooms constructed entirely from raffia-palm branches and fronds. Basic rooms cost US$6 each, and delicious fish and other meals can be prepared with advance notice at around US$2 a plate.

HALF ASSINI

The most westerly Ghanaian port of any substance is the brilliantly named Half Assini, which lies about 5km from the Côte d'Ivoire border and was the main crossing point between the countries prior to the construction of the modern road to Elubo. Now something of a backwater – albeit one accessible by a good surfaced road – Half Assini lies along a wide sandy beach flanked by a pair of lagoons, one of which is said to harbour an evil witch and the other a good witch. It was the battle for dominance between these witches that led to the tragic sinking of a British cargo vessel offshore of Half Assini in 1913 – a show of strength by the evil witch, or so legend has it. Today, the grave of Captain Williams, who went down with the ship, stands in bizarre isolation in the middle of a road running north of and parallel to the main surfaced road through town.

That minor curiosity aside, Half Assini has little in the way of tourist attractions, though you could do worse than spend a few hours exploring the attractive beach and busy fishing harbour. Should you decide to visit, however, there's plenty of public transport running along the surfaced road from 'Tikobo One', at the junction with the road to Beyin. The comfortable **Hotel Gracia**, which lies on the left side of the main road as you enter Half Assini, charges US$13 for a clean carpeted self-contained double with fan.

ANKASA PROTECTED AREA Updated in 2007 by Phil Marshall of the Protected Areas Development Programme

One of Ghana's most exciting emergent ecotourist destinations, the Ankasa Protected Area comprises the contiguous Nini–Suhien National Park and Ankasa Resource Reserve, which together form a highly accessible and well preserved 509km² chunk of wet evergreen rainforest, bounded on the south by the Ankasa River and on the north by the Nini River. Ankasa is regarded as having the greatest biodiversity of any reserve in Ghana. Up to 300 plant species have been counted in one hectare, with over 870 vascular plant species so far on record for the reserve. The list of more than 70 resident mammal species includes forest elephant, bongo antelope, Ogilby's duiker, bay duiker, golden cat, giant forest hog, and red river hog. All ten forest primates known from Ghana have been recorded in the past, including chimpanzee, mona monkey, spot-nosed monkey, black-and-white colobus and the localised Diana monkey and white-crested sooty mangabey, but it is probable that some primate taxa are now extinct. A checklist of 190 bird species – which excludes the many savanna species found in the surrounding farmland – contains more than 100 forest-obligates, with the localised spot-breasted ibis, grey ground thrush, white-crested tiger heron and white-breasted guinea fowl being of particular note, though the latter hasn't been recorded in longer than a decade. The reserve also protects a prodigious variety of butterflies (some authorities estimate more than 600 species), reptiles, and amphibians.

Ankasa currently has few facilities for tourists, but a second phase of support from the EU should provide some improvements. The project is just getting started, but we are told that plans are being developed to attract private sector involvement in the provision of facilities. At the time of going to print it is too early to state exactly what will be provided, but the construction of an observation tower, overnight hiking trails, mountain bike and canoeing trails, and a private camp aimed at upmarket visitors are being considered. An inexpensive overnight camp will be refurbished, while other facilities that are beyond repair will be removed. Guided walks will be improved, and there is a 25km stretch of gravel road along which visitors are free to walk or cycle.

The entrance fee for non-Ghanaian adults currently is US$2.50 and for students US$1. Vehicle entrance costs US$0.50, guide fees work out at US$0.75 per person per hour, and nominal fees for still and video photography are also levied.

GETTING THERE AND AWAY Ankasa gate and campsite lie 6km north of the main Takoradi–Elubo road along a signposted turn-off 21km east of Elubo, and can be reached in any vehicle. The best day to get to the reserve using public transport is Monday (local market day), when you can catch a tro-tro from Aiyinasi or Elubo to Sowodadem, and then another tro-tro from Sowodadem directly to the Ankasa gate. On other days, your options are either to charter a taxi to the gate from Elubo or Aiyinasi (this shouldn't cost more than US$20 one way), or else to ask a tro-tro heading along the main road to drop you at the junction from where you can hitch or walk the last 6km. If you go for the latter option, it's a pleasant walk on gentle slopes and you can break the walk at a small bar in Amokwasuazo.

Do note that when you arrange transport to Ankasa, you should make it clear that you want to visit the reserve and not the eponymous town.

The Elubo Camp and Park Headquarters, which opened in early 2003, can be approached directly from Elubo town. The entrance gate and camp lie 5km from the town: there is no public transport, but you could walk or charter a taxi.

WHERE TO STAY AND EAT A single camp will be refurbished just inside the main gate, where tourists can camp in shelters with mosquito nets.

Private accommodation is available at **Frenchman's Farm**, a short distance outside Ankasa Gate.

Ankasa Camp About 10 mins' walk west of Ankasa gate, this lovely camp lies in a clearing encircled by tall forest & close to a small waterfall. The current project plans to restore & improve this camp by mid-2008. Accommodation consists of 2 open-sided huts designed to sleep a total of 12 people. Camping with your own equipment costs US$3 per person, or the camp staff can provide you with a kerosene lamp, mosquito net & mattress for US$2.50 per person. Either way, you'll need to supply whatever bedding & food you might need in this hot, sticky climate. Other facilities will (by mid-2008) include a toilet, shower & kitchen with gas cooker & utensils supplied. Meals are available from the restaurant 10 mins' walk away. *US$1–2.50.*

Frenchman's Farm Signposted about 500m before Ankasa gate, & reached via a rough 1km dirt road, Frenchman's Farm (☏ *020 841 2085*) is the only private accommodation in the vicinity of the forest reserve, consisting of a row of small rooms on a stilted wooden platform. It feels rather disorganised, & also seems overpriced. Meals are available, but you need to ring ahead to give 24 hours notice of your requirements. *Dbl US$15 with netting, toilet & bucket shower.*

Nkwanta Camp Situated 8km by road from the Ankasa gate, this staff camp is named after the nearby village of Nkwanta, an ancient slave-trading post mentioned in literature dating from 1640. The last inhabitants were compensated & moved out in the late 1990s. The camp lies near a fantastic stand of bamboo forest often referred to as the Bamboo Cathedral, an excellent site for black-&-white colobus monkey in the morning & for potto at night (though you might need a spotlight or a strong torch to see the latter). The nearby forest regularly turns up fresh bongo spoor (though this elusive antelope is very difficult to see). Little more than 100m from the camp, the mango trees & plantains around the abandoned village are a favoured haunt of elephant during the fruiting season of March to May. There used to be some basic accommodation for tourists here, but it is no longer available.

The 3km Paa Ngrant Trail leads out of Nkwanta Camp along an overgrown logging trail last used in the early 1970s. The area for about 2km around Nkwanta was selectively logged & old concrete concession markers can still be seen. The trail currently extends to the high-tension transmission line that bisects the reserve, a good spot for birdwatching. Past the power line, the pristine rainforest reasserts itself. The trail currently goes to Dyer's Camp at the Suhien River Falls (approximately 20m high & truly beautiful). No facilities are yet available at this site though tents are permitted. Two footbridges will be constructed here in 2007, to enable tourists (& wildlife protection staff) to pass into the National Park. The trail will eventually extend northwards to provide a 3–4 hour hike to a granite outcrop known as Brasso Hill, which, at 167m, is the highest point in the reserve.

ELUBO

Everything about Elubo screams 'border town', from the exceptionally chaotic market spilling over on to the main street, to the hissing moneychangers and mandatory clowns who try to overcharge you for everything on the basis that you've probably just crossed into Ghana from Côte d'Ivoire. As a result, Elubo is the sort of place you'll probably want to pass through as quickly as possible. Redeeming features include the street food – the beef kebabs on sale here are as tender, tasty and generous as any we had in Ghana – and (especially if you have come from the more expensive Côte d'Ivoire) a couple of very reasonably priced hotels. Shortly before this fourth edition went to print, we were alerted to rumours of visitors to Elubo (and the Hotel Cocoville in particular) being murdered and their body parts used for witchcraft and fetish rituals. It's certainly not a story that has hit international headlines, and it all sounds rather fanciful, but apparently the locals are convinced.

GETTING THERE AND AWAY Regular tro-tros connect Elubo to Axim and Takoradi, as well as to Abidjan in Côte d'Ivoire. If you are travelling from Elubo to a point before Axim, you may have to change vehicles in Aiyinasi.

WHERE TO STAY AND EAT

Hotel Cocoville 0345 22041/3. This large hotel still accepts guests, but it is barely staffed, the restaurant & bar have closed, there is no electricity or water, & it lies at the centre of rumours about abductions & witchcraft in Elubo. That fairly weighty list of negatives aside, the hotel's location is pleasant – about 200m from the lorry station overlooking the Tano River. *Dbl with fan US$7, with TV US$9, with AC US$13.*

Hotel Falon An adequate budget hotel, situated opposite the lorry station. *Dbl with common bucket showers US$3.50, self-contained dbl with fan US$5.*

The most discerning travel magazine this side of Nanga Parbat
Michael Palin

Every issue includes:
● Stunning photography to entice you ● Expert advice to keep you safe & savvy
● Unique trip ideas to inspire you ● News & reviews to save you time & money

Subscribe today – save 25% UK subscriptions cost only £22.80 for eight issues

TO SUBSCRIBE ● **Call:** 01753 620426 (and quote 'BRADT')
● **Online:** www.wanderlust.co.uk

Wanderlust
SPECIAL ISSUE

Save the WORLD

WIN A TRIP TO BORNEO

8 issues only
£22.80 (UK)

Part Four

EASTERN GHANA

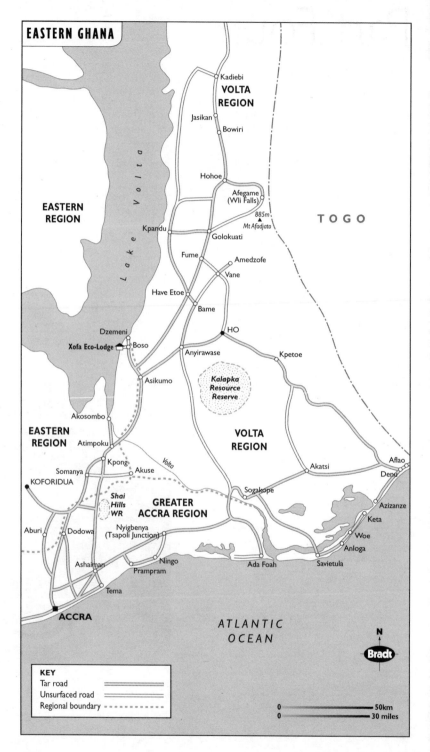

EASTERN GHANA

VOLTA REGION

Kadiebi

Jasikan

Bowiri

Hohoe

Afegame
(Wli Falls)

EASTERN
REGION

885m
Mt Afadjato

TOGO

Kpandu

Golokuati

Fume

Amedzofe

Vane

Have Etoe

Bame

HO

Dzemeni

Xofa Eco-Lodge

Boso

Anyirawase

Kpetoe

Asikumo

Kalapka
Resource
Reserve

Akosombo

EASTERN
REGION

VOLTA
REGION

Atimpoku

Kpong

Volta

Akatsi

Aflao

Somanya

Akuse

Denu

KOFORIDUA

Sogakope

Shai
Hills
WR

GREATER
ACCRA REGION

Azizanze

Aburi

Dodowa

Keta

Nyigbenya
(Tsapoli Junction)

Woe

Ashaiman

Ningo

Anloga

Prampram

Ada Foah

Savietula

Tema

ACCRA

ATLANTIC
OCEAN

N

Bradt

KEY
Tar road
Unsurfaced road
Regional boundary

0   50km
0   30 miles

INTRODUCTION

The east of Ghana, though less geared towards upmarket tourism than the west coast, is a haven for independent travellers, rich in natural beauty and offering a wealth of low-key, low-cost travel possibilities to those with the initiative to take them up. For keen hikers and ramblers, the lush and relatively cool highlands around Ho and Hohoe are studded with the country's highest peaks, as well as a plethora of accessible waterfalls and an excellent little monkey sanctuary at the village of Tafi Atome. The east coast, too, is rich in isolated, out-of-the-way gems, most notably the small ports of Ada and Keta, while the area immediately inland of Accra is notable, among other things, for the tranquil Aburi Botanical Garden and impressive Akosombo Dam on the Volta River.

Travel conditions in eastern Ghana generally conform to those experienced in other parts of the country; a little cheaper perhaps, but no more arduous. Nevertheless, this region will appeal greatly to those travellers for whom travel means travel in the chest-thumping, epic journey sense, rather than, say, soaking up the tropical beach atmosphere at Ada. Two exceptional ferry rides run through this part of Ghana: the daily trip from Ada north to Akuse along the Volta River, and the legendary overnight run from Akosombo to Yeji via Lake Volta. And there is also the bumpy overland trip from Hohoe through to the northern capital of Tamale, the closest thing in Ghana to those interminable bone-crunching trips for which many other African countries are renowned. In short, if the term 'off the beaten track' sets your ears pricking, then this is probably the part of Ghana for you.

A less obvious attraction of the east, but one that strikes us sharply whenever we revisit Ghana, is an almost total absence of hassle. After two weeks on the west coast, where it feels impossible at times to walk a few paces without being subjected to tedious catcalls, we found it immensely refreshing to travel in a region where children tend to greet travellers with an altogether more dignified 'How are you?', 'Mia Woeso', or 'You're welcome!' This is one part of Ghana where the country's reputation as the friendliest in Africa seems fully justified.

Finally, it should be noted that, while eastern Ghana is currently favoured mostly by backpackers, it does boast a nascent upmarket tourist circuit. The Manet Paradise Hotel at Ada and Volta Hotel at Akosombo are the equal of any hotel in the country, and the last few years have also seen the establishment of good tourist-class accommodation in Ho and on the Keta Peninsula.

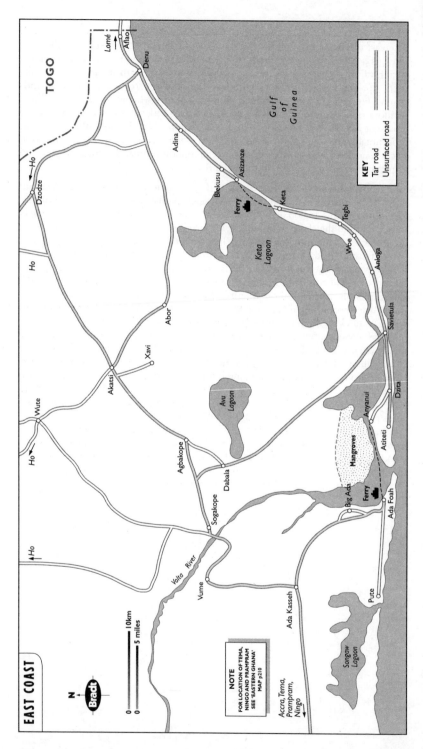

EAST COAST

TOGO

Lomé
Aflao
Denu
_Ho_
Dzodze
Adina
Blekusu
Azizanze
Ferry
Keta
Tegbi
Gulf of Guinea
Keta Lagoon
Woe
Anloga
Savietula
Abor
Xavi
Akatsi
_Ho_
Wute
Avu Lagoon
_Ho_
Agbakope
Dabala
Sogakope
Anyanui
Atiteti
Dzita
Mangroves
Big Ada
Ferry
Ada Foah
Vume
Volta River
Ada Kasseh
Pute
Songaw Lagoon
Accra, Tema, Prampram, Ningo

KEY
Tar road
Unsurfaced road

NOTE
FOR LOCATION OF TEMA,
NINGO AND PRAMPRAM
SEE 'EASTERN GHANA'
MAP p210

N

0   10km
0   5 miles

Bradt

10

The East Coast

Ghana's east coast remains surprisingly underdeveloped for tourism by comparison to the west coast, a situation which – given that Ada or Keta are far closer to Accra than, say, Cape Coast or Elmina – is most probably explained by the relative dearth of landmarks associated with the slave trade. But, while it is true that, the small forts at **Keta** and **Prampram** (see pages 225 and 216) notwithstanding, there is nothing here to compare with the grandiose castles and larger forts to the west of the capital, the east coast does boast at least two very attractive (and very different) beach resorts in the form of **Ada Foah** and the **Keta Peninsula** (see page 219 and 225), as well as a system of vast lagoons and estuaries that offer the country's finest marine birding, and (seasonally) the opportunity to see giant turtles laying their eggs on the beach.

TEMA

Bisected by the Greenwich Meridian, some 25km east of Accra, Tema vies with Takoradi as the third-largest city in Ghana and as the country's most important shipping port. Yet as recently as the 1950s, Tema was an obscure fishing village, founded a few hundred years earlier by Kpeshie fishermen who migrated to the area from present-day Nigeria, and known primarily for its trade in gourds (Tema is said to be a bastardisation of *Torman*, which means 'Town of Gourds'). Then in 1959, Tema was earmarked for development as a deep-water harbour and industrial centre, largely due to its proximity to the Akosombo power station. Today, Tema is a bustling but less than charismatic modern harbour city, supporting a population of greater than 500,000 as well as most of the country's major industries.

Widely overlooked by tourists, Tema is, in all honesty, a rather dull and nondescript city. Its bureaucratic roots are reflected by the division of the city and its suburbs into a series of numbered 'communities', none of which offers much in the way of worthwhile sightseeing. Should you end up in town for some reason, however, it's worth spending some time around the central market area in Community Seven and fishing port, both of which are lively throughout the day. An important landmark is the Kwelitso Tree in the grounds of the disused Hotel Meridian – according to local legend, all attempts to uproot this massive baobab during the construction of the hotel failed, and today it is held sacred by Kpeshie traditionalists. Lovers of geographical trivia might be interested to know that the Presbyterian church in the market reputedly lies right on the Greenwich Meridian. One reader eulogises the vast cylindrical cocoa warehouses constructed under Nkrumah but never used, as having a 'monolithic beauty', while another suggests that a tour through the industrial district might be of interest to those with an interest in Ghanaian economics or its manufacturing industry!

About 2km west of the city centre, the coastal road to Accra crosses the Sakumo Lagoon, a Ramsar wetland site separated from the ocean by a narrow sand dune. In addition to marine turtles, more than 70 waterbird species have been recorded in the lagoon, with seasonal mixed flocks of tens of thousands not unusual. Among the more common species are sandwich, common, little and black tern, spotted redshank, and various egrets and plovers. The Sakuma Lagoon is held sacred by Kpeshie traditionalists, and the striking black heron – also known as the umbrella bird for its habit of opening its wings to form an umbrella-like canopy when it fishes – is protected by local taboos. In the first week of April, the annual Kpledjoo Festival marks the end of a traditional three-month ban on fishing and crab-trapping in the lagoon. The chief priest or priestess performs a series of rites on the lagoon's shore, including casting a symbolic net over the water, and this is followed by a celebratory durbar of local chiefs.

The best beach in the vicinity of Tema is the Regional Maritime Academy Beach – also known as Mighty Beach – which lies along the coastal road to Accra almost immediately past the bridge over the lagoon. Closer to the town centre, a pleasant place to chill out is the Ave Maria Health Centre, which lies on a rough stretch of coast overlooking the small Meridien Rock and has a clean swimming pool and gym open to day visitors for a small fee. Built in the late 1950s by Sir William Halcrow and privatised and restored in 2001, the Ave Maria Centre is of some historical interest thanks to its Nkrumah Room – where the first president of Ghana entertained Queen Elizabeth II on her state visit in 1960.

GETTING THERE AND AWAY Regular tro-tros to Tema leave Accra from Tema Station in the city centre, taking about an hour each way or a lot more in traffic. Travellers staying in the Adabraka area of Accra may find it easier to catch a shared taxi from Nkrumah Circle to Nungua and pick up transport to Tema from there.

WHERE TO STAY
Upmarket

Hotel Marjorie 'Y' \ 022 206947. According to the brochure, the hotel is 'a mere 10-min drive' from Kotoka International airport – but whilst this is clearly a lie, the 2-star hotel does cater well for business travellers. Other facilities inc car hire & an attractive pool area with its own waterfall, which hosts live music on Sun. A range of comfortable rooms are offered with b/fast. *From US$60/70 for sgl/dbl to US$120 for suite.*

Hotel Westgate \ 022 205107/8 or 207074/5; f 022 200470; e Hotelwestgate@4U.gh.com; www.hotelwestgate.com. This bland modern multi-storey hotel in Community Six is hardly very inspiring, but it's one of the best in Tema, & good value by comparison to hotels of a similar standard in Accra. Facilities inc a swimming pool with concreted sundeck & a good restaurant. An excellent car rental & tour company called Afrocentric Ventures (see *Travelling in Ghana*, page 66) is based in the hotel. *Spacious self-contained dbl with AC & DSTV US$70, suite US$110.*

Moderate

Crismon Hotel (20 rooms) \ 022 205547/680; e afedzi@yahoo.com. Small & smart, this friendly hotel in the residential Community Five offers low-key business travellers a good alternative to the proliferation of multi-storey monoliths in town. The staff at Crismon are especially professional & attentive. Around 20 large rooms with hot bath, AC & DSTV & free internet access. *Sgl/dbl US$50/60 inc b/fast.*

Friends Club Hotel \ 022 206575; f 022 205436; e davidakiti2002@yahoo.com. This small hotel in Community Two, close to the town centre, is reasonable value. A restaurant is attached. Clean self-contained rooms with AC & TV. *Sgl/dbl US$24/30.*

Oak Royal Hotel \ 022 206926. This popular little hotel was under renovation at the time of our last visit, but although the work so far looks good it feels a tad overpriced. All rooms will be self-contained with AC & DSTV. *US$70–120.*

Torica Home Lodge (6 rooms) \ 021 813128 or 024 255441; e toricalodge@hotmail.com. Situated on Aviation Road in Manet Gardens outside Tema, this small lodge consists of 6 good-sized, well-maintained & comfortably furnished dbl rooms with hot water, AC & DSTV. A free airport shuttle is available on request. *Dbl US$25.*

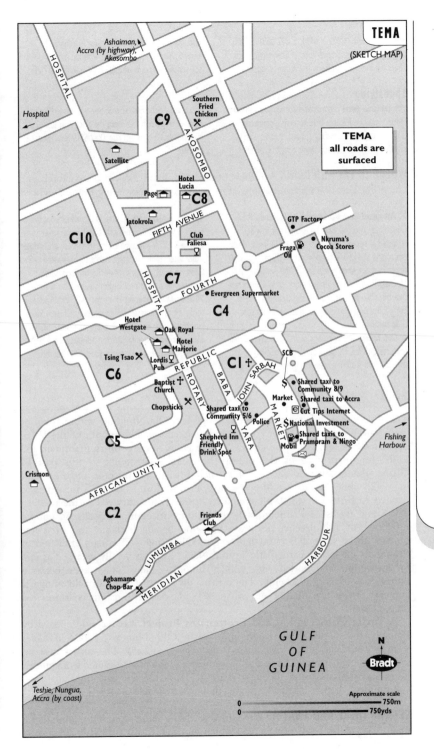

TEMA
all roads are
surfaced

Ashaiman,
Accra (by highway),
Akosombo

Hospital

HOSPITAL

C9

Southern
Fried
Chicken

AKOSOMBO

Satellite

Page

Hotel
Lucia

C8

Jatokrola

FIFTH AVENUE

GTP Factory

Fraga
Oil

Nkruma's
Cocoa Stores

C10

Club
Faliesa

HOSPITAL

C7

FOURTH

Evergreen Supermarket

C4

Hotel
Westgate

Oak Royal

Hotel
Marjorie

Tsing Tsao

Lordis
Pub

REPUBLIC

C1

SCB

SCB

C6

Baptist
Church

ROTARY

BABA

JOHN SARBAH

$

Shared taxi to
Community 8/9

Shared taxi to Accra

Chopsticks

Shared taxi to
Community 5/6

Police

MARKET

Market

Cut Tips Internet

C5

YARA

Shepherd Inn
Friendly
Drink Spot

$ National Investment

Mobil

Shared taxis to
Prampram & Ningo

Fishing
Harbour

Crismon

AFRICAN UNITY

C2

Friends
Club

HARBOUR

LUMUMBA

Agbamame
Chop Bar

MERIDIAN

GULF
OF
GUINEA

N

Bradt

Teshie, Nungua,
Accra (by coast)

Approximate scale
0 ———— 750m
0 ———— 750yds

Budget

🛏 **Hotel Lucia** 📞 022 306134; 📠 022 308142. This long-serving & comfortable hotel in Community Eight offers the best value in town. The attached indoor restaurant is popular with locals for its generously heaped plates of rice & chicken or fish at around US$4. Self-contained rooms with AC & TV. *Sgl/dbl US$17/20.*

Shoestring

🛏 **Jatokron Hotel** Just across the main junction from Hotel Lucia, this friendly little hotel in Community Eight is one of the last shoestring options in town with slightly scruffy rooms set around a kind of indoor courtyard. At the time this edition was researched, plans were afoot to renovate the place & install AC, in which case prices will rise. *Dbl US$10 (may rise to US$30).*

✗ **WHERE TO EAT AND DRINK** A number of the hotels listed above also serve food, with one of the best bets for big portions of inexpensive local fare being **Hotel Lucia.**

✗ **Agbamami Chop Bar** Situated on Lumumba Rd in Community Two, this cavernous chop bar is widely regarded as serving the best local food in Tema. *Meals cost around US$1.50 & it's open from 07.30 to 17.30 daily except Fri & Sat, when it stays open in the evenings.*

✗ **Chopsticks** Situated along Rotary Rd in Community Five, this Chinese restaurant is slightly cheaper than Tsing Tao, though not quite as good. *Count on about US$6 per dish.*

☆ **Club Faliesa** This popular club in Community Seven operates on Wed, Fri, Sat & Sun nights, opening at around 21.00 & staying open all night.

🍷 **Orlando's Jazz Café** Situated in Community Six, this smart new cocktail-cum-sports bar shows Premier League & UEFA games on a large screen, as well as other major international sporting events, supplemented by live Ghanaian music & jazz over weekends. Food is also available, inc a traditional English Sunday b/fast & roast.

✗ **Tsing Tao Restaurant** This smart, AC restaurant, next to the Hotel Westgate, serves excellent Chinese food, inc chicken feet, frogs legs & 'crispy ox penis'. There is also plenty of choice for the less adventurous, & the spring rolls here are especially good. *US$7 per main course, exc rice.*

PRAMPRAM AND NINGO

The small towns of Prampram, New Ningo and Old Ningo lie within 10km of each other on the stretch of coast between Accra and the mouth of the Volta. Separated by a long, sandy beach as attractive as any in the country, Prampram and Old Ningo are two of the oldest European settlements in this part of Ghana. Prampram was the site of a small British trading post and fort built in 1742, while Ningo was the site of a Danish fort from 1735 until it was handed to Britain in 1850. Neither fort, however, has survived to the modern day: some traces of Prampram's Fort Vernon remain in the walls of a more modern, but also derelict resthouse near the fishing harbour, and even less remains to be seen of Fort Fredensborg in Old Ningo. The main attraction of the area is the beach, particularly around New Ningo, generally regarded as safe for swimming and dotted with holiday homes – New Ningo even boasts a rather posh-looking polo club. The estuary on the west flank of Old Ningo is also very pretty, its natural beauty enhanced by the colourful fishing boats moored on the beach.

A **Turtle Conservation and Ecotourism Project** was recently opened by Raleigh International at Kpongunor near Old Ningo (📞 *024 356857;* e *doctor_peacemaker@yahoo.com; kokou_william@hotmail.com*). The turtles nest on the beach here between March and November and the money gained from guided tours and tourists using the new campsite is channelled back into the local community, which it is hoped will give them a sustainable income.

GETTING THERE AND AWAY All three small towns lie about 6km to the south of the main Accra–Aflao road, along a road which on paper forms a roughly 20km-long

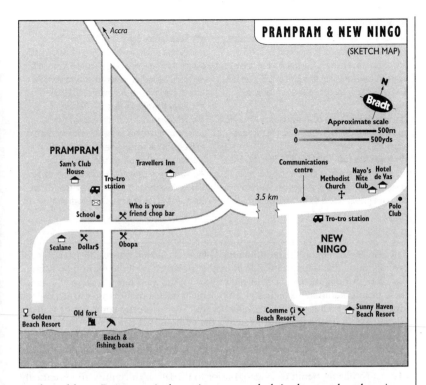

PRAMPRAM & NEW NINGO
(SKETCH MAP)

Approximate scale
0 ——————— 500m
0 ——————— 500yds

PRAMPRAM

Sam's Club House
Tro-tro station
Travellers Inn
Communications centre
Methodist Church
Nayo's Nite Club
Hotel de Vas
School
Who is your friend chop bar
3.5 km
Tro-tro station
NEW NINGO
Polo Club
Sealane   Dollar$ Obopa
Golden Beach Resort
Old fort
Comme Çi Beach Resort
Sunny Haven Beach Resort
Beach & fishing boats

Accra

southward loop. Prampram is the main transport hub in the area, but there is no direct tro-tro transport between it and Accra – you will almost certainly have to change vehicles at Ashaiman, a busy junction town to the north of Tema.

From Tema itself, share taxis run from a rank just by the market and take about 45 minutes (US$1). If you are coming to Prampram from the direction of Ada, ask to be dropped at Dwahenya (also known as Prampram junction) and wait there for a lift to Prampram.

Regular shared taxis connect Prampram to New Ningo and Old Ningo and costs US$0.20.

WHERE TO STAY AND EAT
Prampram

🏠 **Golden Beach Resort** 5 mins' walk from the Sealane Hotel, this rather ambience-deficient bar serves chilled drinks on a desolate beach dominated by the massive hulk of an abandoned cargo ship. *Twin US$10, with TV US$16.*

🏠 **Sam's Club House** Tucked away in the alleys behind the lorry station, this grotty guesthouse has unappealing dbl rooms. In light of the deal to be had at Sealane, this can only be recommended to the severely cash-strapped. *Dbl with shared bath/self-contained US$7/8.*

🏠 **Sealane Hotel** ✆ 024 208830/1. Clearly signposted about 500m from the lorry station, this friendly & professional set-up is definitely aiming for the Accra crowd with green, neat grounds, an attractive bar, & the only restaurant in town serving Western-style food. Other facilities inc a swimming pool & tennis court, complete with eager teen opponents. Self-contained twin rooms with hot water are a bargain, although there has been the occasional complaint about dirty rooms & barely functioning plumbing. *Twin US$10, with TV US$16.*

217

New Ningo

✕ **Comme Çi Beach Resort** This small bar & restaurant is perched on the edge of an enormous beach-front plot, dotted with nim-trees with pink & white stripey trunks. It's a pleasant place to enjoy a beer & a sea view, & is reached along the same path as for the Sunny Haven Resort.

⌂ **Hotel de Vas** On the other side of New Ningo, this small hotel near the Polo Club has basic but adequate rooms. *US$5 per room.*

⌂ **Nayo's Nite Club** ☏ 024 6549877. Basic dbls with a shared bath are on offer at this small bar-cum-hotel. Its nightlife might disturb your sleep, but otherwise Nayo's is a friendly, central choice. *Dbl US$6.*

⌂ **Royal Cariboo Beach** ☏ 024 4723891. The management at this new hotel seems a little unfriendly, but the shady grounds make a pleasant place to sit & the rooms themselves are very clean & comfortable. *Dbl with common showers/self-contained US$25/35.*

⌂ **Sunny Haven Beach Resort** ☏ 024 369134. Reached along a 200m dirt road leading from the communications centre on the main thoroughfare down to the beach, this relatively new resort made a promising start but has since fallen into disrepair. Accommodation is reportedly still available in dbl huts sharing an equipped kitchen with fridge, toilet & bath, but no one was around to say how much it costs.

ADA

The port of Ada lies on the mouth of the Volta River, which was readily navigable for several hundred kilometres inland before the construction of the Akosombo Dam in the 1960s. Among the most celebrated visitors to Ada was Henry Stanley, who sailed there from London in a Thames pleasure launch several months after his renowned 'discovery' of Livingstone in Tanzania. It was Stanley, in the company of Captain Glover, who took the first steamer across the perilous Ada Bar and up the Volta.

Ada is the traditional core of the Ada nation, one of the most important and cohesive empires on the pre-colonial Gold Coast. Oral tradition suggests that the Adali – the people of Ada – arrived in their modern homeland from somewhere to the east (probably Benin or Nigeria) prior to the late 17th century and eventually settled at Big Ada. The nation expanded in the early 18th century, as several lesser chieftaincies in territories along the Volta pledged their allegiance to the Ada Matse (King), who is today the paramount chief over ten major clans occupying an area of almost 20,000km² south and east of the Volta.

The wealth and influence of the Ada Empire was based on its strategic position at the mouth of the Volta River, from where it traded as far upriver as Yeji, and the limitless source of raw salt that is the Songor Lagoon. Both these assets were coveted by neighbouring powers, for which reason the empire spent much of the 18th and early 19th century fighting territorial wars, often with Danish backing. Oddly, despite Ada's significance as a combined river and ocean port, only one rather small fort is ever known to have been built there, Fort Kongensten, constructed by the Danes in 1783 and long since vanished.

Ada probably peaked in importance in the 19th century, but its autonomy became increasingly tenuous after 1850 when the Danes sold their Gold Coast assets to the British. Following the Dutch evacuation of the coast in 1872 and the British victory over Ashanti two years after that, Ada become an *ipso facto* Crown colony, and the traditional role of the Ada Matse was severely compromised. As some indication of how British colonisation neutered the role of the paramount chief, it is said that all but one of the four Matse who were enstooled between 1876 and 1927 died in suspicious circumstances, and the stool was left vacant for 25 of those years. By contrast, only two Matse have ruled since 1927: Dake II (1927–77) and Abram Akuaku III (1977–present day).

Today, Ada is something of a backwater, with nothing but a few faded colonial-era buildings to show for its illustrious past. The superb beach and river-front scenery, however, combined with a range of activities and accommodation to suit all tastes and budgets, make it a worthwhile stop in its own right, as well as the most obvious base from where to explore the lushly vegetated lower regions of the Volta River , whether by chartered canoe or via the public ferry to Akuse.

For more detail about the history of Ada and its surroundings, I recommend C Amate's informative and well-written book *The Making of Ada*, published in 1999 and on sale at the Manet Paradise Hotel.

GETTING THERE AND AWAY Ada consists of three discrete settlements: Ada Kasseh lies on the main Accra–Aflao road, at the junction of the road to Big Ada and Ada Foah, which lie 15km and 20km respectively to its south. From the point of view of travellers, Ada Foah is the most important settlement, since it lies closest to the river mouth as well as to most of the accommodation in the area. If you can't find direct transport to Ada Foah from elsewhere on the coast, you'll have no difficulty getting a tro-tro to drop you at Ada Kasseh, from where regular tro-tros run up and down to Ada Foah.

It is also possible – in theory – to arrive at or leave Ada Foah by river ferry to Akusi near Akosombo, or to catch a motorised canoe across the Volta to Anyanui for Keta (see *Around Ada* page 221). It's best to make this trip on a Wednesday when the Anyanui market is in full swing.

WHERE TO STAY AND EAT All the accommodation listed below lies in or around Ada Foah, the main tourist focus in the area. If, however, you should get stuck at the junction town of Ada Kasseh, the **Garden Club Hotel** is a surprisingly smart-looking local hotel with rooms in the US$5–10 range. There is no accommodation in Big Ada; the closest place is the basic **No Problems Guesthouse** along the road towards Ada Foah.

Upmarket

Manet Paradise Holiday Resort ☎ 096 822276 or 096 22397 or 024 3532587/63; e gabbyaddo@ yahoo.com; www.manet.gh.com. Set in landscaped grounds on the bank of the Volta about 1km from the centre of Ada Foah, this long-standing 3-star hotel is a popular w/end getaway for Accra residents. In addition to a swimming pool area beneath shady palms, the hotel offers good watersport facilities, tennis & volleyball courts, boat trips, deep-sea fishing trips, & other local excursions in the company of knowledgeable guides. The best sea views are to be had on the top floor. The ground-floor restaurant serves a range of excellent Ghanaian, fish & international dishes with prices ranging from around US$7, right up to US$29 for the fabulous mixed seafood grill. Be warned of a hefty premium attached to beer & other alcoholic drinks. Modern AC rooms with DSTV. *Sgl/dbl US$69/81 B&B, suite US$115.*

Tsarley Korpey Hotel ☎ 096 822066; e tsarley_korpey@pransky.com. Nestled in the row of opulent weekend homes that line the riverbank before Manet Paradise, this expensive new hotel has the feel of a private house, & is available for hire in its entirety. On the ground floor, there is a comfortable sitting room & family-style dining area, where excellent food is served, whilst the outside sundeck has a gorgeous pool overlooking the river. *Executive dbl with all mod cons US$110, family suite US$180. Day-visitors are welcome to use the facilities for US$7 a head.*

Budget and shoestring

Brightest Spot Guesthouse ☎ 096 822335. If you don't mind a non-beach-front location, this small, clean guesthouse, which lies a short distance from the town centre along the road back to Big Ada, is one of the best budget deals in the area. Bright self-contained ooms with a fridge & TV & fan or AC. A pleasant garden bar & restaurant in front of the main building serves 'sausage sand wishes' for US$1.50 or 'pasture' (pasta) dishes from US$3. *Dbl with fan US$10, sgl/dbl with AC US$20/25.*

Cocoloko Beach Camp ☎ 096 822356; e cocoloko_info@yahoo.co.uk; www.cocoloko.com. Established in 1999 following the demise of the original Estuary Beach Club, the walled Cocoloko Beach Camp lies about 30 mins' walk west of the town within view of a rather dirty beach where turtles regularly come to nest in Nov/Dec. The restaurant offers a large choice of decent enough food at around US$4 a plate, although whether they actually have the food in stock is another question. Although Cocoloko has been a popular place

The East Coast ADA

10

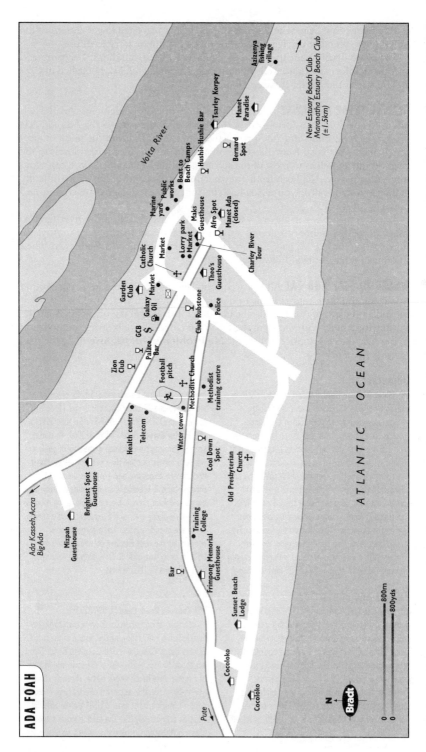

ADA FOAH

Volta River

Ada Kasseh, Accra
Big Ada

Pute

Cocoloko

Cocoloko

Sunset Beach Lodge

Bar

Frimpong Memorial Guesthouse

Training College

Mizpah Guesthouse

Brightest Spot Guesthouse

Health centre

Telecom

Water tower

Football pitch

Methodist Church

Methodist training centre

Cool Down Spot

Old Presbyterian Church

Zion Club

GCB

Palace Bar

Garden Club

Galaxy Market

Oil

Club Rubstone

Police

Theo's Guesthouse

Catholic Church

Market

Lorry park

Market

Maks Guesthouse

Afro Spot

Manet Ada (closed)

Charley River Tour

Marine yard

Public works

Boat to Beach Camps

Hushie Hushie Bar

Bernard Spot

Manet Paradise

Tsarley Korpey

Azizenya fishing village

New Estuary Beach Club
Maranatha Estuary Beach Club
(±1.5km)

ATLANTIC OCEAN

N

Bradt

0 _____ 800m
0 _____ 800yds

to stay over recent years, feedback is very mixed – with regard to the attitude of the staff in particular. The installation of new management at the end of 2006 may signal a change in that respect, but in the mean time, the resuscitated Estuary Beach Club seems a better bet. All the chalets are the same price, regardless of whether they are reed- or brick-built or have fans, although plans to build shower units inside some of the huts themselves is likely to bring a differential. Higher prices are quoted for full-board. *Sgl/dbl/twin (inc b/fast) US$11/21/35.*

⌂ **Dreamland Beach Resort** (4 huts) ☏ 024 4766271; e beate@deam.org. Situated close to Cocoloko Beach Camp, this small, child-friendly new resort opened shortly before we went to print, & it sounds promising, despite a lack of reader feedback. It has a restaurant & offers a variety of activities, inc bike hire, boat trips in the Volta Delta & a visit to a local brewery. *Around US$12 (US$4 per additional person sharing a 4-bed room).*

⌂ **Garden Club Annex** ☏ 024 2746035 or 096 822262. This undistinguished local lodging offers dark, shabby dbls with common showers, or nicer but considerably more expensive self-contained rooms with AC. The owner of the hotel is reputedly a very good cook, & serves uncomplicated, inexpensive meals on request. *Dbl with common shower US$5, self-contained dbl/twin with AC US$15/25.*

⌂ **Maranatha Estuary Beach Club** ☏ 024 3528248. Right next door to New Estuary Beach Club, this copycat resort offers the same reed huts with the added luxury of mosquito nets above the beds & brightly painted world flags on the front doors. Any rivalry between one camp & the other seems to be very friendly. *US$10 pp.*

⌂ **Mizpah Guesthouse** ☏ 096 822014 or 024 2710393. Tucked away among the farms to the right of the main road before you enter town, this friendly family-run guesthouse seems like very good value. Meals are available on request. Rooms are clean self-contained

dbl with fan & tiled floor or with AC. *Dbl with fan/AC US$8/15.*

⌂ **New Estuary Beach Club** (17 huts) Set on a picturesque beach with the lapping Volta on one side & crashing Atlantic waves on the other, the recently re-opened Estuary Beach Club has so far established 17 simple reed huts with bare sand floors, available for hire at US$10 a head. Cold drinks & basic meals are available, although food tends to be slow & overpriced, & shared bucket showers are (theoretically) supplied with fresh non-Volta water. The resort is inaccessible by ordinary car, but can be reached in a 4×4, or by walking for 40 mins through the dunes south of Manet Paradise. Alternatively, a boat from the jetty near the Manet Paradise costs around US$4 one way. Turtles regularly nest on this beach in Nov & Dec, and the staff will wake interested guests when this happens close to the camp. *US$10 pp.*

⌂ **Sunset Beach Lodge** ☏ 096 822376 or 024 2029902. This friendly lodge, set up by former Cocoloko staff in 2006, was still under development when this book was researched. At the time, it had all the charm of a prison camp, with accommodation offered in long concrete blocks & surrounded by a glass topped wall. But the professional managers are eager to listen to customers so it may well develop into something more attractive as time goes on. The menu is a photocopy of the one at Cocoloko but prices for food & accommodation are all very slightly lower.

⌂ **Theo's Guesthouse** Situated on a small lane leading from opposite the tro-tro station, this low-key resthouse, which currently consists of two twin rooms in the private home of its eponymous owner, was warmly recommended by a reader in late 2003. Although rather basic, the twin rooms are clean & have netting (fresh coconuts from the compound inc in the price). Common bucket showers & a flush toilet are also available. *Twin US$6.*

AROUND ADA The main point of interest in Ada itself is of course the beach and river-front, but the town does boast a few minor historical landmarks, notably a 19th-century European cemetery and an attractive Presbyterian church built in 1918. The central market is worth visiting on the main market days of Wednesday and Saturday. An attractive stroll out of town takes you in a south-easterly direction from the Manet Paradise Hotel towards the estuary, through the fishing village of Azizanya. This very friendly village, on a turd-free sandy beach lined with colourful fishing boats and positioned below the tall palms, is a good place to watch rural activities such as smoking and sun-drying fish, and repairing boats and fishing nets. Oddly, the village is also overrun with domestic ducks – the only place I've visited in Ghana (and for that matter in Africa) where this fowl is so prolific.

Ada's main festival is the annual **Asafotufiami Ceremony**, which is held in remembrance of the military achievements of Ada during the 18th and 19th centuries. The festival always begins on the first Thursday of August, when libation is poured at various ancestral shrines, but is far more colourful on Friday, when a succession of traditional military processions are held around the town, starting at dawn and carrying on until late at night. On Saturday, the festival climaxes with the durbar, during which the Matse (paramount chief) and various lesser chiefs are carried through the town on palanquins. Festivities continue until the next Thursday, though these are mostly less traditional and so of less interest to tourists. (As one local brochure puts it 'boat races, river cruises, football matches, and people greeting and bidding goodbye to each other'!)

The **Obonukope Community Zoo**, which lies about 1km from the main road shortly before the turn-off to Big Ada, is possibly a well-intended conservation initiative, but it's also difficult to take entirely seriously. The zoo consists of a small fenced area inhabited by several soporific pythons, an invisible 'alligator' and 'tortoise' (both 'underground' when we visited) and a solitary chameleon. The entrance fee is nominal, but you'll probably be asked for an additional donation towards future development …

SONGOR RAMSAR SITE

This internationally recognised marine wetland site protects the coastline around the 115km^2 Songor Lagoon, running west through Ada Foah to the Volta River estuary. Songor Lagoon is regarded as Ghana's second most important site (after Keta Lagoon) for marine and other water-associated birds, with more than 90 species recorded in the saline marsh and open water, several of which breed around the lagoon or on islands in the Volta estuary. The area is most rewarding for birders during the European winter, when the number of waterbirds present has been known to exceed 100,000, with resident species such as egrets, herons and gulls joined by a host of Palaearctic migrants such as terns, sandpipers and other waders, and waterfowl. Mixed roosts of more than 50,000 terns – most commonly sandwich and black tern, but also royal, roseate and little tern – are frequently seen in September and October. Waders are also well represented, in particular black-winged stilt, avocet, ringed plover, curlew sandpiper, spotted redshank and greenshank. The most interesting mammal found in the area is the manatee, a large aquatic creature whose unusual shape is thought to have given rise to the legend of mermaids.

The area is managed by the Coastal Wetlands Development Project (CWDP), an organisation that has taken an inclusive, community approach to conserving these fragile wetlands. The lagoon is important not only for wildlife, but also as a source of protein and as the base of a traditional salt-production industry involving more than 8,000 people. Tourism is actively encouraged, though the only development to date consists of two bird observation platforms, the most accessible of which is in the village of Pute, on the edge of the lagoon some 9km from Ada (no tro-tros run along this road, but taxis can be chartered). The second observation platform, at Lolonya, offers better birding at present, but it cannot be reached from Ada without returning to the main Accra–Aflao road.

Three species of marine turtle breed on the beaches around Ada. The green and olive ridley turtle are active between March and September, while the leatherback turtle comes to shore between September and January, with sightings most common over November and December. Shortly before going to print, we received news that formal guided excursions to look for nesting turtles can be arranged at the Wildlife Division office, on the east side of the main road from Ada Kasseh after the junction with the road from Big Ada. These cost around US$5 per person, and help fund the petrol and maintenance costs of the motorbike used to patrol the beach in search of illegal poachers. Wildlife Division officers have complained about tourists demanding a refund when they didn't see a turtle, so we should stress that sightings are not guaranteed and that those who do witness the nesting process are very lucky indeed. Turtles generally come to shore to lay eggs between 23.00 and 02.00, so these trips are run only at night. The best time to see nesting turtles is generally from August through to March, with big leatherbacks most likely from November to February. It is hoped, too, that the CWDP will be able to locate the nearest manatee feeding grounds and start running organised boat trips there. For further details contact 024 4843464 or 020 8766237, or check out http://ghanaturtles.spaces.live.com.

BOAT TRIPS Trips on the Volta River can be arranged through the Manet Paradise Hotel or more cheaply with private boat owners at the nearby jetty at a negotiable rate. Popular goals include Crocodile Island, 3–4km from Ada, renowned for its basket-weaving industry, and – although no longer home to crocodiles – a major breeding site for several bird species (including little egret, western reef heron and cormorant) between July and September. Another good excursion is to the mouth of the estuary, about 2km from the town centre, or to Sugar Cane Island (Azikpe) where a group tour of the rum distillery costs the price of a bottle of its produce.

A couple of interesting public-transport options can be used to explore the river cheaply. The first is a somewhat theoretical ferry service that connects Ada and Akuse (15km and a short tro-tro ride south of Kpong) via Sogakope. This consists of two boats, leaving in opposite directions on alternate days. The newer MS *Oko* starts the upriver journey from Ada at 07.00 on Monday, Wednesday and Friday, arriving at Akuse at about 18.00. The same boat leaves from Akuse at 07.00 on Tuesday, Thursday and Saturday, arriving at Ada at about 16.30. The older MS *Sogakope* leaves Ada at 07.00 on Tuesday, Thursday and Saturday, and Akuse at 07.00 on Wednesday, Friday and Monday. Note, however, that this service wasn't running when we visited Ada in 1998 (diesel shortage), nor when we visited again in 2000 (boats being repaired), nor again in 2003, and I've had at least two letters from readers who visited in between and found the ferry was not operational.

A more certain possibility are the boat-taxis that run between Ada Foah and Anyanui on the eastern bank of the Volta on Wednesday (market day in Anyanui). The market here is among the largest in this part of the country, sprawling inland from the riverbank for almost a kilometre, and a great place to seek out anything from authentic local crafts to secondhand T-shirts to, um, fishing nets. The ride across is also fun, leaving from the Ada side at around 08.00, with the option of either returning to Ada by boat or – having crossed the Volta – continuing on the good tar road that connects Anyanui to Keta.

Finally, for serious anglers, the Manet Paradise Hotel offers deep-sea fishing trips in a large motorboat for up to six people at a rate of US$1,000 per day.

SOGAKOPE

On the east bank of the River Volta, some 25km upriver of Ada, the small town of Sogakope forms something of a transport hub, since it lies adjacent to the most southerly bridge across the Volta, making it the sole funnel for road traffic crossing directly between Greater Accra and Volta regions. Sogakope is also the main port stopped at by ferries between Ada and Akuse – at least when these ferries are running.

The Vume area, on the opposite side of the river to Sogakope, is rightfully renowned for its painted **ceramic pots**, which are displayed for sale on the side of the road.

Another attraction along the short stretch of road between Sogakope and Ada Kasseh is an **ostrich farm**, signposted along the main road close to the village of Kpotame; a visit costs less than US$1 per person and can be made independently or through Villa Cisneros.

WHERE TO STAY

Holy Trinity Spa and Health Farm ☎ 024 4838466 or 024 4315160 or 020 8919786; e info@ htmcspa.com; www.htmcspa.com. Right next door to Villa Cisneros, this destination-spa offers an excellent range of beauty & health treatments at Western prices. Accommodation is inc in overnight package deals, & is certainly comfortable, though not quite up to international standards. Other facilities on offer inc tennis courts, horseriding, & boat trips onto the river, as well as a range of restaurants, each specialising in a different cuisine.

Villa Cisneros Resort ☎ 0968 22312; f 0968 22311; e cisneros@africaonline.com.gh. This unexpectedly large & upmarket complex lies on the east bank of the river, about 1km downstream from the bridge. Facilities inc everything from river trips & excursions to the ostrich farm, to a tennis court & swimming pool. Rooms are fair value, ranging from relatively basic sgls with a fan or dbl room with AC & satellite TV to a chalet. *Sgl with fan US$32, dbl with AC US$60, chalet US$72.*

Volta View Hotel ☎ 091 27834/46. Relatively downmarket alternative to Villa Cisneros, which, despite the name, lies on the main road, some 10 mins' walk from the river. The freshly painted rooms, all with TV, are fair value. Should you have to swap vehicles, the garden bar at the Volta View serves ice-cold draught beer & spicy kebabs & is a mere 20m from the tro-tro station. *Dbl with fan US$8 (common shower), US$12 (self-contained).*

AKATSI AND XAVI

This junction town on the Accra–Aflao road is where you might have to change vehicles travelling between Ho and Keta or between Aflao and Sogakope. Akatsi is an unremarkable town, whose sole – and somewhat esoteric – point of interest is the John Klu Wildlife Museum, a collection of skins and trophy heads from various big-game species shot by the late hunter after whom the museum is named. The museum is housed in a room in the former homestead of John Klu, a long pink building which is still lived in by his family and lies about 200m along a dirt road branching from the main road at the police station. Also of interest, 6km from Akatsi, off the main road, is the village of Dagbamate, which is home to a famous fetish priest, Hunya Yao, who performs his services every Sunday from 14:00 onwards. Visitors are welcome to observe traditional rites and rituals.

If Akatsi itself is rather humdrum, the surrounding area is excellent for birdwatchers, comprised as it is of coastal savanna transitional and various wetlands hosting large flocks of resident birds and European migrants. This potential has recently been translated into an ecotourist project by the Akatsi District Assembly in partnership with the NCRC, Peace Corps and the Ewe village of **Xavi** (pronounced 'Havi'), which lies about 10km south of the Accra road along a clearly signposted feeder road about 1km west of Akatsi. Reasonably regular shared taxis leave Akatsi from Xavi Station (opposite the main lorry park), or you can charter a private taxi from the same station. Once in Xavi you will easily find an official guide who will organise a boat and walk you to the river, which lies 15 minutes from the village.

The main attraction at Xavi is the tranquil one-hour tour (US$6.50 for non-Ghanaians) in a traditional dugout canoe on the small and quiet Lotor River, which feeds into the Avu Lagoon to the south. Some 90 bird species have been recorded from the river, with some of the more conspicuous being malachite and pygmy kingfisher, Senegal coucal, emerald cuckoo, yellow-crowned gonolek, pin-tailed whydah, splendid sunbird, yellow-crowned bishop and white-throated bee-eater.

More recently the NCRC has identified the presence of the aquatic sitatunga antelope, long thought to have been extinct within Ghana. Visitors can also observe traditional local fishing practices, and visit a stand of more than 60 baobab trees close to the river.

Another attraction is a new cultural troupe, made up mostly of children, who perform traditional drumming and dancing routines accompanied by an English narration about the history and meaning of each of the dances. The price for a performance is US$8 minimum, but if the group is larger than eight it will be US$1 per person. These services require at least two days' prior notice – contact them at e adamscripps@yahoo.com or ✆ 096 644423.

There are three hotels in Akatsi. The central **Black Cat Hotel** offers simple but clean self-contained rooms at around US$10, while the nearby **Viglin Lodge** has accommodation ranging in price from US$7–20, based on whether rooms come with a refrigerator, large TV or AC. The restaurant provides simple, inexpensive Ghanaian dishes per plate. A little out of town towards Aflao, the **Magava Hotel**, signposted behind the telecommunications aerial, has simple rooms for US$6.50, while self-contained doubles cost US$8.50 or US$21 depending on whether they have a fan only or also have air conditioning. The attached restaurant serves decent Continental and local food.

KETA AND THE FAR EAST COAST

Probably the least-visited part of eastern Ghana, the roughly 100km stretch of coast between the Volta River and the Togolese border is also one of the most rewarding, and highly recommended to travellers with the inclination to spend a few days away from any established travel circuit. A dramatic feature of this region is the Keta Lagoon, which is the largest in the country at 40km long and 8km wide. The lagoon is, generally, a very shallow body of fresh or brackish water, separated from the sea for much of its length by a strip of sand less than 1km wide, causing some concern that many of the settlements on this stretch of coast will eventually be swallowed by the sea.

The main town along the sliver of coast dividing lagoon from ocean is Keta, the site of Fort Pridzenstein, which was built by the Danes in 1784 and sold to the British in 1850. In the colonial era, Fort Pridzenstein served as a prison, a role it continued to serve until it was damaged by waves during a storm in 1980. Until recently, the old fort was essentially a ruin, but it is currently being restored and should start functioning as a guesthouse and entertainment centre in early 2007. For a nominal entrance fee, the caretaker will take you to the old slave chambers, and show you a pile of dusty record books dating from the days when the fort was a prison. The attractive beach immediately in front of the fort is unsafe for swimming due to the large chunks of collapsed wall that jut out of the water, but there is safe swimming about 100m to the west.

The fort aside, Keta seems quite incredibly run-down – a result, presumably, of the water erosion that threatens to engulf the town. The large number of crumbling buildings gives Keta a somewhat bleak mood, one that reminded me of parts of the Tanzanian coast in the 1980s, though based on our experience the advanced urban decay is compensated for by the genuine friendliness you tend to encounter only in places where tourists remain something of a novelty. Further in Keta's favour is its beach, very pretty, relatively turd-free and normally safe for swimming (though you should ask local advice first). And finally, there are the birds, which should hold some interest even for those not normally given to twitching – right in the town centre I saw the largest concentrations of pied kingfisher and avocet that I've ever encountered.

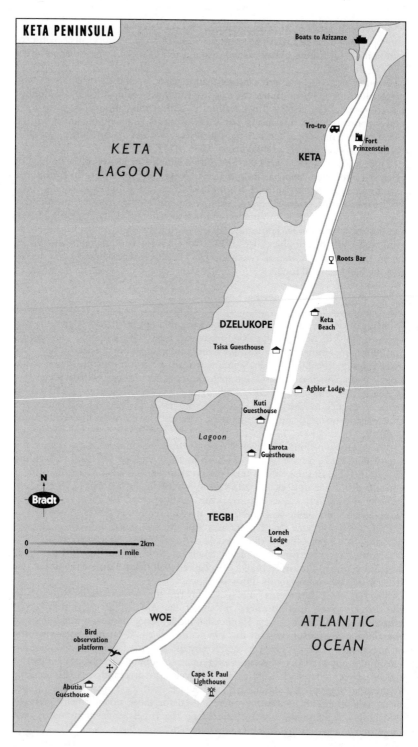

KETA PENINSULA

Boats to Azizanze

Tro-tro

KETA

Fort Prinzenstein

KETA LAGOON

Roots Bar

DZELUKOPE

Keta Beach

Tsisa Guesthouse

Agblor Lodge

Kuti Guesthouse

Lagoon

Larota Guesthouse

N

Bradt

TEGBI

Lorneh Lodge

0 _____ 2km
0 _____ 1 mile

WOE

ATLANTIC OCEAN

Bird observation platform

Cape St Paul Lighthouse

Abutia Guesthouse

While Keta remains the obvious tourist focus in this region, the opportunities for exploration are excellent, aided by the presence of guesthouses or hotels at several points along the coast, including a genuine tourist-class beach resort in the form of the Lorneh Lodge. As far as sightseeing goes, beaches predominate, but there is also Fort Prinzenstein and the lighthouse at Cape St Paul near Woe, reportedly the oldest lighthouse in the country. Extensive shallot farms lie along the edge of the lagoon, especially around Anloga, and the lagoon could reward further exploration by boat – you'll have no difficulty finding somebody to take you out on the water at Keta or elsewhere. The separate Ava Lagoon, the western tip of which lies a mere 50m from the main Keta–Dabala road a few kilometres south of Dabala junction, reputedly harbours a small population of the elusive semi-aquatic sitatunga antelope.

Keta Lagoon is the most important site for marine birds in Ghana, and a genuine birdwatchers' paradise, with 76 water-associated species recorded and concentrations of up to 100,000 individuals not unusual in the European winter. Among the more common species are great white and little egret, western reef heron, fulvous and white-faced duck, black-winged stilt, avocet and a similar range of terns to Songor Lagoon. Several of the islands are important breeding sites for marine birds. A good starting point for birdwatchers is the observation tower in Woe, which lies only 50m from the main road.

GETTING THERE AND AWAY A good tar road connects Keta to the main Accra–Aflao road at Dabala junction. You'll have no problem finding transport to Keta from this direction. Coming from Accra, the best place to find a direct tro-tro to Keta is at Tudu or Ashaiman. Coming from Ho, you'll probably have to catch one tro-tro to Akatsi, then another to Keta. Coming from Ada, you may also have to do the trip in stages, changing vehicles at Kasseh and Sogakope.

A far more interesting way of approaching Keta from the west, however, would be to take a motorised canoe across the Volta River between Ada Foah and Anyanui, from where the occasional tro-tro covers the 10km or so stretch of road to Savietula junction on the main Keta road. Before doing this, it would be wise to check whether any canoes are likely to be leaving the next day, since they generally go only on market days (Wednesday and sometimes Friday and Saturday). Even on these days, there may be only one boat in either direction. The best source of current advice is the tourist centre in Ada.

Heading east from Keta used to be a problem after the sea eroded the main route to Aflao, but an excellent new road has since been built as part of a major land reclamation project. The best day to travel is market day in Keta, every four days, when you'll rarely wait more than about 20 minutes for a tro-tro to leave from the centre of town, although on other days you will still get away with ease.

The route passes through a few small villages, palm-lined havens fringed by both lagoon and ocean, and notable for several large, modern burial shrines reminiscent in style of the *posuban* shrines of the Elmina area (see page 144).

WHERE TO STAY AND EAT
Moderate
Lorneh Lodge 096 642162 or 020 8116748; f 096 64160. This smart lodge, which opened in mid-2000, is situated at Tegbi, 7km from central Keta on the ocean side of the main Dabala road. The main building lies 200m from a safe & very attractive swimming & fishing beach, but a newer row of chalet-like rooms lies right on the beach. Facilities inc a swimming pool & a good restaurant. The large dbl AC rooms with hot water & DSTV are excellent value, or there are beach chalets with similar facilities or suites. *Dbl with shower/bath US$25/35, beach chalet US$40, suite US$40–45.*

Budget

⌂ **Keta Beach Hotel** ☎ 0966 21288. The closest hotel to the town centre, this rather run-down but thoroughly likeable establishment was once popular with Accra weekenders, but these days it sees very little custom. Decent if unspectacular fare is served in the restaurant & pleasantly wooded garden bar, & cold beers are available. Coming by road from the west, ask the tro-tro driver to drop you at the hotel, which is clearly signposted next to the main road some 2km before central Keta. *Sgl/dbl with fan US$6–7.50, self-contained dbl/twin US$9–10, with TV US$18.*

Shoestring

⌂ **Abutia Guesthouse** ☎ 0906 22239. Probably the best deal in this range, the Abutia is situated 500m from the centre of Woe in the direction of Dabala, making it very well positioned for exploring the lagoon & walking out to the lighthouse. It lies in pleasant gardens, signposted 20m from the main road & not much further from the lagoon. A restaurant & bar are attached. The clean dbl rooms with fans are great value. *Dbl (shared bath) US$5.50, self-contained US$7, self-contained with TV US$10.*

⌂ **Agblor Lodge** About 2km further from town than the Keta Beach Hotel, on the seaward side of the main road, this is good value. Has clean self-contained sgls with dbl bed & TV, or a suite with 2 bedrooms. *Sgl US$8.50, suite US$15.*

⌂ **Kuti Guesthouse** ☎ 0966 42987. Don't let the name of this small hotel put you off – the self-contained rooms, though a bit dank & musty, are more than acceptable value. *Sgl/dbl with fan US$6.50–9.*

⌂ **Larota Guesthouse** ☎ 0966 42393. Situated in Tegbi, 4km past the Keta Beach Hotel, this is a clean & secure family set-up. *Dbl with fan US$4.50, self-contained dbl/twin with fan & TV US$7.50/8.*

AFLAO

This typically chaotic border town, the third-largest urban settlement in Volta Region, must be a somewhat disconcerting introduction to Ghana for those coming from Togo. It's one of those places where money-changers yell at you from all directions, and you can expect a few blatant attempts at overcharging, especially when you are walking away from the border. For those travelling entirely within Ghana, Aflao lies off any major trunk route, and the only situation in which you'd be likely to pass through the town is if you'd followed the coastal road from Keta and wanted to pick up transport back towards Accra or Ho. Aflao is not without redeeming features, however, most obviously a variety of street food that's second to none in Ghana – wherever you go you'll see women carrying baskets full of crusty baguettes, betraying your proximity to a francophone country. Readers have passed on stories about 'unofficial officials' hanging around, and shifty 'guides' getting in the middle of things – but if you're reasonably alert, refuse any advances made by prospective guides or money-changers, and walk straight from the lorry park to the border post (you can't miss it), then you shouldn't have any problems. There is no ATM in town so arrive with enough cash to see you through.

GETTING THERE AND AWAY Aflao has a lorry station as crowded as any in Ghana, with all manner of tro-tros heading direct to Accra and most points in between. There are also regular STC and OSA buses to Accra. The most interesting route in or out of Aflao, however, is the coastal one to or from Keta described above.

⌂ **WHERE TO STAY AND EAT** Should you need to stay the night in Aflao, there's no shortage of accommodation. The newly established **Thanks Hotel** is the closest place to the lorry station, and is probably the best deal in town with clean rooms at reasonable rates. Right next door, the **Sanaa Hotel**, has adequate shoestring rooms, but I'll leave it to you to decide whether you transgress the somewhat cryptic ruling that the 'rate applies to one man one flesh only: Gen 2:24'.

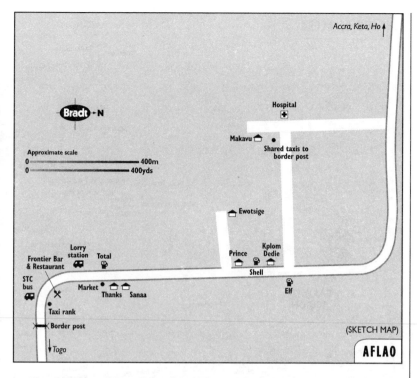

Clustered about 100m apart and roughly 500m back along the road away from the border post, the **Kplom Dedie**, **Prince** and **Ewotsige** hotels all have shoestring rooms with double beds, with the Kplom Dedie definitely the first choice.

The most upmarket place in town is the **Makavu Hotel**, about 1km from the border, which has self-contained rooms with fans for US$12/18 single/double and with AC for US$20. The Makavu has the only restaurant proper in Aflao, as well as an attractive beer garden. Shared taxis run between the border post and a taxi rank in front of the hospital that lies about 50m from this hotel.

The only accommodation along the stretch of road between Keta and Aflao is at Adiafana–Denu, where the one-star **Hotel Vilcabamba** (✆ 0962 354) lies close to the OSA station about 2km before you reach the main junction. Double rooms here start at around US$15.

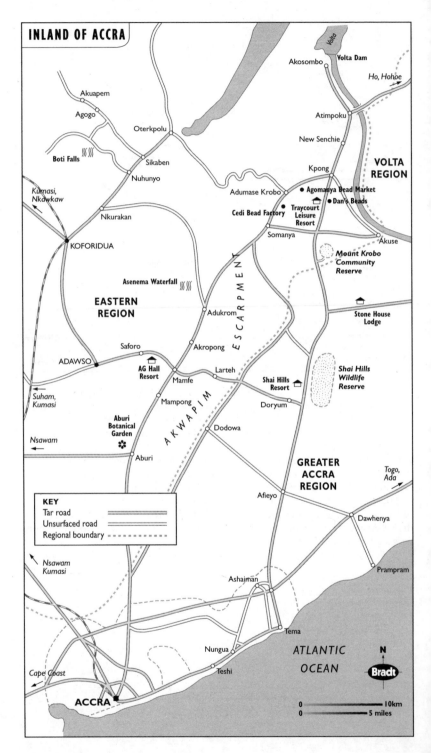

INLAND OF ACCRA

Volta

Akosombo
Volta Dam

Ho, Hohoe

Akuapem

Agogo

Oterkpolu

Atimpoku

New Senchie

VOLTA
REGION

Boti Falls

Sikaben

Kpong

Nuhunyo

Kumasi,
Nkawkaw

Adumase Krobo

● Agomanya Bead Market
● Dan's Beads

Cedi Bead Factory

Traycourt
Leisure
Resort

Nkurakan

Somanya

Akuse

KOFORIDUA

Mount Krobo
Community
Reserve

Asenema Waterfall

EASTERN
REGION

E
S
C
A
R
P
M
E
N
T

Stone House
Lodge

Adukrom

Akropong

Shai Hills
Wildlife
Reserve

Saforo

ADAWSO

AG Hall
Resort

Larteh

Shai Hills
Resort

Mamfe

Suham,
Kumasi

Mampong

Doryum

A
K
W
A
P
I
M

Aburi
Botanical
Garden

Dodowa

Nsawam

Aburi

GREATER
ACCRA
REGION

Togo,
Ada

Afieyo

KEY
Tar road
Unsurfaced road
Regional boundary

Dawhenya

Nsawam
Kumasi

Prampram

Ashaiman

Cape Coast

Tema

Nungua

ATLANTIC
OCEAN

N

Teshi

Bradt

ACCRA

0   10km
0   5 miles

230

above **Pirogues on River Volta, Ada Foah** (AZ) page 218

below left **Kpando market** (AZ) page 265

below right **Bus in Larabanga** (AZ) page 364

above **Cape Coast Castle**
(AZ) page 163

left **Nkrumah Mausoleum,
Accra** (AZ) page 134

above **Mosque, Larabanga**
(AZ) page 366

right **Traditional huts, Nakpanduri**
(AZ) page 380

below **Paga Pia's Palace**
(AZ) page 387

opposite page **Football crazy** (HH)

above left **Drummer, Tafi Atome** (AZ) page 264

above right **Zest for life, Accra** (SP)

below **Beach trade at Kokrobite** (HH) page 141

opposite page   **Wli falls, Agumatsa Wildlife Sanctuary** (AZ) page 271

above   **Green turtle,** *Chelonia mydas* (NHPA) page 196

right   **Blue-bellied roller,** *Coracias cyanogaster*
(AZ) page 47

below   **Nile crocodile,** *Crocodylus niloticus* (AZ) page 386

above **The River Volta at Akosombo** (AZ) page 245

left **Picking coconuts** (AS)

below **Fisherman on Lake Bosumtwi** (WC) page 316

11

Inland of Accra

The area covered in this chapter broadly conforms to Ghana's misleadingly titled Eastern Region (Volta Region lies to its east!) and is bounded by the Volta River to the east, the regional capital of Koforidua to the north, the Akuapem Hills to the west, and the main Accra–Aflao highway to the south. Regional highlights include the Aburi Botanical Garden in the Akuapem Hills, the underrated Shai Hills Reserve, the bead factory and market at Krobo-Odomase, the lovely Boti Falls near Koforidua, and the Akosombo Dam on the Volta River.

Most places detailed in this chapter can be – and regularly are – visited from Accra as a self-standing day or overnight excursion. Equally, the area is well suited to unstructured travel over a few days, with any number of route variations possible, and regular public transport links between practically any two given towns or places of interest. For those travelling further afield, Eastern Region is bisected by a couple of important through-routes. The most significant of these is the road to Akosombo – effectively the gateway to the highlands east of Lake Volta – which bypasses Shai Hills and Krobo Mountain, and comes within a few kilometres of Krobo-Odomase. Also worth noting is that the road between Accra and Koforidua via Aburi could be used as a springboard for travels further north, with regular public transport connecting Koforidua to Kumasi.

THE AKUAPEM HILLS AND ABURI

Situated less than an hour's drive inland of Accra, the green and relatively breezy Akuapem (aka Akwapim) Hills, and in particular Aburi Botanical Garden, have long formed a popular goal for a day trip out of the capital, as well as being an excellent area for travellers to start their exploration of the Ghanaian interior. The hills are named for the Akuapem Kingdom, which was founded in 1733 as a result of a rebellion against the oppressive Akwamu Kingdom of the eastern plains, and today consists of 17 townships ruled over by a paramount chief whose throne lies in Akropong.

The Akuapem Hills were one of the first parts of the Ghanaian interior to be settled by Europeans, starting in 1788 with the short-lived tenancy of the Danish Dr Isert. A permanent European presence was established in 1835 with the arrival of the Basel missionary Andreas Riis, who was warmly accepted by Chief Nana Addo Dankwa I and permitted to build a house in Akropong. One of the appeals of this area to European missionaries was the relatively cool climate and scarcity of malaria in comparison with the coast. During the mid 19th century, Basel missions were founded at Akropong, Aburi, Abetefi and several other townships in the area, manned by the unlikely combination of German and West Indian priests, whose goal was not solely to spread the gospel, but also to provide education and healthcare. The Akropong Seminary, founded by the Basel missionaries in 1848

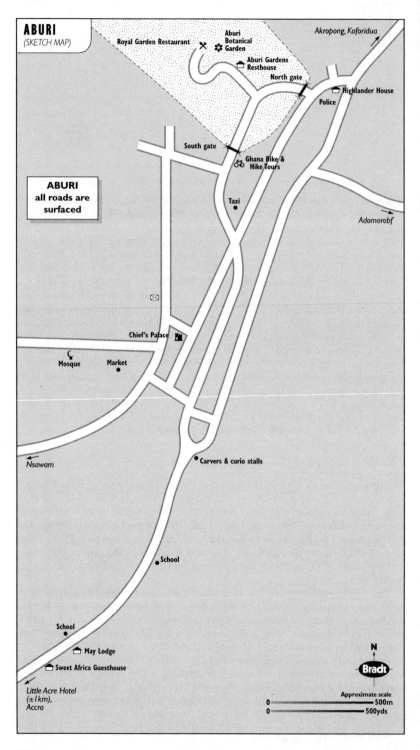

ABURI
(SKETCH MAP)

Royal Garden Restaurant
Aburi Botanical Garden
Aburi Gardens Resthouse
North gate
Akropong, Koforidua
Highlander House
Police
South gate
Ghana Bike & Hike Tours
Taxi
Adomorobf

ABURI
all roads are surfaced

Chief's Palace
Mosque
Market
Nsawam
Carvers & curio stalls
School
School
May Lodge
Sweet Africa Guesthouse
Little Acre Hotel
(± 1km),
Accra

N

Bradt

Approximate scale
0 ——— 500m
0 ——— 500yds

and still active today, is often referred to as the Mother of Ghanaian Schools (sadly, so far as I'm aware, none of the original seminary buildings remain).

The main tourist focus in Akuapem today is the **Aburi Botanical Garden**, founded by Britain in 1890 at a site that had formerly been settled by Basel missionaries and had served as a sanatorium for colonial officials in Accra since 1875. Aburi is still a popular weekend retreat with Accra residents, as much for the relatively bracing montane climate as for the lushly scenic setting. The garden, which covers 65ha and spans an altitude of 370–460m above sea level, is planted with a mixture of indigenous and exotic trees, notably the avenue of tall palms that leads to the guesthouse, and an immense 150-year-old *kapok* on the main lawn. It is riddled with footpaths from where visitors can see a large variety of labelled trees as well as many birds. In clear weather, the views back to Accra can be amazing. Aburi is also an excellent place to buy curios: at the row of stalls on the junction with the Accra road you'll find drums, fertility dolls, stools et al sold in a far friendlier atmosphere than in the capital, and at better prices. Entrance to the botanical garden costs US$2 for non-Ghanaian adults, with a 50% discount available to students. There is no additional charge for still photography, but video cameras attract an absurd fee of US$25!

Aburi's attractiveness to adventure tourists is greatly enhanced by the presence of **Ghana Bike and Hike Tours** (*The office is open from ⊕ 09.00 to 18.00 Thursday to Monday;* ☎ 024 4209587/0277666018; e *kofi@ghanabike.com; www.ghanabike.com*), just outside the southern gate of the botanical garden. The fantastically helpful owner of the company, Kofi, used to work with its Swiss founders who marked out three self-guided mountain bike trails of 2–3 hours' duration in the vicinity of Aburi, as well as a 450km network of guided trails of up to five days in duration. All the mountain bikes have aluminium frames, front suspension forks, and V breaks and are available for hire with helmets, repair kits and maps at US$3 per hour. Guide fees are an additional US$3.50 for up to three hours and US$4.50 for longer, and full rates for longer tours – including one-way trips with baggage transfer to other attractions in Ghana – are posted on the website.

A short tro-tro ride north of Aburi, the small town of Mampong (which, ironically, means 'Large Town', and should not be confused with its more substantial namesake in Ashanti Region) has an important place in Ghana's economic history as the site of the country's first **cocoa farm**, founded by Tetteh Quarshie. Born in what is now Accra in 1842, Tetteh Quarshie was an illiterate but well-travelled Ghanaian who lived on Fernando Po from 1870 to 1876 and brought back with him cocoa seeds that would first bear fruit at Mampong in 1879, revolutionising the national economy. The Gold Coast first exported cocoa in 1891; by 1911, it had become the world's largest cocoa producer, and it remains the world's second-largest producer to this day. While cocoa was Ghana's leading earner of foreign revenue for decades, it has recently been overtaken by gold. Visitors to Tetteh Quarshie's farm and homestead can see Ghana's first cocoa plant, still in good health, and they will be shown how cocoa is planted and picked.

Although few travellers explore the Akuapem Hills beyond Aburi, it is a fascinating area, not only for the scenery, but for the unusual architectural style of the small towns – evidently influenced by the Basel missionaries. Worthwhile goals for day trips include the Asenema Waterfall, which lies along a short signposted footpath off the Koforidua road 5km north of Adokrom, a palm tree with six heads on one stem 2km from Mamfe, and the small town of Larteh, home to one of the most renowned fetish priests in Ghana.

GETTING THERE AND AWAY Aburi lies about 35km from central Accra along the road passing Legon University. The drive generally takes about one hour, depending greatly on the traffic between the city centre and Legon. Regular tro-tros to Aburi leave Accra from Tema Station in the city centre (that's the same station as transport for Tema – you don't actually have to go to Tema to pick up a tro-tro to Aburi, as some readers have). Don't be tempted to go to Aburi from the Circle station, as these tro-tros go to Koforidua via Aburi and take forever to fill up. There are also regular tro-tros from Aburi to Mampong, Adokrom, Larteh and Mamfe, the latter being where you'll find transport to Koforidua.

WHERE TO STAY
Moderate

Jason Lodge 027 574266. This new hotel in Kitase, 5km south of Aburi, is similar in price & standard to the Little Acre.

Little Acre Hotel 021 910121/021 910120. This impressively smart little hotel (dedicated, according to the pamphlet, to the glory of God) is set in neat, green grounds about 2km from Aburi along the Accra road. A restaurant & bar are attached. *Dbl with fan, fridge, & hot shower US$20–25, with AC & TV US$38, large suite US$43.*

Budget

Aburi Gardens Resthouse 0876 22022/37. Housed in a former sanatorium built in 1875, this attractive but rather run-down guesthouse overlooks the main lawns of the botanical garden about 200m inside the northern entrance gate. Accommodation in self-contained chalets or 3-bed dorms. It's advisable to make an advance booking over w/ends & public holidays. *Chalet: dbl US$16, dbl/twin with TV & fridge US$20–26. Dorm US$10 pp.*

Highlander House 027 7547819/087 622114. Situated about 300m outside the botanical gardens' northern entrance gate, this friendly new set-up has exceedingly comfortable self-contained dbls with hot water, TV, fridge, AC, sturdy beds & even duvet covers. Excellent Ghanaian dishes are available for around US$4.50 to US$6.50, & can be served in the neatly tended garden outside. Recommended. *Dbl US$22–25.*

Shoestring

May Restaurant and Lodge 087 622025. This pleasant hotel on the fringe of Aburi village, about 1km south of the southern botanical garden entrance gate, offers simple food & lodging along with fabulous views over a wooded valley. Decent self-contained dbls with fan, although this is one part of Ghana where it does not feel such a necessity. There have been some reports of plumbing problems & a miserly attitude to providing water. Portions in the restaurant seem generous however, with hearty plates of chicken & rice or *fufu* at around US$3 a plate. *Dbl US$10–12.*

Sweet Africa Guesthouse 087 622069. Similarly priced accommodation & views are to be had at this lodge slightly nearer the gardens, although no food is available. Has spacious dbls with common showers, rooms with own bathroom – albeit only screened by a shower curtain, or a truly enormous suite-style room. *Dbl US$10–14, suite-style US$23.*

WHERE TO EAT
The **Rose Plot Restaurant** on the patio of the Aburi Gardens Resthouse sells simple local and Western meals for around US$3.50–4.50, as well as chilled beers, soft drinks, spicy barbecued kebabs and pots of delicious natural honey. More substantial and varied meals are available in the US$5.50–6.50 range at the **Royal Garden Restaurant**, which also lies within the botanical gardens.

For a relaxed drink, **Nora's Spot** above the taxi rank on the road to the south gate of the botanical garden has been recommended. May Restaurant and Highlander House (above) also serve good food.

KOFORIDUA

The capital of Eastern Region, Koforidua was founded in the 1870s by the New Juaben people, who were forced to migrate from Juaben in Ashanti after they staged an unsuccessful (and British-inspired) revolt against the authority of the Ashanti King in Kumasi. Today, Koforidua (or Koff-town, as it's often called locally) is a substantial and busy town, with a lively atmosphere and an important market. It's a pleasant place to spend a few days or use as a base for expeditions to Boti Falls and other nearby attractions, and will be of specific interest to craft lovers for its Thursday morning bead market (on the football field). This assembly of bead makers attracts craftsmen and women from all over Ghana, as well as the occasional merchant from beyond, trading in antique beads from all over west Africa. Strings of new beads are often very inexpensive, but expect to pay considerably more for older pieces, which are often sold individually. There is also a small trade in ready-made pieces of jewellery, which can make good gifts, but steer clear of the ivory stuff for obvious reasons.

GETTING THERE AND AWAY Koforidua is an important transport hub, with good bus and tro-tro connections to and from the GTPU station in Accra, and north towards Kumasi via Nkawkaw and Begoro. The town is also serviced by regular tro-tros and/or shared taxis to other centres in Eastern Region such as Aburi, Somanya (1½ hours; US$1) and Akosombo. There is no STC or OSA bus service linking Koforidua and Kumasi, but the Kingdom Transport Service runs a decent bus between the two towns.

WHERE TO STAY Note that several of Koforidua's best hotels lie in a suburb called Old Estate, about 1.5km northwest of the town centre. Regular minibus public transport runs between the central market and Old Estate, while a dropping taxi should cost no more than US$1. To get there in a private vehicle, follow the Kumasi road out of town for a few hundred metres, then turn left at the poorly signposted junction known locally as Bula Spot junction (after the bar on the corner).

Moderate

Capital View Hotel ☎ 081 26873. This smart, pink double-storey hotel in Old Estate is probably the most upmarket in Koforidua. Clean, comfortable, good-value rooms. Downstairs, the fairly priced restaurant attracts a well-heeled local crowd, with wine & a good range of tasty local, vegetarian & international dishes – although some of them won't bear much resemblance to their namesakes back home. *Self-contained sgl/dbl with AC, DSTV & hot water US$36–45.*

Saint James Hotel ☎ 081 20165; e saintjameshotel@hotmail.com. This stalwart 2-star hotel, built in the 70s, lies about 1km past Old Estate on a dirt track off the Nyamekrom–Densuegya road. A good restaurant is attached, serving pasta, steak & chicken stroganoff in the US$3–6.50 range. Dated, self-contained dbls with AC, DSTV & fridge are not bad value, but a bit rundown compared to the Capital View. *Dbl US$30.*

Budget

Erdrec Hotel ☎ 081 24265. Fashion hasn't been kind to this self-consciously modernist 1970s hotel on the town outskirts, though the open walls & cropped green lawns go some way to offsetting the stark angularity of the architecture. The attached restaurant serves good grilled meats in addition to the ubiquitous 'continental fare'. The large self-contained rooms with TV & fan, though threadbare, seem pretty good value. *Dbl/chalet US$11.50/17, US$21 for a newly spruced-up chalet with AC.*

Partners May Hotel ☎ 081 23138. This pleasant 1-star hotel (where strangers, presumably, may not!) comes highly recommended by many readers for its clean, spacious rooms & beautifully kept grounds. Food is served in a stark but immaculately clean restaurant at around US$3 a dish, making it all round the best budget bet in town. *Costs range from US$11 for a dbl using common showers with fan & TV to US$18–24 for self-contained dbls with AC, depending on size & whether or not they have hot water.*

Shoestring

Eastland Hotel ☎ 081 20216. This quiet, friendly hotel in Old Estate has clean but shabby self-contained dbl with (theoretically) running water & fan. Various

notices warn guests to stay off the 'glass lawns' – which sound hazardous, but even where the grass ones are remains a mystery. The Capital View Hotel and Santa

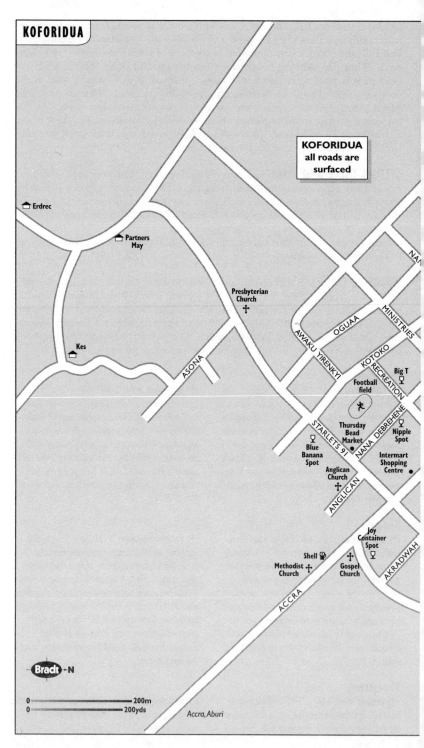

KOFORIDUA

KOFORIDUA
all roads are
surfaced

Erdrec

Partners
May

Presbyterian
Church

Kes

ASONA

AWAKU YIRENKYI

OGUAA

MINISTRIES

NAN

KOTOKO

RECREATION

Big T

Football
field

STARLETS 91

Thursday
Bead
Market

NANA DEBREHENE

Nipple
Spot

Blue
Banana
Spot

Intermart
Shopping
Centre

Anglican
Church

ANGLICAN

Joy
Container
Spot

Shell

AKRADWAH

Methodist
Church

Gospel
Church

ACCRA

Bradt N

0 ────── 200m
0 ────── 200yds

Accra, Aburi

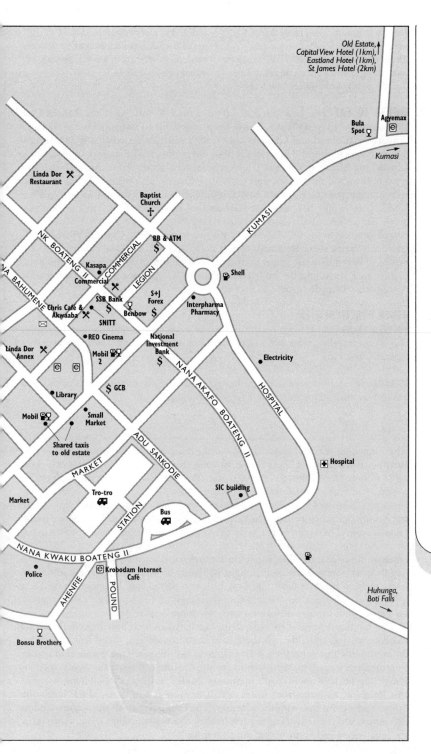

Old Estate,
Capital View Hotel (1km),
Eastland Hotel (1km),
St James Hotel (2km)

Agyemax

Bula
Spot

Kumasi

Linda Dor
Restaurant

Baptist
Church

BB & ATM

KUMASI

Shell

NK BOATENG II

COMMERCIAL

LEGION

Kasapa
Commercial

S+J
Forex

NANA BAHUMENE

SSB Bank

Chris Café &
Akwaaba

Benbow

Interpharma
Pharmacy

SNITT

REO Cinema

National
Investment
Bank

Electricity

Linda Dor
Annex

Mobil
2

NANA AKAFO BOATENG II

HOSPITAL

Library

GCB

Mobil

Small
Market

Shared taxis
to old estate

MARKET

ADU SARKODIE

Hospital

Market

Tro-tro

SIC building

STATION

Bus

NANA KWAKU BOATENG II

Police

AHENFIE

POUND

Krobodam Internet
Café

Huhunga,
Boti Falls

Bonsu Brothers

Rose directly opposite make up for the absence of a restaurant. *Dbl US$8.*

🏠 **Kes Hotel** 📞 081 23326; 📠 081 22534. Probably the closest lodging to the town centre, the pleasant Kes Hotel charges US$9 for an ordinary dbl with fan,

US$10–13 for a self-contained room with TV, or US$18 with AC. There is a restaurant, but the wood panels make it rather gloomy & there's nowhere to eat outdoors. *Dbl from US$9–18.*

✖ **WHERE TO EAT** The best place to eat in central Koforidua is the **Linda Dor Restaurant** on Oguaa Road, which has a varied menu ranging from steaks and burgers to spaghetti and Chinese dishes, with most dishes costing US$4 or less. The portions are big and you can eat in or out of doors. The second, more central, **Linda Dor Annex** next to the Telecom Building has a similar menu, but you can't eat outdoors and the indoor dining room is lit with off-putting blue lights. Also recommended is the nearby **Chris Café**, which serves excellent local meals for US$2–2.50, while the associated **Akwaaba Restaurant** upstairs is best for breakfast, with cornflakes and the usual range of egg dishes priced at US$1–2. The best place to eat in the Old Estate area is the restaurant at the **Capital View Hotel**, while the **Santa Rose Restaurant** next door serves decent local chop and chilled drinks. There's also the usual scattering of bars and drinking spots around the market area, including the bizarrely named **Joy Container Spot** and somewhat more obtuse **Nipple Spot**!

OTHER PRACTICALITIES
Foreign exchange Of the several banks in the town centre, only the Barclays Bank will accept travellers' cheques and has an ATM where local currency can be drawn against a Visa card.

Internet Several internet cafés are dotted around town, concentrated in the area around the Linda Dor Annex and Telecom Building.

BOTI FALLS

This 30m-high seasonal waterfall, one of the most attractive in Ghana, lies on the Pawnpawn River in the Boti Forest Reserve to the northeast of Koforidua. It is most impressive during the rains, as the flow decreases greatly during the dry season, when the waterfall usually splits into two separate streams before drying up altogether. The pool at the base, reached by a sequence of 250 concrete steps, is safe for swimming, provided that you keep clear of the waterfall itself, especially in the rainy season. The scene is made by the surrounding forest, which boasts many enormous trees, including flamboyants with their striking red flowers. A US$1 entrance fee is charged. Do watch out for army ants on the way down – on a bad day they are everywhere, and it might be worth tucking your trousers into your socks to keep them at bay! The Boti Falls is a sacred site, and the setting for a celebration every year on 1 July. Many thousands of Ghanaians visit the waterfall on this day, but foreign visitors are welcome to participate.

The rainforest around the waterfall once harboured chimpanzees and various monkey species, and although these have been hunted out, it still supports many different birds and butterflies. It's no problem to arrange a guided walk along other forest paths for a negotiable fee, or to explore the forest fringing the Agogo road on your own. Further afield, you can arrange guided walks to the anonymous caves that lie about an hour from the waterfall, as well as to the so-called 'Umbrella Stone' and a palm tree with three trunks. The round trip to all three takes around 2–3 hours, and is tough going in parts (take decent walking shoes), but worth it for the great views and atmospheric jungle setting.

According to Lauren Hall-Lew and Jefferson Shirley: 'All your readers should know about an alternative to Boti Falls, which seems rather quiet and undiscovered: Akaa Falls. It's on the way to Boti Falls. Just turn to your left off the road 2km before Boti Falls. The fee is US$0.50–1.00 per person (local vs. non-local price). After seeing the beautiful falls, the tour guides there will show you some unusual rocks, and there is old playground equipment for kids. The falls are great and you can get quite close to them. Some Koforidua locals prefer Akaa Falls to Boti Falls.'

GETTING THERE AND AWAY Boti Falls lies 21km and 30 minutes' drive from Koforidua. To get there, follow the surfaced road northeast to Huhunya via Kurakan, then take the signposted fork to the left, a 7km dirt road that can be driven in any vehicle. If you're using public transport, a tro-tro from Koforidua to Agogo, a small village shown on no maps, will drop you at the entrance to the falls.

WHERE TO STAY AND EAT A self-contained chalet overlooking the waterfall can be rented, and camping is permitted. The friendly caretaker will bring water for washing and arrange for somebody to do your cooking. He keeps two fridges loaded up with ice-cold mineral water, soft drinks and beer, as well as a supply of biscuits and tinned sardines. You can buy other basic foodstuffs at a village 1km up the road, or arrange for the caretaker (who has a car) to run into Agogo to buy you meat or chicken. Plans to build a larger guesthouse may come to fruition during the lifespan of this edition; you can ring ✆ 021 401143 for further information. *Chalet sgl/dbl US$7/10, camping US$2.50 per tent.*

THE ROAD TO AKOSOMBO

If you simply want to get to the town of Akosombo (see page 245), a great many tro-tros head there directly from Accra. For those with time to spare, however, two little-visited nature reserves lie practically alongside the Akosombo road. These are Shai Hills Resource Reserve and the Krobo Mountain Community Reserve, both of which would make for easy day trips for motorised Accra residents. Also very accessible from the Akosombo road are the Agomanya bead market and Cedi Bead Factory on the Kpong–Somanya road.

Note that travellers using public transport to explore this part of Ghana may well end up changing vehicles at **Ashaiman**, a busy little town at the junction of the main Accra–Aflao highway and the roads south to Tema and north towards Akosombo. Regular tro-tros connect Ashaiman with most of the main lorry stations in Accra. There are a few hotels in Ashaiman should you need to spend the night.

Akosombo – and, for that matter, all the other attractions described in this section – can as easily be approached from Aburi (via Dodowa) and/or Koforidua (via Somanya). In both cases, there is plenty of public transport.

SHAI HILLS RESOURCE RESERVE Shai Hills is the closest wildlife sanctuary to Accra, and one of the most accessible in the country, since it is bordered by the main Akosombo road. It protects some 50km² of coastal savanna, broken by a series of scenic granite inselbergs that rise from patches of dry evergreen forest rich in endemic plant species, some of which are threatened by a recent invasion of the exotic Neem tree *Azadirachta indica*. The area now protected within the reserve was home to the Shai people for several centuries until 1892, when they were ejected by the British. There are still a great many traces of Shai occupation in the reserve, including pottery dating to about 1600. Several active Shai shrines lie within the reserve, but the most important are closed to casual visitors.

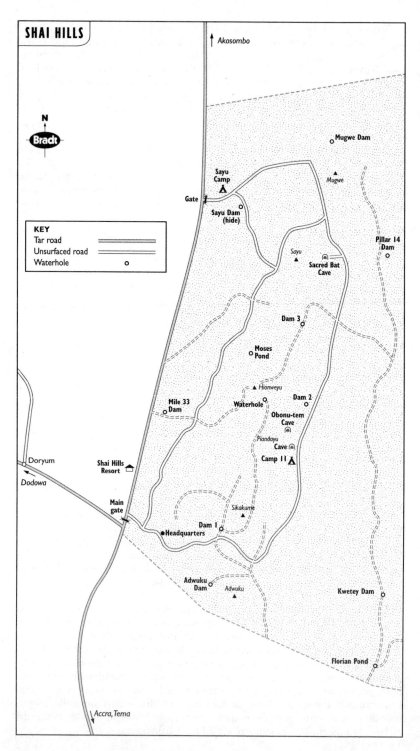

SHAI HILLS

↑ Akosombo

N
Bradt

Mugwe Dam

Sayu Camp

▲ Mugwe

Gate

Sayu Dam
(hide)

Pillar 14
Dam

▲ Sayu

Sacred Bat
Cave

KEY
Tar road
Unsurfaced road
Waterhole   o

Dam 3

Moses
Pond

▲ Hionweyu   Dam 2

Mile 33
Dam

Waterhole

Obonu-tem
Cave

Piandayu
Cave

Doryum

Shai Hills
Resort

Camp 11

Dodowa

Main
gate

Sikakume ▲

Dam 1

●Headquarters

Adwuku
Dam

Adwuku ▲

Kwetey Dam

Florian Pond

↓ Accra, Tema

Originally demarcated as a forest reserve, Shai Hills was listed as a game reserve in 1962 and, uniquely in Ghana, it has since been fenced off to protect the remaining wildlife. Motorised visitors can explore the reserve from a circular 17km road network that used to be adequate for a saloon car, except after heavy rain, but now normally requires a 4×4. Until such time as horseback trails are introduced, other visitors must explore on foot with an armed guide, using a combination of roads and footpaths. The reserve is open to day visits between 06.00 and 17.00. Entrance for a non-Ghanaian adult costs US$2.50 (students US$1), and a small additional fee is charged per vehicle, while a mandatory guide costs USS$0.80 per person per hour. A useful booklet with a map is sometimes sold at the entrance gate.

Wildlife viewing in Shai Hills scarcely compares to Africa's major savanna reserves, but there is a fair amount of game around, most likely to be seen in the early morning. The most common large mammal is the olive baboon, which most visitors will see (one troop often hangs around the entrance gate). About 200 kob antelope are resident, and lucky visitors might also encounter the shier bushbuck, green monkey and spot-nosed monkey. Several years ago, it was planned to reintroduce other antelope species such as roan and hartebeest, but nothing has come to fruition. At the latest count, something like 175 bird species have been recorded, of which some of the more visible and attractive are the black-bellied bustard, Abyssinian ground hornbill, grey hornbill, Senegal parrot and double-spurred francolin.

There are more than ten dams in the reserve, with the one closest to Sayu Camp bordered by an (arguably rather optimistically located) game-viewing hide. Also of interest is the bat cave about 4km east of Sayu Camp, which can be visited from the road through the park following an 800m trail. In addition to the impressive bat colony – several thousands of chirruping individuals, with at least three species represented – this cave once served as the chief's palace, and signs of low protective walls can still be seen.

Getting there and away The main entrance gate is conspicuously signposted on the main Akosombo road opposite Doryumu junction. A second entrance gate, more difficult to pick up, lies about 10km closer to Akosombo at Sayu Camp. On public transport, the best way to get to the main entrance gate is to first take a tro-tro from Accra to Ashaiman, from where any tro-tro heading to Doryumu will drop you outside the reserve. If you want to hire a taxi to explore the reserve, bearing in mind that the internal roads are currently suitable for a 4×4 only, the closest towns from which you could do so are Dodowa, Somanya, Akuse or even Akosombo. Game drives can also be arranged through the nearby Shai Hills Resort.

Where to stay and eat Note that there is no accommodation within the resource reserve, though camping is permitted. Outside the reserve, a hotel recently opened only 500m north of the main entrance gate. Other possible bases from which to explore Shai Hills include the Marina Hotel in Dodowa and Stone Lodge on the Asutsuare road.

Moderate

🏠 **Marina Hotel** 📞 021 767462/220510 or 020 8130467; f 021 775009; e marinahotel@yahoo.com. This gem of a hotel is set in large flowering grounds in the small town of Dodowa on the Accra–Somanya road, about 14km from the main entrance gate to Shai Hills. Comfortable self-contained rooms with AC, fan, satellite TV & hot bath cost around US$30–35 dbl/twin. Good meals are available in the US$3.50–5.50 range. Dodowa is connected to both Accra & Somanya by direct tro-tros. To get to the reserve from Dodowa, follow the Somanya road northwards for 6km to Akiyumu junction, where a right turn will bring you to Doryumu after 6km & the entrance gate at the junction with the Akosombo road after another 2km. *Dbl/twin US$30–35.*

The MV *Yapei Queen*, which has plied the length of Lake Volta from Akosombo to Yeji and back on a weekly basis since the late 1960s, is primarily a cargo vessel, but it also has limited cabin space and deck space for passengers. Its route is the longest followed by any boat in Ghana, and while it's anything but a luxury cruise, many adventurous travellers rank it to be a highlight of travelling around the country.

In theory, the trip takes about 36 hours in either direction, with the boat leaving Akosombo every Monday at about 16.00 and scheduled to arrive in Yeji on Tuesday between 17.00 and 20.00. From Yeji, it leaves at 03.00 on Wednesday to arrive in Akosombo the next day between 11.00 and 19.00. In practice, however, this timetable is not rigidly adhered to, and we've had numerous reports from travellers who were on the boat for 60–70 hours in one or other direction thanks to engine or steering problems or interminable loading stops at villages along the way. Delays seem to be a greater problem on the southbound leg. The boat stops at Keti Krachi on both legs of the voyage and also sometimes stops at Kpando depending on the water level there.

Only two first-class passenger cabins are available on the MV *Yapei Queen*, though the so-called Owner's Cabin will normally be made available to tourists if it is not being used by Volta Lake Transport Company staff. The cabins are quite comfortable, with air conditioning and two beds each, but tickets, which cost US$29 per person, are very difficult to come by. In theory, reservations can be made by ringing ℡ 0251 20686 or 021 665300, but in practice any booking made telephonically will be all but worthless unless you also make an advance payment at the Lake Volta Transport Company office in Akosombo and get a ticket or receipt in exchange (even then, overbooking is not unheard of).

Without a ticket bought in advance, you'll just have to try your chances in what amounts to a 'first on the boat is first to get a cabin' scenario – assuming, that is, there are no other passengers who've paid in advance and have a ticket or receipt. When the ferry arrives, make sure you're in the front of the queue, then take the right entrance, head upstairs, go to the end of the ferry up to the cockpit and ask one of the crew members for the captain. If you're out of luck, buy a second-class ticket (US$7), which means you can sleep in the dining room rather than out on deck – though this distinction between second and third class (US$5) tends to become blurred as the trip progresses and the number of passengers increases.

There is normally plenty of food on the boat, but we've heard of travellers being stuck without food for 24 hours after it ran out. There does always seem to be plenty to drink at all times. If you arrive in Yeji in the late afternoon, don't let the touts convince you to cross to Makongo immediately, as there is nowhere to stay there and there will probably be no transport on to Salaga or Tamale until the next morning – better to overnight in Yeji. For travellers with vehicles, the ferry charges are US$34 for a saloon car, and US$65 for minibus or 4x4. Cheaper fares are available to Keti Krachi (US$23/US$4/US$3 first class/second/third), a trip which can last anything between 12 and 17 hours.

⌂ **Shai Hills Resort** ℡ 024 836883. Opened in 2003, this resort lies in large wooded grounds about 500m north of the reserve's main entrance gate, making it the most convenient overnight base for a visit. The large carpeted self-contained dbls with AC, fan & TV aren't bad value. Facilities inc a restaurant & game drives into the reserve. *Dbl US$20.*

⌂ **Stone Lodge** ℡ 024 4549124; f 024 4303901; e info@stonelodge.biz; www.stonelodge.biz. Probably more suited to a family w/end break from Accra than to overseas tourists, this low-key lodge lies on the Kitoma Stock Farm, 5km from the main Accra–Akosombo road along the side road to Asutsuare. True to the name, accommodation is provided in a range of stone-built chalets, each of which has 2 self-contained dbl rooms & a kitchen (without fan or AC), priced at US$56 for the whole unit or US$30–40 for just 1 room. The Volta River & Shai Hills are both within 15 mins' drive of the lodge, while other activities inc a private 9-hole golf course, bicycle hire at US$4 per day, hiking, croquet, volleyball, & farm tours. The attractively laid-out Kraal Restaurant serves excellent meals & chilled drinks. *Dbl from US$30.*

Shoestring The only option in this range is the **Shai Hills Hotel**, an unsignposted cream building that lies in the small town of Doryumu, some 2km from the entrance gate, on the left side of the Akiyumu road about 100m from the lorry station. It is unclear whether the rooms are still available, as the hotel was deserted when we came past. Even if it is open, a recent correspondent described the hotel as 'unfriendly and filthy' and reckoned it made more sense to ask around for a room in a private house in Doryumu.

Camping Camping is permitted at the main entrance gate for a fee of US$3 per person per night, exclusive of entrance and guide fees. You can also camp at **Sayu Camp** in the north of the park, but you must first report to the headquarters at the main entrance gate. Campers will need to be self-sufficient in terms of food and water.

KROBO MOUNTAIN COMMUNITY RESERVE A craggy inselberg that towers above the eastern side of the Accra–Akosombo road, about 5km south of Kpong, Krobo Mountain is the spiritual home of the Krobo people, who settled there for the natural protection it offered against Ashanti slave raids and whose famous defeat of an Ashanti raid in 1764 led directly to the incumbent Ashanti king being destooled. The Krobo were less fortunate when they resisted a British attempt to impose poll taxes in 1892; they were forced off the mountain, which has remained virtually uninhabited ever since. Among the mountain's natural attractions are the rare charcoal tree *Talbotia genetii*, wild baboons, birds, caves and views across to Lake Volta. Of archaeological interest are the ruins of abandoned Krobo villages, still used to enact sacrificial rites, as well as the former chief's palace and the ceremonial 'Dipo Stone'.

The Krobo Mountain Community Reserve was developed for tourism with the assistance of a Peace Corps volunteer in 1999, when a reception centre with summer huts, shower and flush toilet was constructed at the base of the mountain, and a number of guided walks, ranging from one to five hours in duration and costing US$2–2.50 per person, were demarcated. The project suffered a period of abandonment around the time of the last edition, and – more ominously – one reader wrote in 2002 to say that he had come across a murdered body a few feet from the main path at the reception area.

But Krobo has since returned to life, so if murder stories don't put you off, follow the Akosombo road from Accra/Tema, past Shai Hills until you see the signposted junction to your right (about 2km before Akuse junction), which leads to the reception centre. On public transport, the best option is to catch a bus or tro-tro towards Akosombo and ask to be dropped at the junction, from where it is about ten minutes on foot to the reception area.

AKUSE This small Ewe stronghold on the Volta River is of interest to travellers primarily as the northern terminus of the ferry service to Ada, which departs at around 06.30 every other day (*US$1.50*), and arrives at its destination around 20.00. Situated only 8km from the Accra–Akosombo road, along a turn-off signposted immediately to the north of Krobo Mountain, it would also be as good a base as any from which to visit the mountain and places described under the section *Kpong and the Somanya road* on page 244.

The unexpectedly smart but bland **Volta River Authority Clubhouse**, signposted to the right shortly before you enter Akuse, has self-contained singles with AC, fridge and TV, whilst an enormous family suite with kitchen would make a bargain for four people sharing. The large green grounds outside host an inexpensive restaurant, bar, swimming pool and tennis courts. *Sgl US$10, family suite (for 4) US$15–25.*

KPONG AND THE SOMANYA ROAD Kpong is a small port situated at the junction of the main Accra–Akosombo road and the 10km tar road that leads westward to the large town of Somanya. The Kpong–Somanya road, which is lined with small towns that merge into each other, is best known for the town of Krobo-Odomase. Settled by Krobo people who were evicted from the nearby mountain, this town is regarded to be the centre of the traditional Krobo bead industry. Two good places to buy beads in this area are the **Agomanya Market** (*Wed & Sat*) – a vast expanse of stalls which would rank with Ghana's most worthwhile markets even without the beads – or the sizable Koforidua bead market which gathers on Thursdays.

A great place to see traditional bead-makers at work is **Cedi's Bead Factory**, which despite a rather humble appearance exports its products as far afield as the USA, Europe, Australia and South Africa. Here you can watch the centuries-old process from start to finish: to make new beads, the bead-makers first crush old bottles into small chips, then arrange them in glazed moulds, before placing them in what looks like a fiery pizza oven for about 45 minutes. They also restore worn beads – some of them many centuries old – by placing them intact in an appropriate mould, then baking them at low heat for about 15 minutes so that they come out shiny as new. The Nene Nomoda family, which runs the factory, claims to have been bead-makers for more than 200 years, and visitors appear to be welcome. There's no charge for looking around, and the family is very welcoming, but if you do visit it would be courteous to buy something from the well-stocked showroom, if only to make things easier for those who follow in your footsteps (prices start at around US$1 for enough beads to make a necklace, but the restored old beads are far more expensive). The factory is open daily except for Sunday (✆ *081 24106/8;* f *021 229168*).

Another place to buy beads and see the craftsmen at work is along the Accra road about 3km south of Kpong, where in 2003 a subsidiary branch of Cedi's Bead Factory as well as a new place called **Dan's Beaded Handicraft** opened alongside each other opposite the Traycourt Leisure Centre and next to Starr Villa Lodge and Garage. Both of these places will let you look around with no pressure to buy. Further towards Accra, ten minutes before Adenta junction, is **TK Beads** – a relatively new set up run by Florence Martey, reputedly the first woman in Ghana to set up her own glass bead business. Visits are welcomed at no charge, and Mrs Martey is happy to help you string any purchases into a bracelet or necklace (✆ *024 4727853 or 024 4862809;* e *tkbeads@yahoo.com*).

Getting there and away Good tar roads and regular tro-tros connect Somanya to Accra, Koforidua, Aburi, and most other urban centres in the region, while any public transport on the surfaced road between Accra and Akosombo will be able to drop you at Kpong. Agomanya Market lies on the south side of the road 3km from Kpong; the bead and other craft stalls are at the far end of the market from the main road. Cedi's Bead Factory lies about 500m south of the main road; the signposted turn-off is 3km past Agomanya coming from the direction of Kpong. The road between Kpong and Somanya is serviced by a steady stream of tro-tros that will drop you wherever you want along the way. There is a tro-tro park right next to Agomanya Market, and another at the junction 500m from Cedi's Bead Factory.

Where to stay and eat Using public transport, this area could easily be explored as a day trip from Akosombo, while with a private vehicle it could also be visited as a day trip out of Akuse, any of the hotels mentioned under Shai Hills, or, at a push, Accra, Tema or Ada. I'm not aware of any accommodation in Kpong itself, but there is a fair selection of budget accommodation in the immediate vicinity, including two basic hotels in Somanya, one slightly nicer hotel in Krobo-Odomase, and a pair of smarter hotels about 3km back along the Accra road near Dan's Beaded Handicrafts.

Moderate

🏠 **Starr Villa Hotel** (7 rooms) ☎ 081 91533. Part of a garage complex at Okwenya, 3km south of Kpong next to Dan's and Cedi's Beads, this smart new hotel sits alongside a good restaurant & supermarket, making it a convenient stopover en route to somewhere further north. It's very good value too – with comfortable, self-contained dbls with tiled floor, fan, hot water & TV, some with AC. *Dbl US$14–21.*

Budget

🏠 **Gerted Hotel** Situated in Krobo-Odomase, about 500m south of the main road along a motorable track signposted next to the Manya Krobo Community Bank, this is a comfortable & reasonably priced double-storey building with a good rooftop bar & restaurant. Room prices vary, depending on whether they are sgl or dbl, self-contained, & have TV. *US$10–12.*

🏠 **Traycourt Leisure Centre** ☎ 024 531042 or 024 3160891. Diagonally opposite Starr Villa, this pleasant enough lodge is a bit more run-down than its more expensive neighbour. But the clean rooms are very good value indeed for a self-contained dbl with hot water & fan, some with AC. An attractive garden restaurant at the front serves decent food & cold beer. *Dbl US$7–15.*

Shoestring

🏠 **99 Westend Lane Hotel** ☎ 024 2974525. This hotel in Somanya was recently spruced up & charges are fair: *US$10 for a self-contained dbl with fan.*

🏠 **Palm Hotel** ☎ 024 2522692. Marginally the cheaper & probably the nicer of the two hotels in Somanya, this has small clean rooms with fan or self-contained dbl with or without TV. *Sgl/dbl with fan US$8.50/9.50, self-contained dbl without/with TV US$14–15.*

AKOSOMBO AND SURROUNDS

The township of Akosombo was purpose-built in 1961 to house the workers involved in the creation of Ghana's largest dam, a clay and rock construction that measures 370m across and 124m from top to bottom. The notion of damming the Volta at the Akosombo Gorge for hydroelectric power was first proposed by the Australian geologist Sir Albert Kitson in 1913, but the dam itself is inalienably associated with the late President Nkrumah, who believed its construction would help Ghana's industrial development. Inaugurated by Nkrumah in 1966, Akosombo Dam hems in Lake Volta, the most expansive artificial lake in the world, with a surface area of roughly 850,000ha, a length of 400km, and a shoreline measuring almost 5,000km. Aside from affording an excellent view over the dam, Akosombo is important to travellers as the southern terminus of the weekly Lake Volta ferry to the northern ports of Kete Krachi and Yeji (see page 242).

It is also possible to visit the hydroelectric plant itself – a trip that garners rave reviews from those with an interest in engineering. Visitors should report to the Corporate Services reception in the GCB building just after the police barrier before you reach Akosombo. Tours last approximately 45 minutes, and leave every hour on the hour between 09.00 and 15.00. A US$2.50 fee is charged to non-Ghanaians; call ☎ 0251 20658/0 for details.

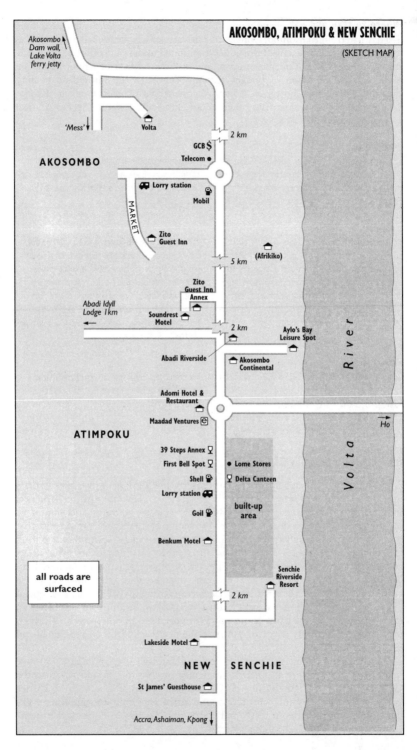

AKOSOMBO, ATIMPOKU & NEW SENCHIE

(SKETCH MAP)

Akosombo
Dam wall,
Lake Volta
ferry jetty

'Mess'

Volta

AKOSOMBO

GCB $
Telecom ●

2 km

Lorry station

Mobil

MARKET

Zito
Guest Inn

5 km

(Afrikiko)

Zito
Guest Inn
Annex

Abadi Idyll
Lodge 1km

Soundrest
Motel

2 km

Aylo's Bay
Leisure Spot

Abadi Riverside

Akosombo
Continental

Adomi Hotel &
Restaurant

River

Maadad Ventures ⓔ

ATIMPOKU

39 Steps Annex ⚲

Ho

First Bell Spot ⚲

● Lome Stores

Shell ⛽

⚲ Delta Canteen

Lorry station

Goil ⛽

built-up
area

Benkum Motel

Volta

all roads are
surfaced

Senchie
Riverside
Resort

2 km

Lakeside Motel

NEW   SENCHIE

St James' Guesthouse

Accra, Ashaiman, Kpong

246

Another popular excursion from Akosombo is the tourist-oriented MV *Dodi Princess*, which undertakes a joyride to the Dodi Islands every Saturday, Sunday and public holiday, leaving at 10.30 and getting back at around 16.00. Tickets are available from the Volta Hotel for US$20 a person and include a good barbecue lunch. The trip draws mixed reactions from readers – many have complained that it's too touristy, but others reckon it's tremendous fun, with the deciding factor probably being one's tolerance for the very loud live band. There's also a plunge pool and upper- and lower-deck bars to enhance the hedonistic pleasure inherent in sailing across this vast, hill-ringed lake on a sunny day. The boat moors at Dodi Island for 45–60 minutes, when you can either splash around on the small beach or allow one of the gang of children who make up the boat's reception party to lead you across the island for a small fee.

For the purpose of orientation, it's worth noting that Akosombo township lies some 8km off the main road between Accra and Ho. The junction to Akosombo is at Atimpoku, a small but impressively chaotic urban sprawl straddling the Accra–Ho road on the west bank of the river next to Adome Bridge, a massive suspension bridge that forms one of only two places where cars are able to cross the Lower Volta. Travellers on a budget are generally better catered for in Atimpoku than in Akosombo, and Aylo's Bay, 500m from the junction, offers perhaps the best access to the river in this area.

There are no foreign exchange facilities in the Akosombo area, though the Volta Hotel will exchange US dollars cash for hotel residents – and sometimes day visitors – at a rather poor rate. Internet facilities are limited to the slow and expensive New Age Café in Akosombo near the lorry station.

GETTING THERE AND AWAY The main regional transport centre is Kpong, situated on the west bank of the Volta some 10km south of Atimpoku and 10km north of the river ferry terminal at Akuse. Kpong is bisected by the main Accra–Ho road, and is connected by regular tro-tros to Ashaiman (for Accra), Ho and Akuse. Regular tro-tros also run up and down from Kpong to Akosombo via Atimpoku and New Senchie, and you'll rarely wait more than five minutes for a seat between any of these places. STC, OSA and other buses travelling between Accra and Ho will generally drop passengers on request at Atimpoku, provided that they don't mind paying the full fare. If you're heading to Ho from Atimpoku, vehicles passing in the right direction might be full when they come past, so it may be quicker in the long run to take a tro-tro to Kpong and board a Ho-bound vehicle there.

Every second Sunday of the month, the *Dodi Princess* is the subject of an organised coach excursion from Accra, leaving from La Beach at 06.30 – for further details, contact Insight Travel on ☎ 028 206541/784267 or ℮ insightghana@ yahoo.com.

Regular shared taxis run around the sprawling hills of Akosombo. From the lorry station, ask for a taxi to 'Mess' for the Volta Hotel, and one to 'Marine' for the ferry jetty and ticket office.

See also the boxed text *The Akosombo–Yeji Ferry* on page 242.

WHERE TO STAY
Upmarket

Afrikiko Set up just a few years ago by the founder of Afrikiko's in Accra, this immaculate & characterful lodge has already gained itself an enviable reputation as one of the best expat escapes in the area. Rooms range from a simple self-contained African-style hut to a gorgeous chalet with AC, DSTV, etc, tastefully decorated with restored colonial furniture & each with its own flower-covered terrace. Camping is permitted, while expensive family facilities under construction at the time of research, are expected to cost around US$100 for a suite with kitchenette. Facilities inc an award-winning 'wellness spa', which offers Western-standard treatments at Western prices, & a 15-man motorboat available for hire at US$20 an hour. There is also a tempting-looking pool & an excellent bar & restaurant, which host cultural displays on Sat & Sun afternoons. *Prices range from US$18–60. Camping US$5 pp.*

🏠 **Akosombo Continental Hotel** ✆ 0251 20091; 📠 0251 20092; e akoscontinentalhotel@yahoo.com. This immaculate hotel has won numerous awards since opening in 2001, no doubt helped by its superb river-front location in Atimpoku. The attractive grounds are set around a large, tempting swimming pool (open to day visitors for US$3), & dotted with zoo exhibits, inc a crocodile pit & a few sad monkeys in cages. The rooms themselves are a bit small, but still very comfortable, & offer reasonable value with AC, DSTV & fridge. Larger chalets are set back away from the pool area. The restaurant serves good food from a varied

Moderate

🏠 **Abadi Riverside** This German-run resort just north of Aylo's Bay is the latest in a string of pleasant travellers' lodges to set up around this area, notable for its paddling pool & child-friendly atmosphere. There is a range of accommodation to suit all budgets & camping is permitted for a small fee. The attached restaurant specialises in barbecued *tilapia*, but also serves chicken, & seafood dishes for around US$6. The lodge's more expensive forerunner, the **Abadi Idyll Lodge**, does not sound as alluring on paper for the simple fact that it is not by the river, but in reality it is an extremely pleasant spot – built on 6 acres of land set well back from the road & offering a good range of accommodation from inexpensive backpacker huts (US$3 a head) to spacious, tourist-class chalets (US$60).

🏠 **Aylo's Bay Leisure Spot** ✆ 0251 20093 or 024 756088; e aylosbay@hotmail.com or aylosbay@yahoo.com; www.aylosbay.com. This gem of a hotel is set in tranquil wooded river-front gardens alongside the Akosombo Continental Hotel, & less than 500m from Atimpoku & the Volta Bridge. Run by a charming Ghanaian couple, it used to function primarily as a restaurant, & is still a great place to eat – in the garden or the floating pontoon out on the river. The largely organic menu offers a good range of chicken & fish dishes at around US$4 a plate, inc unbeatable golden fried shrimps (US$3) fished direct from the Volta. A more recent addition is the row of cosy air-conditioned dbl chalets with kitchenettes & private

menu in the US$5–10 range, & even better cocktails. *US$55–90.*

🏠 **Volta Hotel** ✆ 021 662639/49 or 0251 20777/78/46; 📠 021 663791; e info@voltahotel.net; www.voltahotel.net. The building may not be beautiful, but this 3-star hotel is made genuinely special by its spectacular view over the dam wall. Part of the upmarket international Accor chain, the establishment ranks with the few truly upmarket hotels in the country outside Accra. Facilities inc a large swimming pool area, a good restaurant & nightclub as well as live high-life music in the bar over w/ends. Self-contained rooms with AC & DSTV, and suites available. Extra beds are charged at US$28. The hotel lies more than 1km from Akosombo township; passenger taxis from the lorry station to 'Mess' pass by the bottom of its steep drive. *Sgl/dbl US$98/108, suite US$169.*

balconies. Budget travellers will be able to take a room in the new dormitory-style rooms that were being built when this edition was researched, or pitch their tents for US$3 a person. Swimming is said to be safe in this stretch of the river (the water is remarkably clear) & a canoe hire costs US$10 per hour for up to 4 people. With advance notice, it's possible for groups to organise drumming, dancing & cooking workshops here too. *Dbl with/without seaview US$35/25 inc full cooked b/fast. Camping US$3 pp.*

🏠 **St James' Guesthouse** ✆ 0251 20416. Situated in New Senchie, on the opposite side of the road to the river, this small guesthouse offers comfortable accommodation in large, brightly decorated self-contained dbls with AC & DSTV– it would be a great deal anywhere else, but here the riverside options are more alluring. *Dbl US$30.*

🏠 **Senchie Riverside Resort** ✆ 0251 20097; 📠 0251 20098; e senchirl@africaonline.com.gh. Overlooking the river about 2km from Atimpoku in New Senchie, this is another attractive set-up that started life as a restaurant but has subsequently added good-value accommodation. There are 12 large & immaculate self-contained rooms, all with tiled floor, DSTV & AC. The food is good too, with an extensive menu mostly falling into the US$4–5.50 range. Boat trips to the dam are offered at US$20 per hour for up to 14 people. *Sgl/dbl US$37/46 .*

Budget

🏠 **Adomi Hotel** ✆ 0251 20095. This new hotel, situated on the first floor of a building overlooking the main circle in Atimpoku, offers an excellent compromise

between cost & comfort. The self-contained dbl rooms might be a bit garishly decorated for some tastes, but they are very clean & comfortable, have DSTV, & seem good value. The open-sided restaurant has great views over the bridge & river, & serves a variety of Ghanaian, continental & Chinese dishes in the US$3.50–5 range – although it's more tempting to wander down to Aylo's & enjoy better food on the water. *Dbl with fan US$14, with AC US$21.*

⌂ **Lakeside Motel** ☎ 0251 20310. Situated about 2km south of Atimpoku in New Senchie, this comfortably rustic hotel consists of a rambling old house set in shady, sloping gardens with a rather distant view of the Volta River. A variety of meals are available on request &

you can eat in the garden. The rooms vary considerably in quality & price so it's worth checking a few before you settle. *Sgl/dbl with fan US$5–6, self-contained rooms with AC US$7–13.*

⌂ **Zito Guest Inn** ☎ 0251 20474. The only hotel in central Akosombo, this lies about 500m from the lorry station & is clearly signposted. It has a pleasant small garden & serves meals on request. Large & reasonably clean dbl rooms with hot water, queen-size bed, & fan or AC. *Dbl with fan US$13, with AC US$22.*

Shoestring

⌂ **Benkum Motel** ☎ 0251 20050. Centrally located in Atimpoku, only 50m from the lorry station, this long-serving & friendly hotel is the obvious first choice for backpackers on a tight budget. It looks like a dump from the outside & noise from the bar can be disturbing, but the self-contained dbl rooms with fan are actually very clean & seem good value. There's no restaurant in the hotel, but there's plenty of street food around, & the large courtyard bar can be a lively place for a drink, with occasional live traditional music. *Dbl US$9.50.*

⌂ **Soundrest Motel** ☎ 0251 20288. Situated just off the road connecting Akosombo to Atimpoku, about

5km from the former & 2km from the latter, this long-serving hotel has an attractively rustic setting, a relaxed & friendly atmosphere, & decent restaurant & bar facilities. The rooms are good value. Meals are available on request. *Rooms range from sgl/dbl with fan & common showers US$4, to self-contained dbl with AC US$10.*

⌂ **Zito Guest Inn Annex** ☎ 0251 20474. Situated next to the Soundrest, this newer, more rustic & less expensive cousin of the Zito Guest Inn has a variety of clean dbls. The hotel has no restaurant of its own but food can be ordered from Soundrest & eaten on either site. *Dbl US$8–9.*

✗ **WHERE TO EAT** Several of the hotels listed above have good restaurants. The pick is probably the **Volta Hotel**, which serves European cuisine in the US$10-plus range as well as a variety of cheaper snacks, but **Aylo's Bay** and the **Senchie Riverside Resort** win out for a combination of good food, moderate prices and attractive setting. At the bottom end of the price scale, Atimpoku is a great place for street food: oyster kebabs and packets of smoked shrimp are two of the local specialities, both probably to be approached with some caution, as it takes only one dodgy chunk of shellfish to debilitate you with food poisoning. A pleasant place to drink nearby is the garden bar opposite Adomi Spot, about 100m along the road towards Akosombo.

Also in Akosombo, about 500m from the ferry port, the lakefront **Volta Transport Club** (aka The Maritime Club) consists of a more than decent and very affordable restaurant and bar set in pleasant, shady gardens exuding an air of faded colonial languor – it's a good place to hang out at any time (except Wednesdays, when it is closed), and especially convenient when you are waiting for the ferry.

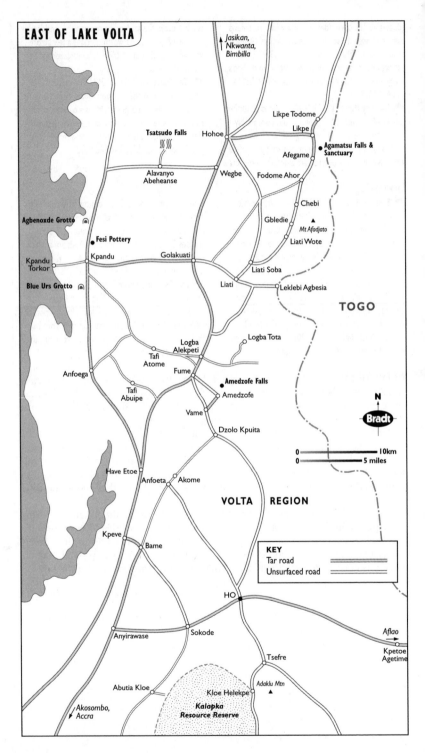

EAST OF LAKE VOLTA

Jasikan,
Nkwanta,
Bimbilla

Likpe Todome

Likpe

Hohoe

Afegame

Agamatsu Falls & Sanctuary

Tsatsudo Falls

Wegbe

Fodome Ahor

Alavanyo Abeheanse

Chebi

Gbledie

Mt Afadjato

Liati Wote

Agbenoxde Grotto

Fesi Pottery

Kpandu

Golakuati

Liati Soba

Kpandu Torkor

Liati

Leklebi Agbesia

Blue Urs Grotto

TOGO

Logba Tota

Logba Alekpeti

Tafi Atome

Fume

Amedzofe Falls

Anfoega

Amedzofe

Tafi Abuipe

Vame

N

Dzolo Kpuita

0   10km
0   5 miles

Have Etoe

Anfoeta   Akome

VOLTA   REGION

Kpeve

Bame

KEY
Tar road
Unsurfaced road

HO

Aflao

Anyirawase   Sokode

Kpetoe
Agetime

Tsefre

Abutia Kloe

Adaklu Mtn

Kloe Helekpe

Akosombo,
Accra

Kalapka
Resource Reserve

12

East of Lake Volta

This chapter covers the interior of Volta Region, a lushly vegetated and relatively mountainous sliver of land bounded by Lake Volta to the west and Togo to the east, and the last region to be annexed to modern-day Ghana. Largely shunned by the package tourist industry – it has been estimated that less than 5% of visitors to Ghana enter Volta Region – this scenic area is increasingly popular with active independent travellers, who are drawn by a compact and generally inexpensive circuit of natural attractions, ranging from the country's tallest waterfall and highest peak to a clutch of obscure but pedestrian-friendly reserves.

A commendable feature of tourism in this part of Ghana is the high concentration of well-run, community based developments. These serve to ensure that virtually all of the revenue raised by tourism is retained locally, to be used for the development of communal resources such as schools and boreholes, while also creating a range of job opportunities at grassroots level. Many of the community projects succeed in subverting the barriers that conventional tourism tends to create between visitors and local people; for instance by offering travellers the opportunity to stay with families rather than in hotels or guesthouses. Perhaps related to this, the ceaseless cat-calls of 'White Man' or 'Obruni' ('Yavoo' in Ewe) that are directed at travellers in areas such as the west coast are notable here by their absence, replaced by altogether more agreeable greetings such as 'Mia Woezor' or 'You're Welcome'.

The main towns in this part of Ghana are Ho, Hohoe and Kpando, all of which form agreeable travel bases and offer good, affordable facilities to backpackers, though they are somewhat lacking in inherent interest. It is the area

VILLAGE NAMES EAST OF LAKE VOLTA

Gerard van de Garde & Sandra Smeets

'It is worth drawing your readers' attention to the system of naming villages to the east of Lake Volta. Most villages have their own local chief and also form part of a cluster governed by a paramount chief, but although there is a main chief, there is not necessarily a main village. In some cases, the history of each village is traced back to separate groups of Ewe settlers, each of which chose its own spot when arriving in this area several centuries ago. Whatever the (pre)history of these clusters, villages of the same cluster now usually have a common first name (Nyagbo, Tafi, Wli, Likpe, Fodome, Liati, etc) and an individual second name. Thus, you get Tafi Atome, Tafi Abuipe, etc. But when asking for directions, asking for tro-tro destinations, etc, people often only refer to the cluster: one asks for the road to Tafi, the tro-tro to Wli etc. After we found out about that, we didn't have to remember long, complex Ewe names anymore. We also understood better where exactly we had to get out of the tro-tro.'

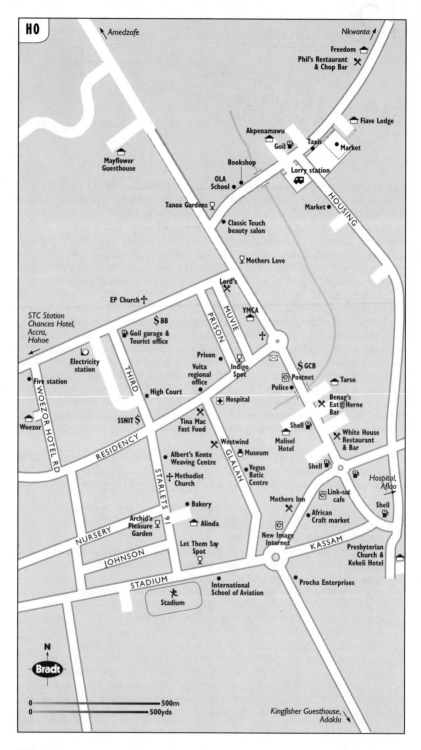

HO

↖ *Amedzofe*

Nkwanta ↗

Freedom 🏨
Phil's Restaurant ✕
& Chop Bar

🏨 Fiave Lodge

Akpenamawu
🏨 Goil 🏧

Taxis
🚕 Market

Bookshop

Lorry station
🚌

OLA
School ●

Market ●

Tanoa Gardens 🍷

● Classic Touch
beauty salon

HOUSING

🍷 Mothers Love

Lord's
✕

EP Church ✝

MUVIE

YMCA

✝

STC Station
Chances Hotel,
Accra,
Hohoe
←

🏧 BB

🏧 Goil garage &
Tourist office

PRISON

✉

🏧 GCB

Electricity
station

Prison ●

Volta
regional
office ●

Indigo
Spot

Police ●

📧 Postnet

🏨 Tarso

Benag's
✕ Eat@Herne
Bar

● Fire station

THIRD

High Court ●

➕ Hospital

Shell 🏧

🏨 White House
✕ Restaurant
& Bar

🏨
Woezor

WOEZOR HOTEL RD

SSNIT 🏧

Tina Mac ✕
Fast Food

GLALAH

Malisel
Hotel

Shell 🏧

🏧

RESIDENCY

✕ Westwind
● Albert's Kente
Weaving Centre

🏹 Museum

Vegus
Batic
Centre

Hospital,
Aflao →

STARLETS

✝ Methodist
Church

● Bakery

91

Archid's
Pleasure 🍷
Garden

🏨 Alinda

Let Them Say
Spot 🍷

NURSERY

JOHNSON

STADIUM

Mothers Inn
✕

📧 Link-sat
cafe

● African
Craft market

Shell 🏧

📧

New Image
Internet

KASSAM

Presbyterian
Church &
Kekeli Hotel

🏃
Stadium

● International
School of Aviation

● Procha Enterprises

N
↑
Bradt

0 ————————— 500m
0 ————————— 500yds

Kingfisher Guesthouse,
Adaklu ↘

between Ho and Hohoe that provides the most rewarding travel circuit in the region, centred around the superb community project at **Tafi Atome** (see page 263), renowned for its sacred mona monkeys and close to a fascinating *kente*-weaving village, and the scenic hilltop town of Amedzofe. Another very popular destination is the **Wli Falls** (see page 271) west of Hohoe – reputedly the tallest in west Africa – while worthwhile goals for relatively off-the-beaten-track exploration include a new community project at Adaklu Mountain, the little-known **Kalapka Resource Reserve** (see page 256), the *kente*-weaving village of **Kpetoe** (see page 259), and a half-dozen small waterfalls in the hills to the south of Hohoe.

HO

The former administrative centre of German Togoland and modern capital of Volta Region, Ho is the largest and busiest town in this part of the country, with excellent facilities for backpackers and good transport connections. Aside from a couple of old colonial buildings (notably the old church and school, and the Evangelical Presbyterian Mission at Wegbe, founded in the 1850s), about the only tourist attraction within the town is the Ho Museum next to the hospital, where an investment of US$1 will gain you entrance to an oddly eclectic and occasionally fascinating collection of photographs and artefacts, including displays on the mud-and-stick mosques of the northwest and Ashanti fetish shrines in the Kumasi area. Otherwise, Ho is of limited interest, though it remains a pleasant, inexpensive and well-organised place to take a day or two's break between exploring the many beauty spots that lie within a couple of hours' radius by tro-tro. It is especially worth spending time here over late September and early October, when the annual Yam Festival takes place, climaxing with a chief's *durbar* in the first week of October.

GETTING THERE AND AWAY Ho is an important transport hub, well connected to most parts of Ghana east of Accra and Lake Volta. Regular tro-tros leave from the central lorry station to destinations such as Kpando, Hohoe, Kpetoe, Akasombo and Accra, where they terminate at the Tudu station just behind Makola Market. Travelling between Ho and eastern ports, such as Keta or Aflao, you'll probably have to change vehicles at Akatsi. There is also one STC bus every day except Sundays, which departs from the STC station near Mother's Love bar at 16.30 and costs US$3 a seat.

WHERE TO STAY
Upmarket

Chances Hotel (100+ rooms/chalets) 091 28344; f 091 27083; e info@chanceshotel.com; www.chanceshotel.com. Set in attractive landscaped grounds at the base of the Kabakaba Hills, on the Accra road about 3km from the town centre, the 2-star Chances Hotel is the only genuinely tourist-class unit in this part of Ghana & it has deservedly won several regional & national awards in recent years. The hotel consists of more than 100 airy & smartly furnished self-contained dbl rooms & chalets, all with AC, DSTV & hot water. Facilities inc a large conference centre, an excellent restaurant serving international & Ghanaian dishes & a children's playground. An AC 10-seat vehicle is available for day & overnight trips at around US$100 per day, as is a 30-seater bus for around US$140 per day, inc driver but exc fuel (rates are quoted in dollars but payable in local currency). Other facilities inc an on-site internet café & swimming pool (open to hotel residents only), while the soundproofed generator & mechanised borehole ensure a 24-hour supply of water & electricity. *Dbl rooms with AC US$33–38, chalets US$43. All rates inc b/fast for one, with a second b/fast charged at US$3. Visa & MasterCard are accepted.*

Moderate

🛏 **Freedom Hotel** ☎ 091 28151/8; e freedomh@ africaonline.com.gh; www.freedomhotel-gh.com. Prices at this excellent 2-star hotel have shot up since the last edition of this guide, jerking it out of reach of most budget travellers, but it remains popular for its friendly atmosphere & convenient location down the road from the lorry station. The garden, dotted with traditional statues, is a relaxing place for a meal or a drink (a good selection of Western dishes is available in the US$3–4 range, inc a delicious take on the traditional club sandwich) & there is also a pool open for use by non-residents for US$2.50. The open-walled bar on the upper floor of the hotel is a good spot to catch the breeze, or, when a Ghanaian football match is showing, to squeeze in with 200 roaring Ghanaians & watch it on the large-screen TV. Ordinary self-contained dbl rooms with DSTV with fan or AC, or suites. *Dbl US$24–27, suite US$37–42.*

🛏 **Woezor Hotel** ☎ 091 28339/26661. Formerly the Government Catering Resthouse, the Woezor Hotel, situated in large overgrown grounds on the outskirts of town, is acceptably comfortable, though the rooms are a little frayed at the seams. Self-contained dbls in the main, utilitarian block, or stone chalets (which, according to the enthusiastic pamphlet, 'fascinate even the best of architects') with AC. A pleasant indoor restaurant serves Ghanaian & continental fare in the US$3.50–4.50 range. *Dbl with fan/AC US$15–25, chalet US$30–40.*

Budget

🛏 **Kekeli Hotel** ☎ 091 26670/26495; e epkeli@ yahoo.com. The formerly Evangelical Presbyterian Social Centre, privatised in 2002, is situated in the pleasant, leafy grounds of Ho's historic Presbyterian church, where it is surrounded by some fine examples of German colonial architecture. The clean & spacious dbl rooms with fans in the old block are good value, self-contained or with common shower, while suites in the new block have AC, TV, hot water & fridge. A bed in the 20-bed dormitory costs US$4 per person. Car rental can be arranged at US$25 per day within a 70km radius of Ho or US$35 further afield, inclusive of driver but exclusive of fuel. *Dbl from US$9, suite up to US$35, dorm US$4 pp.*

🛏 **Malisel Hotel** ☎ 091 26161 or 020 8969622; e jorts2001@yahoo.com. Opened in late 2006 by a well-travelled Ghanaian, this new arrival set back off the main road already ranks as one of the best in its range. Super clean, self-contained dbls with hot water & DSTV, & guests are welcome to help themselves from the mango tree outside. No food is available yet but the hotel has an informal link with the tiny Benag's restaurant across the road, which will send over local dishes priced around US$1 or salads, sandwiches or chicken & rice for US$3. *Dbl US$12–14.*

🛏 **Mayflower Guesthouse** ☎ 091 27265. This very pleasant & reasonably central guesthouse seems very cosy & clean – it's good value. *Sgl with common shower US$6, self-contained dbl with fan/AC US$10/15.*

Shoestring

🛏 **Alinda Hotel** Reached down an unmade track on the outskirts of town, this once popular hotel has seen better days. But what it lacks in fresh paint & location is compensated for by the friendly staff & excellent value for money: plus the bakery opposite might make a good target for b/fast. *Sgl/dbl with fan US$3/4, self-contained dbl/twin with fan US$5/7.*

🛏 **Fiave Lodge** Situated near the main road between the lorry station & the Freedom Hotel, this unpretentious place has a family-run feel. All the rooms have fans, & some have weird blue lights. Food is available on request. Large, clean rooms, prices depending on whether they're self-contained &/or have 1 or 2 dbl beds. *US$5–9.*

🛏 **Tarso Hotel** ☎ 091 26412 or 26732. Established in 1956, the amiable Tarso proclaims itself to be the oldest hotel in Ho, & frankly it looks it, but it still offers good value. The establishment is centrally located, but poor signposting makes it hard to find & the smelly river next door can attract mosquitoes. *Clean, spacious dbl with fan US$7, self-contained US$9–11.*

🛏 **YMCA** (8 rooms) ☎ 091 26374. This centrally located lodge is excellent value, & the 8 rooms are available not only to men but also to couples & single women. Rooms are adequately clean. Guests are also welcome to use the kitchen to prepare their own food. *Sgl US$3, dbl with common shower US$3.50.*

✗ **WHERE TO EAT** A popular place to eat in the town centre is the **White House Bar**, which serves a good selection of chilled drinks – including draught beer – along with a limited but tasty selection of stews, pizzas and other snacks for around

US$2.50–3 per portion, with the added draw of a pool table in the main bar. Also recommended is **Mother's Inn Restaurant**, where a plate of chicken with chips or fried rice costs around US$2.50, and there are similar prices in the new **West Wind Restaurant** opposite the museum. At all of these places you have the option of eating indoors or outdoors, which gives them the edge over the otherwise similar **Lord's Restaurant**, where you are forced to eat indoors (very hot and sweaty). Less central, and more bar than restaurant, **Archid's Pleasure Garden** has an attractively rustic character and gets busy with locals at weekends.

The restaurant at the **Freedom Hotel** is probably the most upmarket eatery in town, serving a good selection of filling snacks at around U$3 and tasty main courses from US$4.50, indoors or in the large gardens. Almost next door to this lies **Phil's Restaurant & Chop Bar**, a lively outdoor bar that also serves filling and inexpensive local meals to background reggae. On the other side of town, the **Woezor Hotel** offers similar dishes at similar prices, but the atmosphere is a little dingy, except perhaps on the rare occasion when there's live music. The food at **Chances Hotel** is excellent and not too expensive at around US$5.50-plus for a main course, but the location isn't very convenient: shared taxis along the route should cost no more than US$0.30 but will be few and far between at night.

For speedy chop, the Queen's Land Fast Food stall at the entrance to the tro-tro station serves excellent salads to go, or you may want to brave the 'Observers Are Worried' chop bar diagonally opposite for its humour value alone!

OTHER PRACTICALITIES

Car hire Ordinary cars can be hired through the Kekeli Hotel, while 10- and 30-seater vehicles are available from Chances Hotel – see *Where to stay* for further details.

Crafts The Ewe, like the Ashanti, are skilled *kente* weavers, and good quality work can be bought at the Albkwas Kente Shop next to the Methodist church on Starlets 91 Road and Africa Craft Market opposite Mothers Inn Restaurant. Better still, head to Kpetoe, 30 minutes away by tro-tro (see page 259) – this is where most of the cloth sold in Ho is weaved, and prices are generally lower. Also worth a look is the Vegus Batik Shop next to the museum.

Cultural performances A renowned Ewe cultural troupe, Ziavi Zigi, is based in the village of Ziavi Dzodze, some 3km northwest of Ho on the other side of the Kabakaba Hills. Performances can be arranged for a negotiable fee through the regional tourist office (see below). Cultural performances are also put on occasionally at the open-air theatre in the grounds of the Woezor Hotel.

Foreign exchange The Barclays Bank offers better rates for cash than the other banks and forex bureaux, and it also accepts travellers' cheques and has an ATM where you can usually draw cash against a Visa card.

Ghana Tourist Board Situated in the SIC Building near the Goil garage, the Volta Region Tourist Office is perhaps the most enthusiastic in the country, and well worth visiting for the latest information on developing tourist attractions throughout the area, especially those with Peace Corps involvement (✆ *091 26560*).

Internet There are a number of internet cafés around town, with the most commonly recommended being the LinkSat near Mother's Inn restaurant, where several computers are available at less than US$1 an hour. The internet cafés at Freedom and Chances Hotels are for hotel residents only.

Swimming pool The only swimming pool open to the public in Ho is at Freedom Hotel, which charges US$2.50 to non-residents and has a good poolside bar.

AROUND HO

XOFA ECO-VILLAGE AND AVAME DZEMENI Situated on the eastern shore of Lake Volta at its approximate widest point, opposite Dodi Island, this 250-acre project was established in the late 1990s by an American-Ghanaian couple as a unique non-profit agroforestry effort, dedicated to replanting the denuded lakeshore with fast-growing fruit trees. In 2001 it also opened to travellers as a supremely chilled-out 'eco-village', where you can relax on the lakeshore with the friendly staff, swim in the (reputedly bilharzia-free) freshwater, explore the nearby islands by canoe, or hike from behind the lodge into dense forested slopes that still harbour a variety of monkeys as well as many forest birds. Sadly, feedback since then has been polarised: many travellers report having had a wonderful time, but others allege that the not-for-profit part of the credo has been forgotten. Shortly before we went to print, we received a report that Xofa is 'virtually defunct' and recommending you attempt to go there only if you have recently spoken to management on the phone. For those that decide to stay, accommodation consists of a cluster of neat, clean and cool stone-and-thatch huts set in a shady fruiting grove about 20m from the lakeshore, and costing US$12 per person per night. Meals are available, although even with a few hours' notice some patience is required, and drinks may also need to be pre-ordered. For more details, log on to www.xofa.org, use ☏ 027 7516222 or e ABSlives@aol.com.

The junction for Xofa is at Asikuma, a large village situated about 40km southwest of Ho along the Accra road, some 25km north of the Adome Bridge and Atimpoku. Coming from Ho, you need to turn right at Asikuma, following the Hohoe road for less than 500m to another junction, signposted for Xofa, where you need to turn left. Follow this road for 16km until you reach the outskirts of the small town of Boso, take a left downhill for a few kilometres, and turn off at the signposted track to the right which runs for 1.5km straight to the eco-village. Using public transport, any transport running between Accra or Kpong and Ho or Hohoe can drop you at Asikuma, and there are also direct tro-tros between Accra and Asikuma, leaving from central Accra's Aflao Station. Public transport between Asikuma and Boso is rather infrequent, except on Thursdays and Fridays (market days in Dzemeni – see below) and there's nothing at all from Boso to Xofa, so the most efficient option is to get a dropping taxi direct from Asikuma to Xofa, which should cost around US$9.

Also worth checking out locally is the village of Avame Dzemeni – the latter word pronounced almost identically to Germany – which lies on the lakeshore about 5km past Boso along a fair dirt road. The lakeshore around Dzemeni is attractive on any day, but the main point of interest is the Thursday and Friday market, one of the largest and most colourful in Volta Region. Plenty of public transport runs between Asikuma and Dzemeni via Boso on market days.

KALAPKA RESOURCE RESERVE Situated no more than 10km south of Ho as the crow flies, this 325km² reserve, gazetted in 1975, has yet to see much in the way of tourist development. It protects an area of gently sloping land, dominated by dry savanna, but with a few patches of forest. Large mammal populations are rather low, though kob antelope, baboon, and green monkey are quite common and likely to be seen by most visitors, at least during the dry season (March to June) when game concentrates around the palm-fringed Kalapka River close to the park headquarters. Less conspicuous species include buffalo, bushbuck, waterbuck,

Maxwell's duiker, patas monkey, and a variety of nocturnal creatures such as bushpig and genet. The area has a reputation for good birding. Although few tourists visit Kalapka at present, and no roads run through the reserve, it is perfectly accessible and day walks can be arranged with the rangers – indeed the small western sector open to tourists has several easy footpaths, wonderful views, and much wildlife. It is worth noting, too, that the owner of Chances Hotel, outside Ho, plans to start running weekend cycling trips into the reserve at some point.

The dirt road to Abutia Kloe passes through some lush semi-forested scenery that is teeming with birds. On the way, it may be worth asking about the traditionally constructed former German governor's residence that lies on a mango-covered hillside near the village of Abutia Agove, also the site of a famous spring which used to draw people from far and wide during periods of drought. Look out, too, for the *kente* weavers who work in some of the villages around Abutia.

Getting there and away The only point of entry is through the village of Abutia Kloe, 18km from Ho by road, and connected to it by regular tro-tros, which take less than half an hour. If you are driving from Ho, head out along the Accra road for 9km to Sokode junction, where a left turn will bring you to Abutia Kloe after another 9km. However you get to Abutia Kloe, you must first visit the Department of Wildlife office on the edge of the village, where you will be asked to pay the nominal entrance fee. A 2.5km side-road branching left from Abutia Kloe leads to the rangers' camp on the edge of the reserve. Here you can arrange game walks into the reserve with one of the rangers, who will expect a tip.

Where to stay There is no formal accommodation at Kalapka or Abutia Kloe, but it is possible to visit Kalapka as a day trip from Ho by tro-tro. In order to get an early start (game being most active in the early morning), it would, however, be preferable to spend the night there. Normally you can pitch your own tent or arrange a room at the friendly rangers' camp for a small fee.

ADAKLU MOUNTAIN Adaklu is the name of the dramatic inselberg that dominates Ho's southern skyline, as well as the collective name for the 40-odd villages that lie around the mountain's base. Oral tradition has it that the Ewe of Adaklu migrated to the area centuries ago, in order to escape the oppressive rule of King Agokoli in what is now Beyin. When they settled around the mountain, they slaughtered and roasted a cow, and divided out the meat – an act of sharing to which the word Adaklu refers.

The Adaklu area has recently been developed as a community ecotourist project, based at Helekpe village, under NCRC and Peace Corps supervision. There are guided hikes to the mountain summit, a reasonably demanding 2–4 hour round trip from Helekpe, along which you should be able to see some monkeys and a variety of butterflies and birds (as well as giant snails, which are held sacred locally and may not be touched!). In addition, several cultural activities are available at Helekpe, ranging from drumming and dancing performances to visits to the sacred bats of Avanyaviwofe, as well as to local *kente* weavers. Costs range from US$0.50 per person for a village tour (plus a tip to the guide) to US$1.50 for a mountain hike or bike tour, or US$5 for a drumming and dancing performance.

Getting there and away Helekpe lies about 15km from Ho along a fair dirt road, regularly plied by tro-tros. In a private vehicle, head out along the Adaklu road past the Kingfisher Guesthouse and Polytechnic, turning right after 12km at Tsrefre, a small village close to the base of the mountain. There is an unmanned visitor centre at Helekpe, but if you arrive with luggage it would make more sense to ask to be dropped at the guesthouse first.

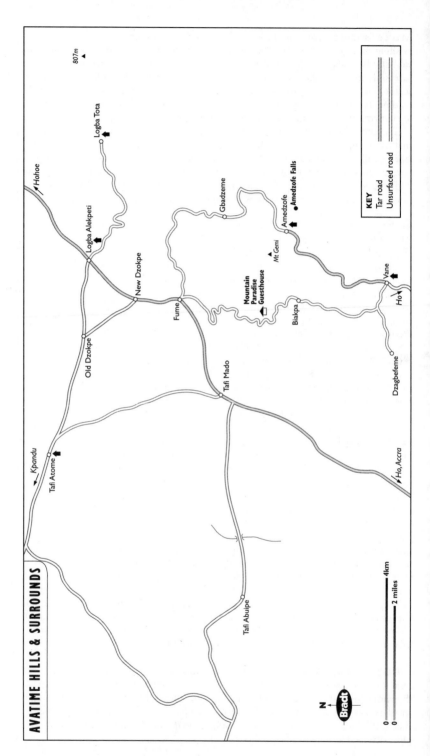

AVATIME HILLS & SURROUNDS

807m ▲

Logba Tota

Hohoe

Logba Alekpeti

Gbadzeme

New Dzokpe

Amedzofe Falls

Old Dzokpe

Fume

Mt Gemi ▲

Amedzofe

Mountain Paradise Guesthouse

Biakpa

Vane

Ho

Kpandu

Tafi Atome

Tafi Mado

Dzagbefeme

Ho, Accra

Tafi Abuipe

N

Bradt

0   4km
0   2 miles

KEY
Tar road
Unsurfaced road

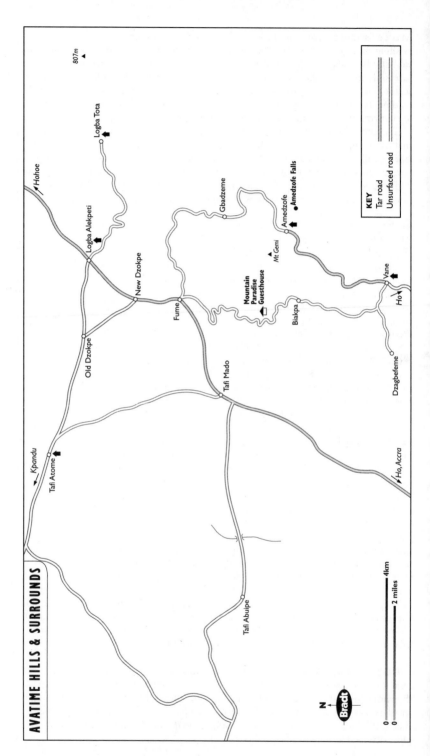

Where to stay and eat Dirt-cheap accommodation is available in Helekpe, in a small and very basic **guesthouse** charging US$1 for a double room with bedding, mosquito nets, communal toilets and bucket showers. **Private homestays** can also be arranged and camping in the village or on the mountain is free of charge. Meals can be provided to visitors with some notice, and a couple of bars sell minerals and beers.

KPETOE AGOTIME

This small town, close to the Togolese border about 30km east of Ho, is renowned throughout Ghana for the quality of its *kente* weavers. Although *kente* weaving is these days largely associated with the Ashanti, the people of Kpetoe claim that the style originated with them and was later adopted further afield after their best weavers were captured during the Ashanti wars. Two types of cloth are made in Kpetoe: the light and popular Ashanti *kente* and the more durable Ewe *agbamevo* (see the *Kente* box on page 330).

The main *kente* factory in Kpetoe, a semi-open concrete construction housing a few dozen weavers, is situated at the barrier outside the village centre, in the direction of Ho. A fee may or may not be asked to look around the factory, but there are also plenty of places where weavers work out in the open, and tourists are still so infrequent that you should have no problems just wandering around the village, taking it all in. If you are thinking of buying, prices are far lower in Kpetoe than in the better-known *kente* villages of Ashanti, and the atmosphere is more laid-back. Desiadenyo Stores and the home of Madame Felicia Kangni are among the better places to choose from a huge range of cloths and designs.

Kpetoe lies along the main tarred road between Ho and Aflao; there is plenty of transport in both directions and it can easily be visited en route between Ho and the coast, or as a day trip from Ho. If you prefer to spend the night, however, decent self-contained rooms are available at the **Buggie Hotel** (✆ *091 28891*) about 1km from town towards Ho from US$5 to US$10, and at the more central and marginally nicer **Friends Lodge Hotel** (✆ *091 27787*) for US$5/9 sgl/dbl.

THE AVATIME HILLS AND SURROUNDS

Rising from the Lake Volta hinterland towards the Togolese border, roughly halfway between the towns of Ho and Hohoe, the beautiful and lushly vegetated Avatime Hills are one of the most popular destinations in Ghana for enthusiastic hikers and budget travellers. With a relatively temperate climate, substantial stands of rainforest, many bird and butterfly species, and inexpensive resthouses, the hills offer excellent opportunities for unstructured hiking and rambling, whether your preference is for day walks or something more ambitious.

The principal town of the Avatime Hills – and main tourist focus – is Amedzofe, which boasts a well-organised tourist office and a good selection of affordable accommodation options. Close to the base of the hills, the village of Tafi Atome – home to several hundred sacred mona monkeys – rivals Amedzofe as the most popular regional travel destination. Less frequently visited attractions include the remote and stunningly situated village of Biakpa, where a former government resthouse has recently been privatised to offer the smartest accommodation in the area, the waterfalls and caves close to Logba Toto, and the fascinating *kente*-weaving village of Tafi Abuipe. While most travellers explore the area on day trips, there are some opportunities for extended hikes – you could, for instance, easily spend a couple of days working your way on foot from Amedzofe to Tafi Atome (see page 260) via Biakpa.

AMEDZOFE A former German mission, Amedzofe is the largest town in the Avatime Hills, and the site of a well-known teacher-training college and attractive century-old church. The town lies at an altitude of more than 600m, and is reached by road via a spectacular 2.5km ascent from Vame. Facing Amedzofe, Mount Gemi is one of the highest mountains in the country, and easily picked out by the 4m tall cross that was erected on its grassy peak in the 1930s by German missionaries – there is a bizarre local legend that the cross doubled as a communication device in World War II!

Tourism in Amedzofe was recently formalised under the auspices of the **Amedzofe Planning and Tourism Council**, which operates a helpful 'welcome' office (0931 22037) in the market square, to which all visitors are expected to report upon arrival to arrange accommodation (unless they're staying at the government resthouse) and pay entrance fees. A good target for a short walk is **Amedzofe Falls** (*US$4 for non-Ghanaians*), 45 minutes from town following a dirt road and then a treacherously muddy footpath through lush forest to come out at the three knee-deep pools separating the upper and lower falls. More ambitiously, ask about visiting the valley at the base of the lower fall, said to harbour a population of black-and-white colobus monkeys. Another worthwhile local goal is the peak of **Mount Gemi** (*US$2 for non-Ghanaians*), which lies about 30 minutes' walk from town and offers tremendous views as far as Lake Volta. The tourist office also arranges guided walks further afield; for instance to Biakpa, Fume (on the main Ho–Hohoe road) and Tafi Atome.

Getting there and away Amedzofe lies about 35km from Ho, and the most normal and direct route is the rough dirt road that runs through Akome and Vame, which you can cover in about one hour in a private vehicle. The most dramatic stretch of this road is the 2.5km ascent from Vame to Amedzofe, but it's also the most dodgy in terms of daft driving – honk on your horn before taking sharp corners. A couple of vehicles plod back and forth between Ho and Amedzofe at least once a day, taking 60–90 minutes in either direction and costing around US$1.50 for a seat, but timings are unpredictable and the only reasonable certainty is that one or all of the vehicles will leave Amedzofe between 05.30 and 06.30 and (assuming there are enough passengers) will be ready to start the return trip from Ho perhaps two hours later. After that, it's not unusual to wait three or four hours for transport in either direction, and there's generally little or no transport out of Amedzofe from around 15.00, after which your options amount to staying the night or hiking the 3km to Fume on the main Ho–Hohoe road. There may be no transport at all on Sundays, unless it falls on Ho's market day (every four days).

Heading northwards from Amedzofe towards Hohoe may look straightforward enough on a map, but the reality is complicated by the absence of public transport between Amedzofe and the junction town of Fume on the main Ho–Hohoe road. The simplest way around this is to walk, with the option of using the road directly connecting Amedzofe to Fume, or else taking a Ho-bound vehicle as far as Vame and using the road that connects Vame and Fume. In terms of distance, the direct route between Amedzofe and Fume is shorter at only 3–4km, but it is steep and slippery in parts and may be tough going with a heavy backpack on. The Vame–Fume road is about double the actual distance, but it's a lot flatter and allows for an overnight stop at Biakpa. When we first visited Amedzofe a few years ago, we found our way to Fume without any problem, but the tourist office in Amedzofe now recommends you take a guide on the pretext you might otherwise get lost. If you feel like taking a guide, all well and good; if not, don't let anybody coerce you – you'll be unlikely to take a wrong turn (there is none!) and will come across plenty of passers-by to confirm you're on the right track.

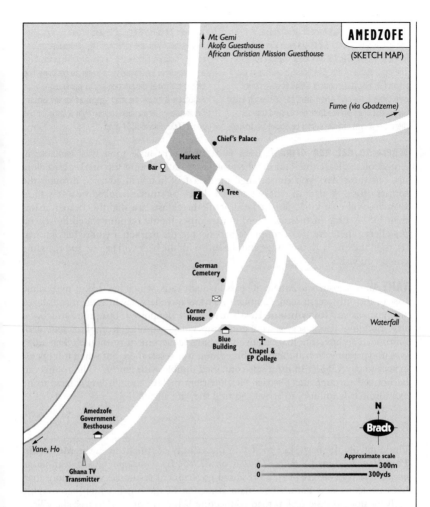

Mt Gemi
Akofa Guesthouse
African Christian Mission Guesthouse

Fume (via Gbadzeme)

Chief's Palace

Market

Bar ♀

ℹ

Tree

German
Cemetery

✉

Corner
House

Waterfall

Blue
Building

✝ Chapel &
EP College

N

Bradt

Amedzofe
Government
Resthouse

Vane, Ho

Ghana TV
Transmitter

Approximate scale
0 ———— 300m
0 ———— 300yds

If you're heading to Hohoe and don't fancy walking, your options are either to catch a tro-tro back to Ho and change vehicles there, or to catch a Ho-bound vehicle as far as Akume, where you should be able to pick up some transport to Vame, 8km away on the main Ho–Hohoe road.

Where to stay In addition to the following, three different families in Amedzofe offer **private homestays** to travellers at a fixed rate of US$6 per room.

🏠 **Akofa Guesthouse** ☎ 020 3011016 or 024 688835. This attractive new guesthouse, operated by the tourist office, has the feel of a family house & also offers stunning views across the valley, & down to the village of Biakpe. The large but cosy rooms are all self-contained & fan-cooled, & priced depending on whether they have a standard or queen size bed. Guests can order meals though the tourist office, or use the kitchen to cook their own & eat at the shared dining table. *US$10 & US$13*

🏠 **African Christian Mission Guesthouse** Also run by the tourist office, this utilitarian-looking lodge lies 10 mins walk from town, next to the football field at the base of Mount Gemi. The rooms are clean & self-contained, but not as comfortable as Akofa's, which is reflected in the price. *Dbl US$8.*

🏠 **Amedzofe Government Resthouse** This pleasant but timeworn resthouse consists of 3 pairs of large self-contained dbl rooms with electricity (there's an outside

261

tap with running water), each of which shares a communal sitting-room & balcony with views over the forest to Mount Gemi & on a clear day to Lake Volta. The exact status of this guesthouse is unclear at the time of writing. It is primarily aimed at government employees & regional government has specifically asked the tourist office in Amedzofe not to send tourists there, but rooms can sometimes be booked in advance at Room 24 in Ho Regional Headquarters, or by arrangement with the caretaker. The guesthouse isn't actually in town, but on top of the same hill as the large & conspicuous TV transmission tower; to get there, hop off the tro-tro at the junction just as you enter Amedzofe & follow the road signposted for the Ghana Broadcasting Corporation to your right & uphill for about 500m. *Rooms US$4–5 pp.*

✗ **Where to eat and drink** It used to be that very little food was available in Amedzofe, at least after sunset when the chop stalls around the market area close up, but these days you can arrange meals a few hours in advance through the tourist office. A plate of chicken and fried rice or similar, cooked by a few local women, will cost US$2.50 per head, while breakfasts are slightly cheaper at less than US$2. One of these women, Betty, comes highly recommended by several travellers. There are also a couple of bars next to the market; if you're luckier than us, then the one with the fridge and the one with the beer will be one and the same when you visit.

VANE All road routes to Amedzofe pass through Vane, which lies 2.5km away at the base of the only ascent road. Although very few travellers stay in Vane, it does boast an inexpensive **Government Resthouse** – not signposted, but pretty much the first building you'll see as you enter the village coming from Ho, and with outmoded architecture that positively screams 'government resthouse'. The lodge was under renovation at the time this edition was researched, but when it reopens, expect to pay US$10/15 for a self-contained double with fan/AC. The rooms can be booked through the District Headquarters in Ho, though you'd have to be extraordinarily unlucky to arrive and find they are all full.

BIAKPA

Undoubtedly the best place to stay in the vicinity of Amedzofe is the **Mountain Paradise Lodge** (☎ *020 8137086 or 8198505;* e *fiakpui@yahoo.com; www. mountainparadise-biakpa.com*), a privatised government resthouse which more than lives up to its new name. The main attraction of the hotel, which lies roughly halfway along on the 6.5km road connecting Vame to Fume, 1km past the village of Biakpa, is the blissfully isolated and scenic location on a grassy knoll overlooking the Kulugu River, facing Mount Gemi, and encircled by lush tropical forest that still harbours small numbers of mona monkey as well as a wide range of forest birds. Accommodation ranges from US$8/12 for single/double occupancy of a double with shared bath, to US$12/17 for a self-contained room. Camping at the guesthouse or at a site on a nearby hill is relatively steep (!) at US$5 per person using the hotel's tent, or US$2 if you have your own gear. There is no electricity at the hotel yet, but fans are in place throughout the building and solar panels are on the agenda for the future. In the meantime, soft drinks and beers are chilled with ice blocks, or you can go for the home-roasted organic coffee. A variety of excellent meals is also available at around US$5, and can be enjoyed on the large porch at the front of the hotel. A three-hour trail following the forest-fringed Kulugu River past five small waterfalls has already been laid out (guided walks cost US$3 per person), and future plans include mountain bike hire (US$3 an hour), abseiling and the construction of a canopy-walk-style bridge to a big tree on a cliff above the river. No public transport runs past the lodge, but the hotel is happy to arrange transfers, or it can be approached on foot from Vane near Amedzofe or from Fume on the Ho–Hohoe road – whichever way you come, the walk will take about 45 minutes or cost about US$6 in a taxi.

FUME This small junction town lies on the main road between Ho and Hohoe at the intersection with the dirt road to Amedzofe via Biakpa and Vame. It's not much of a place, but if you've arrived on foot you'll almost certainly want to down a cold drink at **Hanson's Spot**, under the enormous tree to the left of the road as you come from Hohoe. Should you feel like spending the night, then ask at the spot (✆ *024 4166032*) about the associated, unsignposted guesthouse, which charges US$5 for one of three basic but clean double rooms without fan but with a large balcony facing the nearby hills.

LOGBA ALEKPETI This small, bustling town on the main Ho–Hohoe road is of little inherent interest to tourists, but it has quite a strategic location, on the junction for Tafi Atome (5km to the west) and Logba Toto (7km to the east), and only 3km north of Fume (the turn-off for Amedzofe and Biakpa). Logba Alekpeti also boasts a very decent place to stay in the form of the recently opened **Adzotor Hotel** near the junction, where clean rooms with a fan cost US$6–8 single/double. A bar is attached.

LOGBA TOTA Set on a steep forested slope facing Mount Gemi, the small and attractive town of Logba Tota is yet another site in eastern Ghana undergoing development as a community tourist project. The main local attraction, about 2km from town, is the Apkonu Waterfall, which plunges into a pool where you can swim safely. The cliff above the waterfall is riddled with small caves that house an impressive bat colony and one solitary stalagmite. A guided trip to the waterfall and caves can be arranged for US$1.50, payable at the information centre at the start of town.

Coming in a private vehicle, the 7km turn-off to Logba Tota is signposted eastwards from Logba Alekpeti on the main Ho–Hohoe road. The dirt road initially follows a valley, and is reasonably flat. After about 3km, you'll come to a junction where you need to turn right – from here onwards the road is mostly surfaced, and very steep and winding. Occasional shared taxis run between Logba Alekpeti and Logba Toto, but you could be in for a long wait – it might be worth paying for the extra seats to effectively charter the vehicle. Moderately priced accommodation is available in the community-run guesthouse.

TAFI ATOME MONKEY SANCTUARY Centred around the eponymous village, Tafi Atome Monkey Sanctuary was created in 1993 to protect the sacred monkeys that live in the surrounding forest. The story is that the ancestors of the modern villagers migrated to the area from Brong Ahafo 200 years ago, and brought with them fetishes for monkeys and tortoises in a large pot that still exists today. For many years this taboo protected the monkeys, who were thought to act as spokesmen for the slower tortoises, but numbers had dwindled badly by the late 1980s, largely as a result of the erosion of traditional beliefs by Christianity. Since the creation of the sanctuary, the local monkey population has increased to about 350 monkeys, split across four troops. The habituated troop numbers about 70.

Under Peace Corps guidance, Tafi Atome has developed into the model of a multi-faceted community-based ecotourism project. Naturally enough, the monkeys form the centrepiece of tourist activities; entrance and a guided tour of the sanctuary costs US$6.50 per person, with discounts for students, Ghanaians and volunteers. The monkeys are not nearly as well habituated as their counterparts at Boabeng-Fiema, but they are generally most active before 08.00 and after 16.00, when they often descend to the ground and can be approached quite closely – sometimes feeding out of tourists' hands. Based on recent travellers' reports, you can reasonably expect to have good sightings if you stay here overnight, but are likely to be disappointed on a day trip.

Tafi Atome's importance in conservation terms is that it harbours the only Ghanaian population of the nominate race of mona monkey *Cercopithecus m. mona*, distinguished from the Lowe's mona (*C. m. lowei*) of Boabeng-Fiema by its two white hip discs. Given the confusion that surrounds the classification of the *Cercopithecus* monkeys, it is possible that, as some authorities maintain, these two types of monkey should be treated as discrete species. At Tafi, you'll be told that their monkeys are the only 'true monas' in Ghana, which could come across as hype, but is perfectly accurate – though all it means is that *C. m. mona* was formally described before *C. m. lowei*, so that the latter is regarded as a race of the former.

Several other activities are available to visitors spending a night or two at Tafi Atome. These include a guided walk through the village, drumming lessons, forest walks, and an evening session of storytelling, and drumming and dancing – the latter particularly enjoyable judging by the visitors' book. The guides can also organise inexpensive bicycle hire (US$2 per half day) to explore further afield. Worthwhile objectives, all of which are covered in greater detail elsewhere in this chapter, include the *kente*-weaving village of Tafi Abuipe, as well as Logba Tota and Amedzofe. Another worthwhile project is to plant a tree, in return for a donation which will be directed towards the building of a clinic. The idea is that after the facility is built, the trees will eventually mature and bring in revenue a second time round to help sustain the project.

More generally, we were struck by the lack of hassle that characterises the village. Tafi Atome is a great place to spend a couple of inexpensive and interesting days – and all funds raised from tourism go towards developing the monkey sanctuary or to the development of community. If you are in Ghana at the right time, it's worth knowing that a fetish festival for the monkeys is held in Tafi Atome during the first or second week of February.

Getting there and away Tafi Atome lies about 5km along a good dirt road that leaves the main Ho–Hohoe road at Logba Alekpeti. There is plenty of transport to the village on Logba Alekpeti's market day, which is on a five-day cycle. On other days, there is the occasional shared taxi from Logba Alekpeti, and at US$0.50 a person the fare is so low that you could easily rent the whole vehicle. Alternatively, you can walk out from Logba Alekpeti, an easy hour's trip along a flat road through lush scenery. Heading back, there are the same, sporadic share taxis, and one van leaves from the village to Hohoe on most mornings – though probably before you will have finished the dawn sanctuary tour.

Where to stay and eat A small cluster of guesthouses has been constructed for travellers, some of which are thatched and unexpectedly cool, and others with zinc roofing that smell a bit of damp. All the rooms are clean but sparse – furnished with just beds and nets (something you don't see too often in Ghana)- and share a clean communal ablution block with sit-down toilets and bucket showers. Accommodation costs US$11.50 per person inclusive of breakfast, dinner (both taken at the cook's home at the other end of town) and a guided monkey tour. Lunch can be arranged for around US$2 per plate, and a couple of shops in the village sell warm minerals, beers and pure water.

TAFI ABUIPE This small village to the southwest of Tafi Atome is one of the major *kente*-weaving centres in Ghana. It is also arguably the nicest to visit, as most of the weavers work outdoors, which gives it a far more organic and aesthetically pleasing atmosphere than Bonwire and the other *kente* villages in Ashanti. With the guidance of the people at Tafi Atome, Abuipe is well organised to receive tourists, and once you pay the small entrance fee (US$2 for non-Ghanaians) you are free to walk around and photograph as you like. Outside almost every house in the village you'll see a few weavers at work – they are amazingly quick and dextrous – and when we visited the hassle factor and pressure to buy was zero. Having said that, if you are thinking of buying *kente* cloth, starting prices here are almost half of what you'll be asked in Ashanti or Accra although you will have to allow extra time and possibly money to have the woven strips sewn together into full cloths.

From the main Ho–Hohoe road, the most direct route to Tafi Abuipe is via a 5km dirt road which branches westwards immediately to the south of Tafi Mado. At the time of writing, this road is good for pedestrians only, since a bridge had collapsed, but I'm told the bridge will eventually be repaired. Once this happens, it could be that shared taxis run directly between Tafi Mado and Tafi Abuipe. Tafi Abuipe can also be visited from Tafi Atome on foot or using a rented bicycle following a 7km footpath. By road, the distance between the villages is about 14km – follow the Kpando road for 3–4km, turn left at the first junction, then left again at a small village about 7–8km further on, then continue straight ahead through the last junction, which you'll cross after another 1km or so.

There is no accommodation in Tafi Abuipe at present, though tentative plans exist to build a small resthouse or organise village homestays. The people at Tafi Atome are involved in promoting tourism to Tafi Abuipe, and should have current information.

KPANDO

This small town near Lake Volta is of interest to travellers primarily as the one place on the eastern shore where you can board or disembark from the Lake Volta ferry, at least during the rainy season when the water level is sufficiently high. It is also the leaping-off point for an off-the-beaten-track ferry and road route to Nkawkaw on the Accra–Kumasi road via Donkorkrom, Adawso and Mpraeso (see box *Crossing Lake Volta via the Afram Plains*, page 286). The town centre, set about 4km back from the lake, is notable for several turn-of-the-century German buildings, part of a mission founded there in 1904. The lake port of Kpando Torkor, connected to the town centre by a steady stream of shared taxis, hosts a bustling market selling not only fish but all manner of cloths, garments and other foodstuffs, while Kpando Potters, which lies 4km out of town at Fesi, is a worthwhile excursion for handicraft enthusiasts. And while tourists are an infrequent sight in Kpando District, the same cannot be said of the Virgin Mary, who evidently makes regular appearances and has two grottoes dedicated to her within 10km of the town centre.

Note that the 'K' in Kpando (and in all other place names in this part of the country that begin with 'Kp') is silent – locals pronounce 'Kp' as a slightly more explosive 'P'. It is also sometimes spelt 'Kpandu'.

GETTING THERE AND AWAY Kpando is connected to Ho and Hohoe by regular tro-tros (US$1), while an STC bus to Kpando leaves from Accra's Tudu Station at 15.00 daily except for Sundays.

The daily ferry to Donkorkrom on the Afram Plains on the western lakeshore departs at around 10.00 daily from the jetty at Kpando Torkor – for more details see box *Crossing Lake Volta via the Afram Plains* on pages 286–7. For details of the Lake Volta ferry, which stops at Kpando, see *Getting there and away* under Akosombo on page 242.

KPANDO

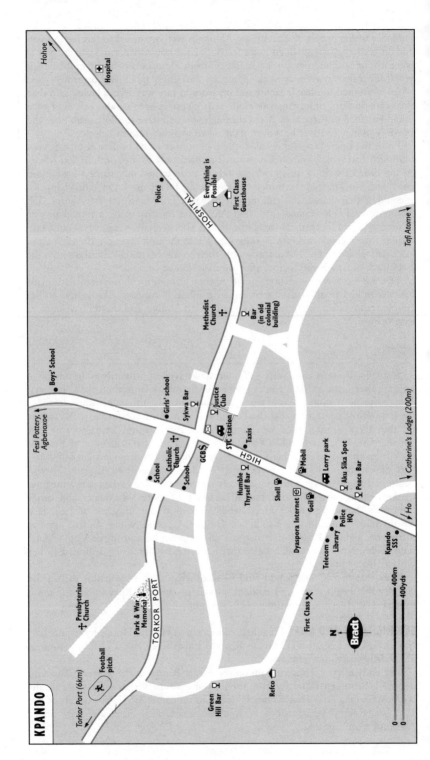

Torkor Port (6km)

Hohoe

Hospital

Police

Everything is Possible

First Class Guesthouse

Boys' School

Methodist Church

Bar (in old colonial building)

Tafi Atome

Fesi Pottery, Agbenoxoe

Girls school

Sykwa Bar

Justice Club

Catholic Church

School

School

GCB $

STC station

Taxis

Humble Thyself Bar

HIGH

Mobil

Shell

Goil

Dyaspora Internet

Lorry park

Aku Sika Spot

Peace Bar

Ho

Catherine's Lodge (200m)

Telecom

Library

Police HQ

Kpando SSS

Presbyterian Church

Park & War Memorial

TORKOR PORT

Football pitch

First Class

N

Bradt

Green Hill Bar

Refco

400m

400yds

WHERE TO STAY

Catherine's Lodge ☏ 0936 50050. Probably the most likeable of Kpando's limited selection of hostelries, this quiet, clean & friendly family-run lodge lies about 700m from the town centre, down an unmade road that branches left off the main route to Accra. There's a beautiful garden where you can enjoy a drink, but you will have to trek back towards town for any food. *Sgl/dbl with common shower US$7.50, self-contained with fan US$9, with AC US$16–20.*

First Class Guesthouse ☏ 0936 50230. Situated just off the road to the hospital, this pleasant & well-established lodge has sgl rooms that could easily sleep 2, or twin rooms that could probably push to 4 (both have fan & use common showers). The rooms in the main house can be noisy when there's music playing in the bar, so try for an outside room (though the blaring hi-fi of old appears to have been usurped by a more subdued TV). Meals are available to residents only. *Sgl US$10, twin US$13, self-contained dbl with AC US$15.*

Refco Hotel ☏ 0936 50336. This once-smart hotel was undergoing renovations in late 2006, after being closed down by the Ghana Tourist Board for failing to comply with standards. The friendly owner expects to finish work by the time you read this. *Dbl with common shower US$6, self-contained US$15.*

WHERE TO EAT Street food is plentiful along the main road between the Ghana Commercial Bank and the lorry station, and there are a couple of indifferent-looking chop bars dotted around town. For a sit-down meal accompanied by cheap, chilled draught beer, try the **Justice Club**, though this evidently doesn't serve food on Sundays.

AROUND KPANDO

Kpando Potters The Kpando area is known for its fine hand-moulded pottery, which is often claimed to be the finest in Ghana and traditionally made by women only. The best place to check it out is the Fesi Shed of Kpando Potters (☏ *0936 50413/4 or 020 8175596;* e *kpandopottery@hotmail.com*), a women's co-operative that exports its work throughout Ghana as well as into some neighbouring countries. To get there, follow the surfaced Ahenkro road north out of town for 4km to the suburb of Fesi, where a signposted dirt road to the right leads to the shed after about 500m. The women who work here seem very friendly and will gladly let travellers watch them at work and look at some of the finished product – which includes hand-modelled sculptures of animals such as tortoises, pigs and snails, as well as pots with designs based loosely on Adinkra symbols. If you're thinking of buying, fist-sized models start at around US$2.

Our Lady of Lourdes Shrine Situated at Agbenoxoe, some 8km north of Kpando on the surfaced Ahenkro road, this unusual hillside shrine to the Virgin Mary – reputedly the third-biggest Christian grotto in the world – was founded by the Dutch Father Van Dyck in the 1950s in homage to the shrine at Lourdes. The grotto consists of 14 life-sized sculptures of scenes related to the crucifixion of Christ, as well as a huge sculpture of the Virgin Mary that attracts Christian pilgrims from all over Ghana. A few years ago, some children allegedly saw the blue robe on this statue blowing in the wind and called the local priest, who decided that the Virgin was pointing towards one specific palm tree. Rumour got around that this palm had healing powers, and so many pilgrims cut off pieces of the sacred tree for medicinal purposes that it eventually died! An all-day vigil and service is held at the open-air church next to the grotto on the first Friday of every month, and there's also a large ceremony there every 11 December. No fee is charged for looking around, but expect to be asked for a donation towards the upkeep of the shrine.

Blues of Ur Meditation Centre Arguably the most bizarre tourist attraction in Ghana, this meditation centre – 'The Property of the Mysterious Marian "Blues of

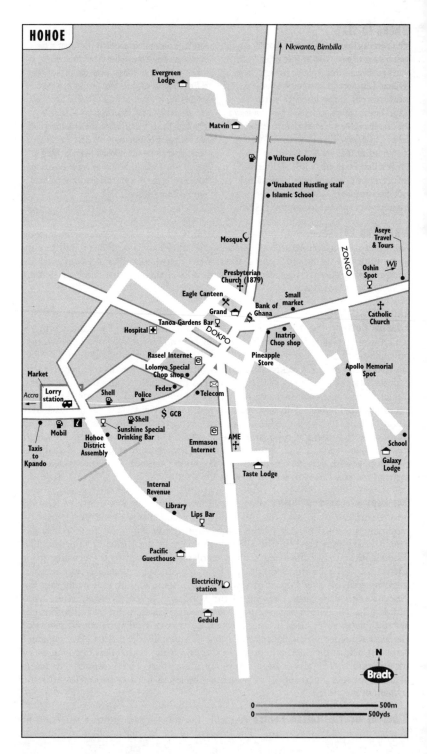

HOHOE

↑ Nkwanta, Bimbilla

Evergreen
Lodge

Matvin

● Vulture Colony

● 'Unabated Hustling stall'
● Islamic School

Mosque ☾

ZONGO

Aseye
Travel
& Tours

Oshin
Spot

Wli

Presbyterian
Church (1879) ✝

Eagle Canteen

Grand

Bank of
Ghana

Small
market

Catholic
Church

Tanoa Gardens Bar

DOKPO

Inatrip
Chop shop

Hospital ✚

Raseel Internet

Pineapple
Store

Apollo Memorial
Spot

Lolonyo Special
Chop shop ●

Market

Shell

Police

Fedex ●

Accra ←

Lorry
station

● Telecom

Mobil

Shell

GCB

Sunshine Special
Drinking Bar

Taxis
to
Kpando

Hohoe
District
Assembly

Emmason
Internet

AME ✝

School

Galaxy
Lodge

Taste Lodge

Internal
Revenue

Library

Lips Bar

Pacific
Guesthouse

Electricity
station

Geduld

N

Bradt

0 ————————————— 500m
0 ————————————— 500yds

268

Ur'" – is situated in Kpando Aziavi, roughly 2km from central Kpando alongside the Accra road. The centre was founded in May 1964 by one Kwame Linus Appaw, who saw a blue star in the sky above Kpando and followed it into the bush until it landed on a large rock outcrop. There it transmitted a message from the Virgin Mary that the surrounding area should be used as a centre for meditation, prayer and tourism dedicated to her name. Thus were born the mysterious Blues of Ur (Ur being the name of the town where Abraham was born), a 200-strong cult centred on the meditation centre, which is owned by the Virgin Mary, and that prays to Mary more than to Jesus because the mother created the son.

The meditation centre is open to all comers (provided that they adhere to a few prominently signposted rules ie: 'don't pluck fruits or hunt for games, no shooting of birds nor picking of flowers, don't throw any missiles into trees and avoid sexy appearances') and is not without a certain offbeat charm, with its cement reliefs of nativity and other biblical scenes (categorised under the 'five sorrowful mysteries' and 'five joyful mysteries') and plentiful statues of Mary and Jesus. The most interesting time to visit is on the first weekend of the month, when the cult gathers on Friday afternoon to hold an overnight vigil, followed by a service on the Saturday morning. Visit at other times and the caretaker will show you around for a small donation.

HOHOE

The sleepy town of Hohoe is the second most populous settlement in Volta Region, and much like the regional capital it is a decidedly amiable place with a good range of amenities for budget travellers. It's a small but pleasant place to pass a day or two, and also makes a useful base from which to explore several local beauty spots (the waterfalls at Agumatsa, Tsatsudo and Liati Wote are all feasible day trips).

GETTING THERE AND AWAY Hohoe is connected by regular tro-tros to Ho (US$1.50), Kpando, Wli, and most other towns in the region, as well as Kpalime across the border in Togo. Travellers coming to Hohoe from Amedzofe should note that there is no direct transport: you will either have to take a tro-tro back to Ho and pick up a Hohoe-bound vehicle there, or else walk from Vame or Amedzofe to Fume on the main Ho–Hohoe road. Coming directly from Accra, the safest option is the STC bus that leaves from the Tudu station every day except Sundays at 16.00 and takes three to four hours (US$4). The bus overnights in Hohoe and returns to the capital in the morning – though the hideous 03.30 departure time may act as something of a deterrent to travellers.

WHERE TO STAY
Moderate

Evergreen Lodge `0935 22254. This smart 2-star hotel on the edge of town may be a bit bland but it is very well priced. A good restaurant & bar are attached. Attractively furnished self-contained rooms with hot shower & bath, DSTV, AC & fridge. US$14– 23, larger deluxe rooms US$29.

Galaxy Lodge (14 rooms) `093 520533. Opened in 2005, this grand-looking hotel with its imposing gates jars with the run-down wooden school just opposite – but as long as you can get over that disparity, the Galaxy is an excellent deal. All 14 rooms are pristinely decorated with high quality furnishings, & fitted with

AC, hot water & DSTV. The friendly, uniformed staff are very attentive & have good information about the local tourist attractions, as well as recommendations for food & drink in town. Alternatively, the hotel can provide Ghanaian dishes at around US$4.50 as well as the usual cold drinks, plus there are a few smart-looking new bars under construction just down the road. At the time of research, guests of the Galaxy could also get a discount at Roseel Internet Café in the centre of town, although this may change with the installation of internet facilities onsite. Sgl/dbl (enormous) US$10/30.

Budget

🏠 **Geduld Hotel** 🕿 0935 22177. This small double-storey hotel is situated around the corner from the Pacific Guesthouse. The furnishings are starting to look a little worn & the location isn't ideal, but otherwise it's very good value. Cold drinks & food from the attached restaurant can be enjoyed in one of a number of outdoor booths. *Sgl with fan US$6; large, clean self-contained dbl with AC & TV US$10–16.*

🏠 **Hotel de Mork** 🕿 0935 22082 or 020 8161380. This large new hotel is situated in Kpoeta, about 2km from the town centre along the Accra road. A decent restaurant & bar are attached. Rooms are comfortable self-contained dbls with hot water & fan, while large suites have AC, TV, fridge & fan. *Dbl US$12, suite US$18–20.*

🏠 **Ma-hill Hotel** (6 rooms) 🕿 0935 22624. Set further out of town, at least 1km along the Wli road, this is a decent little place. The absence of food & the distance from town will put off most backpackers, but it's not a bad choice if you have a vehicle. For those without, shared taxis cost US$0.3 to the town centre. Six clean, self-contained dbls with fan & running water are available. *Dbl US$8.*

🏠 **Matvin Hotel** (27 rooms) 🕿 0935 22134. This was once Hohoe's most upmarket hotel, & it has the grounds to prove it, complete with a large landscaped garden bar overlooking the small Dayi River. Reasonably good food costs around US$3 a dish. With 27 rooms, the Matvin is also by far the largest hotel in Hohoe, & the only one with conference facilities. The rooms are comfortably shabby & very inexpensive: *Dbl with fan US$7, self-contained dbl with fan & hot water US$9, twin suite with TV, AC, fridge & hot water US$15, chalet US$29.*

🏠 **Pacific Guesthouse** 🕿 0935 22146. Situated about 10 mins' walk from the tro-tro station via a dirt road, this is a long-serving favourite with budget travellers. Facilities inc running water, a bar & a cosy TV lounge. Some rooms are self-contained. B/fast & other meals are available on request. *Dbl with fan US$8–12, spacious self-contained chalet with AC & TV US$25.*

🏠 **Taste Lodge** 🕿 0935 22023; e taste_lodge@ yahoo.com. The smartest hotel in central Hohoe, Taste Lodge is a fantastically friendly, family-run set-up with 5 dbl rooms & a popular restaurant set around a central courtyard. Buckets of hot water are available on request. The self-contained rooms all have TV, fridge, fan & AC. *US$15 or US$$18 (depending on whether you switch the AC on or not!).*

Shoestring

🏠 **Grand Hotel** 🕿 0935 22053. The cheapest place to stay in Hohoe, the Grand Hotel is also the most central, situated on the main road directly opposite the prominent Bank of Ghana building. It's a good place to stay if you want to be close to the action: the atmospheric courtyard bar serves cheap draught beer & sensibly priced meals (local dishes from US$3.50), & there are several more bars within a block if you hit a dull night. Fortunately, the noise from the bar doesn't penetrate through to the upstairs rooms to a significant degree. The shabby but very acceptable ground floor dbls with fan, & slightly nicer upstairs twins with fan, attract a lot of shoestring backpackers. *Dbl US$6–8.*

✗ **WHERE TO EAT AND DRINK** The restaurant at **Taste Lodge** has the most varied menu in town, friendly service and good ventilation – most main dishes cost around US$3, and there are cheaper snacks. The **Grand Hotel**, **Matvin Hotel** and **Pacific Guesthouse** (see above) also serve a fair variety of dishes for around US$3 and offer the choice of eating inside or out.

For cheaper fare, there is usually a clutch of reliable kebab stalls just outside the Grand Hotel, and some basic stalls serving tasty omelettes which set up every night by Roseel Internet Café.

There are quite a number of good bars in the town centre. The **Tanoa Gardens Bar** and **Golden Palace Bar** both have cheap chilled draught, and the latter might just serve the spiciest kebabs in Ghana. The **Prestige Bar** has always been very quiet when we visited, but it should liven up when it hosts live music – check the posters around town for the next date.

OTHER PRACTICALITIES

Foreign exchange There is no ATM in Hohoe, and the only money changing facility, at Ghana Commercial Bank, doesn't accept travellers' cheques, so make sure you carry enough cash to see you through to the next town.

Internet At the time of research, there was no broadband in Hohoe, so internet facilities were slow and temperamental. That situation is set to change in the near future, but in the meantime the best service is available at Roseel Internet Café on the main junction, bang in the centre of town.

Tour operators and guides Freelance guides in Hohoe – even those with government cards – have a reputation for misleading travellers to suit their own agenda. We've heard of guides claiming that it's not permitted to visit Wli Falls without a guide from Hohoe, while another common ploy is to claim that Wli Falls is closed due to flooding and to offer travellers an alternative guided trip.

If you do want to arrange guided tours locally, you're best off visiting **Aseye Tours & Travel** (\ *0935 22924;* e *aseyetours2000@yahoo.co.uk*), which is run by a friendly local lady from a small office on the Wli road, a little past the Catholic church, who can set up a variety of local day trips at reasonable rates.

AROUND HOHOE

WLI (AGUMATSA) FALLS The Wli (pronounced 'vlee') or Agumatsa Falls, situated near the village of Wli Agorviefe on the Togo border, is perhaps the most popular tourist attraction in eastern Ghana, consisting of a highly accessible lower fall and more difficult-to-reach upper fall. Wli is often billed as the 'largest waterfall in west Africa', but it is not especially voluminous, and my assumption is that it's the *highest* waterfall in the region. Odd, then, that nobody seems to agree on how high it actually is: local estimates range from 20m via 60m and 600m to 2km, and the only figure I can find in print is 400m (surely a reference to the altitude?). Short of leaping from the top myself with a tape measure attached to my waist, I can only guess, but I would imagine that the lower waterfall is in the region of 50m high. It is certainly the tallest single 'drop' of water that we saw in Ghana.

The falls lie within the 3km² Agumatsa Wildlife Sanctuary, which was set aside to protect the numerous straw-coloured bats that roost colonially on the adjacent tall cliffs. All visits must thus be arranged through the Wildlife Department's tourist information centre in Wli Agorviefe. The relatively undemanding hike to the lower falls costs US$7 for a non-Ghanaian adult or US$5 for a student, to which can be added an optional camera/video fee of US$0.50/3. The more arduous hike to the upper falls costs an additional US$3 for up to three people, or US$5 for groups of four to eight. For safety reasons, the upper falls cannot be visited during the rainy season, from 1 July to 31 December.

As much of an attraction as the waterfall itself is the footpath from Wli village to the base of the lower fall. The flat, easy path leads through thick, semi-deciduous forest for 45 minutes to an hour, fording the Wli and Agumatsa Rivers (the former warmer than the latter) a total of nine times – at the time of writing, there are footbridges at all crossings, but these have been washed away after heavy flooding in the past.

You're unlikely to see large mammals on the waterfall trail, and the small number of monkeys that live deeper in the reserve are reportedly threatened by the hunting activity. Birds are less noticeable than might be expected, but around 75 species have been recorded in this one small forest patch, with greenbuls, barbets, and hornbills particularly well represented. More conspicuous are the forest's dazzling butterflies – a claimed figure of 900 species can safely be dismissed as wild exaggeration, but certainly the variety is impressive. The reserve's most memorable wildlife phenomenon, however, is the bat colony it was set aside to protect – as you approach the waterfall, the roar of plunging water vies with their high-pitched chirping, and it's an awesome sight towards dusk when

The rough but scenic back-country route between Hohoe and Tamale runs to the east and north of Lake Volta via the small towns of Nkwanta and Bimbilla. The trip breaks down into three legs, which collectively take at least two and sometimes three days to cover. Roads are rough throughout: dusty in the dry season, muddy during the rains, and bumpy at all times. There is little point in attempting any leg on a Sunday, since there is even less transport than normal.

The 150km leg from Hohoe to Nkwanta is covered by at least one bus or tro-tro daily. These leave in the mid-morning in either direction, and take up to five hours depending on the current state of the road, which is surfaced for some distance out of Hohoe but deteriorates rapidly after that. Most travellers end up spending the night in Nkwanta. The second leg, the 120km trip to Bimbilla, might entail changing vehicles at Kpaso and/or Damanko, and should take about five hours excluding delays caused by waiting for vehicles (which might well double the duration of the journey). The final 220km leg between Bimbilla and Tamale is covered by two buses daily in either direction; these leave in the early morning and early afternoon, and take around five hours with a stop at Salaga (see page 360) on the Tamale–Yeji road. For travellers tackling this route in a southerly direction, a daily bus reportedly runs between Bimbilla and Accra, leaving Bimbilla at around 08.00 and taking only six hours to get to Hohoe (via Nkwanta). I've not heard of anybody catching this bus in a northerly direction – perhaps it's normally full when it passes through Hohoe, or possibly it runs only seasonally depending on the state of the road.

Nkwanta is a small but lush town, noted for the colourful Yam Festival that takes place in November. The best place to stay here is the Gateway Hotel, which lies on the Hohoe side of town and charges US$25 for a very comfortable self-contained double, and has its own generator to combat the frequent power cuts. The cheaper and more central alternative is the clean and pleasant Kilimanjaro Hotel, which charges US$8 for a self-contained double with a running shower and fan, and has some cheaper rooms too. Both places have restaurants serving decent meals.

Close to Nkwanta, the proposed Kyabobo Range National Park protects a series of wooded ridges and slopes where – unusually – the forest is currently expanding into woodland habitats at a rapid rate, presumably as a result of increased rainfall. Extending over 218km², it is named after the 873m Kyabobo Peak (also spelt Djebobo or Dzebobo), which is Ghana's second-highest massif, but lies outside the proposed park's southern border. Large mammal sightings are scarce, but resident species include buffalo, kob, bushbuck, bushpig, red-flanked duiker and at least four monkeys, while elephant, lion and wild dog might occasionally stray across the Togolese border from

the bats go out to forage. There's a large, rather shallow pool below the falls where you can take a refreshing dip, though the water is chillier than you might expect, and facilities consist of a summer hut and urinal built by the owner of Chances Hotel in Ho. If you spend the night at Wli, you could ask about the fetish shrine in nearby Wli Afegape.

Getting there and away The easiest way to reach the falls is along the surfaced 25km road that runs between Hohoe and Wli Agorviefe, forking right at the junction village of Likpe Bakua. This road is serviced by regular tro-tros and share taxis – you're unlikely to wait more than 30 minutes for a vehicle and the trip out costs US$0.70 and takes less than one hour. The tourist centre lies no more than 100m from where tro-tros stop. Note that the bridge at the Togolese border near Wli was washed away in 1999, so that the border is effectively closed except to pedestrians.

Fazao Malfacassa National Park. Given its small area, the park supports an impressive diversity of birds, with 235 species having been recorded by the Dowsetts during a pioneering expedition in 2005. Although the park has yet to be gazetted (and is unlikely to be in the foreseeable future), guided visits and overnight camping can be arranged at the Wildlife Department in Nkwanta. A good target for birdwatchers is the Laboum Basin, which lies within easy walking distance of the main entrance gate (6km by road from Nkwanta via Odume and best reached by taxi) and hosts an excellent selection of forest birds, including the little-known Baumann's bulbul and Lagden's bush-shrike. The riparian forest near Pawa Satellite Camp also offers excellent birding but requires an overnight stay. Kyabobo has a terrible reputation for biting insects and visitors are advised to wear long sleeves and long trousers (with socks pulled over) at all times.

Also of interest, the small town of Shiyari lies at an altitude of 600m on the slopes of Mount Kyabobo and some 15km from Nkwanta along a very poor road. Shiyari, with a cool, misty climate unusual for Ghana, is known for its picturesque terraced houses, as well as two nearby waterfalls and a local fetish shrine. Shiyari can be reached by bus from Nkwanta on Monday, the local market day, but on other days you'd almost certainly have to charter a taxi (expect to pay around US$25), and either way you'll probably have to walk the last 15- to 20-minute stretch up a steep hill. Before visiting the waterfalls, you must visit the local chief, who may help arrange a guide if he takes a shine to you, but has also been known to refuse access to tourists for no obvious reason. One of the waterfalls can be seen only from a distance, while the other is approachable only via a narrow and rather dangerous (but also very beautiful) 30-minute footpath flanked by a slippery hill to the left and a wooded abyss to the right.

Bimbilla has rather less going for it, but unless you arrive before the afternoon bus to Tamale departs (something that will be largely beyond your control), you might be forced to stay overnight. The only formal accommodation is the basic but friendly Teacher's Hostel, which is situated next to the Goil garage some 20 minutes' walk from the tro-tro station and charges around US$6 for a double room using bucket showers. If it's full, or you want more comfortable accommodation, the private house next door rents out a self-contained room with a fan at a slightly higher price. Reasonable meals are served at the restaurant at the Goil station.

As this fourth edition went to print, we were informed that Kyabobo is currently being developed for tourism as part of a funded project with the backing of SNV – further details will be included in the Bradt update newsletter.

Coming from the south, Wli can also be reached from the Ho–Hohoe road via the scenic side road from Golokwati through Laiti Wote (see page 275), Gbledi, Chebe, and Fodome Ahor. In a private vehicle, this mostly dirt road can be covered in about one hour, but public transport is thin on the ground and may not be available at all between Fodome Ahor and Wli.

Where to stay and eat Although many people visit Wli as a day trip out of Hohoe, there are now several accommodation options in and around Wli. In addition to the places listed below, private homestays can be arranged through the tourist centre for US$6–8, or you could stay at the guesthouse at nearby Likpe Todome (see page 274) instead.

Waterfall Lodge 0935 20057; e bernhard. hagspiel@web.de; www.ghanacamping.com. This new German-run lodge, which opened in June 2003, has a superb location about 500m from the tourist centre in a large green garden offering a view of the upper falls & surrounding hills. The large outdoor bar is a great place to enjoy a drink, or a meal from the restaurant, which serves a good variety of dishes from around US$3. Camping is permitted (4 tents are available for hire). *Self-contained dbl with fan & impressively plumped-up pillows US$11–17 inc breakfast, camping US$2 pp plus US$2.50 for tent hire.*

Wli Water Heights Hotel 020 9119152 or 020 8373163; e psapathy@yahoo.com. About 50m past the turn off for the tourist information centre, this newly established hotel is less pretty than Waterfall Lodge, but has a lovely atmosphere thanks in part to the educated & widely travelled Ghanaian couple who own & manage the place. The attached restaurant serves one of the most imaginative menus outside Accra, drawing on influences from francophone Africa (couscous & Sahel-style rice & fish) as well as local ingredients (ostrich & mushrooms) & the usual 'continental' & Ghanaian standards. Accommodation is in 5 large, clean dbls, some self-contained, set back off a long veranda. The hotel also hosts drumming & dancing displays by local schoolchildren every Fri & Sat evening. *US$10–12.*

LIKPE TODOME One of the most recently developed ecotourism sites in eastern Ghana, Likpe Todome is of interest primarily for the network of six caves – some of which support large colonies of bats, while one contains the ancient stool of the first Likpe chief – that runs through the hills immediately east of the village. The caves lie about 45 minutes' walk from the village and can be explored over a total of up to five hours including a side trip to an exceedingly beautiful waterfall nearby. The steep slopes near the caves also offer great views across to Togo. It used to be necessary to arrange this through the local chief, but guided visits have now been formalised at a cost of US$5 per person or US$4 for volunteers (plus a discretionary tip to the guide) and are best arranged at the tourist centre near the entrance to the town. The path to the caves involves a near vertical climb, and although ropes have been attached to the trees for support, its safety is open to question. If you decide to give it a go, wear strong walking shoes and carry plenty of food and water. The caves are not suitable for vertigo sufferers or claustrophobics.

Getting there and away Likpe Todome lies about 5km north of Wli and some 2km north of Bakwa junction on the road back to Hohoe. There's not too much direct public transport to Likpe Todome, but any transport running between Wli and Hohoe can drop you at Likpe junction, from where you can either wait for a lift, charter a taxi, or, most likely, walk.

Where to stay and eat Some 200m from the main road through the village and clearly signposted after the school, the **government resthouse** – built in the colonial era and re-opened in 2002 to cater to tourists – is really excellent value at US$5 for a very spacious twin suite with TV, fan, fridge and sofa. Meals can be prepared by arrangement with the caretaker.

MOUNT AFADJATO AND LIATI WOTE Mount Afadjato (aka Afadzato) at 885m is generally regarded to be the country's highest peak, and since 1998 its forested slopes have been protected in a community reserve by the village of Gbledi in association with the Ghana Wildlife Society, with funding from the government of the Netherlands. The mountain hosts a remarkable diversity of butterflies (more than 100 species including several endemics), as well as relic populations of localised mammals such as golden cat, bay duiker and black-and-white colobus. Supporting one of the few substantial highland forests anywhere in Ghana, Afadjato is also regarded as a key ornithological site, and although no full checklist has been compiled, a recent four-day expedition identified almost 90 species, of which 10 are uncommon in Ghana, including brown snake eagle, Afep pigeon, green-tailed bristlebill, leaflove and olive-green cameroptera. The Ghana Wildlife Society maintains a conservation office in Gbledi, from where treks of up to three days in duration can be undertaken by arrangement with the rangers.

The most normal base for day hikes on Afadjato is the pretty village of Liati Wote, which lies near the Togolese border 3km south of Gbledi and has recently been developed as a community tourism project in association with the Peace Corps. From Liati Wote, Afadjato can be ascended as a roughly two-hour round trip, with great views as far as distant Lake Volta *en route*, as well as good bird- and butterfly-watching, and very occasional glimpses of monkeys or small antelope. Another worthwhile attraction, reached in 45 minutes along a reasonably flat path through the cocoa fields, is the impressive Tagbo Waterfall, which has a refreshing plunge pool at its base, is surrounded by semi-deciduous forest, and is also likely to be protected as a community reserve in the near future. Guided hikes to both sites must be arranged through the caretaker at Liati Wote's guesthouse, and cost US$2.50 for the waterfall, US$2 to the mountain or US$4 for both, with small discounts available to volunteers.

Getting there and away To reach Liati Wote from Hohoe, drive south to Golokwati junction, then turn left at the signposted turn-off. After about 6km on this surfaced road, turn left at Liati Agbonyra, then after 4km turn right at Liati Soba, from where it's another 4km to the village. Public transport between Hohoe and Liati Wote is limited to a couple of tro-tros daily, which leave Hohoe from Fodome Station near the post office, generally between 12.00 and 14.00. There is also a lorry that leaves Liati Wote once daily between 07.00 and 08.00 and Hohoe daily in the late afternoon or evening.

Where to stay and eat The community-run **Afadjato Guesthouse** (⏍ *028 5085939*) is situated in a forest glade at the entrance of Liati Wote on the left side of the road coming from Golokwati. It has six basic but clean rooms with nets and fans – three doubles & three singles. Camping is permitted. Meals can be arranged with the community project staff for around US$2. *Dbl US$4.50, sgl US$3, camping US$1.50 pp.*

TSATSUDO FALLS This seasonal waterfall on the Tsatsudo River, near the village of Alavanyo Abeheanse, is very accessible to travellers. It is not as spectacular as the Wli Falls but is just as pretty, consisting of five separate falls, each separated from the one above and/or below by a rocky ledge. The pool at the base of the waterfall is deep enough to swim in properly, but do take care not to bump into one of the many large, submerged boulders. We climbed up a steep rock-face to the ledge separating the bottom fall from the one above, where you could also swim in a pool below a pretty overhang. The route we used to get up (and so far as we could tell the only way up) is not recommended unless you're reasonably agile and sure-footed, since there are a couple of spots where a slight slip would almost certainly lead to a broken limb or worse. So far as animal life goes, frogs seem to be particularly abundant and vociferous here, and the riverine vegetation and cliffs harbour quite a number of birds – we saw what appeared without binoculars to be a pair of auger buzzards and an African goshawk.

Alavanyo Abeheanse lies no more than 20km from Hohoe along a dirt road that branches from the main Ho road at Gibi Wegbe, about 7km from Hohoe. Regular tro-tros connect Hohoe to Abeheanse, which is the first of several villages making up Alavanyo. Before you head out to the waterfall, you must visit the chief and pay a fee of around US$4 per head or US$3 for volunteers, which allows you to visit the falls as many times and for as long as you like. The waterfall lies about 1km

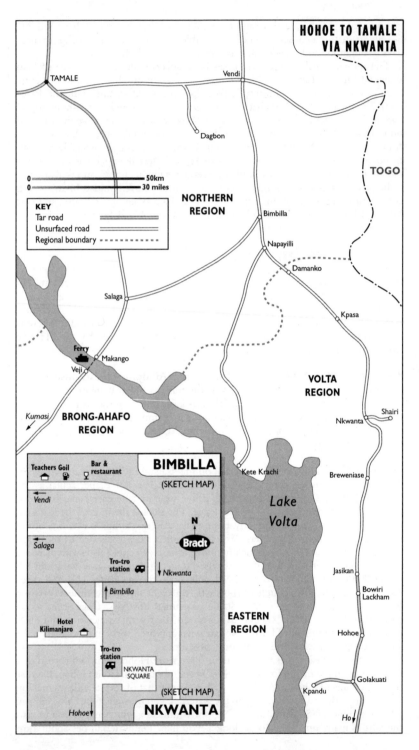

TAMALE

Vendi

Dagbon

TOGO

0   50km
0   30 miles

NORTHERN
REGION

Bimbilla

KEY
Tar road
Unsurfaced road
Regional boundary

Napayilli

Damanko

Salaga

Kpasa

Ferry
Makango

Veji

Kumasi   **BRONG-AHAFO REGION**

VOLTA
REGION

Shairi

Nkwanta

Breweniase

Teachers Goil   Bar &
restaurant   **BIMBILLA**
(SKETCH MAP)

Vendi

Salaga

N
Bradt

Tro-tro
station

↓ *Nkwanta*

Kete Krachi

*Lake
Volta*

↑ *Bimbilla*

**Hotel
Kilimanjaro**

Jasikan

Bowiri
Lackham

Tro-tro
station

NKWANTA
SQUARE

**EASTERN
REGION**

Hohoe

(SKETCH MAP)

Hohoe↓

NKWANTA

Golakuati

Kpandu

Ho↓

from the village; if you have a vehicle, you can drive to within 50m of it. A guide isn't necessary to find the waterfall, but might be a good idea if you want to explore the higher pools. Overnight camping is permitted at no extra charge, assuming that you've paid your entrance fee. Note that there is no public transport along the road connecting Alavanyo directly to Kpando.

LACKHAM LODGE This is a new, multi-faceted community development centred on a 700-acre site called Bowiri Lackham, which lies in an area of lush tropical forest and grassland straddling the tarred Jasikan road some 22km north of Hohoe. Still in its infancy, the tourism aspect of the project is being developed with the assistance of a VSO volunteer, and it promises to open up a part of rural Ghana not currently visited by many tourists. The tourist centre currently consists of a large garden on the roadside, with two summer huts, an ablution block, a bar and a recently constructed six-room guesthouse charging US$9 for a clean double without a fan. The regular tro-tros which run between Hohoe and Jasikan will drop visitors at the lodge (ask for Lackham). It is also possible to pick up transport northwards from Jasikan to Nkwanta; ☏ 021 238192; **f** 021 238192; **e** ckonadu@cel.aau.org.

Among the places of interest to be visited in this area are Tepa Abotoase and Kwamikrom on Lake Volta, both of which are important fish markets and boat-building centres. In the hills above Bowiri Lackham, reached via the district capital of Jasikan, the towns of Bordador and Tetteman boast some interesting German architecture and reputedly can be used as the base from which to visit a little-known crater lake. Organised excursions to these places can be arranged through lodge staff. Other tourist activities include boat cruises at Bowiri Odumasi and Wudormeabra, palm-wine tapping, *kente* weaving and traditional dances.

THE AFRICA IMAGE LIBRARY

The comprehensive source for all images of Africa, including wildlife, nature, scenery, cultures, architecture and people. For further details, visit our website or email photographer Ariadne Van Zandbergen at ariadne@hixnet.co.za

www.africaimagelibrary.com

FCO TRAVEL ADVICE
know before you go
fco.gov.uk/travel

Bradt Travel Guides is a partner to the 'know before you go' campaign, masterminded by the UK Foreign and Commonwealth Office to promote the importance of finding out about a destination before you travel. By combining the up-to-date advice of the FCO with the in-depth knowledge of Bradt authors, you'll ensure that your trip will be as trouble-free as possible.

www.fco.gov.uk/travel

Part Five

CENTRAL GHANA

INTRODUCTION

The following four chapters cover the Ghanaian interior west of Lake Volta, north of Accra, and south of Tamale and Mole National Park. Culturally and geographically, it is a less than cohesive area, but it does tie together in travel terms, since it follows (with only a few diversions) the routes most likely to be taken by travellers heading north from the coast towards Kumasi or on to Tamale and/or Mole National Park.

Within the area described here, all roads seem to lead to Kumasi, Ghana's second-largest city and the most important 'route focus' inland of Accra. Accordingly, this chapter covers the various route permutations between the coast and Kumasi, while the subsequent three chapters, respectively, describe Kumasi itself, the many attractions within day-tripping distance of Kumasi, and finally the main route between Kumasi and the northern 'route focus' of Tamale.

Readers should note that there is arguably far more to be seen within a 50km radius of Kumasi than there is along the roads that connect it to the coast or to Tamale. For this reason, many travellers bus directly between the coast and Kumasi, and between Kumasi and Tamale. If time is a factor, it would be difficult to argue with this course of action, but for those with the time or inclination to explore off the beaten track, areas such as the Kwahu Plateau to the east of the main Accra–Kumasi road, and the excellent monkey sanctuary at Baobeng–Fiema, offer an incentive to break up the inter-city trips.

13

Between the Coast and Kumasi

Three main routes link the coast to Kumasi, with little to choose between them except for how they fit in with the rest of your itinerary. The most popular is the 270km road between Accra and Kumasi, which follows good surfaced roads in its entirety and can be covered in four to five hours on one of the STC buses that leave in both directions every hour. Less popular, but far shorter, is the 220km road connecting Cape Coast to Kumasi via Yamoransa, Foso, and Bekwai, once again surfaced in its entirety and covered by regular buses over three or four hours. The final option is the 225km trip from Takoradi–Sekondi via Tarkwa and Obuasi, which can be covered either by overnight train or by bus along good surfaced roads. A more obscure route to Kumasi, worth looking at if you also intend to explore the area east of Lake Volta, involves using a combination of motor ferries and road transport from Kpando on the eastern lakeshore via the Afram Plains to Nkawkaw on the main Accra–Kumasi road.

ACCRA TO KUMASI

This is another of the many trips in Ghana that could be done as easily in a few hours as over a week. Kumasi lies a mere four hours from Accra by direct STC bus, but there are a number of interesting sights along the way. In addition to the places listed below, it would be feasible to start your trip by travelling from Accra to Aburi and other places of interest covered in the chapter *Inland of Accra* (see page 231), terminating at Koforidua, from where it is easy to pick up transport towards Kumasi, with a possible stop at the Bunso Arboretum en route.

Shortly before going to print, Aruna Subramanian wrote to say: 'An interesting short stop on the way from Akosombo to Kumasi via Koforidua is the village of Awuku Gua. There is a stone here with seven marks apparently made by the heel of the guy who summoned the golden stool from the skies to denote the seven tribes that betrayed him to the Ashanti, who recognised his potential and made him the king's advisor. There is actually another stone beneath this one that apparently has the original secret inscribed by him but he "smashed" the other stone on top after his betrayal so the original secret is lost to the village forever.'

ATEWA RANGE FOREST RESERVE Situated to the west of the main Accra–Kumasi road, near the small junction town of Kibi, the little-known Atewa Range Forest Reserve, which rises to an altitude of 770m and extends over roughly 230km², has been proposed as a Globally Significant Biodiversity Area in recognition of its unusually rich assemblage of forest mammals, birds and butterflies. The reserve was set aside in 1926 to protect one of only two upland evergreen forests in Ghana, and it remains the country's best-preserved example of this habitat, despite reports of extensive logging activity in recent years. For birders, the main attraction here is

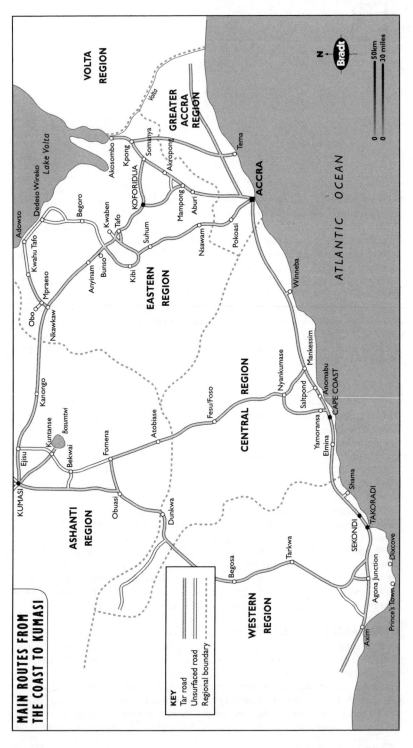

MAIN ROUTES FROM
THE COAST TO KUMASI

VOLTA REGION

GREATER ACCRA REGION

EASTERN REGION

CENTRAL REGION

ASHANTI REGION

WESTERN REGION

ATLANTIC OCEAN

Lake Volta

Volta

N

Bradt

50km

30 miles

0

0

Tema

ACCRA

Akosombo

Kpong

Somanya

Akropong

Mampong

Aburi

KOFORIDUA

Suhum

Nsawam

Pokoasi

Winneba

Mankessim

Nyankumase

Anomabu

CAPE COAST

Saltpond

Yamoransa

Elmina

Shama

SEKONDI

TAKORADI

Dixcove

Agona Junction

Prince's Town

Axim

Tarkwa

Begosa

Dunkwa

Obuasi

Fomena

Bekwai

Kuntanse

Ejisu

Bosumtwi

KUMASI

Kanongo

Nkawkaw

Obo

Mpraeso

Anyinam

Bunso

Kibi

Tafo

Kwaben

Begoro

Kwahu Tafo

Adowso

Dedeso Wireko

Atobiase

Fesu/Foso

KEY

Tar road

Unsurfaced road

Regional boundary

a checklist of 200-plus species, several of which – for instance long-tailed hawk, crowned eagle, Afep pigeon, olive long-tailed cuckoo, African broadbill, Western least honeyguide, spotted honeyguide, yellow-throated olive greenbul, bristlebill and blue-headed crested flycatcher – are highland forest dwellers with a limited distribution within Ghana. Even more remarkable, perhaps, is the total of more than 400 butterfly species, including six endemics, recorded within this relatively small area of forest. Among the more common mammals are black-and-white colobus and Campbell's mona monkey, but half a dozen other monkey species are known to occur, along with four types of duiker. The spectacular bongo antelope used to be common but has been hunted close to extinction.

Before visiting the forest, you need to obtain permission (and a key to the main gate) from the forestry office in Kibi, which is usually a straightforward procedure. From Kibi, drive 8km towards Sagyimase before turning left onto a dirt road at a sign reading 'Save Atewa Forest'. From here, it's another 6km on a bad and steep road (definitely only 4×4 after the first 3km) to the top of the ridge, where there is a network of logging tracks to walk. The birding here is arguably better than at either Kakum or Ankasa, and you don't need to pay the guide fees – which really add up in the national parks. Very basic accommodation can be found in **Ankobea Guest House** for around US$7 a room.

BUNSO ARBORETUM Located only 3km from the main road between Accra and Kumasi and right alongside the surfaced road south to Koforidua, one hour away, the Bunso Arboretum lies in an area of beautiful rolling hills and is home to an extensive variety of plants, trees, and herbs including 70-year-old palms and the country's only Brazil nut trees. The arboretum was founded in the 19th century and is today maintained as a research centre by Ghana's Plant Genetic Resources Centre, which is mandated to undertake the collection and conservation of plant genetic resources in Ghana. Neighbouring fields display identified crop plants, fruit trees and timber species that are either indigenous to Ghana, or which the Plant Genetic Resources Centre is attempting to introduce to the country or region. More than 100 bird species have been recorded, and there's a butterfly sanctuary within the grounds.

The arboretum, which covers 16.5 hectares of land on a steep hill, has recently been developed for tourism with the assistance of the NCRC and Peace Corps. A network of nature trails allow visitors to learn more about local uses for the identified trees, plants and herbs, admire the many species of birds and butterflies, or visit the neighbouring Cocoa College. Check into the visitor centre for an excellent guided tour lasting about 45 minutes and costing US$2 per person. The recently opened **Bunso Arboretum Guesthouse** (⟍ *027 540124*), which charges US$15–20 for an immaculate, self-contained single/double, stands on a hilltop and offers great views from its patio across the surrounding countryside. Reservations are recommended. It may be possible to use the caretaker's kitchen but you should bring your own food.

Local transport from Koforidua or the junction with the main Accra–Kumasi road 3km away is available at any time of the day or early evening. The closest accommodation, aside from the arboretum guesthouse, is in New Tafo, roughly halfway between Bunso and Koforidua. The smartest place to stay here is the **Cocoa Research Institute Guesthouse** (⟍ *024 3344930*), which prepares meals for guests and offers six immaculate doubles in large well-tended grounds for US$15/25 per night depending on whether they have air conditioning. Less expensive at around US$7 for a clean double is the **Echo Guest House**, which also serves meals and drinks on the premises.

ANYINAM It's difficult to imagine why any traveller would want to sleep over at this moderately sized town situated near the junction where the main roads from Koforidua and Accra to Kumasi converge. Should you be that unimaginable traveller, however, you'll be pleased to hear that there are at least two hotels to choose from. The inexpensive **Mensco Hotel**, painted bright blue, is to the left as you enter town from the Accra or Koforidua side, but there is also the newer, rather plush **Stopping Point Hotel** right in the town centre, with rooftop bar and restaurant attached, as well as a supermarket.

ABOMPE Signposted about ten minutes' drive north of Bunso junction on the Accra–Kumasi road, **Abompe Traditional Bead Making & Village Life Tours** is a new community based project that offers tourists a chance to see and try the making of the traditional, rough, brown bauxite beads often worn in Ghana. Activities on offer include half-day tours of the village bead-makers (US$2), full-day bead-making workshops (US$4.50), and half-day guided treks to the escarpment – known as Abompe Hills – where the bauxite is mined (US$2). All fees are directed towards the entire community and payable at the visitor's centre, signposted down a discreet dirt track to the left as you enter the village. Accommodation is also available in two small houses from US$5 per person, with food and drink available upon request. The village is easily accessible but feels very rural once you're there and is a nice place to stay in its own right. The surrounding countryside is worth exploring – aside from the magnificent escarpment, a number of waterfalls make good goals – or you could also visit other local schemes, including a batik and tie dye workshop and professional woodcarving factory at Osino.

NKAWKAW This substantial, readily accessible, but rather scruffy town lies 104km from Kumasi on the main Accra road. Nkawkaw is of interest to travellers primarily as a springboard for visits to Mpraeso and Obo on the northern part of the Kwahu Plateau, but it does boast some memorable features, not least a main street that must rank close to being the most hectic and pedestrian-unfriendly in Ghana. Also noteworthy are the forested mountains rising to the northeast, and the preponderance of fading colonial-era buildings complete with red corrugated-iron roofs and balconies.

There is plenty of transport to Nkawkaw from all directions. STC buses from Accra to Kumasi will drop you at Nkawkaw, assuming that you don't mind paying full fare to Kumasi. The smartest accommodation by far is the **Rojo Hotel** (↘ *0842 22221*), which has self-contained accommodation in the US$10–20 range and offers brilliant views of the escarpment cliffs. Cheaper options include **Bertram's Hotel**, which lies about 500m from the main road off the road to Mpraeso, or the less-appealing **Top Way Hotel**, also on the Mpraeso road.

Plenty of street food is available along the main road through the town centre, but a more attractive option would be to walk out of town about 500m in the direction of Kumasi to the Goil garage. Just behind the garage is a reasonable restaurant with indoor and outdoor seating, serving local fare at around US$2 per plate as well as chilled beers. More fun, perhaps, is to nibble your way around the kiosks and shops that circle the STC parking lot just before the garage – everything from imported biscuits to Californian white wine, as well as the usual grilled chicken and kebabs, chilled sodas and beers, are on offer.

Based primarily on information provided by Frances Bowden and Mike Davies of Raleigh International, and Sam Nash of the Kwahu Ecotourism Project.

The little-visited Kwahu Plateau is an extensive area of elevated hilly country that lies between the main Accra–Kumasi road and the western arm of Lake Volta. Seldom visited by travellers, the area offers some worthwhile opportunities for off-the-beaten track exploration, with the most obvious goals for short forays into the plateau being Begoro and Mpraeso. More adventurously, there is a remote road loop that links these two towns via Abuoso, Adowso, and Kwahu Tafo, while a combined road and ferry trip links Adowso to the eastern shore of Lake Volta and Kpando (see box *Crossing Lake Volta via the Afram Plains,* page 286).

BEGORO This small town, which lies at an altitude of around 500m at the southern end of the Kwahu Plateau, makes for a relatively straightforward stand-alone excursion from the main Accra–Kumasi road. Something of a backwater today, Begoro was chosen as the site of a pioneering Presbyterian mission in 1875 (look for the arch near the Presbyterian church reading 'Presbyterian Boarding School 1885'), a decision influenced by its pleasant and relatively disease-free mid-altitude climate. Also worth a look is Fanteakwa's Palace along the road between the tro-tro station and the Sweet Memories Hotel, easily distinguished by its colonial architecture and the large murals of musicians on the outer wall.

Of greater interest than the town itself, however, is the possibility of using it as a base from which to explore the surrounding countryside, which is great walking country notable for its varied birds and butterflies as well as many streams and waterfalls. An obvious target for day visitors would be the Begoro Falls, which lie less than 20 minutes' walk from town. The Begoro Falls drop about 15m from a large overhang – not much more than a trickle when we visited in the dry season (though even then we were able to wade knee-deep into the muddy pool below the fall for a refreshing natural shower), but reportedly very impressive after the start of the rains.

The junction town for Begoro is Osriem, which lies on the Kumasi road a few kilometres north of where the main surfaced roads from Accra and Koforidua merge. Begoro lies 20km east of Osriem, and coming from Accra your best bet is probably to hop on a bus bound for Kumasi or Nkawkaw and get off at Osriem, where regular shared taxis head up to Begoro. Coming from Koforidua, there are also direct tro-tros to Begoro. To reach Begoro Falls, follow the road leading uphill to your left as you enter the tro-tro station. After about 100m, where a storm drain crosses the road, turn right and uphill towards the Presbyterian church, then after another 50m, just before the church, turn left and follow this road for a few metres until you reach a football field. Immediately before the football field, turn right on to the footpath that runs parallel to it before leaving town to descend into a valley. After about ten minutes' walking downhill, you'll reach the river just below the waterfall.

The only accommodation in Begoro is the aptly named **Sweet Memories Hotel**, which has cosy, clean, self-contained rooms with fan for a couple of dollars, as well as friendly staff and a very effective drinks fridge. For food, you'll find plenty of stalls selling kebabs, bush meat, fried yam and other goodies around the lorry station, all overlooked by the **Dorcas Restaurant**, which does chicken with rice or *fufu* for US$1.50 per plate.

CROSSING LAKE VOLTA VIA THE AFRAM PLAINS

Stephen Gee

The Afram Plains is a sparsely populated and poorly developed part of Eastern Region that has found itself isolated since the creation of Lake Volta, which forms its southern and eastern boundaries. Due to the poor condition of the roads to the north, transport to and from the plains entails crossing the lake by ferry, and electricity is supplied only to those settlements along the route linking the main town of Donkorkrom with the ferry ports of Ekye (for Adowso) and Agordeke (for Kpando). The economy of the area is based on subsistence agriculture, the soil is very fertile and it was once a cocoa-growing region. In recent times, possibly due to the creation of the lake, the climate has changed sufficiently to cause cocoa harvests to fail and leave the population with little or no exportable produce. For these reasons the Afram Plains is considered by the present government to be an underdeveloped region of Ghana.

The Afram Plains lack any tourist attractions of note, but the ferry crossings from Kpando and Adowso can be enchanting in the morning mist, and the sense of isolation from the urbanity of Accra or Kumasi, or even from the relatively cosmopolitan likes of Ho or Hohoe, will provide a more balanced view of modern Ghana. The views across the lake are also very pretty. More pragmatically, for those travelling between the eastern highlands and Kumasi, the route through the Afram Plains offers an appealing and adventurous alternative to the longer road via Koforidua or Accra, one that can be undertaken without having to sit for too many hours in hot and bumpy tro-tros. The route is described below from east to west, but it could as easily be travelled in the reverse direction.

The eastern springboard for the trip across the Afram Plains is Kpando (see page 265), which is connected to the port of Agordeke by a daily ferry service. This leaves Agordeke at 06.00 and 11.00 and Kpando at 08.30 and 13.30 daily, taking about two hours in either direction, and charging US$2.50 per person. If you're travelling with a private vehicle, be at the ferry jetty an hour ahead of the scheduled departure time to be sure of vehicle space on the ferry. If you're not, then when you arrive at Agordeke, which has quite a pleasant beach with a small bar selling drinks and snacks, you'll need to board one of the tro-tros that take about 90 minutes to reach the regional capital, Donkorkrom. In the past, heavy rainfall could transform the poor road from Agordeke to Donkorkrom into an impassable one, but this should have improved following roadworks that began in September 2003.

There are two guesthouses in Donkorkrom, of which the superior Golden Gate charges around US$10 for a self-contained double with fan and en-suite bathroom with a controlled water supply (ie: the staff have to be informed if water is required), although its best avoided if they have plans for a mid-week rave. The cheaper St

ABUOSO AND DODESO Abuoso lies almost directly north of Begoro along the road descending to the village of Dodeso on the Lake Volta shore. From Begoro, Abuoso can be reached via a good unsurfaced road regularly used by shared taxis. Road conditions deteriorate on the descent to Dodeso, but this is compensated for by some fantastic scenery in a rock-strewn valley (with plenty of scenic camping possibilities along with some bouldering options for any climbers) whose head offers a sweeping view across the western arm of Lake Volta to the Afram Plains. There is no formal accommodation in Abuoso but if you report to the police station upon arrival, they are likely to be able to assist in finding a room (and ensuring that any stay in Abuoso is a pleasant one).

An adventurous onward option from Abuoso would be to follow the approximately 35km of rough road along the lakeshore to Adowso, which has regular

Michael's Guesthouse has more basic rooms with fans and electricity, using a shared bathroom and toilet with running water. Both guesthouses serve food but it is advisable to let staff know in advance if you intend to eat there. There are also a number of street vendors and chop bars where you can try the local grasscutter. Fresh produce is also available at Donkorkrom, particularly on the market days of Wednesday and Thursday – enjoyable unless the smell of fish makes you ill – but better markets can be found at Kpando and Nkawkaw before arriving in the Afram Plains.

In Donkorkrom, a very enthusiastic local entrepreneur has set up a tie-dye and batik business called Stephanmanu Enterprises (✆ 0848 22094), where you can buy ready-made fabrics or, if you want a more personal souvenir, create your own unique design at his workshop at very reasonable prices (creating your own design takes up to three hours). The shop can be found in the main market and the workshop is just a ten-minute walk away. There is a bank in Donkorkrom, and public telephones stand outside the post office, but the international lines are often down for weeks on end. Donkorkrom Hospital can cope with many medical problems. Fuel is available in town, as well as in Forefori, Ekye, and Tease.

Donkorkrom is of note as the southern administrative centre for Ghana's second-largest conservation area Digya National Park, which extends over 3,750km² north of the Afram Plains and west of Lake Volta. Proclaimed in 1971, Digya has never formally opened to the public due to difficulty of access, but its potential is enormous, thanks to a remarkable diversity of habitats and a mammal checklist that includes red-flanked duiker, elephant, manatee, hippopotamus, buffalo, lion, leopard, bongo antelope, and half a dozen species of monkey. Until recently, the park was practically unknown in ornithological terms, but its rich biodiversity is reflected by an incredible tally of 236 bird species recorded by the Dowsetts over a pioneering 9-day expedition in January 2005, and a checklist of 300-plus seems more than probable. It is presumably only a matter of time before this alluring park is developed for tourism; check with the wildlife division in Donkorkrom for the current details.

Moving on from Donkorkrom, tro-tros south to the port of Ekye (pronounced 'Eshay') generally take about 90 minutes. Tro-tros in both directions work around the ferry timetable between Ekye and Adowso, which lies at the northern base of the Kwahu Plateau – although locals anywhere north of Nkawkaw tend to refer to both ports as Ekye. Ferries from Adowso to Ekye leave at 09.00, 14.00 and 17.00 daily, while those in the opposite direction leave Ekye at 09.30, 14.30 and 17.30 – the 30-minute ride costs around US$0.80 per person, and once again travellers with private transport should arrive early to be sure of a place for the vehicle. From Adowso, there's plenty of road transport to Mpraeso and on to Nkawkaw on the main Accra–Kumasi road.

tro-tro connections to Nkawkaw (on the main Accra–Kumasi road) and is also the site of the ferry crossing to the Afram Plains. The road between Adowso is very little used, but there is occasional public transport on most stretches, and you could walk the other parts. The road is regularly punctuated by small fishing villages, notably Mpaem, Kwahu Amanforum, New Worobon, Nketepa (very large market with much fresh produce), Asuboni and Okragyei, several of which are resettlements that date to the flooding of the lake. Formal accommodation is not readily available, but requests to the village chief or people you meet along the way may well lead to a room being offered, or church or school buildings being made available.

An even more off-the-beaten-track possibility out of Abuoso would be to follow one of the tracks leading up on to the escarpment to villages almost never visited by outsiders, such as Upper Odede, Amotare, Akumeso and

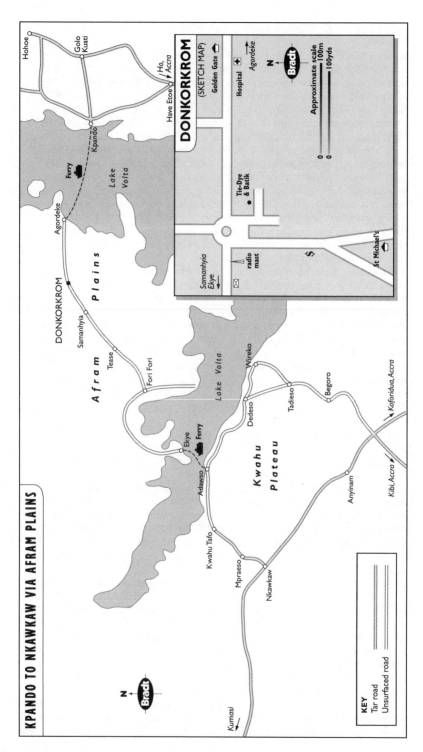

KPANDO TO NKAWKAW VIA AFRAM PLAINS

Hohoe

Golo
Kuati

Ho,
Accra

Have Etoe

Kpando

Ferry

Lake
Volta

Agordeke

DONKORKROM

A f r a m   P l a i n s

Samanhyia

Tease

Fori Fori

Lake Volta

Wireko

Dedeso

Tadieso

Begoro

Koforidua, Accra

Ekye   Ferry

Adawso

K w a h u
P l a t e a u

Anyinam

Kibi, Accra

Kwahu Tafo

Mpraeso

Nkawkaw

Kumasi

N

Bradt

KEY
Tar road
Unsurfaced road

DONKORKROM
(SKETCH MAP)

Golden Gate

Hospital

Agordeke

N

Bradt

Approximate scale
0 ___ 100m
0 ___ 100yds

Tie-Dye
& Batik

radio mast

Samanhyia
Ekye

St Michael's

288

Pamplamantin. Travelling by the bush paths on the escarpment can be very rewarding, but a copy of the (out-of-date) Ordnance Survey map will be required, and be warned that some villages are not in the exact location as shown on the map. Navigation by contours is not too difficult and any locals met along the way are always keen to help travellers on to the right path. There are many opportunities to drop down off the escarpment and head north down towards the road hugging the shore of the lake. Coming down at Mpaem is a pleasant track, as is the steep descent at Adowso. We've also been told that a good track follows the Asuboni River westwards from Asikiman as far as Kwahu Tafo, through an area of the escarpment with teak forests and many other discoveries for the adventurous traveller. Accommodation at escarpment villages is likely to be very basic, if available at all, so it's probably advisable to carry a tent. Having said that, a visit to the chief with a request to camp may well lead to a room in a villager's house, or a community building such as a church.

MPRAESO A district administrative centre, Mpraeso is Nkawkaw's high-altitude twin, perched on top of the sandstone cliffs that lie immediately to the east of Nkawkaw and reached by a road as scenic as any in Ghana, a dramatic series of switchbacks up a jungle-clad slope. Like Begoro to the south, Mpraeso is of less interest in itself than it is for the attractive walking country of the Kwahu Plateau on which it lies. Perhaps 10km northwest of Mpraeso, **Obo** is another quiet small town ringed by forested hills and host to a decidedly odd mixture of dirty old colonial mansions and spanking new, brightly painted holiday homes complete with satellite aerials. It's an unusual town, one that might well appeal to photographers, and the surrounding hills offer some good walking possibilities – any child will act as a guide should you want one. Mpraeso is surrounded by protected rainforests, which can be explored with the permission of the helpful Forestry Services Division office 200m uphill from the roundabout on the Obomen road. In addition to rainforest trips, there may also be an opportunity to visit the self-styled 'bushman' who lives in a cave some four hours' trek into the rainforest from Ntomen – gifts of cigarettes and tuna are much appreciated, in return for which the bushman will share stories and information about the bush.

Regular passenger taxis run along the 10km road between Nkawkaw and Mpraeso. There are also regular passenger taxis between Mpraeso and Obo. There are several inexpensive lodges in Mpraeso of which the **Ohene Nana Classic Hotel** and the **Moonlight Hotel** are currently about the best. In Obo, the **Obo Central Hotel** is a friendly, family-run place with simple rooms. Also in Obo, the recently established **Eagle's Peak Resort**, built by an American Buddhist who fell in love with the surrounds, offers some accommodation and is a good place to stop for a chilled drink and a tasty meal for around US$3 a plate. Another option, in nearby Bepong, is the **Onyame Bekyere Hotel**, which has good self-contained doubles for around US$6, but no food.

ABETIFI Straddling the road between Mpraeso and Adowso, the picturesque small town of Abetifi is reputedly the highest inhabited place in Ghana, and one of the most climatically pleasant, set at an altitude of around 750m. It is the site of one of the country's most important Basel Missions, founded by Fritz Ramseyer, who spent several months there with his family as hostages of the Asante army in 1869, and returned seven years later to build the charming mission house that still stands there today. Also worth a look is the Dutch-style Presbyterian Church, which was built over 1907–10 and has the largest bell in Ghana, a 10-ton artefact that was carried by boat to Adowso and pulled by teams of men along the 50km ascent to Abetifi in 1910. Shoestring accommodation can be found at Abetifi's large

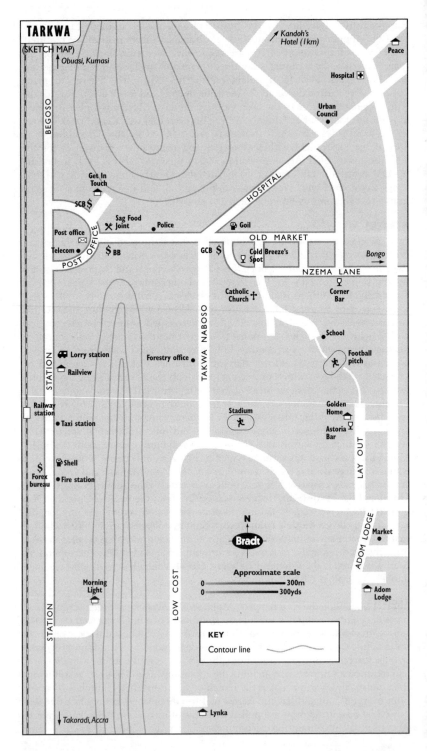

TARKWA
(SKETCH MAP)

↑ Obuasi, Kumasi

↑ Kandoh's Hotel (1km)

Peace

Hospital ✚

Urban Council ●

BEGOSO

HOSPITAL

Get In Touch

SCB $

Sag Food Joint ✕ ● Police

⊠ Goil

OLD MARKET

POST OFFICE

Post office ⊠

Telecom ●

$ BB

GCB $

Cold Breeze's Spot

Bongo →

NZEMA LANE

Catholic Church ✝

Corner Bar

School ●

Football pitch 🏃

STATION

🚌 Lorry station

Railview

TAKWA NABOSO

Forestry office ●

Railway station

● Taxi station

Stadium 🏃

Golden Home

Astoria Bar

LAY OUT

$ Forex bureau

🅿 Shell

● Fire station

N

Bradt

ADOM LODGE

● Market

STATION

Morning Light

LOW COST

Approximate scale
0 ——————— 300m
0 ——————— 300yds

Adom Lodge

KEY
Contour line ～～～

↓ Takoradi, Accra

🏠 Lynka

290

community centre. Other amenities include a library in a wooden chapel, satellite internet café and university.

KWAHU TAFO Called Tafo for short, this busy town marks the end of the surfaced stretch of the road from Mpraeso to Adowso. Mainly a farming town, Tafo is a pleasant place to stroll through in the evening, when the workers return from the fields and the main street bustles with people socialising. Much food is cooked by the roadside for the returning farmers and an evening on the streets is a great opportunity to try the local delicacies of smoked fish, fried yam and sweet potato, and fried plantain. Matthew, from the TV series *Desmonds*, is a son of Tafo. A bust of him sits proudly outside the new community library in Tafo. The library was part-funded by the Friends of Tafo organisation. This is a UK-based charity run by the development chief from Tafo, the TV producer of *Desmonds*, Humphrey Barclay.

Just outside of town on the Kotoso road is a small waterfall that is scenically set in a very shaded spot near a quarry – most locals will be able to point you in the right direction or lead you there when asked. Visits to one of the local priests/priestesses can also be arranged provided they are not busied exorcising a witch.

Situated a few kilometres out of town along the Adowso road, the village of Burukuwa plays host to a 'sacred waterfall and cup-stone', as well as the Buruku Rock Pillar Shrine – an immense and spectacular rectangular rock sitting on a small hill, which is the paramount shrine in the Tafo area. Believed to be home to a powerful god, the rock shrine is shrouded in superstitions and is said to watch over and protect all the villages in the surrounding area like a giant eye. More can be found out from the locals or one of the fetish priests or priestesses in Tafo. The walk to and from Buruku will take about five hours and, with a good guide, it's a great opportunity to find out more about local folklore and wildlife.

Further afield, there's also an attractive waterfall at **Oworobong**, about 90 minutes' drive south along a rough road (shared taxis are erratic but you can hire a private taxi to do the return trip for around US$20). Tafo and Oworobong are the focus of a new ecotourism project that runs overnight trips to the Kwahu Plateau out of Accra, staying in local homesteads and meeting local chiefs at around US$50 a head – ideal for tourists who want to see rural Ghana but have limited time. For further details, check out their website, www.geocities.com/apexmediagh, or use ☏ 024 753755/998136 or 021 242762, or **e** kwasisam@yahoo.com.

Tafo is connected to Mpraeso by regular tro-tros via Asakraka and Bepon, which cost around US$0.50. There are a couple of basic guesthouses in tow, including the shabby **Middle East Hotel**. The Traditional Council Office is a good source of local travel information, as is the Galaxy Bar on the Adowso road, not far from the police station. Otherwise, a trip to the chief's palace may result in one of his sons willingly showing you the highlights of Tafo.

ADOWSO Situated at the northern base of the Kwahu Plateau, Adowso is the most important port on this part of the Lake Volta shore, linked to Ekye on the Afram Plains by a thrice-daily motor ferry (see box *Crossing Lake Volta via the Afram Plains,* page 286). Because of the ferry, Adowso is a busy town, with a constant stream of traffic travelling to and from the ferry jetty along the Kwahu Tafo road, mainly lorries or tro-tros carrying produce or people to and from markets on the Afram Plains. There's no formal accommodation in Adowso, nor any absolute reason why you'd need it, but if you do feel like spending the night, it should be easy enough to arrange a room privately. Canoe trips can be arranged on to the lake (ask down by the ferry terminal) and there may be possibilities of hiring a guide for trips on to the escarpment to see the teak forests and other sites. The chief in Adowso is very welcoming as is the Assembly Man who runs a bar in the main road through the town. For hikers, the escarpment above Adowso can be climbed following a steep track, from where footpaths can be taken to Asikiman then along the Asuboni River to Kwahu Tafo. Alternatively the road can be followed to the last borehole before Tafo at Nkyenenkyene (pronounced 'enchinni-enchinni') and on to Kwahu Tafo itself.

CAPE COAST TO KUMASI

The shortest route between the coast and Kumasi is the surfaced road which branches from the main coastal highway at Yamoransa, about 1km west of Biriwa and 7km east of Cape Coast. Direct buses between Cape Coast and Kumasi take three to four hours. I'm not aware of any sightseeing along the way. At Yamoransa itself, **Sammy's Hillside Lodge** has decent rooms with a fan in the US$3–4 range, though it's difficult to conceive of any circumstance under which a tourist might want to stay here.

TAKORADI TO KUMASI

The port of Takoradi is connected to Kumasi by a popular overnight train service, which currently leaves in either direction at 20.30 , theoretically arriving at 07.30 the following day, stopping at Tarkwa and Obuasi *en route*. In reality, the trains usually leave anything from an hour late, and make so many unscheduled stops that you are more likely to reach your destination just in time for lunch – and we have had one report of a journey that lasted 50 hours – but those with flexible schedules speak highly of the trip. Tickets can be booked only on the day of departure. Unless you are seriously strapped for cash or a hardened masochist, it's well worth paying the additional fare for a first-class sleeper with fan, which costs US$4.50 at the time of writing. The second-class carriages get unbelievably hot and sticky, and all classes are subjected to bone-rattling bumpiness as the train clunks over the tracks.

For those looking for speedier travel, Takoradi and Kumasi are also connected by a good surfaced road passing through Tarkwa, Begoro, and Obuasi. STC and other buses run directly between Takoradi and Kumasi. It is also possible to cover the route in stages using the tro-tros that connect all the towns listed above. The lush scenery along the way is not without some appeal, but none of the towns on this road are regularly visited by tourists, nor do they boast much in the way of recognised attractions.

TARKWA Set in the rainforest inland of Takoradi, this large town is the commercial and industrial hub of a region rich in gold, diamonds and manganese. Although infrequently visited by travellers, Tarkwa has unexpectedly good tourist facilities which cater mainly to local businessmen and the substantial contingent of expatriates who work at the various mines in the area. Lush surrounds and some interesting colonial architecture notwithstanding, it would be difficult to make much of a case for Tarkwa as a tourist attraction, though with advance notice it is possible to arrange tours of the gold mine at Prestea, 18km away, and the manganese works at Nsuta, 6km from Tarkwa.

Should you find yourself in Tarkwa, one possible excursion is to the artificial lake at Tarkwa Banso, 45 minutes' walk (or a short tro-tro ride) from the town centre. The lake itself is nothing very special, but the walk there leads through some attractive green scenery, and a small local bar on the lakeshore is a pleasant place for a drink. A second lake lies another ten minutes' walk from Tarkwa Banso – anybody will be able to direct you.

Getting there and away Tarkwa lies about 90km from Takoradi by road; to get there you need to head westwards along the coastal road before turning right at a signposted junction a short distance past Agona. The surfaced road is in fair condition and can be covered in an hour in a private vehicle, or about 90 minutes by tro-tro. The road between Tarkwa and Kumasi via Obuasi is also surfaced and covered by regular buses and tro-tros. There are direct buses between Tarkwa and Accra, but they are rather slow, so far better to catch a local tro-tro between Takoradi and Tarkwa and use the hourly STC bus between Takoradi and Accra.

All trains between Kumasi and Takoradi stop at Tarkwa. Northbound trains arrive at around midnight, and southbound trains at around 04.30 in the morning. If you want to book a first-class sleeper out of Tarkwa, the station master will phone your reservation through to either Takoradi or Kumasi. The passenger train service between Takoradi, Tarkwa, and Accra was suspended in 2000 and is unlikely to resume in the foreseeable future.

Where to stay
Moderate
🏠 **Lynka Hotel** ☎ 0362 20412. Situated about 1km from the town centre along the bizarrely named Low Cost Road, this 2-star hotel is officially the only tourist-class lodging in Tarkwa – although some reports suggest that the service doesn't quite live up to that standard. Facilities inc a generator & private water supply, as well as a good restaurant. *Comfortable rooms with AC, hot water & DSTV cost a negotiable US$35 inc b/fast.*

Budget
🏠 **Get in Touch Hotel** ☎ 0362 20592. This is another reliable central option offering clean, comfortable self-contained rooms with AC & TV. An attractive feature of this hotel is the rooftop bar & restaurant with views over the surrounding hills. *US$13–21.*

🏠 **J. Tandoah Hotel** ☎ 0362 20387. Well signposted & on a shared taxi route, this is probably the best value of any budget or shoestring hotel in Tarkwa provided you don't mind the location – about 2km from the town centre in the suburb of Kwabedu. There is a bar & restaurant. Clean sgl rooms with a dbl bed & fan, some have DSTV and are self-contained. *Sgl US$10–15, twin with AC & DSTV US$22.*

🏠 **Morning Light Hotel** ☎ 0362 20355. This good budget hotel lies just off the Accra road about 500m from the railway & tro-tro station. B/fast and other meals are available on request, but the dining room is rather cramped & stuffy. Clean, carpeted dbl rooms, all self-contained with AC, hot bath & TV. *US$15–25.*

🏠 **Peace Hotel** ☎ 0362 20557. Comparatively overpriced, this hotel is located on a dirt road behind the hospital. An attraction for some will be the disco, though this functions only at w/ends. *Dbl with AC & fan US$20–30.*

Shoestring
🏠 **Adom Lodge Hotel** Close to the market, this functional multi-storey block lacks character but has very reasonably priced accommodation at similar rates to the Golden Home.

🏠 **Golden Home Hotel** ☎ 0362 20583. The outstanding place in this range, this is set along a side road near the market & has a homely, friendly atmosphere & clean, comfortable rooms with fans. *US$6 with communal showers & US$11 self-contained.*

🏠 **Railview Hotel** The only other option in this range is situated in the heart of the long-haul lorry station & directly opposite the railway station. While this location couldn't be more convenient for catching public transport, it is also very noisy. If that doesn't worry you, the rooms with fan are adequate & acceptable value. Prices vary depending on whether rooms are sgl, dbl or self-contained. *US$6.50–14.*

✖ **Where to eat** The air-conditioned **Sag Food Joint**, which lies along a short side road opposite the Barclays Bank, serves a wide range of Western and Ghanaian dishes (pizzas, pastas, curries and seafood, mostly for less than US$3.50), and is also a good place for breakfast. It stocks a selection of fresh snacks and imported fruit juice and chocolate.

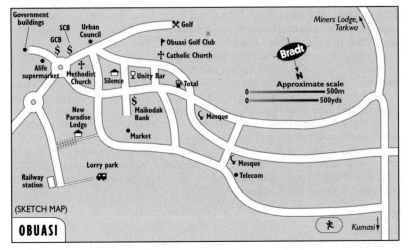

Government
buildings
SCB   Urban
GCB   Council
Alife
supermarket   Methodist
Church   Silence   Unity Bar
New
Paradise
Lodge
Maikodak
Bank
Market
Lorry park
Railway
station

✕ Golf
♭ Obuasi Golf Club
✝ Catholic Church

☾ Mosque

☾ Mosque
● Telecom

Miners Lodge,
Tarkwa

Bradt

N

Approximate scale
0 ━━━━━━━ 500m
0 ━━━━━━━ 500yds

(SKETCH MAP)

OBUASI

Kumasi ▼

Most of the hotels also have restaurants attached – the rooftop at the **Get in Touch Hotel** is perhaps the pick, at least in terms of atmosphere – and there are plenty of chop shops around the lorry station and market. For a night out, check whether the **Astoria Bar** next to the Golden Home Hotel is hosting any live music or other performances.

BEGOSO Straddling the main tar road towards Obuasi, Begoso is a small, bustling market town set in a lushly forested area about 50km north of Tarkwa. I'm not aware of any particular tourist attractions around Begoso, but the surrounding countryside must have some potential for walking and birding well away from any beaten tourist trail. Any road transport between Tarkwa and Obuasi can drop you in Begoso, where the **American House Hotel** offers reasonably priced, self-contained accommodation with air conditioning.

OBUASI Situated some 85km south of Kumasi, Obuasi is Ghana's most important gold-mining centre and the home of the AngloGold Ashanti mining company. Despite an attractive setting in a valley ringed by verdant hills, this town of 400,000 inhabitants couldn't have much less going for it aesthetically, presenting itself to the tourist as a large sprawl of concrete dwellings and 'shops'. It is, however, an excellent place to buy locally produced gold jewellery, or – if you want to steer away from the usual *adinkra* symbols – to buy the gold dust and design it yourself. There's also an attractive golf course behind the Catholic church. In Patakro, on the Kumasi road about 10km north of Obuasi, lies the most southerly of the extant 19th-century *Obosomfies* (Ashanti shrine houses) and, in front of it, four statues of similar vintage.

Interesting guided tours of AngloGold Ashanti can be organised through the visitors' centre, for US$15 for an above ground tour or US$25 below ground. With a private vehicle, this is straightforward, as you can drive directly to the visitors' centre and find a guide there. But taxis are forbidden from driving between the entrance gate and the visitors' centre, and it would be very far to walk (assuming that you are allowed too), which means that you have to wait for an occasional vehicle of the mining company to take you there. The same procedure starts again the moment you want to get from the visitors' centre to the actual mine, and also on the way back out, which can mean a lot of waiting for transport. If you ring in advance (✆ *0582 40494 ext. 4309*), then you may be permitted to drive to the visitors' centre in a taxi.

Getting there and away Obuasi is easy to reach, connected to Kumasi by regular minibus-taxis (*US$1; 1¹/₂ hours*), and to Tarkwa and Takoradi by less frequent buses. All trains between Takoradi and Kumasi stop at the railway station.

Where to stay and eat The best hotel in Obuasi is the two-star Coconut Grove **Miners Lodge** (↘ *0582 40550/1 or 024 4425958;* **e** *minerslodge@coconutgrovehotels. com.gh; www.coconutgrovehotels.com.gh*), the sister hotel of other Coconut Grove establishments in Elmina and Accra. Comfortable rooms with AC, DSTV and hot water are reasonably priced at US$40/50 for single/double, with an additional 5% charge for credit card or travellers' cheque payments. The hotel is also happy to arrange mine tours with AngloGold, and an attached restaurant serves excellent food priced between US$5 and US$10 per main course.

Other tourist-class hotels which have been recommended by readers include **Victoria Gardens Guest House** (↘ *0582 40763*) and the **Anyinam Lodge** (↘ *0582 40439*), which is owned by the mine but run as a private enterprise. The best bet in the budget category is the **Silence Hotel**, which lies no more than five minutes' walk from the lorry station via the market and has a variety of double rooms with fans ranging in price from US$6–12 depending on whether they are self-contained and have a fridge. Cheaper still, **New Paradise Lodge** next to the lorry station is neither new nor conspicuously paradisiacal, but if run-down and seedy don't worry you, it is difficult to argue with a room rate of US$2.50.

The **Silence Hotel** serves decent local grub, while the **Golf Restaurant**, next to the golf course, and the Coconut Grove Miners' Lodge serve more Westernised dishes and are popular with expatriates working at the mines.

13

Volunteer with Onechild

Onechild is a registered charity set up by former British volunteers at schools in the Ashanti Region

We link volunteers with host schools in several villages and support them in helping make a difference to the lives of young Ghanaians

There are no administration fees and we are flexible to the volunteers' needs and wishes

For more information visit **www.onechild.org.uk** email **info@onechild.org.uk**

REG CHARITY No. 1115081

14

Kumasi

Ghana's second city, with a population approaching one and a half million, Kumasi is not only the modern capital of Ashanti Region, but has also for three centuries served as royal capital of the Ashanti state. Tradition has it that the city was founded by the first Asantehene, Nana Osei Tutu, who relocated there from his former capital at Kwaman in 1695. Kumasi rapidly acquired the status of largest and most important city in the Ghanaian interior, and was the inland terminus of most of the major 18th-century slave-trading routes to the coast.

Accounts by early 19th-century visitors to Kumasi suggest it must once have been a spacious, attractive city of whitewashed buildings with steep thatched roofs. In the latter part of the century, however, Kumasi became the focus of hostilities between aspirant British colonists and the Ashanti. The old city was burnt to the ground by Sir Garnet Wolseley in 1873, resulting in the Anglo-Ashanti Peace Treaty of March 1874 and a period of prolonged infighting within the Ashanti state. Following the Yaa Asantewaa War of 1900–01, Kumasi (or Kumase as it was then spelt) was annexed to the British Gold Coast colony on 1 January 1902.

Today, contrary to any expectations conjured up by the epithet 'Ancient Ashanti Capital', your first impression upon arriving in Kumasi, particularly if you disembark near Kejetia Circle, is less likely to be rustic traditionalism than daunting developing world urbanity. Kumasi is one of the most hectic cities I've visited in Africa, far busier than Accra, and the mood is emphatically modern: the surging throngs of humanity and constant traffic jams that emanate in every direction from the market and lorry station feel positively overwhelming if you arrive from the relatively provincial, traditionalist north of Ghana.

Still, Kumasi ranks in most people's books as one of Ghana's 'must-sees', and what the city centre, known as Adum, lacks for in terms of traditional architecture buildings – 'historical Kumasi' amounts to little more than the late 19th-century fort and a cluster of colonial-era buildings in Adum – is made up for by a number of fascinating small museums (see *Exploring Kumasi* on page 307), and any number of day or overnight trips, as detailed in the chapter *Greater Ashanti* (see page 313).

PRACTICAL INFORMATION

GETTING THERE AND AWAY The most reliable road transport between Accra and Kumasi are the STC coaches that leave 13 times daily in either direction, between 04.30 and 16.00 or three times on Sundays at 12.30, 13.30 and 16.00. The standard coaches cost US$6, while express coaches with air conditioning cost US$7.50. The route used by the buses is via Nsawam, Suhum, Kibi and Nkawkaw. You can ask to disembark from the bus before Kumasi, but will still have to pay the full fare. Depending on the traffic in Accra, the journey takes four to five hours.

In addition to the Accra service, two STC buses leave for Tamale daily at 07.00 and 17.00, except on Sundays when the only bus leaves at 10.00. Tickets cost

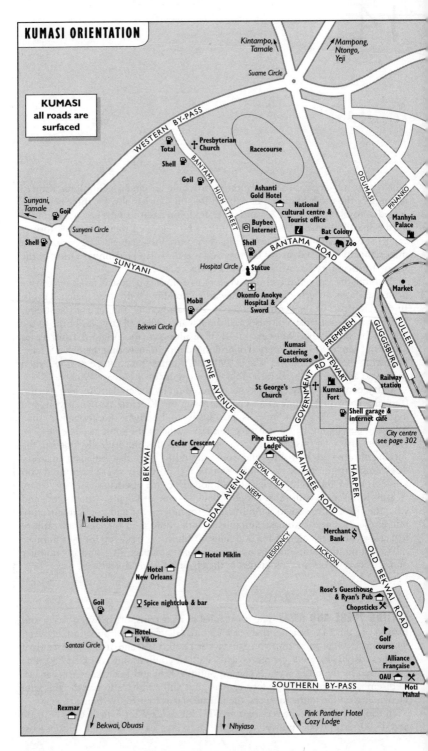

KUMASI ORIENTATION

KUMASI
all roads are
surfaced

Kintampo,
Tamale

Mampong,
Ntongo,
Yeji

Suame Circle

WESTERN BY-PASS

Total

Presbyterian
Church

Racecourse

Shell

BANTAMA HIGH STREET

Goil

Ashanti
Gold Hotel

National
cultural centre &
Tourist office

ODUMASI

PINANKO

Sunyani,
Tamale

Goil

Sunyani Circle

Shell

SUNYANI

Buybee
Internet

Shell

Bat Colony

Zoo

BANTAMA ROAD

Manhyia
Palace

Hospital Circle

Statue

Market

Mobil

Okomfo Anokye
Hospital &
Sword

Bekwai Circle

FULLER

GUGGISBURG

PREMPREH II

Kumasi
Catering
Guesthouse

STEWART

GOVERNMENT RD

Railway
station

PINE AVENUE

St George's
Church

Kumasi
Fort

Shell garage &
internet cafe

BEKWAI

Cedar Crescent

Pine Executive
Lodge

City centre
see page 302

ROYAL PALM

CEDAR AVENUE

NEEM

RAINTREE ROAD

HARPER

Television mast

RESIDENCY

Merchant
Bank

JACKSON

OLD BEKWAI ROAD

Hotel Miklin

Hotel
New Orleans

Rose's Guesthouse
& Ryan's Pub

Chopsticks

Goil

Spice nightclub & bar

Golf
course

Hotel
le Vikus

Santasi Circle

Alliance
Française

OAU

Moti
Mahal

SOUTHERN BY-PASS

Rexmar

Bekwai, Obuasi

Nhyiaso

Pink Panther Hotel
Cozy Lodge

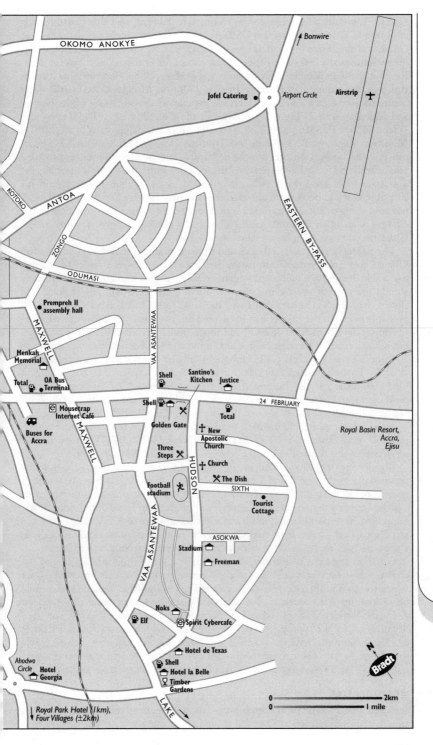

OKOMO ANOKYE

↑ Bonwire

Jofel Catering ● Airport Circle   Airstrip ✈

KOTOKO

ANTOA

ZONGO

ODUMASI

EASTERN BY-PASS

VAA ASANTEWAA

MAXWELL

● Prempreh II assembly hall

Menkah Memorial 🏛

Total 🅿   OA Bus Terminal

ⓔ Mousetrap Internet Café

🚌 Buses for Accra

Shell 🅿

Shell 🅿🏛 Santino's Kitchen   Justice 🅿

24 FEBRUARY

✕
Golden Gate   Total 🅿

† New Apostolic Church

Three Steps ✕

† Church

✕ The Dish

HUDSON

Football stadium 🕴

SIXTH

● Tourist Cottage

VAA ASANTEWAA

ASOKWA

Stadium 🏛

🏠 Freeman

Royal Basin Resort, Accra, Ejisu

Noks 🏠

🅿 Elf   ⓔ Spirit Cybercafe

🏠 Hotel de Texas

Ahodwo Circle Hotel Georgia 🏠

🅿 Shell   🏠 Hotel la Belle
🍷 Timber Gardens

↓ Royal Park Hotel (1km), Four Villages (±2km)

LAKE

N

Bradt

0 ———————— 2km
0 ———————— 1 mile

US$10. Two daily STC buses connect Kumasi to Takoradi via Cape Coast, leaving at 04.00 and 12.00 and charged at US$7.50 taking three to four hours to reach Cape Coast, and about five to reach Takoradi. A daily STC bus to Bawku via Bolgatanga leaves Kumasi at 11.00 (US$14) every day except for Friday, while a bus for Tema leaves at 13.30 on Mondays, Wednesdays and Fridays (US$8). International services run to Ouagadougou in Burkina Faso at 17.00 on Mondays, Wednesdays and Saturdays – costing US$22 plus CFA500 payable on the other side of the border, and taking around 24 hours; to Abidjan in the Côte d'Ivoire at 04.00 every day except Sunday (US$16 plus CFA9,000); and Aflao at the Togo border at 21.00 on Mondays, Tuesdays, Wednesdays and Thursdays for US$12. Seats on STC buses can only be booked on the date of departure, and in my experience, provided you're at the STC station 30 minutes ahead of departure time, you'll normally get a seat. Services are greatly reduced on Sundays and public holidays, and it's advisable to try to book as far ahead as possible over holiday periods. If booking is not your thing or you are keeping a serious eye on costs, the OA bus station on the Accra road is open 24 hours, and runs slightly cheaper services to most major Ghanaian cities on an 'it leaves when its full' basis.

The rail service between Takoradi and Kumasi, stopping at Tarkwa, Dunkwa and Obuasi, was quite popular with travellers prior to its suspension in May 2006, ostensibly due to high fuel costs, which – if true – means it might possibly resume should the current reverse in crude oil prices continue. Assuming it does, it is slower than the STC buses that cover the same route, but also a lot cheaper and probably safer. (In the past, one train covered this route daily in either direction, an overnight sleeper that left at 20.30 and theoretically arrived at 07.30 the next day, but seldom made it through before lunchtime and had been known to take up to 50 hours in total.) Tickets could be bought only on the day of departure, starting at 05.30. First-class sleeper tickets, for a two-berth compartment, cost a bargain US$4.50, although the bumpy tracks and apparent lack of suspension often prevented much sleeping. No meals were available, and the selection of food on sale at stations was limited, though the dining car did sell drinks and biscuits.

An altogether swifter alternative is to take a domestic flight (see *Travelling in Ghana*, page 71). Both Antrak (✆ 051 41296) and CityLink (✆ 051 39267) run twice-daily services between Kumasi and Accra, costing US$84 and US$75, respectively.

Regular tro-tros leave Kumasi in practically every direction. Tro-tros for destinations to the north and west generally leave from Kejetia Station, which is situated below the traffic circle of the same name and – following recent renovations – is also very easy to find your way around, with the termini for all destinations clearly signposted. Transport heading south and east – for instance to Accra, Lake Bosumtwi and Cape Coast – leaves from Asafo Station on Fuller Road, an area known locally as Cape Coast due to the influx of workers from that city who come to live here.

For short trips out of Kumasi, you can waste a lot of time milling around the chaotic bus station (and more still in the constant traffic jams that surround it), for which reason it is often easier to catch a shared taxi to a suitable junction and gamble on picking up a tro-tro there. For Ejisu, Effiduase and other destinations east of Accra, the corner of Fuller Road and the Accra road is a good place to stand. For other destinations, try the appropriate circle on the ring road – Santasi Circle for Bekwai or Obuasi, Sunyani Road Roundabout for Owabi Wildlife Sanctuary, Suame Circle for Mampong, etc. The risk attached to doing this is that everything that comes past will be full, but I've yet to wait more than five minutes for a vehicle to stop.

WHERE TO STAY There must be more than a hundred hotels and guesthouses scattered around Kumasi and its suburbs, most of them smart but bland set-ups aimed at business travellers. The following listings represent a few reliable bets in each category, but new recommendations are welcomed. All the hotels at the upper end of the scale take Visa, and some take MasterCard where mentioned.

Upmarket

🏠 **Cedar Crescent Hotel** ☎ 051 27238; **f** 051 27239; **e** dankaitoo@yahoo.com. Situated off Cedar Av in the leafy suburb of Ridge, this well-managed hotel has large, attractively furnished rooms with AC, satellite TV, & minibar. A good restaurant & bar are attached, & a swimming pool is planned by 2008. *Dbl/suite with balcony US$55/70.*

🏠 **Four Villages Inn** ☎ 051 22682 or 027 7403603; **e** scottash@hotmail.com; www.fourvillages.com. Unless you actively favour the impersonality that characterises most other hotels in this range, the award-winning Four Villages Inn is undoubtedly the most alluring & individualistic upmarket option in Kumasi, & it has received the highest praise from the many readers of previous editions who have stayed there. Situated on the Old Bekwai Rd, 2.8km past Ahodwo Circle, the lodge is owned & managed by a helpful Ghanaian-Canadian couple, & is furnished with books & photographs that give it the feel of a family home. The accommodation consists of 4 spacious self-contained dbl rooms with AC, minibar, DSTV & VCR, as well as a homely common lounge & dining room, & a shady patio overlooking the compact green gardens. Facilities inc on-site internet access, a great selection of free videos, golf cub hire, complimentary tea & coffee, free airport & STC pick-up by prior arrangement, & delicious home-cooked meals by request. *The rates of US$60/70/80 sgl/dbl/trpl inc a substantial b/fast.*

🏠 **Hotel Georgia** ☎ 051 23915. Situated off Ahodwo Roundabout, this multi-storey 3-star monolith is suitable for package groups, with more than 30 rooms, & it has reasonable facilities inc a large swimming pool (open to day visitors for US$5). It is somewhat characterless & frayed. *Self-contained sgl/dbl with DSTV & AC US$50/65, sgl/dbl chalet US$120/150.*

🏠 **Hotel Rexmar** (17 rooms) ☎ 051 29111/181/367; **f** 051 29366; **e** rexmar@africaonline.com.gh. Probably the best of Kumasi's numerous conventional upmarket hotels, the Rexmar is situated a few hundred metres south of Santasi Circle, where its 17 rooms with DSTV, AC & minibar cater primarily to business travellers. Facilities inc a large swimming pool, an efficient business centre & a good restaurant specialising in charcoal-grilled meat. Visa & MasterCard are accepted. *Sgl/dbl US$76/90.*

🏠 **Pink Panther Hotel** ☎ 051 38341; **f** 051 29296; **e** pinkpantherhotel@yahoo.com. Set in large landscaped grounds in the suburb of Adiebra, outside the circle road, this large new 3-star hotel easily matches its more established rivals, provided that you can deal with the eerie blue-lit reception area. Facilities inc a conference centre, international restaurant, jazz bar (occasional live music), business centre & DSTV with in-house video. A swimming pool is planned. *Dbl US$80.*

🏠 **Royal Basin Resort** (15 rooms) ☎ 051 60144/68; **f** 051 60169; **e** rbasin@africaonline.com.gh. This popular 3-star hotel, situated 10km out of town on the Accra road, has comfortable AC rooms with DSTV, & excellent facilities including a swimming pool, gym & jazz club. Highly recommended. *Sgl/dbl US$65/85.*

🏠 **Royal Park Hotel** ☎ 051 33388 or 024 413138; **f** 051 25584. Also in Adiebra, about 500m past Ahodwo Circle, this comfortable new hotel charges US$60/70/80 for a self-contained sgl/dbl/suite with AC & DSTV. The attached Chinese restaurant serves authentic dishes from US$5.50, & an excellent set menu costs US$24 for 2. *US$60/70/80.*

Moderate

🏠 **Ashanti Gold Hotel** (25 rooms) **e** ashgoldhotel@ yahoo.com, www.ashantigoldhotel.com. The winner of several local tourism awards, this affordable 2-star hotel is conveniently located behind the National Cultural Centre. Its self-contained rooms with AC have been praised by several readers. *US$18–35.*

🏠 **Fosua Hotel** ☎ 051 37382/7; **f** 051 37387; **e** fosuahotel@myway.com; www.fosuahotel.com. Situated in Adum, about 100m from the STC bus station, this smart hotel on the fourth floor of Aseda House offers the most central upmarket accommodation in Kumasi. All rooms are clean & comfortable, with hot water, DSTV, minibar & AC, but the sgls are a bit cramped at the price. Facilities inc an elevator & 24-hour standby generator, & the building houses a good restaurant, coffee shop, internet café, travel agent, beauty salon & clinic. Visa accepted. *Self-contained sgl/dbl with glazed balcony US$43/48, suite US$90.*

🏠 **Hotel New Orleans** ☎ 051 25966. Roughly 3km from the city centre along Cedar Av, this is a large & pleasant enough hotel. The garden bar & restaurant look good too. *Large, carpeted, self-contained dbl with AC & DSTV US$30, suite US$40.*

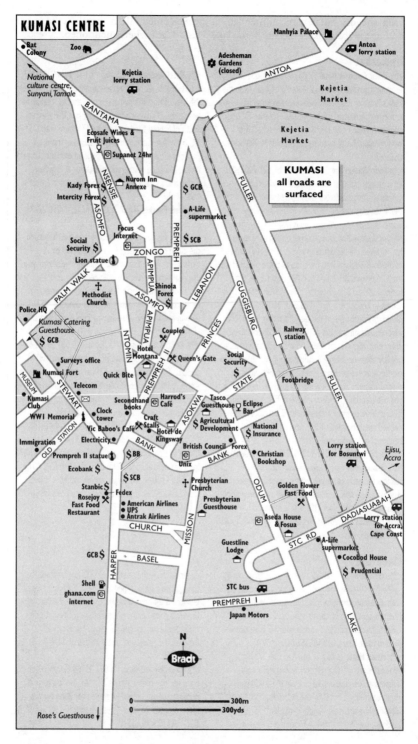

KUMASI CENTRE

Bat Colony
Zoo
National culture centre, Sunyani, Tamale
Kejetia lorry station
BANTAMA
Ecosafe Wines & Fruit Juices
Supanet 24hr
Kady Forex
Intercity Forex
NSENSIE
Nurom Inn Annexe
ASOMFO
Focus Internet
Social Security
Lion statue
ZONGO
APIMPUA
PALM WALK
Methodist Church
Police HQ
ASOMFO
Shinola Forex
Kumasi Catering Guesthouse
GCB
Surveys office
Kumasi Fort
NTOMIN
Telecom
Kumasi Club
WWI Memorial
MUSEUM
STEWART
Clock tower
Secondhand books
Harrod's Café
Vic Baboo's Café
Craft Stalls
Electricity
Hotel de Kingsway
Immigration
OLD STATION
Prempreh II statue
BANK
BB
Ecobank
SCB
Stanbic
Fedex
Rosejoy Fast Food Restaurant
American Airlines
UPS
Antrak Airlines
CHURCH
HARPER
GCB
BASEL
Shell
ghana.com internet
MISSION
Presbyterian Church
Presbyterian Guesthouse
Guestline Lodge
STC bus
PREMPREH I
Japan Motors

Manhyia Palace
Antoa lorry station
Adesheman Gardens (closed)
ANTOA
Kejetia Market
Kejetia Market
FULLER
KUMASI all roads are surfaced
GCB
A-Life supermarket
SCB
PREMPREH II
LEBANON
GUGGISBURG
Railway station
PRINCES
Couples
Hotel Montana
Queen's Gate
Social Security
STATE
Quick Bite
Footbridge
Tasco Guesthouse
Eclipse Bar
ASOKWA
Agricultural Development
National Insurance
British Council Forex
BANK
Unix
Christian Bookshop
ODUM
Golden Flower Fast Food
Aseda House & Fosua
STC RD
A-Life supermarket
Cocobod House
Prudential
DADIASUABAH
Lorry station for Bosuntwi
Ejisu, Accra
Lorry station for Accra, Cape Coast
LAKE

N
Bradt

0   300m
0   300yds

Rose's Guesthouse ↓

Kumasi Catering Guesthouse 051 26506; f 051 23656; e kcrhouse@yahoo.com. This venerable former government hotel lies in an attractive green compound a short walk south of the central Stewart Avenue. An inexpensive restaurant is attached & there are also a pool & beauty salon in the grounds. The large old dbl rooms with fan & DSTV are excellent value. There are also smart chalet-like dbl rooms in the new block with AC & DSTV or suites. It's popular with local businessmen, & quite often full, so it's worth ringing in advance. *Dbl US$20–45, suite US$70–100.*

Noks Hotel 051 24438; f 051 24162. Set in large, flowering gardens in a quiet suburb off Hudson Rd, this 2-star hotel is one of the best deals in its range. A fair restaurant is attached. Visa & MasterCard are accepted. *Dbl with AC & DSTV US$35/44/50 for a sgl/dbl/'executive suite'.*

Budget

Guestline Lodge 051 22128 or 27657; e mahesh161us@yahoo.com. Under the same management as the popular Vic Baboo's Café, this backpacker-oriented lodge attracts plenty of travellers but receives mixed feedback, with the broad consensus being that it is very friendly but the rooms could be cleaner & seem poor value at the asking price. It is conveniently located in an old triple-storey house in Adum, decorated with black stars & accessed through the back of the STC bus station. The dormitories are a better bet than the cell-like, sweaty sgls. Facilities inc a book-swap service, a good gift shop, luggage storage, laundry & 24-hour hot/cold drinks. At the time of writing, b/fast is prepared on site, while lunch & dinner can be delivered from Vic Baboo's, which offers a 5% discount to lodge residents. *Dormitory bed with fan US$5.50, large sgl/dbl with fan US$7/10, self-contained sgl/dbl with AC US$14/30.*

Hotel de Kingsway 051 26228. The most central option in this range, the venerable Hotel de Kingsway lies in the heart of Adum diagonally opposite Vic Baboo's Café. It's an adequate fallback but none too clean & a

Shoestring

Freeman Hotel 051 24880. Situated on Harper Rd, this sprawling guesthouse has a quiet location & its stuffy but clean dbl rooms with fan are good value. *Dbl with common shower US$6, self-contained US$8–12.*

Menkah Memorial Hotel 051 26432. This cheap but rather scruffy hotel lies on the Accra road about 1km from the city centre. Try to get a room facing away from the noisy road below. *Basic dbl rooms with fan & common showers US$6.50, self-contained dbl US$8.50, or US$10 on the top floor.*

Pine Executive Lodge 051 26566; f 051 26103. This very pleasant lodge lies on Pine Rd, a short taxi drive from the city centre. *Huge dbl room with AC, fan, hot bath & DSTV US$25.*

Rose's Guesthouse (14 rooms) 051 32594; f 051 23500; e consulgames@yahoo.com. Situated along the Old Bekwai Rd, a short taxi ride from town, Rose's has long been a popular choice with relatively well-heeled travellers & the large self-contained dbl & twin rooms with AC, DSTV & fridge seem okay value. Following a recent change of management, the adjacent pub has been replaced with the gaudy Vienna City, which serves adequate food & a good range of drinks, but is overrun with prostitutes at night. *US$35–40.*

bit overpriced. Prices vary depending on size & whether they have AC or TV. *Dbl with common shower from US$12, self-contained dbl with fan & hot water US$16–24.*

Justice Hotel 051 22525. More inherently appealing than the Kingsway, the long-serving Justice Hotel lies on the Accra road close to a rank where you can easily pick up shared taxis & tro-tros into the city centre or out towards Ejisu. The attached restaurant & garden bar look at best serviceable, but there are plenty of other places to eat & drink in the area. *Clean self-contained dbls with fan US$12, sgl/dbl with AC US$17–18.*

Sanbra Hotel Several readers have recommended this affordable hotel, which is centrally located on Prempeh II Street, not far from Kejetia Market. The popular restaurant serves Ghanaian & international cuisines. Good value. *Self-contained dbl with AC US$23.*

Stadium Hotel 051 23647; f 051 23730. Situated a short distance south of the stadium down the tree-lined Asokwa Road off Hudson Road, this comfortable hotel is decent value. All rooms have TV & a good restaurant is attached. *Large self-contained dbl with AC US$32, dbl (twin beds) with fan/AC US$22/26.*

Nurom Inn Annexe 024 4383166. Situated on Nsensie Rd closer to Kejetia Market & lorry station, this rather basic but adequately clean hotel offers what is one of the cheapest lodgings in Kumasi. *Sgl US$5.50, dbl US$6.50–8.50.*

Presbyterian Guesthouse 051 23879. With its wide wooden balconies overlooking the leafy grounds of the Basel Mission, this ramshackle, colonial-era building has long been one of the most important backpacker crossroads in the Ghanaian interior. But all that comes at a cost: the basic rooms are not terribly clean, & are certainly steep in price. A number of readers have also complained about grumpy, unwilling staff. *US$8 with fan or US$15 with AC, all using common showers.*

🏠 **Samaritan Villa Guesthouse** ☎ 051 235593. Assuming that you don't mind staying out of town, this

clean little guesthouse in the tranquil, leafy grounds of St Hubert's Seminary, is easily the best value accommodation in the city. Private taxis will drop you to the hotel, or you can get a share taxi 1km south of Santasi Circle down the Obuasi road & ask to drop at the junction. *Immaculate self-contained room with lounge costs US$7–12, & substantial b/fast US$2.*

✕ WHERE TO EAT AND DRINK

Adum (city centre) There are surprisingly few places to eat out in central Kumasi, and most of what is on offer tends to be geared to local rather than international palates and budgets, the main exception – at least where variety is concerned – being the superb Vic Baboo's Café. Most restaurants in Adum close on Sundays.

✕ **Aseda House** This new 4-storey building near the STC bus station contains a few upmarket places to eat & drink, including the AC **Tiwaah Restaurant** (*good Chinese & continental in the US$4–6 range*), the cosy **Second World Coffee Bar** (which does exactly what it says on the tin, with a menu of filter coffee, cappuccino, fruit juice, burgers & sandwiches) & the smart **Appiah Cocktail Bar**.

✕ **Couples Restaurant** This family-run first-floor restaurant on Prempreh II St, accessed up a dark staircase off Apimpua Rd, boasts an extensive menu of Ghanaian & Western dishes for around US$3, together with very friendly staff & a most competent chef. The chicken & jollof rice comes recommended – & do ask to be served on the balcony as the evening draws in & the lights come on.

🍸 **Eclipse Bar** Situated on Adum Rd downhill from the Tasco Guesthouse, this is another pleasant drinking hole that serves reasonable local meals in the US$2–3 range. It's as near as you'll get to an affordable Western-style bar set-up outside Accra, although there is a mark-up on beer prices. It's a mainly local clientele, with a fair bit of dancing.

✕ **Funkies** ☎ 027 7873400. Another highly recommended pizza joint, located at Apino Plaza near Kapital Rd Junction, Funkies is run by a Ghanaian who used to live in the US. The restaurant is known for its excellent pizzas – indeed one reader rates them as the 'best in West Africa' – & a chilled-out local crowd. There's a decent wine shop in the complex if you fancy some wine with your meal. *Expect to pay around US$6 for a pizza.*

✕ **Golden Flower Fast Food** Another good central option, this restaurant on Guggisburg Rd serves the usual combination of Chinese & other meat/chicken dishes. So far as I'm aware, this is the only sit-down restaurant in Adum that opens on Sun (though based on our last Sun visit, you'll need a pretty high tolerance level for wailing cod-gospel music to want to spend much longer here than it takes to gulp down a meal). *Around US$3 per heaped plate.*

🍸 **Kenny Joe's** Situated near the corner of Palm Walk & Nsensie Rd (near Emmanuel Forex Bureau), this pleasant pavement bar also serves decent local meals. *Around US$1.50–2 per plate.*

✕ **Nick's Pizza Place** This new restaurant tucked away behind the Old Bekwai Rd has been recommended by a number of readers for excellent pizzas which are available to eat al fresco at the restaurant or to take away. The restaurant is signposted on the right hand side of Old Bekwai Rd as you come from Ahodwo circle (near the Hotel Georgia). Follow the turn off for 250m, then take a left & walk the same distance again. *Expect to pay US$4.50 for a large pizza.*

🍸 **Old Timer's Bar** Part of the Hotel de Kingsway, this is one of the most pleasant drinking holes in the city centre – admittedly rather dead on w/days, but sometimes thriving on Sat.

✕ **Queen's Gate Restaurant** This is another one accessed up an inauspicious staircase, but the restaurant itself feels surprisingly upmarket in an 1980s kinda way, & is a great spot for people-watching with a cocktail or a cool beer. The restaurant serves Ghanaian standards for around US$3.50, or delicious Chinese & fish for around US$6 – which can be eaten inside where the AC is blasting, or outside on a breezy balcony that runs the length of the restaurant. VAT is charged extra.

✕ **Sweet Bite** This Lebanese restaurant on Ahowjo Rd is a great spot for mezze, or a falafel wrap for around US$4.

✕ **Vic Baboo's Café** This central & perennially popular restaurant has a menu that would take weeks to work through – burgers, pizzas, grills, curries, Chinese, vegetarian, Indian. Although we've had the occasional complaint from readers, we've yet to be disappointed by anything we've ordered. The restaurant is AC, with separate smoking & non-smoking areas, & it serves cocktails & filling fruit lassis as well as the usual range of chilled soft drinks & local beers. There are also plans for an internet café on the first flr open to diners only. The restaurant is open from 11.00 to 21.00 daily except Sun. A 5% discount is available for guests of Guestline Lodge. *All main courses in the US$3.50–5.50 range.*

Suburban Kumasi

Kumasi's pricier eateries lie outside the city centre, and include the restaurants of several of the hotels listed in the upmarket and moderate ranges, notably the **Hotel Georgia** and **Royal Park Hotel** (both Chinese) & **Rexmar** (*grills for US$6–9*). The stand-alone suburban restaurants listed below generally open for lunch and dinner only (typically 12.00–15.00 & 18.30–22.30) but unlike the restaurants in the city centre, they mostly do open on Sundays.

✕ **Abusua Restaurant** Situated on Pine Rd near the Pine Executive Lodge, this is a fine restaurant serving inexpensive continental & Indian food, but not alcohol. There is an internet café in the basement.

✕ **Chopsticks Restaurant** Situated around the corner from Rose's Guesthouse, Chopsticks has long been rated as the best Chinese restaurant in Kumasi, though it does occasionally receive negative feedback. *Main courses start at around US$8.*

✕ **The Dish Restaurant** Situated on Sixth St, 50m from the stadium on Hudson Rd area, this is recommended for its good selection of Chinese, Western & Ghanaian dishes. You can eat on the terrace or in the AC lounge. *Main courses in the US$3.50–5 range.*

✕ **Kentish Restaurant** Situated in the National Cultural Centre near Kejetia Circle, this popular restaurant serves a selection of uncomplicated Western & Ghanaian dishes at reasonable prices, either indoors or in the fairly attractive garden. It's a good place to eat should you be planning on seeing one of the musical concerts or plays that are put on occasionally at the cultural centre.

✕ **Moti Mahal Restaurant** Housed in the OAU Hotel off the Southern Bypass west of Ahodwo Circle, this superb Indian restaurant comes as a refreshing – though by no means inexpensive – treat after the ubiquitous Chinese & Western dishes served in most parts of Ghana. Many readers cite this restaurant as the best Indian food they have had in Ghana, if not the Western world.

✕ **Spice Nightclub & Bar** This popular open-air bar near Santasi Circle is a great place to spend an evening drinking, eating grilled meat & listening to a great selection of local & international music.

✕ **Timber Gardens** For uncomplicated boozing, this busy open-air spot on the junction of Lake & Southern Bypass roads is difficult to beat – cold draught beer, spicy grilled kebabs & chicken, as well as more ordinary chop.

✕ **Vienna City** This gaudy restaurant/bar has about as much to do with Vienna as it has to do with Ghana – & no doubt for some this is part of the attraction. It's a reliable escape if you fancy some acceptable international food in an AC environment, plus the opportunity to play some pool & watch sports on the wide-screen TV. At night, the atmosphere tends to get seriously seedy, when it's largely populated by prostitutes. *Main course upwards of US$5 a plate.*

OTHER PRACTICALITIES

Books and newspapers Following the recent (and hopefully temporary) closure of the secondhand book stalls on Prempreh II Street close to Vic Baboo's Café, and at the Queensway Bookshop near the British Council, reading material is pretty hard to come by in Kumasi. The British Council itself has a stack of fairly recent British newspapers in the air-conditioned reading room, and there is a decent book swap service at Guestline Lodge

Cinema The Roxy Cinema on Maxwell Road, more or less opposite the Prempreh Assembly Hall, is open every day and puts on a diverse selection of African, Western, and Asian films.

Crafts The numerous craft villages around Kumasi are covered in detail in the next chapter (Greater Kumasi) but their products – including *kente* cloth – can easily be bought at Kejetia Market, at the craft shop in the National Cultural Centre where you can also see them being made, at upmarket hotels, or elsewhere in the city centre. Those with an interest in traditional sculpture might want to head out to the small village of Kofofrom, which lies on the Old Bekwai Road roughly 4km past Four Villages Inn. The village is famous for its brass-moulding co-operative, the main product of which is cremation urns, though statues and other figurines are also made and sell from US$3.50 upwards. The craftsmen will gladly show interested visitors how they create the mould, using a combination of beeswax, clay and coconut hairs.

A reader of the first edition met and bought a painting from one of Ghana's leading painters, Ato Delaquis, who heads the painting department at the Kumasi Art College, and encourages visitors with an interest in art to make contact with him (✆ *051 60329*).

Football It can be fun to watch a game at Kumasi Stadium (on Hudson Road) – tickets for league matches cost US$3 and those for more important matches might cost up to US$7. There's a great atmosphere, and armed guards to escort the referee off the pitch, but do watch out for pickpockets, especially on the way in and out.

Foreign exchange The Standard Chartered Bank and Barclays Bank are situated opposite each other off Prempreh II Circle and stay open until 15.00 Monday to Friday. Both exchange travellers' cheques without charging commission, but both impose limits (Barclays up to US$250 in any one transaction, Standard Chartered up to $200) and Standard Chartered normally offers a considerably better rate. An ATM accepting international Visa cards (but not MasterCard) can be found outside both banks. To exchange cash, you're better off heading to any of the numerous private forex bureaux that are dotted around the city centre. Intercity Forex Bureau usually has very good rates, but the Aries Forex Bureau at Asokwa Road is best avoided, as it has a reputation for swindling travellers.

Golf You can get a round of golf in at the Royal Golf Club, a decent 18-hole course with a US$15 green fee. It's not quite up to Western standards but it's a great way to kill a Sunday morning. A caddie costs US$2 and clubs can be rented from US$6–10.

Hassles Kumasi is a reasonably safe city – certainly we've had very few reports of armed crime against tourists – but the hassle factor from aspirant guides and other chancers can be quite high. One reader writes: 'Most of the con-artists hang around the road in front of Vic Baboo's Café, and if you want to avoid them just walk up Bank Road to access this restaurant. Unlike cities like Tamale, where many of the street kids are orphans who sleep overnight at the STC station, these guys aren't needy (they certainly have no trouble affording a few drinks!). More subtle are the chancers who hang around the National Cultural Centre. I let someone sit next to me in the Kentish Kitchen and within a few minutes he wanted to take my photo and offer me various dubious services!'

Another reader writes 'You probably won't spend long in town before you're approached by one of several ingratiating young men who pretend they are bead craftsmen or exiled artists from neighbouring countries – their scam is to befriend you, then to offer you jewellery or other craftwork at a wildly inflated price in the hope you'll not negotiate too hard with a friend. If you can't shake off one of these chancers (and some are really persistent) then do at least check out prices at the market before you buy anything.'

Internet Several internet cafés are dotted around central Kumasi, charging a fairly uniform rate of US$0.50 per hour, and the more reliable ones are all marked on the map. The best internet café in Kumasi is probably the air-conditioned UNIC Internet, next to the British Council, which has about two-dozen fast machines and opens seven days a week. Once it resumes, the internet service at Vic Baboo's Café is also very convenient.

Nightlife Among the livelier weekend nightspots in Kumasi are the **Yegoala Niteclub** close to Kejetia Circle the **Foxtrap Nightclub** next to the Prempreh Assembly Hall on Maxwell Road, and the **Genesis Niteclub** at the Goldengate Hotel, all of which charge an entrance fee of around US$5. The **Old Timer's Bar** below the Hotel de Kingsway is reliably lively on Saturday nights. The best place for live highlife music is the **Jofel Restaurant** near the Airport Roundabout – bands play here most Saturday nights, starting at around 19.00 – while a good spot for contemporary local music is **Spice Nightclub & Bar** at Santasi Circle.

Red tape The visa extension service here is far quicker than in Accra: two or three days as opposed to two weeks, and you may even be able to get it done overnight if you can persuade the immigration officers that it's urgent.

Supermarkets Quite a number of reasonable supermarkets are to be found in the vicinity of Prempreh II Street. By far the most varied selection of groceries in Kumasi is available at the excellent A-Life Supermarket (between the STC and railway stations), which also serves ice-cream cones and other snacks on the veranda café.

Swimming There is no public swimming pool, but the ones at the Hotel Georgia and Rexmar are open to non-residents for a fee of US$5.

Tourist office The Ghana Tourist Board office in the National Cultural Centre is a useful source of current travel information, particularly if you want to head off the beaten track, and depending to some extent with whom you end up speaking. The office also stocks a good map of Kumasi and surrounds.

Tours and guides Accredited local guides speaking most European languages can be arranged at a negotiable fee through the tourist office in the National Cultural Centre (☏ 051 35848 or 024 4202777). Another good place to obtain a knowledgeable guide is Vic Baboo's Cafe, where you can also arrange local day tours using reliable taxi drivers. Most of the upmarket hotels offer day tours in private vehicles, albeit at a higher price.

EXPLORING KUMASI

The **National Cultural Centre** on Bantama Road, about five minutes' walk out of town from Kejetia Circle, is a good place to start your explorations of Ashanti. The helpful regional tourist office can be found here, and the staff are likely to be clued up about any new tourist developments in the region. An excellent craft market in the cultural centre makes goods onsite, and has been recommended by several readers as far friendlier and cheaper than its counterpart in Accra.

Situated within the cultural centre, the **Prempreh II Jubilee Museum** offers a good overview of Ashanti history. The museum is named after the popular Asantehene, Nana Osei Agyeman Prempreh II, who ascended to the Golden Stool in May 1931 and reigned until his death almost 40 years later in 1970. Most of the artefacts in the museum relate to the reign of Prempreh II, a largely peaceful period during which the Ashanti Empire, shattered in several respects by the British colonists, re-established much of its former cultural cohesion. Several black-and-white photos are on display, most strikingly a vibrant portrait of the young Asantehene taken at his coronation. There are also a number of royal stools in the museum, one of which is said to be the fake Golden Stool that was handed to Lord Baden-Powell in an attempt to fool the British authorities in 1900, and a photo of the real Golden Stool, which last appeared in public at the enstoolment of the present Asantehene in 1999. Perhaps the most historically significant artefact in the museum is the royal cask which dates back 300 years to the rule of Nana Osei Tutu; its contents are unknown, since tradition holds that opening it would bring about the fall of Ashanti. The entrance fee of US$2 covers an informative guided tour. Photography is forbidden.

About 500m further out of town along Bantama Road, situated behind Block C of the Okomfo Anokye Hospital on Bantama Circle, the **Okomfo Anokye Sword** has, according to tradition, been stuck in the same position in the ground for 300 years. The sword marks the spot where the Golden Stool initially descended from the sky and – in common with the cask mentioned above – it is an important symbol of Ashanti unity. Legend has it that the state would collapse should it ever be pulled out of the ground. The sword is now housed in a small circular building, and a US$2 entrance fee is charged to see it. The building is in theory open 09.00–17.00 Monday to Saturday, and 09.00–14.00 on Sundays.

Walking back towards town, shortly before Kejetia Circle and lorry station, the **Kumasi Zoo** consists of a few depressingly cramped cages harbouring various primates (many are in solitary confinement, a fate as cruel to a chimp or a monkey as to a person) as well as a rather more aesthetically pleasing duiker-breeding scheme and a few recent additions in the form of chimpanzees and lions. Altogether more phenomenal than the inmates of the zoo are the thousands upon thousands of fruitbats that rest of their own volition in the trees. This is a quite incredible sight (not to say sound – they chatter away like demented mice), and worth the nominal entrance fee if you've never before seen a large bat colony. Even more spectacular is the sight of the hungry fruitbats as they flock through the sky in their thousands towards dusk.

Few people would spend time in Kumasi and not pay a visit to the vast, sprawling **Kejetia Market**, immediately southeast of Kejetia Circle. Reputedly the largest open market in West Africa, this has now been restored to its gloriously hectic former self after it was partially destroyed by fire in 1995. Incredibly, some 10,000 traders operate within the 12-hectare market – many more stalls spill out along the surrounding streets – and excellent overviews can be obtained from the tall building on its western edge. Once inside, the market takes on a labyrinthine aspect, confusing at first, but in fact quite orderly, with clothing, textile and food stalls clustered in the west, pottery and metal in the northeast, and tailors in the southwest. Aside from the decidedly smelly part of the market where fish and meat are sold, this is a fascinating place, well worth dedicating an afternoon or morning to, and a great place to buy curios and crafts in an environment where tourists form a fraction of the clientele. Getting lost is part of the fun – the market isn't so large that you are likely to lose your bearings for long – and there is little cause for concern about hassle or theft, though many travellers do prefer to explore the market with a local guide. For collectors, the market is a great place to buy old trade beads, but you're advised to enter at Roman Hill to avoid a tiresome slog through the main household goods and food sections. There seem to be very few drinking spots in the market, so carry a big bottle of water with you.

On Antoa Road, about 1km from the National Museum, **Manhyia Palace** was built in 1926 following the return from exile of Prempreh II's predecessor and uncle, Asantehene Nana Prempreh I. Surprisingly low-key, the palace remains in use today and houses a small but interesting history museum open 09.00–16.00 on weekdays and 09.00–15.00 at weekends (entrance US$2, photography predictably but for no apparent reason forbidden). The best time to visit the palace is between 10.30 and 13.00 on Adae festival days, which occur every sixth Sunday.

The Adae is when the Asantehene receives homage from his subjects, as well as from subservient chiefs – a truly spectacular occasion, with a variety of traditional dress on show, great drumming displays, traditional horns blaring and all the rest. The Adae dates for any given year are pinned up at the tourist office at the beginning of the year, but unfortunately cannot be predicted further in advance as they are sometimes shifted or cancelled to accommodate other important events. Casual photography was forbidden under the previous Asantehene, at least without written permission, but it is evidently condoned by his successor Osei Tutu II, who ascended to the Golden Stool in 1999 – several tourists were snapping away when we attended the festival in late 2000. A more recent report (July 2003) is that you're allowed to take photos of the drummers and of the audience (including chiefs with their company), but not the Asantehene, whose bodyguards can be quite rude if you point a camera in his general direction. It's not that Osei Tutu II is bothered by cameras, but rather that you're expected to buy pictures of the Asantehene taken by the official court photographer from the palace museum's shop!

Back in the centre, near Prempreh II Circle, is the **Kumasi Fort**, probably the oldest building in the city, though not as old as many of the traditional shrines in rural Ashanti. Some sources suggest – wholly inaccurately – that the foundation of the fort and some of the walls date to 1820, when Asantehene Osei Tutu Kwame decided to build a replica of the fort at Cape Coast. The fort as it stands today was completed in 1897 by the British using granite blocks transported to Kumasi from the coast. The fortress was surrounded in March 1900, during the so-called 'Ashanti Rebellion', and 29 Britons were trapped within its walls for several weeks before they were able to escape. The Queen Mother of Ejisu, Ohemaa Yaa Asantewaa, the prime initiator of the Ashanti Rebellion, was imprisoned here for a week before being exiled to Cape Coast and later the Seychelles, where she died. A well-maintained British Military Cemetery about 200m northwest of the fort contains the graves of British casualties of the Yaa Asantewaa War.

A highly informative guided tour of the fort, which now doubles as an **Armed Forces Museum**, was US$2 for non-Ghanaians at the end of 2006 (plus an additional US$1 for photography) and is well worth the expenditure despite plans to raise the fee in 2007. The tour starts unpromisingly with a collection of weapons and the spoils from various campaigns in which the Gold Coast Regiment has been involved (I was surprised to see how heavily the Gold Coast Regiment had featured in booting the Italians out of Ethiopia during World War II). More interesting, in my opinion, are the many portraits of Ashanti notables (notably Yaa Asantewaa), the first African soldiers to be promoted to various ranks during colonial rule, and two of the World War II veterans who were killed when an anti-colonial protest outside Osu Castle in Accra was fired upon by colonial police. The tour gradually takes on several unexpected dimensions: a potted history of 20th-century conflict, as seen through the collected memorabilia of a relatively obscure African regiment, and, more tellingly, a cruel exposure of the minutiae of colonial arrogance which for many years forbade African soldiers in their regiments to wear shoes. The fort is open 08.00–17.00 on Tuesdays to Saturdays, but closed on Mondays and Sundays.

Also of interest are the two handsome colonial-era **cathedrals** in the city centre and the attractive campus of the **University of Kumasi** (KNUST), with its museum, botanical garden, archaeological site, and Engineering Guest House, A rather more quirky excursion that has also been recommended is to the small **hat**

museum at Nnrom Hotel, just outside Kumasi at New Suame, which claims to house the largest collection of hats in the world, with around 4,000 exhibits dating back to 1927. An engineer writes 'ask any taxi driver to take you to a place called **The Magazine**, a sprawling labyrinthine wrecking yard that houses several hundred mechanics, welders and labourers – here I witnessed the complete construction of a newly painted bus out of the hulks of several wrecked ones, with nothing more than a grinder, a welding rod and a hammer!'

If you are interested in visiting a traditional **fetish priest** operating within suburban Kumasi, one who welcomes foreign visitors is Akwasi Anokye, who is named after Okomfe Anokye, the first priest of Ashanti. Akwasi lives in house DN24 in the suburb of Daban, and he is in session on Fridays and Sundays (though visits can be arranged with prior notice on other days). Although there is nothing preventing you from visiting the priest privately (don't forget to bring a bottle of Schnapps), his house may be difficult to locate without assistance – one of the guides at Vic Baboo's Café set up our visit.

Further afield, Kumasi is the obvious base for numerous **day trips** and **overnight excursions**, most of which are described in the next chapter *Greater Ashanti*.

BIA PROTECTED AREA   Updated in 2007 by Phil Marshall of the Protected Areas Development Programme

This isolated 305km² forest reserve, currently under fresh development but effectively closed to tourists until the guesthouse re-opens in around April 2008, lies on the Ivorian border west of Kumasi. Administratively, Bia falls into Western Region, and logistically it is remote from any other tourist attraction in Ghana, but since it is most easily visited as a round trip from Kumasi, I have chosen to include it in this chapter. Bia protects an important area of virgin rainforest, noted for its enormous biodiversity. In addition to trees reaching a height of 60m, the reserve harbours many mammal species, including forest elephant, but tourists should not expect to see mammals in rainforest conditions. The bird list now stands at 203, while 668 species of butterfly have been recorded.

Until fairly recently, Bia was known to harbour all eight of the forest-associated higher primates that occur in Ghana, ie: mona, Diana and lesser spot-nosed monkeys; chimpanzee; white-naped mangabey; and black-and-white, olive, and red colobus. The red colobus is now thought to be extinct in Bia (it has been declared totally extinct in Ghana by primatologists in the USA), but it might still occur in the adjoining Krokosua Hills Forest Reserve, which is inaccessible at present, and lacks tourist facilities. A large portion of the forest reserve has recently been declared a Globally Significant Biodiversity Area (GSBA) and its protection status is being increased.

Various walking trails have been cut through the Bia Reserve, and it is possible to drive into the reserve from the eastern side. Getting here from Kumasi is straightforward on public transport, but it is a long and for the last part bumpy ride, and probably worth doing only if you intend to spend at least three nights in the reserve.

A 3km loop walk from the guesthouse at Kunkumso takes you to the Apaso Rock, which offers spectacular views of the forest in an area teeming with birdlife. The rock and its pools form a shrine for the local people, who believe it to be the home of spirits which exercise a great deal of power, assisting people to have good fortune and helping barren women procreate. There is an annual yam festival in the honour of these spirits. Visitors are welcome, but are asked to respect the rules and conditions of visiting the rock.

While the reserve is closed, the walking trails are being refurbished and approximately 35km of roads cut. For more details, contact the Regional Manager of Wildlife Division in Takoradi (✆ *031 25322*).

GETTING THERE AND AWAY The main entrance to Bia lies at New Debiso (aka Kunkumso), about 240km west of Kumasi along a road which is surfaced for all but the last 94km. A couple of tro-tros run between Kumasi and Debiso daily, taking about seven hours, and passing through Bibiani (Ashanti Goldfields opencast mine), Sefwi Bekwai and Sefwi Wiawso. The road from Sefwi Wiawso to the Côte d'Ivoire border is now being rebuilt to a very high standard.

From here the road is gravel and can be very bumpy in the wet season. About 2km past the market town of Asawinso you turn right at the police barrier and take the road to Debiso through the Krokosua Hills and the village of Asempanye. The Bia National Park HQ is signposted on the left but the park entrance is at **Kunkumso**, 23km further on. Kunkumso is situated at the north end of Bia National Park on a road junction. The northern road (straight ahead) goes to Debiso (5km) and the western road goes to the border. Both have customs barriers at New Debiso. The entrance gate to Bia National Park is about 20m past the left-hand barrier on the left of the road to the border. (If you miss New Debiso, a taxi back there from Debiso takes about 15 minutes.)

WHERE TO STAY About 100m from the entrance gate lies Kunkumso Guesthouse, a one-storey cabin consisting of two double rooms with bedding provided, en-suite toilet and shower, electricity, and a shared kitchen and dining-room with gas stove, pots, plates and cutlery. Visitors should bring all their own food. Note that the guesthouse is not available until April 2008. Camping is permitted next to the guesthouse.

15

Greater Ashanti

The lush countryside within a 50km radius of Kumasi is regarded to be the core region of Ashanti, since it is occupied by the various states that combined forces under the golden stool in the late 17th century. It is also a region that offers practically limitless opportunities for unstructured travel: not only Ashanti cultural sites such as the new Yaa Asantewaa Museum near Ejisu and a half dozen or so *Abosomfie* (19th-century fetish houses), but also several *kente*-weaving and other craft villages, and natural attractions such as Lake Bosumtwi (the country's largest natural body of water) and several pedestrian-friendly forest reserves.

Travellers generally explore the region using Kumasi as a base (of the places listed in this chapter, only Lake Bosumtwi is more often visited as an overnight excursion than a day trip), and the regional capital is certainly far better equipped than anywhere else in Ashanti when it comes to tourist facilities such as accommodation and restaurants. For those who prefer to get away from tourist hubs, however, a number of small towns might as easily be used as a base for exploring Ashanti, notably Ejisu, Effiduase and to a lesser extent Mampong, and it would also be possible to travel around whimsically staying overnight at wherever you happened to end up. One obvious advantage of steering clear of Kumasi is that it would eliminate the need to navigate the city's legendary traffic jams whenever you want to get out.

Given that tastes and interests differ, I feel it would be restrictive to describe the places listed in this chapter in the form of a prescribed circuit, so I've chosen to follow them in roughly anti-clockwise sequence, starting with **Owabi Wildlife Sanctuary** and **Lake Bosumtwi**. With the exception of Owabi and to a lesser extent Bosumtwi, you can travel between virtually any of the places listed in this chapter without returning to Kumasi, making use of the small tro-tros and shared taxis that connect just about any two villages in the area. Alternatively, if you have time restrictions or can't be bothered with using public transport, you can arrange a taxi for the day out of Kumasi – expect to pay around US$25 for about six hours of driving around.

OWABI WILDLIFE SANCTUARY

One of Ghana's smallest conservations areas, covering a mere 13km², Owabi Wildlife Sanctuary nevertheless protects a good selection of forested and aquatic habitats, making it an excellent day retreat for wildlife lovers seeking respite from the chaos of Kumasi. The sanctuary was gazetted in 1971 to protect the chunk of pristine forest and reedbeds surrounding the Owabi Reservoir, which was constructed by the British on the eponymous rocky river in 1928, and served for many years as Kumasi's sole source of drinking water. Crossed by several footpaths, the sanctuary harbours a great many varieties of butterfly, and more than 100 bird species have been identified – the raucous pied hornbill is among the most

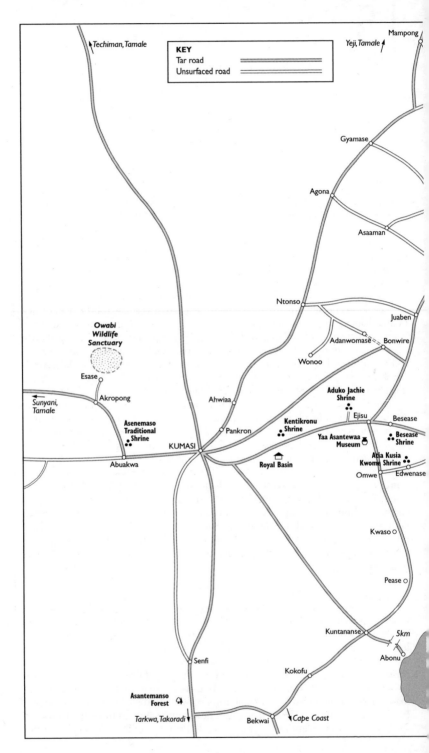

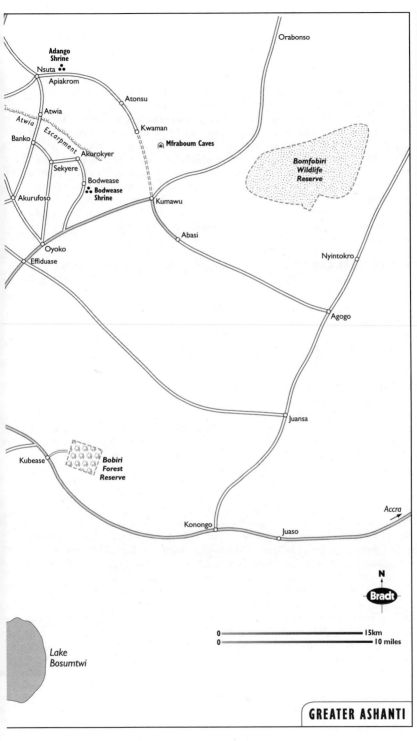

GREATER ASHANTI

Orabonso

Adango
Shrine
Nsuta
Apiakrom
Atonsu
Atwia
Kwaman
Atwia
Mfraboum Caves
Escarpment
Banko
Akorokyer
Sekyere
Akurufoso
Bodwease
Bodwease
Shrine
Kumawu
Abasi
Oyoko
Nyintokro
Effiduase
Agogo
Bomfobiri
Wildlife
Reserve
Juansa
Kubease
Bobiri
Forest
Reserve
Accra
Konongo
Juaso
N
Bradt
Lake
Bosumtwi
0   15km
0   10 miles

conspicuous of the forest birds, while the likes of African finfoot and African jacana might be seen on the reservoir, and kingfishers, barbets, greenbuls, and herons are generally well represented. A fair number of large mammals are present: casual visitors stand a reasonable chance of glimpsing Campbell's mona monkey, the population of which is estimated at 500, as well as the semi-habituated Cusimanse mongoose, but are unlikely to see more secretive terrestrial species such as bushpig, bushbuck, Maxwell's duiker or royal antelope.

Easily visited in conjunction with Owabi, **Asenemaso Traditional Shrine** is one of the most unusual of the old fetish houses in Ashanti, since it consists of one large enclosed building rather than four semi-open rooms around a courtyard. Nevertheless, the murals here are excellent, and it is unique in having retained its original ceiling. Asenemaso lies along the Sunyani/Owabi road, 8km from Kumasi, and perhaps 200m past Akuakwa on the junction of the Bibiani road (see *Where to stay*, below). The shrine itself lies along the road to Akropong and is difficult to find unless you ask around for directions. Last we heard, the old female fetish priest was too ill to perform the rites, and her son had the key. I had seen and heard it all in five minutes however.

GETTING THERE AND AWAY Owabi lies roughly 16km from Kumasi and 3km from the main Sunyani road. The turn-off to the sanctuary is at Akropong, which can be reached by a regular tro-tro service from Kejetia Station. Most tro-tros going from Kumasi to Akropong continue along the Owabi turn-off as far as Esase, from where it's a ten-minute walk to the entrance to the reserve – you may even be lucky and get a lift with a waterworks vehicle. At the entrance gate, you'll have to pay the entrance and guide fees (visitors may not enter the forest without a guide), which work out at less than US$2 per person.

 WHERE TO STAY There's no formal accommodation at Owabi, but for a small fee you can pitch a tent on the lawn between the entrance gate and the dam wall, or use the school dormitory attached to the Owabi water treatment plant. The bar at the entrance sells chilled beers and soft drinks, and you shouldn't have a problem finding food in Akropong – it's a fairly large town with a couple of chop bars. Alternatively, it's easy enough to visit Owabi as a day trip from Kumasi. Otherwise, the closest accommodation is at Abuakwa, about 5km from Akropong back towards Kumasi, at the junction of the Kumasi and Bibiani roads.

LAKE BOSUMTWI

Situated some 30km south of Kumasi in an almost circular crater, Lake Bosumtwi is by far the most expansive natural fresh-water body in Ghana with a surface area of around 25km². It is also the deepest, reaching a maximum depth of about 90m – and steadily rising, a phenomenon that has resulted in the submersion of several lakeshore villages within living memory. Debate about the origin of the crater in which Bosumtwi lies was settled by a recent geological study which confirmed it isn't volcanic but the result of a meteorite impact. The lake is a beautiful spot, encircled by raggedly mountainous, thickly vegetated crater walls that reach an altitude of greater than 600m, and it offers ample opportunities for walking, birding, fishing and canoeing. Boat trips can be arranged through the various lodgings or in the village, while a small passenger boat normally circumnavigates the lake every Sunday ferrying locals between the different villages. It's also possible to rent a bicycle to explore more remote parts of the lakeshore, but not – as locals might tell you – to cycle the whole way round the lake. Plenty of people swim; there is reputedly no bilharzia.

As you might expect, Lake Bosumtwi is held sacred by Ashanti traditionalists, though the finer details of its exalted status are rather elusive. Some claim that Bosumtwi is where a deity called Twi resides, others that it is visited by the souls of the departed on their passage to eternity. It is also the sacred water body of the Bosumtwi (one of five divisions in the patrilineal *nton* system which the Ashanti and other Akan peoples believe passes a father's attributes to his children), on account of it being as round as the sun, the model for members of the Bosumtwi *nton*. There is a taboo on the use of traditional pirogues on the lake; local fishermen get around by lying on customised tree trunks called *padua*, and using their hands as paddles. An important stone shrine is situated at Abrodwum, on the lakeshore about 1km south of Abono, where libation is poured at traditional festivals or when any bad omen concerning the lake is detected.

The normal base for visits to the lake is Abono, a pretty and accessible village on the northern shore, alongside which lies one of the most pleasant upmarket hotels in central Ghana. Unfortunately, Abono is often characterised by unusually high levels of hassle, though this does seem to have abated slightly over the past year or two. Still, you can safely ignore any 'caretaker' who demands a donation before allowing you to walk to the lakeshore, as well as the persistent old fellow who evidently makes a living from persuading gullible tourists that the chief of Abono has nothing better to do with himself than wander around telling gullible tourists that he's the chief of Abono (and while they're about it some cash would be welcome…!). Harder to ignore is the 'toll gate' on the route out of Kuntanase – in reality a rope manned by self-appointed 'officials' who charge non-Ghanaians US$0.50 to get to the lake. This would be fine if funds were used to maintain the area and develop the communities around Bosumtwi, but until that is the case, a request for an official receipt should make them give up pretty sharply.

Country-lovers may want to consider using Bosumtwi as an alternative base to Kumasi, from which to explore the string of rural attractions which surround the city, without having to grapple with Kumasi itself.

GETTING THERE AND AWAY Direct tro-tros from Kumasi to Abono take around 45 minutes, though you may have to wait a while for something to leave. The alternative is to take a tro-tro to Kuntanase, where you can pick up a shared taxi to Abono. Either way, all vehicles leaving Kumasi in this direction leave from Asafo Station, and the total fare to Bosumtwi shouldn't exceed US$1.

Kuntanase can also be approached from Ejisu via a new surfaced road for around US$1. Shared taxis do occasionally cover the whole route, but it's easier to get transport if you do it in short hops, changing vehicles in Piase and Kwaso. A surfaced road and shared taxis connect Kuntanase to Bekwai via Kokofu.

WHERE TO STAY
Moderate

Lake Paradise Resort \ 051 20164 or 051 81470; e lakebpr2@yahoo.com or frontdesk@lakebosumtwiresort.com. This excellent hotel lies to the immediate south of Abono, accessed along a dirt track to the right of the main road just after the school. The landscaped gardens slope down to a secluded beach, & there's a good first-floor restaurant with a view over the water. *Large dbls with AC & DSTV US$51.*

Budget

Lake Bosumtwi Tourist Lodge Situated in Kuntanase, a clean, comfortable, friendly, & reasonably priced guesthouse. It lies in attractive grounds, & meals are served, but is a full 13km by road from the lake, with no view whatsoever. *Dbl with fan using common showers US$4, self-contained dbl US$7.50.*

Lake Point Guesthouse \ 024 3452922 (SMS only) or 008821651074079 (satellite phone so no

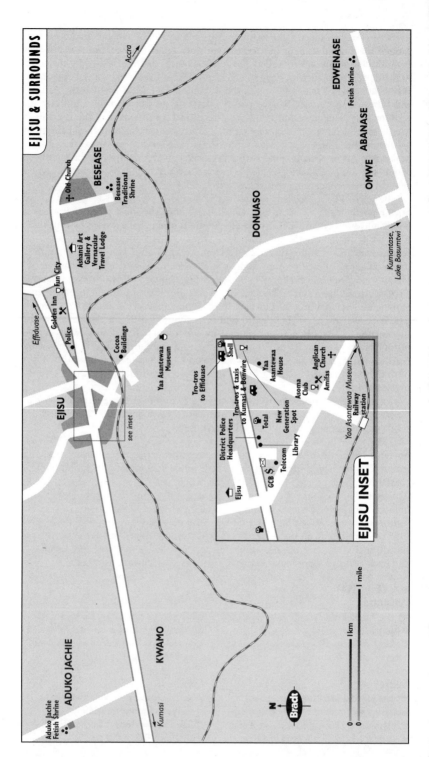

EJISU & SURROUNDS

Accra

BESEASE

† Old Church

Beseease
Traditional Shrine

Effiduase

Golden Inn □ Fun City
✗

Police ●

Ashanti Art
Gallery &
Vernacular
Travel Lodge

Cocoa
Buildings

DONUASO

EJISU

see inset

Yaa Asantewaa Museum

Kumantase,
Lake Bosumtwi

EDWENASE

Fetish Shrine ●●

OMWE ABANASE

ADUKO JACHIE

Aduko Jachie
Fetish Shrine ●●

KWAMO

Kumasi

Kumasi

N
Bradt

0   1km
0   1 mile

EJISU INSET

Tro-tros
to Effiduase

Shell

Tro-tros & taxis
to Kumasi & Boniwire

District Police
Headquarters

New
Generation
Spot

Total ●

GCB $

Telecom

Library

Ejisu

Yaa
Asantewaa
House

Asoma
Club

Amifas
✗

Anglican
Church †

Yaa Asantewaa Museum
Railway station

318

international dialling code required). Set in landscaped gardens with its own private beach a couple of km from Abono, this attractive new lodge fits the backpacker budget but could just as easily please mid-range travellers. Accommodation is provided in traditional-looking huts all with immaculately finished interiors & individual touches, dotted around a pristine garden planted with flowers & coconut trees. Camping is permitted & discounts are available for longer stays. Good meals are available, prepared by the Ghanaian & Austrian owners who will rustle up delicious pancakes & spicy fruit smoothies on demand, or more substantial meals at a few hours' notice. Facilities include paduas which are free to borrow & bicycles available for hire. As you enter Abono, the track to the lodge is signposted in blue to your left – follow the signposted track for 2km, then turn left again at a second signpost & you'll reach it after another 500m. *Dbl US$18–22, trpl US$26. Camping US$4 pp.*

🏠 **Rainbow Gardens Resort** ☎ 0244 869510; e www.rainbowgardenvillage.com. This German-owned, Ghanaian-run resort is not quite as pretty at Lake Point, but has a similarly chilled out atmosphere with a cranked-up Rasta vibe. Three levels of accommodation are available in red-brick huts, ranging from US$6 a head for a spot in the clean 6-man dormitory with shared outside toilets & showers, to US$20 for a comfortable dbl with common showers, or US$25 for a room that is self-contained. Camping is permitted. Food & meals are available at reasonable prices, & day-visitors are welcomed, making the resort a good target for a walk from Abono or elsewhere. Take the road for Lake Paradise Resort & continue for another 4km. If you are arriving with luggage, send a messenger on a bike & the management will come & pick you up. *US$6–25. Camping US$3 pp.*

EJISU AND SURROUNDS

The busy little junction town of Ejisu, which lies some 20km from Kumasi at the intersection of the Accra and Effiduase roads, is best known historically as the birthplace and home of Yaa Asantewaa, the Queen Mother who instigated the Ashanti siege of Kumasi Fort in 1900. It also lies within striking distance of three of the region's most accessible *Abosomfie* shrines, all of which are described fully overleaf. Although the Ejisu area can easily be explored as a day trip out of Kumasi, it boasts a couple of decent budget hotels, and could serve as a useful base for exploring the Kumasi area.

GETTING THERE AND AWAY Ejisu straddles the main road connecting Kumasi to Accra, 20–30 minutes' drive from the regional capital in a private vehicle. It is also serviced by a constant stream of minibuses in both directions. Coming from central Kumasi, rather than head to the tro-tro station, the best place to pick up transport to Ejisu is at the circle west of the railway bridge at the intersection of Fuller Road and the Accra road (you're unlikely to wait more than five minutes for something to come past). Travellers staying at any hotel along or near the Accra road will easily pick up transport to Ejisu from any taxi stop along the eastbound side of the Accra road.

There are also regular minibus tro-tros connecting Ejisu to Effiduase and Kuntanase (the latter more usually via a series of short hops) – just wait at the junction. The taxi station opposite Yaa Asantewaa House is the place to pick up shared taxis to local destinations.

🏠 **WHERE TO STAY AND EAT**

🏠 **Ashanti Art Gallery & Vernacular Travel Lodge** (5 rooms) ☎ 024 4502523. Situated about 1km from Ejisu towards Besease & Accra, this clearly signposted lodge has a rather dismal atmosphere, but the 5 rooms on offer are all clean, comfortable & reasonably priced. No food is served, but the art gallery serves cold drinks & is a good spot for some unpressurised curio shopping. *Sgl with shared bath US$6, self-contained dbl US$10.*

🏠 **Ejisu Hotel** ☎ 024 4036726. This friendly budget hotel, situated in the town centre only 50m from the main Accra road, is one of the best deals in the region. Large, clean self-contained rooms with fan & running water. No meals or drinks are available at the hotel, but plenty of street food can be found in Ejisu, & there are several bars in town. *US$7 or US$8 for a twin.*

The recent renovation of Besease Traditional Shrine near Ejisu, some 20km east of Kumasi, has provided an overdue incentive for tourists to explore aspects of Ashanti tradition which are easily overlooked in the urban bustle of modern Kumasi. The shrine house at Besease, one of ten scattered around rural Ashanti, is a fine example of an *Obosomfie* (plural *Abosomfie*), a building which is traditionally regarded to be the spiritual abode of a particular *Obosom*, the name given to one of the lesser deities who mediate between mortals and the supreme god Nyame. The *Obosom* maintains a permanent presence in its shrine, but manifests itself only on set occasions through the medium of a fetish priest or Okomfo, who becomes possessed by the spirit and acts as its mouthpiece. Traditionally, the *Okomfo* is regarded to be the most important member of a community, and he or she works closely with the chief, who will call on the *Obosom* for advice before any important decision is made.

Over the last century, the importance of the fetish houses has diminished. Speak to many Christians in Ashanti, and they will dismiss their traditional beliefs as superstition, yet it is also the case, particularly in rural areas, that many Ashanti people adhere to both systems of faith concurrently. The ambiguities can be difficult for outsiders to come to grips with. At Bodwease Shrine, for instance, the last fetish priest has been dead for a decade, yet the shrine is immaculately maintained by the local community, who believe that the *Obosom* still lives in the shrine and will eventually settle on a human medium, who will be accepted as the new fetish priest by the community.

Most of the extant shrine houses are still inhabited by a fetish priest, who sits in session on specific days (typically Sunday and/or Friday) and is consulted by a stream of locals requiring spiritual advice. A fetish priest can be male or female, and although the role is occasionally hereditary, it can fall on anybody who is called to service by the resident *Obosom*. There are also many fetish priests in Ashanti who operate outside of a traditional shrine house. Tourists are generally welcome to any priest or shrine house, although they will be expected to offer a libation (a bottle of Schnapps or the money equivalent).

The ten 19th-century *Abosomfie* that remain were listed as UNESCO World Heritage Sites in 1980, not solely for their spiritual significance but also because they form the only surviving examples of traditional Ashanti architecture. Not easy to imagine today, but Kumasi, prior to being razed by the British in 1874, was by all accounts an unusually beautiful city, the wide streets lined by airy houses of a unique architectural style. The typical house of the period consisted of several rooms centred around a quadrangular courtyard and shaded by steep thatched roofs, often rising at an angle of greater than sixty degrees. The lower walls were polished orange, while the upper walls were whitewashed. Another characteristic feature of 19th-century Ashanti homesteads were carved murals of symbols similar to those found on *adinkra* cloth. Much of what is known of pre-colonial Kumasi comes from the verbal accounts of European travellers such as Bowdich (1819) and Winniett (1884), but the handful of black-and-white photographs that survive do provide a visual record of what Kumasi must have looked like in its heyday.

CULTURAL SITES AROUND EJISU

Yaa Asantewaa Museum This monument to Ejisu's most famous daughter was opened in 2003 to commemorate the centenary of the Yaa Asantewaa War, but had sadly burned down by late 2006 when this edition was researched. If and when the museum reopens, expect a faithful mimicry of a 19th-century Ashanti chief's palace, with traditional *adinkra* murals on the walls, covered by a steeply angled thatched roof. In the mean time, visitors are invited to visit Yaa Asantewaa House

The ten extant *Abosomfie*, some of which are said to be more than 200 years old, are of typical pre-colonial Ashanti construction in general appearance, while also boasting certain features unique to fetish houses. With a couple of exceptions, the *Abosomfie* all conform to a ground plan of four rooms facing into a large courtyard. Three of these rooms – the drumming, singing, and cooking rooms – are open on the courtyard side, while the fourth, which houses the actual shrine, is screened off and may be entered only by the priest and his assistants. In the courtyard of all the shrines stands a *Nyame Dua* – the altar to the supreme god, which generally consists of a pot wedged on a forked branch. Many of the shrines are littered with a variety of fetishes, most unexpectedly the tortoises which mill around the base of the *Nyame Dua* ('when they die, they don't need coffins, because they have their own...').

For the casual visitor, the most interesting of the traditional shrines is at Besease, about 1km from Ejisu (see below). This is the only ancient building in Ashanti where the roof has been fully restored, and it also contains a number of informative displays. Besease is easily visited in conjunction with the Yaa Asantewaa Museum in Ejisu. Curious travellers who prefer to visit a shrine under less formal circumstances might want to seek out two further examples in the immediate vicinity of Besease, at Edwenase and Aduko Jachie. There are also superb examples at Bodwease (see *Effiduase*, page 325), Apiakrom (see *Mampong*, page 330), Patakro (see *Obuasi*, page 294), and Asenemaso (see *Owabi Wildlife Sanctuary*, page 316).

With the exception of Besease, which to all intents and purposes functions as a museum, none of the fetish houses is formally established as a tourist site. In most cases, the shrines are held sacred by the surrounding community, and many are still occupied by a priest. No entrance fee is charged, but under no circumstances should you enter a shrine without offering a libation in advance and/or a donation afterwards. The mood differed at every shrine house that I visited, and it might well differ from one day to the next at any given shrine, which makes it difficult to offer hard and fast advice. In hindsight, my feeling is that the best approach is to follow the local custom when visiting a chief or fetish priest, which is to offer a bottle of schnapps as a libation (one bottle would be fine for two people visiting together). Having offered the customary libation, it would not be customary to make an additional cash payment, and I would ignore any hints in that direction (fair enough for them to play the 'customary libation' card, but then they can't have it both ways...). If you prefer to offer a donation, then a reasonable guideline would be the price of a bottle of schnapps (check this in Kumasi) or the entrance fee to Besease Shrine (about US$1 per person at the time of writing). I was asked for further payments under various pretexts at a couple of the shrines, but when I explained that I was paying what I had been asked for when visiting Besease Shrine, this logic was accepted in good grace.

A lavish booklet entitled *Asante Traditional Buildings*, published by the Ghana Museums and Monuments Board in 1999, and available at most museums in the country, as well as at Besease Traditional Shrine, is highly recommended to those with an interest in the local architecture.

opposite the school supplies shop in the centre of town, where one of her ancestors will recount the history for US$2 per person.

Besease Traditional Shrine This lovely shrine, fully restored in 1998, is the most accessible *Obosomfie* in the region, and regarded as one of the most important. It has reputedly existed in some form for at least 300 years; the current building probably dates to around 1850 and is where Yaa Asantewaa consulted the spirits before leading the attack on the British fort in Kumasi. The shrine is still in active use today: the priestess, who was called by the spirit more than 30 years ago, lives right next door.

The restoration of Besease shrine – complete with traditionally thatched roof – means that it is the only authentic building in existence to give a clear idea of what much of Kumasi must have looked like in the late 19th century. Inside the shrine, a series of fascinating photographic displays help to place the shrine in its cultural and architectural context. All of which makes Besease the obvious first port of call among the region's *Abosomfie*, even if – as is so often the case – the transformation from cultural site to Cultural Site has arguably robbed it of some of its immediacy. For this reason, I would recommend that anybody with sufficient interest to visit Besease in the first place should follow it up with an excursion to at least one *Obosomfie* that has not yet been formalised into a tourist attraction.

Entrance to the shrine costs around US$2. If gratuitous tipping isn't your thing, you might think twice about taking up the offer to meet the priestess – a procedure which when we last visited entailed a cursory handshake, followed by a request for money and a turned-up nose when the amount we offered was deemed insufficient compensation for her efforts.

Besease lies about 2km past Ejisu along the main Accra road. The shrine lies about 500m south of the main road and is clearly signposted. If you don't feel like walking from Ejisu, a taxi will cost next to nothing, or you can wait for one of the regular minibus tro-tros that run along this stretch of road towards Konongo.

Atia Kusia Kwame Shrine Situated in the small village of Edwenase (aka Dwenease), some 5km from Ejisu as the crow flies, this is one of the most elaborately decorated *Abosomfie* in Ashanti. The mural on the southeastern outer wall is particularly impressive, depicting a male and a female figure, above which lies the famous relief of a crocodile that has been reproduced on the wall of the Prempreh II Museum in Kumasi and the Ashanti Art Gallery in Besease. The shrine, which dates to the early 19th century, is not particularly geared to receiving tourists, and there is no charge for looking at the outside walls. Should you want to take photographs, however, or to look at the unusually well-preserved interior, then be prepared to give a substantial donation to the priest (who claims to be almost 100 years old and to have served here since his childhood).

To get to Edwenase by road, follow the Kuntanase road out of Ejisu. Shortly after you leave town, you'll pass the Yaa Asantewaa Museum to your right, then perhaps 1km further cross a bridge spanning the Oda River before passing through the small village of Domuaso. Roughly 5km out of Ejisu, you come to the small town of Omwe and a clearly signposted crossroad where you need to turn left (following the signpost for Accra). Edwenase lies a further 2km along this road, and the *Obosomfie* is clearly visible to your left as you enter the village. A private taxi here and back from Ejisu shouldn't cost more than US$4, or you could catch a shared taxi as far as Omwe and walk from there.

In the right frame of mind, a visit to Edwenase might be treated as a pretext for a gentle ramble through the characteristically verdant Ashanti countryside as much as a goal in its own right. The total walking distance is about 7km in either direction, on reasonably flat roads, which shouldn't take longer than 90 minutes to cover. Given that little or no public transport goes as far as Edwenase, best to take a taxi out should you want to walk in only one direction.

Aduko Jachie Despite being situated no more than ten minutes' walk from the main Kumasi–Accra road, this elaborately decorated and well-maintained *Obosomfie* sees very few tourists. It used to be kept by a flamboyantly dreadlocked fetish priest, but it is now in the care of an old lady after he left/was fired/destooled (depending on who you talk to) to become a musician/after an altercation with the queen mother/for fitting the shrine with electric lights. Entrance costs US$2 or a bottle of schnapps.

The junction for Aduko Jachie – to your left coming from Kumasi, and prominently signposted for 'Tikrem' – lies about 3km from Ejisu on the Kumasi road. Any tro-tro heading between the towns will drop you there. Follow the dirt road towards Tikrem for about 1km until you reach Jachie village, and take the first road to your left. The shrine is enclosed within the third building to your right.

BOBIRI FOREST RESERVE

This 21km^2 pocket of near pristine forest, situated some 30km from Kumasi within walking distance of the main Accra road, has been used as a research site by the Forestry Research Institute of Ghana for some 50 years. The forest supports a rich fauna, most prolifically butterflies, of which nearly 400 different species have been recorded. It is also probably the best site in the region for forest birds, while a variety of monkeys – mona, white-nosed, green, and black-and-white colobus – are present in small numbers. An entrance fee of US$1 is levied and an extra US$1 per person for a guide, although occasional reports suggest they do not do a great deal to earn the fee. Discounts are available to students and researchers.

GETTING THERE AND AWAY To reach the forest from Kumasi or Ejisu, ask any Konongo-bound minibus to drop you at Kubease, about 1km past Hwereso and perhaps 8km past Ejisu along the Accra road (US$0.70). The turn-off to the forest is clearly signposted, and it's a lovely 3km walk out. The first part of the road passes through lush, marshy vegetation, dotted with palms and absolutely heaving with birds in the early morning (serious twitchers could spend a happy two hours along this stretch sorting out the myriad weavers, waxbills and bulbuls). The only place where you could go wrong here is at the fork 1km out of Kubease, where you ought to head to the right. About 500m past this fork, a signpost and abrupt change in vegetation and drop in temperature signal your entry to the forest proper, after which it's a straightforward 10- to 15-minute walk to the resthouse.

WHERE TO STAY AND EAT The excellent **Forestry Resthouse**, set in a small clearing in the heart of the forest, charges US$10/15 single/double for comfortable rooms using communal showers, and US$20 for a self-contained double. Beers and soft drinks are normally available, and the staff will prepare any food you bring with you. Simple, inexpensive meals can also be prepared from scratch with a few hours' notice, using ingredients bought fresh in Kubease.

ADANWOMASE

Also known as Adangomase, this peaceful little village is one of the five original *kente* stools founded by Denkyira exiles, who settled around Kumasi shortly after their homeland was conquered by King Osei Tutu in 1701. It is still a good place to see *kente* being made today, and more accessible than in previous years following the set up of a promising new community-based tourism venture with the Peace Corps and NCRC. Two one-hour tours are available, both of them fascinating in their own right and charged at US$2 for non-Ghanaians, with discounts for volunteers and students. The *Kente* tour follows the production of this famous cloth from the spun thread through to the finished strip, weaving around the village where locals work in a new communal workshop or alone under the trees, and comes with explanations of the various types of cloth and the symbolism of their patterns. The village tour takes in the chief's palaces (both old and new), a traditional healer's shrine, local cocoa farms, and the *danwoma* tree for which the village was named: rather chilling local tradition has it that Adanwomase was founded when the seed was planted in the ground along with a human being who was buried alive. Ghoulish tales apart, Adanwomase is a very pleasant place to spend the night, and accommodation is provided in a newly built guesthouse for US$5 a head, or US$10 including breakfast and one other meal; additional meals cost US$3. The community has signed up to a charter which prevents locals from hassling or overcharging tourists, and guarantees them 40% of the profits of the scheme to invest in community projects in return. Adanwomase can be reached in a tro-tro direct from Kumasi's Kejetia Lorry Station, or you can combine it with visits to other artisanal villages in the area and get a share taxi from Bonwire or Ntonso for around US$0.20.

BONWIRE

The village of Bonwire received royal patronage in the time of King Osei Tutu, and for centuries afterwards the village's most skilful weavers were forbidden from selling cloth to anybody else without the express permission of the Ashanti king. Today it remains the best-known of the five original *kente* stools, but perhaps this is why it is also the one where visitors are most likely to be swindled or hassled. All the same, it's a good souvenir pit stop and still a good place to see weavers at work. Several guides are bound to approach you on arrival; they won't ask a fee but will expect a fair tip.

Bonwire lies about 20km northeast of Kumasi, from where it can easily be visited as a self-standing day trip. Direct tro-tros leave Kumasi from Manhyia Station, close to the synonymous palace, and take about 30 minutes in either direction. The village can also be reached from Ejisu (US$0.40 in a shared taxi) along the signposted 3km dirt road that branches west from the Ejisu–Effiduase road a few kilometres south of Juaben. There is no accommodation actually within the village, but the new **Bonwire Guesthouse** (✆ 024 784120), which lies within walking distance along the dirt road back towards the main Ejisu–Effiduase road, charges a reasonable US$7 for a large, clean, self-contained double with fan. Drinks are available but you will have to head into town for food.

WONOO

Less well known is the *kente*-weaving village of Wonoo, which was not one of the original five Ashanti *kente* stools, but also has a long tradition of weaving. The village receives fewer tourists that either Bonwire or Adanwomase, but the quality of cloth is just as good, and the prices are better (though not as good as in Kpetoe or Tafi Abuipe in Volta Region). Woonoo can be reached in a shared taxi from Ntonso, or a dropping taxi from Bonwire or Adanwomase.

EFFIDUASE AND SURROUNDS

Some 40km from Kumasi along a good, surfaced road through Ejisu, the relaxed market town of Effiduase forms a pleasant retreat into small-town Ashanti, away from the main roads and major tourist circuits. Local attractions include the fascinating Bodwease Shrine and scenic Atwia Escarpment, both of which lie to the north of Effiduase towards Nsuta, in an area offering some great off-the-beaten-track walking possibilities. In addition to this, Effiduase is conveniently situated for exploring most other places listed in this chapter: the manic tro-tro station has good tro-tro and/or shared taxi links in every imaginable direction, while a couple of good budget hotels lie on the outskirts of town.

GETTING THERE AND AWAY There are direct tro-tros from Kumasi to Effiduase, but it's just as easy to pick up something going along the Accra road as far as Ejisu and to change vehicles there. From the tro-tro station in Ejisu, you'll find shared taxis or minibuses heading to most local destinations, including Bodwease, Mampong, Nsuta, and Bonwire.

WHERE TO STAY AND EAT A couple of good budget hotels lie on the outskirts of Effiduase. Firstly, about 500m from the lorry station and signposted from the road towards Efface Secondary School, the **Panama Hotel** is a clean, friendly place with a bar and restaurant, running water, and rooms with fan in the US$6.50–9 bracket, depending on whether they are double/twin and self-contained. Another 500m along the same road, opposite the school, the **Lisp Hotel** is not quite as homely, but the large self-contained doubles with fan are even cheaper.

AROUND EFFIDUASE

Bodwease Shrine This large shrine, set in the village of Bodwease, is as architecturally impressive as any *Obosomfie* I have seen, and it houses a marvellous collection of fetishes and other artefacts such as bead necklaces, a clay fertility doll, ancient drums, animal bones and a couple of tortoises. Although the last priest here died some ten years ago, the spirit is still regarded as inhabiting the shrine, and locals say that it will eventually select another priest to act as its medium. Until that happens, the gracious old lady who acts as caretaker is willing to show the occasional tourist around the 150-year-old building; she will expect a fair tip, but nothing absurd. Also worth a look is the neighbouring chief's palace, a 12-room building which is plausibly claimed to be more than a century old. The chief wasn't around when I visited Bodwease, so I was shown only the outer rooms of the palace, but I'm told that he is happy to receive tourists provided they bring the customary bottle of schnapps. To reach Bodwease, you must first follow the surfaced Kwaman road out of Effiduase for about 8km until you reach Akotusu, where a dirt road to your left brings you to Bodwease after another 5–6km. Regular shared taxis connect Effiduase to Bodwease.

To Nsuta via the Atwia Escarpment The winding, 20km dirt road used by tro-tros and shared taxis connecting Effiduase to Nsuta and Mampong passes through a scenic region of hilly jungle, bisected from east to west by the Atwia Escarpment. Studded with several peaks reaching 600m, as well as numerous remote small towns notable for their traditional Ashanti and colonial architecture, this area has much to offer keen hikers and birders. The 1:50,000 survey sheet 0602B1 (on sale at the map office in Kumasi or Accra) shows several tracks and footpaths which link the villages at the base of the escarpment to those above it.

One alluring possibility, coming from Bodwease Shrine, would be to walk or catch a shared taxi 2km further north to Akorokyere. From here, you could follow a rough road along the base of the escarpment for about 5km west to Sekyere, then another 2km north to Banko, which lies on the road used by public transport between Effiduase and Nsuta.

Another interesting goal in the area, relatively accessible if you don't mind a bit of walking, is the Abesua (aka Abasua) Prayer Mountain, a tall part of the escarpment where people from all over Ghana come to take advantage of the mountain's prayer-answering abilities. The mountain is also notable for the virgin forest of the Ongwam II Forest Reserve, home to many species of birds and small mammals, and for magnificent views of the forest and other scarps in the area. To reach the mountain, ask a shared taxi between Effiduase and Nsuta to drop you at Atwia Adutwam, the forest-fringed village after which the escarpment is named and which lies near the base of its tallest peak. From here, a 2km walk takes you to the village of Abesua, right at the base of the mountain, where you will be able to organise a guide to lead you along the one-hour walking trail to the top. A 12-room guesthouse was reputedly under construction in Abesua a couple of years ago, but we've heard nothing to suggest it ever opened. Otherwise. the closest accommodation is 8km away at Nsuta (see *Mampong, Nsuta and Surrounds*, below). The mountain is easily visited as a day trip out of Effiduase, Nsuta or Mampong.

Bomfobiri Wildlife Sanctuary Gazetted in 1975, the 53km² Bomfobiri Wildlife Sanctuary is centred around the seasonal waterfall on the Boumfoum River after which it is named. The sanctuary harbours a variety of forest mammals, including Campbell's mona monkey, buffalo baboon, bushbuck, and black duiker. The rumoured presence of all three west African crocodile species and the rare bare-headed rock fowl have no apparent foundation, but the forest is of great interest to birders for the opportunity to see the likes of great blue turaco, yellow-casqued hornbill, black-and-white casqued hornbill, red-fronted parrot and Johanna's sunbird.

The entrance to Bomfobiri lies around 10–15km from the town of Kumawu along the Drabonso road. Kumawu itself is easy to reach on public transport, only 30 minutes from Effiduase along a good surfaced road. Without private transport, getting from Kumawu to the entrance could be problematic. Or more accurately, you can get to the entrance with ease using one of the tro-tros to Drabonso that leave Kumawu every afternoon between 15.00 and 16.00 – the difficulty is finding transport back, since vehicles returning to Kumawu from Drabonso are generally full when they come past the entrance. Short of walking back, the only viable option at present is to charter a taxi, which will cost around US$15–20 for a round day trip, and double that if you want to be taken out on one day and picked up a day or two later.

Before heading out to the sanctuary, you are obliged to visit the Department of Wildlife office in Kumawu, clearly signposted as you enter town from the direction of Effiduase. This is where you'll pay your entrance fee (US$2) and collect a guide (US$0.80 per hour for a day trip, negotiable for an overnight trip). It is also the best place to seek current advice about accommodation and camping, and to organise a taxi charter to the sanctuary.

There is no formal accommodation in the sanctuary, but travellers with a tent are free to camp with permission from the Department of Wildlife office in Kumawu. The closest accommodation to Kumawu is the **Manhattan Hotel**, which lies about 2km past the town centre on the Bodomase road – it's not signposted, but the bright orange exterior is a giveaway – and charges US$8/10 for a clean self-contained single/double with fan.

MAMPONG, NSUTA AND SURROUNDS

The seat of Ashanti's second most important chieftaincy, the silver stool of the Mamponhene, Mampong is also one of the largest towns in the region, with a population well in excess of 20,000. But unlike the urban sprawl that characterises so many Ghanaian settlements above a certain size, Mampong is centred around a compact, bustling core, dotted with fading colonial-era buildings in the town centre. It is also the site of an important market, but little visited by tourists on account of its notable absence of formal attractions.

There's not a lot to be said about the smaller and quieter junction town of Nsuta, which lies no more than 10km south of Mampong, but it is passed through by all traffic heading to Mampong from Effiduase. Nsuta also offers the closest accommodation to local attractions such as the Atwia Escarpment and Adango Shrine, which makes it a marginally more useful base for exploration than Mampong itself.

GETTING THERE AND AWAY Mampong is connected to Kumasi by a good surfaced road and regular minibus tro-tros, which take about an hour and cost US$1 for a seat. It also has good transport links to Nsuta and Effiduase. If you're thinking of stopping in Mampong en route to Yeji, note that it's actually easier to find direct transport there from Kumasi – most vehicles will be full by the time they pass through Mampong – though you can get from Mampong to Yeji in short hops changing tro-tros or shared taxis at Ejura and Atebubu.

WHERE TO STAY AND EAT By far the most appealing lodging in town is the **Mampong Guesthouse and Restaurant**, established in 2004 down an unmade road to the left of the police

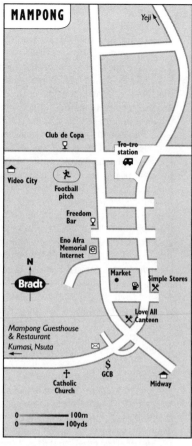

barrier just before you enter town from Kumasi. Nine large, clean and airy rooms are available, all of them self-contained and with a fan, and ranging in price from US$12 for a single big enough for two, to US$13.50 for a double. Share taxis to the town centre costs US$0.20. Cheaper but considerably less appealing rooms are available at the **Midway Hotel** (\ *056 522240*), about 500m from the tro-tro station along the Kumasi road. Expect to pay US$4.50–5.50 for a dark, shabby double using common bucket showers, or US$6 for one that is self-contained. Drinks are available but no food. Closer to the tro-tro station, the conspicuous green **Video City Hotel** next to the football field, was obviously conceived as an upmarket set up, but the peeling reality is notable only for its courtyard centred a around an empty pond, and its comparably dry bar. Hot, stuffy doubles without a fan or private bath facilities cost US$5, while marginally nicer self-contained doubles with running water and fan go for US$8.

The **Simple Stores Restaurant** on the main road between the tro-tro station and the Midway Hotel is very popular with locals for ice-cold drinks and hearty local meals (US$1.50–2.50 a plate) which can be eaten inside or in the courtyard bar.

The closest accommodation to Nsuta is the pleasant **Eldorado Hotel**, which lies about 2km out of town along the Mampong road and charges a bargain US$6 for a clean self-contained double with fan. A bar and restaurant are attached.

The Ashanti (also spelt 'Asante') are one of the few African peoples whose name is instantly familiar to many Westerners. Undoubtedly, this situation is in part a result of the unique role played by Ashanti in the pre-colonial and modern history of Ghana. No less, however, should it be recognised that the Ashanti owe their notoriety to the fact that, like, for instance, the Zulu or the Maasai, they were one of the few sub-Saharan African peoples to provide effective (if ultimately ineffectual) resistance against Britain's late-19th-century drive for colonialism.

The Ashanti Kingdom only started to take a recognisable modern shape under King Osei Tutu of the Oyoko clan in the dying years of the 17th century. What little is known about Ashanti history prior to this is fogged by myth. This is partly as a result of the ban, placed by Osei Tutu on his subject states, on passing down their own foundation legends to subsequent generations. Some oral traditions claim that the Ashanti people emerged from a hole in the ground near Lake Bosumtwi, others that they descended from the sky. More probable than either of the above scenarios is that the ancestral Ashanti, like other Akan peoples, migrated into modern Ghana from its ancient namesake in what is now Mali some time before the 13th century AD. It is likely that they had settled in their modern homeland north of the confluence of the Pra and Oda rivers by the early 17th century. The Oyoko clan, generally seen as the true founders of the Ashanti Kingdom, lived in the vicinity of Lake Bosumtwi, an area they called Amanse ('Beginning of Nations'), where they built a capital called Asantemanso (from which the name Asante or Ashanti derives).

For much of the 17th century, the proto-Ashanti consisted of several loosely linked chieftaincies scattered through an area radiating some 30–50km around modern-day Kumasi. All the evidence suggests that the people of this region enjoyed an immensely high standard of living as a result of the fertility of the soil and their strategic position at the conjunction of the main trade routes to the north and south. In these days, the area was noted particularly for its production of mildly narcotic kola nuts, exported via Salaga to the Muslim states of the Sahel and North Africa. The one thing that these chieftaincies lacked, however, was true political autonomy, since they were all essentially vassal states of the mighty Denkyira Empire, which retained control of the all-important gold trade to the coast throughout the 17th century.

The trend towards Ashanti military unification is thought to have emerged under Oti Akentem, who ascended to the stool of Asantemanso c1650. It continued under his successor Obiri Yeboa, who moved his capital to the more central location of Kwamaan before being killed in battle in 1697. Obiri Yeboa's successor was Osei Tutu, who with the help of the respected priest Okomfo Anokye would become the first true Asantehene (King of Ashanti), and who is still widely regarded as having been the greatest of Ashanti leaders.

In response to the death of his predecessor, Osei Tutu called upon the states of Juaben, Nsuta, Mampong, Bekwai and Kokofu to form a formal confederation with Kwaaman. Legend has it that when the chiefs of the six states assembled to discuss this union, the priest Okomfo Anokye summoned a golden stool from the sky to land in the lap of Osei Tutu, signifying that he should assume the role of paramount king of the new confederation. It is also claimed that the priest planted three palm (*kum*) trees in various parts of the union, and the first one to start growing was nominated as the site of the Ashanti capital, Kumasi (which means 'Under the Kum Tree').

AROUND MAMPONG
Mframaboum Caves These can be reached from Mampong by catching a shared taxi to Kwamang (possibly changing vehicles at Nsuta) where the chief can

When the Denkyirahene (King of Denkyira) heard about the newly formed Ashanti confederation, he responded by increasing tax demands, and dictating that the union should be dissolved, that each of its chiefs should chop off a finger to send him, and that the Asantehene should hand over the golden stool. The chiefs of Ashanti decided to go to war with Denkyira, though Okomfo Anokye warned that the chief who led Ashanti to victory would not live for more than seven days after the battle, and he advised that Osei Tutu should remain in Kumasi. The Mamponhene (King of Mampong) volunteered to serve as general provided that his stool was made second to that of the Asantehene (the silver stool of Mampong is to this day regarded to be second in importance only to the golden stool of Kumasi). In 1701, the Denkyirahene was captured and beheaded at Feyiase, and his kingdom became the first subject by conquest of the Asantehene.

Using revolutionary military tactics, and fuelled by its growing importance in the emergent slave trade, Ashanti grew from strength to strength in the 18th century. Osei Tutu was killed by snipers while crossing the Pra River and, after a brief period of internal instability, his successor Opuku Ware (1720–50) pursued a policy of military expansion that resulted in most of the Akan states of southern Ghana being subject to Ashanti by 1740. In 1744, Accra was briefly captured by the Ashanti army, and later in the same decade much of what is now northern Ghana fell under Ashanti rule. By the time of Osei Bonsu (Asantehene from 1801 to 1824), the kingdom covered an area larger than that of modern Ghana, spilling over into parts of what are now Côte d'Ivoire, Togo and Burkina Faso.

The 19th-century decline of Ashanti is linked to the parallel decline in the trans-Atlantic slave trade, which lay at the heart of the kingdom's economy. It was more or less sealed in 1896 when Britain occupied Kumasi and deported the Asantehene and several other important dignitaries to the Seychelles. In 1900, led by the aged queen mother Yaa Asantewaa, the Ashanti made one last brave but ill-fated attempt to remove Britain from Kumasi Fort, with the net result that even more of its traditional leaders were deported and Ashanti was formally annexed to Britain's Gold Coast colony. However, while this may have resulted in the core states of the Ashanti confederation losing their autonomy, they have never lost their identity – Britain was practically forced to restore the Asantehene to his stool in 1924, and the King of Ashanti is regarded as being the second most important political figure in Ghana to this day.

It is one thing to sum up the history of the Ashanti, another altogether trying to come to grips with their cultural institutions. Every Ashanti is a member of one of seven matrilineal 'families' as well as his or her clan, and of a patrilineal spiritual group known as a *nton*. Like many African cultures, great emphasis is placed on communality and the subservience of the individual to the nation (as an example, until recent times all land was communal, the nominal property of the Asantehene), yet paradoxically the highest of all Ashanti goals is personal power (one classic Ashanti proverb translates thus: 'If power is up for sale, then sell your mother to obtain it – once you have the power there are several ways of getting her back!').

If you are interested in finding out more, seek out one of the books written by Ghanaians and available for next to nothing in bookshops in Accra or Kumasi. Although many of them are based in part on dubious history, they still give insight into the facts and vicarious truths of Ashanti legend. The latest, and I suspect among the more credible, is Nana Otamakuro Adubofour's self-published *Asante: The Making of a Nation*, sold at the Palace Museum in Kumasi.

organise a guide. The caves lie two hours from Kwamang on foot, with the last stretch being rather tough – with luck you'll be offered lunch and liquid at a cocoa farm near the caves. There is nowhere to stay in Kwamang, though vague plans to

Of all the crafts practised in West Africa, few are more readily identifiable with a particular country than *kente* cloth with Ghana. Strongly associated with the Ashanti, modern kente is characterised by intricately woven and richly colourful geometric designs, generally dominated by bold shades of yellow, green, blue, orange and red. However, in its earliest form, before the introduction of exotic fabrics and dyes through trade with the European castles of the coast, kente cloth was somewhat less kaleidoscopic, since white and navy blue were the only available dyes.

According to Ashanti tradition, kente design originated at Bonwire, the small village close to Kumasi which still serves as the one of the main centres of kente production in south-central Ghana. Five kente stools were proclaimed by the first king of Kumasi, of which only Bonwire and Adanwomase remain active. The Ewe people of Volta Region, the country's other important centre of kente production, maintain that they were the first kente weavers, and that their techniques were adopted in Ashanti after some Ewe weavers were captured as slaves. While the Ewe claim has a certain ring of truth, the reality is that most people now associate kente cloth with Ashanti, where the skills of the finest weavers are to this day reserved for the use of royalty.

These days, much of the kente cloth you see on sale in Ghana is mass produced, and considered by experts to have little intrinsic merit. At Bonwire, Adanwomase and Wonoo, however, almost every homestead includes a few traditional weavers, who work at looms of ancient design to produce top-quality cloth. Visitors to Volta Region may also like to visit traditional centres of the kente craft, such as Kpetoe, a small town on the main Ho–Aflao road, or the small village of Tafi Abuipe near Tafi Atome. The best example of kente weaving that you are likely to see in Ghana today is the century-old piece of cloth on display in the National Museum, formerly the property of one of the kings of Ashanti.

Adinkra cloth is popular in many Akan societies, but is most strongly associated with the Ashanti. Like kente cloth, adinkra is generally worn by men in the form of a toga, but

build a resthouse may be abetted by an increase in tourism. Note that Kwamang lies within sight of Kuwamu, but the gorge that separates the towns is passable only on foot, a 5–10km hike depending on who you believe.

Adango Shrine This small *Obosomfie* in the village of Apiakrom is less architecturally interesting than others of its ilk, but it is studded with some impressive statues, notably a singular figure of a person lying on his back on the floor ('this is how you will lie when God punishes you'). The young fetish priest will show you a history of the shrine, written by his predecessor, in which it is claimed it was founded in 1799 by one Nana Akwasi Acheampong. The priest is a really friendly, straightforward guy, who didn't ask me for a libation and – uniquely – accepted my donation without quibbles or requests for extra payments. He is in session on Fridays and sometimes on Sundays, but you can visit the shrine at any time. To get there from Mampong (or for that matter from Effiduase), you must first catch a shared taxi to Nsuta. Apiakrom lies a short distance out of town along the Kwamaan road; any shared taxi heading to Kwaman will drop you there, but it only takes 15 minutes to walk.

NTONSO AND SURROUNDS

Straddling the main Kumasi–Mampong road, Ntonso is the major centre of *adinkra*-cloth design and manufacture in Ashanti. This is the dyed, red-and-black cloth that you often see older Ghanaians wearing draped around them as a toga, especially on Saturdays, since it is the customary attire for funerals. It is not the its use is reserved for funerals and other relatively sombre occasions rather than for celebrations, and adinkra symbolism takes the form of monochrome graphics as opposed to the colourful geometric abstractions of kente. Most contemporary adinkra cloth is made using a plain white calico textile which is then decorated with various ancient designs using calabash stamps and a dye obtained by boiling the bark of the badie tree, *Bridelia micranta*.

More than 60 different adinkra symbols are in use, each of them signifying a specific tradition or proverb. The most popular of these is the rather Chinese-looking *Gye Nyame*, symbolising the omnipotence of God, and is easily recognised since it is depicted on the 100 cedi banknote. Another popular symbol is *sankofa*, heart-shaped with two whirls inside, which has taken on a particular resonance in the post-independence era since it signifies the value of building on one's cultural roots. The *kuntinkantan* design of five interlocking circles depicts the value of pride in one's state or society over pride in oneself, while the *pempansie* (like two opposing figures of '3' linked by a concave bar) symbolises a chain and stresses the importance of each member of a society as part of the whole. While these and other traditional designs remain at the core of most adinkra designs, many modern craftsmen are prepared to experiment with variations reflecting the changing nature of Ghanaian society.

The origin of the adinkra dyeing technique is uncertain. It is thought to have been adopted by the Ashanti in around 1818, when King Osei Bonsu defeated the Gyaman, whose chief at the time was called Adinkra. Oral traditions differ as to whether the craft originated in the neighbouring territory of Denkyira or in the Jaman kingdom in what is now Côte d'Ivoire, both of which were vassal states of Ashanti during its early 19th-century peak. Today, the main centre of adinkra production is the village of Ntonso on the main Kumasi–Mampong road, where it is easy to arrange an informal guide to show you around.

cloth itself – either plain *kente* or imported cotton – that is made in Ntonso, but the dye stamps: it is possible to buy not only stamped cloth here, but also the actual stamps. As is the case in Adanwomase, the mood in Ntonso is welcoming and the pressure to buy is minimal. There are no organised guides, but the dyers are happy for you to watch them as they work in clusters under the trees, and it is easy to find an articulate person to explain the complex symbolism that lies behind the various *adinkra* designs.

South of Ntonso, on the outskirts of Kumasi, the villages of Ahwiaa and Pankrona are known respectively for their woodcarvings and pottery. In both cases, however, you've little chance of seeing the craftsmen at work,. At one point, the level of aggro meant these places were worth visiting only if you planned to buy – but recent reports suggest that Ahwiaa in particular is a worthwhile and pleasant excursion out of Kumasi.

GETTING THERE AND AWAY Any tro-tro heading between Kumasi and Mampong will drop you at Ntonso (or for that matter at Ahwiaa or Pankrona). If you want to continue directly on to Adanwomase or Wonoo, specify this, because the junction lies about 1km from Ntonso town centre in the direction of Mampong. There is a station at the junction from where reasonably regular shared taxis and minibuses head to both the *kente*-weaving villages. There are also shared taxis connecting Adanwomase to Wonoo. Although no public transport runs between Adanwomase and Bonwire, you can walk between the two villages in about half an hour along a little-used dirt road. Note that there is no accommodation in this area.

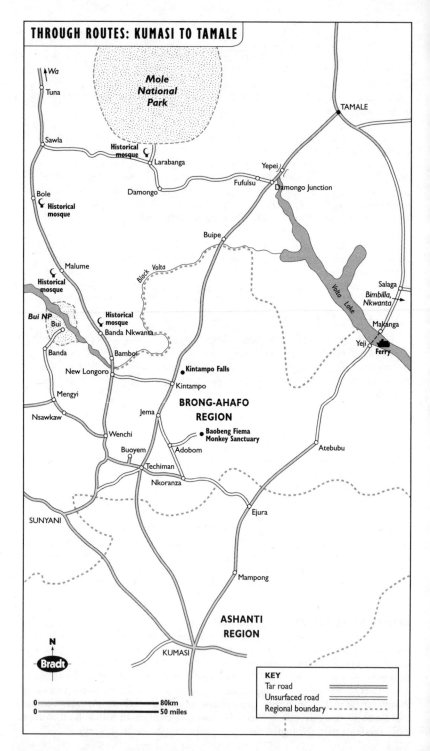

THROUGH ROUTES: KUMASI TO TAMALE

Wa
Tuna

Mole National Park

Sawla

Historical mosque ☾
Larabanga

Yepei

Damongo
Fufulsu
Damongo Junction

TAMALE

Bole
Historical mosque ☾

Buipe

☾ **Historical mosque**
Malume

Black Volta

Salaga
Bimbilla, Nkwanta

Bui NP
Bui

Banda

Historical mosque ☾
Banda Nkwanta

Bamboi

Makanga
Yeji
Ferry

Volta Lake

Banda
New Longoro

● **Kintampo Falls**
Kintampo

Mengyi

Nsawkaw

Wenchi

Jema

BRONG-AHAFO REGION

Buoyem

● **Baobeng Fiema Monkey Sanctuary**
Adobom

Techiman

Nkoranza

Atebubu

Ejura

SUNYANI

Mampong

ASHANTI REGION

N

Bradt

KUMASI

KEY	
Tar road	
Unsurfaced road	
Regional boundary	-----

0 ——— 80km
0 ——— 50 miles

16

From Kumasi to Tamale

Most travellers heading northwards from Kumasi travel along the main north–south highway to Tamale, passing through Techiman and Kintampo. This 400km trip takes about six hours by STC bus, the best way to go if you're doing it in one stretch. Alternatively, it can be broken up using a mixture of shared taxis and tro-tros. The most alluring diversion is the excellent and readily accessible Boabeng-Fiema Monkey Sanctuary, which many visitors have rated as the highlight of their time in Ghana, though the more adventurous might be tempted to divert through Sunyani and Wenchi to the little-visited Bui National Park on the River Volta northwest of Wenchi. Other more low-key attractions include the Tano Sacred Grove and Buoyem Caves near Techiman, and the Kintampo Falls near the town of the same name.

It's worth noting that Mole National Park, covered in the next chapter, does in fact lie along a side road departing from the Kumasi–Tamale road at Fufulsu, on which basis it might reasonably be considered to belong in the present chapter. The reason it has been excluded is that the vast majority of travellers visit Mole on public transport, which is not a realistic option directly from Fufulsu, so that Mole is most often visited in the form of an excursion from Tamale.

SUNYANI *Updated with the assistance of David Thackeray*

Capital of Brong-Ahafo Region since 1909, Sunyani lies at the heart of one of Ghana's main areas of cocoa and kola nut production. The name of the town derives from the Akan phrase '*ason ndwae*', a reference to a time when the elephants that lived in the surrounding forest provided hunters with a rich source of income in the form of ivory. These days, there's not a great deal of virgin forest left in the region, and the elephants have long since been hunted out, but the substantial forest patch about 1km out of town along the same road as the Providence Bar might be worth investigating for birds, butterflies and possibly monkeys. Otherwise there is little of specific interest to travellers – in town or in the immediate vicinity – but it's still a pleasant enough place to spend a couple of days. There are no hustlers, local people tend to be very friendly, and the construction workers (of whom there are many) have a photogenic penchant for perching in long rows on their upended wheelbarrows.

The substantial town of Berekum, which lies one hour west of Sunyani by tarmac road and is regularly connected to it by tro-tros, has an interesting decaying British colonial vibe, quite a good market, a few mediocre hotels, a wackily designed new church, and all the usual banks. It would make a nice short day-excursion by car. Further west, there are quite good hiking opportunities based out of towns such as Adamsu and Zezera on the Côte d'Ivoire border, but there is absolutely no tourist infrastructure in these areas.

333

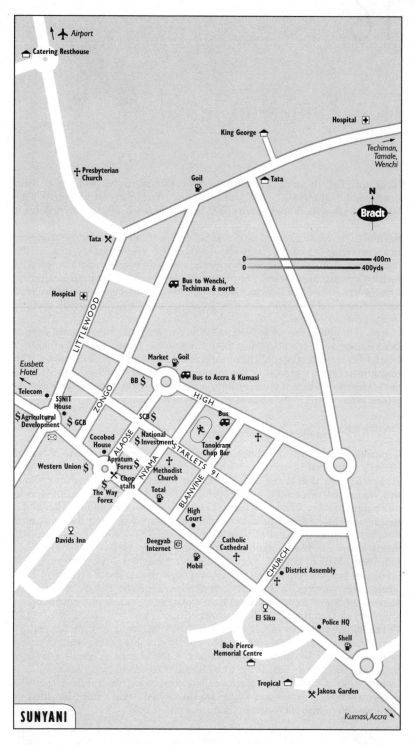

Airport

Catering Resthouse

Hospital

King George

Techiman,
Tamale,
Wenchi

Presbyterian
Church

Goil

Tata

N
Bradt

Tata

Hospital

LITTLEWOOD

Bus to Wenchi,
Techiman & north

0   400m
0   400yds

Eusbett
Hotel

Telecom

Market   Goil

Bus to Accra & Kumasi

ZONGO

BB $

HIGH

SSNIT
House

SCB $

Bus

$ Agricultural
Development

$ GCB

Cocobod
House

National
Investment

Tanokram
Chop Bar

ALAOSE

STARLETS

Western Union $

Apratum
Forex $

Chop
stalls

NYAMA

Methodist
Church

BLANVINE

91

The Way
Forex

Total

Davids Inn

Deegyab
Internet

High
Court

Catholic
Cathedral

Mobil

CHURCH

District Assembly

El Siku

Police HQ

Shell

Bob Pierce
Memorial Centre

Tropical

Jakosa Garden

Kumasi, Accra

SUNYANI

GETTING THERE AND AWAY Regular tro-tros run along the 130km road between Kumasi and Sunyani, taking about two hours either way, and cost around US$2. There is also plenty of transport between Sunyani and Wenchi, Techiman, Tamale and Accra, including a daily STC bus leaving Accra at 15.30 and arriving in Sunyani at around 02.00 the next day. CityLink also runs flights out of the army airport to and from Accra every other day for US$100 (↘ *061 23335* or *021 785725*).

Sunyani will also be a good stopover for the Côte d'Ivoire if and when the conflict in that country settles down. There are quicker road connections to Yammoussoukro via the Ivorian town of Abengourou (if you have your own vehicle) than anywhere else in Ghana at the moment. A good tarmac road runs straight west from Sunyani to Berekum (one hour), from where some 30 minutes of potholed roads lead to Drobo; thereafter it's about 45–60 minutes to the (official) Côte d'Ivoire border at Sampa via a horrendous dirt track. Long-standing plans to surface the Drobo–Sampa road might come to fruition in 2007, making the trip from Sunyani to the border about two hours.

WHERE TO STAY AND EAT
Upmarket

🏠 **Eusbett Hotel** ↘ 061 27116; f 061 24392; e eusbett@etcite.com. An unexpectedly plush modern multi-storey block situated about 1km west of the town centre, the Eusbett Hotel charges US$37 for a small, self-contained 'budget room' or US$60–125 for smart sgls/dbls with AC, DSTV & hot water. Facilities inc a good restaurant, swimming pool, first class gym, onsite internet & a well-stocked supermarket. *US$37–125.*

Budget

🏠 **Bob Pierce Memorial Centre** ↘ 061 27152. Just around the corner from the Tropical, this strange establishment was funded by World Vision (& named after its founder), & turned over to the local community to run. The upshot is a bleak but friendly operation. *Dbl US$10–16.*

🏠 **Catering Resthouse** ↘ 061 27280. Set in large green grounds about 500m from the town centre along the road towards the airport, the Catering Resthouse is undoubtedly the best deal in this range – a carpeted self-contained suite with hot water, AC & TV costs US$18, with discounts often available on request. Some food is available, though the menu is limited to gizzard kebabs & one or two local staples, but chilled drinks are more easily come by. The hotel hosts occasional reggae & highlife dance parties, mainly catering for the crowd from the local polytechnic, every 2–4 weeks (there are fly-posters around town well in advance). *Suite US$18.*

🏠 **Tropical Hotel** ↘ 061 27179/24398. Situated off the Kumasi road about 1km from the main lorry station, this substantial hotel offers self-contained accommodation from US$10 for a timeworn but acceptably clean sgl with fan, to US$10/17 for a sgl/dbl with AC, or a whacking US$25–34 for rooms with AC, TV, hot water & fridge. Local and continental dishes are available on request but the next-door Jakosa Garden Restaurant looks like a better bet. *US$10–34.*

Shoestring

🏠 **Tata Hotel** ↘ 06123511. Situated about 1km from the town centre on the Techiman road, this unpretentious hotel offers the cheapest rooms in town, ranging from US$3 to US$9 & all using common showers. It's probably best to get rooms away from the road, to avoid traffic noise in the early morning. The bar has a good atmosphere, with highlife music played in the evening at the weekend. *US$3–9.*

WHERE TO EAT AND DRINK Sunyani's finest eatery is **Gina's Restaurant**, on the ground floor of the Eusbett Hotel, which serves a good selection of continental, Chinese and Ghanaian dishes in the US$4–7 range. For cheaper eats, the new **Jakosa Garden Restaurant** next to the Tropical Hotel serves traditional Ghanaian dishes for USS$2 a plate, while the **Drop-Inn Bar** on Starlets 91 Av serves similar fare to the nearby chop stalls, with the addition of cheap drinks and a good atmosphere. The **Mandela Restaurant** near the Tata Hotel has also been recommended.

OTHER PRACTICALITIES

Foreign exchange Forex bureaux are unexpectedly prolific in Sunyani (far more so than in larger and more touristed centres such as Tamale or Bolgatanga) but rates are quite variable so do shop around – The Way Forex Bureau diagonally opposite Cocobod House was offering the best rate in town in late 2003, indeed only slightly lower than the rate in Accra or Kumasi. The Barclays Bank opposite the market will accept travellers' cheques but it doesn't have ATM facilities.

Internet Although several internet cafés are marked on the map, the standard browsing rate is high and connections are typically very slow. The air-conditioned internet café on the ground floor of Cocobod House charges US$1.80 per hour, and has cheap telephone and photocopying facilities, but the machines often break down. Also central is the Liberty Internet Café, which lies 200m past Cocobod House near the crossroads with Nyama Road, charges US$1.50 per hour, tends to be slightly quicker than Cocobod, and is the only café open on Sunday. Better still is an obscure internet café next to the computer shop opposite Sunyani Polytechnic (200m past the large church and Mobil station), which offers far better service, is rarely full, and charges US$1 per hour. There are plans to introduce broadband at the Centre for the Empowerment of the Vulnerable (immediately left of Standard Chartered Bank) in 2004, which should result in a far speedier if not cheaper service.

Shopping Cocobod House has a ground-floor supermarket, which stocks a large range of Western imports at prices ranging from reasonable to highly inflated. Eusbett Hotel aside, it's the best place in Brong-Ahafo for essential toiletries and general luxuries.

WENCHI

This reasonably large town, linked by regular tro-tros to Sunyani and Techiman on the main Kumasi–Tamale road, is something of a local route focus, but of interest to travellers mostly as the springboard for visits to Bui National Park. If you need to spend a night, you have the choice of two good-value budget hotels. The friendly blue **Baah Hotel** (℡ 0652 22690), 100m from the bus station along the Wa road, is a bargain: about US$3 for a reasonably clean ground-floor double with fan and shared bucket showers or US$4 for a self-contained upstairs double. The owner seems to keep himself up-to-date with the practicalities surrounding visits to Bui. A definite notch up in both standard and price, the multi-storey **Pony Hotel** (℡ 0652 22343) off the Kumasi road has a wide selection of clean rooms with fans, ranging from a single using common showers at US$5.50 to a self-contained twin with TV and fridge for US$10. Neither of the hotels has a restaurant, and the only possibility for a sit-down meal, so far as I can see, is the less than tempting **Managye Restaurant** – a grand name for a shack in the lorry station. There are a few basic chop stalls around the lorry station; nevertheless Wenchi does come across as something of a culinary black hole.

BUI NATIONAL PARK

The seldom-visited Bui National Park near the Côte d'Ivoire border is the third largest in Ghana, protecting an area of 1,821km² on either side of the Black Volta River, including the large Bui Gorge. The park is best known for its population of roughly 200 hippos, the largest in Ghana, but it also protects small numbers of several terrestrial mammals, including roan antelope, hartebeest, waterbuck, kob,

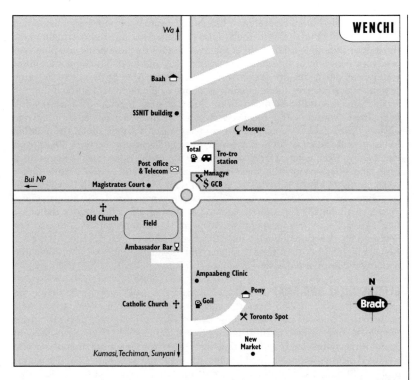

Wa
Baah
SSNIT building
Mosque
Total
Tro-tro station
Post office & Telecom
Managye
GCB
Magistrates Court
Bui NP
Old Church
Field
Ambassador Bar
Ampaabeng Clinic
Pony
Catholic Church
Goil
Toronto Spot
Kumasi, Techiman, Sunyani
New Market
N
Bradt

bushbuck, warthog, and green and patas monkeys. Large carnivores are thinly distributed, but spotted hyena and leopard are probably resident, and a smattering of unverified sight records of lion and African hunting dog over the past 15 years suggest that both species pass through from time to time. Three crocodile species occur in the river, including the localised dwarf and long-snouted crocodiles, but they are seldom observed by casual visitors. More than 220 bird species have been recorded, including several interesting forest species associated with the lush riparian woodland along the river, access to which is more-or-less restricted to the dry months of January to March.

Long mooted as the possible site of an hydro-electric scheme, Bui Gorge is likely to be dammed in the near future, which will cause all land below the 180m contour to be flooded. This will have several implications for the park's ecology. Much of the riparian forest and adjacent woodland will be lost, as will the numerous forested islands in the Volta River, resulting in the likely death of most of the park's monkeys and duikers, and the evacuation of forest-associated birds. The permanent submergence of the fertile seasonal floodplains flanking the Volta is likely to result in the depletion of the park's hippo population, which depends on these plains for grazing. Although there is some talk of extending the park's boundaries in compensation, much of this surrounding land is in poor ecological condition, and it lacks the biodiversity of the riparian woodland and grasslands that will be lost in the flood.

For the time being, however, Bui forms a perfectly feasible goal for backpackers, serviced as it is by basic accommodation built by Raleigh International, and inexpensive overnight camping and hiking trips, which are easily organised through the flexible rangers at Bui Camp. The most popular activity is a river trip with a local fisherman to look for hippos (or at least their ears poking out of the

From Kumasi to Tamale BUI NATIONAL PARK

16

water), as well as monkeys, monitor lizards and a variety of bird species associated with water and riparian forest. You are also permitted to camp out overnight to see the hippos and other wildlife out of the river, but for the time being you'll need to take your own tent or mosquito net, sleeping bag and food. The hippos are most readily seen during the dry season, from December to May. At the end of the rainy season, river trips may not be possible at all due to the high level of the water.

You can also walk unguided from Bui Camp to the top of a nearby hill (signposted 'sunset walk') and get a great view across the whole park and the villages down below – and, possibly, a great sunset. Further afield, the Wildlife Division staff can take you to Banda Ahenkro (a village approximately 10km from Bui Camp), from where a steep climb to the top of the ridge leads to some small caves and offers panoramic views into Côte d'Ivoire and across Ghana. Other walks in the National Park can be arranged with a ranger and will be tailored to suit. Entrance costs US$2 to non-Ghanaians (students pay US$0.80 only), and guides cost US$0.80 per hour. Expect to pay around US$5 per day for the canoe hire. Overall, it's a very inexpensive safari, even if you don't get to see hippos, but reader feedback is split down the middle between three or four travellers who rated Bui as a highlight of their time in Ghana, and a similar number who reckoned the park was a complete let-down.

GETTING THERE AND AWAY The park headquarters at Bui Camp lie 8km from the village of Banda and 2km from the village of Bui on the Black Volta. The best route to the camp is from Wenchi. One large tro-tro daily does the 85km run from Wenchi to Bui village via Bui Camp, leaving Bui at 05.30, arriving in Wenchi about three hours later, and starting the return trip any time after that. The tro-tro is normally only half-full when it passes Bui Camp, so you'll have no problem finding a seat when you leave. If for some reason you can't find direct transport to or from Bui, there are at least three tro-tros daily in either direction between Wenchi and Banda, from where it's a reasonably flat 8km walk to Bui Camp. What you shouldn't do is take a vehicle from Wenchi that's going only as far as Nsoko or Mengyi, since you may well get stuck and neither village has any accommodation.

The only alternative to the Wenchi route is the signposted side-road that leaves the main road to Bole and Wa from near Banda Nkwanta, the site of a well-known mosque (see page 399). Be warned, however, that the signpost at this junction, which blithely proclaims Bui Camp to be 50km away, is not only inaccurate (the distance is more like 15–20km), but it also omits to mention that the Volta River, unbridged and unaffordable by car, lies about 2km before the camp! For those using public transport, this road is a more realistic possibility, but only on Mondays when a few tro-tros leave Banda Nkwanta for the riverbank opposite Bui in the early morning and start the return trip in mid-morning. Passengers can cross the river in a local canoe.

Bui Camp actually lies some 4km outside the national park boundary, so you'll need to arrange to walk there with a guide. Guide fees for day walks into the park cost US$0.75 per hour, while overnight camping trips cost around US$2.50 per day, plus there is a US$1 entrance fee. The alternative to entering the park on foot would be to organise a canoe trip out of Bui village.

WHERE TO STAY AND EAT Two of the wooden chalets at Bui Camp have been upgraded for travellers, and while they are by no means luxurious, they are very clean and comfortable, with beds and bedding provided, netted windows, and hooks for mosquito nets. The cost is US$4 a night for a double room, less for the floor. There's a basic bathroom for bucket showers, with water either collected by yourself or local community members from the borehole, and pit latrines are under construction. There is no electricity but Tilley lamps are provided. Food can be bought from a local lady if there is enough rice available, but there is no choice and no guarantee that there will be any at all. If you take your own food, on the other hand, there are coal pots to cook on. At present, the only possibility for those who enter the park overnight is to camp in their own tent. In the near future, however, it is likely that a few treehouses will be constructed next to some established hippo-viewing sites. There is no accommodation in the villages of Banda, Bui or Banda Nkwanta.

TECHIMAN AND SURROUNDS

Techiman is a substantial and rather ancient junction town straddling the main Tamale road about 60km northeast of Sunyani and 120km north of Kumasi. The long-standing capital of the Techiman-Bono Kingdom, claimed to have been the first of Ghana's centralised Akan states, Techiman is notable today for its sprawling food market – reputedly the largest of its kind in the country – and is passed through by the River Tono with its sacred fishes and crocodiles (the latter sometimes seen along the stretch of river through town). For travellers, Techiman forms a significant route focus, and it has long served as the springboard for visits to the popular Boabeng-Fiema Monkey Sanctuary, though it is also in the process of being developed as a tourist centre in its own right. Two community-based tourist projects have recently started operating in the area – the Tano Sacred Grove and Buoyem Caves – and similar projects have been earmarked for the Kristo Boase Monastery (rocky scenery, occasional monkeys) and a Catholic grotto.

The tourist office close to the main traffic roundabout can provide information about these local attractions, as well as guides if required, and accommodation details and further travel directions. There are also plans to initiate two- and three-day trips out of Boabeng-Fiema or Techiman taking in various combinations of the Bouyem Caves, Tano Sacred Grove, Techiman Catholic Grotto, Kintampo Falls and Boabeng-Fiema Monkey Sanctuary. Visit the tourist office or email ncrckuma@ghana.com for further details.

GETTING THERE AND AWAY You'll have absolutely no problem finding a tro-tro or shared taxi to Techiman from Kumasi, Sunyani, Kintampo, or Tamale. STC buses between Kumasi and Tamale/Bolgatanga pass through Techiman and stop on request, though you will have to pay the full fare. If you're travelling by tro-tro from Kumasi, note that there is another village called Techiman in the area, so do check you're heading to the right one! From Sunyani, look out for Tangoboase, a small town famous in Ghana for its tomato-canning factory.

WHERE TO STAY

Moderate

Dery Hotel 061 91211. This large new hotel is similar in price & standard to the Premier Palace, & probably the better bet these days. It is also notable for a wonderful menu that lists pastas under 'frainaceous dishes' (US$3, incidentally). *Clean, spacious dbl rooms cost US$15/25 depending on whether they have AC, but an extra US$5 charge is levied if 2 people of the same sex share.*

Premier Palace Hotel 061 91299 or 020 8119670. Situated some 1.5km out of town along the Sunyani road, this deceptively smart new hotel is notable for its bright modern décor & attractive grounds, but standards of service & cleanliness have drawn less favourable comments from a few readers. An excellent restaurant serves a wide selection of meals, ranging from US$3.50 for pasta dishes to around US$6 for fish or meat, though there has been the occasional report of poor service. *Self-contained dbl with DSTV & fan US$16–25, depending on size & whether they have a fridge, more luxurious dbl/twin with AC US$35/40.*

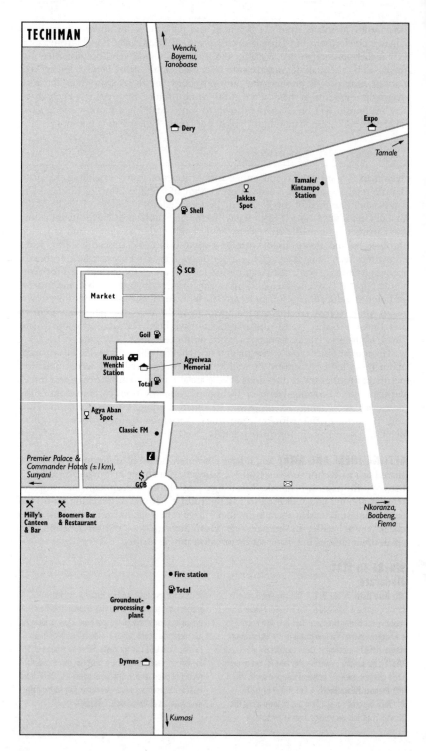

TECHIMAN

Wenchi,
Boyemu,
Tanoboase

Dery

Expo

Tamale

Shell

Jakkas
Spot

Tamale/
Kintampo
Station

$ SCB

Market

Goil

Kumasi
Wenchi
Station

Agyeiwaa
Memorial

Total

Agya Aban
Spot

Classic FM

Premier Palace &
Commander Hotels (±1km),
Sunyani

$
GCB

Nkoranza,
Boabeng,
Fiema

Milly's
Canteen
& Bar

Boomers Bar
& Restaurant

Fire station

Total

Groundnut-
processing
plant

Dymns

Kumasi

Budget and shoestring

🏠 **Agyeiwaa Memorial Hotel** (30 rooms) ☎ 0653 22074. This 2-storey block, centred around a shady garden bar, is conveniently located about 100m from the main lorry station, & the friendly staff & good-value accommodation are routinely praised by readers – though mosquitoes can be a problem. The restaurant serves a good selection of Chinese, continental & local meals in the US$3–4 range. The rooms cater to a wide range of budgets. *Sgl with fan US$5, self-contained dbl with fan US$17, self-contained dbl with AC & TV US$26.*

🏠 **Commander Hotel** ☎ 0653 22360 or 020 82156158. This pleasantly rustic hotel, which lies about 1.5km from the town centre along the Sunyani road, would be good value in most other parts of Ghana at US$10 for a large carpeted dbl with fan, but it doesn't really match up to Techiman's finest. No food is available, but you could eat at the neighbouring Premier Palace Hotel. *US$10.*

🏠 **Dymns Hotel** ☎ 0653 22112 or 024 598291. This pleasant 3-storey hotel lies just off the Kumasi road a few hundred metres south of the main traffic circle. As with the Agyeiwaa, the rooms here cater to a broad range of budgets. The restaurant has a varied menu, with most items falling in the US$2.50–4.50 range, & meals can also be taken in the hotel's large green garden bar, which lies on the opposite side of the road to the main building. Neat & clean self-contained dbls, some with DSTV & fan or AC. *Dbl US$9–18, suite with AC US$35–39.*

✗ WHERE TO EAT The restaurants at the **Premier Palace**, **Agyeiwaa Memorial**, **Dery**, and **Dymns Hotels** are all good. The best stand-alone restaurant in Techiman is **Boomers**, on the Sunyani road, which serves local dishes from US$1.50 and continental meals for around US$3.

TANO SACRED GROVE Of the two eco-tourist sites already operating, the Tano Sacred Grove is the more accessible, situated at the village of Tanoboase on the main Tamale road 15km north of Techiman. It consists of an attractive cluster of sandstone rock formations, now formally protected within a community-run sanctuary, which lie at the source of the Tano River. The stretch of river protected within the sanctuary is believed to house Taakora, the greatest of the earthly Akan gods, and it is the site of an annual cleansing festival called the Apoo in April or May. In addition to its spiritual significance, the sanctuary protects a variety of mammals and birds. Patas monkey and baboon had become very rare here in recent years, but seem to have multiplied in number since the sanctuary was created and a ranger station established. A trip to the grove can incorporate a cultural visit to the village of Baafi, and – assuming you're reasonably fit and fearless – a hike up steep rock surfaces to the top of the escarpment and a stunning lookout point used during the 18th-century Ashanti-Bono Wars. Other attractions include the fruit-bat colony in the trees of the sacred grove, and a tour of historical sites related to the 18th-century Ashanti-Bono Wars.

Tanoboase and Techiman are connected by regular shared taxis. Once in Tanoboase, anybody will be able to point you to the sacred grove or the ranger station on the outskirts of town. A fee of US$0.50 per person is levied for a total hike of one to two hours. It is easy to visit Tano as a day trip from Techiman, but a guesthouse at the site offers inexpensive accommodation in two twin rooms with shower and toilet facilities, or men could try the beautiful Benedictine monastery built into the rock, and signposted from the main road, where you can eat and live with the monks in return for a donation.

BUOYEM CAVES The other developed tourist site near Techiman consists of three large caves situated in a sandstone canyon near the village of Buoyem, where the Bono people retreated in the 18th century after their defeat by the Ashanti at Tano Sacred Grove. A variety of tours is offered by the local community, ranging from a straightforward climb to the caves – one of which harbours a huge colony of Rosetta fruit bats – to a five-hour hike passing through the Mprisi rainforest via the impressive Africa Rock and Bibiri Waterfall (good for a swim), or a highly recommended two-day camping trip with an overnight stay under Canopy Rock. The fee structure is US$2 per person to go to the caves, US$3 to the caves and a waterfall near town, or US$5 to add Africa Rock and Bibiri falls. Discounts are available for larger groups, and trips can be arranged on arrival or in advance by calling the local communication centre (❝ 061 26461) and asking for Nana Adjei Ameyaw.

Buoyem lies approximately 8km from Techiman, along a rough dirt road into the bush, and takes about 30 minutes. Shared taxis cost around US$0.50 and leave Techiman from the Wenchi Station on normal days, or from the main Kumasi/Market Station on market days (Wednesday, Thursday and Friday). If public transport is slow, a charter taxi should cost no more than US$2.50 one-way. The village is reached by following the Wenchi road north, and turning right after about 1.5km at the Buoyem signboard, then continuing straight until the road splits. Take the right fork and continue straight to the village, passing through Mesidan en route. The community-run **guesthouse** in Buoyem consists of five single bedrooms, a lounge, and a shared toilet and showers. There is electricity, and water is supplied daily. Each of the rooms costs US$5 for non-Ghanaians or US$3 for Ghanaians. Meals can be provided on request, or visitors can cook using the guesthouse facilities. You're advised to wear solid shoes and proper trousers for the hike to the bat cave – and a hat to protect against bat poo!

NKORANZA

Until recently, the small town of Nkoranza, set in green wooded hills some 25km east of Techiman, was known to travellers solely as the place to change vehicles en route to Boabeng-Fiema. But this has all changed with the set up of a budget guesthouse at **Operation Hand in Hand**, a community-based project for mentally handicapped children run by a Dutch doctor. The project provides shelter to 30 mentally handicapped children who might otherwise be homeless and lies in a compound on the outskirts of town behind the hospital.

The guesthouse consists of six round, stone-built huts with running water and a double bed, set in a beautiful location a short distance further out towards the hills. Accommodation costs US$4 per room without meals, or US$8 for full-board. Alternatively guests can camp or hire bedding to sleep in the beautiful 'hermitage', a natural rock formation covered over with a roof. Other attractions include an internet café, although it does tend to be rather slow, and a craft shop which sells jewellery, attractive postcards, and items made by the children. Visitors are encouraged to interact with the children, who all seem very happy and stimulated, and you can ask about local cultural points of interest such as the traditional religion and the chief. The guesthouse can also be used as a base to explore Boabeng-Fiema (half an hour away in a private vehicle) and Kintampo Falls (one hour away). The project accepts a limited number of volunteers, who are given free accommodation in return for their help. Placements must last at least two weeks, and should be pre-arranged (❝ 061 24342; **e** handinhand@ghana.com; www.operationhandinhand.nl).

Plenty of tro-tro traffic runs between Techiman and Nkoranza. Direct public transport from Kumasi's Racecourse or Kejetia stations takes about two hours. The Hand in Hand Guesthouse is situated directly behind St Theresa Hospital, and the road there passes through the hospital compound. Arriving on public transport, a dropping taxi should cost around US$0.80, or you can walk there in about ten minutes – ask for directions to the hospital (about 500m from the lorry park), then go through the hospital gate, keeping to the right, and after about 100m cross a bridge over a gutter directly opposite the main hospital building, from where it's another 300m or so to the project.

BOABENG-FIEMA MONKEY SANCTUARY

This wonderful small sanctuary was created in 1974 to protect the monkey population supported within a 35-hectare patch of semi-deciduous forest centred around the villages of Boabeng and Fiema, which lie 1km apart in Nkoranza District. Two monkey species occur here in significant numbers, the mona monkey and black-and-white colobus, but there are also unsubstantiated reports of sightings of green, patas, spot-nosed and Diana monkeys in recent years. The mona monkey population is thought to stand at around 400 individuals, living in troops of 15–50 animals, several of which now have a territory in the forest fringe and adjacent woodland. The black-and-white colobus monkeys, with a population of 200 animals divided into 13 troops, are rarely seen outside the true forest.

The reason why significant monkey populations have survived here but not in most other parts of Ghana is that the inhabitants of both villages regard them as sacred. This tradition has been undermined somewhat in recent years by the rising influence of Christianity, for which reason it is now illegal to hunt monkeys within a 5km radius of either village. Oral tradition dates the monkey taboo to 1831, when the villages were founded, and a special festival is held to this day for the monkeys every November. So serious is the taboo that whenever a monkey dies it is given a formal burial and funeral service by the villagers.

As for how the taboo arose, one story is that Boabeng was founded by a Brong warrior who, seeing two mona and two black-and-white colobus monkeys guarding a piece of white calico, consulted his patron god, Daworoh, and was told that the monkeys would bring him good fortune. Another story is that Daworoh married Abodwo, the patron saint of Ashanti-founded Fiema, and that the monkeys are their offspring. Yet another tradition is that a former chief who had the ability to turn people into monkeys and back at will, something that was useful in battle, died before he was able to transform some 'monkeys' back into human form. According to this version of events, the colobus monkeys are men and the monas are women, and the two interbreed freely!

The main centre for monkey-viewing is Boabeng village, ten minutes' walk from the resthouse, where a one-off entrance fee of US$4 (most of which goes towards community projects) must be paid to the game scouts and is valid for the duration of your stay. The mona monkeys that scavenge from the village are particularly tame and they spend a great deal of time on the ground; it is highly rewarding to be able to watch these normally shy forest monkeys interact at such close quarters. The colobus monkeys are shyer and they stick to the trees, but you should easily get a clear view of them, and it's wonderful to see them leap between trees with their feathery white tails in tow. Although the village is the best place to see monkeys at close range, you can also do a guided walk along some of the 10km of footpaths that emanate from it; an opportunity to see some of the many birds and butterflies in the forest, as well as a giant mahogany tree thought to be more than 150 years old. Small plastic bottles of the excellent local honey are on sale at the entrance.

GETTING THERE AND AWAY The monkey sanctuary lies about 6km along a clearly signposted turn-off running eastwards from the dirt road that connects Nkoranza to Jema. The springboard for visits is Techiman, from where you will first need to take a shared taxi to Nkoranza, 25km to the east. From Nkoranza, you shouldn't have to wait too long for a shared taxi heading directly northwards to Fiema (US$0.90), another roughly 25km trip. Ask to be dropped at the resthouse, on the left side of the road about 1km before you enter Fiema. With luck, you can get from Techiman to Fiema in about one hour, and even on a slow day you should be there in two hours. If you don't mind more frequent changes, one reader recommends doing the trip in a series of shorter tro-tro journeys, along the back roads via Tanoboase, then Kranka, Yeffi and Tanko, for less traffic and dust. Heading back to Nkoranza tends to be a little harder, but one of the Fiema residents recently bought a car to ferry visitors, although you'll have to bargain hard.

Travellers leaving Fiema for points further north should note that, while shared taxis do run along the road connecting Nkoranza to Jema, they are normally full when they pass the Fiema junction. In other words, rather than trying to head directly between Fiema and Jema, you might be better heading back to Techiman and picking up a northbound vehicle there.

WHERE TO STAY AND EAT Established as part of a community project, the recently renovated **resthouse** charges US$6 for a large, double (although you are advised to bring your own sheet as theirs are often a bit dirty) or US$1 per person to camp. Meals can be provided by private arrangement with the caretaker – expect to pay around US$2.50 per substantial plate – and beers and soft drinks are also sold.

A new and evidently nameless hotel recently opened less than 6km from the sanctuary – it consists of seven dirty rooms with fan in the US$4–5 range, and also has an on-site restaurant.

KINTAMPO

This moderately sized town lies on the main north–south road, almost precisely halfway between Kumasi and Tamale, and all STC buses stop here for 10–15 minutes when running between these towns. The town itself is somewhat scruffy and amorphous and of limited interest to travellers – clutching at straws, students of colonial architecture just might want to take a peek at the century-old former prison building that now serves as the police station – but the surrounding area is notable for a couple of waterfalls. Trivia lovers might also relish the knowledge that the official Centre of Ghana, as measured in colonial times, lies a few hundred metres before the STC bus stop as you enter the town from Kumasi. Decorated by a local artist, the exact site lies about 100m left of the main road, behind a football field under a big mango tree.

The best-known attraction in the area is the 25m high Kintampo Falls, known as Saunders Falls in the colonial era (after a British medical officer stationed at Kintampo) and briefly renamed Nkrumah Falls in honour of Ghana's first president shortly after independence. The waterfall lies on the Pumpum River, a tributary of the Black Volta, about 5km from Kintampo alongside the Tamale road, where it was reputedly discovered by local hunters in the 18th century. The waterfall is most impressive during the rains, but is still worth visiting in the dry season. The pool at the base can easily be reached by a concrete staircase that dates from the mid-1960s, when the construction of a State House at the waterfall was aborted following the 1966 coup that ousted Nkrumah. There's a large cave a short distance further upstream, while the fringing riparian forest is dominated by mahogany trees up to 40m high and looks promising for birding. According to a local brochure, the area around the waterfall is home to a large but harmless aquatic snake, which is sometimes seen by visitors, as well as a band of human dwarfs whose existence 'has not been proved yet, since none of them has ever been seen'! An entrance fee of US$2 is charged to non-Ghanaians – although more is occasionally asked for. There's long been talk of a three-star hotel and visitor centre being constructed at the falls, but so far it's no more than talk.

Situated on the Yoko River near the village of Yabraso about 8km from Kintampo, the seldom visited Fuller Falls is named for the British surveyor who 'discovered' it in 1911. The 10m-high upper waterfall is very pretty, and the pool below it is safe for swimming, but the most remarkable feature is that the stream below the waterfall disappears underground for some 40m before re-emerging. A nominal entrance fee is now charged to enter the church-run compound around the waterfall. A primitive camping site and a new two-star guesthouse have been under construction for a number of years, but there is no finish date in sight.

GETTING THERE AND AWAY There is plenty of direct transport between Kintampo and Tamale, Kumasi, Techiman, Wenchi and Nkoranza. The Kintampo Falls lie 5km from town, a short walk from the Tamale road, and are signposted at the 191km marker. Any public transport heading along the Tamale road can drop you at the waterfall, but you'll probably end up paying the full fare to wherever that transport is headed, which may be costly. Better perhaps to charter a taxi from the lorry station in Kintampo – expect to pay US$1 one-way – and either ask the driver to wait for you, or else wait on the roadside for a lift when you're finished. Alternatively it's not too far to walk.

Fuller Falls lie 8km from town along the more obscure side road to New Longoro – there's no public transport so you'll have to charter a taxi.

WHERE TO STAY AND EAT The handful of hotels in Kintampo have generated a fair amount of negative feedback from readers of late, for which reason – unless you arrive too late in the day – you might want to think about popping out to one of the waterfalls and then moving on the same day. If you do decide to stay, the pick of the lodgings, set on a side road to the east of the town centre, is probably the **Life Hotel**, which charges US$12 for a large, clean double room with air conditioning, and also has a restaurant serving a limited range of Ghanaian dishes. Also recommended, and clearly signposted from the main road through town, is the new **Toronto Hotel**, where a reasonably clean self-contained double with TV, fridge and fan costs around US$9. Going down in price and standard, the **Midway Hotel** attracts a lot of custom simply by virtue of its location directly opposite the lorry station, but the scruffy double rooms with fan are nothing to write home about at US$5.50 using common shower or US$9 self-contained. The rather pokey and airless **Midway Restaurant**, opposite the hotel of the same name, charges around US$1.50 for an adequate plate of food, but you're probably better off heading to the row of chop stalls and bars in the lorry station and along the road towards the Shell garage.

THE OLD TAMALE ROAD

Once the main trunk route north from Kumasi to Tamale, the road through Mampong to Ejura and the port of Yeji has only recently been surfaced and is little travelled by tourists. But for those with time to spare, the route offers some stunning scenery and combines well with a trip on the *Nana Besemuna*, a twice daily motor ferry which runs between Yeji and Makongo, and provides an opportunity to spend an hour or so on this vast lake. Yeji is also the main northern terminus of the weekly MV *Yapei Queen* that runs to and from Akosombo (see box *The Akosombo–Yeji Ferry*, page 242).

South of Yeji, the remote Digya National Park is the second-largest sanctuary in Ghana, protecting a 3,478km² knuckle of rolling hills, large, granite inselbergs and varied vegetation jutting into the west shore of Lake Volta. Digya protects one of the most varied faunas of any Ghanaian reserve, including elephant, leopard, possibly lion, warthog, buffalo, bushbuck, waterbuck, reedbuck, kob, roan antelope, six types of duiker and eight primate species. It is rumoured that this part of the lake supports a small population of manatees, large aquatic mammals similar in appearance and closely related to the dugong of the Indian Ocean. The Department of Wildlife office at Ejura must be visited by all prospective visitors to the park, but the park itself is accessible only to self-sufficient campers with a private 4×4. The only accommodation that I'm aware of in Ejura is the basic **Liberty Avenue Hotel**.

Yeji is essentially a port town, and not a particularly attractive one, so there's no reason to spend the night unless you have to. For travellers heading between Kumasi and Tamale, this should be easy enough to avoid, since terrestrial public transport tends to tie in with the crossing times of the *Nana Besemuna*, which typically leaves from Yeji at about 10.00 and 14.00 and from Makango about 08.00 and 12.00, and is supplemented between crossings by small motorised boats that take around 45 minutes between the ports. Tickets for the *Nana Besemuna* cost US$1 per person and vehicles can also be taken. Travellers waiting for the *Yapei Queen* are advised not to head to Yeji until Tuesday, and even then they may be in for a wait – in theory the boat arrives on Tuesday at around 17.00 to 20.00 and departs again at around 03.00 on Wednesday morning, but it can run anything up to 48 hours behind schedule!

There's no shortage of accommodation in Yeji, and it's all pretty grotty – indeed one reader refers to a 'collective conspiracy by hoteliers who know that people boarding or disembarking from the ferry are going to put up with anything for one night, and that nobody will stay longer because Yeji has nothing to offer'. At present, the cream of this poor crop is probably the **Volta Hotel**, which charges around US$5.50 for a basic room, as do the **Alliance**, **Ebenezer** and **Nifanifa** hotels. None of the hotels has running water or a fan, and they are all quite dirty. North of Yeji, regular transport runs along the 160km road between Makongo and Tamale, though you may need to change vehicles at Salaga. There is nowhere to stay in Makongo, and not a great deal to do, so don't cross from Yeji in the afternoon unless you can be sure of reaching Salaga, a further 40km along the Tamale road (see *Around Tamale,* page 360).

Part Six

NORTHERN GHANA

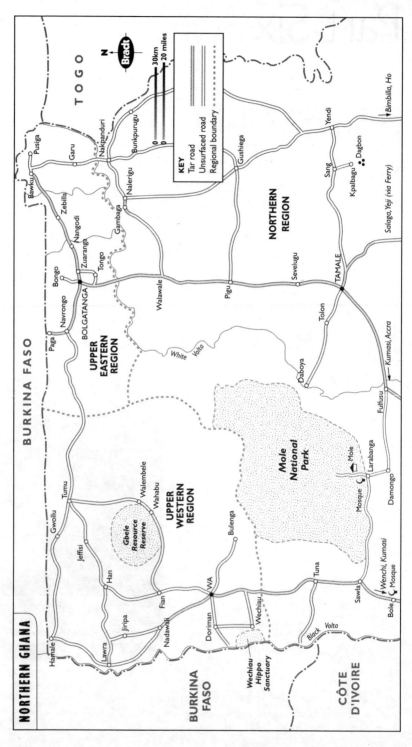

NORTHERN GHANA

INTRODUCTION

The vast and relatively thinly populated savanna country that lies to the north of Lake Volta and the Black Volta River was annexed to the Gold Coast colony in 1902. Formerly known as the Northern Territory, it is now divided into three administrative regions. The Northern Region is the largest of these, covering an area of 70,384km² (more than one quarter of the country's surface area), and its regional capital Tamale boasts a population of roughly 250,000, which puts it in competition with Tema and Takoradi as the country's third most populous city. Much smaller than Northern Region and – somewhat paradoxically – lying to its north are the Upper East and Upper West regions, the respective capitals of which, Bolgatanga and Wa, each support a population of between 45,000 and 60,000.

The north of Ghana can in many respects be viewed as a historically and culturally discrete entity from the southern and central regions. Unlike the various Akan groups who live to the south of the Black Volta, the predominantly Mole-Dagbani groupings of the north generally follow patrilineal lines of inheritance and they share a common oral tradition that suggests they arrived in modern-day Ghana in the 12th or 13th centuries following a militarised migration from the Lake Chad region. Historically, the Mole-Dagbani have had far stronger trade and cultural links with the Islamic world than with the Christian Europeans who settled along the Gold Coast, as witnessed by the large number of mosques throughout the region, including several centuries-old West-Sudanese-style whitewashed mud-and-stick mosques in the northwest.

Not as dense with tourist attractions as the coast, northern Ghana has a relatively untrammelled, parochial atmosphere that seems far removed from the bustle of Accra or Kumasi. Mole National Park is the country's best and most easily visited game reserve: a patch of open, tsetse-fly-infested savanna where close encounters with elephants are an everyday occurrence on what must be about the most affordable guided foot safaris in Africa. Close to the entrance to Mole, at the small village of Larabanga, is the oldest and most famous mosque in the country. Another important attraction of the region is the traditional architecture which reaches its peak at Paga on the Burkina Faso border, where large, flat-roofed mud constructions have grown organically over decades, even centuries, to house as many as a dozen related families. Similar homesteads are to be found around Nakpanduri, on the famed Gambaga escarpment, an area also notable for having some of the best scenery and birding in the country, as well as a magnificently positioned and highly affordable government resthouse.

The city of Tamale has no major attractions, but it's a nice place to hang out all the same and boasts the best facilities in the north. It's also the obvious gateway to the region if only because it's connected to both Accra and Kumasi by daily STC buses and a plethora of tro-tros. Tamale can also be reached by using the weekly ferry service from Akosombo to Yeji on Lake Volta. A second main access road to the north, connecting Kumasi to Wa via Wenchi and Bole, is in worse condition than the main Tamale road, but it's traversed by regular buses and allows you to see several beautiful old mosques. The only entrance gate to Mole National Park lies 5km from Larabanga, along a rough dirt road that runs between Fufulsu on the Kumasi–Tamale road and Sawla on the Kumasi–Wa road.

The following chapter covers Tamale, the economic and administrative capital of Northern Region, and springboard for visits to Mole National Park, the country's premier savanna reserve. Note that while Mole is covered in this chapter, and is most realistically visited out of Tamale on public transport, the main access road to the national park lies along the main Kumasi–Tamale road, which means that visitors with private transport can go there without ever setting foot in Tamale.

17

Tamale and Mole National Park

TAMALE

The cultural divide between northern and southern Ghana really starts to become obvious in this predominantly Muslim city, as bicycles, Sahel-style architecture, striped plastic teapots and the diverse meats (beef and lamb) more usually associated with francophone territories further north start shading into the former British colony. Made regional capital less than a decade after the Northern Territory was annexed to the Gold Coast, Tamale is now the largest and fastest-growing urban conglomeration in northern Ghana, with a population estimated at 350,000. It is also one of the most friendly – engendering more loyalty among locally based volunteers than any major town in the south – and the most rapidly changing. The first edition of this guidebook described Tamale as 'hot, flat and quite incredibly dusty: first impressions are less than flattering, unless perhaps you're a homesick construction worker', but whilst it remains hot and flat, the distinctive red-dirt suspension that once enveloped Tamale is today sealed beneath the grid of freshly tarmacked roads, and the construction of a US$80m football stadium ahead of 2008's Africa Cup has given its 'provincial' feel something of a boost.

Tamale is the most important route focus in northern Ghana – indeed, it would take some effort to travel through the north and avoid passing through it – and although it lacks 'must see' attractions, its friendly, hassle-free atmosphere and good range of inexpensive travel amenities make it a pleasant place to spend a few days. The most noteworthy facet of the city centre is a quite astonishing infestation of bicycles, whose propensity for weaving whimsically between pedestrians can be positively hazardous (a danger only slightly reduced by the recent – and, in my experience of Africa, unique – construction of bicycle lanes running parallel to the main thoroughfares).

As for sightseeing, the large central market itself is worthwhile – in particular the fetish section which sells scraps of tiger skin, leopard skin, horses' tail and other weird animal artefacts for use in traditional medicine. It's also a good spot for fabric and beads, and you'll certainly want to pause to watch the Gonja cloth weavers at work. Another interesting short excursion for craft enthusiasts entails walking south from the Grand Mosque for ten minutes along Zongo Hausa Road to the suburb of Zongo, and then – literally – following your nose to the pungent open-air tannery where hundreds of sheep, goat and cow hides (as well as the odd crocodile skin from the Volta) are pinned down to dry in the sun. The people who work at this extensive tannery seem happy to show tourists the leather-making process from start to finish, and when we visited there was no fee nor any significant pressure to buy from the several nearby stalls that sell sandals and other leatherwork to a predominantly local clientele.

As a taster for architectural styles found to the north, wander past the engagingly low-key palace of the Gulpke Na, which is clearly signposted on Hospital Road near Barclays Bank, and consists of several small, pink, thatched buildings connected by 2m-high walls In previous years, any photography or poking around was met with a certain amount of hostility, but it recently opened to visitors in return for a discretionary donation. You could also try to set up a visit to another chief's palace a few kilometres north of town – in a letter dated January 2001, one traveller mentions being taken there by a local teenager, and being free to explore and photograph the low-key but attractive local architecture after offering the chief a handful of kola nuts and a small donation.

Near to the palace is the Centre for National Culture, mentioned prominently in every piece of travel literature about Tamale that I've come across, but I have no idea why. Further afield, there are a couple of small dams about 1.5km from the town centre along Education Ridge Road, a good place for a walk and highly promising for birds, though the teak forest that once surrounded the dams has evidently been reduced to tinder. Not so the 'mystery tree' in the hospital grounds (about 1km from the town centre along Hospital Road), which – or so legend has it – was pulled down several times during the construction of the hospital, but always resurrected itself overnight. Another botanical attraction in the immediate vicinity of Tamale is Madam Tamaiko's Herbal Garden, where a wide variety of exotic and indigenous herbs are cultivated in a patch of baobab woodland on the Bolgatanga road between the Gariba Hotel and the army barracks.

GETTING THERE AND AWAY Tamale is the pivotal transport hub in northern Ghana, and – unusually for a Ghanaian town of its size – the main tro-tro and STC stations could scarcely be more central, situated right next to the main market. The recently renovated bus station is easy to find your way around, as the individual termini for all destinations are clearly signposted. A great many private tro-tros and/or buses run between Tamale and most other towns along the surfaced road south to Kumasi (7 hours, US$6) and north to Bolgatanga (2½ hours, US$3) – just head to the right terminal and ask for the next vehicle heading there. If you're a glutton for punishment, you could also consider a tro-tro to Accra: these are slightly cheaper than the STC buses at US$9 for a clapped-out death trap, US$12 for an acceptable 'imperial' bus and US$14 with AC.

Much better (and slightly quicker) to take an AC STC bus at US$18, of which there are three daily, except on Sundays, leaving Tamale at 06.30, 07.00 and 08.00 and taking around 11 hours (night services were cancelled after a series of armed robberies on the road between Kintampo and Techiman). Two STC buses also leave daily to Kumasi (US$11), departing at 06.00 and 16.00, or 10.00 at weekends, and taking around six hours, and one bus leaves every Tuesday for Taloradi (US$20) STC buses between Bolgatanga and towns further south pass through Tamale, but are of limited interest to travellers arriving at or leaving Tamale, since they would have to pay the same full fare as those travelling between the start and end destinations. All STC buses leave from the STC bus station (which lies behind the post office and adjacent to the main bus station), where you can also book tickets and make enquiries about current timetables.

Most travellers heading to Mole National Park use the daily Metro Mass bus that leaves Tamale at around 14.00 in theory (but often a few hours later) to overnight at the Mole Motel before heading back to Tamale at 05.30 the following morning. It's advisable to book a seat for this bus at least an hour in advance (tickets cost US$2) and ideally earlier, or you'll probably have to stand most of the way. A good alternative is the daily Metro Mass bus to Wa, which leaves from Tamale at around 06.00 (though you should be at the bus station by 04.30 to book a seat, as reservations cannot be made the day ahead) and passes through Larabanga at around 10.00. Other Metro Mass services run to Makongo (US$2.50, departure 05.00) and Yendi (US$1, departures at 05.00 and 07.00). All Metro Mass buses leave from the southwest corner of the main bus station. See also *Getting there and away* under *Mole National Park* (page 363) for further details of this sometimes problematic trip. A speedy alternative – and definitely an attractive option for travellers who are short of time but want to see the north – is a domestic flight from Accra with Antrak (*Wed, Fri, Sun; US$146*) or CityLink (*Tue, Thu, Sat; US$125*). Contact details are in the *Travelling in Ghana* chapter (pages 71–72).

Travellers coming to Tamale via the Lake Volta ferry are advised to disembark at Yeji rather than Kete Krachi, since the City Express bus from Kete Krachi to Tamale can takes in excess of 15 hours. For details of transport between Yeji and Tamale, see pages 242 and 345. For crossing between Hohoe and Tamale via Bimbilla, see page 272.

If you're staying in one of the Christian guesthouses along the Bolgatanga road, a constant stream of shared taxis runs there from a rank just past the traffic lights diagonally opposite the main lorry and STC station, charging US$0.20 per person at the time of writing.

WHERE TO STAY
Upmarket

Gariba Lodge ☎ 071 23041/2/3; f 071 23040; e garibalodge@yahoo.com. Set on the outskirts of town just north of the police barrier on the Bolgatanga road, this comfortable 3-star lodge is widely regarded as the best hotel in northern Ghana. All rooms have AC, hot showers, DSTV, fridge & international telephone. The hotel also doubles as the booking centre & pick up point for Citylink flights & offers onsite internet access & a Western-standard restaurant. Three types of room are available: single, standard double & executive double. *Sgl US$50, standard dbl US$70 & executive dbl US$90.*

Mariam Hotel ☎ 071 23548/25497; e mariamhotel@yahoo.com. With its grim purple exterior, Mariam's is certainly not as attractive as the Gariba, but its clean rooms & exceptionally helpful staff make it a pleasant enough alternative. An onsite restaurant serves good Ghanaian & international staples, & excellent, locally produced shea butter is on

sale at reception. The hotel also has links with **Daud's Car Rentals** (☎ 027 7168380) which owned one decent AC 2×2 estate at the time of research but has plans to expand. Basic hire costs US$55 a day including driver (compulsory for insurance reasons) but exc fuel. *Spotless rooms with all mod cons cost US$52/72 sgl/dbl.*

Relax Lodge ☎ 071 24981; f 071 24978; e relax@gmail.com. This family-run lodge painted in ice-cream colours, has attractive grounds & a more central location than its main competitor – but the rooms aren't quite to the same standard & feel a touch overpriced. The attached restaurant is known for its speciality Tandoori menu – reflecting the owners' nationality – but also serves a good range of Chinese & other dishes in the US$5–7 range. Expansion plans inc the addition of internet facilities & a conference centre. *Self-contained dbl with AC, hot bath & DSTV US$60, suite US$70.*

Moderate

GILBT Guesthouse Situated 7km out of town in the Bolgatanga road, this quiet guesthouse charges US$22 for a clean self-contained dbl with AC. The food is fair & the staff friendly, but no alcohol is allowed. If you ask at reception, they might be able to organise a taxi to pick you up at the guesthouse so that you don't have to walk the 1.5–2km to the main road to find one.

Picorna Hotel ☎ 071 22070/672; f 071 22062; e picornahotelgh@yahoo.com. Formerly the smartest option in Tamale, the Picorna has certainly seen better days – but it is also the only hotel to bridge the

substantial gap in price & quality between the upmarket & budget ranges, & has a convenient location about 10 mins' walk from the central bus station. The upstairs restaurant serves acceptable Chinese, continental & local dishes priced around US$3.50–5.50, & you can also eat in the garden bar which turns into the popular Club de Classique nightclub at weekends. Reports in 2005 suggested the hotel was 'woefully understaffed' but the situation seems to have improved since then. *Self-contained sgl/dbl with AC & DSTV US$20–30, larger rooms US$38.*

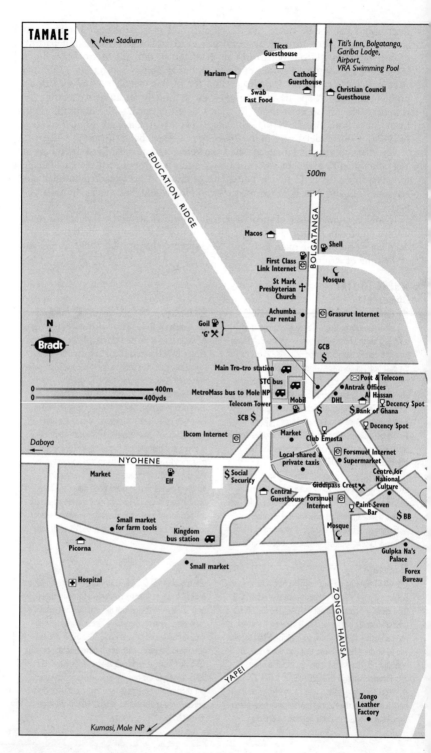

TAMALE

New Stadium

Ticcs Guesthouse

Mariam

Catholic Guesthouse

Swab Fast Food

Christian Council Guesthouse

Titi's Inn, Bolgatanga, Gariba Lodge, Airport, VRA Swimming Pool

EDUCATION RIDGE

BOLGATANGA

500m

Macos

Shell

First Class Link Internet

Mosque

St Mark Presbyterian Church

Achumba Car rental

Grassrut Internet

N

Bradt

Goil 'G'

GCB

Main Tro-tro station

Post & Telecom

Antrak Offices

Al Hassan

STC bus

MetroMass bus to Mole NP

Mobil

DHL

Decency Spot

0   400m
0   400yds

Telecom Tower

SCB

Bank of Ghana

Decency Spot

Daboya

Ibcom Internet

Market

Club Emesta

Forsmuel Internet

Supermarket

NYOHENE

Local shared & private taxis

Centre for National Culture

Market

Elf

Social Security

Central Guesthouse

Forsmuel Internet

Giddipass Crest

Paint Seven Bar

BB

Small market for farm tools

Kingdom bus station

Mosque

Picorna

Gulpka Na's Palace

Small market

Forex Bureau

Hospital

ZONGO HAUSA

YAPEI

Zongo Leather Factory

Kumasi, Mole NP

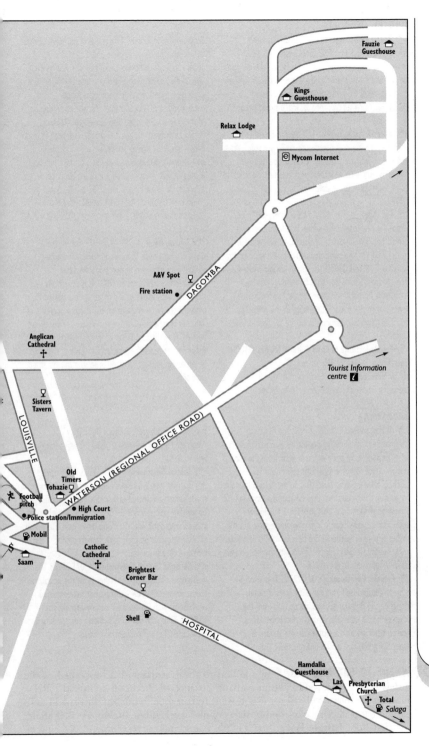

Budget

🏠 **Fauzie Guesthouse** 📞 071 24340. This small, friendly hotel in Kalpohin Estates, seems like good value. It's some distance from the town centre, but can be reached in any shared taxi going to 'Kalpohin Village (just opposite), from the main taxi rank in town (US$0.20). *Clean self-contained dbl with a small front porch & fan US$8.*

🏠 **King's Guesthouse** Also in Kalpohin Estates, the rooms in this low-key guesthouse could use some work – & feel slightly overpriced at US$9 & up – but the owner is very friendly & the place feels safe, making it a good address for those that want to stay out of town. *US$9.*

🏠 **Las Hotel** 📞 071 26097. This comfortable hotel, which lies on Hospital Rd about 1km from the town centre, has quite a variety of rooms, ranging in price from US$8/12 for a self-contained dbl/twin with fan, hot water & GTV, to US$8/15 for similar rooms with AC. The cheapest rooms compare favourably with the shoestring hotels in the town centre, but the more expensive rooms feel a little shabby at the price. The attached Chinese restaurant is one of the best in town. *US$8–15.*

🏠 **Tamale Institute of Cross Cultural Studies (TICCS) Guesthouse** 📞 071 22836; e ticcs@ africaonline.com.gh; www.ticcs.com. Situated in attractive wooded grounds about 200m off the Bolgatanga road & some 2km north of the town centre, this popular budget resthouse offers clean accommodation in boring-looking blocks. Run by TICCS (which despite its right-on name is actually a Christian organisation dedicated to 'fostering a deeper understanding of African culture for the enculturation of the gospel'), the lodge also houses an excellent library relating to northern Ghana & elsewhere in west Africa, while the breezy Jungle Bar serves alcoholic & non-alcoholic drinks as well as decent pizzas, hot dogs & burgers. For guests, a separate dining room serves up a substantial b/fast for around US$2 & a 5-course continental set lunch for US$4. *Sgl/dbl with fan & common showers US$9/11, self-contained sgl/dbl/twin with fan US$13/15/16.*

🏠 **Tohazie Hotel** 📞 071 24174/6/9. Formerly the Catering Resthouse, this recently privatised hotel looked a bit rundown on last inspection, but renovations are planned for 2007. It is potentially very attractive, with thatched & painted chalets dotted among large green grounds on the eastern outskirts of Tamale's town centre. All the rooms are self-contained with AC. The restaurant has an inexpensive b/fast menu & sometimes hosts the popular 'Old Timers' nightclub, or other live music. *US$19–40 depending on room size & state of repair.*

Shoestring

🏠 **Al Hassan Hotel** 📞 071 23638. The Al Hassan owes some of its enduring popularity with backpackers to its location, only a few minutes' walk from the bus station, which makes it especially convenient for catching early-morning buses. But although it's a friendly set-up, the rooms are seriously variable: the large self-contained ground-floor dbls with fan & fabulously enthusiastic shower come highly recommended, but the shabby first-floor hotboxes are best avoided unless you enjoy sweaty, sleepless nights. *Sgl/dbl with common shower US$6–7, self-contained dbl US$14.*

🏠 **Catholic Guesthouse** 📞 071 22265. This clean & popular guesthouse lies in rambling green grounds alongside the Bolgatanga road, about 1km from the town centre, & offers very good value. Inexpensive, hearty meals are also available (the guineafowl is especially good), & – a little unexpectedly – the guesthouse has a great outdoor bar. Highly recommended. *Sgl with fan/AC US$8–10, self-contained dbl with AC US$14.*

🏠 **Central Guesthouse** 📞 071 22135. Aptly named, this discreet little guesthouse lies in a maze of back roads behind the shared-taxi station. It's a great budget option, but probably not the best choice for night-time arrivals who don't want to troop down unlit alleys with all their valuables on their back. *Surprisingly decent self-contained dbl with fan US$7.*

🏠 **Christian Council Guesthouse** 📞 071 23278. The management at this little guesthouse on the Bolga road seems almost comically lethargic, but self-contained twin rooms with fan are a bargain nevertheless at US$6.50. Dbls with common showers are not such a draw but still cheap enough. *From US$6.*

✖️ **WHERE TO EAT AND DRINK** In addition to the restaurants below, several of the hotels serve good food. Within walking distance of the town centre, the Relax Hotel is the place to head for if you want Indian food, while the Picorna Hotel's garden bar is very relaxing and hosts a popular weekend nightclub. Further afield, the first-floor **Jungle Bar** in the TICCS Guesthouse is recommended for pizza, hot dogs and burgers, while the **Sweet Gardens Restaurant** on the first-floor balcony of the Las Hotel serves popular but rather pricey Chinese food.

✗ **Crest Restaurant** Better known as the Giddipass, this popular restaurant occupies the first floor & rooftop of a central, double-storey building, & ranks as the breeziest spot to eat in downtown Tamale. The menu offers a wide selection of continental & Chinese dishes, or set menus. Even if you don't eat here, the rooftop is a great place to people-watch or stargaze with a chilled beer. *Main course around US$4, set menus US$6.50–7.50.*

✗ **G Restaurant** Centrally located in the Goil garage opposite the STC bus station, G's location is hardly the stuff of romance. But the lack of atmosphere is served up with sparklingly clean décor that will win votes of confidence from any travellers suffering with dodgy tummies. There's no outdoor seating, but the ventilation is pretty effective. *Pizzas & other Western meals US$3.50–4.50, Ghanaian dishes are slightly cheaper at around US$2.50.*

✗ **The Novel Restaurant** in the Al Hassan Hotel is supposedly under the same management but the dining room is unbearably hot & the menu is much more basic, with prices to match. *Expect to pay around US$2.*

✗ **Point Seven Bar** Directly opposite the Crest, there's cheaper beer but less breeze at this popular bar, where you have the choice of sitting indoors or on the semi-enclosed pavement.

✗ **Sparkles Restaurant** This friendly restaurant in the National Cultural Centre has improved vastly following a recent change of management, & you can eat inside or outdoors. The menu is small but varied, & standards are generally high. It's also a good place to try guineafowl, a dish that is extremely popular further north. *Most items cost around US$3.50.*

♀ **Sisters Tavern** This pleasant suburban drinking hole lies within easy walking distance of the city centre & serves simple meals as well as chilled drinks indoors or in the neat garden area.

✗ **Sunset Bar** ☎ 024 4201643. Set in open countryside about 12km from Tamale on the Bolga road, this new restaurant serves up excellent tilapia & other Western and Ghanaian dishes, to a well-heeled, mostly business crowd. The varied drinks menu inc a range of wines. *Expect to pay around US$3.50 for meat & an accompaniment (charged separately), or considerably more for the fish.*

✗ **Swab Fast Food** Probably the best affordable eatery in Tamale, this Indian-run gem lies about 1.5km from the town centre off the Bolgatanga road, along the same side road as the Catholic Guesthouse. The extensive menu is vegetarian-friendly with an excellent selection of Indian food – including delicious vegetable samosas with shito (US$1.50 for 2 pieces) – along with the usual Chinese & Ghanaian fare. You can eat indoors or under thatched canopies in the well-kept, shady garden. *Most main dishes cost around US$5.50*

✗ **Titi's** Named after the owner's daughter, this new set-up, past Gumani junction on the Bolga road, has hit the ground running. The place is clean, the food is good, & you can get anything from local dises (around US$2.50) to pizzas (US$6), burger & fries, & Lebanese food. There is also a bar with a pool table & ping-pong, which serves cold beers & mineral water. Take a Gumani shared taxi (US$0.3) & walk a block.

OTHER PRACTICALITIES

Car hire An unsignposted office on the Bolgatanga road about 200m past the main bus station has a few new-looking vehicles for rent, at a cost of US$50 daily for a Suzuki 4×4 or saloon-car self-drive, or US$100 for a larger chauffeur-driven 4×4 (*call Mr Ayoma on* ☎ *024 4452057 or 027 7781635*). I've had no feedback from readers on the quality of service or vehicles, but it might be worth talking to them if you're thinking of taking a vehicle into Mole National Park. Otherwise, **Daud's Car Rentals** (☎ 027 7168380), opposite the Mariam Hotel, offers a decent air conditioned 2×2 estate for US$55 a day including driver but no fuel. The operation has plans to buy a small fleet in the near future, including some 4×4s.

Curios Try the stalls around the Centre for National Culture, which have been recommended as far better than most in the country. The busy market is also a good place to buy local crafts, cloths and beads. Reader Heike Moers recently recommended a little shop called **COLWOD**, which stands for Collaboration with Women in Distress, as follows: 'it is a charity organisation founded in 1995 to help abandoned women. Through teaching them skills, tie-dye, batik and sewing,

COLWOD enables them to achieve economic independence as well as regain their dignity. This is a small organisation, their shop is a little hidden, but they offer really nice goods, like self-made cards, aprons, tablecloths, shirts/blouses, among many other things. We bought most of our Ghana souvenirs there. It would be great if it could be made a bit more known through publications like yours. It is located behind the CVL internet cafe, near the Melcom and Areeba stores; e colwodjacky@ africaonline.com.gh.'

Foreign exchange Oddly, there is no private forex bureau in Tamale, which means that travellers carrying cash will get a better deal if they change it in Bolgatanga (coming from the north) or Kumasi (coming from the south). The Standard Chartered and Barclays Banks in the town centre both have foreign exchange facilities for cash and travellers' cheques, as well as ATMs where local currency can be drawn against a Visa card (assuming that they are working). Should you be heading on to Mole, do make sure you have enough local currency to pay for everything there, as the motel works on a far lower exchange rate than the banks.

Guides and tours A relatively recent development in Tamale is the emergence of a handful of swindling teens – known locally as 419s after the Nigerian penal code for fraud. They tend to hang around the bus station or the Crest bar, trying to latch on to newly arrived travellers and clocking their every move. They're clearly after one thing – cash – but they're a relatively unsophisticated (and good-humoured) bunch and can be shaken fairly easily if you make it clear you're not going to give or buy anything. The best way to get hold of someone reliable is through the tourist board, or you could contact Walisu Alhassan (↘ 024 3822633), who left the tourist office to work at Kalpohin (see opposite) and has been recommended by a number of readers.

Medical care Travellers in need of health care are advised to avoid Tamale Hospital, which is ill-equipped. Instead, visit the British Consulate doctors, who are contactable through the Peace Corps suboffice.

Internet and email There are several internet cafés dotted around Tamale, though most seem to suffer intermittent server problems. The exception is the excellent Forsmuel internet next to the Forsmuel supermarket, which has at least 20 machines, excellent air conditioning and charges US$0.60 an hour. Another branch just underneath the Crest restaurant is almost as good, as is Grasruts on the Bolga road. Agric near the Christian Council Guesthouse is highly unreliable but cheap.

Drumming and dancing Based in the Tamale Youth Home Centre opposite Tohazie Hotel, the established Ddavonet performance group also offers drumming and dancing courses, including traditional dances such as *fume*, *kpalongo*, *pacha*, *bamaaya*, *tora*, *taai* and fast *agbeko*. Lessons are usually taught by Osman or Iddrisu, and can be held at the school itself or elsewhere for groups. Contact Iddrisu on ↘ 020 8077937; e ddavonet@yahoo.com, eddeblai@yahoo.com or rasoscer@hotmail.com.

Books A surprisingly good range of new and secondhand books – including recent bestsellers – is available at Tasneem Bookshop, a short share taxi ride out of town on the Bolga road. Turn left down a dirt road at the Jisonayili junction just after King Daniel bar.

Swimming pool The pool at the Volta River Authority (VRA) clubhouse on the Bolga road is open to the public for US$1.50 per person, every day except

Mondays. It is well maintained with shaded tables and showers, and there are usually a few vendors selling drinks and food.

Tourist information The helpful tourist office (↘ *071 24834*) recently moved out of town, to near the Regional Coordinating Council offices. Any taxi driver will know where this is; ask them to turn right just before the gates and follow the signs to the left. The office stocks a few quite useful brochures and information about new attractions being developed in the region, as well as reliable guides.

AROUND TAMALE

KALPOHIN CULTURAL EXCHANGE PROGRAM (Adapted from information from Bill Reinecke and the Jones-Parry family) One worthwhile tour near Tamale is to the small village of Kalpohin, just a couple of kilometres out of the town centre. Although it's close by it feels very far away, and is a great opportunity to see Ghanaians making traditional produce using the same methods as they have for centuries. The tour consists of watching local women work shea butter, palm oil, groundnut oil and groundnut paste, as well as spinning cotton, which you can see the men making into traditional Dagomba smocks. If you plan in advance, arrangements can be made to enjoy lunch or dinner with entertainment from the local drumming and dancing troupes. Prices depend on the size of the group and activities you want to do, but expect to pay US$5–10 per person. The tour is arranged through Walisu Alhassan (↘ *024 3822633*), who guarantees that a proportion of the proceeds are directed towards the village.

SOGNAAYILLI Shortly before we went to print, Jessica Cornelissen wrote in about another tour programme ten to fifteen minutes' drive from Tamale, in the village of Sognaayilli, being set up by Dutch volunteer organisation Meet Africa: 'We are setting up something similar to a community-based tourism project, offering visitors an experience of local culture and rural life in the north, except that the land and the guesthouse (still to be built) are owned by Meet Africa. The guesthouse will be in the style of a local compound and activities such as shea butter extraction, smock weaving, *dawadawa* processing, traditional cooking and dancing will be developed in collaboration with the community. The name for our project is **Meet Africa Rural Village Experience and Lodging** (MARVEL) and it is likely to open in July 2007. For information, drop into the Meet Africa office at Kanvilli, 7km out of Tamale along the Bolgatanga Road, or visit the Taimako Herbal Centre in the town centre (↘ *024 4824110;* e *info@meetafrica.org; www.meetafrica.org*). A similar project will soon start up close to Bolgatanga; for details pop into the Meet Africa office opposite the Twin Bar in Bolgatanga (↘ *020 8913117*).'

YENDI Situated about 100km east of Tamale, the small town of Yendi is the seat of the Ya Naa of Dagbon (aka Dagomba), who was murdered in 2002 triggering a bitter dispute over who should succeed him. (The situation cooled in 2006 following the enskinment of an acting Ya Naa.) Dagbon is an ancient Mole-Dagbani offshoot of the even older Mamprusi Kingdom, and according to oral tradition it was founded circa 1415 by the militaristic Chief Nyagse. The first Dagomba capital, Yendi Dabari, which lay some 30km southwest of present-day Yendi, was the base from where Nyagse expanded his empire to incorporate a great many smaller kingdoms, most strategically the salt-producing village of Daboya on the White Volta. The Dagomba influence appears to have declined following the rise of the Gonja Kingdom, circa 1620, when Gonja expansionists forced Chief

Dariziogo of Dagomba to relocate his capital to modern-day Yendi. From around 1750 to 1874, Dagomba was a vassal state of Ashanti, and from 1902 until after World War I the state was split between the British Gold Coast and German Togoland, with Yendi falling into the latter territory. Despite the economic ascendancy of Tamale since it was made capital of the Northern Territory in 1907, Yendi remains the traditional centre of Dagomba power.

Yendi is best visited on Monday or Friday mornings, when the paramount chief holds an open court in the company of his two-dozen shaven wives – but inter-clan politics could well flair up at any time so ask around about security before heading out. Assuming that all's well, there are several tro-tros daily from Tamale to Yendi, taking around two and half hours in either direction. The only places to stay are the **Yahaya Iddi Guesthouse**, which charges US$8–12 for clean, self-contained rooms with air conditioning, and the **District Assembly Guesthouse**, which charges US$7 for a more basic room.

DABOYA Set on the northwest bank of the White Volta, 67km west of Tamale, Daboya is the best place to see high-quality *fugu* being made – the hand-spun white and indigo-dyed cloth worn as a smock by men throughout northern Ghana, also known as 'ash and white' – and makes a very pleasant day trip from Tamale. The town might also be the most ancient extant settlement in northern Ghana thanks to its location at a good river crossing close to a salt pond that was of great commercial significance as a source of this precious commodity until very recent times. According to Gonja oral tradition, the present-day settlement at Daboya dates to the mid-17th-century reign of Chief Jakpa Lanta, whose son Denyawuri became Daboya's first *Wasipewura* (chief), a title still in use today. However, Dagomba traditions, backed up by archaeological investigation, indicate that Daboya was probably settled and mined centuries before the arrival of Jakpa Lanta. Although salt is still mined in Daboya today, it happens on a far smaller scale than it did during the pre-colonial era, when salt was a treasured commodity to barter for slaves and other items of trade.

From Tamale, the drive to the eastern riverbank opposite Daboya takes about 60–90 minutes in a private vehicle, while public transport is limited to a daily Metro Mass bus service in either direction, leaving from Tamale at around 05.00 (get there at least an hour early to be sure of a seat) and returning when it feels like it. *En route*, it might be worth checking out the Jaagpo Sacred Grove (near Tali, about halfway between the two towns) and its giant baobab tree indented by the hoofprints of the horse of a local chief who rode up the trunk! A dugout canoe ferries passengers across the river to Daboya itself, for a nominal fee. Homestays can be arranged through the local assembly man or chief.

SALAGA Set roughly 120km southeast of Tamale along the Yeji road, the small town of Salaga, though rather nondescript today, was for several centuries at the commercial hub of northern Ghana, situated at the crossroads of several key caravan routes that ran north towards Burkina Faso, Mali and Nigeria and south to Ashanti. Throughout the 19th century, merchants from the north and the south converged on Salaga – which at its peak reputedly boasted seven different marketplaces – to barter salt, kola nuts, cowries, gold, livestock, gunpowder and guns and other imported European goods and local produce. But the small town is most notorious today for its large 19th-century central market, which served as the most important slave-trading emporium in this part of west Africa, the place where villagers captured in present-day northern Ghana, Burkina Faso and Mali would be offered for sale to coastal and Ashanti traders for eventual resale to the European coastal forts and export to the Americas.

Salaga can easily be visited as an excursion from Tamale or *en route* between Kumasi and Tamale via Yeji. The infamous former slave market isn't difficult to find – it now serves as the central tro-tro station – but there is little there for the untrained eye to see aside from a white signpost reading Salaga Slave Market, and a young baobab that was planted in 1989 on the spot where the original tree to which slaves were once tied had stood before it fell over in 1970. Supported by the friendly chief of Salaga – to whom you might well be introduced before you look around – plans do exist to relocate the tro-tro station elsewhere, fence off the former slave market and construct a museum displaying artefacts related to the slave trade such as metal shackles and old rifles. Until such time as this happens, however, you can arrange to see similar artefacts simply by asking around – rusting relics of the slave trade are still in the possession of many of the town's more established households.

The anthropologist Jack Goody once referred to Salaga as the City of a Thousand Wells, for reasons that aren't immediately evident in the former slave market, where only one such well still stands, protected by a padlocked concrete bunker. But Salaga and its immediate vicinity is indeed studded with a remarkable number of clusters of small wells, most of which were excavated before or during the town's 19th-century commercial peak. The best known of these sites, signposted alongside a river crossing about 2km from the town centre along the Tamale road, is known as 'Ouankan Baya' in the local Hausa dialect, which translates as Bathing Place of Slaves. According to local tradition, these river-fed wells are where newly arrived slave traders from the north would bathe their human captives, rub them with shea butter to make them shine, and feed them up to make them look strong before taking them to the market to be sold. Another network of underground cisterns, together with the remains of 17th-century walls associated with the Chief Jakpa, the founder of the Gonja state, can be seen at Jakpa Wuto near Grushi Zongo, 5km southeast of Salaga.

Reasonably regular public transport runs between Tamale and Salaga throughout the day, taking up to three hours in either direction. If you're planning to visit as a day trip, best get an early start by using the Metro Mass bus to Makongo (the port on the opposite side of the Volta ferry crossing to Yeji) that departs from Tamale at around 05.00 and generally passes through Salaga before 08.00. It would also be possible to stop off in Salaga *en route* between Kumasi and Tamale via the Yeji–Makongo ferry – indeed, northbound travellers might well be forced to change vehicles at Salaga. Should you need accommodation, four self-contained double rooms with air-conditioning and fan are available for US$9 each at the **Salaga Community Centre**, some 200m from the tro-tro station. Slightly cheaper rooms with common showers are available at the **Catholic Guesthouse**.

SAAKPULI The unspoiled village of Saakpuli, located in Savelugu/Nanton District about 15km north of Savelugu on the Tamale-Bolgatanga road, was one of the region's most important slave trading centres in the early 19th century. The village was founded circa 1700 by Asante settlers first stationed in the area during a dispute between the Asantehene and the Dagbon king Naa Gariba, but peaked in importance under a local chief called B'laima during the reign of Naa Yakuba (1824–49). During this period, it doubled as a military base and a slaving market, and is said to have consisted of several hundred 12-pole reception halls, each of which housed a platoon of around 50 young men.

Saakpuli has preserved a great deal of evidence dating from the 19th-century slave trade. A stand of massive baobab trees, to which slaves were chained, still overlooks the former market and several trees are scarred with human marks. A small museum containing some notable slave-trade artefacts was built by Americans in the early 1990s, while relics from other periods include the remains of a slave warehouse and a cluster of water cisterns about 1.5km northwest of the old market. Other local points of interest include the Yoo Naa's palace, built in Savelugu in 1754. A four-page history of Saakpuli is retained at the site.

Saakpuli lies about 7km east of the Tamale–Bolgatanga road along a dirt road signposted with a Ghana Tourism Office logo, 8km north of Savelugu. There are no eateries or lodgings in the village, but it should be easy enough to visit as a day trip out of Tamale, and basic food is available in Savelugu. For further information, contact the District Office on ✆ 071 91092.

MOLE NATIONAL PARK AND LARABANGA

Mole National Park is Ghana's largest wildlife sanctuary, and – when it comes to general game-viewing – the best. It was set aside as a game reserve a year after Ghana attained independence, and gazetted as a national park in 1971 following the controversial resettlement of the relatively few villagers who lived in the area (which had always been thinly populated due to an abundance of tsetse flies). Extended to its present size of 4,840km² in 1991, Mole (pronounced Mo-*lay*) conserves an area of relatively flat savanna, set at an average altitude of about 150m, and bisected by the 250m-high escarpment on which the Mole Motel (the park's only accommodation) is situated. A visit to Mole is easily combined with one to Larabanga, which lies at the junction for the national park entrance gate and hosts the most famous and reputedly oldest of the half dozen or so West-Sudanese-style mud-and-stick mosques dotted around northwestern Ghana.

More than 90 mammal species and at least 344 bird species (the largest bird checklist for any site in Ghana) have been recorded in Mole, though several of the larger mammals are thought to be locally extinct or in critical danger of that fate – there has, for instance, been no trace of an African hunting dog noted in more than a decade. In general, however, populations appear to have increased since the last large mammal census was carried out in 1988, and current estimates for the larger herbivores stand at about 800 elephant, more than 1,000 buffalo, and significant populations of hippo, warthog and antelope species such as kob, Defassa waterbuck, bushbuck, roan, hartebeest, and grey- and red-flanked duiker. Five primate species are present, most visibly the olive baboon, as are 17 carnivores, of which the various mongoose species are most likely to be seen by visitors. Leopard and lion are now mostly known from the occasional spoor, though occasional lion sightings are still reported, possibly of vagrants from better-protected parts of Burkina Faso.

Whether you're travelling on public transport or in a private vehicle, a visit to Mole is well worth the effort for the opportunity to see elephants and other large mammals at surprisingly close quarters. All the same, the park's full tourist potential remains strangely – and sadly – unrealised, which works not only to the detriment of tourists and the tourist industry, but also to the probable advantage of subsistence poachers. As things stand, the game-viewing circuit is effectively limited to a 40km network of poorly maintained roads to the south of the Lovi River (and even this much is inaccessible to the majority of tourists who arrive without vehicles), leaving about 95% of the total area without any of the sort of sustained tourist and ranger presence that tends to discourage poaching. All of which is bizarre when you consider that Mole is the linchpin of the northern tourist circuit, and that development of more varied and widespread amenities – new roads, new campsites, new lodges, overnight walking trails and organised game-drives out of the motel – is integral not merely to the tourist growth in the north but also to the ongoing survival of scarce species such as lion and other predators.

A one-off park entrance fee of US$4 per non-Ghanaian adult (US$2.50 for students with ID) must be paid at the park entrance, as must the video fee of US$2

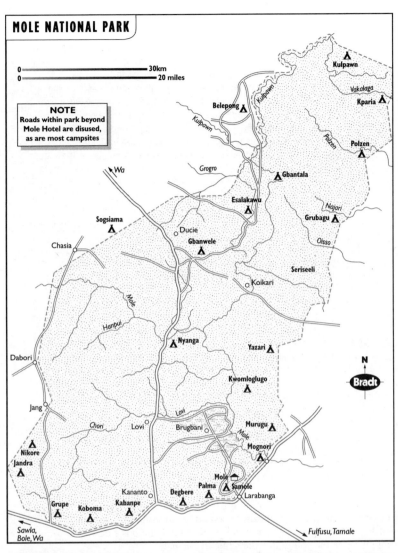

MOLE NATIONAL PARK

NOTE
Roads within park beyond
Mole Hotel are disused,
as are most campsites

Kulpawn

Vakalaga

Kparia

Belepong

Polzen

Polzen

Grogro

Gbantala

Wa

Esalakawu

Najari

Sogsiama

Grubagu

Ducie

Oisso

Gbanwele

Chasia

Seriseeli

Koikari

Mole

Hanput

Nyanga

Yazari

Dabori

Kwomloglugo

Jang

Lovi

Chori   Lovi   Brugbani   Murugu

Nikore
Jandra

Mognori

Mole

Grupe   Koboma   Kabanpe   Kananto   Degbere   Palma   Samole
                                                    Larabanga

Sawla,
Bole, Wa

Fulfusu, Tamale

N

Bradt

17

and camera fee of US$0.20 per person, where appropriate. Guide fees are US$0.80 per person per hour, though students pay only US$0.40. Note that it is mandatory to wear closed shoes (as opposed to sandals or flip-flops) on guided walks; visitors who don't comply with this ruling will be forced to rent bulky (and blister-inducing) rubber boots.

GETTING THERE AND AWAY One of Mole's chief attractions to independent travellers is that it is relatively cheap and easy to reach on public transport, certainly by comparison to the more renowned savanna reserves of eastern and southern Africa, most of which can only be visited on costly organised safaris. Having said that, the trip to Mole is tough going by Ghanaian standards, since the only access road to the park is legendarily dusty and bumpy, and public transport is not only limited in volume but also prone to lengthy delays and breakdowns. Don't let this

READER PERSPECTIVES ON LARABANGA

Larabanga, more than any other site or town in Ghana, draws extremes of positives and negatives from readers, and the following extracts from recent letters may help future travellers get the best from the village:

'My first stay at Larabanga was among the highlights of my year in Ghana, so I was surprised to read your mostly negative assessment. It was only when I went back that I understood why: Larabanga is only a nice place if you stay with the Salia brothers. If you don't say right away that you're going there, you're likely to be mobbed by the irritatingly pushy young men who've made a business of providing homestays to travellers. I literally had to snatch my bag from one of these guys when I alighted from the bus, but I'm glad I did. At various times during my stay I saw sad-looking travellers trudging around with one of these supposed guides, who pass on incomplete information about the points of interest, and charge ridiculous fees for imagined services. The Salia brothers, on the other hand, are extraordinarily friendly and helpful. Best advice: sleep on the guesthouse roof, even though they've finally bought fans!' (Joseph Blocher, April 2002)

'When I arrived, I was swamped by children and adults wanting to show me round. I resented having to hand out money – to the tourist point, the guy at the mosque, and the guides – for what was a dull and boring tour. I wasn't allowed in the mosque. On my return trip I was caught by a youth with a visitors' book. Underneath each entry was written the amount donated by each visitor. I'm fairly sure these amounts hadn't been donated (some were fantastic – like US$50) – but had been written in afterwards. I wonder how many visitors have been duped into giving money away – because they thought others had donated?' (Nick Wood, July 2002)

'If you think of Larabanga as just a cheap place to sleep while visiting Mole, you would be underestimating the charms of the village itself. We had a great time talking with the Salia Brothers, whose young nephews were the perfect guides to the mosque, the local school, the round houses built by immigrants from Burkina Faso, etc.' (Deborah Lerme Goodman, January 2003)

'Salia Brothers Guesthouse is the best! Wow! The night sleeping on their roof is my best African Experience! Count the stars and wake up by sunrise and sounds from the villagers!' (Alice and Joep Manders, November 2004)

'Larabanga we felt is full of hassle, and you have to be very rude in order to get rid of crowds of kids trying to be your guide.' (Chercher Yang, September 2005)

put you off the trip – practically everybody who visits Mole agrees that it is well worth it – but do accept that even on a good day the bus ride will be one of the more memorable you undertake while in Ghana!

Mole lies to the north of a dirt road that connects Sawla on the main Kumasi–Wa road to Fufulsu (or, more accurately, Damongo junction, about 3km north of Fufulsu), on the main Kumasi–Tamale road. The turn-off to the park is in Larabanga village, roughly 50km from Sawla, 80km from Fufulsu, and 20km north of Damongo, the district capital of West Gonja. The entrance gate lies 3km along the turn-off from Larabanga and the motel a further 1.5km past the entrance gate. You can walk there in 60–90 minutes – a trip best undertaken in the cool of the early morning or late afternoon – or you can rent a bicycle from the Salia Brothers Guesthouse in Larabanga for US$2 per day.

Travellers coming from the south might be tempted to catch a Tamale-bound bus as far as Damongo junction or a Wa-bound bus as far as Sawla, and then to try to pick up transport from the junction. My advice to them? Forget It! We tried to do it a few years ago, and eventually had to give up and board a bus to Tamale, and

I've since heard from numerous other travellers who attempted (and failed) to do exactly the same thing. The problem is that no tro–tros run along the Fufulsu–Sawla road and buses are always full by the time they get to the junction. The only place where you can pick up public transport directly to Mole Motel is Tamale, and the only other towns where you can reliably pick up transport as far as Larabanga (within walking distance of the entrance gate) are Bole and Wa.

The only public transport that goes all the way to Mole is the daily Metro Mass service from the main bus station in Tamale, which costs US$2. In theory, this bus departs from Tamale at 14.00 and takes about four hours to get to Mole Motel, but in practice it often leaves later than that (sometimes by a few hours) and occasionally, thanks to breakdowns, it never gets going at all. Seats are almost always fully occupied when the bus leaves Tamale, and often booked up an hour or two in advance, so try to reserve a ticket as early as possible on the day of travel. Once on the road, the bus might arrive at Mole Motel any time between nightfall and midnight, depending on when it left and the extent to which breakdowns extend the duration of the journey. It then overnights at Mole Motel and begins the return trip from the motel at between 05.00 and 06.00, depending on the driver's mood, to arrive back in Tamale anything from four to eight hours later.

Aside from the direct service between Tamale and Mole Motel, at least three other buses daily pass through Larabanga, from where you can walk or cycle to the park, or catch the shuttle service from Larabanga planned by the Salia brothers (see *Where to stay and eat*). The most useful of these services – arguably a better bet than the bus direct to Mole – is the daily Metro Mass bus between Tamale and Wa, which leaves at around 06.00 in either direction and takes about eight hours to cover the full route. Because this bus is faster and in better condition than the direct bus to Mole, and makes fewer gratuitous stops; it reaches Larabanga at around 10.30 – allowing plenty of time to see the mosque, have lunch, and still make it to Mole in time for the afternoon walk (15.30).One disadvantage of this bus is that it entails being at the bus station by 04.30 if you want to be certain of getting a seat, since tickets cannot be booked until the day of travel. There is also at least one bus daily in either direction between Tamale and Bole, also leaving at 06.00 and passing through Larabanga no more than three hours later when coming from Bole.

Leaving Mole in the direction of Bole or Wa, your best bet is to take the Metro Mass Mole–Tamale bus as far as Larabanga, then pick up the first bus heading west, which generally passes through Larabanga between 09.00 and 10.00. If this bus is heading to Wa and you want to go to Bole (or vice versa), disembark at the junction town of Sawla, from where there is plenty of transport in either direction.

Driving to Mole should be straightforward enough in a good 4×4, even though the stretch of road between Fufulsu and Damongo is poorly maintained. A 2×2 vehicle with good clearance should get you through, except after heavy rain, but it cannot be recommended. If time is an issue, consider taking a taxi from Tamale. Extravagant, perhaps (it will cost about US$60), but it takes approximately two and a half hours so you could be in Mole in time to see the animals at dusk. Be warned – it's seriously bumpy and dusty and you'll get filthy, but it's worth it if time is tight.

Another development for the future is the planned set up of a new minibus service by Larabanga's enterprising Salia brothers, who will arrange transfers from Tamale or even direct from Accra.

WHERE TO STAY AND EAT To see Mole at its best but keep costs to a minimum, a good compromise might be to spend your first night at the motel in the park, then spend a second night at one of the villages outside, ie: Larabanga or Mognori. Should you stay in Larabanga, we would advise against taking up the offer of a private homestay made by the throng of so-called guides who meet the bus from Tamale – we've had more than one report of such an offer resulting in theft from the room.

🏠 **Mognori** Reached along the road from Larabanga to Mole, but continuing past the entrance to the park, the small village of Mognori recently started to offer **homestays** to tourists & is the focal point for a number of exciting plans for the future. A new trail is being developed from the village into Mole, together with a Fulani-style campsite for overnight trips, & a short canoe safari is being charted along the pretty river which runs from Mognori into the park. It's still early days, but I'm assured that drumming & dancing performances can already be arranged. Visitors should report to the village chief.

🏠 **Mole Motel** ☎ 027 756 4444, 021 663155 or 027 7120564 or 071 722041; e ha@ghana.com. Built in 1961 on a cliff overlooking 2 watering holes, this idyllically situated hotel is an amazing place to wake up – as likely as not to the sound of baboons clattering over the roof. The accommodation is reasonably priced, & the swimming pool at the edge of the escarpment is a great spot to cool down after a walk in the park itself. In fact, the only major drawback of Mole Motel is its failure

to even attempt to harmonise with the wild surrounds. All that may change: in late 2006, a Tanzanian company was signed up to develop the park, & was rumoured to have plans to raze the whole thing to the ground and start from scratch – but for the time being there are 3 types of room in a series of long white blocks, all with fans that work only while the generator is running (typically between 18.00 & 23.00) & a private bathroom with (usually) running water. A twin costs US$18/24 with fan/AC, while a standard triple costs US$22, & a bed in one of the 2 6-bed dorms costs US$6 – the same price as an extra mattress. A dbl chalet with AC & a private balcony overlooking the waterhole costs US$37. By the pool, which is generally clean & inviting, a bar serves fairly priced sodas, beers & mineral water, the coolness of which depends on whether it was in the fridge while the electricity was running. The restaurant serves good meals starting at around US$4.50 – though service is legendarily slow so it is worth ordering several hours before. Theoretically guests are allowed to camp in the grounds for a fee – either in their own tent or in one of

A NON-HISTORY OF LARABANGA

The mosque at Larabanga may well be the oldest extant building in Ghana. Yet, oddly, nobody seems to agree on just how old it is, or even who built it. Some sources date it to the 13th century, which if not impossible is certainly improbable given that Islam had barely infiltrated the region at that time. In Larabanga itself, locals are fixated on the year 1421 and accredit the construction to an Islamic trader called Ayuba. Meanwhile, a display on Larabanga in the National Museum in Accra states that the mosque was built over the period 1643–75 by Imam Bramah, a theory that seems to be based solely on the somewhat negative evidence that the imam's original illuminated Koran – supposedly delivered to him by angels – is still preserved in the mosque (but don't get excited, because you won't be allowed inside the mosque, let alone be shown the Koran).

Local tradition has it that the mosque's founder was travelling through the region when he found the so-called mystic stone that lies on the outskirts of Larabanga in the direction of Wa, and decided, for some unexplained reason, that he would throw his spear from there and sleep wherever it landed. This he did, and during the night he had a strange dream about a mosque, the foundations of which were mysteriously in place when he awoke. Ayuba completed the construction of the mosque and settled at Larabanga – whose name reputedly derives from the Mole-Dagbani for 'speakers of Arabic'. How the date 1421 arose is anybody's guess. Then again, the early 15th century would tie in with dates given by the imams of other similar mosques, as well as the period that is generally agreed to be when Islam expanded its hold into what is now northern Ghana. And if this is the case, then, yes, visitors to Larabanga are probably looking at the oldest extant building in Ghana, some 50 years old when the Portuguese set about building their first castle at Elmina. But who knows?

the motel's – but in reality the management seems reluctant to let this happen. Booking is advisable, especially over a w/end. Visa, Amex & MasterCard are all accepted. *US$6–37*.

⚑ National Park Campsites In 2003, Raleigh International built a new campsite, just off the road & 10 minutes' walk from the motel in the direction of the entrance gate, with the support of the park rangers. The campsite is made up of 3 camping areas, each able to accommodate 4–5 tents, and parking spaces, & there is a long-drop toilet & water onsite. Camping here costs around US$3 pp. Several other very basic campsites are dotted around the reserve, which can theoretically be visited with a ranger, but many of the roads have become impassable & guides are reluctant to go there. This may well change over the lifespan of this edition, as the new Tanzanian management open up the routes & add new bush camps deeper in the reserve. Ask around for the current situation. *US$3 pp*.

⌂ Salia Brothers Guesthouse ☏ 027 5544071; e save_larabanga@yahoo.com; www.larabanga. netfirms.com. Run by twin brothers, this green guesthouse opposite the visitor's centre in Larabanga is regularly recommended by readers, though single women might take heed of a solitary report of sexual harassment by the staff. Simple accommodation is provided in dbl rooms with fans for US$5 a night, but during the dry season it is much nicer to stay on the roof, at US$2.50 a head, with clean blankets provided if the night turns cold. Good meals are available for around US$3 pp, ideally with an hour or so's notice. Village tours can be arranged & bicycles rented for visits to Mole at US$2 per day, while forthcoming plans inc a minibus shuttle to the park. A proportion of proceeds are ploughed into local community projects inc the prevention of guinea worm. *US$2.50–5*.

⌂ Savannah Lodge This new enterprise on the Larabanga-Mole road is also run by the Salia brothers offers a similar range of services in 5, round, thatched & brightly painted huts, equipped with mosquito nets (but no fan) using shared, outdoor showers. At the time of research, there was also a new dormitory block under construction. Drumming & dancing performances can be arranged on request. Around *US$3 pp*.

It is just as difficult to get to the bottom of Larabanga's status as the oldest and most holy of Ghana's mud-and-thatch mosques. People in Larabanga generally deny the existence of similar mosques elsewhere in the country and, if you say that you've actually seen some of them yourself, they turn up their noses at any suggestion that a 'man-made replica' might be of similar antiquity to their divinely created original. In all probability, the mud-and-stick mosques of Ghana were built in close succession along a well-established trade route through the west. Larabanga's claim to be the oldest of these mosques is supported by its reported status over several centuries as a surrogate Mecca for Ghanaian Muslims but it is difficult to verify. Can it be pure coincidence that 'Ghana's oldest mosque' also happens to be the one that lies a mere 5km from the motel in Mole National Park? The sense that the people of Larabanga aren't above a bit of conscious mythologising is heightened when you are taken to the mystic stone, a frankly very ordinary chunk of rock which caused the road towards Bole to be diverted because it 'mysteriously' reappeared overnight every time that it was removed by the road constructors.

Whenever it was built, Larabanga mosque, like others of its ilk, is obviously very old, and a truly strange and inspiring sight. Since 1995, the mosque has also been the cornerstone of a Peace-Corps-coordinated community-tourism project, one of particular importance in that, by allowing the villagers to benefit from tourism, it has the potential to ease the tension which has marked relations between village and national park ever since the former's traditional hunting grounds were gazetted away without recompense. But it does seem a shame under the circumstances that nobody locally, not even the guides, is able to provide visitors with any objective information whatsoever about its history.

17

WHAT TO DO There would be worse ways to pass a day than sitting on the **viewing platform** at the Mole Motel, cold beer in hand, swimming pool 20 paces away, and two waterholes clearly visible below. In the dry season, even this most passive approach to safari-going should reward you with sightings of elephant, kob antelope, Defassa waterbuck, bushbuck, warthog, olive baboon, green monkey and numerous birds during the course of any given day. While you're hanging around the motel, do drop in at the small museum in the staff quarters, which contains elephant skins, skulls and embryos, as well as some good sketches (but expect a bit of a wait while somebody locates the keys). At around 11.00, some traditional Gonja weavers come to the motel to display their craft – if you watch them, then a donation will be expected.

Far more exciting than the motel grounds, however, is to head down to the base of the cliff on a **guided game-walk** – not that you'll necessarily see a greater variety of mammals, just that you'll get far closer to them, in particular the elephants, which are reasonably habituated to human pedestrians and often allow visitors to approach to within 20m. On foot, you can also be reasonably sure of seeing Nile crocodiles in the dam and of mutually startling a few water monitors – bulky lizards which measure more than 1m long and habitually crash gracelessly to safety when disturbed. A guided walk with an armed ranger costs US$0.75 per person per hour, regardless of group size, and there are enough rangers for every group to have its own guide. It is customary to tip the ranger. The walks generally depart at 06.00 and 15.30, but can be arranged at other times with notice. Note that walking in the park without an armed ranger is forbidden, except along the road between the motel and Larabanga.

If the variety of large mammals is limited, the number and variety of birds to be seen around the waterholes can be fantastic. Most visitors will notice larger birds such as martial eagle (a pair of which currently nest in the area), woolly-necked and saddle-billed stork, white-backed and palmnut vulture, and various herons and egrets. Colour, too, is not lacking: the noisy but elusive yellow-crowned gonolek is something of a speciality, as is the red-throated bee-eater, a colony of which nests in the vicinity. Also worth looking out for are Senegal parrot, Abyssinian roller, green pigeon and violet turaco. All in all, I saw around 60 species in a three-hour walk; a more experienced west African birdwatcher would doubtless have seen more. Another accessible and worthwhile spot for birds is the stretch of riparian forest following the Mole river at Mognori on the road between the motel and Larabanga. Typical gallery forest species likely to be seen here include yellowbill, Narina trogon, blue-breasted kingfisher, shining-blue kingfisher, common wattle-eye, blue flycatcher, blackcap babbler, square-tailed drongo and bar-breasted firefinch. The elusive African finfoot is also resident here, and most likely to seen swimming close to the bank, below overhanging vegetation.

If birds are of specific interest, ask for a ranger who is especially knowledgeable. Binoculars and possibly a copy of the *Collins Field Guide to the Birds of West Africa* can be rented from the tourist centre in Larabanga at a reasonable daily rate. Those with a strong interest in birds should ask to be guided by Zechariah Wareh, one of the best birding guides in Ghana.

Those wishing to see some of the large mammal species that don't frequent the motel area, or who simply want to experience a genuine wilderness atmosphere, will be disappointed to learn that talk of starting up **overnight excursions** with an armed ranger has been going around for years, but we have yet to hear of anyone who has actually experienced one. Likewise, game drives from the motel haven't been operating for some years, nor are they likely to be restarted in the foreseeable future.

Few visitors would want to miss seeing **Larabanga Mosque**, in the village of the same name, some 5km from the motel (see box on page 366). If you're going to be bussing directly in and out of Mole from Tamale, then the best way to do this is to hire a bicycle from the Mole Motel, though you could also walk out in the mid-afternoon and then either walk back or (optimistically) wait to catch the late afternoon bus from Tamale. Otherwise, you'll get a chance to spend time at the mosque while you wait to change vehicles at Larabanga – it's only 50m from the main junction and bus station, and there is no longer any need to take a guide, though plenty of guides will try to latch on to you. If you visit independently, or with a guide arranged through the Salia brothers, you'll need to pay the official entrance fee (or more accurately 'viewing fee' since visitors may not enter the mosque) of US$0.50 as well as a tip of US$0.20 to the imam and something to the guide. Visit with an unofficial guide and you can expect several extra charges and/or optional donations to be introduced.

Larabanga village is itself a fascinating place, with perhaps the most southerly accessible examples of traditional flat-roofed mud *kraals* in the country, of particular interest to travellers who are not exploring other parts of northern Ghana. Through the Larabanga visitor information centre it is possible to take a guided tour of the village and a local farm for US$1 per person. Other activities arranged by the tourist centre include bicycle hire and traditional drumming and dancing evenings.

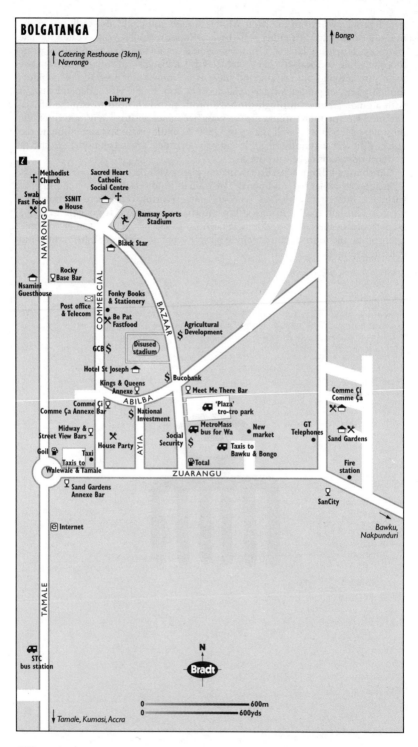

BOLGATANGA

↑ Bongo

↑ Catering Resthouse (3km),
  Navrongo

● Library

ℹ

† Methodist Church

Swab Fast Food ✗
SSNIT House ●

Sacred Heart Catholic Social Centre ⌂ †

🏃 Ramsay Sports Stadium

🏠 Nsamini Guesthouse

Rocky Base Bar ♀

Black Star ◻

NAVRONGO

COMMERCIAL

Post office & Telecom ✉

Fonky Books & Stationery ●
✗ Be Pat Fastfood

BAZAAR

Agricultural Development $

GCB $

Disused stadium

Hotel St Joseph ⌂
Kings & Queens Annexe ♀

Comme Ci Comme Ça Annexe Bar ♀
Comme Ci Comme Ça Annexe Bar $

$ National Investment

Midway & Street View Bars ♀
✗ House Party

AYIA

Social Security
$

Goil ⛽
Taxi ●
Taxis to Walewale & Tamale

Sand Gardens Annexe Bar ♀

ⓔ Internet

$ Bucobank
♀ Meet Me There Bar

🚌 'Plaza' tro-tro park

🚌 MetroMass bus for Wa
● New market
🚌 Taxis to Bawku & Bongo

⌂ ✗ Comme Ci Comme Ça

GT Telephones ●

⌂ ✗ Sand Gardens

♿ Total

ZUARANGU

Fire station ●

♀ SanCity

→ Bawku, Nakpunduri

ABILBA

TAMALE

🚌 STC bus station

N
Bradt

0 ————— 600m
0 ————— 600yds

↓ Tamale, Kumasi, Accra

370

18

Bolgatanga and the Upper East

Because the Upper East Region is so remote from the coast and capital, the few travellers who pass through it are generally backpackers or overlanders travelling between Ghana and Mali or Senegal via Burkina Faso. Those who do visit this region will, however, find it offers much in the way of off-the-beaten-track rewards. Bolgatanga, the regional capital, is a chaotic but somehow rather captivating town, and a good base for day visits to Sirigu, with its wonderful painted houses, as well as the rhyming villages of Bongo and Tongo. Paga, on the Burkina border, is noted for its sacred crocodile pool and striking adobe architecture, while Navrongo, between Paga and Bolgatanga, boasts a beautiful church with a unique mud-sculpted interior. Somewhat more remote, but accessible nonetheless, the pretty Gambaga Escarpment actually lies within Northern Region, but from a travel perspective it slots in more comfortably with Bolgatanga than Tamale.

BOLGATANGA

The burgeoning capital of Ghana's Upper East Region may be smaller than Tamale, but it is no less hectic. Bolgatanga, you can't help but feel, is about to do the urban equivalent of bursting at the seams, and it comes as no surprise to discover that the population of this amorphous, bustling city has grown from fewer than 20,000 in 1970 to about 70,000 today. Like many towns in the north, Bolga (as you'll soon come to call it) lacks for specific tourist attractions, though the small but interesting ethnographic museum behind the Catholic Social Centre is definitely worth an hour or two. You might also want to pop in at the nearby regional library and Ghana Tourist Board office, the latter your best source of current local tourist information. Bolga's most interesting feature, however, is the busy market, which peaks in activity every three days and is best known elsewhere in Ghana for the fine and often very affordable leatherwork, basketry, colourful straw hats and striped cloth shirts produced by the Frafra people for a predominantly local market. Hat salesmen, heads layered high with samples of their wares, are a familiar sight around town.

GETTING THERE AND AWAY Bolga is an important regional transport hub and you'll have little difficulty finding transport in most directions from the recently enlarged station on Bazaar Road. Regular tro-tros and buses also leave for Tamale (a 2½-hour trip costing US$3) from the small station on Zuarangu Road.

For southerly travel beyond Tamale, popular options are the daily STC service that leaves from the STC station on the Tamale road for Kumasi (11.30, US$13) and Accra (09.00, US$20) or the Saturday service to Takoradi, leaving at 13.00 and costing US$22 for a seat. Alternatively you could try the daily OA bus which leaves at 15.00 and goes to Accra (US$19) via Kumasi (US$13). Travellers are advised to turn up at least an hour in advance, but I've had no reader feedback about how reliable the service is.

If the STC bus timetables for Bolga don't suit you, then catch one of the several buses that connect Tamale to Accra and Kumasi daily, and use local transport between Bolga and Tamale. Also recommended are the fairly regular Metro Mass buses that run to Tamale (US$2), Bawku (US$1), Paga (US$0.90), Bongo (US$0.30) and other local destinations. The only direct transport between Bolga and Wa is the clapped out (and somewhat ironically named) City Express bus that runs next to the Social Security Bank outside the new bus station. In theory, these buses leave at 06.00 daily except Sundays in either direction and take about nine hours, but it's not unusual to arrive after dark due to delays and unscheduled stops. Tickets cannot be booked before the departure date, which means you ought to be at the station at 04.30–5.00 to be certain of a seat. It's also possible to travel to or from Wa by tro-tro, changing vehicles at Tumu, but be aware that while it's possible to get through in a day coming from Bolga, you'll almost certainly need to overnight in Tumu coming from Wa.

WHERE TO STAY
Moderate

Comme Çi Comme Ça ☎ 072 22355/16. Bolga's leading eatery also offers what are probably the smartest rooms in town, set in a in leafy gardens behind the main restaurant building. *Self-contained dbl with AC & TV US$28, slightly larger chalet with bath & shower US$30.*

Budget

Black Star Hotel ☎ 072 22346. The central Black Star Hotel was once the most upmarket offering in Bolga, but whilst the restaurant still looks the part – with its blasting AC, swish décor & chattering TV – the rooms are starting to look a little frayed at the seams and it can be noisy on Sat nights when they are infected by blasting highlife from the ground-floor disco. *Sgl/dbl with fan US$12/18 using common showers, self-contained twin with powerful AC US$25.*

Catering Resthouse ☎ 072 22399. This grand folly, situated 3km out of town off the Navrongo road, consists of a massive, partially unfinished concrete monolith with comic modernist pretensions, redeemed from utter absurdity only by the pleasant self-contained chalets with AC (& even the occasional trouser press!), which are very fair value. The bar & restaurant also seem OK, & host the occasional disco, but ultimately the desolate atmosphere & distance from town are a bit of a downer. *Dbl US$9.*

Sand Gardens Hotel ☎ 072 23464. This excellent hotel – which lies off the Bawku road about 15 mins' walk from the town centre & 10 mins from the new lorry park – is difficult to beat at any level. The large gardens – no longer sandy, but grassy & shaded by leafy mango trees – are a pleasant place for a drink, especially as the sound system is played at non-distortive levels until it shuts down at around 10.30, after which the frogs & cicadas take over. Reasonable Chinese, Ghanaian & continental meals cost US$18–27 & can be eaten outdoors or in the AC restaurant, though service can be slow. Tours can be arranged through the reception, including 2-night trips to Mole National Park. The hotel is popular with conferences & travelling professionals, so it's worth booking in advance. A variety of neat, clean, comfortable rooms is available. *Dbl with fan & shared bath US$9, self-contained dbl/twin with fan & TV US$14/22 & similar rooms with AC US$24/25.*

Shoestring

Hotel St Joseph ☎ 072 23214. Tucked away behind the disused stadium, this central multi-storey block is a lot better than its rather sleazy exterior might suggest & is well placed for travellers planning to catch an early morning bus. Better value is to be had elsewhere however. There's a lively outdoor bar, but the noise doesn't permeate to the rooms to a disturbing degree. *Extremely basic sgl with fan US$7, superior self-contained dbl* with fan US$8.50–11.50 depending on whether they have a TV, self-contained dbl/twin with AC US$15–22.

Nsanmini Guesthouse ☎ 072 23403. This 6-room lodge, which lies on the west side of the Navrongo road roughly opposite the Rocky Base Bar, has been recommended by several readers as an excellent shoestring bet. The rooms use a spotless common shower & toilet is spotless. The owner is exceedingly friendly & helpful, & justly proud of the Greek lemon tree in his garden. Booking is recommended. *Neat sgl/dbl with fan & comfortable beds US$4–5.*

⌂ **Sacred Heart Catholic Social Centre** Some might find the aura of shabby institutionalism a little off-putting, but the central location & cheap canteen go a long way to compensating. Clean dbl rooms at this poorly signposted guesthouse are excellent value at US$5, using immaculate common showers, whilst a bed in one of the 6-man dorms is even cheaper. *US$2–5.*

✗ **WHERE TO EAT** The **Comme Çi Comme Ça Restaurant**, on the outskirts of town close to the Sand Gardens Hotel, is not quite as indifferent as the name might suggest – on the contrary, it's perhaps the best restaurant of its sort in northern Ghana, offering a varied selection of tasty, attractively presented and substantial Western and Chinese dishes starting in the US$2.50–4.50 range. You can eat either in the air-conditioned dining hall or in one of several fan-cooled, thatched, outdoor shelters. It's a good place to drink, too, with friendly service and a highly effective fridge. You might want to check the bill, however, as it has a reputation for overcharging.

Good food is also available, at slightly cheaper prices, at the **Sand Gardens Hotel** or at the restaurant in the more central **Black Star Hotel**. Another good place to eat near the town centre is **Swab Fast Food**, which lies in a small garden just off the Navrongo road opposite SSNIT House, and serves a similar range of Indian, Chinese and Western dishes to its namesake in Tamale, as well as the only pizzas in town, with most dishes costing about US$3.50–5. The well-ventilated **Diplomate Restaurant** in SSNIT House serves a more limited range of decent Western and local dishes from US$2.50 upwards.

The courtyard bar at the **St Joseph Hotel** is popular with locally based volunteers, and cheap grilled-beef kebabs and whole guinea fowl can be bought from a vendor at the entrance. The usual range of street food is available around the market and lorry parks. In addition to the hotel and restaurant garden bars, the cluster of down-to-earth local drinking holes that includes the **Midway** and **Street View Bars** (on Ayia Road) serve chilled beer at rock bottom prices, to the usual accompaniment of blaring distorted music.

OTHER PRACTICALITIES

Books The Readwise Bookshop in SSNIT House stocks a reasonable selection of Victorian and older 'classics' for US$1.50 apiece. A far more limited selection, this time of modern novels, is available at the nearby Fonky Book & Stationery for around US$3 each.

Foreign exchange The exchange rates for US dollars cash and other major currencies at the efficient Hopewell Forex Bureau on Afteba Road are only slightly lower than bureau rates in Accra or Kumasi. The rates here are better than any you'll get in Tamale, where there is no private forex bureau at the time of writing, and they are far better than the rates offered at the nearby Burkina Faso border, whether you want to change hard currencies or CFA into cedi (or vice versa). Following the recent closure of the Standard Chartered Bank, however, there is nowhere to exchange travellers' cheques and no ATMs from where you can draw cash against a Visa card – to do this you will need to go to Tamale.

Internet Several internet cafés are dotted around town, charging a uniform and relatively steep rate of US$0.05 per minute.

Tourist information The tourist office (☎ *072 23416;* e *gtuer@ghana.com*) for the Upper West Region lies alongside the Navrongo road a short distance north of Swab Fast Food. The staff seem pretty clued up and helpful, and if nothing else they can give you a selection of pamphlets covering ecotourism sites in and around Bolga.

Ellen Holiday Services (☎ *072 22316/55* or *024 370715*; e *ellenholiday@yahoo.com*), based out of the Comme Çi Comme Ça Hotel, can arrange a variety of day trips around Bolgatanga, as well as longer trips through to Wa, Mole and the Upper West.

Alternatively, a reliable young man called **Mohammed Moro** (☎ *024 6750823*; e *amead2006@hotmail.com* or *contactable through Sand Gardens Hotel*) is willing to purchase tickets on travellers' behalf, lead trips to nearby villages, or further afield into Burkina Faso and Mali for reasonable, negotiable fees.

In early 2007, a Belgian-Ghanaian NGO called **Tanga Tours** (☎ *024 4816767* or *024 6101589*; e *solomon@tangatours.org* or *tom@tangatours.org*; *www.tangatours.org*) opened an office behind the Root Art Shop, opposite the post office on Commercial Road. In addition to scooter and bike hire, it can arrange a variety of guided excursions in the Upper East and further afield.

AROUND BOLGATANGA

In addition to the sites listed below, Paga – about an hour's drive away, and covered under its own heading later in the chapter – would make a perfectly feasible goal for a day trip out of Bolgatanga.

TENGZUG/TONGO The small town of Tengzug, also known as Tongo, lies about 15km southeast of Bolgatanga at the base of a horseshoe-shaped chain of hills known for its striking balancing rock formations and the whistling sound made by the Harmattan wind as it passes through cracks in the rocks from December to February. But most of all, perhaps, these rocky hills are venerated for their many sacred Talensi ancestral shrines, of which the most venerated is Ba'ar Tonna'ab Ya'nee, a popular site of pilgrimage for Ashanti traditionalists, who call it Nana Tongo. The hills and Tengzug, the nearest settlement to Ba'ar Tonna'ab Ya'nee, have recently become the site of a formal ecotourism project initiated by the NCRC, and they are also being proposed as a UNESCO World Heritage Site.

The Talensi people of the Tengzug/Tongo Hills are sedentary agriculturists whose rich oral traditions and unusual agricultural practices – which include stone terracing and strong taboos against starting uncontrollable fires and the felling of trees in certain areas – suggest they have occupied the area for many centuries. For much of the 19th century, the Talensi suffered heavily at the hands of slave raiders, partially because Tongo formed something of a no-man's land between Mossi and Dagbon territory, but they still resisted any significant cultural assimilation into the more powerful neighbouring states. The Talensi also offered staunch resistance to British rule, inspired by the powerful ancestral spirits and oracle housed in Ba'ar Tonna'ab Ya'nee. Even after 1911, when they were finally subjugated by a colonial military expedition and evicted from the hills, the Talensi took little heed of a ban on attending their hilltop shrines, resulting in a second – and essentially ineffective – British military foray into the hills in 1915. Today visitors can see the Hiding Caves, where the chief took shelter and commanded his forces against the British during their attempts to colonise, and the Hyena Caves, where the chief and other figureheads met during their battle with the British. Another attraction well worth a look is the enormous and labyrinthine chief's house, which has at times sheltered more than 300 people and is considered to be the largest of its kind.

If you're in the area at the right time of year, ask about the exact dates of the Boar Dam Festival, which usually occurs over late October to celebrate the harvest and is centred on Ba'ar Tonna'ab Ya'nee and other Talensi ancestral shrines, or about

March's Golob Festival at Nnon Shrine. Also of interest is the sacred bat-tree at **Baare**, 3km from Tengzug, though whether it's worth the hassle is debatable, especially as the bats aren't always there and the numbers pale by comparison with the bat colonies you can see in parts of Accra and Kumasi.

In Tengzug, a community fee of US$3.50 is charged to non-Ghanaian visitors, with discounts for Ghanaians, students, children and volunteers, and includes a visit to the model home, all guide services, hiking in the hills and entrance to the Hiding and Hyena caves. An additional US$1.50 is charged for a tour of the chief's house, and a further US$1.50 to see the shrine.

Tengzug lies 17km from Bolga by road. To get there, follow the Tamale road south for 5km as far as the signposted junction at Winkogo, then turn left, and then – after another 8km – right at another signposted junction. No public transport runs all the way to Tengzug, but you can either charter a direct taxi from Bolga, or else catch a shared taxi or tro-tro from the new bus station to the Tangzug turn off (about 30 minutes), from where it's a 4km walk along a rather steep road. Guides can be arranged and fees paid at the tourist office in Tengzug, from where you can visit Ba'ar Tonna'ab Ya'nee on foot, as well as two other important shrines called Nnoo and Bonab. It might be worth noting that visitors of both genders are permitted to enter the shrine only if topless. In addition to visiting the shrine, it's possible to arrange longer hiking trips into the mountains.

Accommodation is available in a new guesthouse or a model Talensi home (US$5 per person), both of which are built in the traditional northern style and have bath facilities and authentic cooking areas (indoor and out). Food and drinks are available upon request. Alternatively you can camp (US$1.50 per person), stay in the basic Tongo Community Centre, or organise a homestay with an approved family through the tourist office. A new resort, the **Tongo Oasis** just before you reach town from Bolga, was also under construction as this book went to press.

BONGO About 15km north of Bolgatanga, the small town of Bongo lies at the heart of a truly memorable landscape of smooth rocky outcrops, magnificent baobab trees, and round-hutted compounds covered in childish stencil-like painted figures. The main attraction here, the aptly named Bongo Rock, emits a convincingly resonant vibrating boom when struck, while the general landscape offers much to photographers. At the chief's palace, signposted to the right just after the Catholic church, Nana Lemyaarom (aka Baba Salifu), who was enskinned in 2006, is happy to welcome respectful visitors. Donations are welcome but not compulsory. Further along the road back towards Bolga, the Bongo Woman Weavers Association sells well-priced traditional baskets.

Regular tro-tros and Metro Mass buses to Bongo leave Bolgatanga from the central lorry station, taking about 30 minutes and charging around US$0.30 a seat. Bongo Rock lies 20–30 minutes' walk from Bongo; to get there follow the main road back from the tro-tro station past the church, until after about 300m you see a footpath to your left leading to the taller and more distant of two hills. There's no accommodation in Bongo, but cool soft drinks and beers are available from a number of bars in town, including Avag Spot, just past the Goil station.

SIRIGU Nestled against the Burkina Faso border almost directly north of Bolgatanga, Sirigu is known throughout Ghana not only for the superb pottery and basketwork produced by its women, but also for the elaborate symbolic wall paintings with which these female artists decorate their characteristically Sahelian flat-roofed adobe houses. Also very striking is the elaborate facial scarring – almost like a spider's web in complexity – practised by the Nakarisi people who live in and around the village.

Sirigu is also the site of an excellent new community-based tourism project centred on a guesthouse and gallery run by the Sirigu Woman's Organisation for Pottery and Art (SWOPA), a local organisation founded in 1997 with the linked goals of preventing these traditional crafts from dying out, of increasing the income derived from these crafts, and of offering opportunities for social and economic advancement for local women.

Sirigu lies 35km from Bolgatanga by road and can be reached by following the Navrongo road for 18km then turning right into a signposted dirt side road at Kandiga junction. Minibuses to Sirigu leave from Bolga throughout the day, departing from right alongside the disused stadium, and take about one hour. The minibuses can take a while to fill up, so it might be worth paying for some extra seats to get things rolling – the fare is US$0.90 per person. Incidentally, if you're coming from Navrongo, there is no direct public transport to Sirigu and it is difficult to pick up a lift at Kandiga junction, so you'll have to either travel via Bolgatanga or charter a taxi. However you get there, ask to be dropped at the SWOPA Guesthouse and Cultural Centre, about 1km before you reach the village itself. Devotees of house painting might be interested in checking out the village of Kandiga, which lies about halfway along the road between Kandiga junction and Sirigu, where several monochrome exteriors depict animals, people and geometric patterns.

The **SWOPA Guesthouse** consists of four round double huts and a new dormitory, which was still under construction at the time of research. The three huts using common bucket showers cost US$7.50 per unit, while the solitary self-contained hut costs US$11. Camping costs US$1 per person. There is no electricity, but solar lights are available, as are additional mattresses. In theory, breakfast can be provided at US$1.50 per head and other meals cost US$2.50, but all meals need to be ordered a few hours in advance – and the staff won't prepare food at all if they're not in the mood, in which case you'll have to eat at one of the basic chop shops in Sirigu village. Drinks are available at the guesthouse, but if you want them chilled then you'll be better off at one of the bars in Sirigu. Advance bookings can be made by ringing Melanie Kasise, the founder and manager of SWOPA based in Bolga (✆ 072 24378, 024 8222232, 072 23432 or 024 822276).

A tour of two of the traditional painted homesteads dotted around the SWOPA Guesthouse costs US$2 inclusive of guide fee. Village tours of Sirigu itself are available at US$2.50, taking in the chief's palace, market, Catholic Mission and sacred groves, but it is perfectly possible to visit the village independently – indeed, should you be staying at the SWOPA Guesthouse and want to eat, you may need to! There's no official charge for entering the SWOPA Visitors' Centre Gallery, but a donation of US$0.50 is recommended – which seems a bit of a cheek, frankly, as the gallery is basically a shop selling a selection of the superb local pottery and other craftwork. By prior arrangement (see the telephone numbers above), SWOPA can also arrange one-day pottery and basket-weaving workshops (US$5 per person).

VOPAC The Village of Pottery Art and Culture is similar in concept to Sirigu, but considerably easier to get to – set as it is off the main road to Navrongo, 8km west of Bolga. The project offers some excellent examples of traditionally painted mud houses, as well as locally made pottery which is sold to raise funds for the village school. Alanbee, who runs the scheme, is happy to arrange pick up from Bolga (✆ 024 4671562).

WIDNABA Situated in the Red Volta Valley near the Burkina Faso border northeast of Bolgatanga, the remote village of Widnaba, home to the Kusaasi people, was developed for community-based ecotourism by the NCRC with Peace Corps assistance. According to oral tradition, Widnaba – which translates as 'Horse Chief

Palace' – was founded and named by the eldest of a quartet of siblings who migrated to the area from present-day Burkina Faso, and whose horse delivered three foals upon its arrival at the site, a sign of good luck (it is said that Tilli, which you pass through en route to Widnaba, was founded by another one of the siblings).

Widnaba is essentially a cultural site – a guided tour includes the chief's palace, various shrines and sacred groves, and the old slave market with its hollowed-out baobab where slaves were held captive – but there are a few good walking trails along the crest of hills to the north, with a picnic hut overlooking Burkina Faso on the ridge, while the walk between the village and the damn offers excellent savanna birding, and the odd sighting of a non-habituated crocodile. There is also a very slim chance of encountering a herd of elephants on its migratory route through the Red Volta Valley, although poaching and other human disturbances in recent years have diminished sightings to the occasional fresh dung heap. A fee of US$1.50 per non-Ghanaian visitor is charged for each of the following activities: Hills and Burkina Border Tour, Slave Trade & Hidden Place Tour, Town Tour (includes market and chief's palace) and Wildlife Tour. Cultural displays can be arranged for groups.

Widnaba lies 49km from Bolgatanga by road. It can be reached in a private vehicle by following the Bawku road east for 35km as far as Tilli, then turning left along the signposted dirt track to Widnaba. There is no public transport to Widnaba but any vehicle heading from Bolga to Bawku or Zebilla can drop you at Tilli, where it's possible to rent a bicycle to cover the last 14km. Another option would be to charter a private taxi out of Bolga, but this will be relatively costly. If you want to overnight in Widnaba, it's possible to rent a basic room at the **Widnaba Visitors Centre** for around US$6/9 single/double with net, lantern and common bucket showers, or to camp at US$1.50 per tent. Local meals and drinks, including filtered drinking water, are available by arrangement, and served in the communal round eating hall.

THE GAMBAGA ESCARPMENT

The Gambaga Escarpment, which lies to the east of the main Tamale–Bolgatanga road, is the most significant physical feature in northeastern Ghana, measuring more than 60km from east to west and rising several hundred metres above the surrounding plains. The escarpment is named after the town of Gambaga, capital of the ancient kingdom of Mamprusi, which is widely regarded to be the oldest of the Mole-Dagbani states, and whose chief, the Nayiri, is still sometimes called upon to settle internal disputes in neighbouring Mossi and Dagomba. It is probable that Mamprusi is the oldest extant political unit in Ghana. All Mole-Dagbani traditions agree that it was founded before AD1200 by the descendants of a light-skinned chief remembered by the name Toha-jie ('The Red Warrior'), who led his people from somewhere further east to Pusiga on what is now the Ghana–Burkina Faso border. Toha-jie's grandson, Naa Gbewa, is thought to have been the first true Mamprusi chief, settling first at a place called Mamprugu (from which the name Mamprusi derives), then at Gambaga, where he forged a union with the indigenous people by assuming political control but allowing religious power to remain in the hands of traditional Tengdana priests.

Although it is practically undeveloped for tourism, the Gambaga Escarpment can be explored following a circular road route from Walewale (on the main Bolga-Tamale road) via Gambaga and Nalerigu to Nakpanduri at the eastern edge of the escarpment, then returning to Bolga via Bawku and Zebilla. The region does harbour some potential for birdwatching and hiking, while archaeological and cultural interest is provided by the Naa Jaringa Walls at Nalerigu, the Outcast Home (aka Witch Colony) at Gambaga, and the fantastic traditional kraals –

18

extended family homesteads in which each nuclear family unit has its own hut and courtyard area enclosed within one walled compound – of Nakpanduri. All the same, there is an element of travel for its own sake to this trip, the main attraction of which is arguably the sense of being away from any beaten tourist trail.

The road circuit around the escarpment is described below starting at Walewale, running via Gambaga and Nalerigu to Nakpanduri, from where you could either turn back directly towards Walewale or else continue north via Bawku and Zebilla to Bolgatanga.

WALEWALE The unexpectedly substantial town of Walewale sprawls untidily along the main Bolgatanga–Tamale road at the junction of the dirt road to Nakpanduri. There's not much to see in the town itself – the mosque opposite the junction, notable for its Moorish tower, was built in 1961 on the site of an ancient mud-and-stick mosque – but there are plenty of bars and chop shops, and even a few lodgings should the need arise, of which the pick is the new **Masagri Guesthouse** (✆ 071 522076 or 22000), situated about 500m from the junction in the direction of Bolga. Far more interesting than Walewale is the village of Wulugu, which lies about 7km back towards Bolga and is notable for the traditional Zayaa Mosque, a fort-like double-storey construction of rich red earth that rises in mildly surreal isolation some 50m west of the main road like a gigantic sculpted termite mound. There is reputedly also an ostrich farm in the vicinity of Wulugu, but you'll have to ask around locally for details.

Walewale lies some 40km south of Bolgatanga, to which it is connected by a regular stream of minibuses that leave every 15–30 minutes throughout the day from the Tamale Station on Zaurangu Road, taking about one hour and costing US$1. Coming from Tamale, which lies 120km to the south, you can either do the trip in short hops, a somewhat tedious exercise, or – more practically – pay the full fare on a bus or tro-tro heading to Bolgatanga and ask to 'drop' at Walewale.

GAMBAGA It is difficult to determine the historical relationship between Gambaga and Nalerigu, which lies 8km to its east. Most sources refer to Gambaga as the ancient capital of Mamprusi; it was certainly the colonial capital of the Northern Territory until 1907, and it remains district capital to this day. Yet Nalerigu appears to be the older settlement and it houses the palace of the Nayiri (paramount chief of Mamprusi) while Gambaga has its own local chief, called the Gambagarana.

Gambaga's main point of interest is the *kukoa* (witches' camp) on the outskirts of town, which provides refuge to women that have been cast out of their communities after being accused and found guilty of witchcraft. Founded in the 19th century by the Gambagarana, who is accredited with the hereditary power to exorcise evil spirits from alleged witches, the camp today houses an estimated 150–200 women, some from as far afield as Burkina Faso and Togo, and many of whom have lived there for decades. Since 1994, the *kukoa* at Gambaga – one of three left in northern Ghana – has been managed in collaboration with the Presbyterian Church under the euphemistic auspices of the Gambaga Outcast Home Project (GOHP), which has attempted to reduce poverty within the camp by teaching the women income-generating activities such as cotton-spinning and beadmaking. It is also perhaps the only village in Ghana where every homestead has its own 'front garden' – cultivated out of necessity as social convention prevents the 'witches' from inheriting land or buying any nearby

To the casual observer, the women at Gambaga seem very happy – and are clearly delighted when tourists come to visit – but the camp has attracted a great deal of controversy in recent years. Human rights activists and feminists argue convincingly that it essentially functions as a prison wherein hundreds of women charged with imaginary crimes have been detained on what is effectively a life sentence. In most parts of northern Ghana, it doesn't require any effort – just a bit of misfortune – for a woman to find herself stigmatised as a witch. It is customary, for instance, for a charge of sorcery to be levelled at an elder female relative of anybody who dies prematurely of measles, epilepsy, malaria, cholera or any other disease, while elder wives are also often accused of casting a spell to make their polygamous husband impotent or his younger wives barren. The accused will be tried according to local custom, which varies from one community to the next, but is generally somewhat arbitrary – for instance, the chief might strangle a chicken, throw it into the air, and decide the case on the basis of how the fowl lands. If the accused is found guilty, she might at worst be beaten to death by angry relatives of the deceased, but just as often she will be forced to flee and placed by relatives, or take refuge herself, in a witches' camp.

The Gambagarana and church workers associated with the camp reject the charge that it is a prison. Instead, they characterise the *kukoa* as a sanctuary, one that has over several generations offered refuge to social outcasts with nowhere else to go. And they have a point, insofar as attempting to close the witches' camp could be likened to treating the symptom rather than the disease – for so long as the women are stigmatised as witches, then they will need to be afforded some form of refuge, and the *kukoa* at Gambaga is accepted because it is widely believed that the Gambagarana has the power to render the alleged witches harmless whilst they are in his presence. Indeed, in early 1998 more than 100 of the witches held in the camp were formally released, following pressure from outside sources, and they simply refused to leave. The septuagenarian leader of the released women, who had been resident in the camp for more than three decades, said 'We will not go anywhere; we are safe here' – and cited the example of another camp resident who had recently returned home only to come back to the camp a few days later with one ear cut off by angry locals, who told her that if she returned home again, then the other ear would be cut off too.

A visit to the *kukoa* at Gambaga poses a genuine humanitarian dilemma, and there are no easy answers. Expecting the government to close down the camp entirely doesn't appear to be a realistic option, at least not so long as the belief in witchcraft remains rampant in northern Ghana. Equally, the reality is that the camp's inhabitants *are* effectively prisoners, if not of the Gambagarana then certainly of the cruel superstitions that rule their own communities. Perhaps the most immediate need is some sort of official intervention aimed to improve the living conditions within the camp; for instance by providing food rations and piped water to the women. If you want to see it for yourself, visitors are welcome. Ask for the GOHP office, which lies about ten minutes' walk from the lorry station in Gambaga, from where you'll then be taken to the chief to offer him a libation (US$2 is suggested) and obtain permission to enter the camp. You'll also be expected to make a donation directly to the women or to the GOHP office.

Plenty of public transport runs along the unsurfaced 45km stretch of road between Walewale and Gambaga, though do note that Gambaga-bound tro-tros leave Walewale not from the main lorry station but from the main junction, which lies about 500m back towards Bolga – you shouldn't wait more than 45 minutes for something to leave. A steady stream of shared taxis covers the 8km asphalt road between Gambaga and Nalerigu. There are two decent little lodgings in Gambaga, of which your first choice should be the friendly **Norrip Guesthouse** (☎ *071 23812*), where an air-conditioned double room with cold running water costs US$7 and good meals can be prepared with advance notice. The more central **Martha Memorial Guesthouse** charges US$5–7 for a double room depending on its size.

NALERIGU Only 8km past Gambaga, Nalerigu is of some archaeological interest for the remains of the Naa Jaringa Walls, which lie under a grove of trees to the left of the dam wall a short distance from the town centre in the direction of Gambaga. According to local tradition, the walls were built with stones, mud, honey and milk during the 16th-century rule of Naa Jaringa, partly to protect the village from slave raiders, and partly so that Naa Jaringa's name would not be forgotten after his death – the story is that his only son was not accepted as his nominated successor because he was blind in one eye. There's plenty of transport in and out of Nalerigu in all directions, and little reason why you'd be likely to spend the night, but if you do then the **Chesterfield** (❧ 071 24153) is your best bet, with neat, self-contained rooms for US$8–12. The alternative is the very inexpensive **government resthouse** in the school grounds, where for around US$1.50 you'll be offered a bare room with no mattress, no lock and no electricity, as well as the opportunity to watch the schoolchildren doing their early morning thing – national anthem, national pledge, a bit of marching, the *Ghana Wildlife Men* song, etc. A small garden bar next to the bus station sells cool but not chilled drinks, while an adjacent chop stall sells deliciously spicy guineafowl stew.

NAKPANDURI Perched on the highest point on the Gambaga Escarpment, Nakpanduri lies about 25km east of Nalerigu and is connected to it by reasonably regular transport. There's little in the way of sights, but the attractive surroundings and a relatively cool climate make it a pleasant place to settle for a day or two. The town is a striking collection of circular traditional compounds interspersed with massive baobab trees, while the area around the government resthouse affords great views to the northern plains, and is excellent for birdwatching. A good day's walk would be to follow the Bawku road through a forest reserve to the base of the escarpment, where a bridge crosses a forest-fringed tributary of the Volta River. So far as we can ascertain, the locally vaunted seasonal waterfall that lies about 45 minutes' walk from the town centre is actually an artificial drainage ditch that diverts the water from the road down the side of the escarpment. Of greater interest are the caves, about 2km away, where local people once hid from slave raids, as well as a small dam about half an hour's walk from the main traffic circle – the guesthouse staff can direct you or arrange a local guide.

As for practicalities, the first thing you'll want to do upon arrival in Nakpanduri is make certain of a room. The established option is the **government resthouse**, where all but one of the rooms has been occupied by a solar power research group for the past couple of years, a situation that's unlikely to change in the foreseeable future. Assuming you can get that one room, however, the resthouse does have a superb location on the escarpment rim, and it's not bad value at US$4.50 for a double with fan and common bucket showers. To get to the resthouse from the main circle (which is where most tro-tros and buses stop), walk along the Bawku road for about 15 minutes until you pass the Agricultural Rehabilitation Centre for the Blind to your right and see a three-way fork to your left opposite a signpost reading 'Caution: Slow Down'. The guesthouse is about 200m down the central fork.

A more reliable option is the new and privately owned **Sillim Guesthouse**, a bright pink building that lies about 500m from the main circle in the same direction as the government resthouse and charges around US$8 for a clean double room with fan, using common showers and toilets. For food, there are several chop stalls around the main circle where spicy guinea-fowl stew is the local speciality, sold from mid-afternoon until late evening, and stale bread is sold at all times, but be warned that on the basis of our experience *kenkey* (or whatever other hot starchy accompaniment is available) evidently sells out well before nightfall. There are also several bars near the main circle.

Approaching or leaving Nakpanduri in the Walewale direction is very straightforward: a few buses daily run directly to and from Tamale and Bolga, and a steady stream of local transport hops between Nakpanduri, Nalerigu, Gambaga and Walewale. Except on Gambaga's market day (every third day), however, transport to and from Bawku is limited to a solitary bus that leave Bawku at 06.00, passes through Nakpanduri at about 09.00 and terminates at Nalerigu an hour later, starting the return trip at around 16.00 to pass through Nakpanduri at about 15.00 and arrive in Bawku after dark.

BAWKU Heading on from Nakpanduri, your options are to beat a retreat back to Walewale or strike on northwards to Bawku – a large and busy market town whose buildings were left pitted with gun shot after a chieftaincy dispute in 2005. The conflict has since been resolved and some of the damage repaired, restoring Bawku to a low-key but unmemorable town – made more absorbing on market days (every third day), or if you want to buy a sample of the attractive *fugu* shirts that are characteristic of the far northeast. Before you go clothes shopping, however, you'll need to find transport from Nakpanduri through to Bawku, which – as noted above – is less straightforward than local advice ('you get lorry any time') might have you believe. As compensation, once you finally get going the 60km road offers some magnificent views.

Accommodation in Bawku is limited to a few basic lodges. The **Blue Cross Guesthouse** next to the hospital charges about US$3 for a clean room with fan and communal bucket showers, while the nearby **Hospital Guesthouse** is better and more expensive. A more central option is the rather seedy **Paradise Guesthouse**. The best place to eat in the town centre is the **Him Restaurant**, next to the Mobil garage. The only sightseeing in the area that I'm aware of is the ancient shrine to Naa Gbewa, the founder of the Mamprusi state, at nearby Pusiga.

Heading west from Bawku isn't a problem: not only do tro-tros to Bolgatanga leave from in front of the Mobil garage every half hour or so, but there's also a daily STC bus to Kumasi and Accra, leaving at 09.00, which you can use to hop as far as Bolgatanga or Tamale, assuming seats are available. Alternatively, you could also do the trip to Bolgatanga in hops, with one attraction being the geometrically painted family compounds around Zebilla, better examples of which can be seen by 'dropping' from a tro-tro at an appropriate spot along the road than by actually getting off in the town. Still, if for some reason you want to overnight in Zebilla, it does boast a couple of cheap options in the form of the **Friends Garden Hotel** and **Mofa Guesthouse**. About 10km past Zebilla you pass through Tilli, the junction for Widnaba (see page 377).

NAVRONGO

This quiet, rustic town, situated close to the main border crossing into Burkina Faso, is notable for its angular, flat-roofed traditional homesteads, which are typical of northern Ghana, and often painted in monochrome geometric patterns. Coming from Tamale or Bolgatanga, Navrongo also feels remarkably orderly and shady; this, despite the large number of uncompleted concrete buildings dotting the small town centre, skeletal relics of an absurdly ambitious development plan initiated by the short-lived Acheampong government of 1972–75.

According to oral tradition, Navrongo was founded about 200 years ago by three brothers from Zecco, which lies about 25km to the northeast in Burkina Faso. The eldest brother Butto named his new home Nagavoro, meaning 'Soft on the Foot', in reference to its sandy soil, and this was later bastardised to Navrongo. The town's modern-day significance can be traced to 1901, when Chief Kwara invited a British

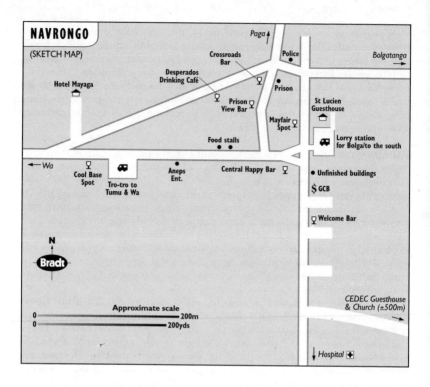

NAVRONGO
(SKETCH MAP)

Paga ↑

Bolgatanga →

Crossroads Bar

Police

Desperados Drinking Café

Prison

Hotel Mayaga

St Lucien Guesthouse

Prison View Bar

Mayfair Spot

Food stalls

Lorry station for Bolga/to the south

← Wa

Cool Base Spot

Aneps Ent.

Central Happy Bar

Unfinished buildings

Tro-tro to Tumu & Wa

$ GCB

Welcome Bar

N

Bradt

CEDEC Guesthouse & Church (±500m) →

Approximate scale

0 ———— 200m
0 ———— 200yds

↓ Hospital ✚

expedition to establish a military encampment next to his palace, in exchange for protection against the slave raiders who still made regular forays into the region.

Navrongo's predominantly Christian feel in an otherwise mostly Muslim part of Ghana reflects its claim to fame as the home of Catholicism in northern Ghana. In 1906, a Catholic mission was founded alongside the British military encampment by a group of pioneering 'White Fathers' led by the Canadian missionary Oscar Morin, who had travelled to the area from Ouagadougou via the then little-known south of Burkina Faso. Now almost a century old, the mission is definitely worth visiting for the Cathedral of Our Lady of the Seven Sorrows, which was built under the supervision of Father Morin in 1920 and dedicated as a cathedral and as the Mother Parish of northern Ghana in 1934. A large, traditionally constructed building with a colonnaded interior, the cathedral is notable above all for the simple but beautiful frescos of biblical scenes, animal forms and geometric patterns, painted on the pillars by women from Sirigu using kerite oil and soil-based pigments. A small museum housing displays on local history and culture stands adjacent to the church. Also in the mission grounds is a remarkable grotto, reportedly a replica of the one at Lourdes, protected by a high stone wall constructed in a manner reminiscent of the Zimbabwe ruins in the country of the same name. The mission lies about 1.5km from the town centre, and is particularly worth visiting when a service is on the go, as the singing can be phenomenal. To get there, follow the main road past the Ghana Commercial Bank, and after the second big tree to your left turn into a vehicle-width track. After perhaps 500m you'll pass a conspicuous blue water tower, then after another 100m you'll see the cathedral in front of you.

GETTING THERE AND AWAY Shared taxis between Navrongo and Bolgatanga and Paga leave every few minutes in all directions throughout the day. Navrongo is one of the few towns in Ghana where shared taxi drivers seem to routinely overcharge tourists, so it's worth knowing that the fare to Bolgatanga is US$1 at the time of writing and the fare to Paga is U$0.80. To get to nearby Lake Tono, the turn-off to which lies 3km along the Wa road, you'll probably have to charter a taxi for around US$5.

If you're heading towards Wa, tro-tros very occasionally ply the whole route for US$6 a seat and the City Express buses from Bolgatanga pass through, but seats are generally full by the time they reach Navrongo, which means standing at least as far as Tumu, three hours away. Far better to go to Bolgatanga and pick up the bus at the terminus. For those prepared to overnight in Tumu, a couple of tro-tros run on market days (every three days) and cost US$3. But be cautious about travelling at night, as the rough, dusty road is a favourite with armed robbers, although recent police patrols have abated the problem considerably.

🏠 WHERE TO STAY

🏠 **CEDEC Guesthouse** 🗮 020 8489858 or 024 3429940 or 0742 22118/864. Situated some distance from the town centre alongside the Catholic Mission, this inexpensive guesthouse is part of the church-affiliated Centre for Development Communications (CEDEC), which also houses a printing press & a small shop stocking religious books. B/fast costs around US$2 & other meals cost US$2.50 – it's worth ordering in advance. The rooms in the main block are very dingy but indisputably cheap. More attractive are the large & reasonably clean self-contained chalets that stand in rambling gardens behind the main building. *Sgl/dbl with common shower US$4.50/5.50, or self-contained US$5/6; chalet US$5.50/7.00 sgl/dbl occupancy.*

🏠 **Hotel Mayaga** 🗮 0742 22327. This likeable family-run hotel, situated at least 500m from the lorry station along the Wa road, & clearly signposted, is a little run down from the outside but has good spacious rooms inside. The restaurant is good & affordable, though the choice is limited & it's worth ordering well in advance as food is cooked from scratch. A shady outdoor bar serves chilled beer & cold drinks. *Sgl/dbl with fan &* common shower US$6.50/8.50, self-contained dbl US$13.50, suite US$18.

🏠 **St Lucien Guesthouse** 🗮 0742 22707. Easily Navrongo's most attractive lodging, this new hotel about 100m from the taxi park offers clean rooms, all of which are centred around a vast courtyard bar where DVDs are played after dark at non-intrusive volumes. The restaurant serves acceptable meals for around US$3–3.50. *From US$7 for a small twin with fan & common showers or US$8 with a TV.*

🏠 **Tono Guesthouse** This is the only accommodation in the vicinity of Lake Tono, an artificial body of water that forms an important source of irrigation for the region, as well as offering good birdwatching to visitors. Unfortunately, the guesthouse lies a good 2km from the lake, it's often full, & without private transport you'll need to charter a taxi or hitch. To get there, follow the Wa road out of town for roughly 3km then turn right on to a surfaced turn-off, which after 5km leads directly to the guesthouse. Meals can be arranged by advance request. Two men are not permitted to share a room. *Rooms cost around US$7.*

✗ WHERE TO EAT

Numerous stalls around the taxi park sell tender grilled chicken and guinea fowl, betraying Navrongo's proximity to Burkina Faso, and the chop bar next door to Cool Bar spot serves incredible, tender chunks of lamb. The best place for a sit-down meal on our most recent visit was **Mayfair Spot** opposite the taxi park, where you can buy a deliciously fiery half-chicken with lettuce (ideally accompanied with bread bought from the stall across the road). Both the hotels in the town centre serve reasonable meals, and the **Crossroads Bar** is also worth trying.

PAGA

Situated only 12km north of Navrongo along a good surfaced road, the border town of Paga is the most popular crossing point between Ghana and Burkina Faso, though you'd scarcely know it from the subdued mood of the somewhat rustic town centre – a chaotic northern counterpart to Aflao or Elubo it most definitely

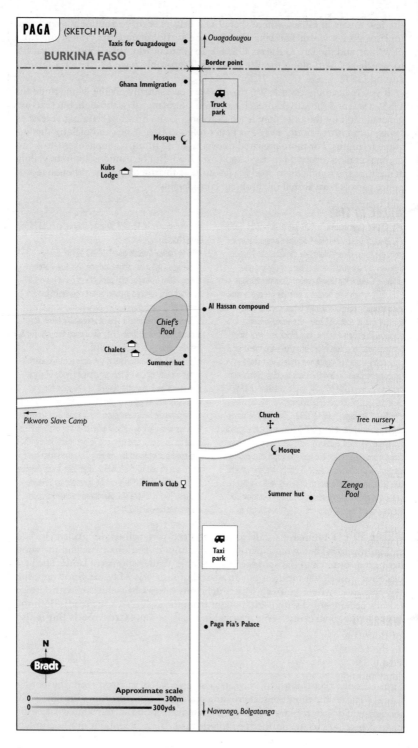

PAGA (SKETCH MAP)

BURKINA FASO

Taxis for Ouagadougou •

↑ *Ouagadougou*

Border point

Ghana Immigration •

Truck park

Mosque ☽

Kubs Lodge ⌂

• Al Hassan compound

Chief's Pool

Chalets ⌂⌂
Summer hut •

← *Pikworo Slave Camp*

Church ✝

Tree nursery →

☽ Mosque

Zenga Pool

Pimm's Club ♀

Summer hut •

Taxi park

• Paga Pia's Palace

N

Bradt

Approximate scale

0 ————— 300m
0 ————— 300yds

↓ *Navrongo, Bolgatanga*

384

isn't. International connections aside, Paga attracts a fair number of Ghanaian and foreign visitors on account of its sacred crocodile pools, which are said to harbour 200 crocs of various ages and sizes, while other attractions include the fascinating Paga Pia's Palace near the taxi park and disused Pikworo Slave Camp 2km from the town centre.

A few years back, the taxi park at Paga was notorious for the pestilence of informal guides whose aggression and dishonesty made many travellers question whether visiting Paga was worth the hassle. This problem has been more-or-less stifled by the incorporation of the crocodile pools and Paga's other attractions into a formal community-based ecotourism project, but we do still receive occasional reports of unpleasant experiences with guides. Travellers are thus advised to ensure that their shared taxi drops them at the summer hut next to the Chief's Pool where photograph sheets help identify official representatives of the eco-tourism project, and to make sure they collect receipts for all payments. Be circumspect, too, in your dealings with the charismatic Al Hassan, whose compound lies opposite the Chief's Pool – his bicycle tours have been highly praised by several readers, but he also has a tendency to pass himself off as an affiliate of the ecotourism project, and to claim his house (just opposite the pool) is the official visitors' centre. A fee of US$2 per person is charged for each of Paga's sites, and sacrificial chickens cost an additional US$2–3.

GETTING THERE AND AWAY Paga is connected to Navrongo and Bolgatanga by regular shared taxis, which cost US$0.30 and US$1 per person and take about 20 minutes and 90 minutes, respectively. If you're coming for the crocodile pools or other facets of the ecotourism project, then ensure you are dropped at the visitors centre, a prominent, traditionally painted building opposite the Chief's Pool. Most shared taxis continue past the visitors centre to terminate at the parking lot next to the border post at the northern end of town, but some will try to drop tourists at the central taxi park, which lies about 500m back towards Navrongo.

The **border with Burkina Faso** lies at the northern end of the town centre, perhaps 500m past the Chief's Pool. Shared taxis from Navrongo or Bolgatanga will drop passengers at the border on request, practically alongside the building where Ghanaian border formalities must be completed. Bush taxis and other transport on to Ouagadougou, the capital of Burkina Faso, line up about 200m into no-man's land, and – because the Burkina Faso border post lies another kilometre or so away – it's conventional for passengers to wait for the vehicle to fill up and leave and then to complete entrance formalities en masse. Most visitors require a visa for Burkina Faso, but this can be bought on arrival for CFA10,000, while transport on to Ouagadougou currently costs CFA5,000. It's easy enough to change money on the street at the border – whether you want to exchange hard-currency cash or change CFA into cedi or vice versa – but the rates are lousy and there is a risk of being conned, so don't change more than you need to see you through to the capital.

WHERE TO STAY AND EAT The vast majority of travellers visit Paga as a day trip out of Bolgatanga or Navrongo, but the new **Kubs Lodge** (↑ 024 3243444) just next to the border is a good bet if you get stuck. Clean sgls with shared bath facilities cost US$8, whilst airy doubles with AC are US$15. The music tends to be a little loud and no food is served, but the management is very professional and friendly and serves cool drinks. Alternatively, there is a somewhat derelict chalet complex behind the Chief's Pool where two units are still in sufficiently good repair to be rented out, albeit without electricity (as negotiated with the caretaker), or you can rent a room or pitch a tent at the Al Hassan compound directly opposite the

Local tradition has it that Paga was founded in 1670 by Naveh Kampala, the grandson of an important chief whose totem was a crocodile. When the old chief died, Naveh's father Paniogo lost out in the succession dispute and he and his followers were forced to flee from their home on horseback with the new chief and his soldiers in hot pursuit. At a place called Tampala, Paniogo's passage was blocked by a raging river, and in desperation he asked a nearby crocodile to help his party across the river, and pledged that in return he and his followers would never again harm a crocodile. Obligingly, the crocodile dived into the water and beat his tail so hard that the water parted, clearing the way for Paniogo to scurry to the safety of the opposite bank before the water rolled back to block his pursuers' path. After this close escape, the exiles settled in a place called Kampala (in present-day Burkina Faso), which lay close to a grove and crocodile pool that Paniogo declared to be sacred.

Many years later, Paniogo's son Naveh was out hunting when he fell into an aardvark hole whose entrance collapsed. Naveh was trapped in the hole for two full days, and his family assumed him to be dead when his dog returned home alone. But then a crocodile living in the hole saw that Naveh was dying, showed him an escape route, and walked him to a pool to quench his thirst. Naveh reaffirmed his father's pledge to the crocodile, but when he returned to Kampala he realised that his people had broken the taboo by killing and eating crocodiles, and he decided to move away with his family. Then, some time in 1670, after several months of searching for an appropriate new home, Naveh arrived at the uninhabited margin of the crocodile-infested Chief's Pool and cried out 'A yi paga ywo!' – this place pleases my eyes – from which the name Paga derives. Naveh became the first Paga Pia (Chief of Paga) and instated crocodiles as the town's totem – it is said that no person has ever been harmed by one of the crocodiles of Paga, and the town's human residents traditionally view killing a croc to be as sinful as homicide.

At least two other conflicting legends are in circulation to explain how the crocodiles of Paga become sacred, though it's possible that these relate to the circumstance under which they originally became the totem for Naveh Kampala's ancestors. One story is that a hunter trapped between a hungry lion and a river asked a crocodile to carry him across to safety in exchange for which he and his descendents would never eat crocodile meat. The other is that a man who left home after his pet dog had been sacrificed by his parents got lost in a dry area and was nearly dying of thirst when a friendly crocodile led him to a pool and saved his life.

Chief's Pool. Eating-out options in Paga are limited to street food and little else, but there are plenty of bars around

WHAT TO SEE

Crocodile ponds There are two main sacred crocodile pools in Paga today, though the resident crocs may disperse into other seasonal pools and swamps during the rains. The ancient Chief's Pool, on the west side of the main road directly opposite the visitors centre, probably harbours the greatest number of crocodiles, but the largest individuals are said to live in Zenga Pond, which lies no more than 500m along a signposted footpath running east from the main road between the taxi park and the visitors centre. The entrance fee is US$2, and live chickens – used to bait the crocs onto *terra firma* – cost US$2–3 each, and can be arranged by the caretaker who stays at each of the ponds. It's a rare treat to be able to touch and photograph crocodiles at such close quarters, though one can't help but feel for them – revered for centuries as vassals for the ancestral spirits, they now suffer the indignity of being leaped on, prodded about and shooed off with a familiarity that might lead a more sceptical observer than myself to form the conclusion they are preserved solely for the money they generate. Still, I'd rather be a crocodile in Paga than a chicken!

Paga Pia's Palace Paga hosts some superb examples of the extended family homesteads that characterise this Burkina Faso border region – fantastic, labyrinthine, fortress-like constructions characterised by their curvaceous earthen walls, flat roofs and cosy courtyards. Many of the complexes are more than a century old, and they may be inhabited by more than ten separate households, each with its own living quarters and courtyards, some marked by rounded mud mounds under which an important family member is buried. The flat roofs are used not only for drying crops, but also as a place to sleep in hot weather, while the mud walls are often covered in symbolic paintings or portraits of animals – a crocodile with a chicken in its mouth being a particular favourite.

It's possible to visit a private compound by arrangement, but the obvious place to start is the Paga Pia's Palace (where the entrance fee is US$2 but donations above US$0.50 are discouraged!), which lies on the east side of the main road a short distance south of the taxi park. Said to have been founded by Naveh Kampala himself (see box opposite), this sprawling complex is now home to his descendent Awia Awampaga, who was enstooled as the 11th Paga Pia in 1971, and more than 300 relatives, including five wives and 15 children. Roughly three-quarters of the buildings in the complex are built in the traditional Sahelian style, several are attractively painted, and some contain centuries-old pottery and other artefacts. The door design of the palace houses, typical of this part of Ghana, is reputedly a relic of the slaving era – the low entrance and high rim immediately inside made it impossible for somebody to enter a house without giving the occupant plenty of time to whack them on the head!

Pikworo Slave Camp Slaving activity around Paga reputedly peaked between 1840 and 1870, when the rocky outcrops of Pikworo – situated some 2km from the town centre – enclosed the most important slave-holding pen in this part of Ghana. At any given time, up to 200 captives from surrounding parts of present-day Ghana and Burkina Faso would be held at Pikworo, eventually to be sold to slave traders from Salaga. Strong local oral traditions relating to the layout of the slave camp suggest that the captives were well looked after – not through any altruism on the part of their captors, but in order that they would fetch a good price – and you can still see their 'eating bowls' carved in neat rows into the rock, as well as the recreational area where they would dance to the accompaniment of a resonant natural rock drum. On the other side of the camp is the cemetery, where dead slaves were buried in mass graves, and the punishment rock on which failed escapees would be seated and bound hand and foot to bake in the heat of the sun. A nearby lookout rock is where the slavers stood guard against attacks – several of which, it is said, were initiated by the Paga Pia, an opponent of slavery who frequently led rescue parties to Pikworo to release captured residents of nearby Paga.

Entrance to Pikworo costs US$2 per person inclusive of an informative guided tour, and a donation (around US$0.40 per person) for the drummers who play on the natural rock drum is expected. The site lies about 2km west of Paga, along a dirt road signposted from the main road perhaps 200m south of the Chief's Pool. You can walk there and back, allowing about 30 minutes each way and an hour to explore the camp, but most people either hire a bicycle for around US$0.70 for a half-day or charter a taxi for the return trip for around US$7.

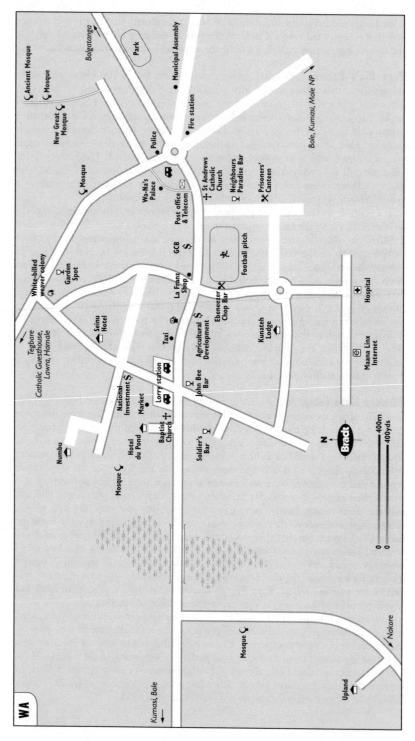

WA

Ancient Mosque ☪
Mosque ☪
Bolgatanga →
Park
Municipal Assembly ●
New Great Mosque ☪
Fire station ●
Police ●
Mosque ☪
Wa-Na's Palace ●
Post office & Telecom ⊠
St Andrews Catholic Church ✝
Neighbours Paradise Bar ⊔
Prisoners' Canteen ✗
Bole, Kumasi, Mole NP →
White-billed weaver colony
Garden Spot ⊔
GCB $
Football pitch 🏃
La Franz Shop ●
Tegbare Catholic Guesthouse, Lawra, Hamale →
Seinu Hotel
Ebeneezer Chop Bar ✗
Taxi
Agricultural Development $
Kunateh Lodge
Maana Linx Internet @
Hospital ✚
National Investment $
Market
Lorry station
John Bee Bar ⊔
Numbu
Hotel du Pond
Baptist Church ✝
Soldier's Bar ⊔
Mosque ☪
N
Bradt
400m
400yds
0
0
Kumasi, Bole ↓
Mosque ☪
Nakore →
Upland

388

19

Wa and the Upper West

The most remote and little-visited of Ghana's administrative regions, the Upper West boasts little in the way of formal tourist development, though in the right frame of mind this absence is amply compensated for by a timeless frontier atmosphere and deep sense of removal from the rest of modern Ghana. The regional capital, Wa, is a sleepily appealing small town, studded with some fine examples of Sudanese-style mud-and-stick architecture, notably the striking Wa-Na's palace and lovely mosque in nearby Nakori. Many similar constructions are found elsewhere in the region, for instance at Bole, on the junction with the main western access point to Mole National Park. A more recent development, one which has received lavish praise from several quarters since its inception in early 1999, is the under-utilised Wechiau Community Hippo Sanctuary on the Black Volta, which not only protects a herd of 50-odd hippos, but also harbours a wide variety of birds and lies in an area rich in traditional Sahelian cultures. Another under-subscribed natural attraction is the little-known Gbele Resource Reserve, which lies to the northeast of Wa on the Tumu road and where several antelope species as well as a rich variety of birds can be found.

WA

The unimposing but thoroughly amiable capital of Upper West Region, Wa is one of the oldest cities in the Ghanaian interior, founded in the mid 17th century by an offshoot of the Dagomba state, since when it has served as the seat of the Wa-Na (the title given to the chief of Wa). This was one of the first parts of the country to adopt the Islamic faith, as evidenced by the extraordinarily high number of mosques dotted in and around Wa, as well as the earthy architecture of the striking Palace of the Wa-Na in the town centre.

Of particular interest to tourists are two disused but reasonably well-preserved mud-and-stick mosques in the West-Sudanese-style situated next to each other behind the modern Great Mosque. The imam at this mosque is usually very welcoming – it's unproblematic to take photos, or to go inside, or even to climb on the roof – and as a coin collector he will be doubly so if you bring him a gift of a foreign coin, no matter how small its value.

Constructed during the 19th century to imitate the architectural style of these ancient mosques, the Wa-Na's Palace is a large fortress-like building situated close to the main traffic circle in the town centre. In front of the palace lie the graves of five former Wa-Nas, starting with Pelpua III, who ruled from 1920 to 1935. The palace was abandoned following the death of the last-but-one Wa-Na in January 1998, an event that also signalled the start of a protracted and sporadically violent succession dispute. The situation stabilised in early 2003 following the formal appointment of a new Wa-Na, who died in late 2006 and whose successor (awaiting enstoolment as we go to print) is said to have plans for renovation.

Somewhat shabbier than it was a few years back, but structurally intact, the traditional palace still lies abandoned, though it is unclear whether this is a result of the last Wa-Na wanting to maintain a low profile or simply because he preferred to live in the more modern house he built behind it. The palace was under armed guard for the duration of the succession dispute, when we received several reports of tourists being hassled by the army, especially if they tried to photograph the palace. By late 2003, however, the armed guards had vanished, to be replaced by the more predictable hopefuls who will offer to liaise with the elders on your behalf to photograph the palace and possibly go inside in exchange for a donation for 'upkeep'. All this will most likely change again if and when the new Wa-Na moves to the palace and assumes the long-standing custom of receiving all visitors when he's in town – but do note that the Wa-Na may not be spoken to directly!

GETTING THERE AND AWAY STC buses from Accra leave at 07.00 on Tuesday, Thursday and Saturday, while buses to Accra leave Wa on Monday, Wednesday and Sunday at 14.00. The trip should take about 13 hours, though delays are quite frequent, and tickets cost US$16. The STC station lies about 100m from the Wa-Na's Palace. There is also a daily service to Kumasi (US$13), or two daily services at 08.00 (US$6.50) and 18.30 (US$6) from EPA transport, on the same roundabout as the police station. In the same direction, plenty of buses travel directly between Wa, Bole, Sunyani and Kumasi, and the medium-sized towns along this route are also connected to each other by localised tro-tro services.

The most reliable transport to Tamale (and to Mole National Park) is the Metro Mass bus via Larabanga, which leaves at around 06.00 in either direction and takes about eight hours. All being well, the bus reaches Larabanga around 10.30, so it is perfectly feasible to look around the village, have a meal, and still make it to Mole in time for the 15.30 walk. Advance bookings cannot be made, which means you'll need to be at the OSA station (the open area in front of the Wa-Na's Palace) at around 04.30 to be certain of a seat.

Coming to or from Bolgatanga, the only direct public transport is a battered City Express bus that theoretically leaves at around 05.00 in either direction (US$5) and arrives nine hours later, but often runs up to six hours late. This bus does stop at Navrongo, but seats to Wa are unlikely to be available here if you're coming from Bolgatanga. The only other scheduled stop is at Tumu, where you can buy chilled soft drinks and make use of a one-time nominee for the category 'Most Disgusting Public Toilet that I've seen in Africa' at the bizarrely vast and empty lorry station. It's also possible to travel between Bolga and Wa in hops. Coming from Bolga, you should get through in one day, since sporadic tro-tros run in either direction between Wa and Tumu throughout the day (US$2.50), but coming from Wa you'll almost certainly have to spend the night in Tumu and be at the station at around 05.30 the next morning to be certain of onward transport.

WHERE TO STAY
Budget

 **Tegbeer Catholic Guesthouse** ✆ 0756 22375. Situated about 3km from the town centre along the Lawra road, this clean guesthouse is popular with volunteers. Reasonable meals are available, but as with the Upland it's not very convenient for dawn buses. *Around US$8.50/11 for a spotless, self-contained sgl/dbl with fan, or US$22 for a dbl with AC.*

🏠 **Upland Hotel** ✆ 0756 22180/701. Set in attractive grounds some 30 mins' walk from the town centre, this large, comfortable & well-run hotel is good value. The restaurant serves a varied menu of continental, Chinese & local dishes in the US$4.50 range, & you can eat indoors or in the garden bar, though everything closes up at 22.00. The DSTV service at reception is the one place in Wa to catch international sporting events. One possible drawback with this hotel, at least if you're thinking of catching the early morning Metro Mass or City Express bus to Bolga, Tamale or Larabanga, is the

out-of-town location. *US$23/26 for an airy self-contained sgl/dbl with fan & hot water, or US$28–US$39 for larger rooms with AC & DSTV.*

Shoestring

⌂ **Hotel du Pond** ↘ 0756 20018. This once-popular shoestring lodge went through a bad patch, but recently made an effort to spruce up its rooms with a lick of fresh paint. It's still a bit grubby & musty, but when a sgl with shared bath facilities costs a knock-down US$2, there's really not much room for complaint. Drinks are available, but it may be noisy on the rare occasions when there's live music. *Self-contained dbls are US$5.50/8.50 depending on whether they have AC.*

⌂ **Kunateh Lodge** ↘ 075 622102. Probably the best central cheapie, & reasonably convenient for catching early-morning buses, this is a clean & friendly lodge. Simple food is available for US$2.50–3 a plate. There are large dbl rooms with fan using common showers, &

self-contained dbls, some of which have a balcony. *US$5–15.*

⌂ **Numbu Hotel** ↘ 075 620460. Set in a maze of unmade roads, this quiet & friendly hotel offers extremely good value. Food & cold drinks are available on request & it's reasonably close to the main tro-tro station. In fact, the only drawbacks are the presence of two forlorn-looking monkeys tethered outside & its distance from the Metro Mass & STC bus stations should you want to make the dawn dash. *Large bright dbl with fan & common showers US$4–5.*

⌂ **Seinu Hotel** ↘ 0756 22010. There's nothing exceptional about this centrally located hotel, but the large, clean rooms seem fair value. *Sgl with fan using common showers US$4, self-contained dbl US$6.*

✕ WHERE TO EAT AND DRINK

The restaurant at the **Upland Hotel** is the best in Wa, serving a selection of generously proportioned main dishes for around US$5 per plate. More centrally, the **Frantech Decent Restaurant** near Kunateh serves excellent cheap local fare, as do the **Soldiers' Bar** and **Prisoners' Canteen**. There are several cheaper chop houses and bars scattered in the town centre, and the usual street food is sold around the market. For chilled beers, try the **Neighbours' Paradise Spot** or **Garden Spot**.

OTHER PRACTICALITIES – INTERNET At the time of research there was just one internet café in town, although if the trends in other towns are anything to go by, this is likely to change dramatically within the lifespan of this edition. Maana Linx Internet, just to the east of the hospital and on the same side of the road, has about ten PCs with reliable connection, and charges US$0.50 for 25 mins.

AROUND WA

WECHIAU COMMUNITY HIPPO SANCTUARY Developed in collaboration with the NCRC to protect a 40km stretch of the Black Volta flowing west of Wa, the Wechiau Community Hippo Sanctuary is a little-visited but relatively straightforward goal for anybody who makes it to this rather remote corner of Ghana. In July 2000, the *Independent* newspaper in the UK ranked Wechiau as the world's third-best conservation holiday, a ranking that might arguably be stretching a point based on mixed (but mostly positive) feedback from readers. Some people have rated Wechiau as the highlight of their trip to Ghana, and it provides a rare opportunity to get close to the wildlife with few or no other tourists around.

The sanctuary's population of 50 hippopotami – the second largest in the country after Bui – is readily seen from a canoe during the dry season, though somewhat more elusive during the rains when visitors might go weeks on end without a sighting. But even if there are no hippos in sight, it's a very beautiful and worthwhile trip: the savanna and riparian forest along the river is offset by some stunning rock formations and it supports small populations of terrestrial mammals, though these are unlikely to be observed by casual visitors. An impressive tally of 250 bird species have been recorded since the sanctuary was founded in February 1999. Among the more interesting species likely to be seen are exclamatory paradise whydah, malachite kingfisher, Senegal parrots, Abyssinian roller and breeding colonies of red-throated bee-eater.

Wechiau, the closest village to the sanctuary and springboard from which it is visited, is also of some cultural and architectural interest. The well-maintained façade of the centuries-old palace here is constructed in typical Sudanese mud-and-stick style, and the chief himself is very welcoming to visitors. The main ethnic groups in the area are the Wala, Lobi and Biri, the last two still often to be seen wearing traditional lip-plugs, especially on market days, which fall every six days. An added incentive to visit is that this is one of the first community-managed ecotourist ventures to be established in the far north of Ghana, and all profits are returned to the local community.

Its not realistic to visit Wechiau as a day trip out of Wa on public transport, so unless you have a private 4×4, plan on spending at least one night there, and better still two nights to be reasonably certain of seeing hippos (at least during the dry season). Public transport from Wa to Wechiau leaves from the main tro-tro station throughout the day, takes roughly one hour, and costs around US$0.80 per person, but it does run rather sporadically, with the most reliable time being from 07.30 to 08.00. If you're heading south from Wechiau and have no reason to return to Wa, note that there might be a direct bus from to Kumasi on Wechiau's market day, or one that necessitates changing at Techiman – ask around for current information.

On arrival at Wechiau, visit the tourist office, where you must pay your fees and will be given a guide to take you to Telewona or Tankara Camp, which respectively lie 19 km and 26km from Wechiau along a sandy track. Unless you have a private 4×4, the best way to get to the lodges is by bicycle, which can be hired at the visitors' centre for US$1.50 per day – the ride takes up to two hours and can be quite tiring. Alternatively, the Visitors Centre can arrange a charter tro-tro to the lodges for around US$12 one-way. You can stash your backpack in their locked reception hut. Canoe safaris leave from close to the lodges. Village homestays in Wechiau are coming soon.

Two low-key lodges have been constructed within the sanctuary, both of them set about 1km back from the river, or you can stay on the single tree platform that remains after the other was destroyed by fire. A rate of US$7 per person for the first night, or US$6 thereafter includes entrance, one night's accommodation, and cooking services (you provide the ingredients). Pure/bottled water is normally but not always available in the village, but it's advisable to bring all the food you need with you from Wa. Bath facilities are an outdoor bucket job – with one wall open to the forest – and there is no electricity. Guided river safari in small dugout canoes cost US$2 per person per hour, and day visitors are charged an additional entrance fee of US$3, with discounts available to Ghanaians and students with ID.

NAKORI With a couple of hours to spare, one very worthwhile and easy short excursion from Wa takes you to Nakori (also sometimes referred to as Dondoli), where there's a very striking mud-and-stick mosque, taller than the one at Larabanga and of a similar vintage. The friendly chief of Nakori, to whom you'll probably be required to pay a call of respect, claims that the mosque was constructed in the 15th century and will usually let visitors climb to the roof and take photographs. Nakori lies within easy walking or cycling distance of Wa, roughly 4km from the town centre along the road passing the Upland Hotel. A taxi charter shouldn't cost more than US$5 for the round trip.

KALEO AND SURROUNDS For travellers interested in a spot of genuinely off-the-beaten-track exploration, a cluster of low-key sites lies in the vicinity of Kaleo, some 10km north of Wa along the Lawra road. The so-called crocodile pool at Kaleo itself probably isn't worth more than a casual look over – the crocs are seldom seen, indeed some say they vanished altogether a few years back – but (after seeking permission from the local chief) keen hikers might enjoy the roughly four-hour round hike from the main road through the village to the top of Kaleo Hill, the tallest point in the region and one clearly visible from Wa itself. The Zumbenti Festival, one of the most important in Upper West Region, is held in the first week of April to thank the ancestors and various deities, and to cleanse evil spirits.

A left fork west from the Lawra road at Kaleo leads after about 10km to Sankana, a small village whose market – every six days – often attracts traditional Lobi women with their characteristic lip plugs. A nearby set of caves was used as a slave hold during the 19th century, while 10km further west there's reputedly an impressive anthill colony at Nanvili. Plenty of transport heads along this road from Kaleo or Wa on market days, but on other days it's pretty quiet. An excellent time to visit Sankana is in the first week of April, when the Kalibi Festival is held to commemorate the village's victory over slave raiders in 1897.

Back on the main Lawra road, some 20km north of Kaleo, the village of Sombo is renowned for its sacred colony of the hammer bat, *Hypsignathus monstrosus*, which as the Latin binomial suggests is a genuinely monstrous creature – at almost a metre long, the largest fruitbat on the African mainland – distinguished by its lopsided hammerhead and a resonant chest cavity producing a booming but eerie call that can carry for kilometres on a still night. We were told that Sombo also harbours a sacred porcupine grove, but were unable to confirm this.

LAWRA   Adapted from information supplied by Paul Ramsbottom

Situated roughly 100km north of Wa along the road to Hamale on the Burkina Faso border, Lawra (pronounced like 'Laura') might be something of a backwater today – Wa looks positively cosmopolitan by comparison – but it actually served as the regional administrative centre before it was superseded by Wa in the early 1980s. Lawra is especially worth a diversion during the post-harvest Kobine Festival (generally in the first week of October, but sometimes later), when it springs into colourful life with music and dancing competitions. At other times of year, market day – the day after Wa's market – is the best time to visit.

The Lobi and Dagati people of Lawra and surrounds are known countrywide for their traditional music, which is based around drumming and a unique type of xylophone called a *gyil*. The Lobi xylophone maker for the region is a fascinating man and worth visiting, but do knock before you enter his workshop – which lies in the last complex of buildings on the Wa side of town – since it doubles as the family residence. The chief and his palace are also certainly worth checking out. The palace is an elaborate, rambling maze of mud buildings, and the chief (a real Anglophile whose day revolves around the BBC World Service) can be met by appointment. The tribal court meets outside the front entrance of the palace.

Directly behind the District Assembly Guesthouse, the mansion that once housed the regional administrator is – somewhat incongruously given its obscure setting – quite possibly the grandest colonial-era building anywhere in Ghana. Pitifully derelict and overgrown today, the residence must have been constructed about 100 years ago and consists of 15–20 rooms, large grounds, servants' quarters,

19

a separate kitchen complex, and an elaborate swimming pool added in the 1950s. The caretaker at the District Assembly Guesthouse is happy to act as a guide, and uniquely capable to do so – he worked as a house servant there in the 1950s and can rattle off some wonderful anecdotes and show visitors a picture of the house in all its glory.

Two other somewhat off-the-beaten-track colonial relics are worth mentioning. The first is the classically stylish Karbo Primary School, situated about 2.5km out of town along the Jiripa road, and noted for its huge underground larder. Second is the overgrown but rather poignant grave of District Commissioner JA Prendergast, who died far from home in 1937 – follow the Hamale road out of Lawra, then take the first right, and the grave is obscured in the undergrowth about 150 metres up the road on the left.

The Black Volta River can be reached by following the dirt track west out of the town for 1–2 miles (1.5–3km). The local ferry boat can be chartered for a very modest fee to sail along the river, which forms the border with Burkina Faso. One is virtually guaranteed to see a variety of wildlife, including snakes and birds, along the riverbank, particularly during the dry season.

Further afield, there is an active sacred crocodile pool in Erimon, about 30km east of Lawra on the Han road. In a northerly direction, the small town of Nandom, which lies along the Hamale road perhaps 15km south of the border, has a guesthouse based on similar lines to the District Assembly Guesthouse in Lawra. Nandom has little else to recommend it except during the last week in November or first in December, when the Kakube Thanksgiving Festival is marked by vibrant xylophone music and Bewaa dancing.

GETTING THERE AND AWAY Tro-tros between Wa and the border town of Hamale, which typically run three times daily in either direction, leave during the morning and will 'drop' passengers in Lawra town centre. The volume of traffic increases significantly on Lawra's market day and during the Kobine Festival.

WHERE TO STAY AND EAT There are two lodgings in Lawra, both on the eastern edge of the town (ie: turn right at the main fork in the town centre). Both are in the US$2 price bracket, but the **District Assembly Guesthouse**, situated just past the hospital, is easily the best, with ceiling fans and shared showers. Food of a decent standard can be served on request. The **Ideas Guesthouse** is more basic (and less clean), though it also has ceiling fans and a rudimentary shower and is seldom used except as an overflow for the District Assembly Guesthouse, which is booked out by visiting officials on a surprisingly regular basis.

The keys for Ideas Guesthouse are kept at **Ideas Restaurant**, which is signposted off the northern end of the main road, and – as the only dedicated eating place in town – serves very acceptable food, alongside the usual range of chilled drinks (yam with spicy *alufo* and boiled egg is a particular favourite). As for bars, the **Lover's Inn** on the main street is worth visiting for its atmospheric outdoor terrace decorated with colourful, lurid murals mixing local religion with AIDS warnings. Its only rival is the **Sika Assembly Square Bar Inn**, signposted west off the high street in the oldest area of Lawra among residential buildings.

TUMU AND SURROUNDS

Possibly the most remote town of its size in Ghana, Tumu lies a few kilometres south of the Burkina Faso border about halfway along the bumpy strip of red dust that passes for the main road between Wa and Bolgatanga. The town itself is friendly but has no specific draw – except over the cusp of January and February

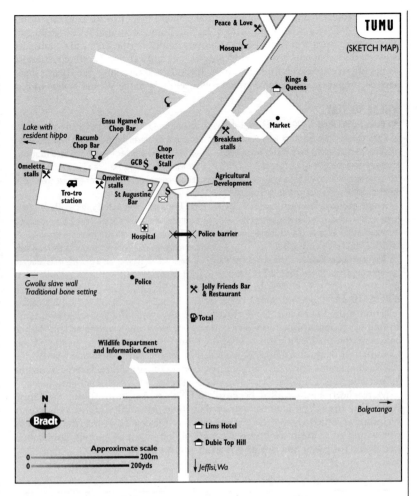

Peace & Love

Mosque

Kings & Queens

Market

Ensu NgameYe
Chop Bar

Lake with
resident hippo
Racumb
Chop Bar

Breakfast
stalls

Chop
Better
Stall

GCB

Omelette
stalls

Omelette
stalls

Agricultural
Development

Tro-tro
station

St Augustine
Bar

Hospital

Police barrier

Gwollu slave wall
Traditional bone setting

Police

Jolly Friends Bar
& Restaurant

Total

Wildlife Department
and Information Centre

N

Bradt

Bolgatanga

Approximate scale

0 ————— 200m
0 ————— 200yds

Lims Hotel

Dubie Top Hill

Jeffisi, Wa

when the Paragbeile Festival is marked by some lively local drumming and dancing – although this may change if plans to establish a hippo sanctuary in the pretty lake at the northern edge of town come to fruition. In this case (or even if not), it may be worth combining a visit with a trip across the border to Burkina Faso's Nazinga game ranch, less than 50km away.

For the moment though, the main reason to stop in Tumu is to overnight on the trip between Wa and Bolga, or to use as a springboard to the under-visited but very worthwhile Gbele Resource Reserve and the slave-protection walls at Gwollo.

GETTING THERE AND AWAY Most travellers pass through Tumu on the laughably named City Express bus between Bolga and Wa, which leaves daily in either direction at around 06.00 and takes anything from nine hours upwards. This bus service should in theory pass through Tumu at around midday, but it's often very late, and you'll probably have to pay full fare even if you plan to disembark at Tumu. Wa and Tumu are also connected by a few clapped-out tro-tros daily, leaving every three hours or so on a good day and taking about four hours (US$2.50). Your best bet is to turn up at about 05.00 – though be warned that dust levels on this road make the Tamale–Mole route seem like child's play. Tro-tros between Tumu and Bolga follow a more rigid pattern, leaving Tumu at around 05.30–06.00 and starting the return trip from Bolga at around midday – the only other transport between the two towns is the City Express bus service to/from Wa, which is almost always full when it passes through Tumu. Try and avoid travelling after dark as there have been reports of occasional armed robberies on both the Wa and Bolga roads.

WHERE TO STAY

Dubie Top Hill Hotel 020 8389453. Situated off the Bolga road 1km from the central lorry station, this reasonably pleasant hotel is by far & away Tumu's best – which says more about the dismal state of accommodation in this town than anything else. Set in large but somewhat desolate gardens, the hotel offers comfortable accommodation in large, clean self-contained fan-cooled rooms. The management is fantastically helpful & friendly, & a restaurant is planned for 2007. *Sgl US$7 or dbl with AC US$15.*

Kings and Queens Hotel For those on a budget, this centrally located hotel charges US$3.50–5 for a large dbl with fan – but the rooms are filthy, the management grumpy, & the shared bath facilities will make you want to avoid them altogether. If you do stay, bag a room on the left of the courtyard or face a 05.15 alarm call from the blaring call-to-prayer speaker right next door. *Dbl US$3.50–5.*

Lims Hotel 020 9383686. This very basic lodge, situated right next door to the Dubie Top Hill, charges US$3.50 for an unappealing sgl room. The shared bathrooms are marginally cleaner than at the Kings and Queens, but the attached bar is probably quite rowdy at night. *Sgl US$3.50.*

WHERE TO EAT
Good question! None of the hotels serves food, and the limited selection at the **Peace and Love Restaurant** serves traditional Ghanaian fare for around US$1 a plate, but it looked less than appetising when we popped in. Rather better are the fried yam chips sold at the **Chop Better Stall** next to the Ghana Commercial Bank, and the kebab stall in front of the Saint Augustine Inn. And if all else disappoints, the stall near the market serves the usual breakfast combination of omelette, bread and tea.

More cheeringly, a chilled beer isn't difficult to locate in Tumu: the **Saint Augustine Inn** is a pleasant enough drinking hole, assuming you're deaf, but until such time as somebody replaces the speakers – or the distortion-tolerant staff – my vote would go to the rustic and shady garden, dominated by an immense mango tree, at the **Jolly Friends Bar and Restaurant** on the Bolga road.

AROUND TUMU

Tumu's Wildlife Office, signposted off the Bolga road, can provide up-to-date information about Gbele Resource Reserve, and the head warden of the park – assuming he's around – is an enthusiastic source of tourist information about other local places of interest.

GBELE RESOURCE RESERVE The 565km² Gbele Resource Reserve, though seldom visited by travellers, is highly accessible by road, particularly for those with private transport, and it offers some excellent birdwatching as well as a fair chance of seeing large mammals on foot. Gbele – silent 'G', incidentally – was set aside in 1975 to protect Ghana's last population of the handsome roan antelope, which is still present there but rather uncommon, and it also supports small numbers of hartebeest, Defassa waterbuck, bushbuck, green and patas monkey, black-and-white colobus monkey, baboon and warthog, all of which are reasonably likely to be seen on guided walks out of the rangers camp at Wahabu. Less readily observed are carnivores such as side-striped jackal, or a rumoured population of the endangered African hunting dog has eluded the rangers for years. The birdlife in the riparian woodland that follows the Kulpawn River at the camp is very varied.

Some 194 species have been recorded, including the rare yellow-billed oxpecker, Willcock's honeyguide, Gambaga flycatcher, black-headed weaver, spotted thick-knee, long-tailed parakeet, Senegal parrot, carmine bee-eater, blue-breasted kingfisher, bearded barbet, Vieillot's barbet, and yellow-crowned gonolek – while the magnificent Egyptian plover is reputedly quite regular along sandy stretches of riverbank. Entrance costs US$2 per person.

The effective entrance to Gbele is the rangers' camp at Wahabu, which lies on the bank of the Kulpawn River some 60km south of Tumu along the route to Wa via Walembele (15km before Wahabu) and Kujopere (20km past Wahabu). In a private vehicle, the drive from either Tumu or Wa shouldn't take much longer than an hour, though high clearance and possibly 4×4 may be a prerequisite during the rains – check first at the very helpful Wildlife Office in Tumu (\ 075 622758; e gbelewd@yahoo.com or gelerr@hotmail.com). Wahabu is quite easy to reach using public transport between Tumu and Wa, but you'll have to check which of three interchangeable routes (via Wahabu or via Jeffisi or via Gwollo) the tro-tro will follow, and you may have a problem finding transport out of the reserve. Alternatively, and especially attractive for small groups, you can sometimes arrange a lift from Tumu with the Wildlife Office 4×4 at a charge of US$9.

It's easy enough to visit the reserve as a day trip out of Tumu with private transport or using the Wildlife Office 4×4, but accommodation is available in three spacious, semi-permanent six-man 'tourist tents' at US$5 per person, and a new tourist centre with accommodation, toilets, running water and a kitchen was under construction in early 2007. Guided walks with the rangers cost US$0.80 per hour, while those with camping gear can arrange overnight hiking and camping trips deeper into the park for a negotiable fee. Future plans for Gbele – part of Ghana's Northern Savannah Biodiversity Conservation Project sponsored by the World Bank – include the erection of two observation towers in 2007, a new game-viewing route planned to take in the entire length of the reserve, and facilities for canoeing and sports fishing.

GWOLLO AND JITTON Situated right on the border with Burkina Faso 32km northwest of Tumu, Gwollo is the site of two concentric walls built in the 18th century under Kuoro (Chief) Tanjia Vanye Mussah to protect his people against slave raids that originated from present-day Mali. The first wall was built to protect the village homesteads, but a more expansive wall, with a perimeter of 3km, was later constructed to protect the surrounding farmland and water sources. Although much of the wall has subsequently collapsed, and parts have now been incorporated into other structures, several sections are still freestanding, notably an 8m-long and 4m-high stretch adjacent to the Chief's Palace.

Gwollo may be developed as a formal ecotourism project with the assistance of the NCRC during the lifespan of this edition, but even if this doesn't go ahead, it is an unusually interesting village. A community museum, housing artefacts relating to the slaving era, is currently under construction, while the baobab tree opposite the Chief's Palace is claimed to be the largest in Upper West Region. The graves of Kuoro Tanjia Vanye Mussah, builder of the walls, can be seen within the chief's living compound, as can that of former President Hilla Limann, brother of the current chief. Also of interest is the Tituobala Bone-Setting Clinic near the Chief's Palace, where the Tituo family (*Tituobola* literally means 'Children of Tituo') practise their hereditary healing craft using traditional and herbal medicines, and a more clandestine impotency clinic near the central market. Locals can also show you some of the 18 shrines dotted around the village – including one at the spot where a spiritual leader called Wasawila is said to have vanished into thin air – and seasonal ponds near the walls that sometimes harbour crocodiles.

There's no accommodation in Gwollo at present, but this could change if the ecotourism project gets going. In a private vehicle, Gwollo can be reached from Tumu in about 45 minutes, and a few tro-tros run there and back from Tumu daily. Tro-tros between Wa and Tumu might go via Gwollo – it's on one of three possible routes so you'll have to check with the driver – which would be useful if you are coming from Wa, but would leave you with a genuine risk of being stranded overnight if you're travelling on to Wa. A visit to Gwollo can easily be combined with one to Jitton, on the Gwollo road about 15km out of Tumu, where a pair of perennial pools harbour an estimated 40 sacred crocodiles, including a few seriously big individuals. The people of Jitton welcome casual visits, and there is some talk of developing the pools for tourism under the Wildlife Department. No fee is charged by either village but it is polite to make a donation to the chief.

WOTUMU CAVES Situated about 10km from Tumu along the Jeffisi road, near the village of Pulima, the Wotumu Caves are associated with an eponymous warrior who, according to tradition, hid all his people in the caves to protect them during a slave raid. This plan is said to have met with partial success, insofar as the hidden people were never found by the slave raiders, but vanished deep into the rocks, never to be seen again. Poor Wotumu waited and waited in vain, for so long that his footprint can still be seen worn into the rocks outside the cave, and it is still believed locally that anybody who enters the cave will never return unless all the local elders are gathered there at the time.

BOLE

This small town on the main Kumasi–Wa road is of interest primarily for its beautiful mud-and-stick mosque, regarded locally as the second oldest of its type in the country, but it also boasts some interesting traditional houses. The ancient mosque isn't visible from the main road, but it's easy enough to find, situated about 50m from the modern mosque, a major landmark with its five-storey parapet. A significant attraction of Bole over Larabanga is that the set-up is so much more casual: the imam seems to be very relaxed about women visitors and photography, and he may well offer to take you inside the mosque and up to the roof. We were asked for a donation, which is only proper – the critical thing is that once we had paid we were left alone to take our time absorbing the atmosphere and photographing the mosque, a far cry from the incessant chit-chat that can characterise the Larabanga experience.

Bole serves as a convenient overnight stop for travellers heading between Kumasi and Mole (see also *Getting there and away* under *Mole National Park*, page 363). Coming from Wa, there are at least three tro-tros daily to Bole. The only place to stay in town is the **Motel Eureka**, a clean, friendly, family-run establishment offering adequate dbl rooms with fan at US$4. There's an outdoor bar on the main road, easily recognised by the tell-tale blue-and-white fence, which serves a good selection of refrigerated drinks as well as tasty chop on some evenings, but not at weekends (when you may have difficulty finding cooked food other than basic chop). For those with private transport, we were told that there's superior accommodation a few kilometres out of town at the **Cocoa Research Centre Guesthouse**.

AROUND BOLE Two further mud-and-stick mosques are clearly visible from the road between Bole and Kumasi, evidence that the modern road approximates a much older Islamic trade route. Both these mosques are fenced, making them less photogenic than the one at Bole. The first mosque is on the east side of the main road through Maluwe, a forest-fringed village which might well hold some interesting walking possibilities. The second mosque, at Banda Nkwanta, lies on the west side of the road and is notable for having very tall parapets relative to the size of the rest of the building. There's no formal accommodation in either of these villages, but it's unlikely you'd have a problem pitching a tent or finding a room in a private house.

There are also a number of low-key community projects currently under development with the Dutch NGO, SNV.

Sonyon is a flat-roofed village about 5km east of Bole, known locally for its annual rabbit-hunting festival said to culminate in lots of informal roof-top wife-swapping! At less exuberant times of year, the roof tops are used as an aerial network of pathways between the houses, which in turn are accessed from above. The community also plays host to the Soonyor Kipo shrine, which is sworn on as one would the bible and is believed to have the power to instantly kill anyone who lies. Visitors should report to the CDC (Care for Deprived Communities) information centre which can organise inexpensive homestays. Meals can also be arranged but it is advisable to bring your own food.

Ntereso Set on the banks of the Black Volta about two hours southwest of Bole, this peaceful village is special simply for its remote riverside location and the possibility of spotting some hippos. The CRC centre in Bole has trained up some of the locals as guides, who will take you around the village – and you can also hire a canoe for an unofficial daytrip into the Côte d'Ivoire. The community is reached along a rough dirt road, regularly plied by tro-tros, and will happily arrange homestays in simple lodgings without electricity. Travellers are advised to bring all their own water and food.

Kulmasa Easily accessible on the main road from Wa, some 20km north of the Bole junction, this village is like a mini-Paga – characterised by a number of seemingly tame crocodiles who live in a nearby dam and regularly wander around the centre of town. Visitors should ask for the chief and offer some kola nuts or gin, in order that the crocodiles' caretaker will call on them not to bite.

Jikankan is another appealing flat-roofed village, 10km northeast of the Sawla junction, where you can also walk over the roofs from one house to the next. Some 15 minutes walk away there is an attractive 'sacred grove' where bushbuck are sometimes seen. The road is good and transport is plentiful, making it a perfectly feasible day trip target – but inexpensive homestays can be arranged if you fancy spending the night. This particular development has been a little wary of opening up for tourism before now, so all visitors should report to the village chief and perhaps offer a donation.

Appendix I

LANGUAGE

English is the official language of Ghana, widely spoken in those parts of the country likely to be visited by travellers, to a standard that is matched in few other anglophone African countries. This means that there is little need for short-stay travellers to try to familiarise themselves with any local tongues, though knowing a few words or greetings in a local language will often help open doors and break through barriers, particularly in rural areas.

Numerous different languages and dialects are spoken in Ghana, but you'll find that most people belonging to one or other of the Akan groups – and that means more than half of the population and practically everybody in southern and central Ghana – will speak Twi (pronounced rather like Chwee) as a first or second language. Twi is the Ghanaian language taught to most Peace Corps and other volunteers spending a lengthy period of time in the country, and it may help travellers to know a few basic words and phrases. Those who speak Twi will also be able to understand Fante, another widely spoken Akan language.

Note that pronunciation of the words listed below, as of most place names in Ghana, is phonetic (eg: 'ache' is pronounced as 'ah-chee' rather than the English word ache), and that spellings have been simplified to make sense to English speakers (eg: 'ch' is often spelt 'ky' in Ghana, while 'dz' is pronounced 'j'). Note, too, that vowel sounds are closer to the soft French vowels than hard English ones.

Those who want to learn more could try getting hold of a copy of *Learning Ghanaian Languages*, available from the University Book Shop at Legon University in Accra (e *Unibks@ug.gn.apc.org*).

PRONUNCIATION
Vowels
a   similar to the 'a' in 'father'
e   as the 'e' in 'wet'
i   as the 'ee' in 'free', but less drawn out
o   somewhere between the 'o' in 'no' and the word 'awe'
u   similar to the 'oo' in 'food'

BASIC WORDS AND PHRASES

Do you speak English?	*Wote Borofo ana?*
equal to	*ya anua*
friend	*madanfo*
Good afternoon	*Mma aha* (response *yemu*)
Good evening	*Mma ajo* (response *yemu*)
Good morning	*Mma ache* (response is *yemu*)
Goodbye	*Nanti ye*

How are you?	*Wo ho te sen?* (response *me ho ye*)
How much?	*Sain Me?*
I'd like...	*Me pe*
man	*oberima*
No	*Dabe*
Please	*Me pawocheo*
Thank you	*Meda ase*
today	*enne*
tomorrow	*echina*
water	*nsuo*
we	*ye*
Welcome	*Akwaaba* (response: *Ya eja* (to older man); *Ya ema* (to older woman)
What's your name?	*Ye frewo sen?*
My name is...	*Ye fre me...*
What is the cost?	*Eyesen?*
Where is....?	*Wo hin...?*
woman	*obaa*
Yes	*Nyew* (Fante) or *aane* (Ashanti)
yesterday	*enra*

NUMBERS

1	*baako*	30	*aduasa*
2	*mienu*	40	*aduanang*
3	*miensa*	50	*aduonum*
4	*enang*	60	*aduosia*
5	*enoum*	70	*aduosong*
6	*nsia*	80	*aduowotwe*
7	*nsong*	90	*aduokrong*
8	*nwotwe*	100	*oha*
9	*nkrong*	1,000	*apem*
10	*edu*	10,000	*pemdu*
11, 12, etc	*dubaako, dumienu, etc*	100,000	*mpemba*
20	*aduono*	1,000,000	*opepe*
21	*aduono baako*		

DAYS OF THE WEEK

Monday	*Uzoada*	Friday	*Fiada*
Tuesday	*Blada*	Saturday	*Memleda*
Wednesday	*Akuada*	Sunday	*Kuasiada*
Thursday	*Yawada*		

EWE The key language to the east of the river Volta is 'Ewe' (pronounced somewhere between 'eh-way' and 'eh-vay'). The main pronunciation points here are that a 'k' before a 'p' is always silent, and makes the 'p' more explosive, and that 'dz' sounds like a soft 'g'.

Useful phrases include:

Good morning	*Ndi* (add-*nami* to end if addressing more than one person)
Good afternoon	*Ndo* (*nami*)
Good evening (after 5pm)	*Fieyi* (*nami*)
Welcome	*Woeso*

Goodbye	*Miadogo*
How are you?	*Eh Foa?* (respond '*Eh*')
Thank you (very much)	*Akpe (ka ka)*
Yes	*Eh*
No	*Ow*
How much?	*Nene?*
Money	*Ga*
White person	*Yavoo* (literally 'trickish dog' – but with no pejorative meaning)
Black person	*Ameyebo*
Fika	*Where*

DAGBANI The main language around Tamale is Dagbani. A 'g' before a 'b' is silent and makes the 'b' explosive – as in Gbele national park. Useful phrases include:

Good morning	*Dasiba naa* (response is *Naa!*)
Good afternoon	*Autine naa*
Good evening	*Aniwula naa*
Welcome	*Maraaba*
How are you?	*A gbihira?*

Please note that where words are properly spelt with local characters, I have given an approximation in English characters. Readers are welcome to submit vocabulary lists for other Ghanaian languages (see *Feedback request*, page i).

GHAN-ENGLISH Travellers whose first language is not English may also appreciate a few 'Ghan-English' phrases – which won't make a lot of sense in English-speaking countries in the Western world, but are useful if you want to make yourself understood in Ghana.

I'll come back later	*I'll go and come/go come*
see you later	*we shall meet*
tip/bribe	*dash*
How are you?	*How? Or How is it?* ('*How are you?*' is also used)
How are things?	*How's back?*
mate	*chalay*
flip-flop/thong	*chalay Wote*
small child	*pekin*

Appendix 2

GLOSSARY

Here follows a glossary of terms and names used in this book and/or in Ghana itself.

abekwan	palmnut soup
Abosomfie	Asante traditional shrines – literally home of a 'bosom' or deity (singular: *Obosomfie*)
AC	air conditioning
acacia woodland	any woodland dominated by thorn trees of the acacia family
Acheampong, Gen Ignatius	military president of Ghana 1972–78, publicly executed in 1979
adinkra	cloth with dyed symbols made in Ashanti, often worn to funerals
adobe	mud building
Afrifa, Brigadier Akwasi	military president of Ghana 1968–69, publicly executed in 1979
Akan	most populous of Ghana's linguistic groupings, includes the Asante and coastal Fante
akpeteshie	local gin
Akuffo, Lt-Gen	military president of Ghana 1978–79, publicly executed 1979
Akwaaba	Welcome
Ancient Ghana	medieval empire centred on present-day Mali for which Ghana was named
Ankrh, Lt-Gen Joseph	military president of Ghana 1966–68
Anokye, Okomfo	spiritual advisor to Asantehene Osei Tutu
Asante	indigenous kingdom centred on Kumasi
Asantehene	King of Asante
Ashanti	*see* Asante
atumpan	talking drum
balance	change (for a payment)
banda	any detached accommodation, such as a hut or chalet
bo froot	deep-fried sweet dough-ball, not unlike doughnuts in taste and texture
boma	colonial administrative office
bosom	god or deity
bubra	draught beer
Busia, Dr Kofi	Prime Minister of Ghana 1969–72

cedi	local unit of currency
cowry	small white shell used as currency in pre-colonial times
Denkyira	dominant empire in central Ghana prior to the emergence of Asante
dropping taxi	charter taxi, as in Europe (but not metered)
DSTV	South African multi-channel satellite television service
Durbar	reception or celebration at the court of a traditional ruler or chief
endemic	unique to a specific area
enstoolment	equivalent of coronation of a chief or king
exotic	not-indigenous, eg: pine plantations
Fante	people of the coast (roughly between Accra and Takoradi)
Ferguson, George Ekem	Ghanaian explorer and colonial political agent; born Ekow Atta, 1864; killed Wa, 1897
forest	wooded area with closed canopy
forex bureau	bureau de change
fufu	popular gooey doughy staple made from ground cassava, plantain, and/or yam
fugu	cloth smock worn in northern Ghana
German Togoland	pre-World War I German territory comprising present-day Togo and Ghana's Volta Region
Ghartey IV, King	King of Winneba 1872–97; founder of Fante Confederation; also referred to as Robert Johnson Ghartey
Golden Stool	ultimate symbol of Asantehene
grasscutter	also known as the cane rat (*Thryonomys* spp.), this rodent, weighing up to 8kg, is popularly eaten as bushmeat in Ghana
guesthouse	cheap local hotel
Harmattan	dry dusty wind blowing across west Africa from the Sahara in the dry season
Hayford, Joseph Casely	Ghanaian barrister who formed NCBWA to resist British rule after World War I
highlife	home-grown style of music fusing traditional and imported rhythms
ice water	chilled tap water sold in packets
indigenous	occurring in a place naturally
jollof rice	tangy, sometimes very spicy, rice, red in colour, cooked with vegetables and/or meat
kenkey	maize-based starch ball, wrapped in banana leaves and usually eaten with tomato relish
kente	national cloth weaved by the Asante and Ewe people
kola nuts	bitter and mildly narcotic nuts chewed throughout west Africa
krom	town
Kufour, John	elected president of Ghana 2000–present
Limann, Dr Hilla	civilian president of Ghana 1979–81
lorry	term used locally for any large passenger vehicle (any bus or tro-tro)

MacLean, Gordon	Governor of the Gold Coast 1830–47, buried in Cape Coast Castle
na	chief (mainly in north)
NCBWA	National Congress of British West Africa
netting	mosquito net
Nkrumah, Kwame	first African prime minister of Gold Coast/Ghana (1952–66); died in exile 1972
Obosomfie	see *Abosomfie*
obruni	white person
Okomfo	Asante fetish priest
omo tua	rice balls
panga	local equivalent of a machete
passenger taxi	public transport taxi that carries a full quota of passengers between two fixed places
pito	millet-based beer
posuban	large shrine associated with relatively urbanised Fante settlements
Prempreh I, Asantehene	king exiled by British to Sierra Leone in 1896; returned to stool, 1926; died, 1931
Prempreh II, Asantehene	popular king of Asante 1931–70
pure water	chilled and sealed filtered water sold cheaply in plastic packets
Quarshie, Tetteh	local blacksmith who introduced cocoa to Ghana from Fernando Po in 1876
Rawlings, Flt-Lt Jerry	military president of Ghana 1979, 1981–92, elected civilian president 1992–2000
riparian/riverine woodland	strip of forest or lush woodland following a watercourse, often rich in fig trees
sahel	dry savanna belt dividing the forested coast of West Africa from the Sahara
savanna	grassland with some trees
self-contained	en-suite (ie: room with private toilet and shower attached)
shared taxi	*see* passenger taxi
station	bus, tro-tro or taxi terminal
STC	State Transport Company, operates a good network of intercity coaches
stool	symbol of chieftaincy
surfaced (road)	road sealed with asphalt or similar
track	motorable minor road or path
tro-tro	passenger vehicle larger than a taxi but smaller than a bus
tuo zafi	stiff millet- or maize-based porridge eaten as staple in parts of the north
Tutu, Osei, Asantehene	first true Asantehene, and some say also the greatest, enstooled 1697
TZ	see *tuo zafi*
West Sudanese	architectural style using mud and wood typical of mosques of the Sahel
woodland	wooded area lacking closed canopy
Yaa Asantewaa	Queen Mother who led resistance to British colonisation in 1900

Appendix 3

FURTHER READING

HISTORY AND BACKGROUND I consulted quite a number of books while researching the general and local history sections included in this guide, all of which I was able to buy in Ghana, though I can't guarantee you'll be able to do the same. I've listed them all below, but it would be pushing it to class most of them as recommended further reading. Buah's *History of Ghana* would be the obvious starting point for those seeking deeper insight into the country's historical background; readable, informative, and of manageable length, without really propelling you to turn to the next page. More compelling, oddly enough, is Agbodeka's *Economic History*, while Gadzekpo's otherwise rather flimsy *History of Ghana* is especially strong on prehistory. Best of all in my opinion – certainly the only substantial book in the collection that I could think about reading from start to finish for pleasure – is *A Thousand Years of West African History*, a collection of essays covering most aspects of the region's history, probably a bit dated by now, but of great value for the lively, questioning style throughout.

Of the more focused titles, van Dantzig's *Forts and Castles* offers a good introduction to coastal history, brought to life by the final chapter on living conditions in and around the forts, and it's readily available in Accra and Cape Coast. Anquandah's *Castles & Forts of Ghana*, sold at the Accra Museum, and at Cape Coast and Elmina castles, covers similar ground with less substantial, but more readable, text and some wonderful photographs. Debrah's *Asante Traditional Buildings*, also sold at most museums, is a lightweight, but beautiful production well worth buying for further detail on the shrines at Besease and elsewhere in Ashanti.

Superficially somewhat esoteric, Schweizer's *Survivors on the Gold Coast* relates the story of the foundation of the Basel Missionaries, but is of greater interest for its 80-plus pages of monochrome photographs, which date from 1860 onwards and document subjects as diverse as the Asantehene in exile in the Seychelles to Accra street scenes – all in all, a fascinating document.

A highly worthwhile new book about the slave trade out of Ghana is St Clair's *The Grand Slave Emporium*, which will be available in an inexpensive paperback edition by the end of 2007. By contrast, Meredith's *State of Africa* is a very readable history of 50 years of African independence, which goes a long way to explaining why Africa is as it is, and Guest's *Shackled Continent* is an excellent book looking at development and economic problems in modern Africa.

Agbodeka, F *An Economic History of Ghana* (Ghana University Press, 1992)
Ajayi, F & Espie, E (Eds) *A Thousand Years of West African History* (Thomas Nelson, 1965)
Amate, C O C *The Making Of Ada* (Woeli Publishing Services, 1999)

Anquandah, K J *Castles & Forts of Ghana* (Ghana Museums & Monuments Board, 1999)

Arhin, K (Ed) *The Cape Coast and Elmina Handbook* (University of Ghana, 1995)

Buah, F *West Africa Since AD1000* (Macmillan, 1974)

Buah, F *A History of Ghana* (Macmillan, 1980)

Davidson, B *A History of West Africa 1000–1800* (Longman, 1977)

Debrah, I N (Ed) *Asante Traditional Buildings* (Ghana Museums & Monuments Board, 1999)

Gadzekpo, S K *A History of Ghana* (Royal Crown Press, 1997)

Graham, J *Cape Coast in History* (Anglican Printing Press, 1994)

Guest, Robert *The Shackled Continent* (Pan, 2005)

Herbstein, M *Ama: A Story of the Atlantic Slave Trade* (ereads.com, 2004)

Kwadwo, O *An Outline of Asante History* (O Kwadwo Enterprises, 1994)

Kyeremateng, K *The Akans of Ghana* (Sebewie Publishers, 1996)

Meredith, Martin *The State of Africa* (Free Press, 2005)

Moxon, J *Volta: Man's Greatest Lake* (André Deutsch, 1969)

Obeng, E *Ancient Ashanti Chieftaincy* (Ghana Publishing Corporation, 1984)

Onwubiko, K *History of West Africa 1000–1800* (Africana FEP, 1982)

Onwubiko, K *History of West Africa 1800–Present Day* (Africana FEP, 1985)

Packenham, T *The Scramble for Africa* (Jonathan Ball, 1991)

St Clair, William *The Grand Slave Emporium: Cape Coast Castle and the British Slave Trade* (Profile Books, 2006)

Sampson, M *Makers of Modern Ghana Volume One* (Anowuo Publications, 1969)

Sarpong, P *Ghana in Retrospect* (Ghana Publishing Corporation, 1974)

Schweizer, P A *Survivors on the Gold Coast* (Smartline Publishing, 2000)

Tufuo, J & Donkor, C *Ashantis of Ghana* (Anowuo Publications, 1989)

van Dantzig, A *Forts and Castles of Ghana* (Sedco, 1980)

Ward, W *Short History of Ghana* (Longman, 1957)

FIELD GUIDES Jonathon Kingdon's superb and dauntingly comprehensive *Field Guide to African Mammals* (Academic Press, 1997) is recommended to serious mammal-watchers, especially for its detail on primates, but it's probably too pricey and bulky for most travellers. A cheaper and more handy volume, just as useful to those visitors whose interest is confined to large mammals, is Chris and Tilde Stuart's *Field Guide to the Larger Mammals of Africa* (Struik, 1997). If you have difficulty locating these, several other inferior guides are more widely available, most visibly those published by Collins. Once in Ghana, you might be able to get hold of Happold's *Large Mammals of West Africa* (Longman, 1973), which, despite being rather dated in some respects, is a very handy, lightweight volume with adequate pictures and descriptions.

A useful starting point for dedicated birders visiting Ghana, Llewellyn Grimes's *The Birds of Ghana* (British Ornithologists Union, 1987) includes a systematic list of all 712 species found in the country, together with details of favoured habitat, relative abundance, and distribution. Unfortunately, it is no longer in print, but you may be able to pick up a copy second-hand or in the library. For identification purposes, however, this list must be supplemented with a field guide, ideally Borrow and Demey's superb (but also very bulky, and, at UK£55, rather costly) new *Field Guide to the Birds of Western Africa* (Helm Identification Guides, 2002). Another useful title, especially for regular visitors to Africa, is Sinclair and Ryan's new, comprehensive, and relatively inexpensive *Field Guide to the Birds of Sub-Saharan Africa* (Struik, 2003). Until recently the only field guide covering the region, Serle, Morel, and Hatwig's *Field Guide to the Birds of West Africa* (HarperCollins, 1977) is best avoided, since full descriptions and illustrations are supplied for only half the species recorded in the region, while almost 400 species are relegated to one line each in an appendix.

TRAVEL GUIDES Highly recommended to those who are spending a while in the capital is the North American Women's Association's *No More Worries: The Indispensable Insiders' Guide to Accra* (1997), an excellent source of advice and contacts in Accra. Also worth buying, though more as a souvenir than a guide, is Mylene Remy's *Ghana Today* (Jaguar, 1977, 1992), a 30cm-long hardback book packed with good photos, but textually tending towards whimsy and hyperbole. Jojo Cobbinah's *Ghana* (Peter Meyer, 1995, 1999) is an established German-language guide written by a Ghanaian resident in Germany. It is popular with Germans and contains lots of useful information, but the recently published English version has been ill-served by the translator.

FICTION AND BIOGRAPHY Ghana has one of the strongest English literary traditions to be found anywhere in Africa, dating back to 1911 and the publication of what is regarded as West Africa's first novel, *Ethiopia Unbound* (Frank Cass Publishers, 1969), by the barrister and nationalist politician Joseph Casely Hayford (see pages 18–19). A fair selection of local novels is available in most bookshops around the country, generally at very reasonable prices. A few better-known novels include B Kojo Laing's *Search Sweet Country* (Farrar, Straus & Giroux, 1998), Ayi Kwei Armah's *The Beautiful Ones Are Not Yet Born* (Heinemann, 1989) and *Healers* (Heinemann, 1979), Ama Ata Aidoo's *Dilemma of a Ghost* and *Our Sister Killjoy* (both Longman, 1995), and Amma Darko's *Beyond the Horizon* (Heinemann, 1995).

Maya Angelou's *All God's Children Need Travelling Shoes* (Virago, 1987) recounts the story of the American author's return to Ghana to search out her roots. *The Narrow Path* by Francis Selormey (Heinemann African Writers Series, 1992) is a vivid and very readable account of a Ghanaian boy's upbringing in the 1920s. And Manu Herbstein's *Ama: A Story of the Atlantic Slave Trade* (Picador Africa, 2001) won the 2002 Commonwealth Writers' Prize for Best First Book, and was nonimated for the 2003 International IMPAC Dublin Literary Award, for its novelisation of one woman's experience of this bleak period.

WEBSITES

Websites worth checking out before you travel to Ghana include the following:

http://uk.geocities.com/davethack/adamsu.html Information for volunteers working in rural Ghana.
http://uk.multimap.com/world/places.cgi Free online maps of countries and major towns.
www.africa-geographic.com Site for the South African publications *Africa Geographic* and *Africa Birds & Birding* – useful news and archives, subscriptions, special offers and tours.
www.africaonline.com.gh General tourist information.
www.brookes.ac.uk/worldwise/directory.html General practical information about visas, costs, transport, etc.
www.bradtguides.com Log on for your free Ghana update newsletter.
www.fco.gov.uk British Foreign & Commonwealth Office site, whose 'Travel Advice by Country' pages contain up-to-date, generally rather conservative information on trouble spots and places to avoid.
www.ghana-com.co.uk Site of the Ghana High Commission in London, with

plenty of background information and details of visa requirements, etc.

www.ghanaweb.com Probably the best site overall for current affairs and sports news, together with a daunting mass of background information and statistics, as well as comprehensive news archives dating back to 1995.

www.graphicghana.com Current and archived news from Ghana's most popular anglophone newspaper, the *Daily Graphic*.

www.ncrc.org.gh Information about ecotourist and community development tourist sites.

https://www.cia.gov/cia/publications/factbook/geos/gh.html Another site focussing on security and safety matters, based on CIA files; judgements tend to be on the conservative side.

www.tougha.com Excellent site of the Tour Operators Union of Ghana (TOUGHA) with good information about all aspects of travel in Ghana; especially strong on wildlife.

www.travelafricamag.com Site for the quarterly magazine Travel Africa – good news, travel archives, and subscriptions.

www.travel.state.gov US State Department equivalent to Dave Thack's site, above.

www.usatoday.com/weather/forecast/wglobe.htm Weather forecasts and archives covering remote parts of Africa; try also www.worldclimate.com or http://weather.yahoo.com/regional/GHXX.html.

www.vibefm.com.gh Music news and views from Accra's most popular radio station.

www.wildlife-ghana.org Detailed website covering the 15 protected areas administered by the Ghana Wildlife Division.

NEWSLETTER

Don't forget to email Bradt (info@bradtguides.com) for your free update newsletter – see page iv for details.

WIN £100 CASH!
READER QUESTIONNAIRE
**Complete and return this questionnaire for the chance to win
£100 cash in our regular draw**

(Entries may be posted or faxed to us, or scanned and emailed.)

Your feedback is important. To help us plan future guides please answer all the questions below. All completed questionnaires will qualify for entry in the draw.

Have you used any other Bradt Guides? If so, which titles?. . . . .

. . . .

Where did you buy this guidebook? . . . .

Your age   16–25 ☐   26–45 ☐   46–60 ☐   60+ ☐

Please send us any comments about this guide or other Bradt Travel Guides. . . . .

. . . .

. . . .

. . . .

. . . .

CLAIM YOUR HALF-PRICE BRADT GUIDE!
Order Form

Please send me one copy of the following guide at half the UK retail price

Title   *Retail price   Half price*

. . .   .

Post & packing (£1/book UK; £2/book Europe; £3/book rest of world) . . . .

Total   . . . .

Name . . . .

Address. . . . .

Tel . . . .   Email . . . .

☐ I enclose a cheque for £ . . . . made payable to Bradt Travel Guides Ltd

☐ I would like to pay by credit card. Number: . . . .

Expiry date . . . . / . . . . 3-digit security code (on reverse of card) . . . .

☐ Please add my name to your mailing/e-newsletter list. (For Bradt use only.)

☐ I would be happy for you to use my name and comments in Bradt marketing material.

Send your order on this form, with the completed questionnaire, to:

Bradt Travel Guides/GHA4
23 High Street, Chalfont St Peter, Bucks SL9 9QE
☏ +44 (0)1753 893444   f +44 (0)1753 892333
e info@bradtguides.com   www.bradtguides.com

Bradt Travel Guides

www.bradtguides.com

Africa

Africa Overland	£15.99
Benin	£14.99
Botswana: Okavango, Chobe, Northern Kalahari	£15.99
Burkina Faso	£14.99
Cameroon	£13.95
Canary Islands	£13.95
Cape Verde Islands	£13.99
Eritrea	£15.99
Ethiopia	£15.99
Gabon, São Tomé, Príncipe	£13.95
Gambia, The	£13.99
Ghana	£15.99
Johannesburg	£6.99
Kenya	£14.95
Madagascar	£15.99
Malawi	£13.99
Mali	£13.95
Mauritius, Rodrigues & Réunion	£13.99
Mozambique	£13.99
Namibia	£15.99
Niger	£14.99
Nigeria	£15.99
Rwanda	£14.99
Seychelles	£14.99
Sudan	£13.95
Tanzania, Northern	£13.99
Tanzania	£16.99
Uganda	£15.99
Zambia	£15.95
Zanzibar	£12.99

Britain and Europe

Albania	£13.99
Armenia, Nagorno Karabagh	£14.99
Azores	£12.99
Baltic Capitals: Tallinn, Riga, Vilnius, Kaliningrad	£12.99
Belarus	£14.99
Belgrade	£6.99
Bosnia & Herzegovina	£13.99
Bratislava	£6.99
Budapest	£8.99
Cork	£6.99
Croatia	£13.99
Cyprus see North Cyprus	
Czech Republic	£13.99
Dresden	£7.99
Dubrovnik	£6.99
Eccentric Britain	£13.99
Eccentric Cambridge	£6.99
Eccentric Edinburgh	£5.95
Eccentric France	£12.95
Eccentric London	£13.99
Eccentric Oxford	£5.95
Estonia	£13.99
Faroe Islands	£13.95
Georgia	£14.99
Helsinki	£7.99
Hungary	£14.99
Kiev	£7.95
Kosovo	£14.99

Krakow	£7.99
Latvia	£13.99
Lille	£6.99
Lithuania	£13.99
Ljubljana	£7.99
Macedonia	£14.99
Montenegro	£13.99
North Cyprus	£12.99
Paris, Lille & Brussels	£11.95
Riga	£6.95
River Thames, In the Footsteps of the Famous	£10.95
Serbia	£14.99
Slovakia	£14.99
Slovenia	£12.99
Spitsbergen	£14.99
Switzerland: Rail, Road, Lake	£13.99
Tallinn	£6.99
Ukraine	£14.99
Vilnius	£6.99
Zagreb	£6.99

Middle East, Asia and Australasia

China: Yunnan Province	£13.99
Great Wall of China	£13.99
Iran	£14.99
Iraq	£14.95
Maldives	£13.99
Mongolia	£14.95
North Korea	£13.95
Oman	£13.99
Sri Lanka	£13.99
Syria	£14.99
Tibet	£13.99
Turkmenistan	£14.99

The Americas and the Caribbean

Amazon, The	£14.99
Argentina	£15.99
Bolivia	£14.99
Cayman Islands	£12.95
Costa Rica	£13.99
Chile	£16.95
Eccentric America	£13.95
Eccentric California	£13.99
Falkland Islands	£13.95
Panama	£13.95
Peru & Bolivia: Backpacking and Trekking	£12.95
St Helena	£14.99
USA by Rail	£13.99

Wildlife

Antarctica: Guide to the Wildlife	£14.95
Arctic: Guide to the Wildlife	£15.99
Galápagos Wildlife	£15.99
Madagascar Wildlife	£14.95
Peruvian Wildlife	£15.99
Southern African Wildlife	£18.95
Sri Lankan Wildlife	£15.99

Health

Your Child Abroad: A Travel Health Guide	£10.95

Index

413

Insight Travel & Tours
Presents
GHANA

Don't Be A Tourist, Be A Guest

DY ALL YEAR ROUND TAILOR MADE INDIVIDUAL AND GROUP TOURS

*Home Stay packages * Whistle-Stop tours * Eco Tourism tours * Educational tours
stival tours * Historical & Heritage tours *Drumming & Dance tours * Honeymoon tours
Just tell us what your expectations are and we will package to suit your budget.

Request information through our website:
www.insighttravelghana.com or email us through
insightghana@yahoo.com or amokyereme@gmail.com

& Bus rentals
vailable

In London talk to Isaac on 07985107650, USA 5103076985
In Ghana call Martina 0277424244 or Nana on (051) 28569
visit the office at Osu Ako Adjei close to Kyns Hotel.

Experience A Different Africa, Where Tourism Makes Sense

NOTES